INDEX to
American
Reference
Books
Annual

2005–2009

A Cumulative Index to
Subjects, Authors, and Titles

INDEX to
American
Reference
Books
Annual

2005–2009

A Cumulative Index to
Subjects, Authors, and Titles

COMPILED BY **Shannon Graff Hysell, Associate Editor**

LIBRARIES
UNLIMITED
A Member of the Greenwood Publishing Group

Westport, Connecticut • London

LIBRARIES UNLIMITED
A Member of the Greenwood Publishing Group, Inc.
88 Post Road West
Westport, CT 06881
www.lu.com

ISBN 978-1-59158-858-0   ISSN 0192-6969

Contents

Preface

American Reference Books Annual (ARBA) is well established as a comprehensive source of reviews for all types of reference books, CD-ROMs, and Websites published or distributed in the United States and Canada. The 40 annual volumes of ARBA, which began in 1970, contain more than 62,000 reviews of reference materials. These titles include books, CD-ROMs, and Websites on almost any topic in a variety of reference formats (e.g., almanacs, bibliographies, catalogs, dictionaries, encyclopedias, handbooks, indexes).

Access to each annual volume is provided through that volume's indexes of authors, titles, and subjects. Offering comprehensive access, the cumulative index brings together five years of ARBA. Joseph Sprug prepared the first 5-year volume, *Index to American Reference Books Annual 1970-1974*; Christine Gehrt-Wynar, *Index to American Reference Books Annual 1975-1979*; Ruth Blackmore, *Index to American Reference Books Annual 1980-1984*; Anna Grace Patterson, *Index to American Reference Books Annual 1985-1989* and *Index to American Reference Books Annual 1990-1994*; Susan Strickland, *Index to American Reference Books Annual 1995-1999*; and Martin Dillon, *Index to American Reference Books Annual 2000-2004*. Although each cumulative index volume contains author, title, and subject indexes, some variations in style and organization showing the unique hand of each volume's individual compiler exists among the volumes.

This cumulative index merges five years of information on reference materials that have appeared in ARBA from 2005-2009. Each entry in ARBA presents full bibliographic information, an evaluative review, and citations to professional journals containing other published reviews. The index is more than a location devise; it is a critical tool for the scholar, librarian, and reader seeking to tap ARBA's wealth of information.

Index to American Reference Books Annual 2005-2009 covers over 7,500 books, CD-ROMs, and Websites reviewed during the 2005-2009 period. In order to offer a reasonable-sized book, short titles and abbreviated words within titles are used.

AUTHORS AND TITLES

The author/title index is arranged alphabetically word by word (when a word is abbreviated it is filed as if it were spelled out). Multiple volumes of the same title are arranged numerically. Books with the same title published in different years are arranged chronologically. Acronyms are filed alphabetically as they appear.

Author entries in the 2005-2009 index contain author's name with year and entry number.

Author's name   ARBA year (2006)   Entry   Number of entry

Abel, Richard, 2006n1148

Authors, editors, and compilers appear in the index as their names are shown on the title page; therefore, if authors have written books under their full names, initials, or parts of both, they will appear under all forms in the index.

Smith, J. L.
Smith, John
Smith, John L.

All single, joint, and corporate authors are individually indexed. Titles appear in a shortened form in title entries. Ordinarily, subtitles are deleted. Usually, abbreviated words are filed as if they were spelled out. Entries show title, year of ARBA, and entry number.

Abbreviated title   ARBA year (2006)   Entry   Number of entry

Hispanics in the American West, 2006n353

SUBJECTS

The subject index, with a few variations, uses terms that are based upon Library of Congress Subject Headings. This format allows easy access to titles from different years of ARBA. The subject terms are arranged alphabetically and ignore punctuation; therefore, one may find the following alphabetical arrangement:

MEDICAL LAWS
MEDICAL TESTS
MEDICINAL PLANTS
MEDICINE—BIBLIOGRAPHY

Each of these entries will have titles with year and entry number appearing beneath them:

MEDICINAL PLANTS
    Medicinal plants in folk tradition, 2005n1347
    Medicinal plants of the world, 2005n1352
    Medicinal plants on N America, 2009n1178

ACKNOWLEDGMENTS

In closing, we wish to express our gratitude to the many talented contributors without whose support these volumes of ARBA could not have been compiled. Many thanks also go out to our distinguished Advisory Board members whose contributions greatly enhance ARBA and ARBAonline. We would also like to thank the members of our staff who were instrumental in this title's preparation.

Author/Title Index

A-Z common symptom answer gd, 2005n1451
A-Z of ...
    chest radiology, 2009n1241
    cool computer games, 2006n1480
    essential oils, 2005n1454
    social research, 2005n65
A to Z gd to American consumers, 2009n157
A to Z of ...
    alternative music, 2005n1141
    American Indian women, rev ed, 2008n317
    American women writers, rev ed, 2008n909
    ancient Greek & Roman women, rev ed, 2009n785
    Byzantium, 2007n382
    feminism, 2008n781
    Latino Americans series, 2008n333
    Lutheranism, 2008n1083
    mathematicians, 2006n1525
    multinational peacekeeping, 2007n633
    new religious movements, 2007n1076
    revolutionary America, 2008n400
    sci fiction lit, 2006n1026
    scientists in space & astronomy, 2006n1503
    Shinto, 2007n1127
    the Civil War, 2007n355
    the French Revolution, 2008n431
    the Holocaust, 2006n499
    the Korean War, 2006n462
    the Olympic movement, 2008n712
    the Persian Gulf War, 1990-91, 2008n586
    the Renaissance, 2007n423
    women in sci & math, rev ed, 2008n780
A to zoo, 7th ed, 2007n897
A to zoo, suppl to the 7th ed, 2009n924
Aaker, Everett, 2007n1044
AARP gd to pills, 2007n1280
Abazov, Rafis, 2005n100, 2006n98
Abbey, Cherie D., 2005n12, 2005n750, 2005n997,
    2006n118, 2006n1250, 2007n669, 2007n875,
    2008n12, 2009n9,
Abbotson, Susan C. W., 2006n1006, 2008n92
Abbott, Damien, 2009n241
ABC Chinese-English comprehensive dict, 2005n970
ABC for bk collectors, 8th ed, 2005n920
ABC of obesity, 2008n1256
Abel, E. Lawrence, 2005n1116
Abel, Ernest L., 2007n1023
Abel, Richard, 2006n1148
Abels, Eileen G., 2006n644
Abert, Allison D., 2009n1171
Abortion in the US, 2008n716

Abou-Zeid, El-Sayed, 2008n170, 2009n147
About.com [Website], 2006n260
Abraham Lincoln companion, 2009n638
Abraham Lincoln on screen, 2d ed, 2009n1059
Abrams ency of photography, 2005n950
Abrams gd to American house styles, 2005n945
Abramson, Glenda, 2007n282
Abramson, Rudy, 2007n61
Abuse & violence info for teens, 2009n764
Aby, Stephen H., 2008n266
ABZU: a gd to study of the ancient Near East on the
    Web [Website], 2005n526
Academic bill of rights debate, 2008n266
Academic lib & the net gen student, 2008n513
Academic lib research, 2009n503
Academic search premier [Website], 2006n1474
Academy of American poets [Website], 2008n952
Access, 2008n49
Access sci [Website], 2009n1124
Access to E European & Eurasian culture, 2009n527
Accident & safety info for teens, 2009n1268
Accidental lib manager, 2006n638
Accredited institutions of postsecondary educ,
    2006-07, 2008n275
ACE electoral knowledge network [Website],
    2008n614
Acharya, Tara, 2006n1359
Achieving diversity, 2008n554
Ackerman, Thomas H., 2007n206, 2007n207
Ackermann, Marsha E., 2009n426
Ackerson, Linda G., 2007n543, 2008n562
ACLS hist e-bk project [Website], 2007n402
ACM digital lib [Website], 2006n1475
Acquiring & organizing curriculum materials, 2d ed,
    2005n624
Acronym finder [Website], 2006n1
Acronyms, initialisms & abbrevs dict, 34th ed, 2005n1
Acronyms, initialisms & abbrevs dict, 39th ed, 2008n1
Across cultures, 2009n921
Acton, Johnny, 2008n1110
Adam, Frederic, 2009n1281
Adam, Thomas, 2006n748
Adamec, Christine, 2005n1439, 2006n1430,
    2008n719, 2009n700, 2009n763
Adamec, Ludwig W., 2006n87
Adams, Bruce F., 2006n480
Adams, Cynthia, 2005n1299
Adams, Dale E., 2005n276
Adams, Denise Wiles, 2005n1309
Adams, J. Q., 2006n1146
Adams, James Eli, 2005n485

Adams, Kathy L., 2005n276
Adams, Simon, 2008n427
Adams, Stephen J., 2006n1068
Adams, Tania, 2008n1110
Adamson, Hugh C., 2007n1093
Adamson, Lynda G., 2007n976
Adamson, Melitta Weiss, 2005n1303, 2009n1145
Addiction counselor's desk ref, 2007n716
Administrative assistant's & secretary's hndbk, 3d ed,
     2009n240
Adolescent health sourcebk, 2d ed, 2007n1254
Adoption, 2d ed, 2008n723
Adrien, Nicolas G., 2009n1327
Adult health concerns sourcebk, 2009n1243
Adult psychopathology & diagnosis, 5th ed,
     2009n708
Advances in enterprise info tech security, 2008n1277
Adventurers of purse & person Va. 1607-24/5, v.1, 4th
     ed, 2008n338
Adventurers of purse & person Va. 1607-24/5, v.2, 4th
     ed, 2008n339
Adventurers of purse & person Va. 1607-24/5, v.3, 4th
     ed, 2008n340
Aerial atlas of the Holy Land, 2009n125
Affirmative action, 2005n587
Afghanistan to Zimbabwe, 2007n58
Afolayan, Funso, 2005n89
Africa & the Americas, 2009n692
Africa & the Middle East: a continental overview of
     environmental issues, 2005n1541
Africa south of the Sahara [Website], 2008n91
Africa south of the Sahara 2007, 36th ed, 2008n96
Africa south of the Sahara 2008, 37th ed, 2009n89
African American almanac, 9th ed, 2005n335
African American almanac, 10th ed, 2008n307
African American biogs, 2007n267
African-American business leaders & entrepreneurs,
     2005n140
African American chronology, 2007n268
African American dramatists, 2005n1034
African American experience [Website], 2009n298
African American hist, 2006n327
African American hist, 2007n269
African-American holidays, festivals, & celebrations,
     2007n272
African American issues, 2007n274
African American lit, 2006n1030
African American lives, 2005n326
African American natl biog, 2009n14
African American pioneers of baseball, 2008n707
African-American pol leaders, 2005n695
African American religious experience in America,
     2006n1216
African American religious experience in America,
     2007n1086

African American women writers of the 19th century
     [Website], 2007n934
African-American writers, 2005n1058
African Americans & pop culture, 2009n1047
African Americans in Congress, 2009n659
African Americans in sports, 2005n749
African Americans in the media today, 2008n310
African Americans in the military, 2005n658
African Americans in the US Army in WWII,
     2009n304
African biogl dict, 2d ed, 2007n79
African children's lit [Website], 2006n989
African folklore, 2005n1153
African households, 2007n723
African letters [Website], 2006n1066
African lit in English [Website], 2006n1052
African mythology A to Z, 2005n1161
African placenames, 2d ed, 2009n342
African states & rulers, 3d ed, 2007n626
African studies center [Website], 2008n93
African studies centre [Website], 2008n94
African timelines [Website], 2005n463
African, Asian, & Middle Eastern artist's signatures &
     monographs from 1800, 2009n853
Africana, 2d ed, 2006n328
Agapanthus for gardeners, 2005n1320
Agata, Burton C., 2007n458
Agata, Seth H., 2007n458
Age of ...
     Milton, 2005n1002
     Napoleon, 2005n481
     Romanticism, 2008n430
     sail, v.2, 2005n672
     the storytellers, 2007n781
     wars of religion, 2008n587
Ageline database [Website], 2005n793
Agent & Web serv techs in virtual enterprises,
     2008n1279
Ager, Simon, 2006n940
AGRICOLA (AGRICultural online access) [Website],
     2006n1279
Aguilar-Moreno, Manuel, 2007n279
Aiken, Charles Curry, 2006n429
Aikin, Jane, 2006n587
AIM/FAR 2006, 2006n1547
AIM/FAR 2008, 2008n1352
Air Univ Lib index to military per [Website],
     2005n670
Aircraft carriers, 2007n571
Aircraft markings of the Strategic Air Command,
     1946-53, 2007n565
Aircraft record cards of the US Air Force, 2009n611
Aitken, Ian, 2007n1045
Akay, Metin, 2007n1222
ALA best free ref Web sites [Website], 2008n7

Albrecht, Gary L., 2006n805, 2007n701
Alciati, Andrea, 2005n942
Alcock, Joan P., 2007n1152
Alcohol & temperance in modern hist, 2005n820
Alcoholism sourcebk, 2d ed, 2007n715
Aldama, Arturo J., 2005n354
Alderfer, Jonathan, 2007n1193, 2007n1194
Alderton, David, 2006n1378
Aldighieri, Ann Marie, 2006n3
Aldrete, Gregory S., 2005n517, 2006n476
Aldwin, Carolyn M., 2008n685, 2009n741
Alessio, Amy J., 2007n510, 2008n534
Alexander, Christine, 2005n1075
Alexander, Dey, 2006n1203
Alexander, Graham, 2009n1210
Alexander, Ivy L., 2006n1433, 2008n1235
Alexander, James, 2005n1535
Alexander Pope ency, 2005n1112
Alexander, S. L., 2005n539
Alexander, Thomas G., 2009n1106
Alexander, Yonah, 2009n695
Alger, Chadwick F., 2006n739
Ali, Mohammad Farhat, 2006n1494
Alice Munro, 2008n937
Alice Walker, 2006n1040
Alicea, Marixsa, 2005n832
Alison, Malcolm R., 2008n1252
Alkire, Leland G., Jr., 2005n57, 2006n55
All-American colleges, 2008n276
All business [Website], 2006n261
All in a day's work, 2d ed, 2009n1140
All movie gd [Website], 2006n1138
All Music gd to classical music, 2007n998
All Music gd to country, 2d ed, 2005n1147
All Music gd to hip-hop, 2005n1148
All of me: the complete discography of Louis
     Armstrong, 2007n992
All the people in the Bible, 2009n1096
All things Austen, 2006n1048
All things Chaucer, 2008n929
All things Darwin, 2008n1163
All things in the Bible, 2007n1100
Allaback, Sarah, 2009n856
Allaby, Michael, 2005n1511, 2007n1132, 2008n1307,
     2008n1314, 2008n1315, 2009n1300
Allan, Tony, 2007n1310
Allee, Nancy J., 2005n1423
Allegretto, Sylvia, 2006n151, 2008n236
Allen, Bob, 2009n1018
Allen, Catherine Judge, 2006n1380, 2007n1212,
     2007n1218
Allen, Craig H., 2006n1553
Allen, Damian, 2008n1275
Allen, David E., 2005n1347

Allen, Gary, 2008n1118
Allen, John O., 2005n454
Allen, Judy, 2007n1017, 2008n695
Allen, Mary Beth, 2006n766
Allen, Paul L., 2009n1114
Allen, Philip M., 2006n83
Allergy info for teens, 2007n1267
Alles, Gregory D., 2007n1081, 2008n1055
Allred, Barry J., 2009n1143
Allyn & Bacon social atlas of the US, 2008n55
Almanac of ...
     American educ 2005, 2006n277
     American educ 2006, 2007n238
     American employers, 2004 ed, 2005n228
     American employers, 2006 ed, 2006n228
     American employers, 2007 ed, 2008n225
     American pol 2008, 2008n619
     famous people, 8th ed, 2005n11
     famous people, 9th ed, 2008n11
     New York City, 2009n76
     state legislative elections, 3d ed, 2008n650
     the 50 states, 2007 ed, 2008n68
     the unelected 2004, 17th ed, 2005n713
     the unelected 2005, 18th ed, 2006n717
     the unelected 2006, 19th ed, 2007n586
     the unelected 2007, 20th ed, 2008n630
     the unelected 2008, 21st ed, 2009n655
Alpine plants of Europe, 2006n1298
Alrich, Peggy, 2009n1183
Alsop, Ronald J., 2007n251
Alternative energy, 2007n1322
Alternative publishers of bks in N America, 6th ed,
     2007n547
Altmaier, Elizabeth M., 2009n701
Altschiller, Donald, 2006n564
Alvarez-Smith, Alma, 2005n354
Alzheimer disease sourcebk, 4th ed, 2009n1260
AMA manual of style, 10th ed, 2008n798
Amazing animals of the world 1, 2008n1169
Amazing animals of the world 2, 2007n1184
Amazing animals of the world 3, 2007n1185
Amazing baby, 2009n1174
Ambrose, Gavin, 2009n842, 2009n861
America: a hist in art, 2009n855
America at the polls 1960-2004, 2007n616
America discovered, 2005n385
America in revolt during the 1960s & 1970s, 2008n405
America speaks, 2006n447
America the beautiful [Website], 2005n422
America votes 2005-06, 2008n643
America votes 25, 2005n719
America votes 26, 2003-04, 2006n732
America's best value colleges, 2007 ed, 2007n247
America's cosmetic doctors & dentists, 2d ed,
     2006n1411

America's founding charters, 2007n362
America's 101 fastest growing jobs, 8th ed, 2006n251
America's top doctors, 5th ed, 2006n1412
America's top doctors, 7th ed, 2008n1208
America's top 100 jobs for people without a 4-yr degree, 7th ed, 2005n241
America's top 101 computer & technical jobs, 2d ed, 2005n242
America's top 101 jobs for college graduates, 6th ed, 2006n252
America's top-rated cities 2004, 11th ed, 2005n852
America's top-rated cities 2005, 12th ed, 2006n847
America's top-rated cities 2006, 13th ed, 2007n751
America's top-rated cities 2007, 14th ed, 2008n769
America's top-rated cities 2008, 15th ed, 2009n778
America's top-rated smaller cities 2004/05, 5th ed, 2005n853
America's top-rated smaller cities 2006/07, 6th ed, 2007n752
America's top-rated smaller cities 2008/09, 7th ed, 2009n779
America's top 300 jobs, 9th ed, 2005n238
American art dir 2007-08, 61st ed, 2008n838
American artists II, 2008n840
American attitudes, 4th ed, 2005n67
American attitudes, 5th ed, 2009n59
American azaleas, 2005n1331
American Bar Assn gd to credit & bankruptcy, 2006n534
American Bar Assn legal gd for women, 2006n535
American bk trade dir 2005-06, 51st ed, 2006n648
American bk trade dir 2006-07, 52d ed, 2007n546
American bk trade dir 2008-09, 54th ed, 2009n590
American cars, 1946-59, 2009n1350
American cars, 1960 to 1972, 2005n1549
American Catholic Bible in the 19th century, 2007n1103
American Civil War, 2005n456
American Civil War, 2009n386
American College of Physicians complete home medical gd, 2d ed, 2005n1442
American colonist's lib [Website], 2005n437
American Congress, 2006n718
American conservatism, 2008n625
American counties, 5th ed, 2006n429
American dict of criminal justice, 3d ed, 2006n554
American dir of writer's gdlines, 5th ed, 2007n769
American environmental leaders, 2d ed, 2009n1331
American ethnic writers, 2009n949
American families in crisis, 2009n748
American first ladies, 2d ed, 2007n587
American folk songs, 2009n1021
American frontiersmen on film, 2006n1158
American generals of the Revolutionary War, 2008n572

American generations, 5th ed, 2006n827
American generations, 6th ed, 2009n770
American govt leaders, 2008n620
American govt on file, rev ed, 2005n714
American health, 2006n1422
American health, 2d ed, 2008n1219
American Heritage 1st dict, 2007n849
American Heritage abbrevs dict, 3d ed, 2006n2
American Heritage children's dict, updated ed, 2007n848
American Heritage college dict, 4th ed, 2008n854
American Heritage college thesaurus, 2005n962
American Heritage desk dict & thesaurus, 2006n941
American Heritage dict define-a-thon for the high school freshman, 2008n855
American Heritage dict define-a-thon for the high school graduate, 2008n856
American Heritage dict of phrasal verbs, 2006n962
American Heritage dict of the English lang, 4th ed, 2007n20
American Heritage gd to contemporary usage & style, 2006n950
American Heritage high school dict, 4th ed, 2008n857
American Heritage medical dict, new ed, 2008n1223
American Heritage sci dict, 2005n1282
American Heritage Stedman's medical dict, 2d ed, 2005n1432
American Heritage student dict, updated ed, 2007n850
American heroes, 2009n362
American hist [Website], 2009n371
American hist album, 2009n838
American hist through lit 1820-70, 2007n937
American hist through lit 1870-1920, 2007n938
American home front in WW II: almanac, 2005n410
American home front in WW II: biogs, 2005n411
American home front in WW II: primary sources, 2005n412
American Horticultural Society AHS great plant gd, rev ed, 2005n1311
American Horticultural Society A-Z ency of garden plants, rev ed, 2005n1310
American Horticultural Society garden plants & flowers, 2005n1319
American icons, 2007n1028
American incomes, 5th ed, 2006n828
American incomes, 6th ed, 2008n747
American Indian biogs, rev ed, 2006n334
American Indian chronology, 2008n320
American Indian contributions to the world series, 2006n338
American Indian culture, 2006n335
American Indian food, 2006n1285
American Indian hist online [Website], 2007n277
American Indian law deskbk, 3d ed, 2005n540
American Indian law deskbk, 2007 suppl, 2008n472

American Indian religious traditions, 2006n336

American Indian themes in YA lit, 2007n913

American Indian wars, 2008n318

American Indians in the early west, 2009n309

American law yrbk 2003, 2005n541

American law yrbk 2005, 2006n536

American law yrbk 2008, 2009n446

American lib dir [Website], 2006n590

American lib dir 2004-05, 57th ed, 2005n596

American lib dir 2005-06, 58th ed, 2006n589

American lib dir 2007-08, 60th ed, 2008n505

American lib dir 2008-09, 61st ed, 2009n491

American marketplace, 7th ed, 2006n829

American marketplace, 8th ed, 2008n748

American Medical Assn concise medical ency, 2007n1245

American Medical Assn family medical gd, 4th ed, 2006n1434

American men & women of sci, 22d ed, 2005n1279

American men & women of sci, 23d ed, 2007n1128

American men, 2d ed, 2007n728

American Midwest, 2008n69

American murder, 2009n471

American music librarianship, 2006n609

American natl biog [Website], 2008n17

American natl biog, suppl 2, 2006n20

American Naval hist, 3d ed, 2005n675

American opera singers & their recordings, 2005n1137

American plays & musicals on screen, 2005n1197

American pol leaders 1789-2005, 2006n719

American pol music, 2006n1072

American pol parties in the 21st century, 2007n593

American popular music: blues, 2006n1099

American popular music: classical, 2006n1088

American popular music: country, 2006n1100

American popular music: folk, 2006n1102

American popular music: jazz, 2006n1105

American popular music: rhythm & blues, rap, & hip-hop, 2006n1104

American popular music: rock & roll, 1109, 2006n1219

American presidents, 3d ed, 2007n588

American presidents attend the theatre, 2007n1058

American presidents in popular culture, 2007n1032

American regional folklore, 2005n1156

American Revolution, 2008n406

American Revolution, updated ed, 2008n407

American Revolutionary War, 2007n345

American rights series, 2006n537

American salaries & wages survey, 8th ed, 2006n235

American scientists, 2006n1251

American sexual behavior, 2007n708

American slang dict, 2007n846

American social reform movements: almanac, 2007n323

American social reform movements: biogs, 2007n324

American social reform movements: primary sources, 2007n325

American soldiers' lives: WW I, 2007n564

American songbk, 2007n1004

American statesmen, 2005n694

American time use, 2008n764

American verse project [Website], 2009n988

American villains, 2009n461

American voices, 2006n870

American wholesalers & distributors dir, 13th ed, 2005n188

American wholesalers & distributors dir, 14th ed, 2006n176

American wholesalers & distributors dir, 16th ed, 2008n190

American wholesalers & distributors dir, 17th ed, 2009n172

American women, 3d ed, 2007n729

American women conservationists, 2005n1536

American women stage directors of the 20th century, 2009n1073

American women's hist [Website], 2005n855

American women's hist online [Website], 2009n786

American writers, 2005n1060

American writers, suppl 17, 2009n950

American writers, suppl 18, 2009n951

Americans & their homes, 2d ed, 2006n830

Americans at war, 2006n439

Amit, Vered, 2005n319

Ammer, Christine, 2005n1118, 2006n1428, 2007n85

Amoia, Alba, 2005n986

Amory, Hugh, 2008n569

Amy Tan, 2005n1071

Analyses of 19th- & 20th-century music, 2008n962

Analytic dict of English etymology, 2009n887

Analyzing lib collection use with Excel, 2008n565

Anan, Ruth, 2007n1269

Anatomy of exercise, 2009n735

Anatomy of wonder, 5th ed, 2006n1018

Ancestors in German archives, 2005n363

Ancestral trails, 2d ed, 2007n290

Ancestry lib ed [Website], 2009n325

Ancient astronomy, 2006n1506

Ancient Canaan & Israel, 2006n116

Ancient Christian commentary on scripture CD-ROM [CD-ROM], 2006n1221

Ancient Greece, 2007n390

Ancient hist, 2006n494

Ancient Indian artifacts, v.1, 2009n837

Ancient Indus Valley, 2008n383

Ancient Mesopotamia, 2006n485

Ancient Mesopotamia, 3300-331 B.C.E., 2005n504

Ancient texts for N.T. studies, 2007n1101
Ancient texts for the study of the Hebrew Bible,
    2006n1220
Ancient world, 2008n451
Andersen, Robin, 2009n795
Anderson, Byron, 2007n541, 2007n547
Anderson, Cynthia, 2009n578
Anderson, D. Brian, 2006n1133
Anderson, Dan, 2008n88, 2009n83
Anderson, Dee, 2009n546
Anderson, Gary L., 2008n59
Anderson, James D., 2005n1114, 2005n1115,
    2006n1071, 2007n982, 2008n96, 2009n1009
Anderson, Malcolm G., 2007n1227
Anderson, Nancy D., 2006n1524
Anderson, Norman B., 2005n1417
Anderson, P. F., 2005n1423
Anderson, Rick, 2005n653
Anderson, Robert B., 2009n294
Andrea, Alfred J., 2005n521
Andrews, Susyn, 2005n1351
Andreychuk, Ed, 2006n1158
Andriamialisoa, Fanja, 2008n1181
Ang, Tom, 2009n866
Angehr, George R., 2009n1195
Angelini, Anthony, 2009n269
Angelo, Joseph A., Jr., 2005n1502, 2006n1265,
    2006n1503, 2007n1299
Angels A to Z, 2d ed, 2009n1091
Anglican young people's dict, 2005n1259
Anglophone & lusophone African women's writing
    [Website], 2006n1053
Anheier, Helmut K., 2008n727
Animal & plant anatomy, 2008n1148
Animal atlas, 2007n1183
Animal rights, 2005n1379
Animal rights, rev ed, 2008n1167
Animals are the issue, 2005n1376
Animated movie gd, 2007n1041
Anime ency, 2008n997
Annals of America, 2005n27
Annenberg pol fact check [Website], 2009n629
Annotated bibliog of works about Sir Winston S.
    Churchill, 2005n721
Annotated bibliog on the Mekong, 2009n94
Annotated computer vision bibliog [Website],
    2006n1471
Annual abstract of stats, no.141, 2005 ed, 2006n835
Annual register 2007, 248th ed, 2008n617
Annual register, 2008, 2009n38
Annual register of grant support 2004, 37th ed,
    2005n809
Annual register of grant support 2006, 39th ed,
    2007n707

Annual register of grant support 2007, 40th ed,
    2008n729
Annual register of grant support 2009, 42d ed,
    2009n750
Annual review of ...
    anthropology, v.32, 2003, 2005n322
    environment & resources, v.28, 2003, 2005n1540
    environmental & resources, v.29, 2004, 2006n1538
    global peace operations 2008, 2009n694
    pol sci, v.6, 2003, 2005n690
    pol sci, v.11, 2008, 2009n622
    psychology, v.55, 2004, 2005n743
    psychology, v.60, 2009, 2009n709
    public health, v.25, 2004, 2005n1427
    public health, v.29, 2009, 2009n1229
    sociology, v.29, 2003, 2005n791
    sociology, v.30, 2004, 2005n792
Ansell, Janis, 2005n1014
ANSS reviews [Website], 2008n295
Answering consumer health questions, 2009n587
Answers to the health questions people ask in libs,
    2009n532
Antarctic fishes, 2008n1182
Antebellum era, 2005n442
Antebellum period, 2005n461
Anthropology of food [Website], 2008n296
Anthropology review database [Website], 2006n320
AnthroSource [Website], 2008n297
Anti-Americanism, 2008n667
Antique & collectible dict, 2009n821
Antique Trader antiques & collectibles price gd 2005,
    20th ed, 2005n912
Antique Trader antiques & collectibles price gd 2006,
    2006n897
Antique Trader antiques & collectibles price gd 2007,
    2008n811
Antique Trader bk collector's price gd, 2d ed,
    2007n797
Antique Trader collectible paperback price gd,
    2009n824
Antique Trader furniture price gd, 3d ed, 2009n814
Antique Trader gd to fakes & reproductions, 4th ed,
    2008n812
Antiques 101, 2006n900
Antiques price gd 2008, 2009n820
Antiques Roadshow 20th-century collectibles,
    2005n910
Antisemitism, 2005n349
Antisemitism, 2006n346
Anton, Mauricio, 2005n1383
Ants of N America, 2008n1185
Anttiroiko, Ari-Veikko, 2007n39, 2008n43, 2009n36
Anzovin, Steven, 2008n26
APA dict of psychology, 2007n649
APA online [Website], 2006n1199

APIS: advanced papryological info system [Website], 2007n407

Appiah, Kwame Anthony, 2006n328

Appiani, Roberto, 2006n1516

Applebaum, Wilbur, 2006n1266

Aquariums, 2006n1381

Arab-American experience in the US & Canada, 2008n312

Arab Americans, 2006n332

Arab folklore, 2009n1032

Arabian Nights ency, 2005n1093

Arana, R. Victoria, 2008n956

Arat, Zehra F. Kabasakal, 2007n489

Archambault, Ariane, 2006n965, 2007n857, 2008n870

Archer, J. Clark, 2007n585

Archetypes & motifs in folklore & lit, 2006n1116

Archiplanet [Website], 2009n857

Architecture, 2007n816

Architecture of ...

England, Scotland, & Wales, 2006n931

France, 2007n817

Greece, 2005n947

Spain, 2006n932

Architectural inspiration, 2008n845

Archival info, 2005n600

Archives & archivists in the info age, 2006n613

Archives & the digital lib, 2008n522

Archives of traditional music [Website], 2008n961

ArchNet [Website], 2008n379

Argentina, 2009n120

Argentina, rev ed, 2006n414

Argote-Freyre, Frank, 2008n440

Ariew, Roger, 2005n1228

Aristotle bibliog [Website], 2006n1180

Arizona breeding bird atlas, 2006n1368

Armageddon now, 2006n764

Armed conflict database [Website], 2008n577

Armenti, Vincent T., 2005n1480

Armes, Roy, 2009n1061

Armitage, Allan M., 2005n1312, 2007n1155

Armitage's garden annuals, 2005n1312

Armitage's native plants for N American gardens, 2007n1155

Armstrong, Jeanne, 2009n769

Armstrong, Patrick H., 2007n308, 2008n1163

Arnesen, Eric, 2007n191, 2008n224

Arnett, Jeffrey Jensen, 2007n720, 2007n764, 2008n737, 2008n791

Arnold, Bill T., 2006n1222

Arnold, Guy, 2007n106, 2009n398

Arnold, James R., 2006n448

Arnold-Scriber, Theresa, 2008n388

Aron, Paul, 2009n47

Aron, Paul D., 2006n507, 2007n428

Around the world with histl fiction & folktales, 2005n1022

Arrighi, Barbara A., 2008n733

Arrigo, Gianni, 2006n227

Art & culture [Website], 2007n762

Art in world hist, 2005n943

Art market research, 2007n815

Art museum image gallery [Website], 2009n848

Art museum libs & librarianship, 2008n518

Art nouveau, 2005n911

Art of the piano, 3d ed, 2005n1134

Art of The Saint John's Bible, 2009n1099

Arthritis, 2009n1261

Arthritis sourcebk, 2d ed, 2005n1460

Arthurian writers, 2009n969

Artist's & graphic designer's market 2005, 2006n923

Artist's & graphic designer's market 2008, 2008n839

Artist's materials, 2006n925

Artists of Colonial America, 2005n932

Artists of the Renaissance, 2005n931

Artists of WW II, 2006n917

Arts & crafts, 2006n896

Arts & humanities through the eras, 2005n880

Artwalks in New York, 3d ed, 2005n940

Asafyev, Boris, 2008n974

Asante, Molefi Kete, 2005n333

Ash, Russell, 2006n51, 2009n40

Ashby, Bonnie Lee, 2008n1232

Ashcraft, W. Michael, 2008n1065

Asher, R. E., 2008n848

Asher, Robert, 2005n324

Ashkenazi, Michael, 2005n1304, 2008n1129

Ashley, Mike, 2007n781

Ashliman, D. L., 2007n1020

Asia-Pacific mktg info sourcebk, 2005n212

Asian American children, 2005n336

Asian American issues, 2005n337

Asian Americans, 2007 ed, 2008n313

Asian databk, 2005n839

Asian mktg data & stats 2007/08, 3d ed, 2009n196

Askeland, Lori, 2006n807

Assessing ref & user servs in a digital age, 2008n557

Assistantships & graduate fellowships in the mathematical scis 2005, 2006n1528

AssocationExecs.com [Website], 2009n134

Associated Press stylebk & briefing on media law, 39th ed, 2005n893

Associated Press stylebk & briefing on media law, 2008n799

Associationexecs.com [Website], 2007n29

Associations Canada 2007, 28th ed, 2008n35

Associations Canada 2008, 29th ed, 2009n27

Associations USA, 2005n37

Associations USA, 2d ed, 2007n30

Associations yellow bk, Summer 2005 ed, 2006n31

Associations yellow book, 2008 ed, 2009n28

Asthma info for teens, 2006n1442

Asthma sourcebk, 2d ed, 2007n1268

Astore, William J., 2008n597

Astronomy, 2005n1505

Astronomy, 2007n1305

At issue series, 2009n60

Athletic dvlpmt, 2009n733

Atkins, Stephen E., 2005n686, 2009n372

Atkinson, Michael, 2008n1013, 2009n1054

ATLA religion database [Website], 2005n1245

Atlantic coast conference men's basketball games, 2008n709

Atlas & survey of Latin American hist, 2007n117

Atlas A to Z, rev ed, 2005n368

Atlas of ...

    African-American hist, rev ed, 2008n308

    American hist, 2007n336

    American hist, 2008n386

    American military hist, 2006n658

    bird migration, 2008n1172

    climate change, 2007n1307

    Egyptian art, paperback ed, 2009n847

    endangered species, rev ed, 2009n1192

    food, rev ed, 2009n1144

    global dvlpmt, 2009n107

    human migration, 2008n740

    mammalian chromosomes, 2007n1207

    the Messier objects, 2009n1303

    race, ancestry, & religion in 21st-century Fla., 2007n64

    Thailand, 2005n101

    the Civil War, 2006n428

    the Middle East & N Africa, 2007n118

    the medieval world, 2006n487

    the world's langs, 2d ed, 2008n848

    the world's religions, 2d ed, 2009n1088

    US hist, rev ed, 2009n359

    woody plant stems, 2009n1180

Atterberry, Tara E., 2005n221, 2007n31, 2008n36

Attorney's ref on human anatomy, 2009n1176

Atwood, Christopher P., 2005n466

Atwood, Jerry L., 2005n1493

Audio dict, 3d ed, 2006n1084

Audio visual market place 2009, 37th ed, 2009n811

Augenbraum, Harold, 2006n350

Augustana Evangelical Lutheran church in print, 2008n1076

Augustine, Todd, 2006n1235

Ausmus, William A., 2009n1149

Aust, Anthony, 2006n538

Austin, Claire, 2006n1295

Austin, Peter, 2009n872

Australia, 5th ed, 2008n370

Australia, rev 4th ed, 2006n404

Australia, New Zealand, & the Pacific, 2006n1542

Australia, Oceania, & Antarctica, 2005n1542

Australian bed & breakfast bk 2007, 2008n371

Australian writers, 1975-2000, 2007n963

Author index to little mags of the mimeograph revolution, 2009n44

Author law A to Z, 2006n876

Authors & artists for YAs, v.55, 2005n877

Authors & artists for YAs, v.56, 2005n878

Authors & artists for YAs, v.57, 2005n879

Authors & artists for YAs, v.73, 2008n787

Author's hndbk, 2d ed, 2007n773

Autism & pervasive developmental sourcebk, 2009n1262

Autobiographical writings on Mexico, 2006n1063

Automotive Websites, 2d ed, 2007n1340

AV market place 2005, 33d ed, 2006n892

AV market place 2006, 2007n784

AV market place 2007, 2008n806

Avallone, Eugene A., 2007n1228, 2008n1200

Avalon project at Yale Law School [Website], 2006n508

Avasthi, Smita, 2005n513

Avery, Laura, 2009n12

Aviation century: the golden age, 2005n1546

Aviation century: war & peace in the air, 2007n1336

Aviation century: wings of change, 2006n1548

Aviation century: WW II, 2005n1547

Aviation security mgmt, 2009n1348

Awards, honors & prizes, 23d ed, 2005n38

Awards, honors & prizes, 24th ed, 2006n32

Awards, honors & prizes, 26th ed, 2008n36

Awe, Susan C., 2007n142

Axelrod, Alan, 2005n662, 2006n660m 2007n338, 2007n424, 2007n561, 2008n389, 2008n452

Axelrod-Contrada, Joan, 2009n213

Aycock, Wendell M., 2005n1052

Ayto, John, 2007n835, 2009n891

Ayurveda, 2009n1256

Ayurvedic herbs, 2008n1243

Aztecs, 2006n341

B-29 Superfortress, 2005n677

Babcock, Robert G., 2005n614

Baber, David, 2008n1012

Baby boom: Americans born 1946 to 1964, 4th ed, 2005n267

Baca, Murtha, 2008n527

Back & neck sourcebk, 2d ed, 2006n1435

Backgrounds to American lit series, 2007n946

Backroads of S Calif., 2006n399

Backsheider, Paula R., 2006n1046

Backyard astronomer's gd, 3d ed, 2009n1307

Bacon's media calendar dir 2004, 22d ed, 2005n902
Bacon's newspaper dir 2004, 52d ed, 2005n903
Bacon's TV/cable dir 2004, 18th ed, 2005n906
Bader, Philip, 2005n1058
Baechle, Thomas R., 2009n732
Baek, John Y., 2009n274
Baergen, Ralph, 2007n1061
Baggini, Julian, 2005n1226
Bahmueller, Charles F., 2008n70
Bahr, Howard M., 2005n346
Bailey, Alison, 2009n99
Bailey, Frankie Y., 2008n484
Bailey, James R., 2009n231
Bailey, Joseph A., Jr., 2007n455
Bailey, Lee W., 2006n1213
Bailey, Rayna, 2009n771
Bailey, Ronald A., 2006n1492
Baird, W. David, 2009n80
Baker, Brian, 2006n986
Baker, Chris, 2009n94
Baker, Deborah J., 2005n161, 2005n810, 2005n1508,
         2005n1509, 2006n143
Baker ency of Bible people, 2007n1096
Baker, John R., 2006n1331
Baker, Lawrence W., 2005n413, 2005n414, 2005n415,
         2005n837, 2005n838, 2005n1508
Baker, Lynda M., 2009n535
Baker, Nancy L., 2007n494
Baker, Patricia L., 2005n1272
Baker pocket gd to new religions, 2007n1074
Baker, William, 2009n973
Bakewell, Lisa, 2009n1231
Bakken, Gordon Morris, 2007n733, 2009n364
Bakker, Peter, 2005n952
Balaban, Naomi, 2005n1287, 2005n1340, 2009n1175
Bald, Margaret, 2007n867
Baldick, Chris, 2009n914
Balding, D. J., 2008n1199
Baldrige, Letitia, 2005n800
Bales, Kevin, 2006n581
Balkun, Mary McAleer, 2007n979
Ball, Howard, 2005n542, 2007n644
Balloffet, Nelly, 2006n612
Ballparks of the deadball era, 2009n719
Bally, John, 2007n1304
Bane, Charles, 2007n925
Banerjee, Kyle, 2009n575
Banking basics [Website], 2009n159
Banking tutor [Website], 2009n160
Banks, Arthur S., 2007n583, 2009n627
Banks, Cyndi, 2006n565
Banks, David P., 2006n1301
Bankston, Carl L., III, 2006n327, 2007n269,
         2007n735, 2008n443
Banned plays, 2005n1039

Barak, Gregg, 2009n465
Barancik, Sue, 2006n990
Barasi, Mary E., 2008n1126
Barber, Raymond W., 2008n515
Barker, Chris, 2007n265
Barker, Nicolas, 2005n920
Barkworth, Mary E., 2008n1150
Barnes-Svarney, Patricia, 2005n1519, 2006n1531
Barnet, Richard D., 2005n1142
Barnett, Colleen, 2007n926
Barnett, Douglas Q., 2009n1075
Barnett, Jeffrey E., 2009n710
Barnhart, Cynthia A., 2008n865
Barnhill, Georgia Brady, 2007n811
Barnhouse, Rebecca, 2005n1015
Barone, Michael, 2008n619
Barr, Catherine, 2005n1017, 2005n1018, 2006n997,
         2006n998, 2007n886, 2007n893, 2007n894,
         2009n284, 2009n919
Barr, Patty, 2007n517
Barr, Ronald G., 2006n822
Barrea-Marlys, Mirta, 2005n1219
Barrett, Carole A., 334, 2006n335
Barrett, Rosemary, 2005n1372
Barron, Neil, 2006n10182007n920
Barron's best buys in college educ, 8th ed, 2005n287
Barron's best buys in college educ, 9th ed, 2007n248
Barron's French-English dict, 2007n858
Barron's gd to …
    graduate business schools, 13th ed, 2005n288
    graduate business schools, 14th ed, 2006n285
    law schools 2005, 16th ed, 2005n289
    the most competitive colleges, 3d ed, 2005n290
    the most competitive colleges, 4th ed, 2006n286
Barron's profiles of American colleges 2005, 26th ed,
         2005n291
Barron's profiles of American colleges 2007, 27th ed,
         2007n243
Barron's Spanish-English dict, 2007n863
Barstow, Barbara, 2009n920
Bartel, Julie, 2005n644
Bartell, Patrice, 2008n515
Bartholomew, Craig G., 2007n1097
Bartle, Lisa R., 2007n889
Bartleby verse [Website], 2009n989
Bartlett, Patricia P., 2007n1215, 2007n1216,
         2007n1217
Bartlett, R. D., 2007n1215, 2007n1216, 2007n1217
Bartlett, Roger, 2007n671
Bartrop, Paul R., 2009n474
Barwick, Margaret, 2005n1369
Baseball bibliog, 2d ed, 2007n675
Baseball bks, 2008n708
Baseball cyclopedia, repr ed, 2006n777
Baseball novel, 2009n939

Baseball prospectus 2005, 2006n779
Baseball's retired nos, 2005n763
Basic lib skills, 5th ed, 2007n498
Basics of ...
   biology, 2005n1342
   economics, 2005n171
   genealogy ref, 2009n537
   physics, 2008n1329
   sociology, 2006n799
   western philosophy, 2005n1234
Basketball, 2006n785
Baskin, Ellen, 2005n1193
Baskind, Samantha, 2008n834
Basnight, Bobby L., 2009n1351
Bassett, Diane S., 2009n281
Bassett, T. D. Seymour, 2007n78
Bastian, Dawn E., 2006n1118
Bastianich, Joseph, 2006n1284
Bates, Gerri, 2006n1040
Batman filmography, 2005n1206
Batten, Donna, 2005n49, 2005n689, 2005n705,
     2006n689, 2008n44, 2008n1214, 2009n37
Battle of Iwo Jima, 2006n488
Battlefield, 2008n590
Battleground: business, 2008n152
Battleground: criminal justice, 2009n465
Battleground: environment, 2009n1332
Battleground: schools, 2009n242
Battleground: sci & tech, 2009n1125
Battleground: the media, 2009n795
Battleground: women, gender, & sexuality, 2009n787
Battleships, 2006n680
Bauer, Laurie, 2006n951
Baughman, Judith S., 2009n957
Baumeister, Roy F., 2008n677
Baumeister, Theodore, III, 2007n1228, 2008n1200
Baxter, Angus, 2009n319
Baxter, Craig, 2005n94
Bayer, Patricia, 2005n929
Bayley, Stephen, 2008n830
Bazirjian, Rosann, 2007n544
Bazler, Judith A., 2005n1335, 2005n1498
BC Almanac bk of greatest British Columbians,
     2007n18
Beach, Sara Ann, 2009n265
Beal, Alison M., 2009n1204
Beat culture, 2006n1033
Beath, Warren, 2006n1147
Beatty, Scott, 2006n1121
Beaty, H. Wayne, 2007n1225
Beaulieu, Elizabeth Ann, 2007n945
Becher, Anne, 2009n1331
Bechtel, Brenda, 2007n805
Beck, Jerry, 2007n1041
Beck, Susan E., 2008n559

Becker, Patricia C., 2007n746
Beckert, Jens, 2006n123
Beckley, L. E., 2009n1208
Beckman, James A., 2005n587
Bed & breakfast Ireland 2006, 2008n372
Bedford, Elizabeth A., 2009n658
Beer, Amy-Jane, 2007n1132
Beer, Jeremy, 2008n625
Beers, Mark H., 2007n1259
Beers, Sue R., 2006n758
Bees of the world, 2d ed, 2008n1186
Behrstock, Robert A., 2009n1199
Beidel, Deborah C., 2009n708
Beik, Millie Allen, 2006n236
Bekoff, Marc, 2006n1364, 2008n1165
Béland, Daniel, 2008n473, 2009n449
Beletsky, Les, 2007n1190
Belknap, Michal R., 2005n543
Bell, Alan W., 2005n1333
Bell, Dana, 2005n676
Bell, Steven M., 2005n121
Bell, Suzanne, 2005n565, 2009n466
Bellamy, Paul, 2009n696
Bellenir, Karen, 823, 2005n1172, 2005n1428,
     2005n1443, 2005n1446, 2005n1448,
     2005n1469, 2006n759, 2006n1442,
     2007n665, 2007n1256, 2007n1260,
     2007n1267, 2007n1268, 2008n183,
     2008n184, 2008n185, 2008n736, 2008n1253,
     2008n1254, 2009n279, 2009n1247,
     2009n1250, 2009n1260, 2009n1268,
     2009n1269
Beller, Susan Provost, 2008n336
Bellori, Giovan Pietro, 2008n832
Bendtsen, Birgitte Husted, 2006n1296
Benedetti, Joan M., 2008n518
Benedetto, Robert, 2009n1111
Benenson, Bob, 2008n628
Benewick, Robert, 2006n90
Benjamin, Carmen, 2006n971
Benjamin, Ruth, 2006n1171
Benjamin, Thomas, 2007n419
Bennett, Jennifer, 2006n1297
Bennett, Jim, 2009n837
Ben's gd to govt for kids [Website], 2008n631
Benson, Sonia, G., 2005n836, 2005n1377, 2006n342,
     2006n343, 2006n420, 2006n421, 2006n422,
     2007n326, 2007n327, 2007n328, 2008n432,
     2009n385
Bentley, Elizabeth Petty, 2006n355, 2006n356
BEOnline: business & economics online [Website],
     2006n125
Berard, Jeanette M., 2007n782
Berardi, Rosemary R., 2005n1481
Bercovitch, Jacob, 2006n741

Bercovitch, Sacvan, 2006n1070, 2007n947
Bergin, Thomas G., 2005n472
Bergquist, James M., 2009n387
Berkin, Carol, 2009n953
Berkowitz, Edward D., 2008n473, 2009n449
Berkshire ency of extreme sports, 2008n697
Berkshire ency of world hist, 2007n416
Berkshire ency of world sport, 2007n670
Berkwitz, Stephen C., 2007n1106
Berlan, Elise, 2009n1236
Berlin, Howard M., 2006n119
Berlitz Chinese dict, 2006n966
Berlitz complete gd to cruising & cruise ships 2008, 2008n363
Berlitz complete gd to cruising & cruise ships 2009, 18th ed, 2009n344
Berlitz Japanese dict, 2006n970
Berman, Alan, 2009n846
Berman, Milton, 2009n374
Berman, Neil S., 2008n820
Bernadowski, Carianne, 2009n936
Bernard, Edina, 2006n924
Bernier, Julie N., 2006n1454
Bernstein, Eckhard, 2005n109
Bernstein, Jared, 2006n151, 2008n236
Bernstein, Mark F., 2008n650
Bernstein, Saul, 2009n1259
Berry, Irene, 2007n483
Berry, S. Torriano, 2008n1014
Berry, Venise T., 2008n1014
Bertland, Linda, 2009n524
Berzok, Linda Murray, 2006n1285
Best bks for ...
    boys, 2009n933
    children, 8th ed, 2007n886
    children, suppl to the 8th ed, 2009n919
    high school readers grades 9-12, 2005n1017
    high school readers grades 9-12, suppl, 2007n894
    middle school & jr high readers grades 6-9, 2005n1018
    middle school & jr high readers, suppl, 2007n895
    YAs, 3d ed, 2008n881
Best bks of football facts & stats, rev ed, 2005n772
Best career & educ Web sites, 5th ed, 2007n205
Best customers, 3d ed, 2005n259
Best customers, 4th ed, 2007n229
Best DVDs you've never seen, just missed, or almost forgotten, 2006n1167
Best entry-level jobs, 2005n237
Best jobs for the 21st century, 4th ed, 2007n199
Best, Laura, 2005n358
Best new media, K-12, 2009n284
Best of hist Web sites, 2008n442
Best 170 law schools, 2007 ed, 2007n244
Best rose gd, 2005n1357

Best, Samuel J., 2006n686
Best songs of the movies, 2006n1164
Best 357 colleges, 2005 ed, 2005n292
Bethell, Leslie, 2009n412
Between you & I: a little bk of bad English, 2006n952
Betz, Hans Dieter, 2008n1059
Beumers, Birgit, 2006n1125
Bevilacqua, Michelle, 2006n942
Bevir, Mark, 2007n641, 2008n671
Beyond Jennifer & Jason, Madison & Montana, rev ed, 2005n367
Beyond picture bks, 3d ed, 2009n920
Beyond the Internet, 2008n560
BFI film & TV hndbk 2004, 21st ed, 2005n1209
Bhatta, Gambhir, 2006n750, 2007n640
Bhattacherje, S. B., 2007n95
Bianchi, Robert Steven, 2005n464
Biblical studies on the Internet, 2d ed, 2009n1095
Bibliographic checklist of African American newspapers, 2009n317
Bibliographic control of music, 1897-2000, 2007n505
Bibliographical hist of the study & use of color from Aristotle to Kandinsky, 2008n831
Bibliography of ...
    Africana per lit [Website], 2008n92
    criticism on S African lit in English [Website], 2006n1054
    medical & biomedical biog, 3d ed, 2007n1230
    modern American philosophers, 2006n1181
    modern British philosophers, 2005n1223
    modern Romani linguistics, 2005n952
    pol sci resources on the study of pol violence [Website], 2008n670
    the Samaritans, 3d ed, 2006n1245
    the writings of Sir Winston Churchill, 2007n627
Bibliography on American prints of the 17th through the 19th centuries, 2007n811
BiblioTravel [Website], 2006n1009
Bickel, Alexander M., 2008n478
Bickford, Charlene Bangs, 2009n365
Bienvenidos! Welcome! A handy resource gd for mktg your lib to Latinos, 2006n633
Bierbrier, Morris L., 2009n414
Big bk of ...
    beastly mispronunciations, 2d ed, 2007n823
    children's reading lists, 2007n515
    lib grant money 2006, 2006n591
    teen reading lists, 2007n516
Big curmudgeon, 2008n53
Bigelow, Barbara C., 2007n718
Biggs, Matthew, 2007n1149
Bignami, M., 2005n1403
Bilingual visual dict: French/English, 2007n859

Bilingual visual dict: German/English, 2007n861
Bilingual visual dict: Spanish/English, 2007n864
Billboard albums, 6th ed, 2007n1003
Billboard ency of classical music, 2005n1136
Billboard hot 100 annual 1955-2005, 2008n981
Billboard illus ency of …
    country music, 2009n1018
    jazz & blues, 2007n1011
    music, 2005n1139
    opera, 2006n1092
Billboard top adult songs 1961-2006, 2008n982
Billboard's hottest hot 100 hits, 4th ed, 2008n983
Bilovsky, Frank, 2005n768
Bingham, Ann, 2005n1157
Binnewies, Stefan, 2009n1303
Bio-bibliography for Biruni, 2007n1060
Bioethics & medical issues in lit, 2006n1012
Biographical connections series, 2007n9
Biographical dict of …
    American economists, 2007n130
    Australian & New Zealand economists, 2008n149
    British economists, 2005n137
    Central & E Europe in the 20th century, 2009n108
    modern world leaders 1900 to 1991, 2005n683
    psychologists, psychiatrists, & psychotherapists,
        2009n698
    Scottish women, 2007n388
    Scottish women, paperback ed, 2008n778
    social & cultural anthropology, 2005n319
Biographical ency of …
    artists, 2006n916
    Islamic philosophy, 1119, 2007n1062
    the modern Middle East & N Africa, 2008n142
    the Supreme Court, 2007n440
Biographies: lib of economics & liberty [Website],
    2005n138
Biographies of women mathematicians [Website],
    2005n1527
Biography ref bank [Website], 2009n7
Biography resource center [Website], 2009n8
Biography today, v.12, 2003, 2005n12
Biography today, v.13, 2006n15
Biography today, v.14—2005 annual cumulation,
    2007n10
Biography today, v.15, 2008n12
Biography today, v.16—2007 annual cumulation,
    2009n9
Biography today: authors, v.16, 2005n997
Biography today: authors, v.18, 2007n875
Biography today: business leaders, 2006n118
Biography today: scientists & inventors, v.10,
    2006n1250
Biography today: scientists & inventors, v.11,
    2007n1129
Biography today: sports, v.12, 2005n750

Biography today: sports, v.13, 2006n767
Biography today: sports, v.14, 2007n669
Biology, 2008n1139
Biology matters! 2005n1339
Biology resources in the electronic age, 2005n1335
Biomes of Earth, 2005n1343
Biotechnology, 2008n1140
Biotechnology & genetic engineering, rev ed,
    2005n1413
Biotechnology & genetic engineering, 3d ed,
    2009n1219
Bird almanac, rev ed, 2005n1384
Bird, David M., 2005n1384
Bird-finding gd to Panama, 2009n1195
Birder's companion, 2008n1179
Birds, 2007n1191
Birds of Australia, 7th ed, 2006n1375
Birds of Costa Rica, 2008n1176
Birds of the Carolinas, 2d ed, 2007n1195
Birds of the raincoast, 2005n1390
Birds of the world, 2007n1190
Birds of the world, 2008n1177
Birds of the world, 2009n1196
Birkland, Thomas A., 2008n610
Birth of stars & planets, 2007n1304
Birth of the Bill of Rights, 2005n701
Birth of the church, 2005n1263
Birx, H. James, 2007n259
Bisbort, Alan, 2009n800
Bischoff, James L., 2009n475
Bishop, A. C., 2006n1515
Bishop, M., 2008n1199
Bispham, Edward, 2007n384
Bitton, Davis, 2009n1106
BizStats.com [Website], 2006n126
Bjarkman, Peter C., 2006n776
Bjerga, Alan, 2006n717, 2007n586
Black academic's gd to winning tenure—without
        losing your soul, 2009n278
Black, Allida, 2008n496
Black American military leaders, 2008n575
Black Americans, 2007 ed, 2008n311
Black, Brian, 2009n1340
Black death, 2005n475
Black, Fiona A., 2006n656
Black lit criticism, 2009n903
Black, Robert J., 2006n1339, 2008n1159
Black stars who made baseball whole, 2006n783
Black submariners in the US Navy, 1940-75,
    2006n672
Blackburne-Maze, Peter, 2005n1367
Black's medical dict, 40th ed, 2005n1433
Black's medical dict, 41st ed, 2007n1246
Blackwell companion to the sociology of families,
    2006n806

Blackwell ency of sociology, 2007n689
Blackwell, Jean, 2009n530
Blair, Jayne E., 2007n363
Blake, N. F., 2005n1079
Blakemore, Robbie G., 2007n810
Blamires, Cyprian P., 2007n632
Blanchard, Mary Loving, 2008n953
Blankman, Drew, 2006n1235
Blechman, Hardy, 2006n908
Bleeding hears, corydalis, & their relatives,
    2009n1160
Bleiler, Richard J., 2005n1046
Blevins, Dave, 2005n56, 2007n593
Bloch, Henry, 2007n987
Block, A. G., 2008n642
Block, Marylaine, 2005n634
Blocker, Jack S., Jr., 2005n820
Blood & circulatory disorders sourcebk, 2d ed,
    2006n1443
Blood, bedlam, bullets, & badguys: a reader's gd to
    adventure/suspense fiction, 2005n1040
Blood on the stage, 2009n1079
Bloom, Ken, 2007n1004
Bloom's literary ref online [Website], 2009n904
Bloomfield, Victor A., 2009n1135
Blowers, Paul M., 2006n1230
Blu-bk production dir 2004, 2005n1182
Blu-bk production dir 2005, 2006n1129
Blu-bk production dir 2006, 2007n1037
Blueberries, cranberries, & other vacciniums,
    2005n1332
Blueprint for your lib mktg plan, 2006n636
Blume, Kenneth J., 2006n742
Blumenfeld, Robert, 2007n1038
Bly, Robert W., 2007n771
BNA's dir of state & fed courts, judges, & clerks,
    2006n522
BNA's dir of state & fed courts, judges, & clerks
    online [Website], 2006n523
Boas, Gideon, 2009n475
Boatner, M. T., 2006n953
Boatner, Mark M., III, 2007n356
Boatner, Maxine T., 2005n959
Bob Dylan, 2d ed, 2009n1023
Bob Dylan ency, 2007n1008
Bob Hope films, 2006n1162
Bobick, James E., 2005n1287, 2005n1340, 2009n1175
Bobick, Sandra, 2005n1340
Bobinski, George, 2008n551
Bockstruck, Lloyd deWitt, 2006n362, 2008n34
Boczek, Boleslaw A., 2006n517
Bodybuilding anatomy, 2009n726
Boersma, P. D., 2007n1169
Boettcher, Jennifer C., 2005n165

Boffey, Julia, 2007n981
Bogar, Thomas A., 2007n1058
Bogart, Dave, 2005n601
Bogdanov, Vladimir, 2005n1147, 2005n1148
Bogucki, Peter, 2008n455, 2009n424
Bolan, Kimberly, 2007n528, 2008n546, 2009n576
Boles, Janet K., 2005n869, 2008n781
Bolton, Lesley, 2008n347
Bomarito, Jessica, 2005n999, 2007n930
Bonewitz, Ronald Louis, 2006n1512
Bonner, Kimberly M., 2007n521
Bonney, Rick, 2005n1386
Book: the life story of a tech, 2006n657
Book crush, 2008n891
Book of ...
    alternative medicine, 2008n1239
    emblems, 2005n942
    rule, 2005n691
    US govt jobs, 9th ed, 2006n245
    US govt jobs, 10th ed, 2008n241
Book review index, 2004 cum, 2005n55
Book review index, 2005 cum, 2006n53
Book review index: 2008 cum, 2009n42
Booker, Bryan D., 2009n304
Booker, M. Keith, 2005n1082, 2007n880
Bookman's price index, v.76, 2005n916
Bookman's price index, v.77, 2005n917
Bookman's price index, v.78, 2005n918
Bookman's price index, v.79, 2005n919
Bookman's price index, v.88, 2009n825
Bookman's price index, v.89, 2009n826
Bookreporter.com [Website], 2006n972
Books & beyond, 2009n938
Books & writers [Website], 2006n975
Books kids will sit still for 3, 2007n891
Books on early American hist & culture 1961-70,
    2008n387
Bookshelf of our own, 2005n1007
Booktalking bonanza, 2009n549
Boomgaard, Peter, 2008n1345
Boon, Brooke, 2005n785
Boon, Heather, 2005n1453
Boorkman, Jo Anne, 2005n1415, 2009n530
Booth, Chris, 2005n254
Booth, Douglas, 2008n697
Booth, Heather, 2008n535
Booth, Wayne C., 2008n801, 2009n807
Borchert, Donald M., 2007n1068
Bordman, Gerald, 2005n1220
Borisenko, Victor E., 2006n1397
Born this day, 2d ed, 2008n1004
Borner, A., 2009n1180
Borrero, Mauricio, 2005n113
Bortz, Alfred B., 2008n1327
Boschung, Herbert T., Jr., 2005n1392

Boslaugh, Sarah, 2008n1225, 2009n1237
Boss, Suzie, 2009n249
Boston symphony orchestra, 2009n1016
Boston women's health bk collective [Website],
    2005n1441
Bosworth Field to Bloody Mary, 2005n486
Bosworth, Mary, 2005n563
Botany for gardeners, rev ed, 2006n1302
Botterweck, G. Johannes, 2005n1249, 2007n1099
Bouchard, Claude, 2005n1447
Boucher, Brian, 2009n801
Boucquey, Thierry, 2006n980, 2006n981
Boughter, Judith A., 2005n340
Boullata, Joseph I., 2005n1480
Boulware, Rick, 2005n145
Boum, Aomar, 2007n88
Boundary-related links [Website], 2008n352
Boundas, Constantin V., 2008n1050
Bounty & donation land grants in British colonial
    America, 2008n341
Bowden, John, 2006n1229, 2009n1105
Bowers, Helen, 2006n912
Bowers, Jennifer, 2006n1047
Bowker annual 2004, 49th ed, 2005n601
Bowker annual lib & bk trade almanac 2007, 52d ed,
    2008n510
Bowker, John, 2009n125
Bowles, E. Joy, 2005n1454
Bowlin, Gary L., 2005n1405
Bowling, Lawson, 2006n694
Bowman, Alan K., 2007n429
Bowman, John S., 2005n666, 2006n389
Bowman, Vibiana, 2005n646, 2008n738
Box full of tales, 2009n554
Boxing filmography, 2005n1207
Boyce, Charles, 2006n1050
Boyd, Todd, 2009n1047
Boyer, Bret A., 2009n711
Boynton, Victoria, 2006n856
Brackett, Virginia, 2006n1044, 2009n1001
Bradfield, Bill, 2006n1224
Bradford, James C., 2007n555
Bradford, Marlene, 2008n1309
Bradley, Carol June, 2006n609
Bragg, Steven M., 2008n173
Braggins, John E., 2005n1374
Brahms & his world, 2007n994
Brahms, William B., 2006n44
Brain disorders sourcebk, 2d ed, 2006n1444
Branch librarians' hndbk, 2005n638
Branch, G. M., 2009n1208
Branch, M. L., 2009n1208
Branch, Robert Maribe, 2005n317, 2006n317,
    2009n288
Brands & their companies, 27th ed, 2006n177

Brands & their companies, 29th ed, 2008n191
Brannen, Daniel E., Jr., 2006n720, 2009n385
Branney, T. M. E., 2006n1344
Brash, Kate, 2009n1321
Brassey's D-day ency, 2005n660
Braukman, Stacy, 2006n851
Braun, Carlos Rodríguez, 2006n120
Brave new words, 2008n903
Bray, George A., 2005n1447
Brazil, 2008n139
Brazin, Lillian R., 2008n1124
Breakup of Yugoslavia & its aftermath, rev ed,
    2005n117
Breast cancer sourcebk, 2d ed, 2006n1445
Breen, Nancy, 2006n879
Bregel, Yuri, 2005n465
Bremer, Francis J., 2007n1115
Brennan, Carol, 2007n324
Brennan, Gerald, 2007n998
Brennan, Scott, 2009n1345
Brereton, Patrick, 2008n1015
Bresler, Robert J., 2005n544
Breuilly, Elizabeth, 2006n1210
Brewer, John D., 2005n65
Brewer, Robert Lee, 2005n892, 2008n796, 2009n804
Brewer's dict of Irish phrase & fable, 2006n1115
Brezianu, Andrei, 2008n125
Brick, Cindy, 2009n840
Brickell, Christopher, 2005n1310
Bridges, Karl, 2008n905
Brief hist of ...
    Afghanistan, 2008n105
    Canada, 2d ed, 2008n426
    Central America, 2d ed, 2008n137
    Egypt, 2009n416
    India, 2006n92
    Iraq, 2009n129
    Israel, 2005n127
    Israel, 2d ed, 2009n131
    Mexico, rev ed, 2005n498
    Pakistan, 2009n105
    Peru, 2005n122
    Russia, 2009n116
    Saudi Arabia, 2005n129
    the Caribbean, 2008n440
    the Netherlands, 2009n409
Brier, Bob, 2009n415
Bright, William, 2005n389
Brignoli, Héctor Pérez, 2005n119
Brill dict of religion, 2007n1075
Briscoe, James R., 2006n1082
Bristow, Barbara A., 2008n512
Bristow, Michael Jamieson, 2008n969
Britain & the Americas, 2006n746
Britannica concise ency, rev ed, 2007n21

Britannica illus sci lib, 2009n1126
Britannica learning zone [Website], 2009n18
Britannica online [Website], 2008n23
British & Irish paintings in public collections, 2008n846
British & Irish poets, 2008n954
British Colonial America, 2009n388
British film noir gd, 2009n1056
British horror film locations, 2009n1058
British military operations in Egypt & the Sudan, 2009n600
British poetry mags 1914-2000, 2008n948
British women romantic poets, 1789-1952 [Website], 2005n1100
British writers, suppl 14, 2009n968
Broadfield, Douglas C., 2007n260
Broadwater, Robert P., 2008n572, 2008n573
Broadway musicals, 1943-2004, 2006n1173
Brock, Jim P., 2007n1204
Brockman, Norbert C., 2007n79
Brody, Lisa R., 2006n474
Brogan, Kathryn S., 2005n891, 2005n892
Bronner, Simon J., 2007n1018
Bronson, Fred, 2008n983
Brooke, Kathleen Lusk, 2007n1224
Brooking, Tom, 2005n469
Brothers grim, 2008n1034
Brothers, Linda, 2006n247
Brotherton, David C., 2009n468
Brottman, May, 2009n1029
Browing, Don S., 2008n1059
Brown, A. Peter, 975, 2008n976
Brown, Anthony Gary, 2007n952
Brown, Bryson, 2008n1144
Brown, George E., 2005n1373
Brown, Gerry, 2005n761
Brown, Gregory S., 2005n480
Brown, Lois, 2006n1034
Brown, Meg Lota, 2006n860
Brown, Nikki L. M., 2009n302
Brown, Paul Martin, 2006n1345, 2008n1153, 2008n1154, 2008n1155
Brown, S. Whittington, 2006n539
Brown, Stephen F., 2008n1044
Brown, Stewart J., 2008n1086
Brown, Stuart, 2006n1189, 2007n1063
Brown v. Board of Educ, 2006n547
Brown-May, Andrew, 2007n104
Browne, Lynn, 2009n444
Brownson, Ross C., 2005n1427
Brownstone, David M., 2005n427
Brucato, Thomas W., 2005n763
Bruccoli, Matthew J., 2009n957
Bruce, Christine Susan, 2009n504

Bruce, Colin R., II, 2006n902, 2007n800, 2009n830, 2009n831
Bruce, Steve, 2007n691
Brukner, Peter, 2007n1277, 2008n1257
Brulotte, Gaëtan, 2007n922
Brumley, Rebecca, 2005n605, 2006n592, 2007n537
Brummitt, R. K., 2008n1157
Brunas, John, 2008n1030
Brunas, Michael, 2008n1030
Brune, Lester, 2006n659
Brunier, Serge, 2006n1507, 2008n1301
Bruns, Roger, 2009n315
Brunsdale, Mitzi M., 2007n927
Brush, Timothy, 2006n1369
Bryan, Cheryl, 2009n509
Bryan, John E., 2006n1300
Bryan, T. Scott, 2009n1322
Bryant, Geoff, 2008n1136
Bryner, John, 2005n612
Bryson, Bill, 2009n802
Bryson, Scott, 2009n952
Bryson's dict for writers & editors, 2009n802
Brzuzy, Stephanie, 2009n787
Buchanan, Colin, 2007n1108
Buchanan, Paul D., 2006n437
Bucher, Greta, 2009n410
Buckland, Raymond, 2005n744, 2006n762
Buckley, Bruce, 2005n1512
BuddhaNet [Website], 2007n1105
BuddhaNet: Buddhist studies [Website], 2005n1252
Buddhism in world cultures, 2007n1106
Buddhist experience in America, 2005n1253
Budgeting & debt mgmt, 2008n183
Buel, Richard, Jr., 2007n346
Buenker, John D., 2006n324, 2006n440
Buenker, Joseph, 2006n440
Buffington, Robert M., 2005n120
Building character through multicultural lit, 2005n611
Building digital libs, 2009n575
Building the world, 2007n1224
Buildings of Rhode Island, 2005n82
Buildings of W.Va, 2006n76
Built in America [Website], 2009n858
Buisseret, David, 2008n359
Bulbs for garden habitats, 2006n1304
Bulbs in containers, 2006n1307
Bull, Stephen, 2005n661
Bulls, bears, boom, & bust, 2007n133
Bullwinkle, Davis, 2008n92
Bulmer-Thomas, Victor, 2007n188
Bumgarner, Jeffrey B., 2005n570, 2009n447, 2009n462
Bunch, Bryan, 2005n1281, 2005n1285
Bungert, Patricia J., 2008n189, 2009n171

Bunson, Matthew, 2005n1262, 2005n1266, 2008n1092, 2009n1101
Bunting, Saskia Schier, 2005n363
Burbidge, John W., 2009n1081
Burchett, Kenneth E., 2008n831
Burg, David F., 2006n449, 2007n344, 2008n407
Burger, Joanna, 2007n1191
Burgess, Michael, 2006n1227, 2007n928
Burgess, Stanley M., 2007n1109
Burgin, Robert, 2006n601, 2007n977
Burke, John Gordon, 2006n59
Burke, John J., 2007n529
Burkhardt, Joanna M., 2007n525
Burki, Shahid Javed, 2007n127
Burleson, Daphne, 2008n1303
Burlingame, Dwight F., 2005n808
Burney, Charles, 2005n500
Burney, William, 2007n567
Burnham, Bill, 2009n349
Burnham, Mary, 2009n349
Burnie, David, 2005n1378, 2005n1522, 2007n1174
Burns, Grant, 2006n1031
Burns, James MacGregor, 2005n147
Burns, Jennifer Bobrow, 2007n208, 2008n240
Burns, Jim, 2009n1197
Burns, Paul, 2006n1226
Burns, Richard Dean, 2006n659, 2008n393
Burns, Tom, 2005n981, 2005n982, 2005n983, 2005n1024, 2005n1025
Burns, Vincent, 2006n566
Burns, William, 2009n862
Burns, William E., 2006n1267
Burrell, Barbara, 2005n715
Burrelle's transcripts [Website], 2005n907
Burstein, Stanley M., 2006n482
Burt, Daniel S., 2005n1062, 2009n906, 2009n937
Burt, Elizabeth V., 2005n438
Burt, Richard, 2007n960
Burton, Orville Vernon, 2008n421
Burton, Patricia A., 2009n1102
Burton, Robert, 2006n1370
Burton, William C., 2007n441m 2008n465
Burton's legal thesaurus, 4th ed, 2007n441
Busby, Mark, 2006n70
Buschman, John E., 2008n553
Buse, Dieter K., 2006n103
Bush, Douglas E., 2007n996
Bush, John, 2005n1148
Business background investigations, 2009n145
Business forms on file, 2004 ed, 2005n166
Business forms on file, 2006n145
Business forms on file, 2006, rev ed, 2007n143
Business forms on file, 2007 ed, 2008n167
Business info resources [Website], 2006n127

Business orgs, agencies, & pubs dir, 16th ed, 2005n148
Business orgs, agencies, & pubs dir, 19th ed, 2006n129
Business plans hndbk, v.14, 2009n230
Business rankings annual, 2004, 2005n168
Business rankings annual, 2006, 2006n147
Business rankings annual, 2007, 2007n144
Business rankings annual, 2009, 2009n143
Business school buzz bk, 2005 ed, 2005n293
Business stats of the US 2004, 9th ed, 2005n169
Business stats of the US 2005, 10th ed, 2006n148
Business stats of the US 2006, 11th ed, 2007n145
Business stats of the US 2007, 12th ed, 2008n168
Business stats of the US 2008, 13th ed, 2009n144
Bussagli, Marco, 2005n946
Bussolini, Karen, 2006n1303
Buta, Ronald J., 2008n1297
Butin, Dan W., 2009n269
Butler, Charles, 2007n911
Butler, Ken, 2008n89
Butler, Marian, 2005n7, 2005n8, 2006n12, 2006n13, 2007n6, 2007n7
Butler, Rebecca P., 2005n608
Butler, Robert J., 2009n967
Butler's lives of the saints, v.1, 2006n1226
Butt, John, 2006n971, 2007n988
Butt, John J., 2007n420
Butterflies of W Africa, 2006n1386
Butterworth, Neil, 2006n1079
Buying & contracting for resources & servs, 2005n653
Buzzacott, Francis H., 2009n728
Bynagle, Hans E., 2007n1059
Bynoe, Yvonne, 2007n1009
Bynum, Helen, 2008n1205
Bynum, W. F., 2008n1205
Byrd, Susannah Mississippi, 2006n633
Byrne, Alex, 2008n548
Byrne, James P., 2009n113
Byrne, Joseph P., 2005n475, 2009n1223
Byworth, Tony, 2009n1018

Cabaniss, Amy D., 2009n1216
Cafferty, Steve, 2006n1352
Cain, Paul D., 2008n725
Cain, Stephen, 2007n822
Cairncross, Bruce, 2006n1513
Calarco, Tom, 2009n363
Caldecott, Julian, 2006n1390
Caldwell, Paul, 2005n1467
Caldwell, Wilma R., 2005n1461
Calhoun, Milburn, 2007n67, 2008n82
Calhoun, Scott, 2009n1157

California cities, towns, & counties, 2007 ed, 2008n74
California pol almanac 2007-08, 2008n642
Calimano, Ivan E., 2009n544
Call to America, 2006n58
Callahan, Daren, 2008n714
Callan, Georgina O'Hara, 2009n845
Callanan, Gerard A., 2007n190
Callary, Edward, 2009n340
Callenbach, Ernest, 2009n1337
Callicott, J. Baird, 2009n1333
Calloway, Stephen, 2006n927
Calore, Michela, 2007n961
Calvert, John, 2008n1096
Camberon, Averil, 2007n429
Cambridge advanced learner's dict, 2d ed, 2006n943
Cambridge aerospace dict, 2006n1400
Cambridge ancient hist, v.12, 2d ed, 2007n429
Cambridge companion to …
     American Judaism, 2006n1244
     Renaissance philosophy, 2008n1049
     the age of Constantine, 2006n477
     the age of Constantine, 2007n394
     20th-century English poetry, 2009n1007
Cambridge dict of …
     classical civilization, 2007n377
     English place-names, 2006n390
     human biology & evolution, 2006n1313
     sociology, 2008n715
Cambridge economic hist of Latin America, 2007n188
Cambridge ency of child dvlpmt, 2006n822
Cambridge ency of hunters & gatherers, paperback ed, 2006n800
Cambridge ency of stars, 2007n1300
Cambridge English pronouncing dict, 17th ed, 2007n825
Cambridge essential English dict, 2006n944
Cambridge gd to English usage, 2006n883
Cambridge gd to lit in English, 3d ed, 2007n878
Cambridge hist of …
     American lit, v.3: prose writing, 2007n947
     American lit, v.4: 19th-century poetry, 2006n1070
     British theatre, 2006n1178
     Christianity, v.6: reform & expansion 1500-1660, 2009n1113
     Christianity, v.7, 2008n1086
     18th-century philosophy, 2007n1072
     18th-century pol thought, 2007n579
     English lit, 1660-1780, 2006n1045
     Irish lit, 2007n965
     Latin America, v.9: Brazil since 1930, 2009n412
     libs in Britain & Ireland, 2007n495
     Russia, v.1, 2007n397
     Russia, v.2: imperial Russia, 2007n398
     Russia: v.3, the 20th century, 2008n438

     sci, v.3: early modern sci, 2007n1140
     17th-century music, 2007n988
     Spanish lit, 2006n1065
     Turkey, v.4, 2009n411
Cambridge hndbk of personal relationships, 2007n662
Cambridge hndbk of the learning scis, 2007n53
Cambridge idioms dict, 2d ed, 2007n841
Cambridge illus dict of astronomy, 2009n1304
Cambridge Mozart ency, 2006n1080
Cambridge phrasal verbs dict, 2007n826
Campaign & election reform, 2005n717
Campaign & election reform, 2d ed, 2009n668
Campaign ads [Website], 2009n630
Campbell, Ballard C., 2009n366
Campbell, Colton, 2006n726
Campbell, Gordon, 2007n790, 2008n835
Campbell, Jonathan A., 2005n1399
Campbell-Jack, Campbell, 2007n1113
Campus legends, 2006n1117
Canada & Arctic N America, 2008n1351
Canada's Prime Ministers, MacDonald to Trudeau, 2008n654
Canadian almanac & dir 2006, 159th ed, 2006n3
Canadian almanac & dir 2007, 160th ed, 2008n3
Canadian almanac & dir 2008, 161st ed, 2009n2
Canadian bks in print, 2004: author & title index, 2005n7
Canadian bks in print, 2004: subject index, 2005n8
Canadian bks in print, 2005: author & title index, 2006n12
Canadian bks in print, 2005: subject index, 2006n13
Canadian bks in print, 2006: author & title index, 2007n6
Canadian bks in print, 2006: subject index, 2007n7
Canadian churches, 2008n844
Canadian environmental dir 2007, 12th ed, 2008n1342
Canadian environmental dir 2008, 13th ed, 2008n1343
Canadian insurance claims dir 2008, 76th ed, 2009n185
Canadian paintings, prints, & drawings, 2008n842
Canadian Parliamentary gd 2008, 2009n669
Canadian romance authors' networks (CRAN) [Website], 2006n1017
Canadian who's who 2004, v.39, 2005n25
Canadian who's who 2005, v.40, 2006n22
Canadian who's who 2006, v.41, 2007n19
Canadian who's who 2007, v.42, 2008n22
Canadian who's who 2008, 2009n16
Canby, Courtlandt, 2008n357
Cancer dict, 3d ed, 2008n1251
Cancer hndbk, 2d ed, 2008n1252
Cancer info for teens, 2005n1461
Cancer sourcebk, 5th ed, 2008n1253
Cancer sourcebk for women, 3d ed, 2007n1270
Cancer survivorship sourcebk, 2008n1254

Candelaria, Cordelia Chavez, 2005n354
Cannings, C., 2008n1199
Cantlon, Marie, 2007n1080
Capital punishment, 3d ed, 2006n570
Capon, Brian, 2006n1302
Cappiello, Paul, 2006n1355
Capturing readers with children's choice bk awards, 2007n517
Car & its future, 2005n1548
Cardiovascular diseases & disorders sourcebk, 3d ed, 2006n1449
Career discovery ency, 6th ed, 2007n198
Career ideas for teens series, 2006n243
Career info center, 9th ed, 2007n209
Career opportunities in ...
    advertising & public relations, 4th ed, 2006n244
    aviation & the aerospace industry, 2006n248
    banking, finance, & insurance, 2d ed, 2008n246
    computers & cyberspace, 2d ed, 2005n249
    conservation & the environment, 2008n247
    educ & related servs, 2d ed, 2007n212
    engineering, 2007n223
    forensic sci, 2009n216
    health care, 3d ed, 2008n245
    journalism, 2008n240
    law & the legal industry, 2d ed, 2008n243
    law enforcement, security, & protective servs, 2d ed, 2006n249
    lib & info sci, 2006n595
    photography, 2007n222
    pol, govt, & activism, 2d ed, 2009n213
    sci, 2d ed, 2009n217
    the nonprofit sector, 2007n208
    the automotive industry, 2006n254
    the armed forces, 2d ed, 2008n249
    the energy industry, 2009n228
    the fashion industry, 2d ed, 2008n253
    the Internet, video games, & multimedia, 2008n251
    the music industry, 5th ed, 2005n245
    the publishing industry, 2006n259
    the sports industry, 3d ed, 2005n246
    the travel industry, 2005n239
    the visual arts, 2007n210
    theater & the performing arts, 3d ed, 2007n221
    TV & cable, 2007n224
    writing, 2007n225
Career resource gd to grants, scholarships, & other financial resources, 2008n286
Careers in business, 5th ed, 2006n258
Careers in intl affairs, 8th ed, 2009n214
Careers in travel, tourism, & hospitality, 2d ed, 2006n247
Carey, Charles W., Jr., 2005n695, 2006n1251, 2007n1130

Caribbean, 5th ed, 2006n415
Caribbean, updated ed, 2008n374
Caribbean & S Asian writers in Canada, 2008n939
Caribbean folklore, 2008n991
Caribbean popular music, 2006n1108
Carland, Maria Pinto, 2009n214
Carlin, Richard, 1100, 2006n1102
Carlisle, Rodney P., 2005n666, 2006n661, 2006n703, 2007n281, 2007n365, 2007n430, 2008n328, 2008n391, 2008n405, 2008n408, 2008n418, 2008n460, 2008n591, 2009n367, 2009n418
Carlito, M. Delores, 2006n1061
Carlson, Delbert G., 2009n1164, 2009n1165
Carlson, Janet F., 2009n262
Carlson, Karen J., 2005n1440
Carlson, Liisa D., 1164, 2009n1165
Carmack, Sharon DeBartolo, 2006n358, 2009n320
Carmack's gd to copyright & contracts, 2006n358
Carmichael, Robert S., 2008n1309
Carnagie, Julie L., 2006n423
Carnes, Mark C., 2006n20, 2008n409
Carnivores of British Columbia, 2009n1204
Carolina starwatch, 2008n1298
Carpan, Carolyn, 2005n1016
Carpenter, Bil, 2007n1015
Carpenter, Richard C., 2006n1549, 2009n1349
Carr, Deborah, 2009n739
Carr, Jo Ann, 2009n522
Carr, William R., 2009n1179
Cars & culture, 2005n1550
Carson, Clayborne, 2009n299
Cartelli, Antonio, 2009n1292
Carter, John, 2005n920
Carter, Ruth C., 2007n509
Carter, Tim, 2007n988
Carter yrs, 2007n590
Cartron, Jean-Luc E., 2009n1189
Cartwright, John H., 2006n986
Carvell, Linda P., 2006n595
Carwile, Mike, 2006n898, 2007n794, 2009n815, 2009n816
Casale, Giuseppe, 2006n227
Cash & credit info for teens, 2006n171
Cashmore, Ellis, 2005n323
Caso, Frank, 2009n129, 2009n485
Caspari, Ann K., 2009n567
Casper, Scott E., 2008n570
Cassell, Dana K., 2006n802, 2007n1272
Cassell, Kay Ann, 2007n538
Cassell's chronology of world hist, 2006n492
Casstevens, Frances H., 2006n450
Castagno, John, 2008n840, 2009n853
Castillo, Susan, 2006n1036
Casting might-have-beens, 2005n1202
Castles of Scotland, 2006n405

Castro, Ivan A., 2008n331

Cat owner's home veterinary hndbk, 3d ed, 2009n1164

Catala, Rafael, 2005n1114, 2005n1115, 2006n1071, 2008n960, 2009n1009

Cataloging & classification, 3d ed, 2008n528

Cataloging & organizing digital resources, 2006n617

Cataloging cultural objects, 2008n527

Cataloging of audiovisual materials & other special materials, 5th ed, 2009n541

Catalogue of Medieval & Renaissance ms in the Beinecke rare bk & ms lib Yale Univ, 2005n614

Catalogue of music for organ & instruments, 2006n1085

Catalysis from A to Z, 3d ed, 2008n1286

CatalB, Rafael, 2007n982

Cates, Jo A., 2005n897

Catherwood, Christopher, 2007n422

Cathey, H. Marc, 2005n1310, 2005n1319

Catholic bk of quotations, 2005n1268

Catholic experience in America, 2006n1238

Catholic schools in the US, 2005n280

Catholic spirit, 2009n1115

Catholicism & sci, 2009n1114

Cathy, Florence, 2008n813

Cats eyewitness companions, 2007n1198

Cats of Africa, 2008n1191

Cattleyas & their relatives, 2005n1359

Causer, Peggy, 2007n743

Causin, Susan, 2009n352

Cave, Alfred A., 2005n439

Cavendish, Richard, 2009n347

Cavin, Andrew I., 2006n16

Cawdrey, Robert, 2008n851

Cawthon, Elisabeth A., 2005n545

Cayton, Andrew, 2008n69

Cazes, Jack, 2006n1401

CD-ROMs in print, 18th ed, 2005n9

Celebration of women writers [Website], 2005n976

Celebrity culture in the US, 2009n1048

Celebrity death certificates 2, 2006n1128

CELT: Corpus of electronic texts [Website], 2005n494

Celt culture, 2007n114

Celtic culture, 2006n104

Celtic mythology A to Z, 2005n1163

Censorship in the Arab world, 2007n120

Censorship, 2009n485

Center for intellectual property hndbk, 2007n521

Central America, 2d ed, 2008n375

Central & S Eastern Europe 2007, 7th ed, 2008n116

Central Asia, 2006n85

Central Intelligence Agency, 2007n605

Cerny, Rosanne, 2007n511

Cervantes ency, 2005n1098

Cesari, Jocelyne, 2008n1098

Cesnola collection: terracottas [CD-ROM], 2005n951

Cetus links [Website], 2006n1470

Chalmers, David, 2006n1182

Chamberlin, Stacey L., 2005n1437

Chambers bk of facts 2006, 2006n4

Chambers concise dict, 2005n953

Chambers dict of literary characters, 2005n1044

Chambers fact finder, 2005n2

Chambers film factfinder, 2007n1050

Chambers hist factfinder, 2006n509

Chambers, Paul, 2007n1315

Chambers ref atlas, 8th ed, 2006n370

Chambers sports factfinder, 2006n773

Chambers synonyms & antonyms, 2005n963

Chambers thesaurus, 2005n964

Champion, Dean John, 2006n554, 2008n491

Chan, Lois Mai, 2008n528

Chan, Ming K., 2007n94

Chan, Simon, 2009n1110

Chance, Rosemary, 2009n547

Chandler, Alfred D., Jr., 2009n635

Chandler, C. Ray, 2008n1145

Chandler, Robin L., 2008n522

Chanes, Jerome A., 2005n349

Chaney, Lillian H., 2009n148

Chang, In-Young, 2007n1167

Chang, Kai, 2006n1395

Chang, Laurence, 2009n360

Change in the weather, 2005n1511

Changing face of govt info, 2008n519

Chape, Stuart, 2009n1347

Chaplik, Dorothy, 2006n919

Chapman, Bert, 2005n730, 2009n603

Chapman, Victoria L., 2005n533

Charles, John, 2007n898

Charton, Barbara, 2008n1324

Charts of modern & postmodern church hist, 2005n1265

Chase court, 2005n552

Chase, Robert, 2008n977

Chase's calendar of events 2006, 49th ed, 2006n5

Chase's calendar of events 2007, 2008n4

Chavalas, Mark W., 2005n515

Cheathem, Mark R., 2009n394

Checks & balances, 2006n720

Chemical & biological warfare, 2d ed, 2007n572

Chemical composition of everyday products, 2006n1497

Chemical compounds, 2007n1292

Chemistry, 2005n1492

Chemistry, 2008n1285

Chemistry matters! 2008n1289

Chermak, Steven, 2008n484

Chernow, Barbara A., 2008n560, 2009n774

Cherokee ency, 2008n322

Chervenka, Mark, 2008n812

Chess results 1947-50, 2009n730

Chess world championships, 3d ed, 2009n731

Chesworth, Ward, 2009n1142

Chi, Tsung, 2006n721

Chicago gd to landing a job in academic biology, 2008n1145

Chicago gd to writing about numbers, 2005n894

Chicago gd to your career in sci, 2009n1135

Chicago manual of style online [Website], 2007n775

Chicano & Chicana lit, 2007n972

Chidester, Jeffrey L., 2006n699

Child abuse sourcebk, 2005n801

Child labor, 2006n237

Child poverty in America today, 2008n733

Childhood sexual abuse, 2d ed, 2008n479

Childhoods of the American presidents, 2006n696

Children & consumer culture in American society, 2009n765

Children & youth in adoption, orphanages, & foster care, 2006n807

Children & youth in sickness & in health, 2005n826

Children with disabilities in America, 2007n698

Children's & YA lit by Native Americans, 2005n1021

Children's & YA lit hndbk, 2007n893

Children's authors & illustrators too good to miss, 2005n1028

Children's bk review index, v.29, 2003, 2005n1032

Children's bks: awards & prizes, 2005 ed, 2006n1003

Children's catalog, 19th ed, 2007n502

Children's folklore, 2009n1033

Children's illus ency, 6th ed, 2007n22

Children's jukebox, 2d ed, 2008n963

Children's lit [Website], 2007n887

Children's lit in action, 2009n557

Children's lit review, v.96, 2005n1023

Children's lit review, v.97, 2005n1024

Children's lit review, v.98, 2005n1025

Children's night sky atlas, 2005n1501

Children's writer's & illus market 2006, 18th ed, 2006n877

Children's writer's & illus market 2008, 2008n793

Chilton, John, 2005n1150

Chilvers, Ian, 2005n937

China, 10th ed, 2006n400

China, 2008n368

China, 2009n99

China today, 2006n89

Chinese mythology A to Z, 2005n1165

Chinese natural cures, 2007n1264

Chinese religions in contemporary societies, 2007n1085

Ching, Francis D. K., 2008n843

Chinua Achebe ency, 2005n1082

Chironis, Nicholas P., 2008n1202

Chisick, Harvey, 2006n496

Choosing the right college 2008-2009, 2008n284

Choron, Harry, 2007n1200

Choron, Sandra, 2007n1200

Choueiri, Youssef M., 2006n483

Chow, Cheryl, 2007n1273

Chow, James H., 2007n1273

Chrisp, Peter, 2007n391

Christensen, Karen, 2007n670

Christensen, Karen, 2008n552, 2008n668

Christian chronology [Website], 2005n1255

Christian philosophy A-Z, 2008n1045

Christian writers' market gd 2005, 2006n880

Christian writers' market gd 2007, 2008n797

Christianity reader, 2008n1087

Christianson, Stephen G., 2006n6

Christmas ency, 2d ed, 2006n1120

Christopher, Connie, 2005n639

Christopher Lee filmography, 2005n1204

Christopher, Peter, 2008n845

Chronic illness dir [Website], 2006n1414

Chronicle of the Roman Republic, 2005n495

Chronologies of modern terrorism, 2009n464

Chronology of ...

American hist, 2009n368

American Indian hist, updated ed, 2007n276

American lit, 2005n1062

communication in the US, 2005n885

educ in the US, 2007n236

housing in the US, 2008n767

immigration in the US, 2009n768

intl orgs, 2009n672

Jane Austen & her family, 2008n928

sci, 2007n1133

the American Revolution, 2009n370

the Cold War 1917-92, 2006n659

the war at sea, 1939-45, 3d rev ed, 2006n669

transportation in the US, 2005n1545

US—Iraqi relations, 1920-2006, 2008n662

world Christianity, 2009n1105

world terrorism, 1901-2001, 2005n562

Chryssides, George D., 2007n1076, 2009n1107

Church, Audrey, 2009n516

Church, Glyn, 2008n1137

Churchill, Nicholas, 2005n1128

CIAO: Columbia Intl Affairs online [Website], 2005n725

Cibulka, James G., 2009n252

Cicciomessere, Roberto, 2008n608

Ciment, James, 2007n52, 2007n347, 2007n358, 2007n554, 2008n308, 2008n402, 2008n582, 2008n584, 2009n376

Cinema review [Website], 2006n1134

Cinema spot [Website], 2006n1152

Cinema yr by yr 1894-2004, 2005n1195

CineMedia [Website], 2006n1153
Cite it right, 2d ed, 2007n778
Cite it right, 3d ed, 2008n800
Cite right, 2007n779
Cities & buildings collections [Website], 2009n859
Cities & growth, 2008n772
Cities & water, 2009n780
Cities of the Middle East & N Africa, 2007n122
Cities of the US, 6th ed, 2009n781
City crime rankings, 10th ed, 2005n571
City crime rankings, 12th ed, 2006n575
City crime rankings, 13th ed, 2007n477
City crime rankings, 14th ed, 2008n492
City profiles USA 2006-07, 8th ed, 2007n319
City profiles USA 2008-09, 9th ed, 2009n350
Civil rights revolution, 2005n421
Civil War, 423, 2005n459
Civil War almanac, 2008n384
Civil War America, 1850 to 1875, 2008n420
Civil War & reconstruction, 2009n367
Civil War Medal of Honor recipients, 2008n573
Civil War navies 1855-83, 2007n568
Civil War suits in the US court of claims, 2007n361
Civil wars of the world, 2008n579
Civilian's gd to the U.S military, 2008n596
Civilizations of Africa, 2009n85
Clamen, Stewart M., 2006n1142
Clancy, Laurie, 2005n103
Clans & families of Ireland, 2005n360
Clark, David S., 2008n466
Clark, George B., 2006n668, 2009n612
Clark, J. Ransom, 2008n592
Clark, Jerome, 2006n763
Clark, John, 2006n763
Clark, John O. E., 2007n1132
Clark, Judith Freeman, 2007n364, 2008n720
Clark, Kelly James, 2005n1229
Clark, Leigh A., 2007n472
Clark, Lewis J., 2006n1346
Clark, M., 2006n968
Clark, Noreen M., 2005n1427
Clark, Richard P., 2007n210
Clark, Robert, 2006n983
Clark, Robin E., 2008n720
Clark, William W., 2007n383
Clarke, Steve, 2006n584, 2006n585
Class & society in Shakespeare, 2009n974
Class in America, 2008n58
Classes in classical ballet, 2008n1011
Classic experiments in psychology, 2006n760
Classic garden plans, 2005n1330
Classic home video games 1972-84, 2008n1272
Classical & medieval lit criticism, v.66, 2005n977
Classical & medieval lit criticism, v.67, 2005n978
Classical & medieval lit criticism, v.68, 2005n979

Classical & medieval lit criticism, v.69, 2005n980
Classical Japanese reader & essential dict, 2008n873
Classical studies, 2d ed, 2007n403
Claudio, Virginia S., 2005n1418
Clausen, Tammy Hennigh, 2005n1050
Clayton-Emmerson, Sandra, 2007n381
Clean air hndbk, 4th ed, 2009n1338
Clegg, Stewart R., 2009n231
Clemens, Raymond, 2009n598
Clements checklist of birds of the world, 6th ed,
    2008n1173
Clements, James F., 2008n1173
Clements, Jonathan, 2008n997
Clements, William M., 2006n1114
Clemson Univ men's basketball games, 2009n720
Clifford, Denis, 2009n484
Clifton, Keith E., 2009n1010
Climate change, 2009n1321
Climate change 2007, 2008n1311
Climate change in context, 2009n1316
Clinical sports medicine, 3d ed, 2007n1277
Clinton yrs, 2005n702
Clive, Peter, 2007n994
Clodfelter, Micheal, 2009n604
Clouds R Us.com [Website], 2009n1310
ClueLass.com & the mysterious home page [Website],
    2005n1047
Coakes, Elayne, 584, 2006n585
Coale, Joseph M., III, 2006n381
Coastal gd to S Africa, 2009n1209
Coates, Paul M., 2006n1282
Coatsworth, John H., 2007n188
Cobb, Boughton, 2006n1333
Cobblestone online [Website], 2009n43
Cochran, Moncrieff, 2008n270
Cochrane, James, 2006n952
Cody, Gabrielle H., 2008n1039
Coenraads, Robert R., 2006n1514
Coerver, Don M., 2005n120
Cogan, Brian, 2007n1013
Cohen, Laura B., 2009n506
Cohen, Norm, 2006n1103, 2009n1021
Cohen, Richard E., 2008n619
Cohen, Ronald D., 2009n1022
Cohen, Ronald I., 2007n627
Cohen, Saul, 2008n349
Cohen, Saul B., 2009n337
Cohen, Selma Jeanne, 2005n1188
Cohn, John M., 2006n634
Cohn, Rella Israly, 2009n328
Cohn-Sherbok, Dan, 2006n347
Coile, D. Caroline, 2006n1376
Colbert, Judy, 2005n239
Cold War, 2007n563
Cold War, 2008n580

Cold War presidency, 2008n649
Colditz, Graham A., 2008n1250
Cole, Forrest, 2008n1222
Cole, James H., 2005n95
Cole, John Y., 2006n587
Coleman, Arthur, 2008n944
Coleman, Bud, 2009n1080
Coleman, Hardin L. K., 2009n257
Coleman, Marilyn, 2008n722
Coleman, Philip, 2009n113
Coleman, Tina, 2009n548
Collaborating for project-based learning for grades
    9-12, 2009n519
Collaboration & the school lib media specialist,
    2006n604
Collaborative strategies for teaching reading
    comprehension, 2009n523
Collection dvlpmt issues in the online environment,
    2007n519
Collection dvlpmt policies, 2005n622
Collection mgmt & strategic access to digital
    resources, 2006n597
Collection mgmt for youth, 2006n605
Collection of computer sci bibliogs [Website],
    2006n1472
Collector's ency of American composition dolls,
    1900-50, v.2, 2006n904
Collector's ency of Depression glass, 18th ed,
    2008n813
Collector's gd to antique radios, 6th ed, 2005n926
Collector's gd to antique radios, 7th ed, 2008n823
Colledge, J. J., 2007n566
College blue bk, 31st ed, 2005n294
College blue bk, 32d ed, 2006n287
College blue bk, 34th ed, 2008n277
College Board bk of majors, 2006n288
College Board college cost & financial aid hndbk
    2005, 25th ed, 2006n311
College Board college hndbk 2005, 42d ed, 2005n295
College Board college hndbk 2006, 43d ed, 2006n289
College Board intl student hndbk 2005, 18th ed,
    2005n310
College Board intl student hndbk 2007, 2007n254
College Board scholarship hndbk 2005, 8th ed,
    2005n307
College Board scholarship hndbk 2006, 9th ed,
    2006n302
College buzz bk, 2005n296
College financing info for teens, 2009n279
College majors & careers, 6th ed, 2009n277
College majors hndbk with real career paths &
    payoffs, 2d ed, 2005n247
College money hndbk 2006, 23d ed, 2006n312
College student's research companion, 4th ed,
    2008n564

Collin, Robert W., 2006n722, 2007n645
Collin, Robert William, 2009n1332
Collins, Deborah, 2009n1259
Collins, Joan, 2009n517
Collins, Ross F., 2009n432
Colomb, Gregory G., 2008n801, 2009n807
Colonial America, 2007n347, 2007n365
Colonial America, 2008n408
Color answer bk, 2006n914
Color ency of hostas, 2005n1350
Columbia companion to American hist on film,
    2005n1210
Columbia companion to 20th-century philosophies,
    2008n1050
Columbia documentary hist of religion in America
    since 1945, 2006n1211
Columbia ency of modern drama, 2008n1039
Columbia gazetteer of the world [Website], 2008n349
Columbia gazetteer of the world, 2d ed, 2009n337
Columbia gd to ...
    African American hist since 1939, 2007n273
    Asian American lit since 1945, 2007n962
    contemporary African American fiction, 2006n1035
    E African lit in English since 1945, 2009n977
    Hiroshima & the bomb, 2008n413
    Irish American hist, 2006n345
    online style, 2d ed, 2007n780
    the Latin American novel since 1945, 2008n942
    W African lit in English since 1945, 2009n978
Columbia Granger's index to poetry in anthologies,
    13th ed, 2008n959
Columbia Granger's index to poetry in collected &
    selected works, 2d ed, 2005n1113
Columbia hist of ...
    American TV, 2008n1031
    Jews & Judaism in America, 2009n313
    Latinos in the US since 1960, 2005n353
    post-WW II America, 2008n409
    20th-century French thought, 2007n1064
    20th-century French thought, paperback ed,
        2008n1051
Columbia lit hist of E Europe since 1945, 2009n980
Columbia River Basin ethnic hist archives [Website],
    2006n432
Columbia world dict of Islamism, 2008n1097
Comaroff, Jean, 2005n322
Combined membership list 2004-05, 2006n1529
Combs, Cindy C., 2008n483
Commins, David, 2005n130
Commire, Anne, 2007n755, 2008n779
Commission on presidential debates [Website],
    2009n631
Commodity yrbk 2003, 2005n260
Common phrases & where they came from, 2d ed,
    2009n894

Commonwealth universities yrbk 2005, 79th ed, 2007n245
Community colleges, 2006n301
Community sourcebk of county demographics 2004, 16th ed, 2005n833
Community sourcebk of county demographics 2006, 18th ed, 2007n730
Community sourcebk of ZIP code demographics 2006, 20th ed, 2007n731
Companies & their brands, 26th ed, 2005n189
Companies & their brands, 29th ed, 2008n192
Companion ency of geography, 2d ed, 2008n358
Companion to …
    American children's picture bks, 2006n1002
    contemporary pol philosophy, 2d ed, 2009n623
    cultural geography, 2005n68
    emblem studies, 2009n327
    Faulkner studies, 2005n1067
    Japanese hist, 2007n372
    19th-century Britain, 2005n487
    sci fiction, 2006n1028
    the American west, 2005n440
    the Civil War & Reconstruction, 2005n441
    the 18th-century English novel & culture, 2006n1046
    the hist of the Middle East, 2006n483
    the lits of Colonial America, 2006n1036
Companions of Champlain, 2009n318
Comparative gd to …
    American elem & secondary schools 2005, 3d ed, 2005n285
    American elem & secondary schools 2006, 4th ed, 2007n241
    American elem & secondary schools 2007, 5th ed, 2008n264
    American hospitals 2005, 2006n1415
    American hospitals, 2d ed, 2008n1209
    American suburbs 2005, 3d ed, 2006n848
    American suburbs 2007, 4th ed, 2008n773
Comparative world atlas, 3d ed, 2006n371
Comparative world atlas, rev ed, 2009n329
Competitive colleges 2006, 2006n300
Complementary & alternative medicine info for teens, 2008n1240
Complementary & alternative medicine sourcebk, 3d ed, 2007n1262
Complete bk of …
    baby names, 2008n347
    business schools, 2004 ed, 2005n297
    law schools, 2004 ed, 2005n298
    medical schools, 2004 ed, 2005n299
Complete compost gardening gd, 2009n1159
Complete copyright, 2006n629
Complete dict of symbols, 2006n920

Complete dir for …
    pediatric disorders 2005, 3d ed, 2005n1457
    pediatric disorders 2008, 4th ed, 2008n1246
    pediatric disorders [Website], 2005n1458
    pediatric disorders [Website], 2008n1247
    people with chronic illness 2005/06, 7th ed, 2006n1413
    people with chronic illness 2007/08, 8th ed, 2008n1210
    people with disabilities 2003/04, 12th ed, 2005n798
    people with disabilities 2005, 13th ed, 2006n803
    people with disabilities 2006, 14th ed, 2007n699
    people with disabilities 2008, 16th ed, 2008n717
    people with disabilities 2009, 17th ed, 2009n744
    people with disabilities [Website], 2005n799
    people with disabilities [Website], 2007n700
    people with disabilities [Website], 2008n718
Complete dir of disabilities [Website], 2006n804
Complete dir of large print bks & serials 2005, 2006n14
Complete ency of natural healing, rev ed, 2007n1265
Complete Fla. beach gd, 2009n349
Complete gd to …
    acquisitions mgmt, 2005n626
    artic wildlife, 2007n1188
    cruising & cruise ships 2006, 16th ed, 2007n318
    market breadth indicators, 2007n153
    nutrition in primary care, 2008n1127
    prehistoric life, 2007n1315
    the snakes of southern Africa, 2d ed, 2006n1391
Complete houseplant survival manual, 2006n1336
Complete hydrangeas, 2008n1137
Complete learning disabilities dir 2004/05, 11th ed, 2005n313
Complete learning disabilities dir 2005/06, 12th ed, 2006n314
Complete learning disabilities dir 2007, 13th ed, 2007n255
Complete learning disabilities dir 2008, 14th ed, 2008n288
Complete learning disabilities dir 2009, 15th ed, 2009n280
Complete learning disabilities dir [Website], 2005n314
Complete learning disabilities dir [Website], 2007n256
Complete learning disabilities dir [Website], 2008n289
Complete mental health dir 2004, 4th ed, 2005n739
Complete mental health dir 2006, 5th ed, 2007n659
Complete mental health dir 2008, 6th ed, 2009n704
Complete mental health dir [Website], 2005n740
Complete mental health dir [Website], 2007n660
Complete natural gd to breast cancer, 2005n1462
Complete natural medicine gd to the 50 most common medicinal herbs, 2005n1453
Complete price gd to watches, 2007 ed, 2007n807

Complete price gd to watches, 2008 ed, 2008n826
Complete RFID hndbk, 2009n559
Complete royal families of ancient Egypt, 2006n484
Complete sportsman's ency, 2d repr ed, 2009n728
Comprehensive, annotated bibliog on Mahatma
    Gandhi, v.2, 2008n109
Comprehensive hndbk of ...
    clinical health psychology, 2009n711
    personality & psychopathology, 2008n683
    psychological assessment, 2006n758
    social work & social welfare, 2009n759
Comprehensive Indonesian-English dict, 2005n973
Compton's by Britannica 2007, 2008n24
Compton's by Britannica 2008, 2009n19
Compton's by Encyclopaedia Britannica 2005,
    2007n23
Computer & info systems abstracts [Website],
    2006n1276
Computer industry, 2006n1482
Computers, 2006n1481
Computing reviews [Website], 2006n1473
Conant, Craig, 2006n514
Concise Corsini ency of psychology & behavioral sci,
    3d ed, 2006n753
Concise dict of Bible origins & interpretation,
    2008n1069
Concise dict of modern medicine, 2007n1250
Concise dinosaur ency, 2005n1522
Concise ency of computer sci, 2006n1476
Concise ency of investing, 2008n174
Concise major 21st-century writers, 2007n871
Concise Oxford American dict, 2007n827
Concise Oxford American thesaurus, 2007n855
Concise Oxford dict of archaeology, 2d ed, 2009n357
Concise Oxford English dict, 11th ed, 2005n28
Concise Oxford-Duden German dict, 3d ed, 2006n968
Concise rules of APA style, 2007n776
Concordance to the major poems of Edward Taylor,
    2009n1008
Conde, Roberto Cortes, 2007n188
Condon, Rebecca A., 2005n1138
Condra, Jill, 2009n844
Conductor's gd to 19th-century choral-orchestral
    works, 2009n1015
Cone, Temple, 2008n957
Confederate sheet music, 2005n1116
Conflict between India & Pakistan, 2009n96
Conflicts over natural resources, 2008n1350
Congdon, Kristin G., 2009n867
Congenital disorders sourcebk, 2d ed, 2008n1233
Congress A to Z, 5th ed, 2009n639
Congress & the nation XI: 2001-04, 2007n606
Congress & the nation series 1945-2004 [Website],
    2007n607
Congress of the US, 3d ed, 2007n620

Congressional districts in the 2000s, 2005n716
Congressional roll call 2004, 2006n723
Congressional roll call 2005, 2007n608
Congressional roll call 2007, 2009n656
Congressional staff dir: summer 2004, 70th ed,
    2005n703
Congressional staff dir [Website], 2005n704
Congressional yellow bk, Summer 2005, 2006n704
Conley, Richard S., 2008n626
Conley, Robert J., 2008n322
Conley, Tim, 2007n822
Conn, P. Michael, 2009n1212
Connecticut municipal profiles, 2007 ed, 2008n77
Connecting YAs & libs, 3d ed, 2005n619
Connell, Royal W., 2005n673
Conner, Susan P., 2005n481
Connor, Brian, 2008n1275
Connor, Elizabeth, 2006n610, 2007n499, 2007n692
Connors, Sarah, 2009n738
Conrad, Tweed, 2007n966
Conran, Terence, 2008n830
Conroy, Mike, 2006n1119
Conservation dir 2005-06, 50th ed, 2007n1326
Conservative Christians & pol participation, 2006n735
Considine, Glenn D., 2006n1493, 2009n1134
Conspiracies & secret societies, 2007n1030
Conspiracy theories in American hist, 2005n424
Constable, Nick, 2006n486
Constitutional amendments series, 2009n448
Constitutional convention of 1787, 2006n446
Constitutions of the world, 3d ed, 2008n481
Consultants & consulting orgs dir, 27th ed, 2005n149
Consultants & consulting orgs dir, 30th ed, 2008n157
Consultants & consulting orgs dir suppl, 27th ed,
    2005n150
Consumer Asia 2004, 11th ed, 2005n213
Consumer Asia 2006, 13th ed, 2006n212
Consumer Asia 2009, 2009n197
Consumer China 2005, 10th ed, 2006n213
Consumer China 2009, 14th ed, 2009n198
Consumer E Europe 2004-05, 12th ed, 2005n216
Consumer E Europe 2005/06, 13th ed, 2006n217
Consumer E Europe 2006/07, 14th ed, 2007n186
Consumer E Europe 2008/09, 2009n199
Consumer Europe 2004/05, 20th ed, 2005n217
Consumer intl 2003/04, 2005n206
Consumer intl 2005/06, 12th ed, 2006n202
Consumer intl 2008/09, 2009n191
Consumer Latin America 2004, 2005n222
Consumer Latin America 2006, 13th ed, 2006n221
Consumer Latin America 2009, 2009n203
Consumer Middle East 2006, 8th ed, 2006n223
Consumer sourcebk, 17th ed, 2005n180
Consumer sourcebk, 18th ed, 2006n160
Consumer sourcebk, 21st ed, 2009n155

Consumer USA 2004, 2005n261
Consumer USA 2006, 10th ed, 2006n268
Consumer USA 2009, 13th ed, 2009n236
Consumer W Europe 2006/07, 22d ed, 2007n187
Consumer W Europe 2008/09, 2009n200
Consumer's gd to dietary supplements & alternative
    medicines, 2008n1241
Consumer's gd to lab tests, 2006n1427
Consumer's gd to mental health servs, 2008n684
Contagious diseases sourcebk, 2005n1443
Contemporary Africa database [Website], 2006n1055
Contemporary American ethnic poets, 2005n1103
Contemporary black biog, v.42, 2005n327
Contemporary black biog, v.43, 2005n328
Contemporary black biog, v.44, 2005n329
Contemporary black biog, v.45, 2005n330
Contemporary Chinese Societies [CD-ROM],
    2008n106
Contemporary ency of herbs & spices, 2007n1150
Contemporary Hindu, 2005n1269
Contemporary literary criticism, v.189, 2005n981
Contemporary literary criticism, v.190, 2005n982
Contemporary literary criticism, v.191, 2005n983
Contemporary Middle East, 2008n146
Contemporary Middle East, 2009n128
Contemporary musicians, v.60,
    2008n964Contemporary musicians, v.61,
    2008n965
Contemporary philosophy of the mind [Website],
    2006n1182
Contemporary postcolonial & postimperial lit in
    English [Website], 2006n973
Contemporary women's issues [Website], 2005n856
Contemporary writers in the UK [Website],
    2006n1042
Contemporary youth culture, 2007n719
Contescu, Christian I., 2005n1401
Conti, Peter S., 2009n1306
Continuum complete intl ency of sexuality, updated
    ed, 2005n816
Continuum ency of ...
    animal symbolism in art, 2005n939
    British philosophy, 2007n1065
    children's lit, 2005n1029
    modern criticism & theory, 2005n1003
    popular music of the world, v.3-7, 2006n1094
    YA lit, 2007n908
Controversial cinema, 2009n1070
Conway, Erik M., 2007n1145, 2008n1114
Cook, Bernard A., 2007n760
Cook, Bruce, 2005n896
Cook, Douglas, 2009n507
Cook, Ian, 2009n773
Cook, James Wyatt, 2006n978, 2007n879, 2009n909
Cook, Karen S., 791, 2005n792
Cook, Rhodes, 2005n719, 2006n732, 2007n609,
    2007n616, 2008n643, 2008n644

Cook, Richard, 2006n1106, 2008n989
Cook's essential kitchen dict, 2006n1283
Cooke, Bill, 2007n1077
Cooke, Nathalie, 2005n1085
Cooking in America 1840-1945, 2008n1131
Cool stuff & how it works, 2006n1275
Coombs, Robert Holman, 2007n716
Coombs, Timothy, 2009n149
Co-op advertising programs sourcebk 2007, 2008n254
Cooper Hill stylebk, 2d ed, 2006n885
Cooper, B. Lee, 2005n1138
Cooper, Bob, 2008n565
Cooper, Bruce S., 2009n252
Cooperative ref, 2005n647
Cope, Kevin L., 2006n10, 2006n11, 2007n4, 2008n8
Copeland, David A., 2005n442, 2007n562
Copper, John F., 2008n107
Copyeditor's hndbk, 2d ed, 2006n884
Copyright catechism, 2007n523
Copyright companion for writers, 2007n522
Copyright for administrators, 2009n561
Copyright for teachers & librarians, 2005n608
Copyright hndbk, 9th ed, 2008n539
Copyright in cyberspaace 2, 2006n628
Copyright law for librarians & educators, 2006n627
Copyright policies, 2009n560
Copywriter's hndbk, 3d ed, 2007n771
Corbeil, Jean-Claude, 2006n965, 2007n857, 2008n870
Corcoran, Neil, 2009n1007
Cordon, Luis A., 2006n754
Cordova, Carlos B., 2007n283
Cordovana, James, 2007n1291
Cords, Sarah Statz, 2007n977
Corduan, Winfried, 2007n1078
Core collection for children & YAs, 2009n930
Coretta Scott King awards 1970-2004, 3d ed,
    2005n1056
Corfield, Justin, 2007n102, 2009n106
Corfield, Robin S., 2007n102
Corman, Troy E., 2006n1368
Cornelison, Pam, 2005n443
Cornelius, Steven H., 2005n1124
Cornell Univ lib of histl mathematics monographs
    [Website], 2005n1529
Cornell Univ Lib of histl mathematics monographs
    [Website], 2008n1330
Cornell, Vincent J., 2008n1099
Cornils, Boy, 2008n1286
Cornog, Mary Wood, 2009n897
Cornwell, Nancy C., 2005n546
Corporate crime, 2009n479
Corporate finance sourcebk 2008, 2008n180
Corporate giving dir, 26th ed, 2005n810
Corporate giving dir, 29th ed, 2008n730
Corporate giving dir, 30th ed, 2009n751
Corporate yellow bk, Summer 2005, 2006n130
Corps, Terry, 2007n348

Correard, Marie-Helene, 2008n872
Corrie, John, 2008n1080
Cortés, Eladio, 2005n1219
Corwin, Harold G., Jr., 2008n1297
Corwin, Kimberley, 2009n1200
Cory, Kathleen B., 2005n359
Cosman, Madeleine Pelner, 2009n401
Cosmeo [Website], 2009n285
Costa Rica 2008, 2008n376
Costa Rica, 2009n121
Coulter, Michael L., 2008n1081
Counseling & psychotherapy transcripts, client
        narrative, & ref works [Website], 2009n699
Counter-creationism hndbk, 2006n1317
Counterterrorism, 2005n583
Counties USA, 3d ed, 2007n732
Countries of the world & their leaders 2009, 2009n616
Countries of the world series, 2005n73
Countryman, Edward, 2009n382
County & city extra 2004, 12th ed, 2005n854
County & city extra 2005, 13th ed, 2006n849
County & city extra 2006, 14th ed, 2007n753
County & city extra 2007, 15th ed, 2008n774
County & city extra 2008, 16th ed, 2009n782
County Longford residents prior to the famine,
        2005n364
Couper, Heather, 2008n1304
Courtney, Angela, 2009n958
Coutts, Brian E., 2005n510
Couzens, Dominic, 2009n1198
Covell, Maureen, 2006n83
Covenants not to compete, 3d ed, 2005n584
Covenants not to compete, 2003 suppl, 3d ed,
        2005n585
Coventry, Martin, 2006n405
Cover, Stefan P., 2008n1185
Cowden, Anthony, 2006n673
Cowlard, Keith A., 2009n117
Cox, Gary, 2009n1082
Cox, Jim, 2006n889, 2006n891, 2007n786, 2008n808,
        2009n812
Cox, Mary, 2006n923
Cox, Michael M., 2009n1173
Cox, Richard J., 2006n613
CQ's pol in America 2006, 2006n724
CQ's pol in America 2006: online ed [Website],
        2007n611
CQ's state fact finder 2004, 2005n846
CQ's state fact finder 2005, 2006n842
CQ's state fact finder 2006, 2007n745
Crabtree, Jaime, 2005n610
Crabtree, Pam J., 2009n425
Crabtree, Phillip D., 2007n989
Craddock, Jim, 2005n1217, 2006n1170, 2007n1053,
        2009n1072
Craft & business of writing, 2009n805
Craft of research, 3d ed, 2009n807

Craig, Edward, 2006n1197
Craig, Raymond A., 2009n1008
Craig, Robert D., 2005n1166
Craighead, W. Edward, 2006n753
Craighead's intl business, travel, & relocation gd
        2004-05, 12th ed, 2005n204
Cramer, Duncan, 2007n738
Crampton, Luke, 2005n1152
Crane, Gregory, 2007n408
Cranshaw, Whitney, 2005n1394
Crash course in ref, 2009n584
Crash course in teen servs, 2009n555
Crawford, Rosemary, 2005n193, 2005n194,
        2005n220, 2005n1490
Crawford, Suzanne J., 2006n336
Crazy quilts, 2009n840
CRC hndbk of chemistry & physics 2007-08, 88th ed,
        2008n1294
Creating a comprehensive info literacy plan, 2007n525
Creating database-backed lib web pages, 2007n527
Creating your lib brand, 2009n581
Creating your library's business plan, 2009n579
Creature features, 2009n1069
Creese, Mary R. S., 2005n1280
Creese, Thomas M., 2005n1280
Creeser, Rosemary, 2005n1323
Cressey, William W., 2005n311
Crew, Danny O., 2006n1072, 2007n985
Crew, David F., 2007n387
Crew, Hilary S., 2008n882
Crews, Kenneth D., 2006n627
Cribb, Robert, 2005n96
Crime & punishment, 2007n478
Crime & punishment in America: almanac, 2005n572
Crime & punishment in America: biogs, 2005n573
Crime & punishment in America: primary sources,
        2005n574
Crime & punishment in the US, 2009n467
Crime fiction Canada [Website], 2006n1013
Crime scene, 2005n581
Crime scene investigations series, 2007n479
Crime scene investigations series, 2008n493
Crime state rankings 2004, 11th ed, 2005n575
Crime state rankings 2005, 12th ed, 2006n567
Crime state rankings 2006, 13th ed, 2007n480
Crime state rankings 2007, 14th ed, 2008n494
Crime state rankings 2008, 2009n476
Crime writers for Canada [Website], 2006n1014
Crimes & trials of the century, 2008n484
Criminal justice, 2006n555
Criminal justice, 2007n468
Criminal justice abstracts [Website], 2005n560
Criminal justice links [Website], 2007n475
Criminal records manual, 2005n577
Criminal records manual, 2d ed, 2006n573
Criminal records manual, 3d ed, 2009n477

CRInfo: the conflict resolution info source [Website], 2008n669
Critical companion to ...
   Arthur Miller, 2008n922
   Charles Dickens, 2008n930
   Chaucer, 2007n957
   Dante, 2009n1005
   Edgar Allan Poe, 2008n923
   Emily Dickinson, 2007n949
   Ernest Hemingway, 2008n920
   F. Scott Fitzgerald, 2008n917
   Flannery O'Connor, 2009n964
   Herman Melville, 2008n921
   James Joyce, 2007n968
   Jane Austen, 2009n973
   John Steinbeck, 2006n1039
   Jonathan Swift, 2007n967
   Kurt Vonnegut, 2009n966
   Mark Twain, 2008n924
   Nathaniel Hawthorne, 2007n951
   Robert Frost, 2008n918
   T. S. Eliot, 2008n916
   Tennessee Williams, 2006n1041
   Toni Morrison, 2009n963
   Walt Whitman, 2007n954
   William Faulkner, 2009n960
   William Shakespeare, 2006n1050
   Zora Neale Hurston, 2009n961
Critical survey of mystery & detective fiction, rev ed, 2009n941
Critical thinking & learning, 2005n275
Crocosmia & chasmanthe, 2005n1361
Croddy, Eric A., 2006n676
Cromley, Elizabeth, 2006n927
Cross, F. L., 2006n1234
Cross, Gary S., 2005n755
Cross, Robin, 2005n519
Crossing boundaries with children's bks, 2007n888
Crow, Gary, 2009n258
Crowe, Judith, 2007n808
Crowley, Rachel, 2009n560
Crown, Alan David, 2006n1245
Crowsey, Linda, 2008n821
Crowther, Paul A., 2009n1306
Cruisers & battle cruisers, 2005n679
Crump, William D., 2006n1120, 2009n1038
Crusades, 2005n530
Crusades, 2007n417
Crusades: almanac, 2005n505
Crusades: biog, 2005n506
Crusades: primary sources, 2005n507
Crystal, David, 2005n1485, 2006n49, 2007n836
Cuba, 2009n122
Cuban-American fiction in English, 2006n1061
Cuban, Larry, 2009n564
Cuban music from A to Z, 2005n1121
Cuban, Sondra, 2009n564

Cuhaj, George S., 2009n832
Culham, A., 2008n1157
Culinary schools 2005, 8th ed, 2006n290
Cullen, Timothy, 2007n531
Cullen-DuPont, Kathryn, 2006n861
Cullin, Robert, 2007n528, 2008n546
Cullinan, Bernice E., 2005n1029, 2007n908
Cullum, Linda, 2005n1103
Cults, 2d ed, 2006n1214
Cultural anthropology, 2d ed, 2009n292
Cultural chronicle of the Weimar Republic, 2009n404
Cultural ency of baseball, 2d ed, 2006n778
Cultural ency of the body, 2009n291
Cultural exchange in early modern Europe, 2008n429
Cultural journeys, 2007n912
Culture & customs of ...
   Afghanistan, 2006n88
   Angola, 2007n83
   Australia, 2005n103
   Botswana, 2007n84
   Cameroon, 2006n80
   Germany, 2005n109
   Ireland, 2007n115
   Israel, 2005n128
   Italy, 2006n105
   Mexico, 2005n121
   Mongolia, 2009n103
   Morocco, 2006n84
   Mozambique, 2007n89
   Pakistan, 2007n99
   Palestinians, 2005n124
   Saudi Arabia, 2007n128
   Senegal, 2009n93
   S Africa, 2005n89
   Thailand, 2005n102
   the Baltic States, 2007n109
   the US, 2008n73
   Zambia, 2007n91
CultureGrams [Website], 2009n67
Cultures & lits of Africa links [Website], 2005n1083
Cultures in conflict: the French Revolution, 2005n480
Culyer, Anthony J., 2006n1410
Cumbler, John T., 2006n1539
Cummins, Alex G., 2006n479
Cumulative index to nursing & allied health lit [Website], 2005n1474
Cunha, Maria Manuela, 2009n1286
Cupito, Mary Carmen, 2006n881
Cure for the common word, 2008n871
Curnow, Trevor, 2005n1237
Curran, Dennis P., 2006n1402
Current biog cumulated index 1940-2005, 2007n42
Current biog illus [Website], 2009n15
Current biog intl yrbk 2003, 2005n13
Current biog intl yrbk 2004, 2006n16
Current biog intl yrbk 2007, 2008n13
Current biog yrbk 2003, 2005n21

Current biog yrbk 2005, 2007n15
Current biog yrbk 2007, 2008n18
Current controversies series, 2008n62
Current controversies series, 2009n61
Current issues [Website], 2009n53
Current medical diagnosis & treatment 2004, 43d ed,
    2005n1444
Current medical diagnosis & treatment 2007, 46th ed,
    2007n1255
Curry, Jennifer, 2006n864, 2007n1167, 2008n876
Curry, Sheryl Moore, 2005n1033
Curtis, Adrian, 2009n1093
Curtis, Bryan, 2006n58
Curtis, Donnelyn, 2006n641
Curtis, Stephen, 2006n882, 2007n777
Curzon, Susan Carol, 2007n532, 2008n544
Cush, Denise, 2008n1094, 2009n1116
Cusick, Tim, 2006n810
Cutler, Deborah W., 2006n670, 2006n671
Cutler, Thomas J., 2006n670, 2006n671
Cutler, Todd, 2005n642
Cutter, Charles, 2005n350
Cutthroat, 2d ed, 2009n1202
Cuvalo, Ante, 2008n119
Cuypers, Martin, 2007n964
Cyber worship in multifaith perspectives, 2007n1087
Cybercrime, 2005n582
Cyclopedia of world authors, 4th rev ed, 2005n984
Cyclopedia of YA authors, 2006n1001
Cyndi's list of genealogy sites on the Internet
    [Website], 2007n286

da Silva, Tony Simoes, 2006n1053
D'Agostino, Ralph B., 2009n1224
D'Ammassa, Don, 2006n1024, 2007n929
D'Amore, Jonathan, 2005n764
Dabydeen, David, 2009n406
Daccord, Thomas, 2008n442
Dahn, Ada P., 2007n1247
Dahn, Russell, 2005n253
Daid, Lynda Lee, 2009n617
Daily life America [Website], 2009n373
Daily life in …
    immigrant America, 1820-70, 2009n387
    Imperial Russia, 2009n410
    the Byzantine Empire, 2007n386
    the early American republic, 1790-1820, 2005n449
    the Hellenistic age, 2009n408
    the industrial US, 1870-1900, 2005n453
    the medieval Islamic world, 2006n1243
    the Mongol Empire, 2007n375
    the N.T., 2009n433
    the Roman city, 2006n476
    the Soviet Union, 2005n114

Daily life of …
    Jews in the Middle Ages, 2006n348
    the Ancient Egyptians, 2d ed, 2009n415
    the Nubians, 2005n464
    the Vikings, 2005n532
Daily life online [Website], 2009n423
Daintith, John, 2006n1491, 2006n1522, 2006n1526,
    2007n1290, 2007n1301, 2009n1296
Dalin, David G., 2009n314
Dalston, Teresa R., 2006n639, 2009n588
Daly, Margo, 2005n402
Daly, Peter M., 2009n327
Daly, Richard, 2006n800
Dalzell, Tom, 2007n845
Damon, William, 2007n663
Damp, Dennis V., 2006n245, 2008n241, 2008n242
Dana, Leo-Paul, 2009n294
Danico, Mary Yu, 2005n337
Daniels, David, 2006n1093
Daniels, Jeffrey J., 2009n1143
Daniels, Peggy, 2009n1040
Danilov, Victor J., 2006n54, 2006n769
Danner, Phyllis, 2006n1078
Darga, Amy, 2005n148, 2005n161
Darga, Amy, 2006n143
Darity, William A., Jr., 2008n61
Darke, Rick, 2005n1368
Darling, Janina K., 2005n947
Darnay, Arsen J., 2005n199, 2007n136, 2008n189,
    2009n171
Darsie, Richard F., Jr., 2006n1384
Darvill, Timothy, 2009n357
Darwin's fishes, 2006n1382
Das, Dilip K., 2007n474
Daston, Lorraine, 2007n1140
Database of award-winning children's lit [Website],
    2007n889
Database of the Calif. Academy of Scis, Dept of
    Anthropology collection, 2005n320
Datapedia of the US 2004, 3d ed, 2005n847
Datapedia of the US 2007, 4th ed, 2009n774
Daugherty, Alice, 2009n566
Davenport, Robert, 2005n1196
Davidson, Frank P., 2007n1224
Davidson, Ivor J., 2005n1263
Davidson, Mark, 2006n963
Davidson, Seth, 2009n1199
Davies, Carole Boyce, 2009n301
Davies, Christopher, 2006n938
Davies, Douglas J., 2007n697
Davies, Peter, 2006n792
Davies, Steve, 2008n602
Davis, Anita Price, 2007n11, 2009n784
Davis, Donald E., 2007n1327
Davis, Kaetrena D., 2008n503
Davis, Larry E., 2009n757

Davis, Lee, 2009n1317
Davis, Lisa Fagin, 2005n614
Davis, Mary Byrd, 2007n570
Davis, Paul, 2008n930
Davis, Paul K., 2007n549, 2007n550
Davis, R. Hunt, Jr., 2006n460
Davis, Ricky, 2007n1195
Davis, Stacy, 2006n876
Davis, Virginia Lee Hutcheson, 2007n292, 2008n342
Davis, W. Marvin, 2008n1241
Dawson, Alma, 2006n1030
Day, Alan, 2007n129
Day by day: the 1930s, 2008n391
Day by day: the nineties, 2005n513
Day by day: the twenties, 2009n418
Day-by-day in NASCAR hist, 2005n783
Day in the life: career options in lib & info sci,
    2008n523
Day, Leslie, 2008n1164
Day, Nicolas, 2006n1375
Day, Simon, 2008n1206
Day, Trevor, 2007n1211, 2008n1323
Daylily, 2005n1328
Daytime serials of TV, 1946-60, 2007n786
DC comics ency, 2006n1121
de Bary, Theodore, 2007n98, 2009n95
de Borst, René, 2006n1393
De Imperatoribus Romani [Website], 2007n395
de Laperriere, Charles Baile, 2005n933, 2007n813
De Leon, Arnoldo, 2006n353
de Mijolla, Alain, 2006n757
de Stricker, Ulla, 2008n524
de Vaucouleurs atlas of galaxies, 2008n1297
de Vries, Ad, 2005n934
de Vries, Arthur, 2005n934
de Wet, Erika, 2007n492
Deal, David, 2008n1024
Deal, William E., 2006n464, 2007n373
Dean, Katharine A., 2005n1101
Dean, Robert, 2008n1176
Dean's hndbk of organic chemistry, 2d ed, 2005n1497
Dear, I. C. B., 2006n1554
Death & dying sourcebk, 2d ed, 2007n696
Death penalty on trial, 2006n541
Death sentences in Mo., 1803-2005, 2007n482
Deaths of the popes, 2005n1267
Debatable issues in US hist, 2005n444
Deboeck, Guido, 2009n321
Debons, Anthony, 2009n571
DeBrandt, Katherine A., 2005n169, 2005n854,
    2006n207, 2006n277, 2006n731, 2006n849,
    2007n238, 2007n736, 2007n753, 2008n771,
    2008n774, 2009n663, 2009n782
Debt info for teens, 2008n184
Decades of American hist series, 2006n438
Decker, Mark D., 2009n1172
Decline & fall of the Roman Empire, 2006n478

DeCotis, Ruth J., 2006n253
Deen, Darwin, 2008n1127
Deering, Kathryn R., 2006n171, 2006n172
Dees, Pamela Youngdahl, 2005n1129
Defendant rights, 2005n579
Defining Latin American art, 2006n919
DeFrancis, John, 2005n970
DeFranco, Laurence J., 2008n650
DeFronzo, James V., 2007n414
Degategno, Paul J., 2007n967
DeHart, Jean, 2006n874, 2007n766
Dehne, Anne, 2005n402
Dekker ency of nanosci & nanotech, 2005n1401
Dekker ency of nanosci & nanotech [Website],
    2005n1402
del Sol Knight, Lucia, 2007n1342
Del Testa, David W., 2005n527
Delahunty, Andrew, 2005n366, 2006n369
Delgado, Mariano, 2008n1089
DeLong, Janice A., 2009n930
DeLong, Marlena C., 2007n618
Delphos, William A., 2005n205
DelPo, Amy, 451, 2007n485
DeMello, Margo, 2009n843
Demin, Vitaliy, 2006n831
Democracy project [Website], 2009n632
Demographic & health surveys [Website], 2008n742
Demographic yrbk 2001, 53d ed, 2005n830
Demographic yrbk 2002, 54th ed, 2006n825
Demographic yrbk 2003, 2007n724
Demographic yrbk 2004, 2008n743
Demographics of the US, 3d ed, 2008n749
Demsky, Aaron, 2005n351
Denbow, James, 2007n84
Denckla, Tanya L. K., 2005n1313
Denison, David, 2008n853
Denizations & naturalizations in the British colonies in
    America, 1607-1775, 2006n362
Dennis, Geoffrey W., 2008n1100
Dennis, Matthew, 2007n1029
Denny, Frederick, 2009n1088
Denny, Mark W., 2008n1166
Dental care & oral health sourcebk, 3d ed, 2009n1257
Denton, Peter H., 2009n1125
Depression sourcebk, 2d ed, 2009n712
Derie, Kate, 2005n1047
Derks, Scott, 2005n170, 2006n149, 2006n238,
    2007n194, 2009n211
Dermatological disorders sourcebk, 2d ed, 2006n1452
DeRouen, Karl, Jr., 2008n579, 2009n696
Descriptionary, 3d ed, 2006n964
Deserts, rev ed, 2008n1315
Design, 2008n830
Designer plant combinations, 2009n1157
Designing a school lib media center for the future, 2d
    ed, 2008n514
Desk & beyond, 2009n583

Destroyers, 2006n679
Detective novels of Agatha Christie, 2009n944
Detrez, Raymond, 2007n112
Deutsch, Jonathan, 2009n1151
Developing an info literacy program K-12, 2d ed, 2005n627
Development of the industrial US: almanac, 2006n420
Development of the industrial US: biogs, 2006n421
Development of the industrial US: primary sources, 2006n422
Deverell, William, 2005n440
DeVito, Carlo, 2006n556
DeVries, Duane, 2005n1077
DeVries, Kelly, 2008n603
Dewey, Barbara I., 2008n554
Dewhirst, Robert E., 2008n627
DeWitt, Larry W., 2008n473, 2009n449
Di Felice, Gino, 2009n730
Diabetes info for teens, 2007n1271
Diabetes ready-ref gd for health professionals, 2d ed, 2005n1466
Diamant-Cohen, Betsy, 2009n549
Diamond, Marie Josephine, 2006n982
Diamonds around the globe, 2006n776
Diaz, Karen R., 2009n505
Dicaire, David, 2007n1012, 2008n987, 2009n1019
Dick, Ron, 2005n1546, 2005n1547, 2006n1548, 2007n1336
Dickens's nonfictional theatrical, & poetical writings, 2008n931
Dickerson, Constance B., 2005n618
Dickerson, Donna L., 2005n445
Dickinson, Terence, 2009n1307
Dickson, Greg, 2007n18
Dickson, Keith D., 2009n419
Dickson-Carr, Darryl, 2006n1035
Dictionary for lib & info sci, 2005n595
Dictionary for theological interpretation of the Bible, 2007n1097
Dictionary of ...
    accounting terms, 4th ed, 2006n155
    African filmmakers, 2009n1061
    alternatives, 2008n1046
    American classical composers, 2d ed, 2006n1079
    American idioms, 4th ed, 2006n953
    American YA fiction, 1997-2001, 2005n1027
    ancient Rabbis, 2005n1275
    antisemitism, 2008n457
    artifacts, 2009n358
    Atheism, skepticism, & humanism, 2007n1077
    banking terms, 5th ed, 2007n162
    battles & sieges, 2007n556
    biblical criticism & interpretation, 2008n1067
    bioinformatics & computational biology, 2005n1411
    biology, 6th ed, 2009n1170
    British classicists, 2006n865
    Canadian biog, v.25, 1921-30, 2006n23
    chemistry, 6th ed, 2009n1296
    civil society, philanthropy, & the nonprofit sector, 2008n727
    clinical trials, 2d ed, 2008n1206
    common wildflowers of Tex. & the Southern Great Plains, 2006n1343
    computer vision & image processing, 2006n1479
    computing, 6th ed, 2009n1285
    concise writing, 2d ed, 2007n768
    contemporary quotations, v.10, 5th rev ed, 2006n59
    continental philosophy, 2007n1066
    disagreeable English, 2005n958
    disruption, 2008n262
    earth scis, 3d ed, 2009n1301
    engineering materials, 2005n1404
    environment & conservation, 2008n1340
    evangelical biog 1730-1860, 2005n1254
    existential psychotherapy & counseling, 2007n658
    finance & banking, 4th ed, 2009n164
    food sci & tech, 2006n1281
    gene tech, 3d ed, 2005n1412
    genocide, 2009n474
    globalization, 2007n577
    gods & goddesses, 2d ed, 2005n1160
    Greek & Roman biog & mythology, 2008n993
    Greek & Roman culture, 2009n407
    Greek & Roman geography, 2007n310
    health economics, 2006n1410
    health economics & finance, 2007n1232
    info sci & tech, 2008n504
    Irish philosophers, 2005n1225
    Islamic philosophical terms [Website], 2006n1239
    Jewish biog, 2006n347
    Jewish-Christian relations, 2006n1246
    linguistics & phonetics, 6th ed, 2009n870
    literary & thematic terms, 2d ed, 2007n882
    literary influences, 2005n998
    major biblical interpreters, 2008n1068
    medical biog, 2008n1205
    microbiology & molecular biology, 3d ed, 2008n1142
    microscopy, 2006n1257
    mission theology, 2008n1080
    mktg communications, 2005n255
    modern American philosophers, 2006n1188
    modern design, 2006n911
    multicultural psychology, 2007n656
    nanotech, colloid & interface sci, 2009n1215
    naval abbrevs, 4th ed, 2006n670
    naval terms, 6th ed, 2006n671
    nonprofit terms & concepts, 2008n728
    orthopedic terminology, 2009n1259
    pharmacy, 2005n1477
    philosophical terms & names [Website], 2006n1190
    physics, 2005n1525
    sociology, 3d ed, 2006n797

stats & methodology, 3d ed, 2007n739
strategy, 2005n254
subjects & symbols in art, 2d ed, 2009n850
the Israeli-Palestinian conflict, 2006n115
the O.T.: histl bks, 2006n1222
the work of W. R. Bion, 2005n736
20th-century British philosophers, 2006n1189
wars, 3d ed, 2007n551
women worldwide, 2007n755
world hist, 2d ed, 2007n418
Diehl, Roberta L., 2008n1354
Diehl, Sarah J., 2008n604
Diet & nutrition sourcebk, 3d ed, 2007n1153
Diet info for teens, 2d ed, 2007n1256
Diethe, Carol, 2007n1067
Digital info & knowledge mgmt, 2008n547
Digital ref serv, 2005n648
Digital resources & librarians, 2005n629
Dikel, Margaret Riley, 2007n211
Dildy, Doug, 2008n602
Dillard, Elsie, 2009n352
Diller, Daniel C., 2006n695
Dimwit's dict, 2d ed, 2007n842
Ding, Kuiling, 2009n1297
Dinosaur atlas, 2007n1316
Dinosauria, 2d ed, 2006n1521
Dinosaurs, 2008n1326
Dinosaurs, suppl 4, 2007n1314
Dinosaurs, suppl 5, 2008n1325
Diotima: materials for the study of women & gender in
     the ancient world [Website], 2005n857
Dirck, Brian R., 2008n645
Direct mktg market place 2008, 2009n234
Direction of trade stats yrbk 2005, 2006n269
Directories in print, 24th ed, 2005n39
Directories in print, 25th ed, 2006n33
Directories in print, 28th ed, 2009n6
Directories in print suppl, 24th ed, 2005n40
Directors up close, 2d ed, 2006n1163
Directory of ...
     biomedical & health care grants 2006, 20th ed,
         2006n811
     business info resources 2005, 12th ed, 2005n151
     business info resources 2006, 13th ed, 2006n128
     business info resources 2007, 14th ed, 2008n158
     business info resources 2008, 15th ed, 2009n135
     business info resources [Website], 2005n152
     business info resources [Website], 2008n159
     business to business catalogs 2004, 12the ed,
         2005n190
     business to business catalogs 2005, 13th ed,
         2006n178
     business to business catalogs [Website], 2005n191
     conductors' archives in American institutions,
         2007n987
     congressional voting scores & interest group
         ratings, 4th ed, 2007n601
     convenience stores, 2005, 2006n179
     convenience stores, 2006, 2007n165
     convenience stores, 2008, 2009n173
     drug & alcohol residential rehabilitation facilities,
         2004, 2005n821
     drug & alcohol residential rehabilitation facilities
         [Website], 2005n822
     executive recruiters, 14th corporate ed, 2006n229
     executive recruiters 2005-06, 34th ed, 2006n230
     executive recruiters 2007-08, 35th ed, 2007n192
     financial aid for women 2005-07, 2006n304
     foreign firms operating in the US, 2007n166
     grants in the humanities 2004/05, 18th ed,
         2005n882
     grants in the humanities 2005/06, 19th ed,
         2006n868
     histl textbk & curriculum collections, 2006n593
     hospital personnel 2006, 18th ed, 2007n1236
     hospital personnel 2007, 19th ed, 2008n1211
     hospital personnel 2008, 20th ed, 2009n1225
     hospital personnel [Website], 2007n1237
     hospital personnel [Website], 2008n1212
     libs in Canada 2008/09, 23d ed, 2009n492
     local court & county retrievers, 2005 ed,
         2006n524
     mail order catalogs 2004, 18th ed, 2005n181
     mail order catalogs 2005, 19th ed, 2006n161
     mail order catalogs 2007, 21st ed, 2007n155
     mail order catalogs 2008, 22d ed, 2008n179
     mail order catalogs online [Website], 2007n156
     physicians in the US 2005 [CD-ROM], 2006n1416
     poetry pubs 2005-06, 21st ed, 2006n649
     poetry pubs 2008-09, 24th ed, 2009n591
     pub 2004, 29th ed, 2005n654
     pub 2008, 33d ed, 2008n566
     publishing 2009, 34th ed, 2009n592
     research grants 2006, 2006n812
     small press/mag editors & pubs 2005-06, 36th ed,
         2006n650
     small press/mag editors & pubs 2008-09, 39th ed,
         2009n593
     special libs & info centers, 30th ed, 2005n597
     special libs & info centers, 34th ed, 2009n493
     state court clerks & county courthouses, 2006 ed,
         2006n525
     theatre training programs 2003-05, 9th ed,
         2006n1175
     trade & investment-related orgs of developing
         countries & areas in Asia & the Pacific
         2003, 2005n214
     univ libs in Europe, 3d ed, 2008n506
     unpublished experimental mental measures, v.9,
         2008n681
     US labor orgs, 2004 ed, 2005n229
     US labor orgs, 2008 ed, 2009n206
     venture capital & private equity firms 2004, 8th ed,
         2005n184

Directory of ... (*Cont.*)
    venture capital & private equity firms 2005, 9th ed,
       2006n167
    venture capital & private equity firms 2008, 12th
       ed, 2009n166
    venture capital & private equity firms [Website],
       2009n167
    women philosophers [Website], 2006n1200
Dirks, Robert, 2008n1117
Dirks, Tim, 2006n1160
Dirr, Michael A., 2005n1324
Disasters, accidents, & crises in American hist,
    2009n366
Disciplinary blueprint for the assessment of info lit,
    2009n570
Discover sci almanac, 2005n1285
Discovering careers for your future series, 2006n246
Discovering careers for your future series, 2009n215
Discovering world cultures: the Middle East,
    2005n123
Discovery & exploration series, 2006n389
Disease mgmt sourcebk, 2009n1244
Diseases, 3d ed, 2007n1248
Diseases & disorders, 2008n1224
Diseases & disorders series, 2009n1245
Disruptive pattern material, 2006n908
Dissertation abstracts intl [Website], 2007n3
Distance educ, 2005n306
Distributed digital lib of mathematical monographs
    [Website], 2005n1530
Ditmore, Melissa Hope, 2007n709
Dittman, Michael J., 2005n1068, 2008n914
Dive, 2005n781
Divided by a common lang, 2006n938
Divorce without court, 2007n460
DK 1st animal ency, 2006n1363
DK 1st atlas, 2006n373
DK compact atlas of the world, 3d ed, 2006n372
DK illus Oxford dict, rev ed, 2005n29
DK Merriam-Webster children's dict, rev ed,
    2006n957
DK online ency, 2007n24
DK ultimate visual dict, 2005n967
DNA evidence & forensic sci, 2009n480
Dobson, John, 2007n133, 2008n153
Docherty, James C., 2005n225, 2007n631, 2008n110
Doctor, Ronald M., 2009n700
Documentary hist of the Supreme Court of the US,
    1789-1800, v.7, 2005n547
Documentary hist of the Supreme Court of the US,
    1789-1800, v.8, 2008n474
Documents from the women's liberation movement
    [Website], 2005n858
Documents of Soviet hist, v.6, 2006n479
Dodds, Steve, 2006n913
Dodgen, Esther Carls, 2005n1247
Dodson, Aidan, 2006n484

Dodson, Carolyn, 2008n1156
Dodson, Peter, 2006n1521
Dog owner's home veterinary hndbk, 4th ed,
    2009n1165
Dogs eyewitness companions, 2007n1199
Dogwoods, 2006n1355
Doherty, Craig A., 2006n458
Doherty, Julie, 2007n244
Doherty, Katherine M., 2006n458
Doing business in 2004, 2005n207
Doland, Michelle, 2007n769
Doll, Carol A., 2006n604
Doll values, 9th ed, 2007n801
Doll values, 10th ed, 2009n834
Dollarhide, William, 2007n288
Dolphin, Jack, 2008n249
Domenico, Roy P., 2007n574
Domestic programs of the American Presidents,
    2009n658
Domestic violence, 2d ed, 2009n747
Domestic violence sourcebk, 2d ed, 2005n802
Donahue, Thomas, 2006n1087
Donald G. Bloesch, 2008n1077
Donald, Graeme, 2009n892
Donald, Stephanie, 2006n90
Donham, Jean, 2005n609, 2009n518
Donnelly, James S., Jr., 2005n110
Donsbach, Wolfgang, 2009n796
Dooley, Patricia L., 2006n451
Doorn, Jorge H., 2006n1486
Dority, G. Kim, 2008n525
Dorling Kindersley concise atlas of the world, 2d ed,
    2005n369
Dorling Kindersley concise atlas of the world, 3d ed,
    2006n374
Dorling Kindersley traveler's atlas, 2006n393
Dorling Kindersley world atlas, 3d ed, 2005n370
Dorling Kindersley world atlas, 6th ed, 2007n297
Dorman, John Frederick, 2008n338, 2008n339,
    2008n340
Doskow, Emily, 2007n459
Dostoevsky ency, 2005n1097
Doty, William G., 2005n1167
Doucett, Elisabeth, 2009n581
Douglas, Ian, 2008n358
Doutrich, Paul E., 2005n696
Douville, Judith A., 2006n1489
Dover, Jeffrey S., 2007n1276
Dover, Michael A., 2008n728
Dow, Andrew, 2007n1338
Dow, James R., 2005n1158
Dow, Kirstin, 2007n1307
Dow's dict of railway quotations, 2007n1338
Dowden, Bradley, 2006n1195
Dowley, Tim, 2005n1263
Dowling, Dave, 2007n838
Dowling, Elizabeth M., 2007n1079

Dowling, Timothy C., 2006n512, 2007n434
Downie, Alex, 2005n1325
Downie, David L., 2009n1321
Downing, David, 2007n839
Downing, Karen, 2006n322
Downing, Thomas E., 2007n1307
Dox, Ida G., 2009n1176
Dr. Seuss catalog, 2006n991
Drabble, Margaret, 2007n955, 2009n971
Drake, Richard L., 2006n1321
Drakeley, Steven, 2007n374
Drama for students, v.18, 2005n1037
Drama for students, v.19, 2005n1038
Drama for students, v.24, 2008n892
Drama 100, 2009n937
Dresang, Eliza T., 2007n512
Drew, Bernard A., 2007n921, 2008n908, 2009n985
Drew, Katherine Fischer, 2005n488
Drexlere, Kateri, 2008n150
Drobner, Hubertus R., 2008n1088
Drone, Jeanette Marie, 2007n991
Drout, Michael D. C., 2008n935
Drowne, Kathleen, 2005n1174
Drug abuse sourcebk, 2d ed, 2006n820
Drug info, 3d ed, 2009n1273
Drug info for teens, 2d ed, 2007n717
Drugs & society, 2006n821
Drugs & sports, 2008n705
Drummond, John J., 2009n1083
Dryland gardening, 2006n1297
Du Noyer, Paul, 2005n1139
du Quenoy, Paul, 2005n477, 2005n478
Dubal, David, 2005n1134
Dubin, Michael J., 2008n624
Dublin, Thomas, 2005n863
Dudden, Rosalind Farnam, 2008n520
Duddy, Thomas, 2005n1225
Dudley, William, 2008n416
Duffes, Melissa Wells, 2009n862
Duffy, Bernard K., 2006n870
Duffy, Sean, 2006n475
Duke, Brad, 2006n1159
Duke ency of new medicine, 2008n1237
Duke Univ men's basketball games, 2009n721
Dulmus, Catherine N., 2009n759
Dumouchel, J. Robert, 2005n817, 2006n817, 2007n712
Dumper, Michael R. T., 2007n122, 2008n143
Duncan, James S., 2005n68
Duncan, Joyce D., 2006n768
Dunlop, Gary, 2005n1361
Dunmire, William W., 2008n1156
Dunn, Jon, 2008n1178
Dunn, Jon L., 2007n1194
Dunn, Loraine, 2009n265
Dunn, Robert, 2007n1306
Dunnavant, Anthony L., 2006n1230

Dunne, Pete, 2007n1192
Dunton-Downer, Leslie, 2005n1080
Dunworth, David J., 2005n1168
Durham, William H., 2005n322
Duriez, Colin, 2005n1078, 2009n945
Durrance, Joan C., 2006n635
Dustman, Karen, 2006n876
DVD & video gd 2004, 2005n1216
Dyer, Alan, 2009n1307
Dyes from American native plants, 2006n1337
Dyja, Eddie, 2005n1209
Dynamic youth servs through outcome-based planning
   & educ, 2007n512
Dyrness, William A., 2009n1110
Dyson, Marianne J., 2008n1302
Dziemianowicz, Stefan, 2007n932

E.encyclopedia animal, 2007n1186
E.encyclopedia sci, 2005n1284
E.guides: Ancient Greece, 2007n391
E.guides: dinosaur, 2005n1523
E.guides: Earth, 2005n1499
E.guides: human body, 2007n1171
E.guides: plant, 2007n1174
E.guides: space travel, 2005n1504
e'Avennes, Prisse, 2009n847
Eaklor, Vicki L., 2009n749
Ear, nose & throat disorders sourcebk, 2d ed,
   2007n1257
Earl, Richard A., 2009n1326
Earle, Roger W., 2009n732
Earley, Chris G., 2006n1371
Earls, Irene, 2005n931
Early American furniture, 2007n805
Early American nature writers, 2009n952
Early Canadiana online [Website], 2005n470
Early childhood educ, 2008n270
Early Christian Greek & Latin lit, 2006n1236
Early civilizations in the Americas: almanac,
   2006n342
Early civilizations of the Americas: biogs & primary
   sources, 2006n343
Early exits: the premature endings of baseball careers,
   2007n682
Early natl period, 2005n458
Early peoples of Britain & Ireland, 2009n405
Early republic, 2006n451
Early republic, 2009n389
Early republic [Website], 2009n365
Early stages of Atlantic fishes, 2006n1379
Earth sci, 2009n1299
Earth sci resources in the electronic age, 2005n1498
Earth's changing environment, 2009n1339
Eason, Cassandra, 2009n1034
East & SE Asia [Website], 2008n102

East Asian Americans & pol participation, 2006n721
East, Kathy, 2009n921
Eastern Europe, 2006n100
Eastern Europe, Russia, & Central Asia 2007, 7th ed, 2008n117
Eastern Europe, Russia, & Central Asia 2009, 2009n109
Eastern Orthodox churches, 2006n1227
Easy info sources for ESL, adult learners, & new readers, 2009n569
Easy orchids, 2006n1305
Eating disorders, rev ed, 2005n1467
Eating disorders info for teens, 2006n1448
Eating disorders sourcebk, 2d ed, 2008n1255
Eaton, Eric R., 2008n1184
Eaton, Katherine B., 2005n114
Eberhart, George M., 2007n497
Eberle, Suzanne Girard, 2008n703
Eberts, Marjorie, 2006n247
Ebner, Aviva, 2005n1289, 2006n1270, 2007n1144
Echaore-McDavid, Susan, 2006n248, 2006n249, 2007n212, 2007n223, 2008n243, 2009n216, 2009n217
Ecker, Richard E., 2005n659
ECO gd to careers that make a difference, 2006n250
Ecology, rev ed, 2009n1337
EconData [Website], 2005n153
ECONlinks [Website], 2005n154
Economic & social survey of Asia & the Pacific 2005, 2006n214
Economic report on Africa 2007, 2008n218
Economic survey of Latin America & the Caribbean, 2004-05, 2007n189
EconWPA [Website], 2005n131
Ecoterrorism, 2005n580
Eco-travel gd, 2009n345
Edelson, Mitchell, 2005n1465
Edgar, Kathleen J., 2005n1, 2005n417, 2007n323
Edge, John T., 2008n1120
Edgerton, Gary R., 2008n1031
Edinburgh companion to Ancient Greece & Rome, 2007n384
Edis, Taner, 2006n1268
Edler, Joel, 2006n903
Edleson, Jeffrey L., 2009n469
Edson, Gary, 2007n258
Education dict [CD-ROM], 2006n274
Education facility security hndbk, 2009n261
Education for lib cataloging, 2007n509
Education state rankings 2003-04, 2d ed, 2005n277
Education state rankings 2005-06, 4th ed, 2006n278
Education state rankings 2006-07, 5th ed, 2007n239
Education state rankings 2008-09, 7th ed, 2009n250
Educational adequacy & the courts, 2006n280
Educational media & tech yrbk 2003, v.28, 2005n317
Educational media & tech yrbk 2005, v.30, 2006n317
Educational media & tech yrbk 2008, v.33, 2009n288

Educational paperback assn Website [Website], 2007n903
Educational rankings annual 2005, 2005n278
Educator's classroom gd to America's religious beliefs & practices, 2008n1064
Educators gd to …
    free Internet resources 2007-08, elem/middle school ed, 7th ed, 2008n291
    free Internet resources 2007-08, secondary ed, 25th ed, 2008n292
    free Internet resources 2008-09, 26th ed, 2009n286
    free Internet resources 2008-09, 8th ed, 2009n287
    free multicultural materials 2007-08, 10th ed, 2008n271
    free sci materials 2007-08, 48th ed, 2008n272
    free social studies materials, 2007-08, 47th ed, 2008n273
    free videotapes 2004-05: elem/middle school, 5th ed, 2005n281
    free videotapes 2005-06: elem/middle school, 6th ed, 2006n318
    free videotapes 2007-08: elem/middle school ed, 8th ed, 2008n293
    free videotapes 2004-05: secondary ed, 51st ed, 2005n282
    free videotapes 2005-06: secondary ed, 52d ed, 2006n319
    free videotapes 2007-08, secondary ed, 54th ed, 2008n294
    solving common behavior problems, 2009n271
Educators resource dir 2007/08, 7th ed, 2008n265
Educators resource dir, 2005/06, 6th ed, 2006n276
Edward, Linda, 2007n801, 2009n834
Edwards, A. S. G., 2007n981
Edwards, Bill, 2006n898, 2007n794
Edwards, Jeffrey K., 2008n684
Edwards, Paul M., 2006n462, 2006n463, 2007n339
Edwards, Todd L., 2008n139, 2009n120
Edwin Arlington Robinson ency, 2008n958
Egan, David R., 2007n974, 2008n439
Egan, Melinda A., 2007n974, 2008n439
Eggers, Ellen K., 2007n85
Eggleston, Merilee, 2007n772
Egyptian mythology A to Z, rev ed, 2007n1027
eHRAF collection of ethnography/archaeology [Website], 2007n262
Ehrlich, M. Avrum, 2009n311
Ehsani, M. Reza, 2009n1143
Eichholz, Alice, 2005n361
Eighteenth-century current bibliog: n.s. v.26 for 2000, 2006n10
Eighteenth-century current bibliog, n.s. v.27 for 2001, 2006n11
Eighteenth-century current bibliog, n.s. v.28 for 2002, 2007n4
Eighteenth-century current bibliog: n.s. v.29-for 2003, 2008n8

Eighties in America, 2009n374
Einsohn, Amy, 2006n884
Eiseman, Leatrice, 2006n914
Eisen, Cliff, 2006n1080, 2007n993
Eisenstadt, Peter, 2007n71
Eisenstat, Stephanie A., 2005n1440
E-journals, 2006n641
Ekarius, Carol, 2008n1175, 2009n1168
Eklund, Robert C., 2008n689
El Ali, Bassam M., 2006n1494
Elbroch, Mark, 2006n795
Eldredge, Debra M., 2009n1164, 2009n1165
Eleanor of Aquitaine, courtly love, & the Troubadours,
    2005n491
Eleanor Roosevelt papers, v.1, 2008n496
Electing Congress, 2d ed, 2009n657
ElectionGd [Website], 2008n615
Elections A to Z, 3d ed, 2008n628
Electoral voter predictor [Website], 2009n633
Electronic govt, 2009n36
Electronic info system for intl law (EISIL) [Website],
    2008n500
Electronic jl mgmt systems, 2006n642
Electronic links for classicists [Website], 2005n876
Electronic poetry center [Website], 2009n990
Electronics, 2005n1292
Elegant glassware of the depression era, 13th ed,
    2009n817
Elegant silvers, 2006n1303
Elementary educ, 2006n283
Elements of …
    design, 2005n929
    lib research, 2009n500
    style, 2006n887
    style, new ed, 2006n927
    visual style, 2008n1276
El-Fakahany, Esam E., 2009n1135
Elgar dict of economic quotations, 2005n173
Elgar ency of comparative law, 2008n501
Elhai, Jon D., 2009n702
Elia, Anthony, 2006n876
eLibrary sci [Website], 2009n1120
Elizabethan poetry, 2005n1102
Elizabethan world: almanac, 2008n432
Elizabethan world: biogs, 2008n433
Elizabethan world: primary sources, 2008n434
Ellis, Barbara W., 2009n1158
Ellwood, Robert S., 2007n1081, 2008n1055
Elphick, Jonathan, 2008n1172
Elsevier's dict of …
    abbrevs, acronyms, synonyms, & symbols used in
        medicine, 2d ed, 2005n1434
    amphibians, 2005n1400
    economics, business, finance, & law, 2005n144
    engineering, 2005n1403
    medicine: Spanish-English & English-Spanish,
        2005n1435

    symbols & imagery, 2d ed, 2005n934
    zoology & general biology, 2005n1380
El-Shamy, Hasan, 2006n1116
Elsie, Robert, 2005n106, 2005n112
Elster, Charles Harrington, 2007n823
Elswit, Sharon Barcan, 2006n1113
Ely, James W., Jr., 2006n519
Emadi, Hafizullah, 2006n88
Embar-Seddon, Ayn, 2009n470
Ember, Carol R., 2006n321, 2006n815, 2006n823
Ember, Melvin, 2006n321, 2006n815, 2006n823
Emergency mgmt, 2009n447
Emerson, William K., 2005n671
Emigration from the UK to America, v.1, 2007n293
Emigration from the UK to America, v.2, 2007n294
Emigration from the UK to America, v.3, 2008n343
Emily Dickinson, 2005n1066
Emmerson, Richard K., 2007n381
Emmett, Ross B., 2007n130
Emmy Award winning nighttime TV shows,
    1948-2004, 2007n1042
Empires at war, 2006n662
Employer legal forms simplified, 2008n235
Employer's legal hndbk, 7th ed, 2007n487
Employment, hours, & earnings 2005, 2006n239
Employment, hours, & earnings 2007 ed, 2008n228
Employment, hours, & earnings 2008, 2009n208
Empowering your lib, 2005n639
eNature.com [Website], 2006n1328
Encountering enchantment, 2008n883
Encyclopaedia Britannica 2005 [CD-ROM], 2005n30
Encyclopaedia Britannica almanac 2004, 2005n3
Encyclopaedia Britannica almanac 2006, 2007n1
Encyclopaedia Britannica bk of the yr 2006, 2007n40
Encyclopaedia Britannica discover America, 2007n60
Encyclopaedia Britannica world atlas, 2007n298
Encyclopaedia Judaica, 2d ed, 2007n1124
Encyclopaedia of Indian events & dates, 5th rev ed,
    2007n95
Encyclopaedia of the hist of sci, tech, & medicine in
    non-Western cultures, 2d ed, 2009n1127
Encyclopedia Americana, 2004 ed, 2005n31
Encyclopedia Americana, intl ed, 2006n24
Encyclopedia Americana [Website], 2006n25
Encyclopedia Americana [Website], 2008n25
Encyclopedia idiotica, 2006n503
Encyclopedia Latina, 2006n350
Encyclopedia mythica [Website], 2007n1024
Encyclopedia of …
    abortion in the US, 2d ed, 2009n740
    activism & social justice, 2008n59
    adoption, 3d ed, 2008n719
    African American business, 2007n134
    African-American culture & hist, 2d ed, 2006n329
    African American hist 1619-1895, 2007n270
    African American hist, 1896 to the present,
        2009n300

Encyclopedia of ... (*Cont.*)

African-American lit, 2009n956
African American military hist, 2005n665
African American society, 2006n330
African American women writers, 2008n911
African hist, 2006n460
African hist & culture, 2006n461
aging, 4th ed, 2007n693
American business, 2005n145
American business hist, 2007n137
American civil liberties, 2007n442
American civil rights & liberties, 2007n490
American educ, 3d ed, 2008n263
American folk art, 2005n935
American folklife, 2007n1018
American folklore, 2008n992
American foreign policy, 2005n726
American gospel music, 2006n1112
American govt & civics, 2009n643
American histl docs, 2005n425
American holidays & natl days, 2008n998
American Indian hist, 2008n323
American Indian lit, 2008n913
American industries, 4th ed, 2006n174
American industries, 5th ed, 2008n186
American Jewish hist, 2008n330
American journalism, 2008n802
American law enforcement, 2008n489
American race riots, 2008n301
American lit, rev ed, 2009n953
American natl parks, 2005n75
American opera, 2007n1002
American radio, 1920-60, 2d ed, 2009n813
American religions, 7th ed, 2005n1241
American social movements, 2005n426
American studies [Website], 2005n76
American studies [Website], 2009n375
American urban hist, 2008n768
American women in business, 2006n124
ancient Asian civilizations, 2005n467
ancient Greece, 2006n473
ancient lit, 2009n909
angels, 2d ed, 2005n1240
animal behavior, 2006n1364
animal sci, 2005n1333
animal sci [Website], 2005n1334
animals, 2005n1381
animals, 2006n1367
animals, 2007n1187
animated cartoons, 3d ed, 2009n1043
anthropology, 2007n259
antislavery & abolition, 2008n394
Appalachia, 2007n61
applied developmental sci, 2005n825
aquarium & pond fish, 2006n1378
Arab American artists, 2009n851
Arab American filmmakers, 2007n1047

Arab-Israeli conflict, 2009n127
Asian American artists, 2008n833
Asian-American lit, 2009n955
Asian theatre, 2008n1040
assns: intl orgs, 42d ed, 2007n31
autism spectrum disorders, 2007n1269
beat lit, 2007n939
behavior modification & cognitive behavior
　　therapy, 2006n755
bilingual educ, 2009n243
biology, 2005n1338
biomaterials & biomedical engineering, 2005n1405
biomaterials & biomedical engineering [Website],
　　2005n1406
bioterrorism defense, 2006n751
birds, 2008n1174
black studies, 2005n333
body adornment, 2009n843
breast cancer, 2005n1464
British writers, 2006n1043
Buddhism, 2008n1075
Buddhism, 2009n1100
business & finance, 2d ed, 2007n160
business ethics & society, 2008n154
business info sources, 19th ed, 2005n135
business info sources, 20th ed, 2006n117
business info sources, 22d ed, 2008n155
business info sources, 23d ed, 2009n133
cancer, 2006n1447
cancer & society, 2008n1250
capital punishment in the US, 2d ed, 2009n473
capitalism, 2005n146
career dvlpmt, 2007n190
careers & vocational guidance, 13th ed, 2006n226
careers & vocational guidance, 14th ed, 2008n223
Caribbean lit, 2007n970
Catholic lit, 2006n979
Catholic social thought, social sci, & social policy,
　　2008n1081
Catholicism, 2008n1082
Celtic mythology & folklore, 2005n1164
censorship, new ed, 2006n632
chemical processing, 2006n1490
chemistry, 2006n1492
Chicago, 2007n65
child abuse, 3d ed, 2008n720
children, adolescents, & the media, 2007n764
children's health & wellness, 2005n1459
Chinese-American relations, 2007n636
Christian theology, 2005n1256
Christianity, 2006n1228
Christianity, v.4, 2006n1229
Christianity, v.5, 2009n1108
chromatography, 2d ed, 2006n1401
civil liberties in America, 2006n582
Civil War medicine, 2009n383
clothing & fashion, 2005n928

coastal sci, 2006n1518
cognitive behavior therapy, 2007n650
Cold War espionage, spies, & secret operations, 2005n664
collectible children's bks, 2009n827
communities of practice in info & knowledge mgmt, 2006n584
communities of practice in info & knowledge mgmt [Website], 2006n585
complementary & alternative medicine, 2005n1455
computational mechanics, 2006n1393
computer sci & tech, rev ed, 2009n1288
conflicts since WWII, 2008n582
conspiracies & conspiracy theories, 2006n559
contemporary Russian culture, 2008n127
corrosion tech, 2d ed, 2005n1414
counseling, 2009n701
cremation, 2007n697
crime scene investigation, 2009n472
criminology, 2006n557
cryptozoology, 2006n1365
Cuban-US relations, 2005n727
dahlias, 2005n1315
data warehousing & mining, 2006n1468
data warehousing & mining, 2d ed, 2009n1280
data warehousing & mining [Website], 2006n1469
database technologies & applications, 2006n1486
death & dying, 2006n802
decision making & decision support technologies, 2009n1281
deer, 2005n1397
diasporas, 2006n823
dietary supplements, 2006n1282
digital govt, 2007n39
disability, 2006n805
disability, 2007n701
disasters, 2009n1318
distance learning, 2006n284
dog breeds, 2d ed, 2006n1376
domestic violence, 2008n721
drug abuse, 2009n763
drugs, alcohol, & addictive behavior, 3d ed, 2009n762
early cinema, 2006n1148
early TV crime fighters, 2007n1044
Earth, 2009n1300
earth & physical scis, 2007n1294
earth & physical scis, 2d ed, 2006n1498
earth sci, 2006n1499
earthquakes & volcanoes, 3d ed, 2008n1318
E-collaboration, 2009n1284
e-commerce, e-got, & mobile commerce, 2007n1286
educ & human dvlpmt, 2006n275
educ law, 2009n244
educl leadership & admin, 2007n237
educl psychology, 2009n245

elder care, 2005n794
electrochemistry, v.7a: inorganic electrochemistry, 2008n1287
electrochemistry, v.7b: inorganic electrochemistry, 2008n1288
Ellis Island, 2005n433
emancipation & abolition in the transatlantic world, 2008n453
emerging industries, 5th ed, 2008n187
endocrine diseases & disorders, 2006n1430
environment & society, 2008n1338
environmental ethics & philosophy, 2009n1333
epidemiology, 2008n1225
erotic lit, 2007n922
European peoples, 2007n111
evaluation, 2005n64
evolution, 2007n1166
evolution, 2008n1141
exploration, 2005n525
family health, 3d ed, 2005n1436
family health & wellness, 2009n1236
fantasy & horror fiction, 2007n929
fed agencies & commissions, 2005n700
feminist lit, 2006n985
feminist lit, 2007n884
fictional & fantastic langs, 2007n822
film noir, 2008n1018
finance, 2007n161
fire protection, 2d ed, 2007n1325
forensic sci, rev ed, 2009n466
gangs, 2009n468
garden design & structure, 2007n1156
gay & lesbian popular culture, 2009n1046
gender & info tech, 2007n1287
genetic disorders & birth defects, 3d ed, 2009n1242
genetics, rev ed, 2005n1375
genocide & crimes against humanity, 2005n588
geomagnetism & paleomagnetism, 2008n1296
geomorphology, 2005n1515
ghosts & spirits, 3d ed, 2008n696
global health, 2009n1222
global industries, 3d ed, 2005n187
global industries, 4th ed, 2008n188
global warming & climate change, 2009n1334
globalization, 2007n135
globalization, 2008n156
gothic lit, 2005n1045
governance, 2007n641
governance, 2008n671
govt & pols, 2d ed, 2005n687
govtl advisory orgs, 19th ed, 2005n705
govtl advisory orgs, 20th ed, 2006n705
govtl advisory orgs, 22d ed, 2008n632
hair, 2007n809
hardy plants, 2008n1134
health & aging, 2008n1207
health & behavior, 2005n1417

Encyclopedia of ... (*Cont.*)

hepatitis & other liver diseases, 2007n1273

high-tech crime & crime fighting, 2005n567

Hinduism, 2008n1094

Hinduism, 2008n1095

Hinduism, 2009n1116

Hispanic-American lit, 2009n984

histl treaties & alliances, 2d ed, 2007n424

historic places, rev ed, 2008n357

holidays & celebrations, 2007n1029

Hollywood, 2d ed, 2005n1199

homelessness, 2005n807

homeopathy, 2007n1263

human-animal relationships, 2008n1165

human computer interaction, 2006n1477

human computer interaction [Website], 2006n1478

human dvlpmt, 2007n651

human geography, 2005n66

human geography, 2007n50

hurricanes, typhoons, & cyclones, new ed, 2008n1308

hydrangeas, 2005n1321

hydrological scis, 2007n1227

immigration & migration in the American west, 2007n733

India, 2006n91

India, 2007n96

indie rock, 2009n1028

industrial & organizational psychology, 2007n652

infectious diseases, 2008n1226

infectious diseases, 3d ed, 2008n1232

info communication tech, 2009n1292

info ethics & security, 2008n1270

info sci & tech, 2006n586

info tech curriculum integration, 2009n1282

intelligence & counterintelligence, 2006n661

interpersonal violence, 2009n469

intl organized crime, 2006n556

intl relations & global pol, 2006n743

intl sports studies, 2007n671

invasions & conquests from the ancient times to the present, 2d ed, 2007n550

Irish hist & culture, 2005n110

Islam in the US, 2008n1098

Italian literary studies, 2008n941

Jewish American artists, 2008n834

Jewish myth, magic, & mysticism, 2008n1100

Judaism, 2006n1248

Judaism, 2007n1126

junk food & fast food, 2008n1122

juvenile violence, 2008n485

kitchen hist, 2005n1302

knowledge mgmt, 2006n1465

Latin American hist & culture, 2d ed, 2009n118

Latin American theater, 2005n1219

Latino popular culture, 2005n354

law & society, 2008n466

law enforcement, 2006n518

leadership, 2005n147

learning disabilities, 2d ed, 2007n257

leisure & outdoor recreation, 2005n754

lesbian, gay, bisexual, & transgender hist in America, 2005n804

libertarianism, 2009n671

life scis, 2d ed, 2005n1336

linguistics, 2006n939

lit & pol, 2007n880

literary modernism, 2005n1004

love in world religions, 2008n1052

magic & alchemy, 2008n694

major league baseball clubs, 2007n678

major mktg campaigns, v.2, 2007n227

mammals, 2d ed, 2007n1208

marine sci, 2009n1323

mathematics, 2006n1527

measurements & stats, 2007n737

measurements & stats, 2008n755

media & pol, 2008n610

medical anthropology, 2006n321

medical devices & instrumentation, 2d ed, 2007n1233

medical genomics & proteomics, 2006n1405

medical orgs & agencies, 14th ed, 2005n1422

medical orgs & agencies, 15th ed, 2006n1417

medical orgs & agencies, 18th ed, 2009n1226

medieval lit, 2006n984

medieval lit, 2007n883

Melbourne, 2007n104

men's health, 2006n1431

men's reproductive cancer, 2005n1463

mental health, 3d ed, 2008n679

mgmt, 5th ed, 2006n262

military tech & innovation, 2005n661

mobile computing & commerce, 2008n1271

modern Christian pol, 2007n574

modern French thought, 2005n1230

modern Greek lit, 2005n1088

modern Jewish culture, 2007n282

modern worldwide extremists & extremist groups, 2005n686

Mongolia & the Mongol empire, 2005n466

multicultural psychology, 2007n653

multimedia tech & networking, 2006n1466

multimedia tech & networking, 2d ed, 2009n1283

multimedia tech & networking [Website], 2006n1467

multiple sclerosis, 2006n1451

muscle & strength, 2008n700

Native American artists, 2009n307

Native American tribes, 3d ed, 2007n278

Native American wars & warfare, 2006n337

native music, 2006n1091

native tribes of N America, 2008n325

networked & virtual orgs, 2009n1286

New England, 2006n69
New Jersey, 2005n81
New Year's holidays worldwide, 2009n1038
N.Y. state, 2007n71
19th-century photography, 2008n847
nonlinear sci, 2006n1394
N American colonial conflicts to 1775, 2009n605
N American immigration, 2006n824
N American railroads, 2008n1354
N. Carolina, 2007n74
novels into film, 2d ed, 2006n1151
obesity, 2009n1265
obesity & eating disorders, 3d ed, 2007n1272
occultism, 2005n745
opera on screen, 2005n1200
Parkinson's disease, 2005n1471
Pentecostal & charismatic Christianity, 2007n1109
pestilence, pandemics, & plagues, 2009n1223
philosophy, 2007n1068
phobias, fears, & anxieties, 3d ed, 2009n700
physics, 2006n1523
physics, 3d ed, 2007n1317
plague & pestilence, 3d ed, 2008n454
plant & crop sci, 2005n1348
plant & crop sci [Website], 2005n1349
police studies, 3d ed, 2008n486
political communication, 2009n617
politics, 2006n703
pol & religion, 2d ed, 2007n575
polymer sci & tech, concise 3d ed, 2008n1196
portal technologies & applications, 2008n1282
prayer & praise, 2005n1257
prisoners of war & internment, 2d ed, 2007n552
prisons & correctional facilities, 2005n563
privacy, 2007n443
privacy, 2008n467
products & industries—manufacturing, 2008n189
products & industries—manufacturing, 2009n171
prostitution & sex work, 2007n709
Protestantism, 2005n1258
Protestantism, 2006n1233
psychoactive plants, translated ed, 2006n1331
psychological trauma, 2009n702
public admin & public policy, 2005n733
public admin & public policy, 1st updated suppl,
   2006n752
public relations, 2005n886
punk music & culture, 2007n1013
race & ethnic studies, 2005n323
race & racism, 2008n302
race, ethnicity, & society, 2009n293
racism in the US, 2007n263
rap & hip hop culture, 2007n1009
rape, 2006n558
real estate terms, 3d ed, 2009n241
recorded sound, 2d ed, 2005n1119
recreation & leisure in America, 2005n755

religion, 2d ed, 2006n1207
religion & nature, 2006n1208
religion & nature, paperback ed, 2009n1090
religion & spiritual dvlpmt, 2007n1079
religion & war, 2005n1238
religion, communication, & media, 2008n1053
religious phenomena, 2008n1056
religious revivals in America, 2008n1054
Renaissance lit, 2006n978
RF & microwave engineering, 2006n1395
rural America, 2009n71
schizophrenia & other psychotic disorders, 3d ed,
   2007n657
school psychology, 2006n756
sci fiction, 2006n1024
sci, tech, & ethics, 2006n1254
scientific principles, laws, & theories, 2009n1129
serial killers, 2d ed, 2007n470
sex & gender, 2006n815
sex & gender, 2008n732
sexually
Singapore, 2007n102
skin & skin disorders, 3d ed, 2007n1276
slave resistance & rebellion, 2008n395
small business, 3d ed, 2007n136
social problems, 2009n55
social psychology, 2008n677
social theory, 2007n690
social welfare hist in N America, 2006n818
social work, 20th ed, 2009n757
society & culture in the ancient world, 2008n455
society & culture in the medieval world, 2009n425
soil sci, 2009n1142
soil sci, 2d ed, 2007n1148
space & astronomy, 2007n1299
special educ, 2008n290
sports medicine, 2005n1473
Sri Lanka, 2d rev ed, 2007n103
statl scis, 2d ed, 2007n1134
stats in behavioral sci, 2007n654
stats in quality & reliability, 2009n1220
stem cell research, 2009n1171
stress & stress-related diseases, 2d ed, 2007n1247
superheroes on film & TV, 2005n1198
superheroes on film & TV, 2d ed, 2009n1044
supramolecular chemistry, 2005n1493
supramolecular chemistry [Website], 2005n1494
survey research methods, 2009n56
survival techniques, new ed, 2009n729
swearing, 2007n844
tarot, v.4, 2007n667
terrorism, rev ed, 2008n483
the African diaspora, 2009n301
the age of Imperialism, 1800-1914, 2009n402
the age of pol revolutions & new ideologies
   1760-1815, 2008n657
the American armed forces, 2006n660

Encyclopedia of ... (*Cont.*)

the American presidency, 2005n698

the American Revolution, 2d ed, 2007n350

the American Revolutionary War, 2007n349

the ancient Greek world, rev ed, 2006n474

the Antarctic, 2008n148

the Arctic, 2005n90

the atmospheric environment [Website], 2005n1513

the back & spine systems & disorders, 2008n1248

the blues, 2007n1007

the Byzantine empire, 2005n473

the Chicago literary renaissance, 2005n1064

the Cold War, 2008n583

the crusades, 2005n521

the developing world, 2007n107

the digestive system & digestive disorders, 2005n1439

the documentary film, 2007n1045

the elements, 2005n1495

the Enlightenment, rev ed, 2005n524

the FBI's 10 most wanted list, 2005n569

the 1st amendment, 2009n437

the French Revolutionary & Napoleonic wars, 2007n553

the gilded age & progressive era, 2006n440

the global economy, 2007n138

the great black migration, 2007n271

the great plains, 2005n77

the great plains Indians, 2008n324

the Harlem literary renaissance, 2006n1034

the Harlem renaissance, 2006n866

the heart & heart disease, 2005n1468

the hist of American mgmt, 2006n263

the India Diaspora, 2009n100

the jazz age, 2009n376

the Jewish diaspora, 2009n311

the Lib of Congress, 2006n587

the life course & human dvlpmt, 2009n739

the middle passage, 2008n396

the modern Olympic movement, 2005n777

the modern world, 2008n456

the muscle & skeletal systems & disorders, 2006n1432

the new American nation, 2007n351

the Palestinians, rev ed, 2006n354

the peoples of Asia & Oceania, 2009n305

the Renaissance & the Reformation, rev ed, 2005n472

the romantic era, 1760-1850, 2005n881

the social & cultural foundations of educ, 2009n246

the Stone-Campbell movement, 2006n1230

the Supreme Court, 2006n520

the Supreme Court of the US, 2009n438

the Underground Railroad, 2008n399

the United Nations, 2d ed, 2009n673

the US Congress, 2008n627

the Victorian era, 2005n485

the world's endangered langs, 2008n850

the world's minorities, 2006n323

the world's nations & cultures, 2008n64

tidepools & rocky shores, 2008n1166

title IX & sports, 2009n717

tracks & scats, 2005n776

transcendentalism, 2007n944

TV shows, 1925-2007, 2009n1065

TV subjects, themes, & settings, 2008n1023

20th century architecture, 2005n948

20th-century photography, 2007n819

20th-century tech, 2006n1255

unsolved crimes, 2005n568

US campaigns, elections, & electoral behavior, 2009n640

US labor & working class hist, 2007n191

US labor & working class hist, 2008n224

US natl security, 2007n642

vampires, werewolves, & other monsters, 2005n1154

visual effects, 2008n1275

vitamins, minerals, & supplements, 2d ed, 2005n1419

war & American society, 2007n352

war crimes & genocide, 2007n422

war movies, 2005n1196

warrior peoples & fighting groups, 2d ed, 2007n549

wars, 2005n662

water garden plants, 2005n1318

weather & climate, rev ed, 2008n1307

western colonialism since 1450, 2007n419

white-collar & corporate crime, 2005n564

white collar crime, 2008n487

witchcraft, 2007n666

witches, witchcraft & Wicca, 3d ed, 2009n716

women & American pol, 2009n641

women & baseball, 2007n679

women & Islamic cultures, v.1, 2005n870

women & Islamic cultures, v.2, 2006n854

women & Islamic cultures, v.3, 2006n855

women & Islamic cultures, v.4, 2007n757

women & Islamic cultures, v.5: practices, interpretations, & representations, 2008n782

women & Islamic cultures, v.6: suppl & index, 2008n783

women & religion in N America, 2007n1080

women in the renaissance, 2008n784

women's autobiog, 2006n856

women's health, 5th ed, 2006n1428

women's reproductive cancer, 2005n1465

wood, 2006n910

world biog suppl, v.24, 2005n14

world biog suppl, v. 27, 2009n10

world climatology, 2007n1308

world constitutions, 2007n444

world geography, 2006n387

world hist, 2009n426
world poverty, 2007n713
world religions, rev ed, 2007n1081
world scientists, rev ed, 2008n1105
world trade, 2006n200
world writers: beginnings through the 13th century, 2006n980
world writers: 14th through 18th centuries, 2006n981
world writers: 19th & 20th centuries, 2006n982
world's fairs & expositions, 2009n1039
WW I, 2006n497
WW II, 2006n498
WW II, 2008n452
yacht designers, 2007n1342
Encyclopedic dict of polymers, 2009n1213
Encyclopedic dict of women in early American films 1895-1930, 2005n1189
Encyclopedic gd to searching & finding health info on the Web, 2005n1423
Encyclopedic ref of immunotoxicology, 2007n1251
Encyclopedic sourcebk of new age religions, 2005n1239
Encyclopedic sourcebk of Satanism, 2009n715
Endangered species, 2d ed, 2005n1377
Endurance sports nutrition, 2d ed, 2008n703
Energy stats yrbk 2002, 2006n1534
Energy stats yrbk 2003, 2007n1323
Energy stats yrbk 2004, 2008n1334
Energy supply, 2006n1536
Energy supply & renewable resources, 2008n1335
Energy use worldwide, 2008n1336
Engel, Michael S., 2007n1205
Enghag, Per, 2005n1495
Engle, Tom, 2007n807, 2008n826
Engleman, Dodge, 2009n1195
Engleman, Lorna, 2009n1195
English China, 2009n819
English, Fenwick W., 2007n237
English glee in the reign of George III, 2005n1126
English, June A., 2005n1259
English lang arts units for grades 9-12, 2009n270
English lit in context, 2009n970
English, Lyn D., 2009n1325
Englund, Klaudia, 2007n782
Engs, Ruth Clifford, 2006n1191
Enhanced occupational outlook hndbk, 5th ed, 2005n233
Enhanced occupational outlook hndbk, 6th ed, 2008n229
Enhancing teaching & learning, 2d ed, 2005n609
Eniclerico, Ronald, 2007n648
Ennis, Lisa A., 2009n717
Enser's filmed bks & plays, 6th ed, 2005n1193
Enter the players: N.Y. stage actors in the 20th century, 2005n1218
Enter the playmakers, 2007n1055

Entertaining from ancient Rome to the Super Bowl, 2009n1145
Entertainment awards, 3d ed, 2005n1183
Entrepreneur's info sourcebk, 2007n142
Environment: the sci behind the stories, 2009n1345
Environmental disasters series, 2006n1540
Environmental engineering dict, 4th ed, 2006n1404
Environmental issues, 2007n1328
Environmental issues in American hist, 2008n1346
Environmental law hndbk, 18th ed, 2007n488
Environmental law hndbk, 19th ed, 2009n481
Environmental Protection Agency, 2006n722
Environmental regulatory calculations hndbk, 2009n1342
Environmental regulatory dict, 4th ed, 2006n579
Environmental resource hndbk 2005/06, 3d ed, 2006n1541
Environmental resource hndbk 2008-09, 4th ed, 2008n1344
Environmental sci in context, 2009n1335
Environmental statutes, 2004 ed, 2005n586
Environmental statutes, 2005 ed, 2006n580
Environmental statutes, 2008 ed, 2009n482
Epic films, 2d ed, 2005n1214
Epidemics, 2005n1445
Epidemics & pandemics, 2006n1423
EpistemeLinks.com: philosophy resources on the Internet [Website], 2006n1183
Eponymous dict of economics, 2006n120
Epps, Edwin C., 2005n1059
Epstein, Irving, 2009n767
Epstein, Lee, 2008n475
Erb, Uwe, 2005n1404
Erchul, William P., 2009n255
Erikson, Rolf, 2008n514
Erin's sons, 2009n326
Erlewine, Stephen Thomas, 2005n1147, 2005n1148
Ermatinger, James W., 2006n478, 2009n433
Ernest, Douglas J., 2006n683
Erratic impact's philosophy research base [Website], 2006n1184
Ervin, Justin, 2009n192
Erwin, Wallace M., 2005n969
ESPN pro football ency, 2d ed, 2008n711
ESPN sports almanac 2004, 2005n761
Esposito, John L., 2005n1274
Espy, Willard R., 2008n866
Essential atlas of biology, 2005n1341
Essential atlas of mathematics, 2006n1532
Essential atlas of physical geography, 2005n383
Essential Civil War, 2007n363
Essential gd to becoming an expert searcher, 2009n531
Essential gd to fed employment laws, 2007n485
Essential gd to prescription drugs, 2004 ed, 2005n1479
Essential gd to prescription drugs, 2006 ed, 2006n1461
Essential herb-drug-vitamin interaction gd, 2008n1261

Essential ref servs for today's school media specialists, 2005n612

Essential school lib glossary, 2006n606

Essential Shakespeare hndbk, 2005n1080

Essentials of elem school lib mgmt, 2005n613

Essentials of forensic sci series, 2009n478

Essentials of strength training & conditioning, 3d ed, 2009n732

Establishment of the Han Empire & Imperial China, 2006n465

Estate planning simplified, 2007n463

Estaville, Lawrence E., 2009n1326

Estes, Kenneth W., 2006n481

Estrada, Larry J., 2009n769

Ethics, rev ed, 2006n1192

Ethics desk ref for psychologists, 2009n710

Ethics updates [Website], 2006n1201

Ethnic bk awards, 2006n1004

Ethnologue [Website], 2008n849

ETHX on the Web [Website], 2006n1185

Etulain, Richard W., 2005n22

Eubanks, Ted Lee, Jr., 2009n1199

Eugenics movement, 2006n1191

EuroDocs [Website], 2005n476

Eurominority [Website], 2008n114

Europa dir of intl orgs 2005, 7th ed, 2006n740

Europa dir of intl orgs 2007, 2008n658

Europa dir of intl orgs 2008, 2009n676

Europa intl foundation dir 2005, 2006n813

Europa intl foundation dir 2007, 2008n731

Europa intl foundation dir 2008, 17th ed, 2009n752

Europa world of learning 2008, 58th ed, 2008n278

Europa world of learning 2009, 59th ed, 2009n273

Europa world yr bk 2005, 2006n45

Europa world yr bk 2007, 48th ed, 2008n45

Europa world yr bk 2008, 49th ed, 2009n39

Europe since 1914, 2007n379

Europe, 1789-1914, 2007n378

European integration current contents [Website], 2008n113

European mktg data & stats 2004, 39th ed, 2005n218

European mktg data & stats 2006, 41st ed, 2006n218

European mktg forecasts 2004/05, 8th ed, 2005n219

European mktg forecasts 2005/06, 9th ed, 2006n219

European mktg forecasts 2009, 12th ed, 2009n201

European Union, 2006n738

European Union ency & dir 2008, 2008n115

Eury, Michael, 2007n1031

Euthanasia, 2d ed, 2008n498

Evaluation of lib collections, access, & electronic resources, 2005n593

Evangelicals & sci, 2009n1138

Evans, Arthur V., 2006n1385, 2007n1213

Evans, Craig A., 2007n1101

Evans, G. Edward, 2005n640, 2006n646, 2008n555, 2008n556

Evans, James Allan, 2009n408

Evans, Martin Marix, 2008n590

Evans, Nick, 2009n726

Evans-Romaine, Karen, 2008n127

Evans-Walls, Tonya M., 2007n522, 2008n538

Even more great ideas for libs & friends, 2009n515

Evens, Jules G., 2009n1190

Events that changed Germany, 2006n472

Events that changed Great Britain from 1066 to 1714, 2005n489

Everett, Deborah, 2009n307

Everett, William A., 2008n1041

Everitt, Brian S., 2007n654

Everyday biblical literacy, 2008n1070

Everyday finance, 2009n165

Everyone & everything in George Eliot, 2007n958

Everyone & everything in Trollope, 2005n1081

Everything Irish, 2005n111

Evidence explained, 2008n563

Evolution, 2007n1167

Evolution, 2008n1144

Evolution & creationism, 2008n1147

Evolution of the insects, 2007n1205

Evolution of US counterterrorism policy, 2009n695

Evolution vs. creationism, 2005n1235

Evolving Eden: an illus gd to the evolution of the African large-mammal fauna, 2005n1383

Evolving Internet ref resources, 2007n539

Ewan, Elizabeth, 2007n388, 2008n778

Ewert, Sara Dant, 2005n75

Executive branch of state govt, 2007n612

Executive branch of the fed govt, 2008n645

Exner, Carol R., 2006n618

Experiment central, v.5 & 6, 2005n1293

Exploration & sci, 2007n1145

Explore Canada, rev ed, 2005n404

Explorer atlas, 2007n312

Explorers & exploration, 2005n382

Exploring American hist, 2008n397

Exploring American hist, 2009n377

Exploring careers, 3d ed, 2005n240

Exploring gun use in America, 2005n548

Exploring Haydn, 2006n1081

Exploring health care careers, 3d ed, 2007n213

Exploring mammals, 2008n1188

Exploring tech careers, 4th ed, 2007n214

Exploring technology, 2005n1283

Exploring the geology of the Carolinas, 2008n1321

Exploring the Middle Ages, 2006n467

Expository dict of Bible words, 2006n1223

Extraordinary animals, 2008n1168

Extraordinary jobs in . . . series, 2007n215

Extrasolar planets, 2006n1504

Extreme birds, 2009n1198

Extreme searcher's Internet hndbk, 2005n1486

Extreme weather, 2008n1313

Extreme weather & climate events [Website], 2009n1311

Extremist groups, 2007n576
Exum, Kaitlen Jay, 2005n1548
Eye care sourcebk, 3d ed, 2009n1258
Eye on art series, 2008n841
Eye on art series, 2009n854
Eyes like butterflies: a treasury of similes &
    metaphors, 2007n853
Eyewitness accounts [Website], 2005n514
Eyewitness to Watergate, 2008n410
EZ occupational outlook hndbk, 2008n230
Ezra Pound ency, 2006n1068
Ezra, Marni, 2006n726

F & S index—US, v.46, no.3, 6, 9, 10, 2007n151
F-15 Eagle engaged, 2008n602
Faber, Candace, 2009n214
Faber, Richard B., 2009n658
Fabry, Heinz-Josef, 2005n1249, 2007n1099
Fabulous creatures, mythical monsters, & animal
    power symbols, 2009n1034
FACCTs [Website], 2006n1463
Facts on File biology hndbk, rev ed, 2007n1168
Facts on File chemistry hndbk, rev ed, 2007n1293
Facts on File children's atlas, 2006 ed, 2007n299
Facts on File companion to …
    American poetry, 2008n957
    British poetry before 1600, 2009n1001
    British poetry: 17th & 18th centuries, 2009n1002
    British poetry: 1900 to the present, 2009n1003
    classical drama, 2006n1005
    the American novel, 2007n940
    the British novel, 2006n1044
    the British short story, 2008n927
    the French novel, 2008n940
    the world novel, 2009n910
    20th-century American poetry, 2006n1069
    world poetry 1900 to the present, 2008n956
Facts on File dict of …
    allusions, 2009n911
    astronomy, 5th ed, 2007n1301
    biology, 4th ed, 2006n1314
    chemistry, 4th ed, 2006n1491
    cliches, 2d ed, 2007n854
    computer sci, rev ed, 2007n1290
    earth sci, rev ed, 2007n1295
    environmental sci, 3d ed, 2008n1339
    foreign words & phrases, 2d ed, 2009n893
    forensic sci, 2005n565
    marine sci, new ed, 2008n1324
    mathematics, 4th ed, 2006n1526
    music, 2005n1118
    physics, 4th ed, 2006n1522
    proverbs, 2d ed, 2008n869
    space tech, rev ed, 2005n1502
    weather & climate, rev ed, 2007n1309

Facts on File earth sci hndbk, rev ed, 2007n1297
Facts on File ency of art, 2006n921
Facts on File ency of health & medicine, 2008n1227
Facts on File ency of word & phrase origins, 4th ed,
    2009n885
Facts on File ency of world mythology & legend, 2d
    ed, 2005n1158
Facts on File gd to good writing, 2006n882
Facts on File gd to research, 2006n46
Facts on File gd to style, 2007n777
Facts on File physics hndbk, rev ed, 2008n1328
Facts on File student's dict of American English,
    2008n865
Facts on File student's thesaurus, 3d ed, 2006n958
Facts on intl relations & security trends (FIRST)
    [Website], 2008n661
Fagan, Deirdre, 2008n918
Fahey, David M., 2005n820
Fahlbusch, Erwin, 2006n1228, 2009n1108
Fairrosa cyber lib of children's lit [Website],
    2007n890
Fairy lore, 2007n1020
Faith reads, 2009n986
Faith seeking action, 2008n1090
Falcetti, Cara, 2008n953
Falconer's new universal dict of the Marine, repr ed,
    2007n567
Falola, Toyin, 2005n83, 2008n396
Faltin, Frederick W., 2009n1220
Family-centered lib hndbk, 2009n551
Family in society, 2007n703
Family life in 17th- & 18th-century America,
    2006n809
Family life in 20th-century America, 2008n722
Family spending, 2005 ed, 2007n725
Famous 1st facts, 6th ed, 2008n26
Famous 1st facts, 6th ed, 2008n26
Fantastic fiction [Website], 2006n1010
Fantasy ency, 2007n1017
Fantasy lit for children & YAs, 5th ed, 2006n992
Farenga, Stephen J., 2006n275
Fargnoli, A. Nicholas, 2007n968, 2009n960
Farmer, Lesley S. J., 2009n550, 2009n565
Farnsworth, Elizabeth, 2006n1333
Farr, Michael, 2005n241, 2005n242, 2006n251,
    2006n252, 2007n199, 2007n200, 2007n216,
    2007n217, 2007n218, 2007n219, 2008n244
Farrell, Susan, 2009n966
Farrington, Karen, 2007n1073
Farris, June Pachuta, 2008n775
Farsoun, Samih K., 2005n124
Farwell's rules of the nautical road, 8th ed, 2006n1553
Fatal Army Air Forces aviation accidents in the US
    1941-45, 2007n548
Fathers of the church, 2008n1088
Fattah, Hala, 2009n129
Favorite children's authors & illustrators, 2005n1026

Favorite children's authors & illustrators, 2d ed, 2007n904

Favorite poem project [Website], 2009n991

Fawcett, Jan, 2008n679

FaxUSA 2005, 12th ed, 2005n41

FaxUSA 2006, 13th ed, 2006n34

FBI careers, 2d ed, 2007n206

FDR yrs, 2008n621

Fearn-Banks, Kathleen, 2006n1149, 2007n1046

Federal law enforcement careers, 2d ed, 2007n207

Federal leadership dir online [Website], 2009n649

Federal regional yellow bk, Summer 2005, 2006n706

Federal regulatory dir, 12th ed, 2007n598

Federal regulatory dir, 13th ed, 2008n633

Federal Reserve educ [Website], 2009n161

Federal Reserve system, 2006n166

Federal resume gdbk, 4th ed, 2008n237

Federal staff dir, Fall 2004, 46th ed, 2005n706

Federal staff dir [Website], 2005n707

Federal yellow bk, Summer 2005, 2006n707

Federalism in America, 2007n594

Feener, R. Michael, 2006n1242

Fehl, Pamela, 2007n210, 2007n222, 2008n249

Feiertag, Joe, 2006n881

Feinberg, Beth, 2006n611

Feinberg, Sandra, 2009n551

Feintuch, Burt, 2006n69

Felder, Deborah G., 2005n1007

Fell, Derek, 2007n1156, 2008n1134

Felton, John, 2008n146, 2009n128

FemBio [Website], 2005n866

Feminism & women's issues [Website], 2005n859

Feminism in lit, 2005n999

Feminist ency of Spanish lit, 2005n1089

Feminist theory Website [Website], 2006n850

Fenner, Audrey, 2005n625, 2007n533

Ferguson career coach: managing your career in educ, 2009n218

Ferguson career coach: managing your career in law enforcement, 2009n219

Ferguson career coach: managing your career in the art industry, 2009n220

Ferguson career coach: managing your career in the health care industry, 2009n1230

Ferguson career coach: managing your career in the music industry, 2009n221

Ferguson career coach: managing your career in the sports industry, 2009n223

Ferguson career coach: managing your career in theater & the performing arts, 2009n222

Ferguson career resource gd for people with disabilities, 3d ed, 2007n702

Ferguson career resource gd for women & minorities, 2007n201

Ferguson career resource gd to apprenticeship programs, 3d ed, 2007n202

Ferguson career resource gd to internships & summer jobs, 2007n203

Ferguson career skills lib series, 2005n243

Ferguson, Dana, 2005n55, 2005n1032, 2006n53

Ferguson gd to resumes & job-hunting skills, 2006n241

Ferguson, Margaret R., 2007n612

Ferguson, Rebecca, 2006n510

Ferguson's career guidance center [Website], 2008n239

Ferguson's careers in focus series, 2005n244

Ferguson's careers in focus series, 2007n220

Ferguson's careers in focus series, 2009n224

Fergusson, Rossalind, 2008n869

Fernando, 2005n936

Ferraggine, Viviana E., 2006n1486

Ferrara, Miranda H., 2005n1000, 2006n977

Ferro, David L., 2006n1481

Ferro, Jeffrey, 2006n568, 2006n569, 2007n481

Feuer, Bryan, 2005n492

Fichtelberg, Susan, 2008n883

Fiction catalog, 15th ed, 2007n916

Fiction catalog, 2007 suppl, 2008n529

Field gd to …

    airplanes of N America, 3d ed, 2007n1337

    animal tracks, 3d ed, 2006n795

    butterflies of the San Francisco Bay & Sacramento Valley regions, 2008n1187

    cattle, 2009n1167

    ferns & their related families, 2d ed, 2006n1333

    freshwater fishes of Calif., rev ed, 2007n1203

    geology, new ed, 2008n1319

    gold, gemstone, & mineral sites of British Columbia, v.2, rev ed, 2007n1312

    insects of southern Africa, updated ed, 2006n1387

    mammals of N America N of Mexico, 4th ed, 2007n1210

    owls of Calif. & the west, 2008n1180

    Narnia, 2005n1078

    N Atlantic wildlife, 2006n1366

    Potter, 2009n945

    rocks & minerals of southern Africa, 2006n1513

    southern New England railroad depots & freight houses, 2008n1356

    the fungi of Australia, 2006n1350

    the natural world of NYC, 2008n1164

    the plants & animals of the Middle Rio Grande Bosque, 2009n1189

    the wild orchids of Tex., 2008n1153

    the wild orchids of Thailand, 4th ed, 2006n1348

Field, Shelly, 2005n245, 2005n246, 2006n244, 2007n221, 2008n245, 2009n218, 2009n219, 2009n220, 2009n221, 2009n222, 2009n223, 2009n1230

Fielding, Jonathan E., 2005n1427

Fields, Anne M., 2009n505

Fields, Armond, 2007n1054

Fierro, Pedro, Jr., 2008n1337

Fieser, James, 2006n1195

Fifties in America, 2006n441

50 aircraft that changed the world, 2008n1353

50 states, 2d ed, 2008n70

Figueredo, D. H., 2007n970, 2008n332, 2008n440

Filby, P. William, 2006n364, 2006n365, 2006n366, 2006n367

Film & media resources from Artslynx [Website], 2009n793

Film, folklore, & urban legends, 2008n1032

Film in Latin America [Website], 2006n1135

Film stars & their awards, 2009n1062

Film studies resources—academic info [Website], 2006n1154

Filmography of social issues, 2006n1161

Filmography of world hist, 2008n1028

Filson, Lawrence E., 2008n476

Financial aid for …
  Hispanic Americans 2003-05, 2006n305
  Native Americans 2003-05, 2006n306
  research & creative activities abroad 2006-08, 2006n307
  studying & training abroad 2006-08, 2006n308
  veterans, military personnel, & their dependents 2004-06, 2006n309
  the disabled & their families 2004-06, 2005n316
  the disabled & their families 2006-08, 2007n252

Financial hist of modern US corporate scandals, 2007n148

Financial servs Canada 2007/08, 10th ed, 2008n181

Financial Times world desk ref, 6th ed, 2005n51

Financial yellow bk, Summer 2005, 2006n169

Financial yellow bk, 2008 ed, 2009n168

Find it online, 4th ed, 2006n1483

Find someone who: introducing 200 favorite picture bks, 2009n928

Finding an online high school, 2007n242

Finding birds of the great Tex. Coastal birding trail, 2009n1199

Findling, John E., 2005n489, 2005n777, 2009n1039

Fink, Donald G., 2007n1225

Finkelman, Paul, 2006n866, 2007n270, 2007n351, 2007n442, 2008n464, 2009n300, 2009n395, 2009n436

Finkelstein, Richard, 2006n869

Finley, Laura L., 2008n485

Fiore, Carole D., 2006n619

Fiore's summer lib reading program hndbk, 2006n619

Firearms, 2005n680

Firefly atlas of N America, 2007n300

Firefly atlas of the universe, 3d ed, 2006n1500

Firefly ency of astronomy, 2005n1503

Firefly ency of trees, 2006n1352

Firefly 5 lang visual dict, 2006n965

Firefly great world atlas, 2006n375

Firefly gd to …
  deserts, 2007n1310
  gems, 2005n1516
  global hazards, 2005n1514
  minerals rocks & fossils, 2006n1515
  mountains, 2007n1311
  seashells of the world, 2005n1398
  the human body, 2005n1345
  the oceans, 2005n1521
  the state of the world, 2006n67
  weather, 2006n1509

Firefly jr visual dict, 2008n870

Firefly world factbk, 2d ed, 2008n360

Firefly's world of facts, 2d ed, 2009n40

First American women architects, 2009n856

First ascent, 2009n737

First Bank of the US [Website], 2009n162

First English dict, 1604, 2008n851

First generation of country music stars, 2008n987

First human body ency, 2006n1320

First ladies fact bk, 2006n698

First name reverse dict, 2d ed, 2008n348

1stHeadlines [Website], 2005n898

Fischbach, Michael R., 2008n142

Fischel, Jack R., 2006n499

Fischman, Josh, 2006n291, 2008n283

Fisher, Brian L., 2008n1185

Fisher, Celia B., 2005n825

Fisher, David G., 2007n1302

Fisher, James, 2009n1074

Fisher, Karen E., 2006n635

Fisher, Patricia H., 2006n636

Fisher, R. B., 2006n1479

Fisher, Steven, 2005n600

Fishes of Ala., 2005n1392

Fishes of the Tex. Laguna Madre, 2009n1201

Fishman, Stephen, 2007n152, 2008n539

Fiske gd to colleges 2006, 22d ed, 2007n246

Fiske gd to colleges 2008, 24th ed, 2008n279

Fiske, Edward B., 2007n246, 2008n267, 2008n279, 2009n254

Fiske, Robert Hartwell, 2005n958

Fiske, Susan T., 2005n743

Fitch, Thomas, 2008n246

Fitch, Thomas P., 2007n162

Fitness & exercise sourcebk, 3d ed, 2008n706

Fitness info for teens, 2005n1428

Fitness info for teens, 2d ed, 2009n1231

Fitness professional's hndbk, 5th ed, 2009n734

Fitzgerald, Mary Ann, 2005n317

Fitzgerald, Terence J., 2009n1048

Fitzhenry & Whiteside bk of Canadian facts & dates, 3d ed, 2006n47

Fitzmyer, Joseph A., 2009n1094

Fitzpatrick, Patrick J., 2006n1510

Fitzpatrick, Tony, 2008n672

500 best ways for teens to spend the summer, 2005n283

500 cacti, 2008n1160
500 comic bk villains, 2006n1119
500 freshwater aquarium fish, 2007n1202
500 great bks for teens, 2007n902
Fixico, Donald L., 2008n326
Flags of all countries [Website], 2005n365
Flanagan, Constance A., 2006n688, 2007n578
Flash focus: the one-stop study gd to American pol,
    2006n725
Flayderman, Norm, 2009n835
Flayderman's gd to antique American firearms, 9th ed,
    2009n835
Fleming, E. J., 2005n1203
Fleming, Patricia Lockhart, 2005n656, 2006n655,
    2006n656
Flemish DNA & ancestry, 2009n321
Fletcher, Nick, 2005n1393
Fletcher-Janzen, Elaine, 2008n290
Flickipedia, 2008n1013
Flinn, Frank K., 2008n1082
Fliotsos, Anne, 2009n1073
Flocker, Michael, 2005n1175
Flood, Michael, 2008n726
Flora of N America: N of Mexico, v.4, pt.1,
    2005n1360
Flora of N America: N of Mexico, v.19, 2007n1176
Flora of N America: N of Mexico, v.20, 2007n1177
Flora of N America: N of Mexico, v.21, 2007n1178
Flora of N America: N of Mexico, v.24, 2008n1150
Flora, Joseph M., 2007n936
Flora's orchids, 2006n1342
Florence, Cathy, 2009n817, 2009n818
Florence, Gene, 2008n813, 2009n817, 2009n818
Flores, Juan Carlos, 2008n1044
Florida almanac 2007-08, 17th ed, 2008n80
Florida landscape plants, 2d rev ed, 2006n1339
Florida municipal profiles, 2007 ed, 2009n72
Florida starwatch, 2008n1299
Flory, J. "Kelly", Jr., 2005n1549, 2009n1350
Flory, Sean M., 2007n925
Flowerdew, Bob, 2007n1149
Flowering plant families of the world, 2008n1157
Flowering plants of the neotropics, 2005n1356
Flowers, John, 2005n1194
Fluent in fantasy, 2009n946
Flute on record, 2007n995
Flygare, Halle, 2008n1158
Flying solo: a survival gd for the solo & small firm
    lawyer, 4th ed, 2006n540
Flynn, Roderick, 2008n1015
Flynn, Tom, 2008n1058
Focus groups, v.1, 2009n5
Focus on freshwater aquarium fish, 2005n1393
Fodor's Caribbean 2006, 2006n416
Fodor's Costa Rica 2006, 2006n417
Fodor's escape to nature without roughing it,
    2005n395

Fodor's Hawai'i 2006, 2006n396
Fodor's Italy 2006, 2006n406
Fodor's Mexico 2006, 2006n418
Fodor's San Francisco 2005, 2005n396
Fodor's Spain 2006, 2006n407
Fogelson, Raymond D., 2005n345
Fogg, Neeta P., 2005n247
Fogle, Bruce, 2007n1198, 2007n1200
Folk music, 2006n1103
Folkard, Claire, 2005n52
Follstad, Virginia P., 2008n1076
Folmer, Henk, 2007n1330
Folsom, W. Davis, 2005n145, 2006n121
Fomerand, Jacques, 2008n659
Fonseca, Anthony J., 2007n931
Fontenoy, Paul, 2007n571
Fontenoy, Paul E., 2008n605
Food & beverage market place 2007, 6th ed, 2007n167
Food & beverage market place 2008, 7th ed,
    2008n1125
Food & beverage market place 2009, 2009n174
Food & drug dict, 2005n1299
Food alert! 2d ed, 2009n1153
Food biotech, 2d ed, 2006n1286
Food culture in …
    Great Britain, 2005n1306
    Italy, 2005n1307
    Japan, 2005n1304
    Mexico, 2006n1289
    Russia & Central Asia, 2006n1291
    Spain, 2006n1292
    S America, 2006n1290
    Sub-Saharan Africa, 2006n1294
    the Caribbean, 2006n1288
    the Near East, Middle East, & N Africa, 2006n1287
Food ency, 2007n1151
Food in colonial & fed America, 2006n1293
Food in medieval times, 2005n1303
Food in the ancient world, 2007n1152
Food plants of the world, 2006n1338
Food safety, 2d ed, 2008n1132
Foodways & folklore, 2009n1154
Forbes bk of business quotations, repr ed, 2006n154
Ford, Charlotte, 2009n584
Ford, Julian D., 2009n702
Ford, Lacy K., 2005n441
Ford, Lynne E., 2009n641
Foreign relations of the US (FRUS) [Website],
    2009n678
Foreign representatives in the US yellow bk, Summer
    2005, 2006n708
Forensic art [Website], 2006n577
Forensic sci, 2007n472
Forensic sci, 2009n470
Forensic sci experiments on file, 2005n1286
Forensic sci timelines [Website], 2006n553
Forest fires, 2006n1544

Former Yugoslavia's diverse peoples, 2005n339
Forms of local govt, 2008n646
Forster, Roy, 2005n1325
Forsythe, Mark, 2007n18
Fortress America, 2005n455
Forts of the US, 2007n353
Fortune-telling bk, 2005n744
40 best fields for your career, 2007n218
Foss, William O., 2006n696
Foster, Donald H., 2007n989
Foster, Douglas A., 2006n1230
Foster, Gerald L., 2007n1337
Foster, Lynn V., 2005n498, 2008n137
Fostering community through digital storytelling, 2009n505
Foundation reporter, 37th ed, 2005n811
Foundation reporter 2008, 40th ed, 2009n753
Foundations of lib & info sci, 2d ed, 2005n602
Founders on religion, 2007n1092
Four British fantasists, 2007n911
Four-yr colleges 2006, 36th ed, 2006n292
Fouracre, Paul, 2007n432
Fournier, Valerie, 2008n1046
Fourth of July ency, 2008n1000
Fox, Barry, 2008n1261
Fox, N. J., 2007n1063
Fox, Tom, 2008n800
Foxhall, Lin, 2007n377
Foyle, Christopher, 2009n888
Foyle's philavery, repr ed, 2009n888
Frader, Laura L., 2007n366
Fraioli, Deborah A., 2006n471
Frame by frame III, 2008n1025
France & the Americas, 2006n747
Francis, J. Michael, 2006n749, 2007n637
Franck, Irene M., 2005n427
Francoeur, Robert T., 2005n816
Franek, Robert, 2005n292
Frank, Andrew K., 2008n406, 2009n389
Frank, Ben G., 2005n408
Frank, Diane, 2009n874
Frank, Frederick S., 2006n1016
Frank, Lisa Tendrich, 2009n789
Frank Lloyd Wright comp, rev ed, 2007n818
Frankental, Sally, 2007n90
Franklyn, David J., 2005n590
Franks, B. Don, 2009n734
Franks, Don, 2005n1183
Franz Kafka ency, 2006n1058
Fraser, Catherine C., 2007n1033
Frauds against the elderly, 2005n797
Frazier, Harriet C., 2007n482
FRBR, 2008n530
Frederick, Julia C., 2006n109
Fredricksen, John C., 2008n384, 2009n368
Fredriksen, John C., 2005n683, 2007n340

Free African Americans of N.C., Va., & S.C., 5th ed, 2006n357
Free jazz & free improvisation, 2005n1151
Free stuff for baby! 2006-07 ed, 2007n158
Free trade, 2006n203
Freedman, Eric, 2009n659
Freedman, Lew, 2008n707
Freedom of association, 2005n544
Freedom of the press, 2005n546
Freeman, Arthur, 2007n650
Freeman, Brush, 2005n1387
Freeman, Judy, 2007n891, 2009n552
Fremont-Barnes, Gregory, 2007n345, 2007n349, 2007n553, 2008n392, 2008n657
French & Indian War, 2005n439
French Revolution, 2005n482
Fretter, Judith, 2006n741
Frey, Linda S., 2005n482
Frey, Marsha L., 2005n482
Frey, Rebecca Joyce, 2008n1061
Frey, William H., 2008n55
Fridman, Eva Jane Neumann, 2005n1278
Friedberg, Arthur L., 2005n921, 2007n799
Friedberg, Ira S., 2005n921, 2007n799
Friedman, Lisa, 2009n655
Friedman, Norman, 2005n678, 2007n573
Friedrich, Marty, 2007n676
Friedrich, Susanne, 2009n1303
Frisbie-Fulton, Michelle, 2005n88
Fritz, Harry William, 2005n446
Fritze, Ronald H., 2005n510
Frizler, Paul, 2005n1194
Frodeman, Robert, 2009n1333
Frohne, Dietrich, 2006n1334
Frohnen, Bruce, 2008n625
Frois, Jeanne, 2007n67
Frolund, Tina, 2008n895, 2009n927
From A to Zine: building a winning zine collection in your lib, 2005n644
From Agincourt to Zanzibar, 2009n346
From daytime to primetime, 2006n1165
From luminous hot stars to starburst galaxies, 2009n1306
From outreach to equity, 2005n641
From suffrage to the senate, 2d ed, 2007n596
From the ends to the beginning: a bilingual anthology of Russian verse [Website], 2005n1095
Frontier America, 2005n427
Frontiers of space exploration, 2d ed, 2005n1506
Frost, William J., 2007n542
Frost-Knappman, Elizabeth, 2006n861
Frucht, Richard, 2006n100
Fruit & nuts, 2007n1180
Fruit, 2005n1367
Fruit, 2009n1184
Frumkin, Norman, 2007n146
Fuad-Luke, Alastair, 2009n345

FUBAR: soldier slang of WW II, 2008n868
Fuchs, Jurgen, 2006n1405
Fukuchi, Mitsuo, 2008n1182
Fulton, Len, 2006n649, 2006n650, 2006n651,
    2008n10, 2009n591, 2009n593, 2009n594
Functional requirements for bibliog records (FRBR),
    2006n616
Fundamentalism, 2008n1061
Fundamentals of ...
    children's servs, 2006n623
    collection dvlpmt & mgmt, 2005n623
    collection dvlpmt & mgmt, 2d ed, 2009n558
    info studies, 2d ed, 2008n545
    lib supervision, 2006n637
    photography, 2009n866
    tech servs mgmt, 2009n538
Funding sources forchildren & youth programs 2004,
    3d ed, 2005n812
Funding sources for community & economic dvlpmt
    2004/05, 10th ed, 2005n813
Funding sources for K-12 educ 2004, 6th ed,
    2005n284
Fundukian, Laurie J., 2005n811, 2008n678, 2009n703,
    2009n1255
Fung, Karen, 2008n91
Funnell, John, 2006n1164
Fusarelli, Lance D., 2009n252
Future demographic, 2005n831
Future of state [Website], 2008n634
Fyle, C. Magbaily, 2009n87

G. K. Hall annual bibliog of modern art 2001-02,
    2005n930
G. K. Hall bibliog gd to ...
    anthropology & archaeology 2002, 2005n318
    Latin American studies 2002, 2005n118
    Latin American studies 2003, 2006n107
    maps & atlases 2002, 2005n381
    maps & atlases 2003, 2006n383
    Slavic, Baltic, & Eurasian studies 2002, 2005n104
    Slavic, Baltic, & Eurasian studies 2003, 2006n101
Gabby's wordspeller phonetic dict, 2d ed, 2009n874
Gabler-Hover, Janet, 2007n937
Gabra, Gawdat, 2009n1109
Gabriel, Joseph, 2005n1292
Gabriel, Richard A., 2006n662, 2008n593
Gadgil, Ashok, 2005n1540, 2006n1538
Gagne, Louise, 2005n1491, 2008n1284, 2009n597,
    2009n797
Gaines, Leonard M., 2005n165
Gaines, Steven D., 2008n1166
Galambose, Louis, 2009n635
Galbraith, Steven K., 2005n1074
Galbraith, Stuart, IV, 2009n1067
Gale dir of databases, 2004, 2005n1489

Gale dir of databases, 2009 ed, 2009n29
Gale dir of publications & broadcast media, 138th ed,
    2005n887
Gale dir of publications & broadcast media, 140th ed,
    2006n872
Gale dir of publications & broadcast media, 143d ed,
    2009n797
Gale ency of ...
    alternative medicine, 2d ed, 2006n1439
    alternative medicine, 3d ed, 2009n1255
    cancer, 2d ed, 2006n1446
    children's health, 2006n1440
    diets, 2008n1119
    everyday law, 2d ed, 2007n445
    genetic disorders, 2d ed, 2006n1360
    medicine, 3d ed, 2007n1249
    mental health, 2d ed, 2009n703
    neurological disorders, 2005n1437
    nursing & allied health, 2d ed, 2007n1278
    sci, 4th ed, 2008n1107
    surgery & medical tests, 2d ed, 2009n1238
    US hist: govt & politics, 2009n642
    US hist: war, 2009n378
    world hist: govts, 2009n618
    world hist: war, 2009n427
Gale, Robert L., 2005n1069, 2008n958
Galens, David, 2005n1037, 2005n1108, 2005n1109
Galens, Judy, 2005n19, 2007n323
Gallagher, Eugene V., 2005n1244, 2008n1065
Gallagher, Lisa A., 2006n761
Gallagher, Marsha V., 2009n396
Gallaudet dict of American sign lang, 2007n852
Gallery of best resumes, 4th ed, 2008n232
Gallichan, Gilles, 2005n656, 2006n655
Gallico, Alison, 2005n215
Gallup, Alec M., 62, 2009n63
Gallup, George, Jr., 2005n69
Gallup poll, 2007, 2009n62
Gallup poll: pubic opinion 2003, 2005n69
Gallup poll cumulative index, 1998-2007, 2009n63
Gambetta, Vern, 2009n733
Gamers in the lib?! 2008n537
Ganeri, Anita, 2007n1183
Gange, Louise, 2006n654
Gannon, Michael B., 2005n1040
Ganong, Lawrence H., 2008n722
Ganz, David L., 2009n828
Gaquin, Deirdre A., 2005n854, 2006n277, 2006n731,
    2006n849, 2007n238, 2007n753, 2008n771,
    2008n774, 2009n663, 2009n782
Garcha, Rajinder, 2007n892
Garcia, Ageo, 2009n544
Garcia, Frank, 2009n1055
Garcia, Peter J., 2005n354
Garden, Don, 2006n1542
Garden insects of N America, 2005n1394
Garden plants of Japan, 2005n1314

Gardener's A-Z gd to growing flowers from seed to bloom, 2005n1317

Gardener's A-Z gd to growing organic food, 2005n1313

Gardener's peony, 2006n1309

Gardening with hardy geraniums, 2006n1296

Gardiner, Judith Kegan, 2008n726

Gardinier, David E., 2007n86

Gardner, Alfred L., 2009n1205

Gardner, Catherine Villanueva, 2007n758

Gardner, Jo Ann, 2006n1303

Garlick, Mark A., 2005n1505

Garner, Carolyn, 2005n610

Garnsey, Peter, 2007n429

Garratt, Richard, 2008n1316, 2008n1317

Garrett, Benjamin C., 2008n601

Garriguies, Richard, 2008n1176

Garry, Jane, 2006n1116

Garvin, Peggy, 2005n710, 2006n713, 2007n602, 2008n638

Gary, Ralph, 2009n390

Gaschnitz, K. Michael, 2008n698

Gassmann, Gunther, 2008n1083

Gaston, Mary Frank, 2009n819

Gastrointestinal diseases & disorders sourcebk, 2d ed, 2007n1258

Gates, Alexander E., 2008n1318

Gates, Henry Louis, Jr., 2005n326, 2006n328, 2008n915, 2009n14

Gates, J. E., 2006n953

Gates, John E., 2005n959

Gates, Pamela S., 2007n912

Gaulin, David E., 2007n455

Gay & lesbian issues, 2005n806

Gay detective novel, 2005n1048

Gay, Kathlyn, 2007n272

Gay male sleuth in print & film, 2006n1015

Gay rights, rev ed, 2006n810

Gaydosik, Victoria, 2006n1044

Geaves, Ron, 2007n1082, 2007n1107, 2007n1110, 2007n1118, 2007n1120, 2007n1125

Gebel, Doris, 2007n888

Geer, John G., 2005n688

Geeseman, Peggy, 2008n190

Geisinger, Kurt F., 2009n262

Geisst, Charles R., 2007n137

Geist, Helmut, 2007n1332

Gelling, Margaret, 2006n390

Gelo, James H., 2009n731

Gems in myth, legend, & lore, rev ed, 2008n996

GenBank [Website], 2006n1361

Gender issues & sexuality, 2007n710

GenderReach [Website], 2005n860

GenderWatch [Website], 2005n861

Genealogist's address bk, 5th ed, 2006n355

Genealogist's address bk [CD-ROM], 5th ed, 2006n356

Genealogy for the first time, 2005n358

Genealogy of the wives of the American presidents & their 1st two generations of descent, 2006n359

General social survey bibliog [Website], 2005n62

General studies of Charles Dickens & his writings & collected eds of his works, 2005n1077

Generali, Joyce, 2007n1281

Generation X, 4th ed, 2005n262

Genetic disorders sourcebk, 3d ed, 2005n1446

Genetic engineering, 2d ed, 2007n1226

Genetics revolution, 2006n1362

Genghis Khan & Mongol rule, 2005n468

Genovese, Michael A., 2005n698, 2009n643

Genrefied classics, 2008n895

Genreflecting, 6th ed, 2007n917

Gensler, Harry J., 2007n1069, 2009n108

Gentle reads, 2009n925

Gentry, April, 2008n921

Genus lavandula, 2005n1351

Genus paeonia, 2005n1362

Geographers, v.25, 2007n308

Geographic gd to uncovering women's hist in archival collections, 2005n862

Geographic info, 2005n387

Geography action [Website], 2008n353

Geography basics, 2005n384

Geography of presidential elections in the US, 1868-2004, 2006n730

Geography of religion, 2006n1212

Geography on file, updated ed, 2007n313

Geography zone [Website], 2008n354

Geography4Kids [Website], 2008n355

Geology of southern Vancouver Island, rev ed, 2006n1517

George H. W. Bush yrs, 2007n589

George, Mary W., 2009n500

Georgia Tech men's basketball games, 2009n722

Geostat Center: histl census browser [Website], 2006n433

Gerbert, Jurg, 2008n487

Gerding, Stephanie K., 2007n524

Gerhart, Mary, 2008n1087

Geriatric physical diagnosis, 2008n1245

German-American names, 3d ed, 2007n296

Germans to America series II, v.7, 2006n363

Germany, 3d ed, 2006n408

Germany & the Americas, 2006n748

Gershman, Gary P., 2006n541, 2009n660

Gerson, Carole, 2008n571

Gerstenfeld, Phyllis B., 2006n555, 2007n468, 2009n467

Gerstner, David A., 2007n706

Get connected, 2008n536

Get up & move with nonfiction, 2009n556

Getting started in genealogy online, 2007n288

Getty thesaurus of geographic names online [Website], 2007n315
Gewehr, Markus, 2009n1298
Geysers of Yellowstone, 4th ed, 2009n1322
Ghaoiu, Claude, 2006n1478
Ghareeb, Edmund A., 2005n125
Ghazanfar, S. M., 2007n1123
Gibbins, Catherine, 2007n725
Gibbons, Susan, 2008n513
Gibney, Matthew J., 2006n832
Gibson, K. William, 2006n540
Gies, David T., 2006n1065
Giesecke, Joan, 2006n637
Giesen, Rolf, 2009n1053
Giesso, Martin, 2009n413
Giffin, James M., 2009n1164, 2009n1165
Gifford, Clive, 2007n302
Gifford, Court, 2005n229
Giggle poetry [Website], 2008n947
Gikandi, Simon, 2009n977
Gilbert, Geoffrey, 2007n721, 2009n760
Gilbert, George, 2007n222
Gilbert, Mark F., 2008n124
Gilbert, Nedda, 2005n297
Gilbert, Richard E., 2007n807, 2008n826
Gilbert, Steve, 2007n462
Gilded age, 2005n460
Gilded age, rev ed, 2007n364
Gilded age & progressive era, 2007n368
Gilded age & progressive era: almanac, 2007n329
Gilded age & progressive era: biogs, 2007n330
Gilded age & progressive era: primary sources, 2007n331
Gill, Baljit, 2006n837
Gill, Kay, 2006n19, 2007n13, 2008n701
Gillespie, Carmen, 2009n963
Gillespie, Gordon, 2008n437
Gillespie, John T., 2005n1017, 2005n1018, 2007n886, 2007n893, 2007n894, 2007n895, 2008n88, 2009n919, 2009n922
Gillespie, Michael Patrick, 2007n968
Gillette, Gary, 2007n685
Gilley, Sheridan, 2007n1116
Gilliatt, Mary, 2006n928
Gilmore, Alec, 2008n1069
Gilmore, John, 2009n406
Gilton, Donna L., 2008n889
Gin, Ooi Keat, 2005n92
Ginther, Catherine, 2006n820
Giordano, Ralph G., 2007n1039
Giovan Pietro Bellori: lives of the modern painters, sculptors, & architects, 2008n832
Girl culture, 2009n766
Girsberger, Russ, 2008n521
Gisler, Ann, 2006n247
Giuliani, George, 2009n283
Given, Lisa M., 2009n57

Givens, Terryl L., 2005n1264
Giza archives program [Website], 2006n419
Gladysz, John A., 2006n1402
Glancey, Jonathan, 2007n816
Glasse, Cyril, 2009n1117
Glattstein, Judy, 2006n1304
Glazier, Ira A., 2006n363, 2006n364, 2006n365, 2006n366, 2006n367, 2007n293, 2007n294, 2008n343, 2008n344, 2008n345
Glazier, Michael, 2005n1261
Gleaves, David H., 2007n1272
Gledhill, David, 2009n1177
Glenn, Richard A., 2006n546
Glick, Thomas, 2006n1260
Glickman, Sylvia, 2005n1117, 2007n984
Glimpses of God through the ages, 2005n1247
Glischinski, Steve, 2008n1355
Global AIDS crisis, 2006n1441
Global business etiquette, 2009n148
Global climate change, 2007n1329
Global dict of theology, 2009n1110
Global economic prospects 2006, 2007n147
Global epidemics, 2008n1220
Global evolution, 2008n503
Global gateway: world culture & resources [Website], 2008n299
Global hist, 2005n527
Global hist of architecture, 2008n843
Global issues in context [Website], 2009n68
Global legal info network [Website], 2008n470
Global librarianship, 2005n633
Global market share planner, 4th ed, 2007n181
Global market share planner, 6th ed, 2009n193
Global perspectives on the US, v.3, 2008n668
Global terrorism, rev ed, 2005n576
Globalization, 2007n180
Globalization, 2009n192
Globalization & free trade, 2008n258
Globe trekker's world, 2006n394
Gloria Steinem, 2005n867
Glossary of labour law & industrial relations, 2006n227
Glossary of morphology, 2006n951
Glossary of netspeak & textspeak, 2005n1485
Glossary of poetic terms [Website], 2009n1004
Glover, Linda K., 2006n1505
Gluck, Carol, 2007n98
Glut, Donald F., 2007n1314, 2008n1325
Goble, Danney, 2007n76, 2009n80
Gods, goddesses, & mythology, 2005n1159
Goebel, Rolf J., 2006n1058
Goethals, George R., 2005n147
Goethals, Jozef J., 2009n322
Goetting, Denise, 2005n1033
Goetz, Susan Gibbs, 2008n274
Goff, Philip, 2006n1211
Going places with youth outreach, 2006n621

Goins, Charles Robert, 2007n76
Gokel, George W., 2005n1497
Golay, Michael, 2009n960
Goldberg, David H., 2009n130
Goldblatt, David, 2006n796
Goldblatt, Peter, 2005n1361
Golden, Janet, 2005n826
Golden, Jonathan M., 2006n116
Golden, Richard M., 2007n666
Goldenballs & the iron lady: a little bk of nicknames, 2006n369
Goldfield, David, 2008n768
Goldie, Mark, 2007n579
Goldman, Bert A., 2008n681, 2009n705
Goldman, Jan, 2007n595
Goldman, Paul, 2007n814
Goldman, Yosef, 2007n545
Goldmann, David R., 2005n1442
Goldschmidt, Arthur, Jr., 2005n85, 2009n416
Goldstein, Gerald, 2006n758
Goldstein, Natalie, 2008n258
Goldstein, Norm, 2005n893, 2008n799
Goldwag, Arthur, 2008n60
Golf Digest best places to play, 2005n773
Golf Digest's golf weekends, 2006n793
Golfing communities in the SE, 2005n774
Goloboy, Jennifer L., 2009n393
Golson, J. Geoffrey, 2007n281, 2007n365, 2008n328, 2008n405, 2008n408, 2008n418
Gomez, Gay M., 2009n1191
Gonzalez, Alexander G., 2006n1059, 2007n969
Gonzalez, Deena J., 2006n351
Gonzalez, Josue M., 2009n243
Gonzalez, Julio, 2009n1259
Gooch, Jan W., 2009n1213
Good match, 2008n526
Good, C. Edward, 2009n896
Goodin, Robert E., 2009n623
Goodman, Jordan, 2005n824
Goodman, Robert M., 2005n1348
Goodman, Ted, 2006n154
Goodrich, Jeanne, 2009n510
Goodsell, Joan, 2005n617
Gordon, Matthew S., 2006n1241
Gordon, Rachel Singer, 2006n638, 2007n507
Gore, Chris, 2005n1201
Gore Vidal, 2008n925
Goreham, Gary, 2009n71
Gorman, Martha, 2008n498
Gorman, Michele, 2005n619
Gorman, Robert F., 2008n450, 2008n497, 2009n417, 420, 2009n421
Goscilo, Helena, 2008n127
Gosler, Andrew, 2008n1177
Goss, K. David, 2009n379
Gothic lit, 2007n930
Gotlin, Robert S., 2009n1271

Goudie, A. S., 2005n1515
Gough, Julie A., 2005n149, 2005n150
Gould, William, 2007n1301
Goulder, Naomi, 2007n1065
Government affairs yellow bk, Summer 2005, 2006n709
Government assistance almanac 2004-05, 18th ed, 2005n817
Government assistance almanac 2005-06, 19th ed, 2006n817
Government assistance almanac 2006-07, 20th ed, 2007n712
Government assistance almanac 2009, 21st ed, 2009n758
Government, pol, & protest, 2007n580
Government phone bk USA 2004, 12th ed, 2005n708
Government phone bk USA 2005, 13th ed, 2006n710
Government phone bk USA 2007, 15th ed, 2008n635
Government phone bk USA 2008, 16th ed, 2009n30
Government research dir, 18th ed, 2005n689
Government research dir, 19th ed, 2006n689
Government research dir, 21st ed, 2008n616
Government research dir, 22d ed, 2009n620
Governments of the world, 2006n685
Govignon, Brigitte, 2005n950
Gowing, Sir Lawrence, 2006n916, 2006n921
Graduate study in psychology 2008, 2008n682
Graepel, Julia, 2008n966
Graf, Olivia, 2009n862
Graff, Keir, 2005n6
Grafov, Andrei, 2009n1214
Graham, Timothy, 2009n598
Gramercy family world atlas, 2008n350
Grange, William, 2007n1056, 2009n404
Grant, Barry Keith, 2008n1021
Grant, Edward, 2006n1269
Grant, H. Roger, 2006n1550
Grant, R. G., 2009n609
Grants for libs, 2007n524
Grants register 2004, 22d ed, 2005n308
Grants register 2006, 24th ed, 2006n303
Graphic novels, 2007n900
Graphic war, 2006n666
Grasses of Colo., 2009n1185
Grassian, Esther S., 2006n630
Grasslands of the US, 2008n1347
Gratton, Chris, 2007n671
Grawemeyer award for music composition, 2008n966
Gray, Daniel, 2007n1071
Gray, Douglas, 2005n1076
Gray, Jeffrey, 2007n979
Gray, Jonathan, 2009n795
Gray, Michael, 2007n1008
Gray, Richard T., 2006n1058
Grayling, Anthony, 2007n1065
Gray's anatomy for students, 2006n1321
Great American hist fact-finder, 2d ed, 2005n443

Great American hot rods, 2007n1339
Great American judges, 2005n535
Great Canadian vacations, 2005n403
Great careers with a high school diploma series, 2009n225
Great composers portrayed on film, 1913-2002, 2005n1190
Great debates in American environmental hist, 2009n1340
Great Depression, updated ed, 2006n449
Great Depression & the New Deal, 2009n391
Great Depression in America, 2008n404
Great dinosaur controversy, 2005n1524
Great empires of the past series, 2005n528
Great events from hist: gay, lesbian, bisexual, transgender events, 2007n705
Great events from hist: the ancient world, prehist-476 CE, 2005n515
Great events from hist: the middle age 477-1453, 2005n516
Great events from hist: the Renaissance & early modern era, 2006n500
Great events from hist: the 17th century, 2006n493
Great events from hist: the 17th century, 2007n409
Great events from hist: the 18th century, 2007n410
Great events from hist: the 19th century, 2007n411
Great events from hist: the 19th century, 2008n449
Great events from hist: the 20th century, 1940-70, 2009n421
Great events from hist: the 20th century, 1971-2000, 2009n420
Great events from hist: the 20th century, 2008n450
Great Hispanic-Americans, 2006n349
Great instrumental works, 2006n1089
Great jobs for biology majors, 2005n248
Great jobs for chemistry majors, 2d ed, 2006n257
Great jobs for math majors, 2d ed, 2006n253
Great jobs for pol sci majors, 2d ed, 2005n250
Great lives from hist: notorious lives, 2008n443
Great lives from hist: the ancient world, prehist-476 CE, rev ed, 2005n511
Great lives from hist: the Middle Ages, 477-1453, 2005n512
Great lives from hist: the renaissance & early modern era, 1454-1600, 2006n489
Great lives from hist: the 17th century, 2006n490
Great lives from hist: the 17th century, 2007n404
Great lives from hist: the 18th century, 2007n405
Great lives from hist: the 19th century, 2007n406
Great lives from hist: the 19th century, 1801-1900, 2008n444
Great lives from hist: the 20th century, 1901-2000, 2009n417
Great observatories of the world, 2006n1507
Great pictorial hist of world crime, 2005n566
Great Plains illus index, 2005n348

Great quotations that shaped the western world, 2009n48
Great radio sitcoms, 2008n808
Great Spanish films since 1950, 2009n1071
Great stories of WW II, 2008n944
Great thinkers A-Z, 2005n1226
Great voyages [Website], 2005n1224
Great world atlas, 3d ed, 2005n371
Great World Series games, 2006n784
Great world writers: 20th century, 2005n985
Greatest films [Website], 2006n1160
Greece, 5th ed, 2005n405
Greek mythology link [Website], 2007n1025
Green, David L., 2008n54
Green design, 2009n846
Green, Don W., 2008n1197, 2009n1217
Green, Jonathon, 2006n632
Green, Jonathan D., 2009n1015
Green papers [Website], 2009n634
Green, Richard, 2009n672
Green, Simon, 2005n224
Green, Stephen W., 2006n683
Green, Thomas A., 2007n1021, 2009n1031
Greenberg, Arthur, 2008n1285
Greenberg, Gerald S., 2006n1186
Greenberg, Yudit Kornberg, 2008n1052
Greenberger, Robert, 2006n1121
Greene, Jack R., 2008n486
Greene, John Robert, 2007n589
Greene, Roger L., 2009n714
Greenfield, Edward, 2006n1090
Greenfieldt, John, 2005n1222, 2007n916, 2008n529
Greenhaus, Jeffrey H., 2007n190
Greenhaven ency of …
    Ancient Greece, 2008n436
    Ancient Mesopotamia, 2008n441
    capital punishment, 2007n469
    paranormal phenomena, 2007n668
    terrorism, 2008n488
    the Civil War, 2005n428
    the Vietnam War, 2005n429
Greening your business, 2009n233
Greenland, Paul R., 2008n247
Greenwood companion to Shakespeare, 2006n1051
Greenwood daily life online [Website], 2005n508
Greenwood dict of world hist, 2007n420
Greenwood ency of …
    African American civil rights, 2005n334
    African American folklore, 2007n1019
    African American lit, 2007n941
    American folktales, 2007n1021
    American poets & poetry, 2007n979
    American regional cultures, 2006n70
    children's issues worldwide, 2009n767
    clothing through world hist, 2009n844
    daily life, 2005n517
    folktales & fairy tales, 2009n1030

homes through American hist, 2009n862
Latino lit, 2009n982
love, courtship, & sexuality through hist, 2009n755
multiethnic American lit, 2007n942
rock hist, 2007n1014
sci fiction & fantasy, 2006n1025
world folklore & folklife, 2006n1114
world popular culture, 2008n999
Greenwood lib of American war reporting, 2007n562
Greenwood lib of world folktales, 2009n1031
Gregory, Gwen Meyer, 2007n501
Gregory, Richard L., 2005n737
Gregory, Vicki L., 2007n520
Greig, Denise, 2005n1326
Greiner, Tony, 2008n565
Grenfell, Diana, 2005n1350
Grenham, John, 2005n360, 2007n289
Greve, Bent, 2007n714
Greve, Jennifer, 2008n892
Grey House biometric info dir 2006, 2006n180
Grey House biometric info dir online [Website],
    2006n181
Grey House homeland security dir 2005, 2d ed,
    2005n43
Grey House homeland security dir 2006, 3d ed,
    2006n35
Grey House homeland security dir 2007, 4th ed,
    2007n32
Grey House homeland security dir 2008, 5th ed,
    2008n37
Grey House homeland security dir [Website], 2005n44
Grey House homeland security dir [Website], 2007n33
Grey House homeland security dir [Website], 2008n38
Grey House performing arts dir 2005, 4th ed,
    2005n1184
Grey House performing arts dir 2007, 5th ed,
    2008n1005
Grey House performing arts dir 2009, 6th ed,
    2009n1050
Grey House performing arts dir [Website], 2005n1185
Grey House rare disorders dir 2006-07, 2007n1238
Grey House safety & security dir, 2004 ed, 2005n182
Grey House safety & security dir, 2006 ed, 2006n162
Grey House safety & security dir, 2007 ed, 2007n157
Grey House safety & security dir, 2008, 2009n156
Grey House safety & security dir [Website], 2006n163
Grey House transportation security dir & hndbk,
    2006n1546
Grieve, K., 2007n655
Griffin, William D., 2008n131
Griffith, Priscilla L., 2009n265
Griffith, Susan, 2008n248
Griffiths, C. L., 2009n1208
Griffiths, Charles, 2006n1387
Griffiths, Mark, 2007n1158
Griffiths, Martin, 2006n743
Griffiths, Paul, 2007n999

Grigg, John A., 2009n388
Grimaldi, David, 2007n1205
Grizzard, Frank E., Jr., 2008n398
Grobman, Paul, 2006n48
Groden, Michael, 2005n1005, 2009n913
Grohol, John M., 2005n741
Gross, Alan M., 2009n713
Gross, Ann D., 2008n1251
Gross, Ernie, 2009n369
Gross, Herbert, 2006n1407, 2006n1408
Gross, Melissa, 2007n512
Gross, Ruth V., 2006n1058
Grossberg, George T., 2008n1261
Grosser, George S., 2006n274
Grossman, James R., 2007n65
Grossman, Joel B., 2006n519
Grossman, Mark, 2005n699, 2008n574, 2009n644
Groundbreaking scientific experiments, inventions, &
    discoveries of the Middle Ages & the
    Renaissance, 2005n1290
Grove bk of operas, 2d ed, 2007n1001
Grove ency of classical art & architecture, 2008n835
Grove ency of decorative arts, 2007n790
Grove ency of materials & techniques in art, 2009n849
Groves, Jeffrey D., 2008n570
Growing & knowing: a selection gd for children's lit,
    2005n620
Growing hardy orchids, 2006n1310
Growing up with sci, 3d ed, 2007n1141
Gruenberg, Leif A., 2005n447
Grumet, Bridget Hall, 2005n415
Grundy, Valerie, 2008n872
Grzimek's student animal life resource: amphibians,
    2007n1218
Grzimek's student animal life resource: birds,
    2005n1385
Grzimek's student animal life resource: corals,
    jellyfishes, sponges, & other simple animals,
    2007n1212
Grzimek's student animal life resource: crustaceans,
    mollusks, & segmented worms, 2007n1213
Grzimek's student animal life resource: fishes,
    2006n1380
Grzimek's student animal life resource: insects &
    spiders, 2006n1385
Grzimek's student animal life resource: mammals,
    2006n1388
Guastoni, Alessandro, 2006n1516
Gubbins, David, 2008n1296
Guerilla film makers hndbk, 2005n1211
Guerin, Lisa, 2007n451, 2007n485
Guide & ref to the amphibians of E & Central N
    America, 2007n1215
Guide & ref to the crocodilians, turtles, & lizards of E
    & Central N America, 2007n1216
Guide & ref to the snakes of E & Central N America,
    2007n1217

Guide to ...
    America's fed jobs, 3d ed, 2006n255
    backyard birds, 2006n1373
    Civil War Philadelphia, 2005n436
    coin collecting, 2009n828
    collective biogs for children & YAs, 2006n990
    Congress, 6th ed, 2008n647
    developing end user educ programs in medical libs, 2006n610
    distance learning programs 2005, 2006n293
    documentary sources for Andean studies, 1530-1900, 2009n119
    economic indicators, 4th ed, 2007n146
    literary agents 2005, 2005n891
    info sources in mathematics & stats, 2006n1524
    Internet job searching, 2006-07 ed, 2007n211
    literary agents 2007, 2007n770
    microforms in print 2007, 2008n9
    musical temperament, 2006n1087
    off-label prescription drugs, 2007n1281
    pol campaigns in America, 2006n726
    Slavic collections in the US, 2006n611
    the birds of the SE states, 2007n1196
    the Dead Sea Scrolls & related lit, 2009n1094
    the gothic 3, 2006n1016
    the lit of art hist 2, 2005n592
    the presidency, 4th ed, 2009n645
    the reptiles of southern Africa, 2009n1210
    the U.S. Supreme Court, 4th ed, 2005n556
    the world bank, 2005n722
    US govt pubs, 2005 ed, 2005n49
    US govt pubs, 2007 ed, 2008n44
    US govt pubs, 2008 ed, 2009n37
    US map resources, 3d ed, 2006n384
    US map resources, 2007n309
Guided inquiry, 2009n567
Guiley, Rosemary Ellen, 2005n1154, 2005n1240, 2008n694, 2008n696, 2009n716
Guillermo, Artemio R., 2006n95
Guinness world records 2004, 2005n52
Gulevich, Tanya, 2005n1273
Gulla, Bob, 2009n1024
Gulls of N America, Europe, & Asia, 2005n1389
Gulls of the Americas, 2008n1178
Gumshoes: a dict of fictionary detectives, 2007n927
Gun control, rev ed, 2006n571
Gunaratna, Rohan, 2005n583
Gunawardena, C. A., 2007n103
Gunn, Angus M., 2009n1318
Gunn, Drewey Wayne, 2006n1015
Gunnell, John, 2006n1551
Gunston, Bill, 2006n1400
Gunter, Michael M., 2005n352
Gura, Mark, 2009n266
Gutierrez, David G., 2005n353
Gutierrez, Margo, 2005n355
Guynup, Sharon, 2007n1334

Gwinnell, Esther, 2009n763
Gymnosperm database [Website], 2006n1340

Haakonssen, Knud, 2007n1072
Haas, David, 2008n974
Haase, Donald, 2009n1030
Habegger, Jerryll, 2006n915
Habitats of the world, 2006n1511
Habitats of the world, 2007n1296
Hacht, Anne Marie, 2005n1038, 2005n1110, 2007n872, 2007n923, 2007n924, 2008n877, 2008n896, 2008n933
Haeger, John Winthrop, 2009n1150
Hafer, R. W., 2006n166
Hagan, John, 2005n791, 2005n792
Hage, Christine Lind, 2005n606
Hager, Alan, 2005n1002, 2006n1043
Hahn, Peter L., 2008n663
Haines, Tim, 2007n1315
Hake, Ted, 2007n792
Halda, Josef J., 2005n1362
Haldon, John, 2006n466
Halfdanarson, Gudmundur, 2009n112
Hall, Carolyn, 2005n119
Hall, David D., 2008n569
Hall, Dennis R., 2007n1028
Hall, Doris, 2007n769
Hall, James, 2009n850
Hall, Kermit L., 2006n519
Hall, Lena E., 2007n656
Hall, Linda D., 2005n189, 2008n155
Hall, Susan, 2009n923
Hall, Susan Grove, 2007n1028
Hall, Timothy L., 2005n536, 2008n1062
Hallam, Arlita W., 2006n639
Halliday, Fred, 2007n125
Halliday, James, 2008n1116
Hallmark, Kara Kelley, 2008n833, 2009n867
Halls, Monty, 2005n781
Halls of fame, 2005n56
Haltof, Marek, 2008n1017
Hamadeh, Samer, 2005n232
Hamblin, Jacob Darwin, 2006n1256
Hamblin, Robert W., 2005n1067, 2009n960
Hamilton, Allen Lee, 2007n549
Hamilton, Neil A., 2006n697, 2007n341
Hamilton, W. R., 2006n1515
Hammond, Andrew, 2006n1126
Hammond essential world atlas, 2009n330
Hammond world atlas, 5th ed, 2009n331
Hammond world travel atlas, 2005n392
Hamowy, Ronald, 2009n671
Han, Lori Cox, 2009n643
Hanby, Bernard P., 2007n1214
Hancock, John M., 2005n1411

Hand, John Oliver, 2006n934
Handbook for media librarians, 2009n528
Handbook of ...
　　agricultural geophysics, 2009n1143
　　ancient religions, 2008n1063
　　asymmetric heterogeneous catalysis, 2009n1297
　　bird biology, 2d ed, 2005n1386
　　child psychology, 6th ed, 2007n663
　　clinical psychology, 2009n713
　　commonly used American idioms, 4th ed,
　　　　2005n959
　　data-based decision making in educ, 2009n251
　　design research methods in educ, 2009n274
　　drug-nutrient interactions, 2005n1480
　　educ pol & policy, 2009n253
　　fluorous chemistry, 2006n1402
　　food analytical chemistry, 2005n1305
　　food products manufacturing, 2008n1128
　　gay, lesbian, bisexual, & transgender admin &
　　　　policy, 2005n805
　　genome research, 2006n1406
　　health psychology & aging, 2008n685
　　Inca mythology, 2005n1169
　　industrial chemistry: organic chemicals, 2006n1494
　　info & computer ethics, 2009n1287
　　intl law, 2006n538
　　intl research in mathematics educ, 2d ed,
　　　　2009n1325
　　ion chromatography, 2006n1403
　　moral & character educ, 2009n254
　　multicultural assessment, 3d ed, 2008n686
　　N American Indians, Southeast, v.14, 2005n345
　　N American Indians, v.3: environment, origins, &
　　　　population, 2008n327
　　Native American mythology, 2006n1118
　　nonprescription drugs, 14th ed, 2005n1481
　　obesity, 2d ed, 2005n1447
　　optical systems, v. 1, 2006n1407optical systems,
　　　　v.2, 2006n140
　　patristic exegesis, 2005n1250
　　personality assessment, 2009n714
　　plant biotech, 2005n1353
　　plant sci, 2008n1151
　　polymer reaction engineering, 206n1398
　　Polynesian mythology, 2005n1166
　　proteins, 2009n1173
　　psychiatric drugs, 2007n1283
　　psychological assessment, case conceptualization,
　　　　& treatment, 2008n687
　　psychopathy, 2008n688
　　research in educ finance & policy, 2008n267
　　research in school consultation, 2009n256
　　research in social studies educ, 2009n252
　　research on instructional systems & tech,
　　　　2008n1273
　　research on mobile multimedia, 2d ed, 2009n1293
　　research on open source software, 2008n1278
　　research on wireless security, 2009n1294
　　rhetorical devices [Website], 2009n803
　　school counseling, 2009n257
　　sexual & gender identity disorders, 2009n756
　　sport psychology, 3d ed, 2008n689
　　statl genetics, 3d ed, 2008n1199
　　U.S. labor stats 2004, 7th ed, 2005n234
　　US labor stats 2005, 8th ed, 2006n240
　　US labor stats 2006, 9th ed, 2007n195
　　US labor stats 2007, 10th ed, 2008n231
　　US labor stats 2008, 11th ed, 2009n209
Handbook on household hazardous waste, 2009n1216
Handbook to ...
　　life in medieval & early modern Japan, 2006n464
　　life in prehistoric Europe, 2007n385
　　life in renaissance Europe, 2006n470
　　life in the Aztec world, 2007n279
　　life in the medieval world, 2009n401
Handy anatomy answer bk, 2009n1175
Handy astronomy answer bk, 2009n1308
Handy biology answer bk, 2005n1340
Handy geology answer bk, 2005n1519
Handy hist answer bk, 2d ed, 2006n510
Handy math answer bk, 2006n1531
Handy presidents answer bk, 2006n728
Handy sci answer bk, centennial ed, 2005n1287
Handy Supreme Court answer bk, 2008n477
Hanes, Richard C., 2005n410, 2005n411, 2005n572,
　　　　2005n573, 2006n424, 2006n425, 2006n426,
　　　　2007n332, 2007n333, 2007n334, 2008n304,
　　　　2008n305, 2008n306
Hanes, Sharon M., 2005n410, 2005n412, 2005n572,
　　　　2005n574, 2006n424, 2006n425, 2006n426,
　　　　2007n332, 2007n333, 2007n334, 2008n304,
　　　　2008n305, 2008n306
Hank Aaron, 2006n775
Hankins, Barry, 2005n448
Hankins, James, 2008n1049
Hanks, Reuel R., 2006n85
Hanlan, James P., 2005n226
Hanley, Mark Y., 2007n574
Hanna, Robert C., 2008n931
Hannah, John D., 2005n1265
Hannah, Sue M., 2007n158
Hannavy, John, 2008n847, 2009n868
Hannings, Bud, 2007n353, 2008n578, 2009n370
Hansen, Laurel, 2009n1203
Hansen, Randall, 2006n832
Hanser, David A., 2007n817
Hanson, Paul R., 2005n483, 2008n431
HAPI: Hispanic American per index online [Website],
　　　　2008n50
Haque, Saira N., 2006n644
Harada, Violet H., 2009n519
Harcourt, Nic, 2007n990
Harding, Les, 2007n1111
Harding, Patricia A., 2005n1359

Hardy bamboos, 2006n1357
Hardy gingers, 2006n1344
Hardy, Grant, 2006n465
Hareas, John, 2005n771
Hares-Stryker, Carolyn, 2009n935
Hark, Lisa, 2008n1127
Harker, Christa, 2009n520
Harkness, Peter, 2005n1363
Harkness, Philip, 2005n1364
Harlem renaissance, 2009n959
Harman, Keith, 2007n1339
Harmon, Deborah A., 2006n283
Harner, James L., 2009n902, 2009n976
Harper, Dave, 2006n903, 2009n833
Harper, Judith E., 2008n785
Harper, Kristine C., 2008n1306
Harrap's French & English college dict, 2007n860
Harrap's Spanish & English business dict, 2006n122
Harriman, Joy HP., 2009n579
Harrington, Austin, 2007n690
Harrington, Matthew P., 2009n450
Harrington, Paul E., 2005n247
Harrington, Thomas F., 2005n247
Harris, Bill, 2006n698
Harris, Joseph R., 2007n257
Harris, Paul, 842, 2009n861
Harris, Robert L., Jr., 2007n273
Harris, Robert W., 2008n1276
Harrison Ford, 2006n1159
Harrison, James, 2007n302
Harrison, Lorraine, 2006n925
Harrison, Marina, 2005n940
Harrison, Marion, 2005n404
Harrison, Maureen, 2007n462
Harrison, Thomas, 2007n384
Harrod's librarian's glossary & ref bk, 10th ed,
    2006n588
Hart, Craig, 2006n359
Hart, George, 2005n1008
Hart, John, 2008n601
Hart, Tony, 2005n1337
Hartemann, Frederic V., 2006n794
Harter, Christopher, 2009n44
Harter, Jim, 2006n1552
Hartley, Alan H., 2005n430
Hartley, Richard D., 2009n479
Hartman, Gary, 2005n549
Harui, Hisashi, 2008n171
Harvard dict of music, 4th ed, 2005n1120
Harvey, Carl A., II, 2009n521
Harvey, Clare G., 2008n1238
Harvey, Graham, 2008n1103
Harvey, Paul, 2006n1211
Haskell, Jean, 2007n61
Hass, Andrew W., 2009n972
Hassel, R. Chris, Jr., 2007n959
Hastedt, Glenn, 2005n726

Hatch, Charles R., 2008n1161
Hatch, Stephan L., 2005n1355
Hatchwell, Emily, 2008n373
Hate crimes, 2d ed, 2006n564
Hatfield, Gabrielle, 2005n1347
Hatfield, John T., 2008n1064
Hatha yoga illustrated, 2005n785
Hatler, David F., 2009n1204
Hattendorf, John B., 2008n600
Haugen, David M., 2007n687, 2009n745
Haugen, Peter, 2008n1139
Hauptman, Robert, 2006n794
Hauser, Christopher, 2007n677
Hausrath, Don, 2007n847, 2009n346
Haven, Kendall, 2007n1142, 2008n1111
Haverstick, Dolores A., 2006n1145
Havlice, Patricia Pate, 2006n1098
Hawkes, Peter W., 2007n1229, 2008n1203
Hawkesworth, Mary, 2005n687
Hawkins, Lawrence E., 2006n1519
Hawkins, Walter L., 2008n575
Hawley's condensed chemical dict, 15th ed,
    2008n1292
Hay, Jeff T., 2005n429
Hay, Keith G., 2005n397
Haycock, Ken, 2009n502
Hayes, Derek, 2005n385, 2007n335, 2008n75,
    2008n385
Haynes, Elizabeth, 2009n543
Hays, J. N., 2006n1423
Haywood, John, 2007n401
Hazardous Earth series, 2009n1302
Head, Dominic, 2007n878
Headquarters USA 2005, 27th ed, 2005n45
Headquarters USA 2006, 28th ed, 2006n36
Headquarters USA 2007, 29th ed, 2007n34
Healey, Paul D., 2009n501
Health care job explosion! 4th ed, 2008n242
Health care policy & politics A to Z, 3d ed, 2009n697
Health care state rankings 2004, 12th ed, 2005n1429
Health care state rankings 2005, 13th ed, 2006n1424
Health care state rankings 2006, 14th ed, 2007n1241
Health care state rankings 2007, 15th ed, 2008n1221
Health care state rankings 2008, 16th ed, 2009n1232
Health professions career & educ dir 2005-06, 33d ed,
    2006n1418
Health ref center [Website], 2008n1228
Healthcare reform in America, 2005n1431
Healthy woman, 2009n1246
Healthy work, 2006n225
Heaphy, Leslie A., 2007n679
Hearn, Daniel Allen, 2007n467
Heart of the community, 2008n552
Heat & thermodynamics, 2009n1136
Heath, Anthony W., 2008n684
Heath, Julian P., 2006n1257
Heath, Robert L., 2005n886

Hebrew printing in America 1735-1926, 2007n545
Hedblad, Alan, 2005n9, 2005n258, 2005n304, 2005n599, 2005n887
Heidler, David S., 2005n449, 2006n452
Heidler, Jeanne T., 2005n449, 2006n452
Heine, Peter, 2006n1287
Heinegg, Paul, 2006n357
Heinle picture dict, 2005n968
HeinOnline [Website], 2008n462
Heintze, James R., 2008n1000
Heintzelman, Greta, 2006n1041
Helbig, Alethea K., 2005n1027
Helicopters, 2006n677
Hellebust, Lynn John, 2008n673
Hellemans, Alexander, 2005n1281
Hellenistic bibliog [Website], 2007n964
Heller, Ruth, 2006n961
Hellmann, Paul T., 2005n386
Hellwig, Monika K., 2005n1261
Helms, Marilyn M., 2006n262, 2007n226
Hemmer, Kurt, 2007n939, 2008n912
Hemphill, Ian, 2007n1154
Hempstead, Colin A., 2006n1255
Henbest, Nigel, 2008n1304
Henderson, Ashyia N., 2005n327
Henderson, C. J., 2008n249
Henderson, Harry, 2005n249, 2005n576, 2005n717, 2005n899, 2006n570, 2006n571, 2006n572, 2007n1288, 2009n1288
Henderson, Helene, 2006n1122, 2006n1123, 2009n638, 2009n1042
Hendricks, Bonnie, 2008n1189
Hendrickson, Kenneth E., Jr., 2006n692
Hendrickson, Robert, 2009n885
Hendry, Maggy, 2006n852
Hengen, Shannon, 2008n938
Henken, Ted A., 2009n122
Henn, Robert L., 2009n1181
Henri, James, 2009n565
Henritze, Barbara K., 2009n317
Henry Wadsworth Longfellow companion, 2005n1069
Hensley, Thomas R., 2007n452
Henson, Robert, 2008n1312
Heo, Uk, 2008n579
Hepatitis sourcebk, 2006n1450
Hepatitis, 2007n1274
Herald, Diana Tixier, 2007n917, 2009n946
Herb, Guntram H., 2009n434
Herbalist in the kitchen, 2008n1118
Herber, Mark, 2007n290
Herbst, Ron, 2005n1300
Herbst, Sharon Tyler, 2005n1300
Herer, Kathryn G., 2008n59
Herman, David, 2006n871
Hermsen, Sarah, 2005n836, 2005n1507, 2005n1508, 2005n1509
Herrero-Berveera, Emilio, 2008n1296

Herrick, John M., 2006n818
Herrmann, Francine, 2008n1277
Herrmann, Wolfgang A., 2008n1286
Herrnson, Paul S., 2006n726
Hersen, Michel, 2006n755, 2008n683, 2008n687, 2009n708, 2009n713
Hess, Mickey, 2008n988
Hess, Peter M. J., 2009n1114
Hesse, Rayner W., Jr., 2008n829
Hetherington, Cynthia, 2009n145
Hetico, Hope Rachel, 2007n1232
Hey, David, 2009n324
Heywood, Leslie L., 2006n859, 2007n761
Heywood, V. H., 2008n1157
Heyworth, Gregory, 2006n885
Hibler, Harold E., 2009n829
Hickman, M., 2006n1316
Hidalgo, Danielle Antoinette, 2007n735
Higdon, Pamela L., 2006n1373
Higginbotham, Evelyn Brooks, 2005n326, 2009n14
Higgins, Katherine, 2008n809
Higgins, MaryEllen, 2008n1016
Higgins, Wesley, 2009n1183
High definition, 2007n1285
High impact quotations, 2007n45
High school journalism, 2008n803
High tech, high touch: lib customer serv through tech, 2005n642
High-volume retailers 2005, 2005n192
High-volume retailers 2006, 2006n182
Higham, Charles F. W., 2005n467
Higham, Robin, 2005n531
Hill, Anthony D., 2009n1075
Hill, Brad, 2006n1088
Hill, Christopher V., 2009n1341
Hill, Daniel J., 2008n1045
Hill, Donald R., 2008n991
Hill, Gerald N., 2005n700
Hill, Jane, 2005n322
Hill, Jeff, 2006n453, 2006n862, 2007n431, 2009n1040
Hill, Kathleen Thompson, 2005n700
Hill, Samuel S., 2007n1083
Hill, Sonya D., 2005n1422, 2008n163, 2008n507, 2009n141
Hill, Susan, 2005n1322
Hill, Tony, 2007n1150
Hill wars of the Korean conflict, 2006n463
Hillauer, Rebecca, 2007n1047
Hille, Jenny, 2006n612
Hillerbrand, Hans J., 2005n1258
Hillmann, Diane I., 2005n630
Hillstrom, Kevin, 2005n12, 2005n450, 2005n750, 2005n997, 2005n1541, 2005n1542, 2005n1543, 2006n456, 2006n767, 2006n1484, 2007n10, 2007n563, 2007n1129, 2008n411, 2008n412, 2009n391, 2009n959

Hillstrom, Laurie Collier, 2005n667, 2005n668,
    2005n669, 2005n1541, 2005n1542,
    2005n1543, 2006n118, 2006n456,
    2006n1250, 2007n787, 2007n788, 2007n789,
    2008n411, 2008n412, 2008n1001, 2009n392,
    2009n451, 2009n1041
Hilton, Dyan, 2006n484
Himma, Kenneth Einar, 2009n1287
Hindi-English, English-Hindi: dict & phrasebk,
    2005n972
Hinds, Maurene J., 2006n241
Hine, Brent, 2006n1311
Hine, Robert, 2006n1314
Hinks, Peter, 2008n394
Hinman, Lawrence M., 2006n1201
Hinnells, John R., 2008n1063
Hinson, Maurice, 2005n1135, 2007n997
Hinton, Derek, 2005n577, 2006n573
Hip hop culture, 2007n1010
Hipster librarian's gd to teen craft projects, 2009n548
Hiremath, Uma, 2007n538
Hirko, Buff, 2005n649
Hirsch, E. D., Jr., 2005n325
Hischak, Thomas S., 2005n1197, 2005n1218,
    2005n1220, 2006n1179, 2007n1055,
    2008n1042, 2009n1077
Hispanic American biogs, 2007n284
Hispanic Americans, 2007 ed, 2008n334
Hispanic Americans, 2008n335
Hispanic lit of the US, 2005n1065
Hispanics in the American West, 2006n353
Historian's toolbox, 2d ed, 2009n435
Historic cities of the Americas, 2006n845
Historic docs of 2005, 2007n582
Historic docs of 2006, 2008n618
Historic docs of 2007, 2009n624
Historic documents cumulative index 1972-2005,
    2007n581
Historic events of the 20th century [Website],
    2005n522
Historic movie theatres in Ill., 1883-1960, 2008n1010
Historic preservation tech, 2009n865
Historical atlas of ...
    American crime, 2006n560
    Ancient Greece, 2007n392
    ancient Mesopotamia, 2005n502
    ancient Rome, 2006n486
    Calif. with original maps, 2008n75
    Central America, 2005n119
    central Asia, 2005n465
    Islam, 2005n1271
    Okla., 4th ed, 2007n76
    religions, 2007n1073
    the Islamic world, 2005n1270
    the Renaissance, 2005n471
    the US, 2007n335
    US presidential elections, 1789-2004, 2007n585

Historical companion to postcolonial thought in
    English, 2006n1193
Historical dict of ...
    Afghan wars, revolutions, & insurgencies, 2d ed,
        2006n87
    African American cinema, 2008n1014
    African American theater, 2009n1075
    African-American TV, 2006n1149
    Albania, new ed, 2005n106
    Algeria, 3d ed, 2007n82
    American propaganda, 2005n432
    American radio soap operas, 2006n891
    American theater: modernism, 2009n1074
    ancient Egypt, 2d ed, 2009n414
    ancient Greek philosophy, 2008n1047
    ancient India, 2009n399
    ancient Israel, 2005n126
    ancient S America, 2009n413
    ancient SE Asia, 2008n100
    Anglicanism, 2007n1108
    Angola, new ed, 2005n84
    architecture, 2009n863
    arms control & disarmament, 2006n744
    Australia, 3d ed, 2008n110
    Australian & New Zealand cinema, 2006n1150
    Australian radio & TV, 2008n1019
    Bangladesh, 3d ed, 2005n94
    Belarus, 2d ed, 2008n120
    Belgium, 2d ed, 2008n118
    Bosnia & Herzegovina, 2d ed, 2008n119
    Botswana, 4th ed, 2009n90
    British intelligence, 2006n665
    British radio, 2007n783
    Brussels, 2005n107
    Bulgaria, 2d ed, 2007n112
    Burma (Myanmar), 2007n93
    Burundi, 3d ed, 2007n85
    Chinese theater, 2009n1078
    Civil Wars in Africa, 2d ed, 2009n398
    Cold War counterintelligence, 2008n588
    contemporary Germany, 2008n123
    Denmark, 2d ed, 2009n111
    Descartes & Cartesian philosophy, 2005n1228
    early N America, 2005n344
    Egypt, 3d ed, 2005n85
    epistemology, 2007n1061feminist philosophy,
        2007n758
    ethics, 2009n1084
    Ethiopia, new ed, 2005n87
    existentials, 2009n1086
    fantasy lit, 2006n1027
    feminism, 2d ed, 2005n869
    Finland, 2d ed, 2008n121
    France, 2d ed, 2009n403
    French cinema, 2008n1016
    Gabon, 3d ed, 2007n86
    Georgia, 2008n122

German cinema, 2009n1064
German theater, 2007n1056
Ghana, 3d ed, 2006n81
golfing terms, repr ed, 2006n792
Guinea, 4th ed, 2006n82
Hegelian philosophy, 2d ed, 2009n1081
Hong Kong cinema, 2008n1022
human rights & humanitarian orgs, 2d ed,
    2008n497
Hume's philosophy, 2009n1085
Husserl's philosophy, 2009n1083
Iceland, 2d ed, 2009n112
India, 2d ed, 2007n97
Indonesia, 2d ed, 2005n96
intl intelligence, 2007n560
Iran, 2d ed, 2007n126
Iraq, 2005n125
Irish cinema, 2008n1015
Israel, 2d ed, 2009n130
Israeli intelligence, 2007n629
Italian cinema, 2009n1063
Japanese business, 2008n220
Japanese traditional theatre, 2007n1057
Jehovah's Witnesses, 2009n1107
Judaism, 2d ed, 2008n1102
Kant & Kantianism, 2006n1194
Kosova, 2005n112
Kyrgyzstan, 2005n100
Laos, 3d ed, 2009n102
Latvia, 2d ed, 2009n114
Leibniz's philosophy, 2007n1063
lesbian lit, 2007n881
Lesotho, new ed, 2005n88
Libya, 4th ed, 2007n87
logic, 2007n1069
Madagascar, 2d ed, 2006n83
Mali, 4th ed, 2009n92
Marxism, 2007n1071
Mauritania, 3d ed, 2009n86
medieval China, 2009n400
medieval India, 2009n101
medieval philosophy & theology, 2008n1044
Methodism, 2d ed, 2006n1231
modern Italy, 2d ed, 2008n124
Moldova, 2d ed, 2008n125
Mormonism, 3d ed, 2009n1106
Morocco, 2d ed, 2007n88
multinational peacekeeping, 2d ed, 2005n723
Native American movements, 2009n308
NATO & other intl security orgs, 2009n674
new age movements, 2005n1243
New England, 2005n78
New Zealand, 2d ed, 2007n105
Nietzscheanism, 2d ed, 2007n1067
Norway, 2009n115
nuclear, biological, & chemical warfare, 2008n601
old-time radio, 2008n805

organized labor, 2d ed, 2005n225
Pakistan, 3d ed, 2007n127Russian & Soviet
    intelligence, 2007n55
Polish cinema, 2008n1017
postmodernist lit & theater, 2008n789Renaissance
    art, 2008n837
Russian theater, 2008n1043
revolutionary America, 2006n442
Rwanda, new ed, 2008n98
sacred music, 2007n1016
Scandinavian lit & theater, 2007n975
sci fiction lit, 2005n1051
Seventh-day Adventists, 2006n1232
Shamanism, 2008n1103
Sierra Leone, new ed, 2009n87
Sikhism, 2d ed, 2006n1249
Slovakia, 2d ed, 2008n129
socialism, 2d ed, 2007n631
Sufism, 2006n1240
Sweden, 2d ed, 2007n116
Switzerland, 2008n132
Syria, 2d ed, 2005n130
Taiwan, 3d ed, 2008n107
Thailand, 2d ed, 2006n97
the Arab-Israeli conflict, 2007n123
the Baha'i faith, 2d ed, 2007n1093
the Berbers (Imazighen), 2009n306the
    contemporary United Kingdom, 2009n117
the Broadway musical, 2008n1041
the Central African Republic, 3d ed, 2006n77
the Chinese cultural revolution, 2007n371
the Civil War & Reconstruction, 2005n434
the Coptic Church, 2009n1109
the "Dirty Wars," 2005n499
the discovery & exploration of the NW coast of
    America, 2009n380
the discovery & exploration of the NW passage,
    2007n129
the discovery & exploration of the Pacific Islands,
    2006n99
the early American Republic, 2007n346
the Eisenhower era, 2009n646
the enlightenment, 2006n496
the European Union, 2007n110
the French Revolution, 2005n483
the Gambia, 4th ed, 2009n91
the gilded age, 2005n431
the green movement, 2d ed, 2008n1341
the Gulf Arab States, 2d ed, 2008n144
the Gypsies, 2d ed, 2008n314
the Hittites, 2005n500
the Hong Kong SAR & the Macao SAR, 2007n94
the Inuit, 2005n343
the Jacksonian era & Manifest Destiny, 2007n348
the Kennedy-Johnson era, 2008n393
the Kurds, 2005n352
the League of Nations, 2007n635

Historical dict of ... (*Cont.*)
  the Netherlands, 2d ed, 2008n126
  the 1940s, 2007n354
  the non-aligned movement & third world, 2007n106
  the Northern Ireland conflict, 2008n437
  the Old South, 2006n443
  the peoples of the SE Asian massif, 2007n264
  the People's Republic of China, 2d, 2008n108
  the Philippines, 2d ed, 2006n95
  the Puritans, 2008n1084
  the Reagan-Bush era, 2008n626
  the Renaissance, 2005n474
  the Republic of Cape Verde, 4th ed, 2008n97
  the Republic of Korea, 2d ed, 2005n98
  the Roosevelt-Truman era, 2009n648
  the Russo-Japanese War, 2007n557
  The Salvation Army, 2007n1112
  the Shakers, 2009n1112
  the Tamils, 2008n424
  the UN, new ed, 2008n659
  the US diplomacy since the Cold War, 2008n664
  the War of 1812, 2007n357
  the welfare state, 2d ed, 2007n714
  Turkmenistan, 2006n98
  Ukraine, 2006n106
  US-China relations, 2006n745
  US diplomacy from the Civil War to WWI, 2006n742
  US intelligence, 2006n663
  US-Japan relations, 2008n666
  US-Latin American relations, 2007n638
  US-Middle East relations, 2008n663
  US-SE Asia relations, 2009n693
  utopianism, 2005n1232
  Western Sahara, 3d ed, 2007n80
  westerns in cinema, 2009n1066
  Wittgenstein's philosophy, 2005n1233
  women in sub-Saharan Africa, 2006n858
  WW II intelligence, 2008n589
  Zambia, 3d ed, 2008n99
  Zionism, 2d ed, 2009n1119
Historical dir of trade unions, v.5, 2008n226
Historical ency of American labor, 2005n226
Historical fiction, 2007n918
Historical fiction for young readers (grades 4-8), 2009n922
Historical gazetteer of the US, 2005n386
Historical map & chart project [Website], 2006n376
Historical maps on file, updated ed, 2006n454
Historical maps online [Website], 2005n372
Historical maps online [Website], 2007n301
Historical sites of Egypt, v.1, 2008n378
Historical who's who of the automotive industry in Europe, 2007n1341
History for kids [Website], 2005n523
History highway, 4th ed, 2007n427

History in dispute, v.14: the Middle East since 1945, 2005n501
History in dispute, v.16: 20th-century European social & pol movements, 1st series, 2005n477
History in dispute, v.17: 20th-century European social & pol movements, 2d series, 2005n478
History in dispute, v.18: The Spanish Civil War, 2006n481
History in dispute, v.19: the red scare after 1945, 2005n451
History in lit, 2005n1001
History in the media, 2007n1051
History of ...
  astronomy, 2008n1304
  Central America, 2007n399
  Christianity in Asia, Africa, & Latin America, 1450-1990, 2008n1089
  Egypt, 2005n86
  fashion & costume, 2006n909
  folk music festivals in the US, 2009n1022
  food, new ed, 2009n1155
  Great Britain, 2005n490
  Indonesia, 2007n374
  interior design & furniture, 2d ed, 2007n810
  invention series, 2005n1288
  Iraq, 2006n114
  issues series, 2008n461
  Korea, 2006n93
  mathematics series, 2005n1534
  New Zealand, 2005n469
  Pakistan, 2009n104
  sci & tech, 2005n1281
  sci, tech, & medicine [Website], 2005n1297
  the American West [Website], 2006n434
  the ancient & medieval world, 2d ed, 2009n428
  the bk in America, v.1: the Colonial bk in the Atlantic world, 2008n569
  the bk in America, v.3: the industrial bk, 1840-80, 2008n570
  the bk in Canada, v.1, 2005n656
  the bk in Canada, v.1, 2006n655
  the bk in Canada, v.2 1840-1918, 2006n656
  the bk in Canada, v.3, 2008n571
  the English lang, 2008n853
  the lib in western civilization, 2005n637
  the lib in western civilization, 2007n531
  the N.Y. Court of Appeals, 1932-2003, 2007n458
  the world in photographs, 2009n422
  Venezuela, 2006n109
  Vietnam, 2009n106
  women in the US, 2005n872
  world trade since 1450, 2006n265
  WW II, 2005n529
History resource center [Website], 2007n421
Hit records, 1950-75, 2006n1097
Hit singles, 5th ed, 2006n1095
Hitchcock, Susan Tyler, 2006n1212

Hitler & the Nazis, 2007n387
Hixon, Donald L., 2006n1073
HMO/PPO dir 2005, 17th ed, 2005n1424
HMO/PPO dir 2006, 18th ed, 2007n1239
HMO/PPO dir 2007, 19th ed, 2008n1213
HMO/PPO dir 2009, 21st ed, 2009n1227
HMO/PPO dir [Website], 2005n1425
HMO/PPO dir [Website], 2006n1420
HMO/PPO dir [Website], 2007n1240
Hmong-related works, 1996-2006, 2008n315
H-NET reviews in the humanities & social scis
    [Website], 2007n5
Hoare, James E., 2005n98
Hoare, Peter, 2007n495
Hoare, Timothy D., 2006n96
Hobbs, Hoyt, 2009n415
Hobbs, James B., 2007n840
Hochadel, MaryAnne, 2007n1280
Hochmuth, George J., 2008n1138
Hock, Randolph, 2005n1486
Hodge, Carl C., 2007n592, 2008n622
Hodge, Carl Cavanagh, 2009n402
Hodgson, Leslie, 2005n359
Hodgson, Terence, 2007n853
Hoek, D. J., 2008n962
Hoernig, Susan, 2005n185
Hoeveler, Diane Long, 2005n869, 2008n781
Hoffman, Penny J., 2005n756
Hoffman, Tom, 2009n829
Hoffmann, Dierk O., 2007n1033
Hoffmann, Frank, 2005n1119, 2006n1104
Hoffmann, Gretchen McCord, 2006n628
Hoffmann, Susanne M., 2006n1501
Hogan, Sean O., 2007n454
Hogg, Richard, 2008n853
Hohler, Sharon E., 2009n1261
Hoig, Stan, 2007n320
Hole, Georgia, 2007n843
Holiday symbols & customs, 4th ed, 2009n1042
Holidays, festivals, & celebrations of the world dict,
    3d ed, 2006n1123
Holiness-Pentecostal movement, 2009n1103
Holland, James, 2006n1086
Hollands, Neil, 2008n904
Holley, Pam Spencer, 2005n1014
Hollingsworth, Mary, 2005n943
Holloran, Peter C., 2005n78
Holloway, Joel E., 2006n1343
Holloway, Ralph L., 2007n260
Hollywood creative dir, Spring 2004, 50th ed,
    2005n1186
Hollywood creative dir, Spring 2006, 56th ed,
    2006n1130
Hollywood creative dir, Spring 2008, 62d ed,
    2008n1006
Hollywood creative dir, Spring 2009, 65th ed,
    2009n1051

Hollywood creative dir online [Website], 2008n1007
Hollywood creative dir online [Website], 2009n1052
Hollywood distribution dir 2005, 16th ed, 2006n1131
Hollywood distribution dir 2007-08, 18th ed,
    2008n1008
Hollywood music industry dir, premier ed 2004,
    2005n1122
Hollywood music industry dir 2006, 3d ed, 2006n1076
Hollywood music industry dir 2008, 5th ed, 2008n968
Hollywood representation dir, Summer 2004, 27th ed,
    2005n1187
Hollywood representation dir, 30th ed, 2006n1132
Hollywood representation dir, Winter 2007, 34th ed,
    2008n1009
Holmes, Deborah E., 2005n1421
Holmes, Gillian, 2005n142
Holmes, Madelyn, 2005n1536
Holmes, Richard, 2008n590
Holmes, Thom, 2006n1105
Holocaust, 2007n431
Holocaust lit, 2009n912
Holocaust survivors, 2008n447
Holt, Leslie Edmonds, 2007n512
Holtz, Thomas R., Jr., 2008n1326
Holtz-Bacha, Christina, 2009n617
Holy bingo, the lingo of Eden, jumpin' jehosophat, &
    the land of nod, 2007n1111
Holy people of the world, 2006n1206
Holzhey, Helmut, 2006n1194
Home front ency, 2007n554
Home front heroes, 2007n337
Home Planner's ency of home designs, 3d ed,
    2006n929
Home Planner's ultimate home plan ref, 2006n930
Homeland security, 2005n550
Homeland security, 2006n729
Homeland security hndbk for citizens & public
    officials, 2007n646
Homeland security law hndbk, 2005n551
Homeowner's complete tree & shrub hndbk,
    2008n1162
Homophones & homographs, 4th ed, 2007n840
Honderich, Ted, 2006n1196
Honnold, RoseMary, 2007n513, 2008n536
Hook, Richard, 2008n325
Hooper, Brad, 2008n901
Hooper, Kaye D., 2006n1451
Hoover's hndbk of ...
    American business 2004, 2005n155
    American business 2005, 15th ed, 2006n131
    emerging companies 2004, 2005n156
    emerging companies 2005, 2006n132
    emerging companies 2007, 2008n160
    private companies 2004, 9th ed, 2005n157
    private companies 2006, 2006n133
    private companies 2007, 2008n161
    world business 2004, 2005n208

Hoover's hndbk of ... (*Cont.*)
   world business 2005, 12th ed, 2006n201
   world business 2007, 2008n213
   American business 2007, 2007n139
Hoover's MasterList of major US companies 2006,
   2006n134
Hoover's MasterList of US companies 2007, 2007n140
Hoover's MasterList: Ca. ed 2004, 2005n158
Hoover's MasterList: N.Y. metro ed 2004, 2005n159
Hopkins, Brian, 2006n822
Hopkins, Edward J., 2005n1512
Hoppenstand, Gary, 2008n999
Hopper, Leonard J., 2008n1135
Horak, Ray, 2008n1283
Horn, David, 2006n1094
Horn, Henrik, 2009n488
Horowitz, David A., 2005n1442
Horowitz, Maryanne Cline, 2006n501
Horror films of the 1980s, 2008n1026
Horror readers' advisory, 2005n1050
Horseman's illus dict, 2005n1391
Horvath, Istvan T., 2006n1402
Horvitz, Leslie Alan, 2007n422
Hosansky, David, 2008n410
Hot dance disco 1974-2003, 2005n1143
Hothem, Lar, 2005n925, 2008n822
Houlden, Leslie, 2005n1260
Household spending, 9th ed, 2005n834
Household spending, 11th ed, 2007n734
Household spending, 12th ed, 2008n750
Household surveys in developing & transition
   countries, 2006n836
Houston, Lynn Marie, 2006n1288
Houtman, Ronald, 2005n1370
Hovey, Harold A., 2005n846, 2006n842, 2007n745
Hovey, Kendra A., 2005n846, 2006n842, 2007n745
How Congress works, 4th ed, 2009n661
How it happens, 2006n1271
How libs & librarians help, 2006n635
How to plan & develop a career center, 2d ed,
   2008n234
Howard, Caroline, 2006n284
Howard, Nicole, 2006n657
Howatt, William A., 2007n716
Howe, Randy, 2009n52
Howell, David C., 2007n654
Howell, James W., 2009n755
Howell, Steve N. G., 2008n1178
Howells, Cyndi, 2007n286
Howes, Kelly King, 2005n413, 2006n423
Howitt, Dennis, 2007n738
Howley, Edward T., 2009n734
HQ online [Website], 2005n46
HQ online [Website], 2006n37
Hsia, R. Po-Chia, 2009n1113
Huang, Guiyou, 2007n962
Hubbard, Benjamin J., 2008n1064

Hubble, Deborah, 2009n267
Huber, Jeffrey T., 2005n1415, 2009n530
Huber, Patrick, 2005n1174
Huck, James D., Jr., 2009n123
Hudson, Brian P., 2006n71
Hudson, David L., Jr., 2008n477, 2009n437
Hudson, J. Blaine, 2008n399
Hudson, Randolph H., 2005n1064
Hudson, Rick, 2007n1312
Hudson's Washington news media contacts dir 2008,
   41st ed, 2009n798
Huets, Jean, 2007n667
Huff, Randall, 2006n455, 2008n957
Huggett, Richard, 2008n358
Hughes, Arnold, 2009n91
Hughes, Geoffrey, 2007n844
Hughes, J. Donald, 2006n1543
Hughes, Kerry, 2008n1242
Hughes, Thomas J. R., 2006n1393
Hughes-Hassell, Sandra, 2006n605
Hui, Y. H., 2008n1128
Huling, Nancy, 2007n494
Hull, Caroline, 2007n376
Human, 2005n53
Human & civil rights, 2007n491
Human body, 2007n1172
Human body systems, 2005n1346
Human dvlpmt report 2007/08, 2009n64
Human evolution, 2006n1319
Human fossil record, v.3, 2007n260
Human fossil record, v.4, 2007n261
Human genome sourcebk, 2006n1359
Human resources for results, 2009n510
Human rights worldwide, 2007n489
Humbul humanities hub [Website], 2005n883
Humphrey, Carol Sue, 2005n452
Humphreys, Patrick, 2009n1281
Hundert, Gershon David, 2009n312
Hunefeldt, Christine, 2005n122
Huneker, James, 2006n935
Hunt, Courtney, 2006n114
Hunt, Kim, 2005n38
Hunt, Louise, 2009n784
Hunt, Norman Bancroft, 2005n502
Hunt, Thomas C., 2005n280
Hunter, Jeffrey W., 2005n981, 2005n982, 2005n983,
   2005n999
Hunter, Luke, 2008n1191
Hunter, Nan D., 2006n583
Hurricanes, 2d ed, 2006n1510
Hurvitz, Mitchell M., 2006n1248, 2007n1126
Hurwitz, David, 2005n1130, 2006n1081
Husband, Julie, 2005n453
Husfloen, Kyle, 2005n912, 2006n897, 2008n811,
   2009n814
Hussain, Syed B., 2005n146
Hutchings, Jane, 2008n369

Hutchings, Kevin, 2005n1390
Hutchinson, Peter, 2009n354
Hutchinson, Stephen, 2006n1519
Hutson, James H., 2007n1092
Huussen, Arend H., Jr., 2008n126
Huxford, Bob, 2005n914
Huxford, Bob, 2006n901, 2006n907
Huxford, Sharon, 2005n914, 2006n901, 2006n907
Hyatt, Wesley, 2007n1042
Hydrangeas for American gardens, 2005n1324
Hydrangeas, rev ed, 2006n1306
Hypertension sourcebk, 2005n1469

Iber, Jorge, 2006n353
Iberia & the Americas, 2006n749
Ibrahim, Ismail Khalil, 2009n1293
Icons of ...
    business, 2008n150
    crime fighting, 2009n462
    evolution, 2009n1169
    hip-hop, 2008n988
    horror & the supernatural, 2008n902
    Latino America, 2009n315
    R&B & soul, 2009n1024
    rock, 2009n1027
    the American west, 2009n364
    unbelief, 2009n1089
IDEAS (Internet docs in economics access serv)
    [Website], 2005n132
Identification & geographical distribution of the
    mosquitoes of N America, 2006n1384
Ihrie, Maureen, 2005n1089
Ilahiane, Hsain, 2009n306
Illegal immigration, 2008n480
Illicit trafficking, 2006n574
Illustrated atlas, rev ed, 2005n373
Illustrated dict of gardening, 2007n1158
Illustrated ency of Confucianism, 2006n1198
Illustrated ency of orchids, repr ed, 2007n1179
Illustrated ency of Scotland, 2005n116
Illustrated ency of trees, 2d ed, 2006n1353
Illustrated gd to the Bible, 2009n1098
Illustrated gd to veterinary medical terminology, 2d ed,
    2006n1312
Illustrated great decisions of the Supreme Court, 2d ed,
    2007n457
Illustrated pocket dict of chromatography, 2007n1223
Illustrators of The Wind in the Willows 1908-2008,
    2009n935
Image of librarians in cinema, 1917-99, 2006n1166
Images of the Trojan War myth [Website], 2008n994
Imbarrato, Susan Clair, 2009n953
Imhoff, Kathleen R. T., 2009n582
Immigration, 2007n722
Immigration, 2008n741

Immigration, 2009n772
Immigration & asylum, 2006n832
Immigration & migration, 2009n771
Immigration & multiculturalism, 2008n751
Immigration in America today, 2009n769
Immigration in US hist, 2007n735
Immigration to the US series, 2005n324
Immune system disorders sourcebk, 2d ed, 2006n1436
Impact of tech on Asian, African, & Middle Eastern
    lib collections, 2008n549
Imperato, Gavin H., 2009n92
Imperato, Pascal James, 2009n92
Imperialism & sci, 2007n1147
Improving Internet ref servs to distance learners,
    2006n598
In search of your German roots, 4th ed, 2009n319
Incas, 2007n280
Incense bible, 2008n1242
Incrocci, Luca, 2009n756
Index of ...
    American per verse 2001, 2005n1114
    American per verse 2002, 2005n1115
    American per verse 2003, 2006n1071
    American per verse 2004, 2007n982
    American per verse 2005, 2008n960
    American per verse 2006, 2009n1009
    Native American bk resources on the Internet
        [Website], 2006n1037
IndexFungorum [Website], 2006n1349
India, 5th ed, 2005n401
India, 7th ed, 2006n401
India, 8th ed, 2008n369
Indian artifacts, 2005n925
Indian placenames in America, v.2, 2005n390
Indigenous peoples & environmental issues,
    2005n1538
Indonesia, 2005n97
Industiral commodity stats yrbk 2002, 2006n188
Industrial commodity stats yrbk 2003, 2007n177
Industrial commodity stats yrbk 2004, 2008n208
Industrial revolution, 2006n448
Industrial revolution, 2007n366
Industrial revolution, 2009n393
Industrial revolution in America, 2006n456
Industrial revolution in America, 2008n411, 2008n412
Industry research desk [Website], 2006n175
Industry research using the economic census,
    2005n165
Infectious diseases in context, 2008n1229
Infectious diseases sourcebk, 2005n1448
Information & communications for dvlpmt 2006,
    2007n182
Information industry dir, 27th ed, 2005n598
Information industry dir, 28th ed, 2006n594
Information industry dir, 30th ed, 2008n507
Information literacy assessment, 2008n543

Information literacy assessment in K-12 settings, 2009n565

Information literacy collaborations that work, 2008n542

Information literacy programs in the digital age, 2009n566

Information operations—doctrine & practice, 2009n610

Information sci 101, 2009n571

Information security & ethics, 2008n1274

Information sources of pol sci, 5th ed, 2006n683

Information tech & economic dvlpmt, 2008n171

Informed learning, 2009n504

InfoTrac kids [Website], 2008n51

Inglis, Robin, 2009n380

Ingram, David, 2007n1070

Ingrassia, Catherine, 2006n1046

Inman, David, 2006n1139

Innes, Paul, 2009n974

Innes, Sue, 2008n778

Innis, Sue, 2007n388

Innovations in sci & tech libs, 2005n615

Insects, 2007n1206

Inside Wash.: govt resources for intl business, 2005n205

Insider's gd to graduate programs in clinical & counseling psychology, 2004/05 ed, 2005n742

Insider's gd to graduate programs in clinical & counseling psychology, 2006-07 ed, 2007n661

Insider's gd to graduate programs in clinical & counseling psychology, 2008/09 ed, 2009n706

Insider's gd to mental health resources online, rev ed, 2005n741

Insley, John, 2006n390

Institute of museum & lib servs [Website], 2009n489

Integrating print & digital resources in lib collections, 2007n533

IntelCenter al-Qaeda messaging/attacks timeline 1992-2007, 2009n683

IntelCenter terrorism incident ref (TIR): Afghanistan: 2000-07, 2009n685

IntelCenter terrorism incident ref (TIR): Algeria, 2000-07, 2009n687

IntelCenter terrorism incident ref (TIR): Arabian Peninsula, 2000-07, 2009n686

IntelCenter terrorism incident ref (TIR): Iraq: 2000-05, 2009n689

IntelCenter terrorism incident ref (TIR): Iraq: 2006, 2009n690

IntelCenter terrorism incident ref (TIR): Iraq: 2007, 2009n691

IntelCenter terrorism incident ref (TIR): Pakistan: 2000-07, 2009n684

IntelCenter terrorism incident ref (TIR): Philippines, 2000-07, 2009n688

IntelCenter terrorist & rebel logo identification gd, 2009n679

IntelCenter words of Ayman al-Zawahiri, v.1, 2009n680

IntelCenter words of Osama Bin Laden, v.1, 2009n681

Intellectual freedom manual, 7th ed, 2007n530

Intellectual property, 2009n562

Intellectual property, 2008n482, 2008n541

Intelligence & natl security, 2008n592

Interactive Mediterranean project [Website], 2005n374

Interactive weather maker [Website], 2009n1312

Interior materials & surfaces, 2006n912

International Assn of Forensic Linguists [Website], 2006n552

International bk of days, 2006n6

International children's digital lib [Website], 2005n1019

International children's digital lib [Website], 2007n896

International criminal law practitioners lib, v.1, 2009n475

International dict of psychoanalysis, 2006n757

International dict of public mgmt & governance, 2006n750

International dict of public mgmt & governance, 2007n640

International dir of …
    arts 2003, 27th ed, 2005n884
    business biogs, 2005n139
    co hists, v.71, 2006n135
    co hists, v.72, 2006n136
    co hists, v.73, 2006n137
    co hists, v.74, 2006n138
    govt 2008, 5th ed, 2009n621
    little mags & small presses 2005-06, 41st ed, 2006n651
    little mags & small presses 2008-09, 44th ed, 2009n594

International ency of …
    adolescence, 2007n720
    communication, 2009n796
    dance, paperback ed, 2005n1188
    econ sociology, 2006n123
    ergonomics & human factors, 2d ed, 2007n1220
    ergonomics & human factors, 2d ed [CD-ROM], 2007n1221
    horse breeds, paperback ed, 2008n1189
    men & masculinities, 2008n726
    military hist, 2007n555
    organization studies, 2009n231
    social policy, 2008n672
    the social scis, 2d ed, 2008n61

International environmental disputes, 2007n1333

International environmental law reports, v.5, 2009n483

International glossary of place name elements, 2006n391

International govt info & country info, 2005n50

International histl stats: Africa, Asia & Oceania 1750-2000, 4th ed, 2005n840

International histl stats: Europe 1750-2000, 5th ed, 2005n841

International histl stats: the Americas 1750-2000, 5th ed, 2005n848

International hndbk of …
    creativity, 2007n664
    research on indigenous entrepreneurship, 2009n294
    stepfamilies, 2009n746
    univs, 17th ed, 2005n300
    univs, 18th ed, 2006n294
    univs, 19th ed, 2008n280

International hndbk on the preparation & dvlpmt of school leaders, 2009n258

International investment agreements, 2006n204

International law, 2006n517

International law in domestic courts [Website], 2007n492

International lib of the new institutional economics, 2006n150

International librarianship, 2008n550

International literary market place 2004, 2005n655

International literary market place 2006, 2006n652

International literary market place 2008, 2008n567

International literary market place 2009, 2009n595

International mktg data & stats 2004, 2005n263

International mktg data & stats 2006, 30th ed, 2006n270

International mktg forecasts 2003/04, 2005n264

International mktg forecasts 2005/06, 9th ed, 2006n271

International orgs, 6th ed, 2007n634

International perspectives on educ, 2008n268

International plant names index [Website], 2006n1341

International relations, intl security, & comparative pol, 2009n677

International research centers dir, 18th ed, 2005n47

International research centers dir, 19th ed, 2006n38

International research centers dir, 21st ed, 2008n39

International security & counter terrorism ref center [Website], 2009n682

International security & the US, 2009n696

International trade stats yrbk 2002, 51st ed, 2005n265

International trade stats yrbk 2003, 2006n272

International trade stats yrbk 2004, 2007n183

International travel & health, 2005n1430

International who's who 2006, 69th ed, 2006n17

International who's who 2008, 2009n11

International who's who [Website], 2008n14

International who's who in …
    classical music 2006, 2007n1000
    poetry 2005, 13th ed, 2006n1067
    poetry 2007, 14th ed, 2007n978

poetry 2009, 2009n987
    popular music 2006, 8th ed, 2007n1005
    popular music 2009, 2009n1017

International who's who of authors & writers 2005, 2006n976

International who's who of authors & writers 2007, 22d ed, 2007n876

International who's who of authors & writers 2009, 24th ed, 2009n907

International yrbk of environmental & resource economics 2006/07, 2007n1330

International yrbk of industrial stats 2005, 2006n189

International yrbk of industrial stats 2008, 2009n183

Internet, 2006n1485

Internet & society, 2008n1281

Internet & the law, 2006n521

Internet ency of philosophy [Website], 2005n1231

Internet ency of philosophy [Website], 2006n1195

Internet gd to anti-aging & longevity, 2007n692

Internet gd to cosmetic surgery for men, 2007n1253

Internet gd to herbal remedies, 2008n1236

Internet gd to medical diets & nutrition, 2008n1124

Internet lib for librarians [Website], 2009n494

Internet movie database [Website], 2006n1155

Internet predators, 2006n572

Internet public lib [Website], 2009n495

Internet revolution, 2006n1484

Internet sacred text archive [Website], 2005n1246

Internet sources on each US state, 2006n71

Internet speculative fiction database [Website], 2006n1019

Internet tech hndbk, 2005n1487

Internships 2005, 2006n231

Interpreting the Bible, 2007n1098

Intner, Sheila S., 2006n646, 2009n538

Intoxication in mythology, 2007n1023

Introducing issues with opposing viewpoints series, 2009n65

Introduction to …
    birds of the S Calif. Coast, 2006n1372
    health scis librarianship, 2009n529
    manuscript studies, 2009n598
    new & alternative religions in America, 2008n1065
    public librarianship, 2005n607
    ref servs in academic libs, 2007n499
    ref sources in the health sci, 5th ed, 2009n530
    ref sources in the health scis, 4th ed, 2005n1415
    ref work in the digital age, 2005n650
    tech servs, 7th ed, 2006n646
    the world's major religions, 2006n1213
    to serials work for lib technicians, 2005n645

Intute: arts & humanities [Website], 2009n794

Intute: social scis [Website], 2008n56

Invasion of privacy, 2006n542

Invasive species in the Pacific NW, 2007n1169

Inventors & inventions, 2008n1108

Inventory of paintings of Cardinal Pietro Ottoboni
    (1667-1740), 2005n949
Investor's gd to US coins, 2d ed, 2008n820
i-Quote, 2008n54
Iran's diverse peoples, 2006n344
Iraq War, 2005n666
Iraq War, updated ed, 2008n591
Ireland, 2007n393
Ireland, 6th ed, 2006n409
Ireland & the Americas, 2009n113
Irises, 2006n1295
Irish bed & breakfast bk, 2009n352
Irish, Mary, 2007n1157
Irish women writers, 2006n1059
Irish women writers, 2007n969
Iron men of baseball, 2007n676
Irons, Edward A., 2009n1100
Irons-Georges, Tracy, 2005n1438, 2008n1230,
    2009n1240
Irving, Jan, 2009n553
Irwin, Raymond D., 2008n387
Is consulting for you? 2008n524
Isaak, Mark, 2006n1317
Islam & the religious arts, 2005n1272
Islam in world cultures, 2006n1242
Islamic civilization, 2007n1123
Islamic world, 2005n1274
Islamism, 2008n1096
Isms & ologies, 2008n60
Isserman, Maurice, 2006n389
Issues [Website], 2008n57
Issues & controversies in American hist [Website],
    2009n381
Issues in Germany, Austria, & Switzerland, 2005n105
Issues in the French-speaking world, 2005n108
Issues on trial series, 2009n452
Italian horror film directors, 2005n1191
Italian lit & its times, v.7, 2006n1060
Italians to America, v.17, 2006n364
Italians to America, v.18, 2006n365
Italians to America, v.19, 2006n366
Italians to America, v.20, 2006n367
Italians to America, v.21, 2008n344
Italians to America, v.22, 2008n345
Italy, 2005n406, 2005n497
Italy, new ed, 2008n373
Italy, updated ed, 2006n410
Ives, Gary, 2006n642
IVP atlas of Bible hist, 2007n1094
IVP dict of the N.T., 2005n1248
IVP intro to the Bible, 2008n1073
Izzo, David Garrett, 2005n1111

J. R. R. Tolkien companion & gd, 2008n934
J. R. R. Tolkien ency, 2008n935

Jack Aubrey commands, 2005n1070
Jack Kerouac, 2005n1068
Jack the Ripper suspects, 2005n561
Jackson, Keith, 2007n105
Jackson, Kenneth T., 2007n16, 2009n76
Jackson, Nicky Ali, 2008n721
Jackson, Paul, 2008n978
Jackson, Roland, 2006n1074
Jackson, Tom, 2005n235, 2008n1289
Jackson, Yo, 2007n653
Jacksonian & antebellum age, 2009n394
Jacob, Jeanne, 2005n1304, 2008n1129
Jacobs, Eva E., 2005n234, 2006n240, 2008n231,
    2009n209
Jacobs, Steven, 2009n1092
Jacobson, Lisa, 2009n765
Jacobson, Trudi E., 2005n628. 2008n542
Jacoby, Joann, 2009n292
Jade garden, 2006n1311
Jaeger, Paul T., 2009n512
Jahn, Manfred, 2006n871
Jahrbuch-Project, electronic research archive for
    mathematics [Website], 2005n1531
Jaine, Tom, 2009n1147
Jamaica Kincaid, 2009n962
James Dean in death, 2006n1147
James Welch, 2005n1073
James, Delores C. S., 2005n1420
James, W. Martin, 2005n84
Jameson, E. W., Jr., 2005n1396
Jamestown ancestors 1607-99, 2007n292
Jamestown colony, 2008n398
Janer, Zilkia, 2009n1152
Janes, Joseph, 2005n650
Jankowski, Terry Ann, 2009n531
Janowski, Bernd, 2008n1059
Japanese American relocation digital archives
    [Website], 2006n333
Japanese-English chemical dict, 2009n1298
Jaques, Tony, 2007n556
Jarman, Beatriz Galimberti, 2009n901
Jarzombek, Mark M., 2008n843
Jasper, David, 2009n972
Jay & Ellsworth, the 1st courts, 2009n450
Jay, Elisabeth, 2009n972
Jaycox, Faith, 2006n457
Jaynes, Gerald D., 2006n330
Jazz: a regional exploration, 2006n1107
Jazz fiction, 2008n990
Jazz musicians, 1945 to the present, 2007n1012
Jeffrey, Harry P., 2006n736
Jemmott, LarShone, 2007n141
Jenkins, Fred W., 2007n403
Jenkins, John M., 2005n754
Jenkins, Martin, 2009n1347
Jenkins, Simon P. R., 2006n1455
Jenkins, Todd S., 2005n1151

Jennex, Murray E., 2008n169, 2009n146

Jennings, Greg, 2007n1202, 2008n1183

Jensen, Eric L., 2008n487

Jensen, Todd A., 2007n1340

Jermyn, Jim, 2006n1298

Jestice, Phyllis G., 2006n1206

Jesus in hist, thought, & culture, 2005n1260

Jeweler's dir of gemstones, 2007n808

Jewell, Elizabeth, 2007n613

Jewelrymaking through hist, 2008n829

Jewett, Clayton E., 2005n454

Jewish American food culture, 2009n1151

Jewish American lit, 2006n1032

Jewish story finder, 2006n1113

Jewish values finder, 2009n931

Jewish yr bk 2004, 2005n1276

Jewish yr bk 2005, 2006n1247

Jewish yr bk 2007, 2008n1101

Jian, Guo, 2007n371

Jim Burns' Ariz. birds, 2009n1197

Jim Crow ency, 2009n302

Jimenez, Phil, 2006n1121

Joan of Arc & the hundred yrs war, 2006n471

Job hunter's sourcebk, 6th ed, 2005n230

Job hunter's sourcebk, 7th ed, 2007n193

Job hunter's sourcebk, 8th ed, 2009n207

Jobs & careers abroad, 12th ed, 2006n232

Jobs in America, 2007n196

Joel Whitburn presents Christmas in the charts 1920-2004, 2005n1144

Joel Whitburn presents hot country albums, 2009n1020

Joel Whitburn presents rock tracks 1981-2008, 2009n1025

Joel Whitburn presents top R&B/hip-hop singles 1942-2004, 2005n1149

Joel Whitburn's music yrbk 2005-06, 2008n984

Joel Whitburn's music yrbk, 2003, 2005n1145

Joel Whitburn's top country songs 1944-2005, 2006n1101

Joel Whitburn's top pop singles 1955-2006, 2008n985

Joel Whitburn's 2004 music yrbk, 2006n1096

Johann Nepomuk Hummel, 2008n972

Johansen, Bruce E., 2005n1538, 2008n323, 2008n329

John Buchan, 2009n942

John Donne, 2006n1049

John Paul II & the Jewish people, 2009n314

John Steinbeck bibliog 1996-2006, 2009n965

John Steinbeck ency, 2007n953

John Wayne filmography, 2005n1205

John Wesley's ecclesiology, 2008n1091

Johns Hopkins gd to literary theory & criticism, 2d ed, 2005n1005

Johns Hopkins gd to literary theory & criticism [Website], 2009n913

Johns Hopkins medical gd to health after 50, 2005n1449

Johns, Julia, 2007n778, 2008n800

Johnson, Anne Janette, 2007n453

Johnson, Benjamin H., 2008n414

Johnson, Claudia Durst, 2005n1030, 2006n1038, 2007n885

Johnson, David, 2006n1193

Johnson, Ellen, 2008n852

Johnson, Galen K., 2008n1084

Johnson, Jenny Marie, 2005n387

Johnson, Judith L., 2005n306

Johnson, Liz, 2006n1305

Johnson, Michael G., 2008n325

Johnson, Nuala C., 2005n68

Johnson, Peggy, 2005n623, 2009n558

Johnson, Sarah L., 2007n918

Johnson, Tom, 2005n1204

Johnson, W. Brad, 2009n710

Johnson yrs, 2007n591

Johnston, Philip S., 2008n1073

Johnston, Robert, 2005n85

Johnston, Sarah Iles, 2006n1217

Jolliffe, Genevieve, 2005n1211

Jones, Andrew, 2007n577

Jones, Cecily, 2009n406

Jones, Charles Edwin, 2006n1225, 2009n1103

Jones, Chris, 2005n1211

Jones, Constance, 2005n395

Jones, Constance A., 2008n1095

Jones, Diane McClure, 2009n827

Jones, George F., 2007n296

Jones, J. Sydney, 2005n506, 2005n507, 2007n1088, 2007n1089, 2007n1090

Jones, Linda Gale, 2009n401

Jones, Nigel R., 2006n931

Jones, Patrick, 2005n619

Jones, Rosemary, 2009n827

Jones, Sharon L., 2009n961

Jones, Stephen A., 2009n659

Jones, Terry L., 2007n355

Jones, Toni Stokes, 2006n283

Jordan, David, 2005n765

Jordan, Michael, 2005n1160

Jordy, William H., 2005n82

Joseph Stalin, 2008n439

Joseph, Ellis A., 2005n280

Joseph, Suad, 2005n870, 2006n855, 2007n757, 2008n782, 2008n783

Joshi, S. T., 2007n932, 2008n902, 2008n925, 2009n1089

Joslin, Courtney G., 2006n583

Jost, Kenneth, 2007n446

Jotischky, Andrew, 2007n376

Journalism, 3d ed, 2005n897

JournalismNet [Website], 2005n900

Juang, Richard M., 2009n692

Judaica ref sources, 3d rev ed, 2005n350

Judd, Sandra J., 2006n1444, 2006n1445, 2006n1449, 2006n1450, 2007n1257, 2007n1258, 2007n1262, 2008n1233, 2009n712, 2009n1243, 2009n1262, 2009n1266
Judicial branch of state govt, 2007n454
Judicial branch of the fed govt, 2008n648
Judicial staff dir, Winter 2005, 25th ed, 2006n526
Judicial staff dir online [Website], 2006n527
Judicial yellow bk, 2008 ed, 2009n441
Judicial yellow bk, Spring 2005, 2006n528
Judiciary & responsible govt 1910-1921, v. 9, 2008n478
Julian, Beatrice, 2005n499
Julian, Georgina, 2007n725
Julier, Guy, 2006n922
Jungel, Eberhard, 2008n1059
Junior nature experiments on file, 2007n1143
Junior sci experiments on file, new ed, 2005n1289
Junior sci experiments on file, v.2, 2006n1270
Junior sci experiments on file, v.3, 2007n1144
Junior Worldmark ency of ...
    the Canadian provinces, 5th ed, 2008n111
    the Mexican states, 2006n108
    the Mexican states, 2d ed, 2008n140
    the nations, 4th ed, 2005n71
    the nations, 5th ed, 2008n65
    the states, 4th ed, 2005n79
    the states, 5th ed, 2008n71
Jupp, Victor, 2007n51
Jurewicz, Lynn, 2005n642
Jurkowski, Odin L., 2007n503
Justice, Douglas, 2006n1311
Juvenile justice, 2006n576
Jweid, Rosann, 2005n611

K & W gd to colleges for students with learning disabilities or attention deficit disorder, 7th ed, 2005n315
Kabatchnik, Amnon, 2009n1076, 2009n1079
Kagan, Alfred, 2006n78
Kagan, Jeremy, 2006n1163
Kagan, Neil, 2007n412
Kahana, Ephraim, 2007n629
Kahin, Audrey, 2005n96
Kahl, Chad M., 2009n677
Kahl, Gunter, 2005n1412
Kahn, Ada P., 2008n679, 2009n700
Kahn, Cynthia M., 2007n1164
Kahn, Miriam B., 2005n631, 2009n577
Kailbourn, Thomas R., 2006n936
Kaiser, Harvey H., 2009n864
Kalb, Deborah, 2007n624
Kalck, Pierre, 2006n77
Kalck, Xavier-Samuel, 2006n77
Kale, Tessa, 2008n959

Kaler, James B., 2007n1300
Kaliski, Burton S., 2007n160
Kalte, Pamela M., 2005n1279
Kalu, Anthonia C., 2008n936
Kamae, Hiroshi, 2008n171
Kameny, Fred, 2009n76
Kamiar, M., 2007n1060
Kamien, David G., 2007n647
Kammen, Daniel M., 2005n1540, 2006n1538
Kan, Katharine L., 2007n514
Kanduik, Mary, 2008n939
Kane, Joseph Nathan, 2006n429, 2008n26
Kane, Laura Townsend, 2009n532
Kanellos, Nicolas, 2005n1065, 2009n982
Kannengiesser, Charles, 2005n1250
Kanner, Aimee, 2007n110
Kaplan, Dana Evan, 2006n1244
Kaplan, David H., 2009n434
Kaplan, Steven M., 2005n1410
Kaplan, Stuart R., 2007n667
Kaplin, William A., 2009n275
Kaplowitz, Joan R., 2006n630
Kappen, Charles V., 2009n829
Karesh, Sara E., 2006n1248, 2007n1126
Karges, Ken, 2005n180, 2006n160
Karkkainen, Veli-Matti, 2009n1110
Karolides, Nicholas J., 2006n632, 2007n868
Karpuk, Deborah J., 2009n539
Kars, Marge, 2009n535
Karsten, Peter, 2007n352
Karwowski, Waldemar, 2007n1220, 2007n1221
Kasaba, Resat, 2009n411
Kasbekar, Asha, 2007n1034
Kaser, James A., 2007n919
Kasetsiri, Charnvit, 2009n94
Kashatus, William C., 2005n766
Kassel, Richard, 2007n996
Kassimir, Ron, 2006n688, 2007n578
Kastan, David Scott, 2007n956
Katz, Bill, 2005n648
Katz, Ellis, 2007n594
Kaufman, Burton I., 2007n590, 2009n646
Kaufman, Diane, 2009n646
Kaufman field gd to butterflies of N America, 2007n1204
Kaufman field gd to insects of N America, 2008n1184
Kaufman, James C., 2007n664
Kaufman, Kenn, 2007n1204, 2008n1184
Kaufman, Will, 2006n746
Kaufmann, H. W., 2005n455
Kaufmann, J. E., 2005n455
Kaur, Sat Dharam, 2005n1462
Kaye Gibbons, 2008n919
Kaywell, Joan, 2005n1031
Kayyali, Randa A., 2006n332
Kazensky, Michelle, 2007n877
Keane, Nancy J., 2007n515, 2007n516

Keaney, Michael F., 2009n1056
Keating, Ann Durkin, 2007n65
Keating, Chris, 2008n1019
Keefe, Simon P., 2006n1080, 2007n993
Keeley, Jack, 2006n1533
Keenan, Kevin M., 2006n542
Keene, Jennifer D., 2007n564
Keeran, Peggy, 2006n1047, 2008n561
Kehde, Ned, 2006n59
Keith, Michael C., 2005n909
Kelleher, Margaret, 2007n965
Keller, Harald, 2005n1404
Keller, Kathleen, 2009n1265
Keller, Rosemary Skinner, 2007n1080
Keller, Sarah, 2007n778, 2008n800
Kelley, Dennis F., 2006n336
Kellman, Steven G., 2007n935, 2007n948, 2008n878, 2008n910
Kelly, Anthony E., 2009n274
Kelly, Eugene, 2005n1234
Kelly, Louise, 2005n254
Kelly, Patrick, 2005n13
Kelly, Regina Anne, 2008n1335
Kelly, Robert J., 2006n574
Kelsey, Ann L., 2006n634
Kelsey, Paul, 2005n604
Kelsey, Sigrid, 2005n604
Kemmerling, Garth, 2006n1190
Kemp, Donna R., 2008n690
Kemp, Peter, 2005n1013, 2006n1554
Kemp, Roger L., 2007n646, 2008n646, 2008n772, 2009n536, 2009n780
Kenett, Ron S., 2009n1220
Kennedy, G. Michael, 2006n254
Kennedy, James R., 2005n636
Kennedy, Sydney H., 2009n1279
Kennedy yrs, 2005n697
Kenrick, Donald, 2008n314
Kent, Jennifer, 2006n1537
Kenward, Raymond, 2007n658
Keogh, Patricia, 2009n560
Keoke, Emory Dean, 2006n338
Keown, Damien, 2008n1075
Kepner, Terry L., 2006n1504
Kerfoot, Alicia L., 2009n979
Kerkhoff, Ingrid, 2006n1052
Kermel-Torres, Doryane, 2005n101
Kern, M. Kathleen, 2009n585
Kershner, Bruce, 2005n399
Kersting, M. Patricia, 2006n1313
Kessel, William B., 2006n337
Kesseler, Rob, 2009n1184
Kesselman, Martin Alan, 2005n633
Kesselman-Turkel, Judi, 2007n773, 2007n774
Kessler, Edward, 2006n1246
Keurentjes, Jos, 2006n1398
Kevane, Bridget, 2005n1090

Key figures in Medieval Europe, 2007n381
Key population & vital stats, 2007n740
Key terms in syntax & syntactic theory, 2009n871
Key topics in sports medicine, 2009n1270
Key words in …
    Buddhism, 2007n1107
    Christianity, 2007n1110
    Hinduism, 2007n1118
    Islam, 2007n1120
    Judaism, 2007n1125
    religious studies, 2007n1082
Keylor, William R., 2008n456
Keys to the rain: the definitive Bob Dylan ency, 2006n1111
Khadraoui, Djamel, 2008n1277
Khan, Ahmed S., 2006n1487
Khan, Iqtidar Alam, 2009n101
Khan, Karim, 2007n1277, 2008n1257
Khan, Namir, 2006n225
Khosrow-Pour, Mehdi, 2006n586, 2007n1286, 2008n504
Kibbee, Josephine Z., 2009n292
Kidbits, 3d ed, 2005n54
Kidd, Terry T., 2008n1273
KidHaven sci lib, 2008n1112
Kids.gov [Website], 2008n636
KidzCat, 2009n539
Kiernan, Vincent, 2007n242
Killam, Douglas, 2006n1056, 2009n979
Killinger, Charles, 2006n105
Kim, Djun Kil, 2006n93
Kimmelman, Burt, 2006n1069, 2008n957
Kincheloe, Joe L., 2005n275
Kindell, Alexandra, 2007n733
King, C. Richard, 2005n752
King, J. E., 2008n149
King, James J., 2006n579
King, Jason, 2009n113
King, John A., Jr., 2007n614
King, Kimball, 2008n894
King, Peter J., 2005n1227
King, Russell, 2008n740
Kingfisher atlas of the medieval world, 2008n427
Kingfisher 1st dict, 2006n959
Kingfisher 1st thesaurus, 2006n960
Kingfisher illus nature ency, 2005n1378
Kingfisher student atlas of N America, 2007n302
Kingsbury, Noel, 2006n1308
Kingseed, Cole C., 2005n456
Kinnamon, Keneth, 2008n926
Kinnear, Karen L., 2008n479
Kinney, Anne Behnke, 2006n465
Kinsbruner, Jay, 2009n118
Kinshasa, Kwando M., 2007n268
Kipfer, Barbara Ann, 2006n1271, 2007n41, 2007n824, 2009n358
Kirchner, Frank, 2005n815

Kirio, Carolyn H., 2009n519
Kirk, Connie Ann, 2005n1066, 2005n1072, 2006n1002, 2009n964
Kirk, Martin, 2005n785
Kirk-Othmer chemical tech & the environment, 2008n1290
Kirk-Othmer concise ency of chemical tech, 5th ed, 2008n1291
Kirk-Othmer food & feed tech, 2008n1130
Kirkham, Mirjam J., 2005n363
Kirkham, Tony, 2005n1373
Kirkpatrick, Jim, 2005n1467
Kirkpatrick, Zoe Merriman, 2009n1182
Kirschbaum, Stanislav J., 2008n129
Kislenko, Arne, 2005n102
Kistler, John M., 2005n1376
Kitchell, Catherine A., 2006n522
Kittleson, Mark J., 2005n827
Klages, Mary, 2008n790
Klein, Barry T., 2005n342
Klemencic, Matjaž, 2005n339
Klezmer, Deborah, 2007n755, 2008n779
Kline, Michael B., 2005n108
Klingler, Mark A., 2008n1164
Klossner, Michael, 2007n1043
Klotz, John, 2009n1203
Knapp, Bettina L., 2005n986
Knight, Jeffrey A., 2005n1375, 2009n1264
Knight, Peter, 2005n424
Knights Templar ency, 2008n428
Kniskern, Nancy V., 2006n846
Knobock, Glenn A., 2006n672
Knop, Kathi, 2009n578
Knott, Stephen F., 2006n699
Knott's hndbk for vegetable growers, 5th ed, 2008n1138
Knowledge mgmt & business strategies, 2008n170
Knowledge mgmt, 2008n169
Knowledge mgmt, 2009n146, 2009n573
Knowles, Elizabeth, 2005n61, 2006n867, 2007n46
Knowles, Leo, 2005n1268
Knuth, Bruce G., 2008n996
Koch, John T., 2006n104, 2007n114
Kochhar-Bryant, Carol, 2009n281
Kock, Ned, 2009n1284
Koehler, Wallace C., Jr., 2008n545
Koelb, Clayton, 2006n1058
Koelling, Holly, 2008n881
Koerige, Noretta, 2008n1104, 2009n1123
Kofman, Jan, 2009n108
Kogan, Lee, 2005n935
Kogan, Maurice, 2005n687
Kohn, George Childs, 2007n551, 2008n454, 2008n581
Kohut, David, 2005n499
Kohut, Zenon E., 2006n106
Kok, B., 2005n1354
Kokkonen, Jouko, 2009n736

Kolb, Robert W., 2008n154, 2009n132
Kolencik, Patricia Liotta, 2009n936
Kolin, Philip C., 2005n1036
Komara, Edward, 2007n1007
Konstam, Angus, 2007n392
Kontos, Louis, 2009n468
Koontz, Trish Yourst, 2005n1295
Koopmans, Joop W., 2008n126
Korach, Myron, 2009n894
Korea, updated ed, 2006n402
Korean battle chronology, 2005n659
Korean War, 2005n447
Korean War, 2008n578
Korean War almanac, 2007n339
Korenman, Joan, 2005n273, 2007n235
Kornbluh, Peter, 2009n360
Korom, Frank J., 2007n1022
Korrol, Virginia Sánchez, 2007n285
Korsmeyer, Pamela, 2009n762
Kort, Carol, 2008n909
Kort, Michael, 2008n413, 2009n116
Koschorke, Klaus, 2008n1089
Koszczuk, Jacki, 2007n611
Koszczuk, Jackie, 2006n724
Koth, Michelle, 2009n533
Kotin, Alison G., 2006n1441
Kovac's gd to electronic lib collection dvlpmt, 2005n591
Kovach, Robert, 2005n1514
Kovacs, Diane K., 2005n591
Kovel, Ralph, 2006n899, 2008n814
Kovel, Terry, 2006n899, 2008n814
Kovels' American antiques 1750-1900, 2006n899
Kovels' American Collectibles 1900 to 2000, 2008n814
Kovels' antiques & collectibles price list 2006, 38th ed, 2007n795
Koven, Mikel J., 2008n1032
Kowalski, Theodore J., 2009n251
Kowalsky, Daniel, 2006n481
Kowner, Rotem, 2007n557
Koza, Darrell, 2006n1497
Krabbenhoft, Herman O., 2007n681
Kraft, Michael B., 2009n695
Krag, Karen, 2005n1464
Kranz, Rachel, 2005n140, 2006n810
Kranzler, Henry R., 2009n762
Krapp, Kristine, 2005n735, 2006n1440
Krason, Stephen M., 2008n1081
Krauss, Jane, 2009n249
Kravets, Marybeth, 2005n315
Krebs, Robert E., 2005n1290, 2009n1129
Kreisel, Martha, 2007n820
Kreiswirth, Martin, 2005n1005, 2009n913
Kresh, Diane, 2008n511
Kress, Stephen W., 2006n1370
Krieger, Jan, 2009n263

Krismann, Carol H., 2006n124
Kritzman, Lawrence D., 2007n1064, 2008n1051
Kroll, Gary, 2007n1145, 2008n1114
Kroll, Mark, 2008n972
Kronenfeld, Jennie Jacobs, 2005n1431
Kronenfeld, Michael R., 2005n1431
Kronenwetter, Michael, 2005n578
Kroski, Ellyssa, 2009n572
Kross, Andrea L., 2005n1232
Krowchuk, Daniel P., 2007n1266
Krstovic, Jelena, 2005n977, 2005n979, 2005n980,
    2009n903
Kruger, Betsy, 2007n493
Ku Klux Klan, 2007n367
Kuenstle, Michael W., 2009n261
Kuhlthau, Carol C., 2009n567
Kulik, Peter H., 2009n1134
Kumar, Lisa, 2009n908
Kumar, Suhasini L., 2008n519
Kumaraswamy, P. R., 2007n123
Kunzel, Bonnie, 2009n946
Kunzel, Bonnie L., 2007n908
Kupietzky, Allison Siffre Guedalia, 2009n540
Kurian, George Thomas, 2005n847, 2007n473,
    2008n64, 2009n774
Kurihara, Yutaka, 2008n171
Kusha, Hamid R., 2005n579
Kusky, Timothy, 2006n1499
Kutz, Myer, 2008n1201
Kvasnicka, Robert M., 2009n361

La nueva enciclopedia cumbre [Website], 2009n20
Labor & workplace issues in lit, 2007n885
Labor relations, 2006n236
Lacoste, Jean-Yves, 2005n1256
Ladd, Helen F., 2008n267, 2009n254
Ladies in the lab II, 2005n1280
Laffaye, Horace A., 2005n779, 2008n713
LaFond, Deborah M., 2006n79
Lagowski, J. J., 2005n1492
Lagrange, Anne-Marie, 2006n1507
Lagua, Rosalinda T., 2005n1418
Laing, Dave, 2006n1094
Laird, Paul R., 2008n1041
Lal, Brij V., 2009n100
Lal, Rattan, 2007n1148
Lamar, William W., 2005n1399
Lamb, Andy, 2007n1214
Lamb, Peter, 2007n631
Lamb, Vickie, 2007n1201
Lambdin, Laura Cooner, 2009n969
Lambdin, Robert Thomas, 2009n969
Lambert, David, 2008n1319
Lambert, Olga Demin, 2006n831
Lambert, Stephen E., 2006n253

Lamonde, Yvan, 2005n656, 2006n655, 2006n656
Lamoureux, Florence, 2005n97
Lampert, Lynn D., 2008n544
Lancashire, Ian, 2009n869
Land battles in 5th century BC Greece, 2009n602
Land, Gary, 2006n1232
Landau, Herbert B., 2009n511
Lande, Andrew, 2007n317
Lande, Nathaniel, 2007n317
Landesman, Fred, 2005n1205
Landholt, L. M., 2005n1355
Landis, William E., 2008n522
Landlord legal forms simplified, 2008n261
Landmark decisions of the US Supreme Court, 2d ed,
    2008n464
Landmark Supreme Court cases, 2005n549
Landmarks of American women's hist, 2005n873
Landmarks of the American Revolution, 2d ed,
    2007n356
Landow, George, 2006n973
Lands & peoples, 2006n65
Landsberg, Brian K., 2005n553
Landscape architectural graphic standards, 2008n1135
Lane, Chris, 2006n1356
Lane, George, 2005n468, 2007n375
Lang, J. Stephen, 2006n1377, 2008n1070
Lang, Tom, 2009n1144
Langer, Erick D., 2009n118
Langer, Howard J., 2006n459
Lange's hndbk of chemistry, 16th ed, 2006n1495
Langhorne, Mary Jo, 2005n627
Langrand, Olivier, 2008n1181
Langston, Thomas S., 2008n649
Language of tennis, 2005n784
LANIC: Latin American network & info center
    [Website], 2008n134
Lanigan, Ernest J., 2006n777
Lankes, R. David, 2006n644, 2008n558
Lanning, Scott, 2005n612
Lansford, Tom, 2008n397, 2008n664, 2009n377
Lantz, Kenneth, 2005n1097
Lanzi, Gioia, 2005n936
Lapunzina, Alejandro, 2006n932
Lare, Gary A., 2005n624, 2007n240
Large, Mark F., 2005n1374
Largent, Mark A., 2008n1147
Larosa, Michael J., 2007n117, 2008n133
Larousse unabridged dict: Spanish-English,
    English-Spanish, 2005n974
Larsen, Anne R., 2008n784
Larsen, Jeffrey A., 2006n676, 2006n744
Larsen, Torben B., 2006n1386
Larson, Catherine, 2007n493
Larson, Denise R., 2009n318
Larson, Desi, 2006n237
Larsson, Hans, 2005n1389
Lasley, Thomas J., II, 2009n251

Last word, 2009n886

Laster, James H., 2006n1085

Laszloffy, Tracey, 2009n278

Later swing era, 1942 to 1955, 2005n1140

Latham, Kevin, 2008n1002

Lathrop, Charles E., 2005n59

Latin America & the Caribbean, 2005n1543

Latin American database (LADB) [Website], 2008n135

Latin American mktg data & stats 2007/08, 2009n204

Latin American mktg info sourcebk, 2005n223

Latin American network info center (LANIC) [Website], 2008n136

Latin American sci fiction writers, 2005n1091

Latin American women writers, 2008n943

Latinas in the US, 2007n285

Latino American experience [Website], 2009n316

Latino Americans & pol participation, 2006n727

Latino & African American athletes today, 2005n751

Latino chronology, 2008n332

Latino food culture, 2009n1152

Latino lit in America, 2005n1090

Latino media resource gd 2004, 2005n908

Latino media resource gd 2005, 2d ed, 2006n873

Latitia Baldrige's new manners for new times, 2005n800

Latter-day Saint experience in America, 2005n1264

Laughlin, Sara, 2009n580

Launius, Roger D., 2005n1506

Lavery, Brian, 2005n1070, 2005n1551

Lavin, Stephen J., 2007n585

Lavrakas, Paul J., 2009n56

Law: key concepts in philosophy, 2007n1070

Law & legal info dir, 15th ed, 2005n538

Law & legal info dir, 16th ed, 2006n529

Law & legal info dir, 18th ed, 2008n471

Law & legal info dir, 19th ed, 2009n442

Law firm accounting & financial mgmt, 3d ed, 2007n455

Law firms yellow bk, 2008 ed, 2009n443

Law firms yellow bk, Summer 2005, 2006n530

Law of higher education, 4th ed, 2009n275

Law school buzz bk, 2005 ed, 2005n301

Lawler, Jennifer, 2005n473

Lawlor, William T., 2006n1033

Lawrence of Arabia, 2005n503

Lawrence, Paul, 2007n1094

Lawson, Russell, 2009n1137

Lawson, Russell M., 2006n1258

Lawson-Hall, Toni, 2006n1306

Lawton, Sandra Augustyn, 2006n316, 2006n1448, 2007n717, 2007n1271, 2008n1240, 2009n764, 2009n1251, 2009n1267

Layton, Robert, 2006n1090

Lazarus, Richard S., 2008n692

Lazich, Robert S., 2006n156, 2009n150

Le Boeuf, Patrick, 2006n616

Le Faye, Deirdre, 2008n928

Leach, Tam, 2005n782

Leaders of men, 2009n613

Leaders of the info age, 2005n1482

Leadership, 2008n446

Leadership basics for librarians & info professionals, 2008n555

Leadership for excellence, 2009n522

Leadership networks [Website], 2009n31

Leading the parade, 2008n725

Leadoff batters of major league baseball, 2007n681

Leahy, Todd, 2009n308

Leaman, Louisa, 2008n262

Leaman, Oliver, 2007n1062, 2007n1119, 2007n1122

Lean, Mike, 2008n1256

Learner, Adrienne Wilmoth, 2007n710

Learner, Brenda Wilmoth, 2008n1107, 2009n1335

Learner, K. Lee, 2009n1335

Learning disabilities dir [Website], 2006n315

Learning disabilities info for teens, 2006n316

Learning disabilities sourcebk, 3d ed, 2009n282

Learning to lead & manage info literacy instruction, 2006n630

Learning to learn, 2d ed, 2007n526

Least developed countries report 2006, 2007n108

Least developed countries report 2007, 2008n112

Leckie, Gloria J., 2008n553

Lee, Alice C., 2007n161

Lee, Barbara A., 2009n275

Lee, C. C., 2006n1404

Lee, Cheng-Few, 2007n161

Lee, Karen, 2009n483

Lee, M. Owen, 2006n1089

Lee, Philip Yungkin, 2005n971

Lee, Richard B., 2006n800

Lee, Steven W., 2006n756

Lee, Sul H., 2006n597, 2008n547

Lee, Sunggyu, 2006n1490

Leeds, Rod, 2006n1307

Leeman, Richard W., 2006n870

Leeming, David, 2007n1026

Leeper, Angela, 2007n980

Leffel, Gregory P., 2008n1090

Leffman, David, 2005n402

Legal executions in Calif., 2007n483

Legal executions in N.J., 1691-1963, 2007n467

Legal forms for starting & running a small business, 4th ed, 2007n465

Legal terminology, 2006n539

Legalized gambling, 2007n687

Legault, Thierry, 2008n1301

Legislative branch of fed govt, 2009n660

Legislative branch of state govt, 2007n615

Legislative drafter's desk ref, 2d ed, 2008n476

Legislative women, 2009n662

Legrand, Gerard, 2005n944

Lehman, Jeffrey, 2005n335

Lehr, Janet, 2006n1533
Lehr, Jay H., 2005n1408
Lehr, Jay, 2006n1533
Leibs, Andrew, 2005n762
Leiter, Brian, 2006n297
Leiter, Richard A., 2005n554, 2009n457
Leiter, Samuel L., 2007n1057, 2008n1040
Leiter, Sharon, 2007n949
Leitherer, Claus, 2009n1306
Leitz, Robert C., III, 2006n10, 2006n11, 2007n4,
    2008n8
LeMay, Michael C., 2008n480
Lemberg, David S., 2008n357
Lemche, Niels Peter, 2005n126
Lemoine, Florence, 2005n527
Lenburg, Jeff, 2006n46, 2009n1043
Lenfestey, Thompson, 2005n780
Lenski, Noel, 2006n477, 2007n394
Lentz, Harris M., III, 2005n1180, 2006n1127,
    2007n1036, 2008n620, 2009n1049
Lentz, Joan Easton, 2006n1372
Leo Tolstoy, 2007n974
Leonard, Kathy S., 2008n943'
Leonard Maltin's movie gd, 2006 ed, 2006n1168
Leonard, Natacha, 2005n160, 2005n712
Leonard, Thomas M., 2005n727, 2007n107
Leong, Frederick T. L., 2009n701
Leopold, Donald J., 2006n1335
Lerner, Adrienne Wilmoth, 2007n54, 2007n491,
    2007n580, 2007n703, 2008n751
Lerner, Brenda Wilmoth, 2005n1539, 2006n563,
    2007n54, 2007n478, 2007n484, 2007n491,
    2007n580, 2007n672, 2007n703, 2007n710,
    2007n1242, 2007n1321, 2007n1328,
    2008n699, 2008n751, 2008n1140,
    2008n1229, 2009n1133, 2009n1316
Lerner, K. Lee, 2005n1539, 2006n563, 2007n54,
    2007n478, 2007n484, 2007n491, 2007n580,
    2007n672, 2007n703, 2007n710, 2007n1242,
    2007n1321, 2007n1328, 2008n699,
    2008n751, 2008n1107, 2008n1140,
    2008n1229, 2009n1133, 2009n1316
Lerner, Marcy, 2005n232
Lerner, Richard M., 2005n825, 2007n663
Lerner, Rita G., 2007n1317
Lesch, David W., 2005n501
Lesh, Richard A., 2009n274
Leslie, Catherine Amoroso, 2008n827
Leslie, Roger, 2009n1062
Lesser, M. X., 2009n1104
Lester, June, 2008n545
Leverett, Robert T., 2005n399
Levering, Matthew, 2009n314
Levi, Selma K., 2009n549
Levin, Carole, 2008n784
Levin, Robert E., 2006n1286
Levine, Charles M., 2007n767

LeVine, Harry, III, 2007n1226
Levinson, David, 2005n807, 2007n670, 2008n552,
    2008n668
Levinson, David L., 2006n301
Levstik, Linda S., 2009n256
Levy, Richard S., 2006n346
Levy-Yamamori, Ran, 2005n1314
Lewis & Clark Columbia River water trail, 2005n397
Lewis & Clark expedition, 2005n446
Lewis & Clark lexicon of discovery, 2005n430
Lewis Carroll among his bks, 2006n647
Lewis, Christopher J. T., 2009n1136
Lewis Clark's field gd to wild flowers of the sea coast
    in the Pacific NW, 3d ed, 2006n1346
Lewis, D. S., 2008n617, 2009n38
Lewis, Derek, 2008n123
Lewis, Donald M., 2005n1254
Lewis, James R., 2005n1239, 2006n1214, 2009n715,
    2009n1091
Lewis, Linda K., 2005n626
Lewis, Richard J., 2005n1407, 2008n1292
Lewis, Thomas Tandy, 2008n469
Lexicons of early modern English [Website],
    2009n869
Li, Luchen, 2006n1039
Liberman, Anatoly, 2006n948, 2009n887
Liberman, Rosette, 2006n885
Librarian's career gdbk, 2006n614
Librarian's gd to developing Christian fiction
    collections for adults, 2006n624
Librarian's gd to developing Christian fiction
    collections for children, 2006n625
Librarian's gd to developing Christian fiction
    collections for YAs, 2006n626
Librarian's gd to genealogical servs & research,
    2005n603
Librarian's Internet survival gd, 2d ed, 2007n540
Librarian's yellow pages [Website], 2009n497
Librarians' Internet index [Website], 2008n46
Librarians' Internet index [Website], 2009n496
Libraries & librarianship, 2008n551
Libraries beyond their institutions, 2006n645
Libraries within their institutions, 2006n599
Library as place, 2008n553
Library contests, 2009n582
Library of American laws & legal principles,
    2007n456
Library of the 9 planets, 2006n1508
Library research with emergent readers, 2009n520
Library security & safety gd to prevention, planning,
    & response, 2009n577
Library 2.0, 2009n506
Library Web sites, 2005n635
LibrarySpot [Website], 2009n498
Libutti, Patricia O'Brian, 2005n629
Liddle, Andrew, 2009n1305
Lide, David R., 2008n1294, 2009n1295

Liden, Magnus, 2009n1160
Lieber, Ron, 2005n237
Lieberman, Jeffrey A., 2007n1283
Lieberman, Robbie, 2005n451
Lieven, Dominic, 2007n397
Life & presidency of Franklin Delano Roosevelt, 2006n692
Life events & rites of passage, 2009n1040
Life in the sea series, 2006n1520
Life of lang, 2007n824
Life on Earth series, 2005n1291
Light, Jonathan Fraser, 2006n778
Lightman, Benjamin, 2009n785
Lightman, Marjorie, 2009n785
Lilies, 2005n1366
Lille, William, III, 2008n650
Lima, Carolyn W., 2007n897, 2009n924
Lima, John A., 2007n897
Lind, Amy, 2009n787
Lindberg, Christine A., 2005n965, 2009n895
Lindemann, Richard H. F., 2006n991
Lindroth, David, 2005n533
Lindsay, Elizabeth Blakesley, 2009n948
Lindsay, James E., 2006n1243
Lindsell-Roberts, Sheryl, 2005n272
Line, Scott, 2007n1164
Linge, Mary Kay, 2006n774
Lints, Richard, 2005n1229
LiPera, William, 2006n1447
Lipow, Anne Grodzins, 2005n651
Lipsky, Martin S., 2007n1245
Lipson, Charles, 2007n779, 2009n276
Lipton, Laura, 2009n267
List, Regina A., 2008n727
Literacy for young children, 2009n265
Literary ency [Website], 2006n983
Literary filmography, 2007n1049
Literary market place 2006, 2006n653
Literary market place 2007, 67th ed, 2008n568
Literary market place 2009, 2009n596
Literary newsmakers for students, 2007n872
Literary newsmakers for students, v.2, 2008n877
Literary newsmakers for students, v.3, 2009n915
Literary 100, rev ed, 2009n906
Literary ref center [Website], 2009n905
Literary ref online [Website], 2007n873
Literary research & Irish lit, 2009n981
Literary research & the American modernist era, 2009n948
Literary research & the British Romantic Era, 2006n1047
Literary research & the era of American nationalism & romanticism, 2009n958
Literary research gd, 5th ed, 2009n902
Literary S Carolina, 2005n1059
Literary spy, 2005n59

Literary themes for students: race & prejudice, 2007n923
Literary themes for students: the American dream, 2008n896
Literary themes for students: war & peace, 2007n924
Literary theory, 2008n790
Literature & sci, 2006n986
Literature & the environment, 2005n1008
Literature criticism from 1400 to 1800, v.100, 2005n1009
Literature criticism from 1400 to 1800, v.101, 2005n1010
Literature criticism from 1400 to 1800, v.102, 2005n1011
Literature criticism from 1400 to 1800, v.103, 2005n1012
Literature of Africa, 2006n1056
Literature of chemistry, 2006n1489
Literature of Islam, 2007n973
Literature of Latin America, 2005n1092
Literature of the Caribbean, 2009n983
Literature search strategies for interdisciplinary research, 2007n543
Literature suppressed on pol grounds, rev ed, 2007n868
Literature suppressed on religious grounds, rev ed, 2007n867
Literature suppressed on sexual grounds, rev ed, 2007n869
Literature suppressed on social grounds, rev ed, 2007n870
Litt, Jerome Z., 2008n1262
Little, Karen R., 2008n966
Little Oxford dict of quotations, 3d ed, 2006n60
Little Oxford dict of quotations, 4th ed, 2009n49
Little Oxford English dict & thesaurus, 2d ed, 2009n875
Little, Thomas H., 2007n615
Litt's drug eruption ref manual including drug interactions, 13th ed, 2008n1262
Liu, Charles, 2009n1308
Lives & times of the great composers, 2005n1133
Livesey, Steven J., 2006n1260
Livezeanu, Irina, 2008n775
Living green, 2009n1336
Livingston, Steven G., 2009n453
Livingstone, E. A., 2006n1234
Llanes, Peggie, 2009n548
Lo, Shiu-hing, 2007n94
Lobban, Richard A., Jr., 2008n97
Lobbyists.info [Website], 2007n599
Lobbyists.info [Website], 2009n654
Local & regional govt info, 2006n43
Lockhart, Darrell B., 2005n1091
Lockie, Andrew, 2007n1263
Lockwood, Mark W., 2005n1387
Locus online [Website], 2006n1020

Loertscher, David V., 2006n607, 2008n517
LogEc [Website], 2005n133
Logue, Calvin M., 2005n890, 2006n874, 2007n766
Londre, Felicia Hardison, 2009n1074
Lonergan, David, 2006n1097
Long, David E., 2007n128
Long, Douglas, 2005n580
Long, Jeffrey E., 2008n945
Long, Jonathan, 2008n704
Longe, Jacqueline L., 2006n1439, 2006n1446,
    2007n1249, 2008n1119
Longshore, David, 2008n1308
Long-Solis, Janet, 2006n1289
Looking at prints, drawings, & watercolours,
    2007n814
Loomis, Frank Farmer, IV, 2006n900
López-Corvo, Rafael E., 2005n736
Lord, Rexford D., 2008n1192
Lorentz, John H., 2007n126
Losch, Richard R., 2009n1096
Lou Gehrig, 2005n766
Loucky, James, 2009n769
Loughlin, Kevin, 2007n1281
Louie, Gary J., 2006n1084
Louis Armstrong, 2005n1132
Louisiana almanac, 2006-07 ed, 2007n67
Louisiana almanac, 2008-09 ed, 2008n82
Louisiana coast, 2009n1191
Loveday, Jon, 2009n1305
Lovera, José Rafael, 2006n1290
Lovett, Charlie, 2006n647
Lovisi, Gary, 2009n824
Lowe, Cheryl, 2006n1333
Lowe, Denise, 2005n1189
Lowe, Joy L., 2005n1176
Lower taxes in 7 easy steps, 2007n152
Lowery, Charles D., 2005n334
Lu, Henry C., 2007n1264
Lubenow, Gerald C., 2008n642
Lubliner, Shira, 2009n259
Ludman, Mark D., 2009n1242
Ludwig, Frieder, 2008n1089
Luebking, Sandra Hargreaves, 2007n291
Lumber, Terry, 2005n1466
Lumby, Jacky, 2009n258
Lumley, Elizabeth, 2005n25, 2006n22, 2007n19,
    2008n22, 2009n16
Luo, Jing, 2006n89
Lupi, Luca, 2005n1520
Lupton, Mary Jane, 2005n1073
Luraghi, Silvia, 2009n871
Lurie, Jonathan, 2005n552
Lurie, Maxine N., 2005n81
Luscombe, David, 2006n511
Lybecker, Donna L., 2009n1340
Lye, Keith, 2008n360
Lyle, Susanna, 2007n1180

Lynch, David, 2006n1284
Lynch, Mike, 2008n1298, 2008n1299, 2008n1300
Lynch, Patricia Ann, 2005n1161, 2005n1162
Lynch, Patrick J., 2006n1366
Lynn, B., 2009n1270
Lynn, Ruth Nadelman, 2006n992
Lyon, Peter, 2009n96
Lyons, Peg, 2006n1177
Lyon's Press horseman's dict, rev ed, 2008n1190

Ma, Miao, 2009n1294
Mabry, Celia Hales, 2005n647
MacDonald, David W., 2007n1208
Macdonald, Kate, 2009n942
MacDonald, Mary C., 2007n525
MacDougal, John M., 2005n1358
Macey, J. David, Jr., 2007n941
Machine guns, 2006n682
Mack, Daniel C., 2005n622
Mack, Glenn R., 2006n1291
Mack, William P., 2005n673
Mackay, Richard, 2009n1192
MacKellar, Pamela H., 2007n524
MacKenzie, David S., 2007n1160
MacKenzie, John M., 2006n325
Mackey, Thomas P., 2008n542
MacLeod, Iseabail, 2005n116
MacMillan, Kathy, 2009n554
MacNaughton, Daniel Bruce, 2007n1342
Macomber, Roger S., 2006n1496
Macpherson, Gordon, 2005n1433
MacPherson, Heidi Slettedahl, 2006n746
MacQuitty, Miranda, 2009n1324
MacShamhrain, Ailbhe, 2006n475
MacTutor hist of mathematics [Website], 2005n1528
MacTutor hist of mathematics archive [Website],
    2008n1332
Macy, Laura, 2007n1001
Madame Alexander, 2008n821
Madden, David, 2007n925
Madden, M. Leslie, 2009n583
Maddex, Robert L., 2006n543, 2008n481, 2009n439,
    2009n625
Maddox, Gregory H., 2007n1331
Maddox, Taddy, 2009n707
Made in the 20th century, 2006n895
Madin, Mike, 2006n1154
Maestros in America, 2009n1013
Mafia ency, 3d ed, 2006n562
Magazine writer's hndbk, 2d ed, 2007n774
Maggie L. Walker natl historic site [Website],
    2009n163
Maghan, Jess, 2006n574
Magic Dragon Media, 2005n1049
Magill, Frank N., 2005n511, 2005n984

Magill's cinema annual 2004, 23d ed, 2005n1212
Magill's cinema annual 2008, 27th ed, 2009n1057
Magill's literary annual 2006, 2007n948
Magill's literary annual 2007, 2008n878
Magill's medical gd, 3d rev ed, 2005n1438
Magill's medical gd, 4th rev ed, 2008n1230
Magill's survey of American lit, 2007n935
Magna Carta, 2005n488
Magna Carta ancestry, 2006n361
Magoc, Chris J., 2008n1346
Maher, Andrea K., 2008n1133
Maher, Paul E., 2008n1077
Mahler symphonies, 2005n1130
Mai, Larry L., 2006n1313
Mainline Christians & US public policy, 2008n676
Maitre-Allain, Thierry, 2006n1381
Major acts of Congress, 2005n553
Major chemical & petrochemical companies of the
        world 2004, 8th ed, 2005n193
Major companies of …
    Africa S of the Sahara 2004, 9th ed, 2005n211
    Africa S of the Sahara 2005, 10th ed, 2006n211
    Central & E Europe & the Commonwealth of
        Independent States 2005, 14th ed,
        2006n220
    Central & E Europe & the Commonwealth of
        Independent States 2008, 2008n221
    Europe 2005, 24th ed, 2005n220
    Latin America & the Caribbean 2004, 2005n224
    Latin America & the Caribbean 2005, 10th ed,
        2006n222
    SW Asia 2004, 8th ed, 2005n215
    SW Asia 2005, 9th ed, 2006n215
    the Arab world 2006, 29th ed, 2006n224
    the Arab world 2008, 31st ed, 2008n222
    the Far East & Australasia 2008, 2008n219
    the world 2005, 8th ed, 2006n183
Major financial institutions of the world 2004, 7th ed,
        2005n185
Major financial institutions of the world, 9th ed,
        2007n163
Major info tech companies of the world, 5th ed,
        2005n194
Major info tech companies of the world 2005, 7th ed,
        2006n184
Major info tech companies of the world 2007, 9th ed,
        2008n193
Major pharmaceutical & biotech companies of the
        world 2005, 7th ed, 2006n1459
Major telecommunications companies of the world
        2004, 7th ed, 2005n1490
Major telecommunications companies of the world
        2007, 10th ed, 2008n194
Making of America—Cornell [Website], 2006n435
Making of America—Michigan [Website], 2006n436
Making of the American West, 2008n414
Makkai, Adam, 2005n959, 2006n953

Malam, John, 2007n1316
Malatesta, Victor J., 2008n691
Malcomson, Robert, 2007n357
Malik, Iftikhar H., 2007n99, 2009n104
Malin, Jo, 2006n856
Mälkiä, Matti, 2007n39, 2008n43
Mallegg, Kristin B., 2005n39, 2005n40, 2005n904,
        2006n33
Mallon, Bill, 2008n712
Maloney, David J., Jr., 2005n913
Maloney's antiques & collectibles resource dir, 7th ed,
        2005n913
Malsberger, Brian M., 2005n584, 2005n585
Malti-Douglas, Fedwa, 2008n732
Maltin, Leonard, 2006n1168
Mammal species of the world, 2007n1209
Mammals of Calif., rev ed, 2005n1396
Mammals of Costa Rica, 2008n1193
Mammals of Ind., 2009n1207
Mammals of S America, 2008n1192
Mammals of S America, v.1, 2009n1205
Man, John, 2008n364
Management basics for info professionals, 2d ed,
        2008n556
Manager's legal hndbk, 3d ed, 2007n451
Managing budgets & finances, 2006n639
Managing change, rev ed, 2007n532
Managing electronic govt info in libs, 2009n534
Managing facilities for results, 2009n509
Managing the 21st-century ref department, 2005n652
Managing 21st century libs, 2006n640
Mancall, Jacqueline C., 2006n605
Mancing, Howard, 2005n1098
Mancini, Anthony J., 2007n1266
Mancini, Julie R., 2006n1373
Mandel, David, 2009n1118
Mandel, Howard, 2007n1011
Maniotes, Leslie K., 2009n567
Mann, Barbara J., 2005n50
Mann, Joel F., 2006n391
Mann, Robert A., 2005n677, 2009n611
Mann, Thomas, 2006n596
Manners & customs in the Bible, 3d ed, 2007n1102
Manning, John, 2005n1361
Manning, Martin, 2005n432
Mano, Eloisa B., 2009n1214
Manocchia, Pat, 2009n735
Manser, Martin H., 2005n964, 2006n882, 2007n777,
        2008n869, 2009n893, 2009n911
Mansingh, Surjit, 2007n97
Manual for the performance lib, 2008n521
Manual for writers of research papers, theses, &
        dissertations, 7th ed, 2008n801
Manuel, Kate, 2008n559
Manual to online public records, 2009n454
Manufacturing & distribution USA, 3d ed, 2005n199
Manufacturing & distribution USA, 5th ed, 2009n184

Maples, 2005n1372
Mappen, Marc, 2005n81
Mapping the silk road & beyond, 2006n385
Maps in the atlases of the British Lib, 2006n386
Maps on file, 2005 ed, 2005n375
Maps on file, 2008 ed, 2008n361
Marais, Johan, 2006n1391, 2009n1210
Marbach, Joseph R., 2007n594
Marcello, Patricia Cronin, 2005n867
March, Ivan, 2006n1090
Marchant, Harvey J., 2008n1182
Marcinko, David Edward, 2007n1232
Marcovitch, Harvey, 2007n1246
Marcus, Maeva, 2005n547, 2008n474
Maretti, Silvia, 2006n86
Margaret Atwood, 2005n1085
Margaret Atwood, 2008n938
Margolis, Lewis, 2007n651
Margolis, Nadia, 2005n871
Margolis, Simeon, 2005n1449
Marguilies, Phillip, 2009n614
Mari, Christopher, 2008n1220, 2009n1309
Marie Selby Botanical Gardens illus dict of orchid
    genera, 2009n1183
Marill, Alvin H., 2006n1140
Marine life of the Pacific NW, 2007n1214
Marinelli, Janet, 2006n1330
Marion, Allison, 2005n1023
Mark, Dianne L. Hall, 2007n912
Mark Twain, 2005n1072
Market scope 2004, 2005n200
Market share reporter 2005, 2006n156
Market share reporter 2009 ed, 2009n150
Marketing gdbk 2005, 2005n256
Marketing gdbk 2008, 2008n255
Marketing gdbk 2009, 2009n235
Marketing guidebk 2006, 2006n266
Markey, Penny, 2007n511
Markham, Jerry W., 2007n148
Markides, Kyriakos S., 2008n1207
Markoe, Arnold, 2007n16
Markoe, Karen, 2007n16
Markowitz, Harvey, 2006n334, 2006n335
Markowitz, Judith A., 2005n1048
Marks' standard hndbk for mechanical engineers, 11th
    ed, 2007n1228
Marksmanship in the US Army, 2005n671
Markusen, Bruce, 2005n767
Markuson, Carolyn, 2008n514
Marley, David F., 2006n845, 2009n601
Marlink, Richard G., 2006n1441
Marmor, Max, 2005n592
Marquis who's who on the Web [Website], 2008n15
Marriage customs of the world, 2006n808
Marriage on trial, 2006n551
Marrone, Gaetana, 2008n941
Marsh, Arthur, 2008n226

Marshall, Barbara I., 2007n690
Marshall, Bill, 2006n747
Marshall Cavendish digital [Website], 2009n21
Marshall, Gordon, 2006n797
Marshall, Stephen A., 2007n1206
Marszalek, John F., 2005n334
Martin, Alfonso Velasco, 2008n900
Martin, Clemens, 2005n582
Martin, Deborah L., 2009n1159
Martin, Geoffrey J., 2007n308
Martin, Harold, 2005n896
Martin, Iain C., 2009n50
Martin, Jeanette S., 2009n148
Martin Luther King, Jr., ency, 2009n299
Martin, Mary, 2006n43
Martin, Mick, 2005n1216
Martinez, Juan Francisco, 2009n1110
Martirosyan, Tigran, 2006n86
Martis, Kenneth C., 2007n585
Maruca, Regina Fazio, 2009n205
Marvel graphic novels & related pubs, 2009n1037
Mary Gilliatt's dict of architecture & interior design,
    2006n928
Maryland State Archives atlas of histl maps of Md.
    1608-1908, 2006n381
Marzolph, Ulrich, 2005n1093
Masks & masking, 2007n258
Maslin, Ruthie, 2009n582
Mason, Catherine, 2007n111
Mason, Fran, 2008n789
Mason, Laura, 2005n1306
Massachusetts municipal profiles, 2007 ed, 2008n83
Massaro, Joseph, 2009n1224
Massil, Stephen W., 2005n1276, 2006n1247,
    2008n1101
Mastering N.T. Greek, 2007n1104
Masterpieces of beat lit, 2008n914
Masterpieces of classic Greek drama, 2006n1007
Masterpieces of French lit, 2005n1087
Masterpieces of modern British & Irish drama,
    2006n1008
Masterpieces of 20th-century American drama,
    2006n1006
Masterplots II: African American lit, rev ed, 2009n954
Masterplots II: Christian lit, 2008n879
Masterplots II: short story series, rev ed, 2005n1053
Masterson, Joanna, 2007n770, 2008n796
Material culture in America, 2008n1003
Math archives [Website], 2005n1532
Math forum Internet mathematics lib [Website],
    2005n1533
Math forum Internet mathematics lib [Website],
    2008n1333
Math on file: calculus, 2005n1535
Mathematical scis professional dir 2005, 2006n1530
Mathematics on the Web [Website], 2005n1526
Mathematics on the Web [Website], 2007n1320

Mathison, Sandra, 2005n64, 2009n242
Mathews, Sandra K., 2009n309
Matras, Yaron, 2005n952
Matson, Gienna, 2005n1163
Matson, Pamela A., 2005n1540, 2006n1538
Mattar, Philip, 2006n354
Matthew, Kathryn I., 2005n1176
Matthews, Dawn D., 2005n801, 2005n802, 2005n1469
Matthews, J. Greg, 2009n981
Matthews, Tracey L., 2007n871
Matthews, Victor H., 2007n1102
Mattingly, David, 2007n377
Mattison, Chris, 2008n1194
Mattox, Henry E., 2005n562, 2008n662
Matuozzi, Robert N., 2009n948
Matuz, Roger, 2005n414, 2005n837, 2006n728, 2007n325
Matviko, John W., 2007n1032
Matyszak, Philip, 2005n495
Matz, Allan, 2009n628
Mauch, Peter, 2008n666
Maude, George, 2007n113, 2008n121
Maume, David J., 2008n733
Maunder, Andrew, 2008n927
Mauro, Tony, 2007n457
Mauroni, Al, 2007n572, 2008n606
Maven in blue jeans, 2009n1092
Mavroidis, Petros C., 2009n488
Max Planck ency of public intl law online [Website], 2009n486
Maxmen, Jerrold S., 2009n1279
Maxwell, Bruce, 255, 2006n729
Maxwell, Robert L., 2005n616, 2008n530
Maxwell-Long, Thomas, 2006n736
Maxwell's hndbk for AACR2, 4th ed, 2005n616
Maxymuk, John, 2006n788
May, Charles, 2005n1053
May, Charles E., 2008n875, 2009n947
May, Mel Anthony, 2007n679
May, Steven W., 2005n1102
May, Timothy Michael, 2009n103
Mayden, Richard L., 2005n1392
Mayer, Geoff, 2008n1018
Maynard, Donald N., 2008n1138
Mayne, Tracy J., 2005n742, 2007n661, 2009n706
Mayo, Diane, 2006n600
Mayo, Mike, 2009n471
Mays, Dorothy A., 2006n857
Mays, Terry M., 2005n723, 2006n442, 2007n633, 2008n400
Mazama, Ama, 2005n333
Mazur, Carol, 2008n937
Mazzocchi, Jay, 2007n74
MBA programs 2006, 11th ed, 2006n295
Mbaku, John Mukum, 2006n80
McAleer, Dave, 2006n1095
McBride, Dorothy E., 2008n716

McBride, Kari Boyd, 2006n860
McCabe, Gerard B., 2005n636
McCabe, Timothy L., 2005n1338
McCafferty, Michael, 2009n341
McCaffrey, Paul, 2005n720, 2006n549, 2007n1329, 2008n335, 2009n1330
McCallum, Jack E., 2009n606
McCann, Charles Robert, Jr., 2005n173
McCants, Clyde T., 2005n1137
McCarthy, Helen, 2008n997
McCarthy, J. Thomas, 2005n590
McCarthy, John P., 2007n393
McCarthy's desk ency of intellectual property, 3d ed, 2005n590
McCartney, Martha W., 2008n346
McChristian, Douglas C., 2008n607
McClaren, Bill, 2005n1315
McClellan, Lawrence, Jr., 2005n1140
McClendon, Jo, 2006n317
McClendon, V. J., 2009n288
McClinton-Temple, Jennifer, 2008n913
McCloskey, Barbara, 2006n917
McClure, Charles R., 2009n512
McCluskey, Audrey Thomas, 2008n1025
McClymond, Michael, 2008n1054
McColl, R. W., 2006n387
McConnaughy, Rozalynd P., 2009n532
McConnell, Andy, 2008n818
McCook, Kathleen de la Pena, 2005n607
McCorkle, James, 2007n979
McCue, Margi Laird, 2009n747
McCulloch, Graham, 2009n841
McCusker, John J., 2006n265
McCutcheon, Marc, 958, 2006n964
McDaniel, Deanna J., 2009n925
McDavid, Richard A., 2007n223, 2009n216
McDermott, Irene E., 2007n540
McDonnell, Brian, 2008n1018
McDonnell, Jeffrey J., 2007n1227
McDougall, Jennifer Fecio, 2008n498
McDougall, Len, 2005n776
McElmeel, Sharron L., 2005n1028
McElroy, Tucker, 2006n1525
McEwan, Gordon F., 2007n280
McGeorge, Pamela, 2005n1366, 2007n1161
McGeough, Kevin M., 2005n496
McGhee, Karen, 2007n1187
McGillivary, Gregory K., 2006n578
McGillivray, Alice V., 2005n719, 2006n732, 2007n616, 2008n643
McGinnis, Carol, 2006n360
McGinnis, Samuel M., 2007n1203
McGovern, Bernie, 80, 2008n82
McGowan, Kevin J., 2009n1200
McGowan, Sharon M., 2006n583
McGowen, Stanley S., 2006n677
McGrath, Anne, 2007n249

McGrath, Anne F., 2005n305, 2005n916, 2005n917, 2005n918, 2005n919

McGrath, Gavin J., 2007n1113

McGraw-Hill concise ency of …
    biosci, 2006n1315
    chemistry, 2005n1496
    engineering, 2006n1396
    physics, 2007n1318
    sci & tech, 5th ed, 2006n1259

McGraw-Hill desk ref for editors, writers, & proofreaders, 2007n772

McGraw-Hill dict of electrical & computer engineering, 2005n1409

McGraw-Hill dict of misspelled & easily confused words, 2007n839

McGraw-Hill ency of sci & tech, 10th ed, 2008n1109

McGraw-Hill hndbk of business letters, 4th ed, 2007n233

McGraw-Hill Homeland Security hndbk, 2007n647

McGraw-Hill yrbk of sci & tech 2005, 2006n1272

McGraw-Hill yrbk of sci & tech 2008, 2008n1113

McGraw-Hill's American idioms dict, 4th ed, 2008n862

McGraw-Hill's dict of American idioms & phrasal verbs, 2006n954

McGuire, Bill, 2005n1514

McGuire, Michael, 2008n456

McHenry, Ellen Johnston, 2007n1100

McIntosh, Jane R., 2006n485, 2008n383

McIntosh, Jane, 2007n385

McIntyre, Roger S., 2009n1279

McKay, George, 2007n1187

McKean, Erin, 2006n28

McKee, David A., 2009n1201

McKenna, Brian, 2007n682

McKim, Donald K., 2008n1068

McKitterick, Rosamond, 2006n487

McKivigan, John, 2008n394

McLaughlin, Eugene, 2007n471

McLaughlin, Stephen, 2005n674

McLean, Alice L., 2008n1131

McLeod, Hugh, 2007n1117

McLeod, W. H., 2006n1249

McMahon, Sean, 2006n1115

McMillan, Beverly, 2007n1172

McNally, Robert Aquinas, 2005n1450

McNeil, Beth, 2006n637

McNeil, W. K., 2006n1112

McNeill, Allison, 2005n410, 2005n411, 2005n412, 2005n416, 2005n418, 2005n1293

McNeill, William H., 2007n416

McNiece, Matthew A., 2009n615

McNulty, Tom, 2007n815

McPhee, Stephen J., 2007n1255

McRobie, Alan, 2007n105

McVicar, Jekka, 2005n1316, 2007n1149

McVicker, Mary F., 2009n783

Meagher, Timothy, 2006n345

Means, Marcia Merryman, 2005n505, 2005n506, 2005n507

Mechanical engineers' hndbk, 3d ed, 2008n1201

Mechanisms & mechanical devices sourcebk, 4th ed, 2008n1202

Meckel, Richard A., 2005n826

Meckna, Michael, 2005n1131

Medal of Honor citations [Website], 2008n576

Media & American courts, 2005n539

Media scandals, 2009n800

Medical & health care bks & serials in print 2005, 2006n1409

Medical & health info dir, 16th ed, 2005n1426

Medical & health info dir, 17th ed, 2006n1421

Medical & health info dir, 20th ed, 2008n1214

Medical & health info dir, 21st ed, 2009n1228

Medical device register 2007, 27th ed, 2008n1216

Medical device register 2008, 28th ed, 2008n1215

Medical Lib Assn gd to cancer info, 2008n1249

Medical Lib Assn gd to health literacy, 2009n535

Medical marvels, 2007n1261

Medical tests sourcebk, 3d ed, 2009n1247

Medicina Antiqua [Website], 2007n1244

Medicinal plants in folk tradition, 2005n1347

Medicinal plants of N America, 2009n1178

Medicinal plants of the world, 2005n1352

Medicine, health, & bioethics, 2007n1242

Medicine on trial, 2005n545

Medieval castles, 2006n513

Medieval cathedrals, 2007n383

Medieval city, 2006n469

Medieval feminist index or Feminae [Website], 2005n874

Medieval Ireland, 2006n475

Medieval Islamic civilization, 2007n1121

Medieval sci & tech, 2005n1296

Medieval sci, tech, & medicine, 2006n1260

Medieval weapons, 2008n603

Medina, F. Xavier, 2006n1292

Mediterranean cruises, 2005n407

Mediterranean: an environmental hist, 2006n1543

Medoff, Rafael, 2009n1119

Medvic, Stephen K., 2006n726

Mehno, John, 2005n772

Meho, Lokman I., 2007n120

Meier, Matt S., 2005n355

Meinstereifel, Ronald L., 2005n783

Mejia, Armando Xavier, 2006n727

Mejía, Germán R., 2007n117, 2008n133

Mell, Eila, 2005n1202

Mellerski, Nancy C., 2005n108

Mellinger, Axel, 2006n1501

Melloni, B. John, 2009n1176

Melloni, H. Paul, 2009n1176

Melloni, June L., 2009n1176

Melton, Buckner F., Jr., 2005n462

Melton, J. Gordon, 2005n1241, 2006n1233, 2008n1056

Meltzer, Peter E., 2007n856

Meltzer, Tom, 2005n237m 2007n247

Memento mori, 2008n977

Menard, Claude, 2006n150

Mencos, M. Isidra, 2005n1099

Mendelsohn, Hillary, 2006n164, 2007n159

Menendez, Albert J., 2006n730

Menninger, Joan C., 2007n1207

Menopause bible, 2006n1437

Men's health concerns sourcebk, 2d ed, 2005n1450

Mental health disorders sourcebk, 3d ed, 2006n759

Mental health in America, 2008n690

Mental health info for teens, 2d ed, 2007n665

Mental health issues of older women, 2008n691

Mercatante, Anthony S., 2005n1158

Merce Rodoreda, 2005n1099

Merck index, 14th ed, 2007n1284

Merck manual of diagnosis & therapy, 18th ed, 2007n1259

Merck manual of diagnosis & therapy [Website], 2008n1234

Merck veterinary manual, 9th ed, 2007n1164

Meredith, James H., 2006n987

Meri, Josef W., 2007n1121

Merriam-Webster's advanced learner's English dict, 2009n876

Merriam-Webster's medical desk dict, rev ed, 2006n1429

Merriam-Webster's primary dict, 2006n961

Merriam-Webster's visual dict, 2007n857

Merrill, Kenneth R., 2009n1085

Merriman, John, 2007n378, 2007n379

Merriman, Scott A., 2007n427, 2008n1057

Merritt, John G., 2007n1112

Merry, Bruce, 2005n1088

Mersky, Roy M., 2005n549

Mertz, Leslie A., 2007n1218

Mertz, Ursula R., 2006n904

Mesa, Franklin, 2008n979

Messenger, Charles, 2005n519

Messerer, Aasaf, 2008n1011

Messer-Kruse, Timothy, 2009n295

Messiahs & Messianic movements through 1899, 2006n1218

Messina, Lynn M., 2005n550, 2005n890, 2005n1548, 2006n6, 2006n549, 2006n874, 2007n766

Metacritic [Website], 2006n1169

Metadata, 2009n574

Metadata in practice, 2005n630

Metrosexual gd to style, 2005n1175

Mettee, Stephen Blake, 2007n769

Metzer, Greg, 2009n1026

Meuninck, Jim, 2009n1178

Mexican American experience, 2005n355

Mexican War, 2006n452

Mexico, 2005n120

Mexico, 2009n123

Mexico & Central America hndbk 2009, 17th ed, 2009n354

Meyer, Bernard S., 2007n458

Meyer, Michael J., 2007n953, 2009n965

Meyer, Thierry, 2006n1398

Meyers, Elaine, 2005n621

Mezey, Mathy D., 2005n794

Mgadla, Part Themba, 2009n90

Michael, Robert, 2008n457

Michaud, Jean, 2007n264

Michel, George F., 2006n822

Michelman, Stephen, 2009n1086

Michener, Charles D., 2008n1186

Michigan genealogy sources & resources, 2d ed, 2006n360

Michon, Jacques, 2008n571

Mickolus, Edward F., 2009n463

Microterrors, 2005n1337

Middle Ages in lit for youth, 2005n1015

Middle & jr high school lib catalog, 9th ed, 2006n993

Middle & jr high school lib catalog, 2006 suppl, 2008n531

Middle & jr high school lib catalog, 2007 suppl, 2008n532

Middle East, 10th ed, 2006n110

Middle East, 11th ed, 2008n147

Middle East conflict: almanac, 2006n111

Middle East conflict: biogs, 2006n112

Middle East conflict: primary sources, 2006n113

Middle East strategic balance 2004-05, 2008n656

Middle East studies Internet resources [Website], 2008n141

Middle Eastern lit & their times, 2005n1094

Middleton, Carl H., 2009n48

Middleton, John, 2006n504, 2008n95, 2009n88

Middleton, Ken, 2005n855

Middleton, William D., 2008n1354

Mieder, Wolfgang, 2005n1155

Migration & immigration, 2005n832

Miguez, Betsy Bryan, 2005n1033

Mihalkanin, Edward S., 2005n694, 2008n497

Mikaberidze, Alexander, 2008n122

Mikics, David, 2008n880

Miksic, John N., 2008n100

Miler, Joseph C., 2008n95, 2009n88

Miles, Lera, 2006n1390

Milestone docs in American hist, 2009n395

Milestones in archaeology, 2008n381

Military aircraft, 1919-45, 2009n615

Military aircraft, origins to 1918, 2006n678

Military communications, 2008n594

Military ink [Website], 2009n599

Military medicine, 2009n606

Millard, Scott, 2005n645

Millennials: Americans born 1977 to 1994, 2d ed, 2005n266

Miller, Alan V., 2009n45
Miller, David, 2008n948
Miller, Donna P., 2009n555
Miller, Eugene, 2005n288, 2006n285
Miller, Harry, 2009n833
Miller, Hope H., 2007n1181
Miller, J. Mitchell, 2006n557
Miller, James, 2007n342, 2007n1085
Miller, Jane E., 2005n894
Miller, Joseph, 2005n617, 2008n512
Miller, Judith, 2005n911, 2006n896, 2007n791,
    2009n820
Miller, Laurie C., 2008n719
Miller, Mark A., 2005n1204, 2005n1487
Miller, Meredith, 2007n881
Miller, Orson K., 2007n1181
Miller, Page Putnam, 2005n873
Miller, Robert L., 2005n65
Miller, William, 2005n615, 2006n598, 2006n599,
    2006n645, 2007n539
Miller's antiques price gd 2007, 2008n815
Miller's buying affordable antiques, 2008n816
Miller's ceramic figures buyer's gd, 2008n817
Miller's collectibles price gd 2007, 2008n809
Miller's companion to antiques & collectables,
    2008n810
Miller's 20th-century glass, 2008n818
Milling, Jane, 2006n1178
Mills, Elizabeth Shown, 2008n563
Millstone, Erik, 2009n1144
Milne, G. W. A., 2005n1298
Milne, Ira Mark, 2005n1054, 2005n1055, 2008n892,
    2008n897, 2008n898
Min, Pyong Gap, 2007n263
Miner, Jeremy T., 2005n812, 2005n813, 2005n882,
    2006n811, 2006n812, 2006n868, 2009n754
Miner, Lynn E., 2005n812, 2005n813, 2005n882,
    2006n811, 2006n812, 2006n868, 2009n754
Miner, Margaret, 2006n61
Minerals, 2006n1516
Minigh, Jennifer L., 2008n1258
Mink, Gwendolyn, 2005n818
Minocha, Anil, 2005n1439
Minoli, Daniel, 2007n1291
Minoli-Cordovana's authoritative computer & network
    security dict, 2007n1291
Mireles, Anthony J., 2007n548
Mirris, Desmond, 2009n1174
Misakian, Jo Ellen Priest, 2006n606
Mishel, Lawrence, 2006n151, 2008n236
Misiroglu, Gina, 2005n1173, 2007n1031
Miskelly, Matthew, 2005n309, 2005n597, 2008n257,
    2009n155
Misra, Rakesh R., 2009n1241
Mitcham, Carl, 2006n1254
Mitchell, Adam W. M., 2006n1321
Mitchell, Anne M., 2006n617

Mitchell, B. R., 2005n848
Mitchell, Brian, 2009n323
Mitchell, Charles P., 2005n1190, 2006n1161
Mitchell, Claudia A., 2009n766
Mitchell, David F., 2008n681, 2009n705
Mitchell, Judy K., 2006n1118
Mitchell, Meg Tyler, 2009n121
Mitchell, Nicole, 2009n717
Mitton, Jacqueline, 2009n1304
Mizrahi, Terry, 2009n757
MLA style manual & gd to scholarly publishing, 3d
    ed, 2009n808
Moan, Jaina L., 2008n1336
Modern American communes, 2006n801
Modern American poetry [Website], 2009n992
Modern art: 1905-45, 2006n924
Modern Catholic ency, rev ed, 2005n1261
Modern guns, 15th ed, 2005n922
Modern guns, 16th ed, 2007n803
Modern guns, 17th ed, 2009n836
Modern paganism in world cultures, 2006n1215
Modern world hist online [Website], 2009n429
Moe, Barbara A., 2008n723
Moffitt, John F., 2005n942
Mogil, H. Michael, 2008n1313
Mohan, Giles, 2008n674
Mohiuddin, Yasmeen Niaz, 2007n100
Molin, Paulette F., 2007n913
Moliterno, Gino, 2009n1063
Molnar, Leslie, 2009n920
Moltz, James Clay, 2008n604
Monaghan, Patricia, 2005n1164
Monat, Alan, 2008n692
Monger, George P., 2006n808
Mongillo, John, 2005n1544
Monroe, Dan, 2006n430
Montagu, Jeremy, 2008n973
Montgomery, M. R., 2007n1337
Montgomery, Michael, 2008n852
Monthly bulletin of stats [Website], 2008n756
Mood, Terry Ann, 2005n1156
Mook, Douglas, 2006n760
Moore, David W., 2007n389
Moore, Elaine A., 2005n1472, 2007n1274
Moore, John Allphin, Jr., 2009n673
Moore, John Hartwell, 2008n302
Moore, Patrick, 2006n1500
Moore, Peter D., 2008n1316, 2008n1317
Moore, Randy, 2009n1172
Moore, Robert J., 2007n1230
Moorman, John A., 2007n534
Moose, Christina J., 2006n489, 2006n500
Moral educ, 2009n260
Moran, Albert, 2006n1150, 2008n1019
More bk lust, 2006n1011
More, David, 2006n1353
More Okla. Renegades, 2008n89

More outstanding bks for the college bound, 2006n620
More teen programs that work, 2006n622
More than Darwin, 2009n1172
More than 100 brain friendly tools & strategies for literacy instruction, 2009n268
More than 100 ways to learner-centered literacy, 2d ed, 2009n267
More than silence: a bibliog of Thomas Merton, 2009n1102
More word histories & mysteries, 2007n837
More words you should know, 2d ed, 2006n942
MoreBusiness.com [Website], 2006n264
Moreillon, Judi, 2009n523
Moreno, Barry, 2005n433
Moreschini, Claudio, 2006n1236
Morgan, Ann Lee, 2008n836, 2009n852
Morgan, Diane, 2005n1253
Morgan, Kathleen O'Leary, 2005n277, 2005n571, 2005n575, 2005n1429, 2006n278, 2006n567, 2006n575, 2006n843, 2006n844, 2006n1424, 2007n239, 2007n477, 2007n480, 2007n747, 2007n748, 2007n1241, 2008n492, 2008n494, 2008n765, 2008n1221, 2009n250, 2009n476, 2009n775, 2009n776, 2009n1232
Morgan, Pamela J., 2009n586
Morgan, Rose M., 2006n1362
Morgan, Rosemarie, 2008n932
Morgan, Scott, 2005n277, 2005n571, 2005n575, 2005n1429, 2006n278, 2006n567, 2006n575, 2006n843, 2006n844, 2006n1424, 2007n239, 2007n477, 2007n480, 2007n747, 2007n748, 2007n1241, 2008n492, 2008n494, 2008n765, 2008n1221, 2009n250, 2009n476, 2009n775, 2009n776, 2009n1232
Morgan, William, 2005n945
Morris, Gregory L., 2007n153
Morris, James M., 2005n1232
Morrison, Andrea M., 2005n50, 2009n534
Morrison, Craig, 2006n1109
Morrison, Michael, 2005n761
Morrissette, Noelle, 2009n692
Mort, John, 2007n933
Morton, Brian, 2006n1106
Morton, David L., Jr., 2005n1292
Morton, Fred, 2009n90
Morton, Joseph C., 2006n431
Morton, Leslie T., 2007n1230
Mosby's diagnostic & lab test ref, 7th ed, 2006n1425
Moseley, C. J., 2008n848
Moseley, Christopher, 2008n850
Mosko, Lauren, 2008n794
Mosko, Lauren, 2006n878, 2006n923
Moskowitz, David V., 2006n1108, 2007n1006
Mosley, Anthony D., 2005n1471
Mosley, Shelley, 2007n898
Moss, Joyce, 2005n1094, 2006n1060
Moss, Rita W., 2005n136

Moss, Stephen, 2008n1179
Mossman, Jennifer, 2005n11
Motivating readers in the middle grades, 2009n517
Motivating students in info literacy classes, 2005n628
Moulder, Cathy, 2008n937
Mountain ency, 2006n794
Mountain wildflowers of the southern Rockies, 2008n1156
Movers & shakers, 2005n141
Movers & shakers, 2007n835
Movie archive [Website], 2006n1141
Movie review query engine (MRQE) [Website], 2006n1142
Movie tome [Website], 2006n1156
Movieland dir, 2005n1203
Movies made for TV 1964-2004, 2006n1140
Moving & relocation dir 2005-06, 5th ed, 2006n846
Moving & relocation dir 2007-08, 6th ed, 2008n770
Moving image cataloging, 2009n545
Moyer, Jessica E., 2009n513
Moynes, James, 2006n475
MSN Encarta [Website], 2008n27
Mudroch, Vilem, 2006n1194
Mueckenheim, Jacqueline K., 2005n1489
Mugridge, Rebecca, 2007n544
Muhler, Martin, 2008n1286
Muir, John Kenneth, 2005n1198, 2008n1020, 2008n1026, 2008n1033, 2009n1044
Mulcahy, Kathryn, 2005n1466
Mulhearn, Chris, 2007n131
Muller, Hans-Peter, 2007n690
Muller, Roy, 2006n1054
Muller, Thomas C., 2007n583, 2009n627
Mulligan, Timothy P., 2009n608
Multicultural & ethnic children's lit in the US, 2008n889
Multicultural films, 2006n1146
Multicultural writers since 1945, 2005n986
Multiculturalism in the US, rev ed, 2006n324
Multiracial America, 2006n322
Mumford, Russell E., 2009n1207
Muncie, John, 2007n471
Municipal yellow bk, Summer 2005, 2006n711
Muray, Christopher John, 2005n881
Murder in retrospect, 2007n928
Murdin, Paul, 2005n1503
Murie, Olaus J., 2006n795
Murphy, Diane R., 2005n160, 2005n712
Murphy, Justin D., 2006n678, 2009n615
Murphy, Russell Elliott, 2008n916
Murphy, Sam, 2009n738
Murray, Alan V., 2007n417
Murray, Christopher John, 2005n1230
Murray, Lynda, 2005n933
Murray, Richard A., 2008n523
Murray, Stuart, 2006n658
Murray, Tim, 2008n381

Muscular dystrophy sourcebk, 2005n1470
Museum of Broadcast communications ency of radio, 2005n909
Museums, libs, & urban vitality, 2009n536
Museums of the world, 14th ed, 2008n47
Mushrooms & other fungi of N America, repr ed, 2007n1182
Music abbrevs, 2006n1073
Music in Shakespeare, 2007n961
Music lust, 2007n990
Music of the Civil War era, 2005n1124
Music of the colonial & revolutionary era, 2005n1125
Music of the counterculture era, 2005n1146
Music of the Great Depression, 2006n1077
Music of the postwar era, 2008n971
Music publishers' intl ISMN dir 2003, 4th ed, 2005n1123
Music radio, 2006n889
Musical AKAs, 2007n991
Musical biog, 2007n983
Mustazza, Leonard, 2007n1049
MVR bk, 2006 ed, 2006n544
MVR bk, 2008 ed, 2009n455
MVR decoder digest, 2006 ed, 2006n545
MVR decoder digest, 2008 ed, 2009n456
Mwangi, Evan, 2009n977
My Family.com [Website], 2007n287
My 1st Britannica, 2005n32
Mycenaean civilization, rev ed, 2005n492
Myers, Hardy, 2005n540
Myers, Norman, 2006n1537
Myers, Richard L., 2008n1293
Myers, Richard S., 2008n1081
Myers, Rusty L., 2008n1329
Myerson, Joel, 2007n950
Mysteries in hist, 2006n507
Mystery women, rev ed, 2007n926
Myth: a hndbk, 2005n1167
Mythology in our midst, 2005n1168

Naden, Corinne J., 2008n884
Nagel, Rob, 2005n1377, 2005n1507, 2005n1517
Nagorsen, David W., 2009n1204
Nahm, Andrew C., 2005n98
Nakajima, Nina, 2006n225
Names & naming in YA lit, 2008n890
Names of plants, 4th ed, 2009n1177
Nanji, Azim, 2005n1271
Nardo, Don, 2008n436, 2008n441
Narins, Brigham, 2005n1437, 2006n1360, 2008n307, 2009n296, 2009n1238
Narizny, Susan, 2005n1322
Narvaez, Darcia, 2009n253
Narvani, A. A., 2009n1270
Nash, Gary B., 2007n336, 2008n386

Nash, Jay Robert, 2005n566
Nash, William G., 2007n1207
National accounts stats 2001, 2005n209
National accounts stats 2003-04, 2007n741
National accounts stats 2004-05, 2008n757
National accounts stats 2004, 2008n758
National anthems of the world, 11th ed, 2008n969
National archeological database (NADB) [Website], 2008n380
National archive of criminal justice data (NACJD) [Website], 2007n476
National Archives & Records Admin (NARA) [Website], 2005n718
National Basketball Assn ultimate basketball, 2005n771
National Center for Education Stats [Website], 2005n279
National dir corporate public affairs 2004, 22d ed, 2005n160
National dir of …
    corporate public affairs 2005, 23d ed, 2006n139
    corporate public affairs 2006, 24th ed, 2007n141
    corporate public affairs, Fall 2008, 2009n136
    minority-owned business firms, 13th ed, 2006n140
    minority-owned business firms, 14th ed, 2009n137
    nonprofit orgs, 18th ed, 2006n39
    nonprofit orgs, 20th ed, 2008n40
    woman-owned business firms, 13th ed, 2006n141
    woman-owned business firms, 14th ed, 2009n138
National dir to college & univ student records, 2005n302
National e-mail & fax dir 2005, 18th ed, 2006n40
National e-mail & fax dir 2006, 19th ed, 2007n35
National e-mail & fax dir, 21st ed, 2009n32
National faculty dir, 35th ed, 2005n303
National faculty dir, 37th ed, 2006n296
National faculty dir, 39th ed, 2008n281
National Gallery of Art: master paintings from the collection, 2006n934
National Geographic almanac of American hist, 2007n342
National Geographic almanac of geography, 2007n314
National Geographic atlas of the world, 8th ed, 2006n377
National Geographic complete birds of N America, 2007n1193
National Geographic concise hist of the world, 2007n412
National Geographic ency of space, 2006n1505
National Geographic family ref atlas of the world, 2d ed, 2007n303
National Geographic field gd to the birds of N America, 5th ed, 2007n1194
National Geographic gd to the natl parks of the US, 5th ed, 2007n321
National Geographic histl atlas of the US, 2006n427

National Geographic natl park trail gds [CD-ROM], 2005n775

National Geographic ref atlas to the birds of N America, 2006n1374

National Geographic US atlas for young explorers, updated ed, 2006n378

National Geographic visual hist of the world, 2007n413

National park architecture sourcebk, 2009n864

National party conventions 1831-2004, 2007n617

National security archive: the Cuban missile crisis, 1962 [Website], 2009n360

National survey of state laws, 5th ed, 2005n554

National survey of state laws, 6th ed, 2009n457

National trade & professional assns of the US 2008, 2009n139

Nationalism & ethnicity terminologies, v.3, 2006n63

Nation-building, 2005n729

NationMaster.com [Website], 2008n759

Nations & nationalism, 2009n434

Nations of the world 2005, 5th ed, 2005n74

Nations of the world 2006, 6th ed, 2007n57

Nations of the world 2007/08, 7th ed, 2008n66

Nations of the world 2009, 8th ed, 2009n69

Native America from prehist to first contact, 2007n281

Native American issues, 2d ed, 2006n340

Native American mythology A to Z, 2005n1162

Native American place-names of Ind., 2009n341

Native American placenames of the US, 2005n389

Native American sites [Website], 2008n316

Native Americans & pol participation, 2006n339

Native Americans in sports, 2005n752

Native plants of the northeast, 2006n1335

Native trees for N American landscapes, 2005n1371

Native web [Website], 2008n300

Natural disasters, new ed, 2009n1317

Natural hist of the Point Reyes Peninsula, rev ed, 2009n1190

Natural resources & sustainable dvlpmt, 2009n1328

Nature's children, 2005n1382

Nature's children, set 1, rev ed, 2008n1170

Nature's children, set 2, 2008n1171

Nature's children, set 3, 2009n1193

Nature's children, set 4, 2009n1194

Nauert, Charles G., 2005n474, 2007n423

Navajo as seen by the Franciscans, 1898-1921, 2005n346

Navajo code talkers' dict [Website], 2008n585

Navajo/English dict of verbs, 2007n862

Naval ceremonies, customs, & traditions, 6th ed, 2005n673

Naval Institute almanac of the US Navy, 2006n673

Naval Institute gd to combat fleets of the world 2005-06, 2006n674

Naval Institute gd to combat fleets of the world, 15th ed, 2008n599

Naval Institute gd to the ships & aircraft of the US Fleet, 18th ed, 2006n675

Naval Institute gd to world naval weapon systems, 5th ed, 2007n573

Navarra, Tova, 2005n1419, 2005n1455

Navarro, Sharon Ann, 2006n727

Navarro, Yvonne, 2008n348

Nawalinski, Beth, 2009n515

Naxos music lib [Website], 2009n1011

Naylor, Phillip C., 2007n82

Ndege, George O., 2007n89

Neal-Schuman dir of public lib job descriptions, 2006n592

Neal-Schuman gd to celebrations & holidays around the world, 2005n1176

Neal-Schuman lib tech companion, 2d ed, 2007n529

Nebenzahl, Kenneth, 2006n385

Nebesio, Bohdan Y., 2006n106

Needlework through hist, 2008n827

Neel, Hildy, 2008n944

Neely, Teresa Y., 2008n543

Negro Leagues chronology, 2007n677

Nehmer, Kathleen Suttles, 2005n281, 2005n282, 2006n318, 2006n319, 2008n272, 2008n273, 2008n291, 2008n292, 2008n293, 2008n294, 2009n286, 2009n287

Neibaur, James L., 2006n1162

Neiburger, Eli, 2008n537

Neill, Amanda, 2006n1343

Nelson, Arnold G., 2009n736

Nelson, Emmanuel S., 2005n1002, 2005n1034, 2007n942

Nelson, Jeffrey O., 2008n625

Nelson, M. Rae, 2005n1293

Nelson, Michael, 2008n629, 2009n645

Nelson, Sandra, 2009n514

Nelson, Susan, 2007n995

Nemati, Hamid, 2008n1274

Nemeh, Katherine H., 2005n1279, 2007n1128

Nemeroff, Charles B., 2006n753

Nemerov, Bruce, 2005n1142

Ness, Bryan D., 2005n1375

Ness, Daniel, 2006n275

Ness, Immanuel, 2005n426

Nesting birds of a tropical frontier, 2006n1369

Nestor, Sandy, 2005n390, 2008n401

Net effects, 2005n634

Netter, Frank H., 2006n1322

Netter's atlas of the human body, 2006n1322

Netzley, Patricia D., 2005n428, 2007n668, 2008n488

Neubert, Michael, 2007n506

Neundorf, Alyse, 2007n862

Neusner, Jacob, 2005n1275

New atlas of planet mgmt, 3d ed, 2006n1537

New atlas of the moon, 2008n1301

New atlas of the stars, 2006n1501

New biographical dict of film, updated ed, 2007n1040

New biology series, 2006n1318
New bk of herbs, 2005n1316
New bk of knowledge, 2006n26
New bk of knowledge, 2007, 2007n25
New bk of knowledge, 2008 ed, 2008n28
New bk of knowledge online [Website], 2006n27
New bk of popular sci, 2007n1135
New bk of popular sci, 2008 ed, 2009n1131
New bk of popular sci [Website], 2009n1132
New Cambridge medieval hist, 2007n432
New Cambridge medieval hist, v.4, 2006n511
New chemistry series, 2008n1295
New concise world atlas, 2d ed, 2007n304
New Deal network [Website], 2005n420
New dict of Christian apologetics, 2007n1113
New dict of saints, 2008n1079
New dict of scientific biog, 2008n1104
New dict of the hist of ideas, 2006n501
New directions in ref, 2007n541
New 1st dict of cultural literacy, 2005n325
New ency of ...
    Africa, 2008n95
    flower remedies, 2008n1238
    Islam, 3d ed, 2009n1117
    snakes, 2008n1194
    southern culture, v.1: religion, 2007n1083
    southern culture, v.2: geography, 2007n311
    southern culture, v.3: history, 2007n62
    southern culture, v.4: myth, manners, & memory, 2007n63
    southern culture: v.5, lang, 2008n852
    southern culture, v.6: ethnicity, 2008n303
    southern culture, v.7: foodways, 2008n1120
    the saltwater aquarium, 2008n1183
    unbelief, 2008n1058
New gd for occupational exploration, 4th ed, 2007n218
New generation of country music stars, 2009n1019
New Harvard gd to women's health, 2005n1440
New histl anthology of music by women, 2006n1082
New hndbk of literary terms, 2008n880
New index of middle English verse, 2007n981
New interpreter's dict of the Bible, v.1, 2008n1071
New Jersey municipal data bk, 2007 ed, 2008n78
New librarian, new job, 2007n508
New makers of modern culture, 2008n445
New media, 2007n1289
New on the job: a school lib media specialist's gd to success, 2008n516
New OPL sourcebk, 2007n496
New Oxford American dict, 2d ed, 2006n28
New Partridge dict of slang & unconventional English, 2007n845
New Penguin factfinder, 2006n49
New, Rebecca S., 2008n270
New ref grammar of modern Spanish, 2006n971

New religious movement experience in America, 2005n1244
New research centers, 36th ed, 2009n247
New slavery, 2d ed, 2006n581
New traveler's atlas, 2008n364
New views of the solar system, 2008n1305
New Westminster dict of Christian spirituality, 2007n1114
New Westminster dict of church hist, v.1, 2009n1111
New wine lover's companion, 2d ed, 2005n1300
New York City, 2005n398
New York City 2008, 2008n366
New York philharmonic, 2007n986
New York Public Library American hist desk ref, 2d ed, 2005n457
New York state dir, 2005-2006, 2006n833
New York state dir, 2006-07, 2007n72
New York state dir, 2007/08, 2008n84
New York state dir, 2008-09, 2009n77
New York Times almanac 2005, 2006n7
New York Times almanac 2008, 2008n5
New York Times gd to essential knowledge, 2006n50
New York Times 1000 gardening questions & answers, 2005n1327
Newbery & Caldecott awards, 2005n1033
Newbery & Caldecott awards, 2006 ed, 2007n899
Newbery & Caldecott awards, 2007 ed, 2008n885
Newbery & Caldecott awards, 2008 ed, 2009n926
Newbery/Printz companion, 3d ed, 2008n884
Newell, Clayton R., 2008n586
Newell, Josh, 2005n115
Newlands, Anne, 2008n842
Newlin, George, 2005n1081, 2007n958
Newman, Oksana, 2009n140
Newport, Frank, 2009n62, 2009n63
News media leadership dir online [Website], 2009n810
News media yellow bk, Summer 2005 ed, 2006n888
Newsletters in print, 18th ed, 2005n904
Newsmakers 2005 cum ed, 2006n18
Newsmakers 2007, 2009n12
Newton, David E., 2007n1292, 2007n1324, 2008n1146, 2008n1295, 2009n480
Newton, Keith, 2005n1113
Newton, Michael, 2005n567, 2005n568, 2006n559, 2006n1365, 2007n367, 2007n470, 2008n415, 2008n489, 2009n472
Next space age, 2009n1309
NextGen librarian's survival gd, 2007n507
Ng, Franklin, 2005n337
Ng, Kwong Bor, 2008n533
Nichols, C. Reid, 2009n1323
Nichols, Darlene, 2006n322
Nichols, Peter M., 2006n1167
Nicholson, Helen, 2005n530
Nicknames of places, 2007n316
Nicolle, David, 2005n1270

Nielsen, Leon, 2008n906
Niemi, Richard G., 2006n734, 2007n622, 2008n651
Niemi, Robert, 2007n1051
Nieminen, Gayla S., 2006n97
Night sky atlas, 2006n1502
Nijboer, Donald, 2006n666
Nilsen, Alleen Pace, 2008n890
Nilsen, Don L. F., 2008n890
Nilsson, K. Robert, 2008n124
9/11 ency, 2009n372
Nine-lang dict of polymers & composites, 2009n1214
1990s, 2005n1177
1990s, 2007n343
1920s, 2005n1174
1940s, 2005n1178
1950s, 2005n1179
1970s, 2007n341
1980s, 2007n344
19th century French art: 1848-1905, 2006n926
Nineteenth-century lit criticism, v.138, 2005n987
Nineteenth-century lit criticism, v.139, 2005n988
Nineteenth-century lit criticism, v.140, 2005n989
Nineteenth-century lit criticism, v.141, 2005n990
Ninivaggi, Frank John, 2009n1256
Ninth bk of jr authors & illustrators, 2006n1000
Nisonger, Thomas E., 2005n593
Nissenbaum, Stephen W., 2008n570
Njoku, Raphael Chijioke, 2006n84
No school lib left behind, 2009n521
Nobel: a century of prize winners, 2009n13
Nobel e-museum [Website], 2005n15
Nobel e-museum [Website], 2007n12
Nobel memorial laureates in economics, 2007n131
Noble, David F., 2008n232
Nogowski, John, 2009n1023
Nolan, Cathal J., 2007n592, 2008n587, 2008n622
Nolan, Dennis P., 2007n1325
Noll, Richard, 2007n657
Nollen, Scott Allen, 2005n1132
Nollkaemper, Andre, 2007n492
Nolo's essential gd to divorce, 2007n459
Nonfiction readers' advisory, 2006n601
Non-governmental orgs research gd [Website], 2008n660
Nonprofit sector yellow bk, Summer 2005, 2006n142
Nonverbal dict of gestures, signs, & body lang cues [Website], 2007n765
Noonan, Raymond J., 2005n816
Norbye, Jan P., 2007n1341
Norcross, John C., 2005n742, 2007n661, 2009n706
Norelli, Enrico, 2006n1236
Norfolk, Elizabeth, 2008n815
North American birdfeeder gd, 2006n1370
North American jls of Prince Maximilian of Wied, v.1, 2009n396
North American mushrooms, 2007n1181
North American wildland plants, 2005n1355

North Carolina cities, towns & counties, 2007 ed, 2008n86
North Carolina State Univ men's basketball games, 2009n723
North, James H., 2007n986, 2009n1016
North Korea in quotation, 2006n94
Northeast & Midwest United States: an environmental hist, 2006n1539
Northern Europe: an environmental hist, 2006n1545
Northrup, Cynthia Clark, 2006n200
Northwest hist database [Website], 2006n72
Norwood, Stephen H., 2008n330
Notable African American writers, 2007n943
Notable American novelists, rev ed, 2008n907
Notable American women, 2006n851
Notable black American men, bk 2, 2009n297
Notable black American women, bk 3, 2005n331
Notable last facts, 2006n44
Notable Latino writers, 2006n1062
Notable natural disasters, 2008n1309
Notable playwrights, 2005n1035
Nourishing vocabulary, 2009n259
Novel & short story writer's market 2006, 25th ed, 2006n878
Novel & short story writer's market 2007, 2008n794
Novels for students, v.19, 2005n1043
Novels for students, v.25, 2008n897
November, Alan, 2009n289
Novotny, Eric, 2008n557
Nowak, Ronald M., 2006n1389
Nowlan, Robert A., 2008n1004
Nsouli, Mona A., 2007n120
NTIS [Website], 2006n1277
Nucci, Larry P., 2009n253
Nuclear nonproliferation, 2009n614
Nuclear power, 2007n1324
Nuclear tech, 2006n1265
Nuclear weapons & nonproliferation, 2d ed, 2008n604
Null, Gary, 2007n1265
Nunnally, Michael L., 2008n318
Nursery rhymes [Website], 2009n993
Nursing programs 2006, 11th ed, 2006n1456
Nutrition & diet therapy ref dict, 5th ed, 2005n1418
Nutrition & well-being A to Z, 2005n1420
Nutrition at a glance, 2008n1126
Nuttall, Mark, 2005n90
Nuzzi, Ronald J., 2005n280
Nyer, Evan K., 2008n1337

Oakes, Elizabeth H., 2005n63, 2005n1060, 2005n1473, 2007n202, 2008n1105
Obbard, John W., 2007n805
Obert, Beverly J., 2007n517
Obituaries in the performing arts, 2003, 2005n1180
Obituaries in the performing arts, 2004, 2006n1127

Obituaries in the performing arts, 2005, 2007n1036
Obituaries in the performing arts, 2007, 2009n1049
Oboler, Suzanne, 2006n351
O'Brien, Joanne, 2006n1210
O'Brien, Karen, 2005n927, 2009n839
O'Brien, Stephen J., 2007n1207
O'Brien's collecting toys, 12th ed, 2009n839
Ocasio, Rafael, 2005n1092
Occupational outlook hndbk 2004-05 ed, 2005n236
Occupational outlook hndbk 2006-07, 2007n197
Occupational outlook hndbk 2008-09, 2009n210
Ocean, 2009n1324
Ocean cruising & cruise ships 2005, 2006n395
Oceans, 2006n1519
Oceans, 2007n1313
Oceans, rev ed, 2008n1323
O'Connell, Matthew J., 2006n1236
O'Connor, Alice, 2005n818
O'Connor, Brendon, 2008n667
O'Connor, David E., 2005n171, 2007n138
O'Connor, Kevin, 2007n109
Oddy, Christine, 2005n211
O'Dea, Suzanne, 2007n596
Odekon, Mehmet, 2007n713
Oden, Thomas C., 2006n1221
Odewahn, Stephen C., 2008n1297
O'Donoghue, Jo, 2006n1115
O'Donovan, Diarmuid, 2009n1221
OECD factbk 2006, 2007n742
Ofcansky, Thomas P., 2005n87
Official Catholic dir 2007, 2008n1085
Official Gun Digest bk of guns & prices, 2007n802
Official Major League baseball fact bk, 2005 ed,
    2006n780
Official museum dir 2007, 37th ed, 2008n48
Official price gd to Disney collectibles, 2007n792
Official price gd to pottery & porcelain, 9th ed,
    2007n793
Official YALSA awards gdbk, 2009n927
Ogasapian, John, 2005n1125
Ogle, David B., 2007n615
Oglesby, D. W., 2008n174
O'Gorman, Jack, 2009n4
Oh, Gwang Seok, 2008n1091
Oh, Seiwoong, 2009n955
O'Hara, Michael E., 2008n709, 2008n710, 2009n720,
    2009n721, 2009n722, 2009n723, 2009n724,
    2009n725
O'Hare, Sheila, 2007n483
Ohlhausen, Sidney K., 2007n1103
Oklahoma, 2009n80
Oklahoma breeding bird atlas, 2005n1388
Old West, 2009n382
Older Americans, 4th ed, 2005n835
Older Americans info dir 2005, 5th ed, 2005n795
Older Americans info dir 2007, 6th ed, 2007n694
Older Americans info dir 2008, 7th ed, 2009n742

Older Americans info dir [Website], 2005n796
Oldershaw, Cally, 2005n1516
Old-fashioned & David Austin roses, 2005n1365
Oldman, Mark, 2005n232
O'Leary, Philip, 2007n965
Oliver, A. P. H., 2005n1398
Oliver, Charles M., 2007n954, 2008n920
Oliver, Evelyn Dorothy, 2009n1091
Oliver, John E., 2007n1308
Oliver, Sandra L., 2006n1293
Olofsson, Gwyneth, 2005n393
O'Loughlin, Jim, 2005n453
Olsen, Kirstin, 2006n1048
Olsen, Klaus Malling, 2005n1389
Olson, Christi A., 2005n643
Olson, Nancy B., 2009n541
Olson, Richard G., 2005n1294
Olszewski, Edward J., 2005n949
Olympic Games, 2005n778
O'Malley, James A., 2005n111
O'Malley, Vincent J., 2008n1078
Omi, Philip N., 2006n1544
Omniglot [Website], 2006n940
On account of sex: an annotated bibliog on the status
    of women in librarianship, 2007n493
On reading the Bible, 2006n1224
On the trail of the buffalo soldier, 2005n657
Once upon a time, 2009n552
100 albums that changed popular music, 2008n980
100 Americans making constitutional hist, 2005n534
100 best family resorts in N America, 7th ed,
    2006n397
100 best resorts of the Caribbean, 6th ed, 2005n409
100 best resorts of the Caribbean, new ed, 2009n356
100 experiential learning activities for social studies,
    lit, & the arts, grades 5-12, 2009n269
100 great American novels you've (probably) never
    read, 2008n905
100 greatest sci discoveries of all time, 2008n1111
100 greatest sci inventions of all time, 2007n1142
100 Hispanics you should know, 2008n331
100 most important chemical compounds, 2008n1293
100 most popular African American authors,
    2008n908
100 most popular genre fiction authors, 2007n921
100 most popular nonfiction authors, 2009n985
100 myths about the Middle East, 2007n125
100 Okla. Outlaws, gangsters, & lawmen 1839-1939,
    2008n88
One hundred philosophers, 2005n1227
100 ready-to-use pathfinders for the Web, 2005n594
100 sci words every college graduate should know,
    2007n1136
100 words almost everyone confuses & misuses,
    2005n960
100 words almost everyone mispronounces, 2009n889
100 words every word lover should know, 2006n955

100 words for lovers, 2009n890
100 words to make you sound smart, 2007n828
One hundred yrs of world military aircraft, 2005n676
101 key terms in philosophy & their importance for theology, 2005n1229
109th congressional district atlas, 2006n731
110th Congressional district atlas, 2009n663
145 things to be when you grow up, 2005n253
150 best jobs through military training, 2008n250
150 best jobs through military training, 2009n226
150 great tech prep careers, 2d ed, 2009n227
175 best jobs not behind a desk, 2008n244
One thousand langs, 2009n872
1,000 places to see before you die, 2005n394
1001 computer words you need to know, 2005n1483
1001 events that made America, 2007n338
1001 historic sites you must see before you die, 2009n347
1001 movies you must see before you die, 2005n1213
1001 people who made America, 2008n389
1001 things everyone should know about African American hist, 2d ed, 2007n275
1001 things you always wanted to know about cats, 2006n1377
1001 things you didn't know about the Civil War, 2008n423
O'Neal, Michael J., 2005n505, 2007n1088, 2007n1089, 2007n1090
O'Neil, Maryadele J., 2007n1284
O'Neil, Patrick M., 2005n985
Online & distance learning, 2008n269
Online bks page [Website], 2005n10
Online bks page [Website], 2007n8
Online business sourcebk, 8th ed, 2009n140
Online papers in philosophy [Website], 2006n1202
Online ref bk for medieval studies [Website], 2005n479
Online resources for senior citizens, 2d ed, 2007n695
Onorato, Ronald J., 2005n82
Ontario legal dir 2005, 80th ed, 2006n531
Ontario legal dir 2008, 83d ed, 2009n444
Opera, 2008n979
Opportunity for leadership, 2009n563
Opposing viewpoints in American hist, 2008n416
Oracles of the ancient world, 2005n1237
Oran, Daniel, 2008n468
Oran's dict of law, 4th ed, 2008n468
Orchestral music, 4th ed, 2006n1093
Orchid grower's companion, 2006n1301
Orchids to know & grow, 2008n1159
Orchin, Milton, 2006n1496
Orey, Michael, 2005n317, 2006n317, 2009n288
Organ, 2007n996
Organic gardener's hndbk, 2009n1161
Organized crime, 2008n490
Origin of everyday things, 2008n1110

Original Dr. Steve's almanac of Christian trivia, 2008n1093
Origins & dvlpmt of musical instruments, 2008n973
Ornamental foliage plants, 2005n1326
Orovio, Helio, 2005n1121
Orr, Tamra, 2006n349
Ortiz-Griffin, Julia, 2008n131
Osborne, Eric W., 2005n679, 2006n679
Osborne, Kenneth W., 2005n428
Osborne, Robin, 2005n641
Oscar Wilde in quotation, 2007n966
Oscherwitz, Dayna, 2008n1016
O'Shea, Mark, 2007n1219
Osif, Bonnie A., 2008n1195
Osman, Joseph H., 2006n915
Osmolska, Halszka, 2006n1521
Osseo-Asare, Fran, 2006n1294
Ossicini, Stefano, 2006n1397
Ostrom, Hans, 2007n941
O'Sullivan, Penelope, 2008n1162
OSV's ency of Catholic hist, rev ed, 2005n1262
Other British Isles, 2007n389
O'Toole, Thomas, 2006n82
Oudolf, Piet, 2006n1308
Our Earth's changing land, 2007n1332
Our living world: Earth's biomes, 2007n1298
Our own voices [Website], 2009n45
Our Sunday Visitor's Catholic almanac 2004, 2005n1266
Our Sunday Visitor's Catholic almanac 2007, 2008n1092
Our Sunday Visitor's Catholic almanac 2008, 2009n1101
Out of the Mouth of Hell: Civil War prisons & escapes, 2006n450
Outline maps on file, rev ed, 2008n362
Outman, James L., 2005n837, 2005n838
Outreach servs in academic & special libs, 2005n604
Outstanding lib serv to children, 2007n511
Overstreet, William R., 2007n583, 2009n627
Oweis, Fayeq S., 2009n851
Owen, David J., 2008n1236
Owens, Eric, 2005n298, 2007n244, 2007n247
Owens, John, 2007n244
Owl, Marcus Young, 2006n1313
Owomoyela, Oyekan, 2009n978
Owusu-Ansah, David, 2006n81
Oxford African American studies center [Website], 2009n303
Oxford American large print dict, 2007n829
Oxford American large print dict, 2009n877
Oxford American large print thesaurus, 2007n830
Oxford American writer's thesaurus, 2005n965
Oxford American writer's thesaurus, 2d ed, 2009n895
Oxford atlas of ...
    exploration, 2d ed, 2009n332
    N America, 2006n379

the US, 2009n333
the world, 12th ed, 2005n376
the world, 13th ed, 2007n305
the world, 14th ed, 2008n351
the world, 15th ed, 2009n334
the world, deluxe ed, 2006n380
Oxford Bible atlas, 4th ed, 2009n1093
Oxford color Italian dict plus, 2009n899
Oxford companion to ...
    American food & drink, 2009n1146
    American theatre, 3d ed, 2005n1220
    black British hist, 2009n406
    Chaucer, 2005n1076
    cosmology, 2009n1305
    English lit, 6th rev ed, 2007n955
    family & local hist, 2009n324
    food, 2d ed, 2009n1147
    Italian food, 2009n1148
    philosophy, 2d ed, 2006n1196
    ships & the sea, 2d ed, 2006n1554
    the American musical, 2009n1077
    the Brontes, 2005n1075
    the mind, 2d ed, 2005n737
    the Supreme Court of the US, 2d ed, 2006n519
    wine, 3d ed, 2008n1121
    world exploration, 2008n359
    world mythology, 2007n1026
Oxford concise companion to English lit, 3d ed,
    2009n971
Oxford concise ency, 2d ed, 2008n29
Oxford dict of ...
    American art & artists, 2008n836
    American quotations, 2006n61
    art, 3d ed, 2005n937
    Civil War quotations, 2007n370
    contemporary world hist, 3d ed, 2009n430
    humorous quotations, 3d ed, 2006n62
    humorous quotations, 4th ed, 2009n51
    idioms, 2d ed, 2006n956
    literary quotations, 2d ed, 2005n1013
    literary terms, 3d ed, 2009n914
    natl biog, new ed, 2005n16
    natl biog [Website], 2005n17
    nicknames, 2005n366
    phrase & fable, 2d ed, 2006n867
    phrase, saying, & quotation, 3d ed, 2007n47
    plays, 2006n1172
    proverbs, new ed, 2005n60
    quotations, 6th ed, 2005n61
    stats, 2009n773
    the Christian church, 3d ed, 2006n1234
    the classical world, 2006n468
    the classical world, 2008n458
Oxford-duden German dict, 3d ed, 2006n969
Oxford ency of ...
    American lit, 2005n1063
    British lit, 2007n956

children's lit, 2007n909
    food & drink in America, 2005n1301
    Latinos & Latinas in the US, 2006n351
    maritime hist, 2008n600
    women in world hist, 2009n788
Oxford English dict, 2d ed on CD-ROM, 2006n29
Oxford essential world atlas, 2009n335
Oxford gd to lib research, 3d ed, 2006n596
Oxford Hachette French dict, 4th ed, 2008n872
Oxford hist of Christian worship, 2006n1237
Oxford hist of western music, 2005n1127
Oxford hndbk of English lit & theology, 2009n972
Oxford lang dicts online [Website], 2009n898
Oxford large print thesaurus, 2005n966
Oxford-Paravia Italian dict, 2d ed, 2009n900
Oxford rhyming dict, 2005n956
Oxford Spanish dict, 4th ed, 2009n901
Oxford spellchecker & dict [CD-ROM], 2009n878
Oxford W. E. B. Du Bois, 2008n915
Oxoby, Marc, 2005n1177
Oyebade, Adebayo O., 2007n83

Pach, Chester, 2007n591
Pacific pinot noir, 2009n1150
Packer, Matt, 2008n1110
Paddock, Lisa, 2008n921
Padro, Fernando F., 2006n819
Pagana, Kathleen Deska, 2006n1425
Pagana, Timothy J., 2006n1425
Pagani, Margherita, 2006n1466, 2006n1467,
    2009n1283
Page, Martin, 2006n1309
Page, Willie F., 2006n460
Page, Yolanda Williams, 2008n911
Paharia, M. Indira, 2009n711
Pahigian, Joshua R., 2005n769
Paietta, Ann C., 2006n1143, 2008n1027
Pain sourcebk, 3d ed, 2009n1248
PAIR: portal to Asian Internet resources [Website],
    2008n103
Pakistan, 2007n100
Palgrave atlas of Byzantine hist, 2006n466
Palgrave Macmillan dict of women's biog, 4th ed,
    2006n852
Paliyath, Gopinadhan, 2006n1286
Palma, Marco, 2009n1292
Palmer, Allison Lee, 2009n863
Palmer, Colin A., 2006n329
Palmer, Douglas, 2007n322
Palmer, Louis J., Jr., 473, 2009n740
Palmer, Martin, 2006n1210
Palmer, Pete, 2007n685, 2008n711
Palmer, Xuyan Z., 2009n740
Palmer-Fernandez, Gabriel, 2005n1238
Palmowski, Jan, 2009n430

Palmquist, Peter E., 2006n936
Pampel, Fred C., 2008n705, 2009n743
Pandemics & global health, 2009n1254
Pandiri, Ananda M., 2008n109
Panno, Joseph, 2006n1318
Pantelia, Maria C., 2009n792
Panton, Kenneth J., 2009n117
Papadakis, Alexandra, 2009n1184
Papadakis, Elim, 2008n1341
Papadakis, Maxine A., 2007n1255
Papale, Paulo, 2005n1520
Papenfuse, Edward C., 2006n381
Paper money of the US, 17th ed, 2005n921
Paper money of the US, 18th ed, 2007n799
Papers of Dwight David Eisenhower [Website],
     2009n635
Papers of James Monroe, v. 2, 2007n618
Papineau, David, 2005n1236
Parada, Carlos, 2007n1025
Parasecoli, Fabio, 2005n1307
Paravisini-Gebert, Lizabeth, 2009n983
Parham, Loretta, 2008n554
Parini, Jay, 996, 2005n1063
Parish, James Robert, 2007n224, 2007n225,
     2008n251, 2009n228
Park, Chris, 2008n1340
Park, Crystal L., 2008n685, 2009n741
Park, Katharine, 2007n1140
Park, Thomas K., 2007n88
Parker, Bernard S., 2008n970
Parker, Martin, 2008n1046
Parker, Tracey, 2009n1186
Parkinson's disease, 2009n1234
Parks dir of the US, 4th ed, 2005n756
Parks dir of the US, 5th ed, 2008n701
Parmar, Priya, 2007n719
Parnell, James F., 2007n1195
Parodi, Claudia, 2009n871
Parrillo, Vincent N., 2009n55
Parsons, Keith M., 2005n1524
Partners in literacy, 2009n564
Partnership, 2006n152
Party affiliations in the state legislatures, 2008n624
Pashiardis, Petros, 2009n258
Pass, Allan D., 2009n470
Passiflora, 2005n1358
Pastoor, Charles, 2008n1084
Pasztor, Suzanne B., 2005n120
Paterwic, Stephen J., 2009n1112
Patrick, Christopher J., 2008n688
Patrick, James A., 2007n425
Patrick, John J., 2009n458
Patrick O'Brian Muster bk, 2007n952
Patriotic holidays of the US, 2006n1122
Patterns of global terrorism, 1985-2005, 2007n433
Patterson, Dan, 2005n1546, 2005n1547, 2006n1548,
     2007n1336, 2008n1353

Patterson, Daniel, 2009n952
Patterson, Dick, 2008n1353
Patterson, Michael, 2006n1172
Patterson, Tom, 2006n933
Patton, Kimberly A., 2007n510, 2008n534
Paul, Christopher, 2009n610
Paul, Larry, 2006n895
Paul, Louis, 2005n1191
Pauly, Daniel, 2006n1382
Pauly, Roger, 2005n680
Pavlac, Brian A., 2005n516
Pavlovski, Linda, 2005n992, 2005n993
Pawnee nation, 2005n340
Pawuk, Michael, 2007n900, 2008n886
Pazzanita, Anthony G., 2007n80, 2009n86
PDR concise drug gd for …
     advanced practice clinicians, 2008n1263
     advanced practice clinicians, 2d ed, 2009n1274
     pharmacists, 2008n1264
     pediatrics, 2008n1265
     pediatrics, 2d ed, 2009n1275
PDR drug gd for mental health professionals, 2d ed,
     2006n1460
PDR drug gd for mental health professionals, 3d ed,
     2008n1266
PDR for herbal medicines, 4th ed, 2008n1267
PDR for nonprescription drugs, dietary supplements,
     & herbs 2008, 29th ed, 2009n1276
PDR for ophthalmic medicines 2007, 35th ed,
     2008n1268
PDR gd to drug interactions, side effects, &
     indications, 61st ed, 2008n1260
PDR gd to drug interactions, side effects, &
     indications, 63d ed, 2009n1277
PDR lab advisor 2007, 2008n1217
PDR nurse's drug hndbk, 2005 ed, 2005n1475
PDR nurse's drug hndbk, 2006 ed, 2006n1457
PDR nurse's drug hndbk, 2007 ed, 2007n1279
PDR nurse's drug hndbk, 2008 ed, 2008n1259
PDR nurse's drug hndbk, 2009 ed, 2009n1272
Peacock, Kathy Wilson, 2009n1328
Pearce, Lynn M., 2006n174, 2009n230
Pearcy, Thomas L., 2007n399
Pearl, Nancy, 2006n1011, 2008n891
Pease, Bob, 2008n726
Peat, John P., 2005n1328
Peck, Malcolm C., 2008n144
Pederson, William D., 2008n621
Pediatric dermatology, 2007n1266
Peek, Charles A., 2005n1067
Peek, Philip M., 2005n1153
Peeters, Alain, 2006n1351
Peeters, Hans, 2008n1180
Peeters, Hans J., 2005n1396
Pekacz, Jolanta T., 2007n983
Pelle, Kimberly D., 2005n777, 2009n1039

Pellen, Rita M., 2005n615, 2006n598, 2006n599, 2006n645, 2007n539
Peloponnesian War, 2005n493
Peloso, Jennifer, 2005n99, 2006n203
Pendergast, Sara, 2005n416, 2005n417, 2005n418, 2005n485, 2006n111, 2006n112, 2006n113, 2007n910, 2008n888
Pendergast, Tom, 2005n416, 2005n417, 2005n418, 2005n485, 2006n111, 2006n112, 2006n113, 2007n910, 2008n417, 2008n888
Penguin companion to classical music, 2007n999
Penguin dict of biology, 11th ed, 2006n1316
Penguin gd to blues recordings, 2008n986
Penguin gd to compact discs & DVDs, 2003/2004 ed, 2006n1090
Penguin gd to jazz on CD, 7th ed, 2006n1106
Penguin histl atlas of ancient civilizations, 2007n401
Penguin histl atlas of the medieval world, 2007n376
Penny, David, 2006n835
Penrith, Deborah, 2006n232
Penston, Margaret, 2005n1503
Pentzer, Scott, 2009n121
Peonies, 2007n1161
People at the center of ... series, 2006n491
People at work! A student's A-Z gd to 350 jobs, 2006n256
People in power [Website], 2008n609
Peoples, nations, & cultures, 2006n325
People of the Underground Railroad, 2009n363
Peoples of E Asia, 2005n91
Peoples of the Caribbean, 2006n352
Peoples of the N.T. world, 2009n1097
Peoples of W Asia, 2007n92
Perennial vegetables, 2009n1156
Perennials for the SW, 2007n1157
Perez, Alice J., 2006n643
Perez, Janet, 2005n1089
Perez, Kathy, 2009n268
Perfect, David, 2009n91
Perfect resume, rev ed, 2005n235
Performance mgmt & appraisal, 2005n640
Performance practice, 2006n1074
Periodical title abbrevs, 15th ed, 2005n57
Periodical title abbrevs, 16th ed, 2006n55
Periodicals index online [Website], 2007n43
Perkins, Agnes Regan, 2005n1027
Perkins, Chris, 2008n358
Perlman, Daniel, 2007n662
Pernetta, John, 2005n1521
Perone, James E., 2005n1146, 2006n1075
Peroni, Gwen, 2009n185
Perrie, Maureen, 2007n398
Perry Castaneda lib map collection [Website], 2005n377
Perry, Elisabeth Israels, 2007n368
Perry, Glenn E., 2005n86
Perry, Jason, 2008n820

Perry, Robert H., 2008n1197, 2009n1217
Perry's chemical engineers' hndbk, 8th ed, 2008n1197
Perseus digital lib [Website], 2007n408
Person, Diane G., 2005n1029
Personal & business forms online [Website], 2007n150
Personal forms on file, 2004 ed, 2005n167
Personal forms on file, 2006n146
Personal forms on file, 2006, rev ed, 2007n149
Personal forms on file, 2007 ed, 2008n172
Personal perspectives: WW I, 2007n434
Personal perspectives: WW II, 2006n512
Personal versus private: presidential records in a legislative context, 2006n693
Persoon, James, 2009n1002
Perspectives on diseases & disorders series, 2009n1249
Peru, 5th ed, 2009n355
Pesce, August J.Itzo, 2006n274
Pesticides, 2d ed, 2005n1298
Pete Dunne's essential field gd companion, 2007n1192
Pete Rose, 2005n765
Peters, Gerhard, 2007n624, 2009n647
Peters, Pam, 2006n883
Petersen, Jesper Aagaard, 2009n715
Peterson, Amy T., 2005n1168
Peterson, Elizabeth, 2008n508
Peterson, Franklynn, 2007n773, 2007n774
Peterson, Kate Dempsey, 2006n566
Petheram, R. J., 2005n1354
Petit, Ted L., 2005n1328
Petit, William, Jr., 2006n1430
Petri, Liukkonen, 2006n975
Petroleum tech, 2008n1198
Petruzzelli, Barbara Whitney, 2007n500
Pettit, Philip, 2009n623
Pew Internet & American life project [Website], 2009n1289
Pfander, Hans Jurgen, 2006n1334
Pfeifer, Jessica, 2007n1137
Pfeifer, Mark Edward, 2008n315
Pfeil, Angela B., 2006n621
Phifer, Paul, 2009n277
Philander, S. George, 2009n1334
Philanthropy in America, 2005n808
Philippines, 2007n101
Phillies ency, 3d ed, 2005n768
Phillips, Charles, 2005n662, 2007n424
Phillips, Dennis J., 2005n774
Phillips, George N., Jr., 2009n1173
Phillips, John, 2007n922
Phillips, Kendall R., 2009n1070
Phillips, Mark, 2009n1055
Phillips, Robin N., 2006n1437
Phillips, Roger, 2005n1357, 2007n1182
Phillpotts, Greg, 2007n743
Philosophical gourmet report [Website], 2006n297
Philosophy, 3d ed, 2007n1059

Philosophy in cyberspace [Website], 2006n1203
Philosophy of mind A-Z, 2008n1048
Philosophy of sci, 2007n1137
Philpott, Don, 2009n261
PHILTAR: philosophy, theology, & religion
    [Website], 2006n1204
Photographer's market 2006, 29th ed, 2006n937
Photographic gd to the birds of the Indian Ocean
    islands, 2008n1181
Photography bks index 3, 2007n820
Photosynthesis & the Web [Website], 2006n1323
Phylogeny of life [Website], 2006n1329
Physicians' desk ref 2006, 2006n1462
Physicians' desk ref 2007, 61st ed, 2008n1269
Physicians' desk ref 2009, 63d ed, 2009n1278
Physics, 2008n1327
Pianist's dict, 2005n1135
Piano in chamber ensemble, 2d ed, 2007n997
Piano music by women composers, v.2, 2005n1129
Picken, Stuart D. B., 2007n1127, 2008n220
Picker, Mike, 2006n1387
Pickering, David, 2008n869
Pickering, David H., 2006n882, 2009n911
Pickett, Christopher J., 2008n1287, 2008n1288
Piednoir, Christian, 2006n1381
Pierangelo, Roger, 2009n283
Pigram, John J., 2005n754
Pike, Jon, 2009n1087
Pikiewicz, Kristi, 2009n263
Pilch, Richard F., 2006n751
Pill bk, 11th ed, 2005n1478
Pillsbury, Joanne, 2009n119
Pillsbury, Richard, 2007n311
Pinhas, Allan R., 2006n1496
Pinkerton, Jan, 2005n1064
Pinn, Anthony B., 2006n1216, 2007n1086
Pioneer photographers from the Miss. To the
    Continental Divide, 2006n936
Piotrowski, Nancy A., 2005n738
Piper, Ross, 2008n1168
Pitts, Michael R., 2009n1068
Pitts-Taylor, Victoria, 2009n291
Pitzl, Gerald R., 2005n66
Piwowarski, Joyce, 2005n199
Place names of Ill., 2009n340
Placenames of France, 2005n391
Placenames of the world, 2d ed, 2006n392
Places, towns, & townships 2007, 4th ed, 2008n771
Plagiarism plague, 2005n646
Plakans, Andrejs, 2009n114
Plake, Barbara S., 2009n262
Plan your estate, 9th ed, 2009n484
Planet dog, 2007n1200
Planner, Andrew, 2009n1241
Planning the modern public lib bldg, 2005n636
Plant, 2006n1330
Plant finder, 2008n1136

Plant locator: western region, 2005n1322
Plant ontology consortium (POC) [Website],
    2006n1325
Plantagenet ancestry, 2005n362
PlantGDB [Website], 2006n1324
Planting design, 2006n1308
Plants of the Kimberley region of W Australia, rev ed,
    2005n1354
PlantStress [Website], 2006n1326
Plato & popcorn: a philosopher's gd to 75
    thought-provoking movies, 2005n1215
Platt, Richard, 2005n581
Play index 1998-2002, 2005n1222
Play index [Website], 2008n893
Pleasant, Barbara, 2006n1336, 2009n1159
Pletcher, James R., 2008n99
Plumb, Donald C., 2007n1165, 2009n1166
Plumb's veterinary drug hndbk, 5th ed, 2007n1165
Plumb's veterinary drug hndbk, 6th ed, 2009n1166
Plunkett, Jack W., 2005n195, 2005n196, 2005n197,
    2005n198, 2005n228, 2005n231, 2005n257,
    2005n888, 2006n157, 2006n170, 2006n190,
    2006n191, 2006n192, 2006n193, 2006n194,
    2006n195, 2006n196, 2006n228, 2006n233,
    2006n273, 2006n770, 2006n1399,
    2006n1426, 2006n1488, 2006n1535,
    2007n154, 2007n164, 2007n168, 2007n169,
    2007n170, 2007n171, 2007n172, 2007n173,
    2007n174, 2007n175, 2007n179, 2007n228,
    2008n162, 2008n195, 2008n196, 2008n197,
    2008n198, 2008n199, 2008n200, 2008n201,
    2008n202, 2008n203, 2008n204, 2008n205,
    2008n206, 2008n225, 2008n227, 2008n256,
    2008n260, 2008n1218
Plunkett's advertising & branding industry almanac
    2005n257
Plunkett's advertising & branding industry almanac
    2006, 2007n228
Plunkett's advertising & branding industry almanac
    2007, 2008n256
Plunkett's airline, hotel, & travel industry almanac
    2006 ed, 2006n190
Plunkett's airline, hotel, & travel industry almanac
    2007, 2008n195
Plunkett's almanac of middle market companies 2007,
    2008n162
Plunkett's apparel & textiles industry almanac,
    2005n195
Plunkett's apparel & textiles industry almanac,
    2007n168
Plunkett's apparel & textiles industry almanac, 2008
    ed, 2009n175
Plunkett's automobile industry almanac 2005,
    2005n196
Plunkett's automobile industry almanac 2007,
    2007n169

Plunkett's automobile industry almanac 2009 ed, 2009n176

Plunkett's banking, mortgages, & credit industry almanac 2005, 2006n170

Plunkett's banking, mortgages, & credit industry almanac 2006, 2007n164

Plunkett's banking, mortgages, & credit industry almanac 2009 ed, 2009n169

Plunkett's biotech & genetics industry almanac 2006 ed, 2006n191

Plunkett's biotech & genetics industry almanac 2007, 2007n170

Plunkett's biotech & genetics industry almanac 2009 ed, 2009n177

Plunkett's chemicals, coatings, & plastics industry almanac 2007, 2008n196

Plunkett's companion to the almanac of American employers, 2004-05 ed, 2006n233

Plunkett's companion to the almanac of American employers: mid-size firms, 2007 ed, 2008n227

Plunkett's consulting industry almanac 2005, 2006n192

Plunkett's consulting industry almanac 2006, 2007n171

Plunkett's consulting industry almanac 2008 ed, 2009n178

Plunkett's e-commerce & Internet business almanac 2006, 2007n172

Plunkett's e-commerce & Internet business almanac 2008, 2009n179

Plunkett's employers' Internet sites with careers info 2004-05, 2005n231

Plunkett's energy industry almanac 2006, 2006n1535

Plunkett's energy industry almanac 2007, 2008n197

Plunkett's engineering & research industry almanac 2005, 2006n1399

Plunkett's engineering & research industry almanac 2007, 2008n198

Plunkett's entertainment & media industry almanac 2004, 2005n888

Plunkett's entertainment & media industry almanac 2006, 2007n173

Plunkett's entertainment & media industry almanac 2007, 2008n199

Plunkett's food industry almanac 2007, 2008n200

Plunkett's health care industry almanac 2006, 2006n1426

Plunkett's health care industry almanac 2007, 2008n1218

Plunkett's infotech industry almanac 2006 ed, 2006n193

Plunkett's infotech industry almanac 2007, 2008n201

Plunkett's insurance industry almanac 2005, 2006n196

Plunkett's insurance industry almanac 2006, 2007n179

Plunkett's insurance industry almanac 2009, 2009n186

Plunkett's investment & securities industry almanac 2005, 2006n157

Plunkett's investment & securities industry almanac 2006, 2007n154

Plunkett's nanotech & MEMS industry almanac, 2005n197

Plunkett's nanotech & MEMS industry almanac 2006, 2007n174

Plunkett's nanotech & MEMS industry almanac 2008, 2009n180

Plunkett's outsourcing & offshoring industry almanac 2007, 2008n202

Plunkett's real estate & construction industry almanac 2005, 2006n273

Plunkett's real estate & construction industry almanac 2007, 2008n260

Plunkett's retail industry almanac 2006, 2006n194

Plunkett's retail industry almanac 2007, 2008n203

Plunkett's sports industry almanac, 2006n770

Plunkett's sports industry almanac 2007, 2008n204

Plunkett's telecommunications industry almanac 2006, 2006n195

Plunkett's telecommunications industry almanac 2008, 2008n205

Plunkett's transportation, supply chain, & logistics industry almanac, 2005n198

Plunkett's transportation, supply chain, & logistics industry almanac 2007, 2007n175

Plunkett's transportation, supply chain, & logistics industry almanac 2008, 2009n181

Plunkett's wireless, WI-FI, RFID, & cellular industry almanac, 2006n1488

Plunkett's wireless, WI-FI, RFID, & cellular industry almanac 2008, 2008n206

Plunkett's wireless, WI-FI, RFID, & cellular industry almanac 2009 ed, 2009n182

Plut-Pregelj, Leopoldina, 2008n130

Pocket dict of N American denominations, 2006n1235

Pocket gd to depression glass & more 1920s-60s, 2009n818

Pocket gd to Irish genealogy, 3d ed, 2009n323

Pocket gd to legal writing, 2006n886

Pocket gd to world religions, 2007n1078

Pocket Oxford American dict, 2d ed, 2009n880

Pocket Oxford thesaurus, 2d ed, 2009n879

Podda, Maurizio, 2006n1405

Poddar, Prem, 2006n1193

Podell, Janet, 2008n26

Podiatry sourcebk, 2d ed, 2008n1235

Podulka, Sandy, 2005n1386

Poe, Roy W., 2007n233

Poehner, Donna, 2006n937

Poems, plays, & prose [Website], 2005n1006

Poetry archive [Website], 2009n994

Poetry archives [Website], 2009n995

Poetry criticism, v.54, 2005n1104

Poetry criticism, v.55, 2005n1105

Poetry criticism, v.56, 2005n1106
Poetry criticism, v.57, 2005n1107
Poetry daily [Website], 2008n949
Poetry daily [Website], 2009n996
Poetry for students, v.18, 2005n1108
Poetry for students, v.19, 2005n1109
Poetry for students, v.20, 2005n1110
Poetry in lit for youth, 2007n980
Poetry 180 [Website], 2008n950
Poetry people, 2008n955
Poetry Society of America [Website], 2009n997
Poets & writers [Website], 2009n998
Poet's corner [Website], 2008n951
Poets for YAs, 2008n953
Poet's market 2006, 21st ed, 2006n879
Poet's market 2008, 2008n795
Poets.org [Website], 2009n999
Pogge, Thomas, 2009n623
Pohanish, Richard P., 2009n1218
POIESIS: philosophy online serials [Website],
    2006n1187
Poisonous plants, 2d ed, 2006n1334
Poisons in mystery lit, 2008n900
Polelle, Mark Robert, 2008n446
Polette, Nancy, 2009n556, 2009n928
Policing in America, 2008n495
Political corruption in America, 2005n699
Political corruption in America, 2d ed, 2009n644
Political databases of the Americas (PDBA) [Website],
    2008n655
Political hist of America's wars, 2007n561
Political hndbk of …
    Africa 2007, 2007n625
    Asia 2007, 2008n653
    Europe 2007, 2007n628
    the Americas 2008, 2009n626
    the Middle East 2006, 2007n630
    the Middle East 2008, 2009n670
    the world: 2005-06, 2007n583
    the world 2008, 2009n627
    the world online ed [Website], 2007n584
Political parties [Website], 2008n611
Political parties of the world, 6th ed, 2006n687
Political philosophy A-Z, 2009n1087
Political resources on the net [Website], 2008n608
Politics & population control, 2005n734
Politics of promoting freedom of info & expression in
    intl librarianship, 2008n548
Polk, Danne, 2006n1184
Pollack, Eunice G., 2008n330
Pollack, Neuman F., 2006n285
Polling America, 2006n686
Polling the nations [Website], 2008n744
PollingReport.com [Website], 2009n636
Pollock, Bruce, 2006n1110
Pollock, Michael, 2007n1158
Polmar, Norman, 2005n676, 2006n675

Polo ency, 2005n779
Polsby, Nelson W., 2005n690
Pometto, Anthony, 2006n1286
Pond, Wilson G., 2005n1333
Ponterotto, Joseph G., 2008n686
Poole, Hilary W., 2006n1485
Poole, Jackie M., 2009n1179
Pop culture Arab world! 2006n1126
Pop culture China!2008n1002
Pop Culture Germany! 2007n1033
Pop culture India! 2007n1034
Pop culture Russia! 2006n1125
Pop culture universe [Website], 2009n1045
Pope, Alice, 2006n877
Poplawski, Paul, 2005n1004, 2009n970
Popular contemporary writers, 2006n974
Popular music teaching hndbk, 2005n1138
Popular psychology, 2006n754
Popular series fiction for K-6, 2006n997
Popular series fiction for middle school & teen readers,
    2006n998
Popular song index, 4th suppl: 1988-2002, 2006n1098
Population index on the Web [Website], 2005n828
Population ref bureau [Website], 2005n829
Portable MLIS, 2009n502
Portantiere, Michael, 2006n1174
Porter, David L., 2005n751, 2006n785
Porter, J. R., 2009n1098
Porter, Marsha, 2005n1216
Porter, Stanley E., 2008n1067
Porter, Valerie, 2009n1167
Porterfield, Kay Marie, 2006n338
Pospischil, Reiner, 2009n1203
Postma, Johannes, 2009n397
Poststructuralism & communication, 2006n1186
Postwar America, 2007n358
Potter, Eloise F., 2007n1195
Pound, Charles R., 2005n1463
Pound, Richard W., 2006n47, 2007n45
Pounds, Norman, 2006n469
Pournelle, Jerry, 2005n1483
Poverty in America, 2008n734
Poverty in the US, 2005n818
Powell, Eileen, 2005n1317
Powell, John, 2005n998, 2006n824, 2007n405,
    2007n406, 2007n411, 2007n722, 2008n444,
    2008n449, 2008n741
Powell, William S., 2007n74
Power, F. Clark, 2009n260
Power of the news media, 2005n899
Powers of the presidency, 2009n664
Poynter online [Website], 2005n901
Practical gd to info literacy assessment for academic
    librarians, 2009n568
Practical gd to the Indian Child Welfare Act,
    2009n310
Practical pedagogy for lib instructors, 2009n507

Practical percussion, rev ed, 2006n1086
Practical puppetry A-Z, 2006n618
Practical research methods for librarians & info
    professionals, 2008n559
Praeger hndbk on contemporary issues in Native
    America, 2008n329
Praeger hndbk on stress & coping, 2008n692
Praeger security intl online [Website], 2008n665
Prahlad, Anand, 2007n1019
Prakash, Vikramaditya, 2008n843
Prebish, Charles S., 2008n1075
Pregnancy & birth sourcebk, 2d ed, 2005n1456
Prehistoric humans in film & TV, 2007n1043
Prejudice in the modern world: almanac, 2008n304
Prejudice in the modern world: biogs, 2008n305
Prejudice in the modern world: primary sources,
    2008n306
Premila, M. S., 2008n1243
Prescott, Heather Munro, 2005n826
Preservation & conservation for libs & archives,
    2006n612
Presidency A to Z, 4th ed, 2009n647
Presidency, the public, & the parties, 3d ed, 2009n665
Presidential elections, 1789-2004, 2007n619
Presidential facts, 2007n621
Presidents, 2d ed, 2006n697
Presidents, first ladies, & vice presidents, 2006n695
Presidents from Adams through Polk, 1825-49,
    2006n733
Presidents from Eisenhower through Johnson,
    1953-69, 2007n614
Presidents were here, 2009n390
Preston, Daniel, 2007n618
Preston-Mafham, Ken, 2008n1160
Preus, Anthony, 2008n1047
Price, Anne, 2006n993, 2007n502, 2008n531,
    2008n532
Price, Dana M., 2009n1179
Price, Emmett G., III, 2007n1010
Price, Massoume, 2006n344
Price, Monica T., 2008n1320
Price, Richard, 2008n948
Price, Steven D., 2005n1391, 2008n1190
Pride, Marseille M., 2006n636
Pridgeon, Alec, 2007n1179
Primate family tree, 2009n1206
Primer of the novel, rev ed, 2007n925
Primm, E. Russell, III, 2005n1026, 2007n904
Princeton Review gd to college majors, 2006 ed,
    2008n285
Princeton Review gd to studying abroad, 2005n311
Pringle, Keith, 2008n726
Pringle, Robert W., 2007n558
Prisant, Carol, 2005n910
Prisons, 2006n568
Prisons, 2007n481
Prisons & prison systems, 2006n561

Pritzker, Barry M., 2008n323
Privacy in the info age, rev ed, 2007n1288
Private secondary schools 2006, 2006n281
Pro/con 3, 2005n692
Pro/con 4, 2006n691
Pro football prospectus 2005, 2006n789
Processing water, 2009n1327
Proctor, Noble S., 2006n1366
Professional degree programs in the visual &
    performing arts 2006, 2006n298
Professional liability issues for librarians & info
    professionals, 2009n501
Profiles in polo, 2008n713
Profiles of …
    Calif., 2007, 2008n76
    Conn. & R.I., 2008n79
    Fla., 2006n73
    Fla., 2009n73
    Ill., 2006, 2007n66
    Ill., 2009n74
    Ind., 2008n81
    Mass., 2006, 2007n68
    Mich., 2007n69
    Mich. 2008, 2d ed, 2009n75
    N.C. & S.C., 2008n87
    N.J., 2006, 2007n70
    N.Y. 2006, 2007n73
    N.Y. state, 2005-06, 2006n834
    N.Y. state, 2007/08, 2008n85
    N.Y. state, 2008-09, 2009n78
    Ohio, 2006, 2007n75
    Ohio, 2d ed, 2009n79
    Ohio women 1803-2003, 2005n868
    Pa., 2006, 2007n77
    Tex. 2005-06, 2006n74
    Tex. 2008, 2009n81
    Va., 2009n84
    Wis., 2008n90
    worldwide govt leaders 2004, 2005n684
Profiling & criminal justice in America, 2005n570
Programming for adults, 2006n602
Progressive era, 2005n438
Progressive era, 2006n457
Prohibition, 2006n453
Project euclid [Website], 2005n842
Project vote smart [Website], 2009n637
Promislow, Daniel E. L., 2008n1145
Prono, Luca, 2009n1046
Pronunciation of placenames, 2009n343
Proposal planning & writing, 4th ed, 2009n754
ProQuest AP sci [Website], 2009n1121
ProQuest histl newspapers [Website], 2005n905
ProQuest histl newspapers [Website], 2008n804
Prostate & urological disorders sourcebk, 2007n1260
Protecting your library's digital sources, 2005n631
Protevi, John, 2007n1066
Protogeros, Nicolaos, 2008n1279

Proven strategies for building an info literacy program, 2008n544
Provenzo, Eugene F., 2009n246, 2009n269
Proverbs, 2005n1155
Prucher, Jeff, 2008n903
Pruning of trees, shrubs, & conifers, 2d ed, 2005n1373
Pryor, Jan, 2009n746
Prytherch, Ray, 2006n588
PSI hdnbk of business security, 2009n149
Psychologists & their theories for students, 2005n735
Psychology basics, rev ed, 2005n738
Psychotherapists on film, 1899-1999, 2005n1194
Psychotropic drugs, 4th ed, 2009n1279
Pubantz, Jerry, 2009n673
Public debate over controversial Supreme Court decisions, 2007n461
Public interest group profiles 2004-05, 11th ed, 2005n731
Public interest group profiles 2006-07, 2007n600
Public libs & Internet serv roles, 2009n512
Public lib catalog, 12th ed, 2005n5
Public lib manager's forms, policies, & procedures hndbk w/CD-ROM, 2005n605
Public lib start-up gd, 2005n606
Public opinion & polling around the world, 2005n688
Public record research system-Web [Website], 2007n449
Public record research tips bk, 2009n460
Public records online, 5th ed, 2005n732
Public records online, 6th ed, 2007n643
Publishers dir 2005, 28th ed, 2006n654
Publishers dir 2009, 32d ed, 2009n597
Publishing, bks, & reading in Sub-Saharan Africa, 2009n589
PubMed [Website], 2008n1204
Puebloan society of Chaco Canyon, 2005n347
Pugh, Lyndon, 2006n640
Puhl, Maureen, 2005n188, 2005n598, 2006n176, 2006n594
Pulliam, June Michele, 2007n931
Pullin, Michael, 2009n588
Pummer, Reinhard, 2006n1245
Punch, Terrence M., 2009n326
Punishment in America, 2006n565
Puppa, Paolo, 2008n941
Pura Belpre awards, 2007n906
Purcell, Arthur H., 2007n570
Purcell, L. Edward, 2006n701
Purcell, Sarah J., 2005n458
Purdy, Dennis, 2007n680
Puritans & Puritanism in Europe & America, 2007n1115
Purple bk, 2005 ed, 2006n164
Purple bk, 2006 ed, 2007n159
Putman, William H., 2006n886
Putnik, Goran D., 2009n1286
Putonti, Dorette, 2009n520

Putyera, Karol, 2005n1401
Pybus, Victoria, 2006n242
Pykett, Derek, 2009n1058
Pyle, Andrew, 2007n1065

Quality lib, 2009n580
Quanchi, Max, 2006n99
Quaratiello, Arlene Rodda, 2008n564
Queen Victoria, 2005n484
Queer America, 2009n749
Queer ency of film & TV, 2007n1048
Queer ency of music, dance, & musical theater, 2005n1181
Queer ency of the visual arts, 2005n938
Quertermous, Russell, 2005n922, 2007n803, 2009n836
Quertermous, Steve, 2005n922, 2007n803, 2009n836
Quick, Amanda C., 2005n187, 2005n1426, 2006n1421
Quick ref dict for athletic training, 2d ed, 2006n1454
Quick ref for health care providers, 2005n1421
Quigley, Marian, 2008n1270
Quilt, 2008n828
Quin, Jian, 2009n574
Quinlan, David, 2005n1192
Quinlan's character stars, rev ed, 2005n1192
Quinn, Edward, 2005n1001, 2007n882
Quinn, John P., 2007n455
Quinn, Mary Ellen, 2005n6
Quint, Barbara, 2005n1488, 2007n540
Quirk, Tom, 2007n938
Quotable American Civil War, 2009n50
Quotable founding fathers, 2005n462
Quotable John Adams, 2009n52
Quotable soldier, 2006n667
Qur'an, 2007n1122

Rabelais ency, 2005n1086
Rabin, Jack, 2006n752
Race & racism in lit, 2006n988
Race for the presidency, 2008n644
Race relations in the US, 2006n437
Race relations in the US, 1980-2000, 2009n295
Racial & ethnic diversity, 5th ed, 2007n266
Radcliff, Benjamin, 2006n686
Radcliff, Carolyn J., 2009n568
Radford, Marie L., 2009n503
Radio, 2006n894
Radio series scripts, 1930-2001, 2007n782
Rahman, Syedur, 2005n94
Railroad, 2006n1550
Railroad atlas of the US in 1946, v.2: N.Y. & New England, 2006n1549
Railroad atlas of the US in 1946, v.3, 2009n1349
Railroad in American fiction, 2006n1031

Railsback, Brian, 2007n953
Railton, Jack, 2006n1480
Rainey, Buck, 2006n1136
Rainey, David, 2009n986
Rajtar, Steve, 2008n824
Rakipov, Nazib G., 2005n144
Rakipova, Anna N., 2005n144
Rakova, Marina, 2008n1048
Ralls, Karen, 2008n428
Ramaswamy, Vijaya, 2008n424
Ramirez, Luz Elena, 2009n984
Ramm, David, 2007n196, 2008n876
Ramsay, Jeff, 2009n90
Ramsby, Kari L., 2008n650
RAND pubs [Website], 2007n44
Randall, Otelio S., 2005n1468
Randel, Don Michael, 2005n1120
Randolph, Sallie, 2006n876
Random House atlas of the world, 2005n378
Random House concise dict of sci & computers, 2006n1261
Random House Webster's large print crossword puzzle dict, 2008n858
Random House world atlas & ency, 2008n30
Random House writer's ref, rev ed, 2005n895
Ranier, Raymond, 2006n602
Raphael, Marc Lee, 2009n313
Rappaport, Helen, 2005n484
Rappole, John H., 2007n1196
Raptors of N America, 2007n1197
Rare & unusual Indian artifacts, 2008n822
Rare plants of Tex., 2009n1179
Raskin, Jamin B., 2009n459
Rasmussen, Kristin, 2007n737, 2008n755
Rasmussen, R. Kent, 2006n441, 2008n924
Ratcliffe, Susan, 2006n60, 2007n47, 2009n49
Rathemacher, Andre J., 2007n525
Ratner, Lorman A., 2006n324
Ratsch, Christian, 2006n1331
Ratzan, Lee, 2005n632
Raugh, Harold E., Jr., 2005n663, 2009n600
Rausch, John David, Jr., 2008n627
Rauser, Randal D., 2008n1045
Rautman, Marcus, 2007n386
Rawson, Hugh, 2006n61
Ray, Celeste, 2008n303
Ray, Fred Eugene, 2009n602
Raymond, Gino, 2009n403
Reaching financial goals, 2008n185
Read on . . . crime fiction, 2009n943
Read on . . . fantasy fiction, 2008n904
Read on . . . histl fiction, 2008n901
Read on . . . horror fiction, 2007n931
Read the high country, 2007n933
Readers' advisory gd to nonfiction, 2008n946
Readers' advisory serv in the public lib, 3d ed, 2006n603

Reader's Digest illus world atlas, 2007n306
Reading about children's lit [Website], 2007n901
Reading is funny! 2009n546
Reading Jonathan Edwards, 2009n1104
Reading, Mario, 2008n680
Reading women writers & African lits [Website], 2006n1057
Reagan era, 2008n418
Reagan yrs, 2006n699
Real estate forms simplified, 2007n234
Real-life math, 2007n1321
Real-life mktg & promotion strategies in college libs, 2007n500
Real McCoy: the true stories behind our everyday phrases, 2007n843
Real story, 2007n977
Real-world network troubleshooting manual, 2005n1484
Realms of the sacred in daily life [Website], 2005n321
Reardon, Wendy J., 2005n1267
Recent American art song, 2009n1010
Recommended bks in Spanish for children & YAs, 2006n994
Recommended bks in Spanish for children & YAs 2004-08, 2009n929
Reconstruction era, 2005n445
Reconstruction era: almanac, 2005n413
Reconstruction era: biogs, 2005n414
Reconstruction era: primary sources, 2005n415
Red bk, 3d ed, 2005n361
Redman, Nina E., 2008n1132
Redmond, Ian, 2009n1206
Reed, Christina, 2009n1299
Reed, Claudette, 2009n821
Reed, Fred, 2006n1144
Reed, Paul F., 2005n347
Reed, Robert, 2009n821
Reed, Sally Gardner, 2009n515
Reeder, DeeAnn M., 2007n1209
Reedy, Patrick, 2008n1046
Reef, Catherine, 2005n658, 2008n233, 2008n734
Reel women, 2008n1029
Rees, Dafydd, 2005n1152
Reese, Terry, Jr., 2009n575
Reeves, Diane Lindsey, 2006n243
Reevy, Gretchen, 2008n692
Refdesk.com: ref desk [Website], 2008n1280
Reference & info servs in the 21st century, 2007n538
Reference & research gd to mystery & detective fiction, 2d ed, 2005n1046
Reference Bks Bulletin 2002-03, 2005n6
Reference collection, 2007n542
Reference collection dvlpmt, 2006n643
Reference ency of the American Indian, 11th ed, 2005n342
Reference gd to Africa, 2d ed, 2006n78

Reference librarian's policies, forms, guidelines, & procedures hndbk, 2007n537

Reference sources for small & medium-sized libs, 7th, 2009n4

Reference sources in hist, 2d ed, 2005n510

References on chilly climate for women faculty in academe [Website], 2005n286

Reformation, exploration, & empire, 2006n502

Regal, Brian, 2006n894, 2006n1319, 2009n1169

Regional gd to intl conflict & mgmt from 1945 to 2003, 2006n741

Regional railroads of the Midwest, 2008n1355

Regional theatre dir 2003-04, 2006n1176

Regional trends, 2007n743

Regions of Germany, 2006n103

Rehnquist Court, 2007n452

Reich, Bernard, 2005n127, 2009n130, 2009n131

Reich, Steven A., 2007n271

Reichard, S. H., 2007n1169

Reichardt, Mary R., 2006n979

Reichling, Steven B., 2009n1211

Reid, Daniel G., 2005n1248

Reid, Fiona A., 2007n1210

Reid, Luc, 2008n867

Reid, Natalie L., 2009n475

Reid, Rob, 2008n963

Reid-Walsh, Jacqueline, 2009n766

Reidy, Michael S., 2007n1145, 2008n1114

Reiff, Janice L., 2007n65

Reign of Cleopatra, 2006n482

Reiley, H. Edward, 2005n1329

Reill, Peter Hanns, 2005n524

Reilly, Edwin D., 2006n1476

Reimer, Carol J., 2009n1064

Reimer, Robert C., 2009n1064

Reinehr, Robert C., 2008n805

Reingold, Beth, 2009n662

Reinhart, Mark S., 2005n1206, 2009n1059

Reinking, Dan L., 2005n1388

Reinventing project-based learning, 2009n249

Reipurth, Bo, 2007n1304

Reisner, Rosalind, 2006n1032

Reitz, Joan M., 2005n595

Reliable roses, 2005n1364

Religion & the law in America, 2008n1057

Religion bk, 2005n1242

Religion in America, 2008n1062

Religion past & present, v.1, 2008n1059

Religions of the ancient world, 2006n1217

Religions of the world, rev ed, 2006n1210

Religious holidays & calendars, 3d ed, 2005n1172

Religious right, 3d ed, 2008n1066

Remembered childhoods, 2008n945

Remler, Pat, 2007n1027

Remnek, Miranda, 2009n527

Renaissance & reformation, 2007n425

Renaissance art, 2005n944

Renard, John, 2006n1240

Renewable & alternative energy resources, 2009n1329

Renn, Stephen D., 2006n1223

Rennie, Richard, 2006n1522, 2006n1526

Renstrom, Peter G., 2005n555

Renzetti, Claire M., 2009n469

Repa, Barbara Kate, 2007n486

RePEc (Research papers in economics) [Website], 2005n134

Representative American speeches 2002-03, 2005n890

Representative American speeches 2004-05, 2006n874

Representative American speeches 2005-06, 2007n766

Representative American speeches 2007-08, 2009n801

Reptiles & amphibians of the southern pine woods, 2009n1211

Resch, John P., 2006n439

Research & discovery, 2009n1137

Research-based readers' advisory, 2009n513

Research centers dir, 31st ed, 2005n304

Research centers dir, 35th ed, 2008n282

Research centers dir, 36th ed, 2009n248

Research gd for undergraduate students, 6th ed, 2007n494

Research gd to US & intl interest groups, 2005n728\

Research, ref serv, & resources for the study of Africa, 2006n79

Research skills for policy & dvlpmt, 2008n674

Research within the disciplines, 2008n561

Researching leisure, sport, & tourism, 2008n704

Researching natl security & intelligence, 2005n730

Researching WW I, 2005n531

Resources for school librarians [Website], 2007n504

Resources for school librarians [Website], 2009n524

Resources for teachers & students of the DDC [Website], 2009n542

Respiratory disorders sourcebk, 2d ed, 2009n1266

Restivo, Sal, 2006n1262, 2009n1125

Restoring American gardens, 2005n1309

Retail tenant dir 2006, 2007n176

Retail tenant dir 2008, 2008n207

Retail trade intl 2005, 14th ed, 2006n205

Retail trade intl 2007, 15th ed, 2008n214

Rethinking info work, 2008n525

Reverse acronyms, initialisms, & abbrevs dict, 39th ed, 2008n2

Revolutionary & dissident movements of the world, 4th ed, 2005n693

Revolutionary era, 2005n452

Revolutionary movements in world hist, 2007n414

Revolutionary War almanac, 2007n340

Revolutionary War era, 2006n455

Rey, Luis V., 2008n1326

Reyes, Gilbert, 2009n702

Reynolds, Cecil R., 2008n290

Reynolds, Dwight F., 2009n1032

Reynolds, Ross, 2006n1509

Reynolds, Sian, 2007n388, 2008n778

Rezende, Lisa, 2007n1133
Rice, Stanley, 2008n1141
Rice, Stanley A., 2007n1166
Rich & poor in America, 2009n760
Rich, Mari, 2008n876
Rich register 2004, 2005n814
Rich register 2006, 2006n814
Richard, Birgit, 2007n719
Richard Cook's jazz ency, 2008n989
Richard, Susan Marshall, 2005n1033
Richard Wright, 2008n926
Richard Wright ency, 2009n967
Richards, Lynne, 2006n1337
Richards, Martin, 2006n806
Richards, William J., 2006n1379
Richardson, Douglas, 2005n362, 2006n361, 2008n844
Richardson, Peter, 2008n844
Richetti, John, 2006n1045
Richey, Joseph, 2009n1331
Richter, Barbara, 2006n1054
Richter, Duncan, 2005n1233
Richter, William L., 2005n434, 2006n443, 2007n359
Rickards, Steven L., 2009n1012
Ricotta, Mary C., 2006n1427
Riding, Alan, 2005n1080
Ridpath, Ian, 2007n1305
Riechel, Rosemarie, 2009n569
Riedling, Ann Marlow, 2006n71, 2007n526
Riendeau, Roger, 2008n426
Rienner anthology of African lit, 2008n936
Riess, Steven A., 2007n678
Rife, David, 2008n990
Riffenburgh, Beau, 2008n148
Riffle, Robert Lee, 2009n1187
Rifles, 2006n681
Riggle, Judith, 2009n920
Riggs, Thomas, 2006n1209, 2007n227, 2007n1084
Right to counsel & privilege against self-incrimination, 2005n559
Right to die & euthanasia, rev ed, 2008n499
Right, wrong, & risky: a dict of today's American English usage, 2006n963
Rights of lesbians, gay men, bisexuals, & transgender people, 4th ed, 2006n583
Rights of the disabled, 2009n745
Rights of the elderly, 2009n743
Riley, Gillian, 2009n1148
Riley, Noël, 2005n929
Riley, Sam G., 2008n310
Riley-Smith, Jonathan, 2006n511
Rimanelli, Marco, 2009n674
Rinehart, Robin, 2005n1269
Ringgren, Helmer, 2005n1249, 2007n1099
Ringler, William A., Jr., 2005n1102
Rise of Islam, 2006n1241
Risley, Ford, 2005n459
Ritchie, David, 2008n1318

Ritchie, Donald A., 2007n620
Ritchie, Robert, 2005n471
Ritchie, Roy, 2007n806
Rittner, Don, 2005n1338, 2006n1492
Ritzer, George, 2005n788, 2007n689
River systems of the world [Website], 2005n1518
Rivero, Laura C., 2006n1486
Rivers, Vickie, 2005n638
Riverside dict of biography, 2005n18
Rives, Nathan S., 2005n363
Rix, Martyn, 2005n1357
Rizzo, Margaret, 2005n611
Roaring 20s, rev ed, 2008n422
Roaring twenties ref lib, 2006n423
Roark, Elisabeth L., 2005n932
Robbers, Gerhard, 2007n444
Robbins, Paul, 2008n1338
Roberson, Mary-Russell, 2008n1321
Robert E. Howard, 2008n906
Roberts, Elise Schebler, 2008n828
Roberts, Gary Boyd, 2005n356
Roberts, J. M., 2006n494
Roberts, Jeremy, 2005n1165
Roberts, John, 2006n468, 2008n458
Roberts, John R., 2006n1049
Roberts, Keith, 2008n1151
Roberts, Kevin D., 2007n274
Roberts, Laurel Bridges, 2005n1340
Roberts, Michael, 2009n1138
Roberts, Tim S., 2008n540
Roberts, Wesley, 2007n997
Robertson, Ann E., 2008n675
Robertson, Roland, 2007n135, 2008n156
Robertson, Stephen L., 2006n695
Robin, Diana, 2008n784
Robinson, Catherine, 2008n1094, 2009n1116
Robinson, Jancis, 2008n1121
Robinson, Kara L., 2005n591
Robinson, Thomas A., 2007n1104, 2008n1074
Robson, John, 2006n99
Robson, Martin, 2005n672
Rochat, Philippe, 2006n822
Rocheleau, Kathleen, 2005n54
Rock & gem, 2006n1512
Rock & roll film ency, 2008n1020
Rock & roll yr by yr, 2005n1152
Rock band name origins, 2009n1026
Rock song index, 2006n1110
Rocked by romance, 2005n1016
Rockets & missiles, 2005n682
Rockman, Connie C., 2006n1000, 2009n934
Rockquemore, Kerry Ann, 2009n278
Rocks & fossils, 2006n1514
Rodd, Tony, 2008n1136, 2009n1188
Rodgers & Hammerstein ency, 2008n1042
Rodrick, Anne Baltz, 2005n490
Rodrigues, Rick, 2007n565

Rodriguez, Junius P., 2008n395, 2008n403, 2008n453
Rodriguez, Robert, 2006n349
Roe v. Wade, 2009n451
Roehm, Frances E., 2007n211
Rogel, Carole, 2005n117, 2008n130
Rogelberg, Steven G., 2007n652
Roger Hornsby, 2005n764
Rogers, Clifford J., 2008n595
Rogers, Geoff, 2005n1393
Rogers, Pat, 2005n1112
Rogers, Shannon L., 2008n929
Rohrbaugh, Ronald W., Jr., 2005n1386
Rohwer, Jurgen, 2006n669
Rolf, Christer G., 2007n671
Rolland, Jacques L., 2006n1283, 2007n1151
Rollins, Peter C., 2005n1210
Rolls, Albert, 2007n1289, 2008n268, 2008n876
Rollyson, Carl, 2005n1035, 2008n907, 2008n921,
    2009n941
Romaine, Deborah S., 2005n1468, 2005n1471,
    2006n1431
Roman army, 2007n396
Roman, James, 2006n1165
Romaniuk, Bohdan, 2006n39, 2009n207
Romano, Frederick V., 2005n1207
Romans, 2005n496
Romich, Janet Amundson, 2006n1312
Ronald Reagan, 2009n628
Room, Adrian, 2005n391, 2006n392, 2007n316,
    2009n342, 2009n343
Roots for kids, 2008n336
Roper, Fred W., 2005n1415
Rose, 2005n1363
RoseMary, Honnold, 2006n622
Rosen, Fred, 2006n560
Rosen, Joe, 2006n1523
Rosen, Lester S., 2009n232
Rosen, Marie Simonetti, 2006n518
Rosen, Philip, 2008n457
Rosenberg, Scott, 2005n88
Rosenblatt, Arthur, 2006n1171
Rosenblum, Joseph, 2006n1051
Rosenfeld, Esther, 2008n517
Rosenfeld, Lucy D., 2005n940
Rosenfeld, Susan, 2005n425
Rosenkrantz, Linda, 2005n367
Rosi, Mauro, 2005n1520
Rosqvist, Johan, 2006n755, 2008n687
Ross, Alex, 2005n592
Ross, E. Wayne, 2009n242
Ross, Eric S., 2009n93
Ross, Mary Bucher, 2005n649
Rosser, John H., 2007n382
Rosser, Sue V., 2009n790
Rossignol, Rosalyn, 2007n957
Rosson, Joe L., 2007n793
Roszkowski, Wojciech, 2009n108

Roth, John K., 2006n1192, 2008n879, 2009n912,
    2009n916
Roth, Mitchel P., 2006n561
Roth, Norman, 2006n348
Rothera, Brian, 2006n1306
Rothfeld, Glenn S., 2006n1431
Rothman, Hal K., 2005n75
Rotole, Jennifer K., 2006n71
Rottman, Gordon L., 2008n868
Rough gd to Australia, 6th ed, 2005n402
Rough gd to climate change, 2008n1312
Rough gd to skiing & snowboarding in N America,
    2005n782
Routledge ency of narrative theory, 2006n871
Routledge ency of philosophy [Website], 2006n1197
Routledge intl ency of queer culture, 2007n706
Routledge pol & intl relations resource [Website],
    2008n612
Routledge religion resource [Website], 2008n1060
Rovner, Julie, 2009n697
Rowell, Erica, 2008n1034
Rowh, Mark, 2005n250, 2006n257
Rowland, David L., 2009n756
Rowland, William G., Jr., 2005n325
Roy, Christian, 2006n1124
Roy, Joaquín, 2007n110
Roy, John H., Jr., 2008n1356
Roy, Kumkum, 2009n399
Royal descents of 600 immigrants to the American
    colonies or the US, 2005n356
Royal families, v.3, 2008n337
Royster, Jacqueline Jones, 2005n868
RSP funding for nursing students & nurses 2004-06,
    4th ed, 2005n1476
RSP funding for nursing students & nurses 2006-08,
    2007n253
Ruan, Jiening, 2009n265
Rubin, Barry, 2009n464
Rubin, Emanuel, 2005n1126
Rubin, Judith Colp, 2009n464
Rubin, Richard E., 2005n602
Ruckenstein, Lelia, 2005n111
Rucker, Walter, 2008n301
Rudd, Kelly, 2005n411, 2005n573, 2006n424,
    2006n425, 2006n426, 2007n332, 2007n333,
    2007n334, 2008n304, 2008n305, 2008n306
Rue, Leonard Lee, III, 2005n1397
Ruether, Rosemary Radford, 2007n1080
Ruggeri, Fabrizio, 2009n1220
Ruggles, Clive, 2006n1506
Ruiz, Vicki L., 2007n285
Rumney, Thomas A., 2006n1280
Running a small lib, 2007n534
Running well, 2009n738
Rusche, Philip G., 2005n614
Russell, Carrie, 2006n629
Russell, Cheryl, 2005n267, 2009n157

Russell, Patricia Yates, 2007n892
Russell, Richard, 2007n797
Russell, Roy, 2009n901
Russell, Tony, 2008n986
Russia, 2005n113
Russia, updated ed, 2006n411
Russia: Belarus & Ukraine, updated ed, 2009n353
Russian & Soviet battleships, 2005n674
Russian far east, 2d ed, 2005n115
Russian lit pages at Northwestern Univ early
     20th-century Russian drama [Website],
     2005n1096
Russo, Charles J., 2009n244
Russo, Michael F., 2009n566
Russo, Stan, 2005n561
Rust, Michael, 2009n1203
Rutherford, Donald, 2005n137
Rutherford, Scott, 2008n368
Ruthven, Malise, 2005n1271
Ruud, Jay, 2006n984, 2007n883, 2009n1005
RX list [Website], 2007n1282
Ryan, James D., 2008n1095
Ryan, James G., 2005n431, 2007n354
Ryan, Marie-Laure, 2006n871
Ryan, Mary Meghan, 2005n169, 2005n234, 2006n207,
     239, 2006n240, 2007n195, 2007n750
Rybacki, James J., 2005n1479, 2006n1461
Ryerson, Richard Alan, 2007n345, 2007n349,
     2008n392
Ryle, Martin, 2006n323
Rymsza, Guy A., 2005n364

Saari, Peggy, 2005n1508, 2005n1509
Sabasteanski, Anna, 2007n433
Sachedina, Abdulaziz, 2005n1274
Sacks, David, 2006n474
Sadegh, Ali M., 2007n1228, 2008n1200
Sadek, Paul C., 2007n1223
Sadie, Stanley, 2005n1136, 2006n1092, 2007n1001
Safe hiring audit, 2009n232
Safford, Elizabeth J., 2007n698
Safford, Philip L., 2007n698
Safire, William, 2009n619
Safire's pol dict, updated ed, 2009n619
Sage dict of ...
     criminology, 2d ed, 2007n471
     cultural studies, 2007n265
     health & society, 2007n1234
     social research methods, 2007n51
     sociology, 2007n691
     stats, 2007n738
Sage ency of qualitative research methods, 2009n57
Sailor's illus dict, 2005n780
Sainsbury, Diana, 2008n1142
Saints & their symbols, 2005n936

Saints of Asia, 2008n1078
Saints, clergy, & other religious figures on film & TV,
     1895-2003, 2006n1143
Sakenfeld, Katharine Doob, 2008n1071
Saks, Rachel D., 2009n1151
Sale, Richard, 2007n1188
Salem health [Website], 2008n1231
Salem health: cancer, 2009n1263
Salem witch trials, 2009n379
Salinas, Robert C., 2006n802
Salinger, Lawrence M., 2005n564
Salisbury, Joyce E., 2005n517
Salkind, Neil J., 2007n651, 2007n737, 2008n755,
     2009n245
Salowey, Christina A., 2005n511
Salvadoran Americans, 2007n283
Sammons, Eddie, 2005n1208
Sampson, Henry T., 2006n890
Samuels, Richard J., 2007n642
Samuels, Selina, 2007n963
Samuels, Wilfred D., 2009n956
Sandberg, Walt, 2006n488
Sandler, Stanley, 2006n680
Sanga, Jaina C., 2005n1084
Sankaran, Neeraja, 2006n1359
Sankey, Michael, 2009n460
Sankey, Michael L., 2005n577, 2009n455, 2009n456
Santi, Steve, 2007n798
Santucci, James A., 2008n1064
Sarg, Michael J., 2008n1251
Sargent, Frederic O., 2005n421
Saricks, Joyce G., 2006n603
Sarkar, Sohotra, 2007n1137
Sarkodie-Mensah, Kwasi, 2005n652
Sarti, Roland, 2005n497
Satchmo: the Louis Armstrong ency, 2005n1131
Satija, M. P., 2009n543
Satin, Morton, 2009n1153
Satran, Pamela Redmond, 2005n367
Satre dict, 2009n1082
Sattar, Naveed, 2008n1256
Sattelmeyer, Robert, 2007n937
Saucier, Paul Khalil, 2008n97
Sauer, Michelle M., 2009n1003
Saunders, Nicholas J., 2006n352
Savage, David G., 2005n556
Savage, Kathleen A., 2007n472
Savings & investment info for teens, 2006n172
Sawyer, R. Keith, 2007n53
Sax's dangerous properties of industrial materials, 11th
     ed, 2005n1407
Sayette, Michael A., 2005n742, 2007n661, 2009n706
Sayler, Mary Harwell, 2006n1432, 2008n1248
Scagell, Robin, 2005n1501, 2006n1502
Scammon, Richard M., 2005n719, 2006n732,
     2007n616, 2008n643
Scanlan, Margaret, 2007n115

Scarlett, W. George, 2007n1079
Schacter, Daniel L., 2005n743
Schading, Barbara, 2008n596
Schaefer, Richard T., 2009n293
Schaefer, Todd M., 2008n610
Schaffner, Herbert A., 2005n227
Scharnhorst, Gary, 2007n938
Schatz, Aaron, 2006n789
Schatzmann, Siegfried S., 2008n1088
Schaus, Margaret, 2007n759
Scheb, John M., II, 2007n490
Schecter, Roger E., 2005n590
Schein, Richard H., 2005n68
Schelbert, Leo, 2008n132
Schell, Bernadette H., 2005n582, 2008n1281
Scheller, W. G., 2009n855
Scheuering, Rachel White, 2005n1537
Schiecke, Konrad, 2008n1010
Schinder, Scott, 2009n1027
Schirmer ency of film, 2008n1021
Schlachter, Gail Ann, 2005n316, 2005n1476,
    2006n304, 2006n305, 2006n306, 2006n307,
    2006n308, 2006n309, 2007n252, 2007n253
Schlager, Neil, 2005n139, 2005n506, 2005n507,
    2007n1292, 2007n1322, 2008n613
Schleifer, Martha Furman, 2005n1117, 2007n984
Schlup, Leonard, 2005n431, 2007n354
Schmid, W. George, 2006n1299
Schmidgall-Tellings, A. Ed., 2005n973
Schmidt, Benno C., Jr., 2008n478
Schmidt, Tracy L., 2007n796, 2009n823
Schmitz, Cathryne L., 2006n237
Schneider, Carl J., 2007n369, 2008n419
Schneider, Dorothy, 2007n369, 2008n419
Schneider, Joanne, 2008n430
Schneider, Steven Jay, 2005n1213
Schoell, William, 2009n1069
Schoenberg, Thomas J., 2005n1009, 2005n1010,
    2005n1011
Schoenfeld, Brad, 2009n727
Scholarly resources for children & childhood studies,
    2008n738
Scholarly sport sites [Website], 2005n757
Scholars' gd to Washington, D.C. for Central Asian &
    Caucasus studies, 2006n86
Scholarships, fellowships, & loans, 21st ed, 2005n309
Scholarships, fellowships, & loans, 22d ed, 2006n310
Scholarships, fellowships, & loans, 23d ed, 2008n287
Scholastic children's ency, 2005n33
Scholastic new headline world atlas, 2006n382
Scholte, Jan Aart, 2007n135, 2008n156
Scholz, Fritz, 1287, 2008n1288
Schon, Isabel, 2006n994, 2009n929
School lib media manager, 2009n526
School lib media manager, 3d ed, 2006n608
School-Libraries.net [Website], 2009n525
Schopflin, Katharine, 2009n528

Schramm, Laurier L., 2009n1215
Schraufnagel, Noel, 2009n939
Schreurs, Miranda, 2008n1341
Schroeder, Klaus-Peter, 2009n1303
Schroeder-Lein, Glenna R., 2009n383
Schroeder's antiques price gd 2005, 23d ed, 2005n914
Schroeder's antiques price gd 2006, 24th ed, 2006n901
Schroeder's antiques price gd 2008, 26th ed, 2008n819
Schroeder's antiques price gd 2009, 27th ed, 2009n822
Schroeder's collectible toys 2006, 10th ed, 2006n907
Schroeder's collectible toys antique to modern price gd
    2008, 11th ed, 2008n825
Schrott, Allen, 2007n998
Schroy, Ellen T., 2005n915, 2007n796, 2009n823
Schubert, Frank N., 2005n657
Schubert, Irene, 2005n657
Schulman, Bruce J., 666, 2009n667
Schultz, David, 2005n733, 2006n520, 2006n582,
    2009n437
Schultz, Deanne, 2008n1028
Schultz, Jeffrey, 2006n1039
Schultz, Patricia, 2005n394
Schulz, Richard, 2007n693
Schulze, E.-D., 2009n1180
Schusterbauer, Noah, 2005n1279
Schutt, Donald A., Jr., 2008n234
Schwabach, Aaron, 2006n521, 2007n447, 2007n1333,
    2008n482
Schwartz, Andy, 2009n1027
Schwartz, David G., 2006n1465
Schwartz, Jeffrey H., 2007n261
Schwartz, Maurice L., 2006n1518
Schwartz, Richard A., 2007n343
Schwartz, Ronald, 2009n1071
Schwarz, James A., 2005n1401
Schwedt, Rachel E., 2009n930
Schweer, Michael, 2008n794
Schweingruber, F. H., 2009n1180
Schweitzer, Ivy, 2006n1036
Schweitzer, Philip A., 2005n1414
Schwenk, James L., 2009n1115
Schwing, Ned, 2005n923, 2005n924, 2006n905,
    2007n804
Science & nonbelief, 2006n1268
Science & religion, 400 BC to AD 1550, 2006n1269
Science & religion, 1450-1900, 2005n1294
Science & scientists, 2007n1138
Science & society in the 20th century, 2005n1295
Science & tech in Colonial America, 2006n1267
Science & tech in modern European life, 2009n1141
Science & tech in 19th-century America, 2006n1273
Science experiments on file, v.2, 2006n1274
Science experiments on file, v.4, 2008n1115
Science experiments on file, v.5, 2009n1139
Science fact & sci fiction, 2007n1139
Science fiction & fantasy research database [Website],
    2006n1021

Science fiction quotations, 2006n1029
Science fiction studies [Website], 2006n1022
Science fiction TV series, 1990-2004, 2009n1055
Science for girls, 2008n274
Science in the ancient world, 2006n1258
Science in the contemporary world, 2006n1263
Science in the early 20th century, 2006n1256
Science of microscopy, 2007n1229
Science, tech, & society, 2006n1262
Scientific revolution & the foundations of modern sci, 2006n1266
Scientific thought, 2009n1133
SciJinks weather laboratory [Website], 2009n1313
Sclater, Neil, 2008n1202
Scobbie, Irene, 2007n116
Scopes "Monkey Trial," 2007n453
Scotland, Nigel, 2007n1074
Scott, Allen, 2007n989
Scott, Alwyn, 2006n1394
Scott, Caroline Radula, 2008n374
Scott, Chris, 2005n402
Scott, Doug, 2007n1311
Scott, Eugenie C., 2005n1235
Scott, Jacqueline, 2006n806
Scott, John, 2006n797
Scott, Judith A., 2009n259
Scott, Monica, 2005n211
Scott's Canadian sourcebk 2005, 40th ed, 2006n8
Scotter, George W., 2008n1158
Scriber, Terry G., 2008n388
Scribner ency of American lives, v.7, 2007n16
Scudiere, Todd, 2005n972
Sculpting her body perfect, 3d ed, 2009n727
Search engine watch [Website], 2009n1290
Search it! Science [Website], 2009n1122
Searching for Flemish (Belgian) ancestors, 2009n322
Sears, James T., 2006n816
Sears list of subject headings, 18th ed, 2005n617
Sears list of subject headings, 19th ed, 2008n512
Sears lista de encabezamientos de materia, 2009n544
Seberg, O., 2008n1157
Sebesta, Judith A., 2009n1080
Second atlas of breeding birds in N.Y. state, 2009n1200
Second great awakening & the transcendentalists, 2005n448
Seed, David, 2006n1028
Seekins, Donald M., 2007n93
Segal, Jeffrey A., 2008n475
Segan, Francine, 2009n1145
Segel, Harold B., 2009n980
Segen, Joseph, 2007n1250
Segura, Julio, 2006n120
Selcer, Richard F., 2008n420
Selecting & managing electronic resources, rev ed, 2007n520
Selecting materials for lib collections, 2005n625

Selesky, Harold E., 2007n350
Selin, Helaine, 2009n1127
Selter, Ronald M., 2009n719
Selvidge, Marla J., 2007n11
Senechal, Diana, 2005n293, 2005n296, 2005n301
Senelick, Laurence, 2008n1043
Senior high core collection, 17th ed, 2008n515
Sennott, R. Stephen, 2005n948
Sensen, Christoph W., 2006n1406
Sentencing, 2008n491
Serial film stars, 2006n1136
Serio, Joseph D., 2006n574
Serlin, Ilene Ava, 2008n1244
Serving teens through readers' advisory, 2008n535
Seventeenth mental measurements yrbk, 2009n262
Seventies in America, 2006n444
Severson, Marilyn S., 2005n1087
Sex from Plato to Paglia, 2007n711
Sexual harassment decisions of the US Supreme Court, 2007n462
Sexual health info for teens, 2d ed, 2009n1267
Sexual misconduct & the clergy, 2006n569
Sexually transmitted diseases sourcebk, 3d ed, 2007n1275
Sezzi, Peter, 2006n693
SF Canada [Website], 2006n1023
Sfeir, Antoine, 2008n1097
Shade, 2007n1162
Shadow, Don, 2006n1355
Shadrack, Michael, 2005n1350
Shakespeare: a hundred urs on film, 2005n1208
Shakespeare for students, 2d ed, 2008n933
Shakespeares after Shakespeare, 2007n960
Shakespeare's lang, 2d ed, 2009n975
Shakespeare's non-standard English, 2005n1079
Shakespeare's religious lang, 2007n959
Shamanism, 2005n1278
Shamburg, Christopher, 2009n270
Shanahan, Mike, 2008n1168
Shannon, John R., 2009n1014
Shannon, Joyce Brennfleck,
Shannon, Joyce Brennfleck, 2005n1470, 2006n1436, 2006n1453, 2007n696, 2007n1153, 2007n1254, 2008n1255, 2009n282, 2009n1244, 2009n1248
Shannon, Mike, 2008n708
Shanty, Frank G., 2008n490
Shapers of the great debate at the Constitutional Convention of 1787, 2006n431
Shapers of the great debate on conservation, 2005n1537
Shapers of the great debate on Jacksonian democracy, 2005n696
Shapers of the great debate on the Civil War, 2006n430
Shapers of the great debate on the freedom of religion, 2006n516

Shapers of the great debate on the great society, 2006n694

Shaping of America, 1783-1815: almanac, 2006n424

Shaping of America, 1783-1815: biogs, 2006n425

Shaping of America, 1783-1815: primary sources, 2006n426

Shapir, Yiftah S., 2008n656

Shapiro, Arthur M., 2008n1187

Shapiro, Fred R., 2007n48

Share, Bernard, 2005n957

Sharma, Nutan, 2009n1234

Sharma, R. N., 2008n549

Sharp, J. Michael, 2007n601

Sharp, Michael D., 2006n974

Sharpe, Charles C., 2005n797, 2007n695

Sharpe, Roderick L., 2009n1013

Shatkin, Laurence, 2007n216, 2007n217, 2007n218, 2008n244, 2008n250, 2009n226

Shaw, Robert B., 2009n1185

Shearer, Benjamin F., 2005n80, 2007n337, 2008n73, 2008n390

Sheehan, Michael J., 2009n881

Sheehan, Thomas J., 2006n1339, 2008n1159

Sheffield, Suzanne Le-May, 2006n863

Sheldon, AnnaMarie L., 2008n247

Sheldon, Brooke E., 2009n502

Sheldon, Kathleen, 2006n858

Sheldrake, Philip, 2007n1114

Shelley, Fred M., 2007n585

Shelton, Dinah L., 2005n588

Shepherd, John, 2006n1094

Sher, Julian, 2005n900

Sheridan, Susan M., 2009n255

Sheridan, Valerie S., 2005n160, 2005n712, 2006n716, 2007n141, 2007n604

Sherlock Holmes on the stage, 2009n1076

Sherman, Carol, 2007n1151

Sherman, Fraser A., 2006n995

Sherman, Josepha, 2009n1035

Sherman, Wendy R., 2005n1295

Sherow, James E., 2008n1347

Sherrin, Ned, 2006n62, 2009n51

Sherrod, Lonnie R., 2006n688, 2007n578

Sherrow, Victoria, 2007n809

Shetty, Kalidas, 2006n1286

Sheumaker, Helen, 2008n1003

Shewmaker, Eugene F., 2009n975

Shiavone, Giuseppe, 2007n634

Shideler, Dan, 2007n802

Shiers, Jessie, 2008n1190

Shifrin, Laurel, 2008n1013, 2009n1054

Shillington, Kevin, 2006n461

Shim, Jae K., 2006n155

Shine, Ossian, 2005n784

Shinn, David H., 2005n87

Ship, 2005n1551

Ship Island, Miss., 2008n388

Shipley, Graham, 2007n377

Shipp, Steve, 2006n94

Ships of the Royal Navy, rev ed, 2007n566

Shirane, Haruo, 2008n873

Shirley, Rodney, 2006n386

Shoemaker, Donald J., 2006n576

Shoemaker, Rebecca S., 2005n557

Shontz, Priscilla K., 2006n614, 2008n523

Shook, John R., 2006n1188

Short ref grammar of Iraqi Arabic, repr ed, 2005n969

Short stories for students, v.19, 2005n1054

Short stories for students, v.20, 2005n1055

Short stories for students, v.25, 2008n898

Short story index [Website], 2008n899

Short story writers, rev ed, 2008n875

Shorter Oxford English dict, 6th ed, 2008n31

Shostak, Elizabeth, 2008n433, 2008n434

Show me the money! 2006n1144

Showalter, Dennis, 2008n597

Showker, Kay, 2005n409, 2009n356

Shrock, Joel, 2005n460

Shtauber, Zvi, 2008n656

Shugart, Cooksey, 2007n807, 2008n826

Sibbick, John, 2005n1522

Sichone, Owen B., 2007n90

Sickels, Robert, 2005n1178

Sider, Sandra, 2006n470

Siefring, Judith, 2006n956

Siegal, Mark, 2005n169, 2006n148, 2006n207, 2007n145

Siegel, Barbara, 2005n1199

Siegel, Brian V., 2008n99

Siegel, Joel G., 2006n155

Siegel, Scott, 2005n1199

Siegmund, Marianne, 2006n1135

Sienkewicz, Thomas J., 2007n390, 2008n435

Sierra Club gd to the ancient forests of the NE, 2005n399

Sies, Luther F., 2009n813

Siess, Judith A., 2007n496

Sifakis, Carl, 2006n562

Signorielli, Nancy, 2006n875

Silent cinema in song, 1896-1929, 2009n1060

Silitski, Vitali, 2008n120

Silva, Jesse, 2007n483

Silver & gold mining camps of the old west, 2008n401

Silver, Linda R., 2009n931

Silverman, Harold M., 2005n1478

Silverstone, Paul H., 2007n568

Silvey, Anita, 2007n902

Simkin, Joyce P., 2006n235, 2009n184

Simmons, William A., 2009n1097

Simon, Ana Hidalgo, 2005n1435

Simon, David J., 2008n99

Simplified diet manual, 10th ed, 2008n1133

Simpson, Carol, 2007n523, 2009n561

Simpson, Jack, 2009n537

Simpson, John, 2009n891
Simpson, Ken, 2006n1375
Sinclair, Ian, 2008n1181
Singer, Paula M., 2009n510
Singhurst, Jason R., 2009n1179
Single action sixguns, 2006n906
Singleton, Paul, 2008n1142
Sinha, Reeta, 2007n508
Sink, Susan, 2009n1099
Siracusa, Joseph M., 2005n697, 2008n393
SIRC's sport quest [Website], 2005n746
SIRS researcher [Website], 2009n58
Sisler, Timothy J., 2005n1104, 2005n1105
Sisler, Timothy, 2005n1055
Sisson, Richard, 2008n69
Sisung, Kelle S., 2005n19
Sitarz, Daniel, 2005n558, 2006n152, 2006n153, 2007n234, 2007n463, 2008n235, 2008n261, 2009n233
Sittig's hndbk of toxic & hazardous chemicals & carcinogens, 5th ed, 2009n1218
Sittler, Ryan L., 2009n507
Sixties in America: almanac, 2005n416
Sixties in America: biogs, 2005n417
Sixties in America: primary sources, 2005n418
60 years of notable children's bks, 2005n1020
Sizzling summer reading programs for YAs, 2d ed, 2007n514
Sjavik, Jan, 2007n975, 2009n115
Skinner, Edward S., 2007n621
Skinny about dollies, best boys, green rooms, leads, & other media lingo, 2007n767
Skinulis, Richard, 2008n845
Sklar, Kathryn Kish, 2005n863
Skoggard, Ian, 2006n823
Skreslet, Paula Youngman, 2007n973
Skreslet, Rebecca, 2007n973
Skutsch, Carl, 2006n323
Slanguage, new ed, 2005n957
Slann, Martin, 2008n483
Slater, John G., 2005n1223
Slater, Judith J., 2005n93
Slater, Wendy, 2009n38
Slave revolts, 2009n397
Slavery in America, 2007n369
Slavery in America, 2008n419, 2008n421
Slavery in the south, 2005n454
Slavery in the US, 2008n403
Sleep disorders sourcebk, 2d ed, 2006n1438
Sleep info for teens, 2009n1250
Sloan, Jane, 2008n1029
Slocum, Perry D., 2006n1347
Slovic, Scott, 2005n1008
Slusser, John, 2005n926, 2008n823
Small business legal forms simplified, 2005n558
Small business sourcebk, 18th ed, 2005n161
Small business sourcebk, 20th ed, 2006n143

Small business sourcebk, 22d ed, 2008n163
Small business sourcebk, 24th ed, 2009n141
Small change, big problems, 2007n535
Small press record of bks in print 2008, 33d ed [CD-ROM], 2008n10
Small public lib survival gd, 2009n511
Smallwood, Carol, 2006n71
Smart, Ninian, 2009n1088
Smead, Robert N., 2005n975
Smerk, George M., 2008n1354
Smethurst, John B., 2008n226
Smiraglia, Richard P., 2007n505
Smirnov, N. N., 2005n1380
Smith, Andrew F., 2005n1301, 2008n1122, 2009n1146
Smith, Bonnie G., 2009n788
Smith, Carter, 2007n336, 2008n386
Smith, Chris, 2008n980, 2008n986
Smith, Clay, 2005n540
Smith, D. Boyd, 2008n398
Smith, Dan, 2007n119, 2009n126
Smith, Darren L., 2005n756, 2008n701
Smith, David A., 2006n733
Smith, David Horton, 2008n728
Smith, David J., 2005n185
Smith, Gary Alden, 2005n388
Smith, Gary Allen, 2005n1214
Smith, Harold E., 2006n97
Smith, Helaine L., 2006n1007, 2007n915
Smith, Henrietta M., 2005n1056
Smith-Howard, Alycia, 2006n1041
Smith, Jacqueline, 2007n1295, 2007n1309
Smith, James K. A., 2005n1229
Smith, James M., 2006n744
Smith, Jennifer, 2005n1043
Smith, Jessie Carney, 2005n331, 2007n134, 2009n297
Smith, Joseph, 2007n638
Smith, Karen Manners, 2007n368
Smith, Kerry L., 2009n1028
Smith, Margaret, 2005n1075
Smith, Merril D., 2006n558
Smith, Michael, 2005n1453
Smith, Myron J., Jr., 2007n675
Smith, Nathan, 2005n1356
Smith, Norris, 2005n550, 2006n738
Smith, Robert Barr, 2009n83
Smith, Robert D., 2008n603
Smith, Susan Sharpless, 2006n631
Smith, Tony, 2006n149
Smith, Troy E., 2007n594
Smith, William, 2007n310, 2008n993, 2009n407
Smith, William G., 2005n1215
Smith, Zachary A., 2008n1336, 2009n192, 2009n1329
Smithsonian global sound [Website], 2008n967
Smits, Jan M., 2008n501
Smoking concerns sourcebk, 2005n823
Smorodinskaya, Tatiana, 2008n127

Snelson, Pamela, 2009n503
Snodgrass, Mary Ellen, 2005n1045, 2005n1071,
        2005n1302, 2006n388, 2007n884, 2008n919,
        2009n384, 2009n962
Snow, Bonnie, 2009n1273
Snyder, Christopher A., 2009n405
Snyder, Helen, 2007n1197
Snyder, Herbert, 2007n535
Snyder, Noel, 2007n1197
Soanes, Catherine, 2005n28
Soble, Alan, 2007n711
So-called dollars, 2009n829
Soccer yrbk 2004-05, 2006n796
Social change in America, 2006, 2007n746
Social dancing in America, 2007n1039
Social issues firsthand series, 2009n66
Social issues in America, 2007n52
Social issues in lit series, 2009n917
Social panorama of Latin America 2006, 2008n138
Social policy, 2007n54
Social sci research network (SSRN) electronic lib
        [Website], 2007n49
Social sci resources in the electronic age, 2005n63
Social Security, 2008n473
Social Security, 2009n449
Social Security hndbk 2005-06, 15th ed, 2007n464
Social studies teaching activities bks, 2007n240
Social trends, no.35, 2005 ed, 2006n837
Social work dict, 5th ed, 2005n819
Sociological collection [Website], 2005n786
Sociological tour through cyberspace [Website],
        2005n789
Sociology: a Sage full-text collection [Website],
        2005n787
SocioWeb [Website], 2005n790
SocioWeb [Website], 2006n798
Soldiers' lives through hist: ancient world, 2008n593
Soldiers' lives through hist: the early modern world,
        2008n597
Soldiers' lives through hist: the Middle Ages,
        2008n595
Sole proprietorship, 2006n153
Sollars, Michael D., 2009n910
Solomon, Norman, 2008n1102
Solomon, Susan, 2008n1311
Solorzano, Lucia, 2005n287, 2007n248
Somervill, Barbara A., 2007n1298
Somigli, Luca, 2008n941
Song, Holim, 2008n1273
Song, Yongyi, 2007n371
Song, Yuwu, 2007n636
Sonn, Tamara, 2005n1274
Sonneborn, Liz, 2007n276, 2008n317, 2008n319
Sora, Joseph W., 2005n895
Sorenson, Georgia J., 2005n147
Sotheby's wine ency, 4th ed, 2008n1123
Soule, David C., 2007n754

Source, 3d ed, 2007n291
Sourcebook for genealogical research, 2005n357
Sourcebook for research in music, 2d ed, 2007n989
Sourcebook of decorative stone, 2008n1320
Sourcebook of models in biomedical research,
        2009n1212
Sourcebook of modern furniture, 3d ed, 2006n915
Sourcebook to public record info, 5th ed, 2005n709
Sourcebook to public record info, 6th ed, 2006n532
Sourcebook to public record info, 7th ed, 2007n448
Sourcebook to public record info, 9th ed, 2009n445
Sources of E Asian tradition, 2009n95
Sources of Japanese tradition, v.2, 2d ed, 2007n98
Sousa at Ill.: a catalogue of the collections, 2006n1078
South Africa's diverse peoples, 2007n90
South & meso-American mythology A to Z,
        2005n1157
South Asia 2007, 4th ed, 2008n104
South Asia 2009, 2009n98
South Asia: an environmental hist, 2009n1341
South Asian folklore, 2007n1022
South Asian lit in English, 2005n1084
Southeast Asia, 2005n92
Southeast Asia, 2008n1345
Southern, Pat, 2007n396
Southern US, 2007n1327
Southern writers, 2007n936
Sova, Dawn B., 2005n1039, 2007n869, 2007n870,
        2008n923
Sowards, Adam M., 2008n1348
Sowers, Karen M., 2009n759
Space & astronomy, 2008n1302
Space exploration: almanac, 2005n1507
Space exploration: biogs, 2005n1508
Space exploration: primary sources, 2005n1509
Space sci, 2005n1510
Space warfare & defense, 2009n603
Spacecraft launch sites worldwide, 2008n1303
Spaeth, Harold J., 2008n475
Spafford, Carol Sullivan, 2006n274
Spain 2008, 2008n377
Spain & Portugal, 2008n131
Spalding, Mark, 2009n1347
Spanish ref center [Website], 2009n23
Spanish word histories & mysteries, 2008n874
Spanu, Vlad, 2008n125
Sparkes, Brian A., 2007n384
Sparks, Kenton L., 2006n1220
Spatz, Michele, 2009n587
Speake, Jennifer, 60, 2005n472
Spears, Richard A., 2006n954, 2007n846, 2008n862
Special effects artists, 2009n1053
Speichert, Greg, 2005n1318
Speichert, Sue, 2005n1318
Speight, James G., 2006n1494, 2006n1495
Spence, Charles F., 2006n1547, 2008n1352
Spence, Ian, 2005n1319

Spence, John C. H., 2007n1229, 2008n1203
Spence, Lewis, 2005n745
Spice & herb bible, 2d ed, 2007n1154
Spies, Robert A., 2009n262
Spira, Thomas, 2006n63
Spirit bk, 2006n762
Spiro, Avron, III, 2008n685, 2009n741
Sport discus [Website], 2005n747
Sport in American culture, 2006n768
Sporting News archives [Website], 2005n748
Sporting News baseball gd 2005, 2006n781
Sporting News baseball gd 2006, 2007n683
Sporting News baseball register 2005, 2006n782
Sporting News baseball register 2007, 2007n684
Sporting News hockey gd & register 2006-07, 2007n688
Sporting News official NBA gd 2006-07, 2007n686
Sporting News pro football gd, 2005 ed, 2006n790
Sporting News pro football register, 2005 ed, 2006n791
Sports & games of the renaissance, 2005n762
Sports cinema 100 movies, 2007n1052
Sports, exercise, & fitness, 2006n766
Sports in America, 2005n753
Sports injuries gdbk, 2009n1271
Sports injuries info for teens, 2d ed, 2009n1269
Sports market place dir 2004, 2005n758
Sports market place dir 2005, 2006n771
Sports market place dir 2006, 2007n673
Sports market place dir 2007, 2008n702
Sports market place dir 2008, 2009n718
Sports market place dir [Website], 2005n759
Sports market place dir [Website], 2006n772
Sports market place dir [Website], 2007n674
Sports medicine, 2008n1258
Sports museums & halls of fame worldwide, 2006n769
Sports sci hndbk, 2006n1455
Spratford, Becky Siegel, 2005n1050
Spratto, George R., 2005n1475, 2006n1457, 2007n1279
Sprinchorn, Evert, 2008n1039
Spring training hndbk, 2005n769
Springhouse nurse's drug gd, 7th ed, 2006n1458
Spurgin, Earl W., 2009n1084
St. Amant, Kirk, 2008n1278
St. Clair, Anthony, 2006n716, 2007n141
St. John, Ronald Bruce, 2007n87
St. Petersburg, new ed, 2006n412
Stableford, Brian, 2005n1051, 2006n1026, 2006n1027, 2007n1139
Stackhouse, Jennifer, 2009n1188
Staff of U.S. News & World Report, 2005n305
Staffing the modern lib, 2006n634
Staikos, Konstantinos, 2005n637, 2007n531
Stair, Leslie, 2006n258
Stair, Lila B., 2006n258
Stallaerts, Robert, 2008n118

Stan Getz, 2005n1128
Standard & Poor's MidCap 400 gd, 2003 ed, 2005n174
Standard & Poor's small cap 600 gd, 2003 ed, 2005n175
Standard catalog of …
    firearms 2004, 14th ed, 2005n923
    firearms 2005, 15th ed, 2006n905
    military firearms 1870 to the present, 2d ed, 2005n924
    military firearms, 3d ed, 2007n804
    world coins, 2006, 33d ed, 2006n902
    world coins, 2009, 2009n831
    world coins: 1901-2000, 34th ed, 2007n800
    world coins: 2001-date 2009, 3d ed, 2009n830
    world paper money, 14th ed, 2009n832
Standard ency of carnival glass price gd, 16th ed, 2009n816
Standard ency of carnival glass, 11th ed, 2009n815
Standard ency of pressed glass 1860-1930, 4th ed, 2006n898
Standard ency of pressed glass 1860-1930, 5th ed, 2007n794
Standard gd to American muscle cars, 4th ed, 2006n1551
Standard hndbk for electrical engineers, 15th ed, 2007n1225
Standard knife collector's gd, 5th ed, 2007n806
Standard per dir 2004, 27th ed, 2005n58
Standard per dir 2008, 31st ed, 2009n46
Stander, Leo, 2009n1342
Standish, Peter, 2005n121
Stanford, Claire, 2008n735
Stanford, Michael, 2005n325
Stangroom, Jeremy, 2005n1226
Stanley, Brian, 2007n1116
Stanley, Bruce E., 2007n122, 2008n143
Stanley, Harold W., 2006n734, 2007n622, 2008n651
Staples, William G., 2007n443, 2008n467
Stars & stripes on screen, 2006n1145
Start-up at the new Met, 2008n978
State & natl boundaries of the US, 2005n388
State & regional assns of the US 2008, 2009n33
State constitutions of the US, 2d ed, 2006n543
State houses, 2006n933
State of China atlas, 2006n90
State of health atlas, 2009n1221
State of the environ in Asia & the Pacific 2005, 2008n1349
State of the Middle East, 2007n119
State of the Middle East, updated 2d ed, 2009n126
State of the Union, 2007n624
State of the wild 2006, 2007n1334
State of working America 2004/05, 2006n151
State of working America 2006-07, 2008n236
State profiles, 3d ed, 2007n736
State rankings 2005, 16th ed, 2006n843

State rankings 2006, 2007n747
State rankings 2007, 2008n765
State rankings 2008, 2009n775
State trends, 2005n849
State trends, 2d ed, 2006n844
State trends, 3d ed, 2007n748
State trends, 4th ed, 2009n776
State yellow bk, Summer 2005, 2006n712
State yellow bk, 2008 ed, 2009n650
State, Paul F., 2005n107, 2009n409
Statesman's yrbk 2004, 140th ed, 2005n70
Statesman's yrbk 2006, 2006n64
Statesman's yrbk 2008, 2008n63
Statistical abstract of the US 2003, 123d ed, 2005n850
Statistical abstract of the US 2004-05, 124th ed,
    2007n749
Statistical abstract of the US 2007, 126th ed, 2008n766
Statistical abstract: geography & environment
    [Website], 2008n356
Statistical abstracts of the US 2009, 128th ed,
    2009n777
Statistical ency of N American professional sports, 2d
    ed, 2008n698
Statistical hndbk on the social safety net, 2006n819
Statistical indicators for Asia & the Pacific, v.34,
    2006n838
Statistical yrbk 2001, 48th ed, 2005n843
Statistical yrbk 2002-04, 49th ed, 2006n839
Statistical yrbk, 50th ed, 2008n760
Statistical yrbk for Asia & the Pacific 2003, 2006n216
Statistics sources 2005, 28th ed, 2005n844
Statistics sources 2006, 29th ed, 2006n840
Statistics sources 2008, 31st ed, 2008n761
Stavans, Ilan, 2006n350
Stebbins, Robert A., 2008n728
Stec, David M., 2005n1251
Steed, Jonathan W., 2005n1493
Steele, Paul R., 2005n1169
Steele, Valerie, 2005n928
Steen, M. F., 2006n1128
Steen, Michael, 2005n1133
Steiger, Brad, 2007n1030
Steiger, Sherry, 2007n1030
Stein, Erwin, 2006n1393
Stein, Marc, 2005n804
Stein, Richard Joseph, 2009n1344
Steinberg, Shirley, 2007n719
Steinberg, Shirley R., 2006n102
Steiner, Sarah K., 2009n583
Steingold, Fred S., 2007n465, 2007n487
Steinmetz, Sol, 2007n824
Steinway collection, repr ed, 2006n935
Stem cell research, 2008n1146
Stentiford, Barry M., 2009n302
Stephens, Otis H., 2006n546
Stephens, Otis H., Jr., 2007n490
Sterling, Christopher H., 2005n909, 2008n594

Stern, H. Amy, 2006n724, 2007n611
Stern, Pamela R., 2005n343
Stern, Steven B., 2008n365
Sternberg, Guy, 2005n1371
Sternberg, Robert J., 2007n664
Sternlicht, Sanford, 2006n1008
Stern's gd to the cruise vacation 2008, 2008n365
Steven, Graeme C. S., 2005n583
Stevens, Alan M., 2005n973
Stevens, Jen, 2006n996
Stevenson, Angus, 2005n28
Stevenson, L. Harold, 2008n1339
Stevenson, Tom, 2008n1123
Steverson, Leonard A., 2008n495
Stewart, Chuck, 2005n806
Stewart, Jeffrey C., 2007n275
Stewart, John, 2006n1173, 2007n626
Stewart, Kevin G., 2008n1321
Stewart, Ron, 2007n806
Stewart, William, 2008n954, 2009n698
Sticklers, sideburns & bikinis, 2009n892
Stierman, Jeanne Koekkoek, 2009n1013
Still, Brian, 2008n1278
Stilwell, Alexander, 2009n729
Stock, Jennifer York, 2006n420, 2006n421, 2006n422,
    2007n326, 2007n327, 2007n328
Stockwell, Foster, 2005n357
Stokes, Lisa Odham, 2008n1022
Stokstad, Marilyn, 2006n513
Stoll, Malaika, 2005n299
Stolley, Kathy S., 2006n799
Stone, Carol Leth, 2005n1342
Stone, Sally, 2009n861
Stone the crows: Oxford dict of modern slang, 2d ed,
    2009n891
Stone, Thomas Ryan, 2006n1183
Stoner, Katherine E., 2007n460
Stookey, Lorena, 2005n1170
Stooksbury, Kara E., 2007n490
Stoppani, Jim, 2008n700
Stoppato, Marco, 2005n1520
Storey, John W., 2008n1066
Storey's illus breed gd to sheep, goats, cattle, & pigs,
    2009n1168
Storey's illus gd to poultry breeds, 2008n1175
Storrer, William Allin, 2007n818
Story behind the song, 2005n1142
Story celebrations, 2009n553
Storytelling, 2009n1035
Stout, Daniel A., 2008n1053
Stow, Dorrik, 2007n1313
Stoyan, Ronald, 2009n1303
Straley, Dona S., 2006n1064
Strategic business letters & e-mail, 2005n272
Strategic planning for results, 2009n514
Straus, Alex, 2007n1261
Straus, Eugene W., 2007n1261

Strauss's hndbk of business info, 2d ed, 2005n136
Strawser, Cornelia J., 2005n169, 2006n148, 2007n145, 2008n168, 2009n144
Strazny, Philipp, 2006n939
Street, Seán, 2007n783
Streisel, Jim, 2008n803
Streissguth, Tom, 2008n422
Stress info for teens, 2009n1251
Stress-related disorders sourcebk, 2d ed, 2008n693
Stretching anatomy, 2009n736
Strickland, John, 2005n527
Strickland, Ruth Ann, 2009n668
Stringer, Jenny, 2009n971
Stripling, Mahala Yates, 2006n1012
Strmiska, Michael F., 2006n1215
Stroke sourcebk, 2d ed, 2009n1252
Strokoff, Sandra L., 2008n476
Stroman, James, 2009n240
Struglinski, Suzanne, 2008n630
Strunk, William, Jr., 2006n887
Stuart, David, 2005n1330
Stuart-Fox, Martin, 2009n102
Stuart, Paul H., 2006n818
Stuart, Sally E., 2006n880, 2008n797
Stubben, Jerry D., 2006n339
Stubbendieck, James, 2005n1355
Stubblefield, R. Jay, 2007n967
Student almanac of Asian American hist, 2005n338
Student atlas, 3d ed, 2005n379
Student companion to Thomas Hardy, 2008n932
Student ency of African lit, 2009n979
Student plagiarism in an online world, 2008n540
Student's A-Z of psychology, 2007n655
Student's ency of American literary characters, 2009n957
Student's ency of Judaism, 2005n1277
Student's gd to Congress, 2009n666
Student's gd to earth sci, 2005n1500
Student's gd to elections, 2009n667
Study abroad 2004-05, 32d ed, 2005n312
Study abroad 2006, 13th ed, 2006n313
Study of agricultural geography, 2006n1280
Stueart, Robert D., 2008n550
Stuppy, Wolfgang, 2009n1184
Sturtevant, William C., 2005n345, 2008n327
Su, Di, 2007n519
Suad, Joseph, 2006n854
Subject access to a multilingual museum database, 2009n540
Subject dir of special libs, 34th ed, 2009n499
Subject dir of special libs & info centers 29th ed, 2005n599
Submarines, 2008n605
Sub-Saharan Africa, 2007n1331
Succeeding as an intl student in the US & Canada, 2009n276

Success with rhododendrons & azaleas, rev ed, 2005n1329
Successful academic librarian, 2007n501
Suellentrop, Tricia, 2005n619
Suffragists in lit for youth, 2007n898
Sugano, Alan, 2005n1484
Sugita, Yoneyuki, 2008n666
Suid, Lawrence H., 2006n1145
Suleiman, Michael W., 2008n312
Sullivan, K. D., 2007n772, 2008n871
Sullivan, Larry E., 2006n518
Sullivan, Lawrence R., 2008n108
Sullivan, Lisa, 2009n1224
Sullivan, Megan, 2009n1140
Sullivan, Michael, 2006n623
Sullivan, Thomas F. P., 2007n488, 2009n481
Summer jobs abroad 2005, 36th ed, 2006n242
Summer opportunities for kids & teenagers 2006, 2006n282
Summer theatre dir 2004, 2005n1221
Summer theatre dir 2005, 2006n1177
Summerfield, Carol, 2006n837
Summers, Claude J., 2005n938, 2005n1181, 2007n1048
Sumner, Ray, 2005n384
Sun, Dajin D., 2007n509
Sundem, Garth, 2009n263
Suny, Ronald Grigor, 2008n438
Super, John C., 2006n441, 2006n444, 2006n664, 2007n360
Superhero bk, 2005n1173
Supernatural lit of the world, 2007n932
Supervillain bk, 2007n1031
Supervising staff, 2007n536
Supplement to Ralph Waldo Emerson, 2007n950
Supplement to The Modern Ency of Russian, Soviet & Eurasian Hist, v.5, 2006n480
Supreme Court A to Z, 4th ed, 2007n446
Supreme Court compendium, 4th ed, 2008n475
Supreme Court of the US, 3d ed, 2009n458
Surgery sourcebk, 2d ed, 2009n1253
Surina, Asele, 2006n1291
Surratt, Brian E., 2006n617
Sutter, Robert, 2006n745, 2007n639
Sutton, Amy L., 2005n1452, 2005n1456, 2005n1460, 2006n1435, 2006n1438, 2006n1443, 2006n1452, 2007n715, 2007n1270, 2007n1275, 2008n693, 2008n706, 2009n1252, 2009n1253, 2009n1257, 2009n1258
Sutton, Robert P., 2006n801
Suzuki, Lisa A., 2008n686
Svarney, Thomas E., 2005n1519, 2006n1531
Svendsen, Clive N., 2009n1171
Swabey, ffiona, 2005n491
Swain, Joseph P., 2007n1016
Swain, Shurlee, 2007n104

Swaine, Rick, 2006n783

Swan, James, 2005n603

Swan, Wallace, 2005n805

Swartout, Kristy, 2005n230, 2007n193

Swartz, Jon D., 2008n805

Swedin, Eric G., 1263, 2006n1481

Sweet, Kathleen M., 2006n1546

Sweetman, Jack, 2005n675

Swierczynski, Duane, 2005n569

Swingin' on the ether waves, 2006n890

Switala, Kristin, 2006n850

Symphonic etudes, 2008n974

Symphonic repertoire, v.3, pt.A, 2008n976

Symphonic repertoire, v.3, pt.B, 2008n975

Syon, Guillaume de, 2009n1141

Syvertsen, Amy K., 2006n688, 2007n578

Szajkowski, Bogdan, 2005n693, 2006n687

Szeman, Imre, 2005n1005, 2009n913

Szucs, Loretto Dennis, 2007n291

Taaffe, Gerard, 2005n1314

Tabachnick, Stephen E., 2005n503

Tabak, John, 2005n1534

Tablet PCs in K-12 educ, 2009n264

Tackett, Timothy, 2008n1086

Taffin, John, 2006n906

Taft court, 2005n555

Taher, Mohamed, 2007n1087

Taitz, Emily, 2008n447

Takaya, Sadayoshi, 2008n171

Tales online [Website], 2009n1029

Talk the talk: the slang of 65 American subcultures,
    2008n867

Tanenhaus, David S., 2009n438

Taniar, David, 2008n1271

Tanks, 2005n681

Tanton, James, 2006n1527

Tap, Bruce, 2006n430

Tappenden, Curtis, 2006n925

Targum of Psalms, 2005n1251

Taruskin, Richard, 2005n1127

Tarver, H. Micheal, 2006n109

Tasman, Allan, 2007n1283

Tassie, Gregor, 2006n1083

Tate, C. Neal, 2006n685

Tate, Cindy L., 2005n549

Tate, Mary Jo, 2008n917

Tate, W. Randolph, 2007n1098

Tatnall, Arthur, 2008n1282

Tattersall, Ian, 2007n261

Tatum, Charles M., 2007n972

Tavani, Herman T., 2009n1287

Taylor, Allan, 2007n224, 2007n225, 2008n251,
    2009n228

Taylor, Barbara Lea, 2005n1365

Taylor, Bron, 2009n1090

Taylor, Bron R., 2006n1208

Taylor, John B., 2005n559

Taylor, Karen L., 2008n940

Taylor, Katrina D., 2009n1329

Taylor, Larissa Juliet, 2006n490, 2006n493,
    2007n404, 2007n409

Taylor, Mayo R., 2005n1142

Taylor, Rodney L., 2006n1198

Taylor, Scott D., 2007n91

Taylor, Steve, 2005n1141

Taylor, Todd, 2007n780

Teachers in the movies, 2008n1027

Teaching bks [Website], 2007n905

Teaching lib media skills in grades K-6, 2005n610

Teaching literacy, 2009n508

Teaching students with learning disabilities, 2009n283

Teaching with bks that heal, 2009n936

Team-by-team ency of major league baseball,
    2007n680

Teams in lib tech servs, 2007n544

Tebbitt, mark, 2009n1160

TechInfoSource [Website], 2006n1464

Technology & the school lib, 2007n503

Technology for results, 2006n600

Technology made simple, 2007n528

Ted Williams, 2005n767

Teen bk discussion groups @ the lib, 2005n618

Teen gds to environmental sci, 2005n1544

Teen girls & tech, 2009n550

Teen health & wellness [Website], 2007n1235

Teen life in Africa, 2005n83

Teen life in Asia, 2005n93

Teen life in Europe, 2006n102

Teen reader's advisor, 2007n513

Teen spaces, 2d ed, 2009n576

Teens & libs, 2005n621

Teen's gds series, 2008n739

Telecommunications & data communications hndbk,
    2008n1283

Telecommunications dir, 14th ed, 2005n1491

Telecommunications dir, 17th ed, 2008n1284

Telecommunications fact bk & illus dict, 2d ed,
    2006n1487

Television characters, 2006n1137

Television fright films of the 1970s, 2008n1024

Television game show hosts, 2008n1012

Television in American society: almanac, 2007n787

Television in American society: biogs, 2007n788

Television in American society: primary sources,
    2007n789

Television variety shows, 2006n1139

Telgen, Diane, 2006n547

Temperate forests, rev ed, 2008n1314

Tempting tropicals, 2006n1332

10 best of everything: an ultimate gd for travelers,
    2007n317

10 langs you'll need most in the classroom, 2009n263
Tenenbaum, Gershon, 2008n689
Tennessee Williams ency, 2005n1036
Tenth bk of jr authors & illustrators, 2009n934
Terborg-Penn, Rosalyn, 2007n273
Terrace, Vincent, 2006n1137, 2008n1023, 2009n1065
Terranova, Florence, 2005n693
Territories of the Russian Federation 2007, 8th ed,
    2008n128
Terrorism, 2005n578
Terrorism, 2006n566
Terrorism, 2007n484
Terrorism 2005-07, 2009n463
Terrorism & global security, 2008n675
Tesar, Jenny, 2005n54, 2005n1285
Tests, 6th ed, 2009n707
Teulings, Robert P., 2007n1195
Tevis, Brenda, 2006n1166
Tevis, Ray, 2006n1166
Texas almanac 2006-07, 2006n75
Texas almanac 2008-09, 64th, 2009n82
Texas league in baseball, 1888-1958, 2005n770
Texas starwatch, 2008n1300
Texas water atlas, 2009n1326
Thackeray, Frank W., 2005n489, 2006n472
Thailand, 2006n96
Thain, M., 2006n1316
Thames & Hudson dict of ancient Egypt, 2007n400
Thames & Hudson dict of design since 1900, 2d ed,
    2006n922
Thames & Hudson dict of fashion & fashion designers,
    2d ed, 2009n845
Thanksgiving bk, 2008n1001
Theater mania gd to musical theater recordings,
    2006n1174
Theatre as human interaction, 2006n1179
Thebe, Phenyo C., 2007n84
Thelen, Laurie Noble, 2005n613
Thematic gd to biblical lit, 2008n1072
Thematic gd to popular nonfiction, 2007n976
Thematic gd to world mythology, 2005n1170
Thematic gd to YA lit, 2007n914
Theodor de Bry's engravings of Native American life
    [Website], 2005n341
Theodore, Louis, 2009n1342
Theoharis, Athan, 2007n605
Theological dict of the O.T., v.14, 2005n1249
Theological dict of the O.T., v.15, 2007n1099
Theories for everything, 2007n1146
Therrien, Patricia, 2009n1236
Thesaurus of psychological index terms, 10th ed,
    2006n761
These are the names: studies in Jewish onomastics,
    v.4, 2005n351
TheStreet.com ratings' consumer box set, 2008 ed,
    2009n158

TheStreet.com ratings' gd to …
    banks & thrifts, Fall 2007, 2008n182
    banks & thrifts, Spring 2008, 2009n170
    bond & money market mutual funds, Summer 2007,
        2008n176
    bond & money market mutual funds, Spring 2008,
        2009n151
    common stocks, Summer 2007, 2008n177
    common stocks, Spring 2008, 2009n152
    exchange-traded funds, Summer 2007, 2008n178
    exchange-traded funds, Spring 2008, 2009n153
    health insurers, Summer 2007, 2008n210
    health insurers, Spring 2008, 2009n187
    life & annuity insurers, Fall 2007, 2008n211
    life & annuity insurers, Spring 2008, 2009n188
    property & casualty insurers, Fall 2007, 2008n212
    property & casualty insurers, Spring 2008,
        2009n189
    stock mutual funds, Summer 2007, 2009n154
TheStreet.com ratings' ultimate guided tour of stock
    investing, 2008n175
Think tank dir, 2d ed, 2008n673
Thinker's thesaurus, 2007n856
Thirteen colonies series, 2006n458
Thiry, Christopher J. J., 2006n384, 2007n309
This day in American hist, 3d ed, 2009n369
This day in network radio, 2009n812
THOMAS: legislative info on the Internet [Website],
    2008n637
Thomas, Alan, 2008n674
Thomas, Alastair H., 2009n111
Thomas, Andrew R., 2009n1348
Thomas, Carol G., 2006n514
Thomas, Clive S., 2005n728
Thomas, Cullen, 2005n724
Thomas food & beverage market place 2005, 4th ed,
    2006n185
Thomas food & market place online [Website],
    2006n186
Thomas, Jay C., 2008n683
Thomas, P., 2009n1270
Thomas, Rebecca L., 2006n997, 2006n998, 2009n921,
    2009n924
Thommasen, Harvey, 2005n1390
Thompson, Bruce E. R., 2007n469
Thompson, Clifford, 2005n21, 2007n15
Thompson, John, 2007n342
Thompson, Peter, 2005n404
Thompson, Roger, 2009n952
Thompson, Sally Anne, 2005n1020
Thompson, William N., 2006n340
Thoms, Peg, 2008n152
Thomsen, Natasha, 2008n786
Thomson, Ashley, 2008n938
Thomson, David, 2007n1040
Thomson, Peter, 2006n1178

Thorburn, John E., Jr., 2006n1005
Thorpe, Holly, 2008n697
Thrane, Susan W., 2006n933
300 astronomical objects, 2007n1306
300 best jobs without a 4-yr degree, 2d ed, 2007n217
Thursby, Jacqueline S., 2009n1154
Thyen, O., 2006n968
Thyroid disorders sourcebk, 2006n1453
Tibayrenc, Michel, 2008n1226
Tibbetts, John C., 2006n1151
Tice, Janet, 2006n397
Tiedemann, Arthur E., 2007n98
Tierney, Lawrence M., Jr., 2007n1255
Tietenberg, Tom, 2007n1330
Tillman, Barrett, 2005n660
Tilstone, William J., 2007n472
Timber Press pocket gd to …
    bulbs, 2006n1300
    clematis, 2007n1159
    ground covers, 2007n1160
    ornamental grasses, 2005n1368
    palms, 2009n1187
    shade perennials, 2006n1299
Timblin, Stephen, 2005n782
Timeless Earth, 2009n348
Timelines of hist, 2006n495
Timelines of sci & tech, 2007n1132
Timelines on file: nations & states, updated ed,
    2007n415
Timmons, Todd, 2006n1273
Tischler, Nancy M., 2007n1100, 2008n1072
Titanic in print & on screen, 2006n1133
Tobacco in hist & culture, 2005n824
Tobacco info for teens, 2008n736
Tobias, Russell R., 2007n1302
Tobin, Kathleen A., 2005n734
Todd, Deborah, 2006n1503
Todd, Robert B., 2006n865
Toedt, John, 2006n1497
Toensmeier, Eric, 2009n1156
Toft, Marie C., 2005n988
Toho studios story, 2009n1067
Tokyo, 2006n403
Toll-free phone bk USA 2005, 9th ed, 2005n42
Toll-free phone bk USA 2006, 10th ed, 2006n41
Toll-free phone bk USA 2007, 11th ed, 2007n36
Toll-free phone bk USA 2008, 12th ed, 2008n41
Tomaiuolo, Nicholas G., 2005n1488
Tomaselli, Valerie, 2005n714
Tomassini, Christine, 2005n1212
Tomei, Lawrence, 2008n269
Tomei, Lawrence A., 2009n1282
Tomelleri, Joseph, 2009n1202
Tomelleri, Joseph R., 2005n1392
Tomlins, Christopher, 2006n548
Tong, Benson, 2005n336
Tools, 2006n913

Tools & techniques for character interpretation,
    2007n1038
Toomer, Simon, 2006n1354
Toomey, Mary, 2007n1159
Toor, Ruth, 2008n516
Top careers in 2 yrs series, 2008n252
Top 100: the fastest growing careers for the 21st
    century, 4th ed, 2009n229
Top 10 of everything 2006, 2006n51
Top 300 careers, 10th ed, 2007n204
Toro-Morn, Maura I., 2005n832
Torstrick, Rebecca L., 2005n128
TOS hndbk of Tex. birds, 2005n1387
Totten, Samuel, 2009n474
Tourist trains gdbk, 2008n367
Toussaint-Samat, Maguilonne, 2009n1155
Toward a 21st-century school lib media program,
    2008n517
Towe, L. Clarence, 2005n1331
Toys & prices, 12th ed, 2005n927
Tozer, Frank, 2009n1161, 2009n1162, 2009n1163
Tracing your Irish Ancestors, 3d ed, 2007n289
Tracing your Scottish ancestry, 3d ed, 2005n359
Tracy, Nicholas, 2005n672
Trade & dvlpmt report, 2005, 2006n206
Trade & dvlpmt report, 2007, 2008n215
Trade assns & professional bodies of Continental
    Europe, 2005 ed, 2005n221
Trade assns & professional bodies of the Continental
    European Union, 5th ed, 2009n202
Trade shows worldwide, 20th ed, 2005n258
Trade shows worldwide, 22d ed, 2006n267
Trade shows worldwide, 23d ed, 2008n257
Traditional festivals, 2006n1124
Trager, Oliver, 2006n1111
Trahair, Richard C. S., 2005n664
Training paraprofessionals for ref serv, 2d ed,
    2009n586
Transition to postsecondary educ for students with
    disabilities, 2009n281
Transitioning to college [Website], 2009n272
Trans-Mississippi West 1804-1912, 2009n361
Trauth, Eileen M., 2007n1287
Travel gd to the Jewish Caribbean & Latin America,
    2005n408
Travel gd to the Plains Indian wars, 2007n320
Traver, Elizabeth Kim Jin, 2006n237
Travers, Len, 2008n998
Treas, Judith, 2006n806
Treasury of black quotations, 2006n331
Treaties & alliances of the world, 8th ed, 2009n675
Treaties & intl agreements online [Website], 2008n502
Treaties with American Indians, 2008n326
Tree ferns, 2005n1374
Trees, 2009n1188
Trees for the small garden, 2006n1354
Trees of Guatemala, 2009n1186

Trees of the Calif. landscape, 2008n1161
Trees, shrubs, & vines of the Texas Hill Country, 2006n1358
Trehane, Jennifer, 2005n1332
Treier, Daniel J., 2007n1097
Trelawny, John G., 2006n1346
Tresidder, Jack, 2006n920
TreviZo, Rose Zertuche, 2007n906
Tribal art, 2007n791
Tribal libs in the US, 2008n508
Trigg, George L., 2007n1317
Trim, Mary, 2005n620
Trinkle, Dennis A., 2007n427
Tritle, Lawrence, 2005n493
Trivia lover's lists of nearly everything in the universe, 2007n41
Trojan War, 2006n514
Tropical & subtropical trees, 2005n1369
Tropical forests, 2008n1316
Tropical plants of Costa Rica, 2008n1152
Trott, Barry, 2009n943
Trotta, Marcia, 2007n536, 2009n536
Trotter, Patrick, 2009n1202
Troutman, Kathryn Kraemer, 2008n237
Trudeau, Lawrence J., 1009, 2005n1107
True, James L., 2006n735
Truman yrs, 2006n700
Trupe, Alice, 2007n914
Truth about series, 2005n827
Tryphonopoulos, Demetres P., 2006n1068
Tsur (Mansoor), Samuel A., 2005n1434
Tsutsui, William M., 2007n372
Tucker, Cory, 2007n508
Tucker, Elizabeth, 2006n1117, 2009n1033
Tucker, Karen B. Westerfield, 2006n1237
Tucker, Martha A., 2006n1524
Tucker, Spencer C., 2005n681, 2006n497, 2006n498, 2006n505, 2006n506, 2007n426, 2008n580, 2008n583, 2009n127, 2009n605
Tuffelli, Nicole, 2006n926
Tulips, 2007n1163
Tulloch, Alexander, 2006n949
Tullock, John, 2006n1310
TumbleBooks [Website], 2009n932
Tumielewicz, P. J., 2005n1221, 2006n1177
Tundra, 2008n1317
Turabian, Kate L., 2008n801
Turk, Eleanor L., 2005n105
Turkington, Carol, 2005n1459, 2005n1463, 2005n1464, 2005n1465, 2006n1447, 2006n1451, 2007n203, 2007n257, 2007n1269, 2007n1276, 2008n1232
Turner, Alan, 2005n1383
Turner, Barry, 2005n70
Turner, Bryan S., 2008n715
Turner, Jeffrey S., 2009n748
Turner, Michael A., 2006n663, 2007n559

Turner, Samuel M., 2009n708
Turner, Thomas R., 2008n423
TV yr, v.1, 2008n1033
TV.com [Website], 2006n1157
Twagilimana, Aimable, 2008n98
Twentieth century China, 2005n95
Twentieth-century countertenor repertoire, 2009n1012
Twentieth-century literary criticism, v.149, 2005n991
Twentieth-century literary criticism, v.150, 2005n992
Twentieth-century literary criticism, v.151, 2005n993
Twentieth-century short story explication new series, v.6, 2005n1052
Twentieth century US photographers, 2009n867
200 best jobs for college graduates, 3d ed, 2007n200
200 Tex. Outlaws & lawmen 1835-1935, 2009n83
250 essential Chinese characters for everyday use, 2005n971
Two Koreas, 2005n99
Two oceans, 2009n1208
2006 ESPN baseball ency, 2007n685
225 best jobs for baby boomers, 2007n219
Two-yr colleges 2005, 36th ed, 2006n299
Tyler, Colin, 2006n1205
Tyler, Don, 2008n971
Tyrl, Ronald J., 2006n1337
Tyrrell, Ian R., 2005n820
Tyson, Cynthia A., 2009n256
Tzeel, Albert, 2005n1459

Ubelaker, Douglas H., 2008n327
Udoh, Fabian E., 2008n1087
Uebelhor, Tracy S., 2006n700
Ulmer, Torsten, 2005n1358
Ulrich's per dir 2005, 44th ed, 2006n56
Ulrich's per dir [Website], 2006n57
Ulrich's per dir [Website], 2008n52
Ultimate accountants' ref, 2d ed, 2008n173
Ultimate field gd to photography, 2007n821
Ultimate film festival survival gd, 3d ed, 2005n1201
Ultimate gd to medical schools, 2006n291
Ultimate hunting dog ref bk, 2007n1201
Ultimate mystery/detective Web gd [Website], 2005n1049
Unbound Bible [Website], 2007n1095
Uncloudy days: the gospel music ency, 2007n1015
UNCTAD hndbk of stats 2003, 2005n845
UNCTAD hndbk of stats 2004, 2006n841
UNCTAD hndbk of stats 2006-07, 2008n762
Undergraduate's companion to Arab writers & their Web Sites, 2006n1064
Undergraduate's companion to children's writer & their Web sites, 2006n996
Undergraduate's companion to English Renaissance writers & their Web sites, 2005n1074

Undergraduate's companion to women poets of the world & their Web sites, 2005n1101

Underground Railroad, 2009n384

Understanding American business jargon, 2d ed, 2006n121

Understanding architecture, 2005n946

Understanding info systems, 2005n632

Understanding Islam & Muslim traditions, 2005n1273

Understanding Melville's short fiction, 2006n1038

Understanding the lit of WW I, 2006n987

Understanding the pipe organ, 2009n1014

Underwood, Lamar, 2006n667

Unearthing the past, 2007n322

Unexplained: an ency of curious phenomena, 2008n695

Unfinished business: race, equity, & diversity in lib & info sci educ, 2006n615

Unger, Harlow G., 2008n263

Uniform numbers of the NFL, 2006n788

Uniform titles for music, 2009n533

Uniforms, arms, & equipment, 2008n607

United Nations system, 2006n739

United States as depicted on its postage stamps, 2008n824

United States at war, 2006n664

United States at war [Website], 2009n607

United States election system, 2005n720

United States foreign trade highlights, 2006n207

United States foreign trade highlights 2007, 2d ed, 2008n216

United States geography [Website], 2009n338

United States govt Internet manual 2003-04, 2005n710

United States govt Internet manual 2004-05, 2006n713

United States govt Internet manual 2005-06, 2007n602

United States govt Internet manual 2007, 2008n638

United States govt Internet manual 2008, 2009n651

United States Holocaust Memorial Museum [Website], 2008n448

United States Marine Corps Generals of WWII, 2009n612

United States Marine Corps Medal of Honor recipients, 2006n668

United States presidential primary election 2000-04, 2007n609

United States Supreme Court, 549, 2006n548

United States west coast, 2008n1348

Uniting states, 2005n80

Universal horrors, 2d ed, 2008n1030

University of Maryland men's basketball games, 2009n724

University of N.C. men's basketball games, 2008n710

University of Va. men's basketball games, 2009n725

Unnatural phenomena, 2006n763

Unpublished ms in British idealism, 2006n1205

Unreasonable searches & seizures, 2006n546

Uozumi, Yasuhiro, 2009n1297

Upchurch, Thomas Adams, 2005n334

UPI stylebk & gd to newswriting, 4th ed, 2005n896

Upson, Tim, 2005n1351

Upton, Clive, 2005n956

Upton, Eben, 2005n956

Upton, Graham, 2009n773

Upton, James Nathaniel, 2008n301

Urban ants of N America & Europe, 2009n1203

Urban educ, 2005n276

Urban sprawl, 2007n754

Urbanic, Allan, 2006n611

Urdang, Laurence, 2009n886

Urinary tract & kidney diseases & disorders sourcebk, 2d ed, 2006n1433

Urofsky, Melvin I., 2005n534, 2007n440, 2007n461, 2008n464, 2009n436

U.S. coin digest 2006, 2006n903

U.S. coin digest 2009, 7th ed, 2009n833

U.S. Constitution A to Z, 2d ed, 2009n439

US destroyers, rev ed, 2005n678

U.S. govt manual [Website], 2008n639

US Homeland Security, 2007n644

U.S. immigration & migration: almanac, 2005n836

U.S. immigration & migration: biogs, 2005n837

U.S. immigration & migration: primary sources, 2005n838

U.S. industry & market outlook 2007, 2008n209

U.S. legal system, 2005n536

US military serv, 2008n598

U.S. natl debate topic 2004-05: the United Nations, 2005n724

U.S. natl debate topic 2005-06: US civil liberties, 2006n550

U.S. natl debate topic 2006-07: natl service, 2007n648

U.S. natl debate topic 2007-08: health care in Sub-Saharan Africa, 2008n1222

U.S. natl debate topic 2008-09: alternative energy, 2009n1330

US natl parks west, 2006n398

U.S. natl security, 2d ed, 2008n652

U.S. News & World Report ultimate college dir, 2004 ed, 2005n305

U.S. News & World Report ultimate college dir, 2007 ed, 2007n249

U.S. News & World Report ultimate gd to becoming a teacher, 2006n279

U.S. News & World Report ultimate gd to medical schools, 2d ed, 2008n283

US presidents & foreign policy, 2007n592

US presidents factbk, 2007n613

US social security, 2009n453

U.S. Supreme Court, 2008n469

USA: the new south, 2005n400

USA & Canada 2008, 2009n70

USA fifties, 2006n445

USA in space, 2007n1302

USA Patriot Act of 2001, 2005n542

USA twenties, 2005n435

USA.gov [Website], 2008n640
USCivilWar.Net [Website], 2005n419
User's gd to Sears list of subject headings, 2009n543
Uses of wild plants, 2009n1162
USGS educ resources for teachers [Website], 2008n1322
Using benchmarking, needs assessment, quality improvement, outcome measurement, & lib standards, 2008n520
Using lit to help troubled teenagers cope with abuse issues, 2005n1031
Using picture story bks to teach literary devices, v.4, 2009n923
Using the engineering lit, 2008n1195
Using XML, 2008n533
Uthappa, Mangerira C., 2009n1241
Utter, Glenn H., 2006n735, 2008n676, 2008n1066, 2009n668
U*X*L ency of …
    drugs & addictive substances, 2007n718
    landforms & other geologic features, 2005n1517
    US hist, 2009n385
    water sci, 2005n1539
    weather & natural disasters, 2008n1310
    world mythology, 2009n1036
U*X*L graphic novelists, 2007n910
U*X*L newsmakers, 2005n19

Vaddhanaphuti, Nantiya, 2006n1348
Vaidya, Ashish K., 2007n180
Valelly, Richard M., 2007n466
Valentine, Rebecca, 2005n837, 2007n329, 2007n330, 2007n331, 2009n385
Valli, Clayton, 2007n852
Value of a dollar, 3d ed, 2005n170
Value of a dollar: Colonial era to the Civil War, 2006n149
Van Buren, A. N., 2007n1169
Van Cleef-Toedt, Kathleen, 2006n1497
van de Walle, Etienne, 2007n723
van Deurzen, Emmy, 2007n658
van Deventer, V., 2007n655
van Dijk, Hanneke, 2005n1320
Van Ee, Daun, 2009n635
Van Fleet, Connie, 2006n1030
van Gelderen, C. J., 2005n1321
van Gelderen, D. M., 2005n1321
van Ginneken, Anique H. M., 2007n635
Van Horn, Carl E., 2005n227
van Leeuwen, Richard, 2005n1093
van Mantgem, Mike, 2009n264
Van Nostrand's ency of chemistry, 5th ed, 2006n1493
Van Nostrand's scientific ency, 10th ed, 2009n1134
Van Riper, A. Bowdoin, 2005n682
Van Sant, John, 2008n666

Van Tuerenhout, Kirk R., 2006n341
van Wyk, Ben-Erik, 2005n1352, 2006n1338
Van Zandt, Eleanor, 2007n302
Van, Balen John, 2005n348
Vance, Jonathan F., 2007n552
VandenBos, Gary R., 2007n649
Vanderburg, Willem H., 2006n225
Vandergrift, Kay, 2007n907
Vandergrift's children's & YA lit pages [Website], 2007n907
Vanderspoel, John, 2007n377
Vane, Howard R., 2007n131
Vangelisti, Anita L., 2007n662
Vanhoozer, Kevin J., 2007n1097
Varacalli, Joseph A., 2006n1238, 2008n1081
Vardell, Sylvia M., 2008n955, 2009n557
Vargas, Luis Alberto, 2006n1289
Variegated trees & shrubs, 2005n1370
Varieties of English, 2009n873
Varner, Paul, 2009n1066
Vascellaro, Charlie, 2006n775
Vassilakos, Jill H., 2007n928
Vaughan, Catherine, 2009n1321
Vaughn, Jacqueline, 2008n1350, 2009n1343
Vaughn, Stephen L., 2008n802, 2009n809
Vault college career bible, 2005 ed, 2005n251
Vault gd to top internships 2005, 2005n232
Vault gd to top internships 2006, 2006n234
Vault MBA career bible, 2005 ed, 2005n252
Vegetable grower's hndbk, 2009n1163
Vegetables, herbs, & fruit, 2007n1149
Veggie gardener's answer bk, 2009n1158
Velie, Alan, 2008n913
Venables, Stephen, 2009n737
Venice, 4th ed, 2006n413
Venomous reptiles of the western hemisphere, 2005n1399
Venomous snakes of the world, 2007n1219
Ventimiglia, Justine, 2005n162, 2005n163
Venture capital dir [Website], 2006n168
Venzon, Anne Cipriano, 2009n613
Vermont, 2007n78
Verse—anthologies [Website], 2009n1000
Vice Presidents, 3d ed, 2006n701
Victor, Terry, 2007n845
Victorian lit hndbk, 2009n918
Victorian women writers project [Website], 2005n994
Victorians at war 1815-1914, 2005n663
Video source bk, 34th ed, 2006n893
Video source bk, 36th ed, 2007n785
Video source bk, 38th ed, 2008n807
VideoHound's golden movie retriever, 2005, 2005n1217
VideoHound's golden movie retriever, 2006, 2006n1170
VideoHound's golden movie retriever, 2007, 2007n1053

VideoHound's golden movie retriever, 2008, 2008n1038

VideoHound's golden movie retriever, 2009, 2009n1072

Vierow, Wendy, 2009n1073

Vieth, Errol, 2006n1150

Vietnam online [Website], 2008n425

Vietnam War, 2006n459

Vietnam War, 2008n417

Vile, John R., 2005n535, 2006n446, 2006n582, 2009n437

Vilella, Olga, 2005n499

Vino Italiano buying gd, 2006n1284

Vinson court, 2005n543

Violence against women online resources [Website], 2005n803

Violence in the media, 2006n875

Virginia immigrants & adventurers 1607-35, 2008n346

Virtual ref best practices, 2009n585

Virtual ref desk, 2006n644

Virtual ref librarian's hndbk, 2005n651

Virtual ref on a budget, 2009n588

Virtual ref serv, 2008n558

Virtual ref training, 2005n649

Virtual Slavica, 2007n506

Visual Anthropology.net [Website], 2008n298

Visual arts units for all levels, 2009n266

Visual dict of architecture, 2009n861

Visual dict of fashion design, 2009n842

Visual ency of space, 2007n1303

Vital stats, 2006n48

Vital stats of the US 2004, 2005n851

Vital stats of the US 2006, 2d ed, 2007n750

Vital stats on American pol 2005-06, 2006n734

Vital stats on American pol 2007-08, 2008n651

Vital stats on American pol [Website], 2007n623

Vitruvio.com [Website], 2009n860

Vlahakis, George N., 2007n1147

Vocabulario Vaquero/cowboy talk, 2005n975

Vocabulary & concepts of organic chemistry, 2d ed, 2006n1496

Vocabulary of success, 2009n896

Vogel, Amber, 2007n936

Vogl, Wayne, 2006n1321

Vogt, Peter, 2008n253

Vogt, W. Paul, 2007n739

Vohr, Hans-Werner, 2007n1251

Vohs, Kathleen D., 2008n677

Voices of Islam, 2008n1099

Vok, Ruti Malis, 2008n1249

Volcanoes, 2005n1520

Volet, Jean-Marie, 2006n1057

Voll, John O., 2005n1274

Volo, Dorothy Denneen, 2005n461, 2006n809, 2007n704

Volo, James M., 2005n461, 2006n809, 2007n704

Volti, Rudi, 2005n1550

Von Alt, Kenneth A., 2008n275

von Stuckrad, Kocku, 2007n1075

Voting rights act, 2007n466

Voting rights act of 1965, 2009n392

Vyhnanek, Louis A., 2005n510

W. H. Auden ency, 2005n1111

Wage & hour laws, 2006n578

Wagner, John A., 2005n486

Wahab, Shaista, 2008n105

Wainwright, Geoffrey, 2006n1237

Wainwright, Mark, 2008n1193

Wajda, Shirley Teresa, 2008n1003

Wakelyn, Jon L., 2005n701, 2007n362

Walden, Graham R., 2009n5

Walden, Michael, 2008n152

Waldman, Carl, 2005n525, 2007n111, 2007n278

Waldrup, Carole Chandler, 2007n597

Walker, Aidan, 2006n910

Walker, Barbara J., 2006n624, 2006n625, 2006n626

Walker, David, 2007n1071

Walker, Elaine M., 2006n280

Walker, Janice R., 2007n780

Walker, Pam, 2006n1520

Walker, Pamela, 2006n1274, 2007n1143, 2008n1115, 2009n1139

Walker, Richard, 2005n1345, 2007n1171

Walker, Thomas G., 2008n475

Walker's marsupials of the world, 2006n1389

Wall Street Jl gd to the top business schools 2006, 2007n251

Wallace, Dan, 2006n1121

Wallace, Danny P., 2009n573

WallBioNet [Website], 2006n1327

Wallenfels, Ronald, 2005n504

Waller, Raymond J., 2009n271

Wallis, Faith, 2006n1260

Wallis, Robert J., 2008n1103

Walsh, Gretchen, 2006n79

Walsh, Judith E., 2006n92

Walsh, Michael, 2008n1079

Walter, Mariko Namba, 2005n1278

Walter, Scott, 2009n508

Walter, Virginia A., 2005n621, 2008n887

Walzer, Lee, 2006n551

Wang, John, 2006n1468, 2006n1469, 2009n1280

Want, Robert S., 525, 2006n533

Want's fed-state court dir, 2006 ed, 2006n533

War & peace, 2008n887

War in the Persian Gulf: almanac, 2005n667

War in the Persian Gulf: biogs, 2005n668

War in the Persian Gulf: primary sources, 2005n669

Ward, Diane Marie, 2009n559

Ward, Douglas, 2006n395, 2007n318, 2008n363, 2009n344
Ward, Gerald W. R., 2009n849
Ward, Jerry W., Jr., 2009n967
Ward, Patricia Layzell, 2008n555, 2008n556
Ward, Ronald A., 2006n1384
Ward's business dir of US private & public companies, 47th ed, 2005n162
Ward's business dir of US private & public companies, 48th ed, 2006n144
Ward's business dir of US private & public companies, 51st ed, 2009n142
Ward's business dir of US private & public companies, suppl, 47th ed, 2005n163
Ware, Susan, 2006n851
Warf, Barney, 2007n50
Warfare & armed conflicts, 3d ed, 2009n604
Warlow, Ben, 2007n566
Warman's antiques & collectibles price gd, 38th ed, 2005n915
Warman's antiques & collectibles price gd, 40th ed, 2007n796
Warman's antiques & collectibles 2009 price gd, 42d ed, 2009n823
Warman's Little Golden Bks, 2007n798
Warnau, Genevieve, 2006n1367
Warner, Dorothy Anne, 2009n570
Warnock, Amanda, 2008n396
Warren, Andrew, 2007n1310
Warren, Kenneth F., 2009n640
Warren, Lynne, 2007n819
Warrick, Susan E., 2006n1231
Warrior, 2009n609
Wars of the Americas, 2d ed, 2009n601
Warshaw, Shirley Anne, 2005n702
Warwick, Alexandra, 2009n918
Warzinik, Kelly, 2008n722
Was there a Trojan War? [Website], 2008n995
Washington assns contacts dir 2008, 2009n34
Washington D.C., 5th ed, 2009n351
Washington, D.C. of fiction, 2007n919
Washington info dir 2004-05, 2005n711
Washington info dir 2005-06, 2006n714
Washington info dir 2006-07, 2007n603
Washington info dir 2007-08, 2008n641
Washington info dir 2008-09, 2009n652
Washington info dir online [Website], 2006n715
Washington representatives 2004, 28th ed, 2005n712
Washington representatives 2005, 2006n716
Washington representatives 2006, 30th ed, 2007n604
Washington representatives, Spring 2008, 2009n653
Wasserman, Paul, 2007n847, 2009n346
Wasserman, Steven R., 2005n844
Wasson, John H., 2005n1451
Waste mgmt, 2009n1343
Water ency, 2006n1533
Water ency, 3d ed, 2008n1337

Water supply, 2009n1344
Water, Mark, 2005n1257, 2007n1096
Waterfowl of eastern N America, 2006n1371
Watergate & the resignation of Richard Nixon, 2006n736
Watergate, 2005n450
Waterlilies & lotuses, 2006n1347
Watkins dict of dreams, 2008n680
Watkins, John V., 2006n1339
Watson, Cynthia A., 2005n729, 2008n598, 2008n652
Watson, Marston, 2008n337
Watson, Robert P., 2007n587, 2007n588, 2009n1002
Watson-Boone, Rebecca A., 2008n526
Watters, David H., 2006n69
Watts, Linda S., 2008n992
Watts, Victor, 2006n390
Wauson, Jennifer, 2009n240
Wax, Imy F., 2005n315
Waxman, Chaim I., 2009n1119
Way we work, 2009n205
Wayne, Tiffany K., 2007n944
We hold these truths, 2009n47
We the students, 3d ed, 2009n459
Weapons of mass destruction, 2006n676
Weasel words, 2007n847
Weather, 2005n1512
Weather & climate, 2008n1306
Weather glossary [Website], 2009n1319
Weather underground [Website], 2009n1314
Weather watch [Website], 2009n1315
Weatherbee, Donald E., 2009n693
Weatherford, Doris, 2005n872
Weatherson, Brian, 2006n1202
Weaver, Tom, 2008n1030
Weaving, Alan, 2006n1387
Web based instruction, 2d ed, 2006n631
Web lib, 2005n1488
Web literacy for educators, 2009n289
Web of sci [Website], 2006n1278
Web site source bk 2004, 9th ed, 2005n48
Web site source bk 2005, 10th ed, 2006n42
Web site source bk 2006, 11th ed, 2007n37
Web site source bk 2007, 12th ed, 2008n42
Web site source bk 2008, 13th ed, 2009n35
Web 2.0 for librarians & info professionals, 2009n572
Webb, Kristine W., 2009n281
Webb, Paul T., 2007n541
WebChron [Website], 2005n518
Weber, Peter J., 2005n577
Weber, R. David, 2005n316, 2005n1476, 2006n304, 2006n305, 2006n306, 2006n307, 2006n308, 2006n309, 2007n252, 2007n253
WebJunction [Website], 2009n490
Webster, John G., 2007n1233
Webster, Kelly, 2006n322
Webster, Tom, 2007n1115
Webster's all-in-one dict & thesaurus, 2009n882

Webster's contemporary school & office dict, 2009n883

Webster's contemporary school & office thesaurus, 2009n884

Webster's desk ref set, 2007n831

Webster's dict & thesaurus for students, 2007n832

Webster's dict for students, new ed, 2008n859

Webster's family Spanish-English dict, deluxe ed, 2007n865

Webster's French-English dict, 2006n967

Webster's new explorer college dict, new ed, 2008n861

Webster's new explorer crossword puzzle dict, 2d ed, 2007n833

Webster's new explorer dict, new ed, 2006n945

Webster's new explorer dict & thesaurus, new ed, 2006n946

Webster's new explorer dict of American writers, 2005n1061

Webster's new explorer dict of word origins, 2005n954

Webster's new explorer encyclopedic dict, 2007n26

Webster's new explorer gd to English usage, 2005n961

Webster's new explorer large print dict, new ed, 2007n834

Webster's new explorer medical dict, new ed, 2007n1252

Webster's new explorer Spanish-English dict, new ed, 2007n866

Webster's new explorer student dict, new ed, 2007n851

Webster's new explorer vocabulary skill builder, 2009n897

Webster's thesaurus for students, new ed, 2008n860

Webster's II new college dict, 3d ed, 2006n947

Wee, Patricia Hachten, 2006n999

Wee, Robert James, 2006n999

Weibgen, Lara, 2006n550

Weihs, Jean, 2006n646

Weil, Danny, 2005n275

Weil, David, 2005n1482

Weiner, Irving B., 2009n714

Weiner, Richard, 2007n767

Weiner, Robert G., 2009n1037

Weintraub, Irwin, 2005n633

Weir, Robert E., 2005n226, 2008n58

Weir, Stephen, 2006n503

Weir, William, 2005n665

Weisbard, Phyllis Holman, 2005n273, 2007n235

Weisblatt, Jayne, 2007n1292, 2007n1322

Weisblatt, Jayne, 2008n613

Weisburg, Hilda K., 2008n516

Weisfelder, Richard F., 2005n88

Weishampel, David B., 2006n1521

Weiss, Brett, 2008n1272

Weiss, Joachim, 2006n1403

Weiss, Jodi, 2005n253

Weiss Ratings' gd to ...
　banks & thrifts, Summer 2004, 2005n186
　banks & thrifts, Fall 2005, 2006n173
　bond money market mutual funds, Spring 2004, 2005n176
　bond & money market mutual funds, Summer 2005, 2006n158
　brokerage firms, winter 2003-04, 2005n177
　HMOs & health insurers, summer 2004, 2005n201
　HMOs & health insurers, Winter 2005-06, 2006n197
　life, health, & annuity insurers, Summer 2004, 2005n202
　life, health, & annuity insurers, Fall 2005, 2006n198
　property & casualty insurers, Spring 2004, 2005n203
　property & casualty insurers, Fall 2005, 2006n199
　stock mutual funds, Spring 2004, 2005n178
　stock mutual funds, Summer 2005, 2006n159

Weiss Ratings' ultimate guided tour of stock investing, summer 2004, 2005n179

Weissman, Dick, 2006n1099

Welcome to America: the complete gd for immigrants, 2006n831

Welsch, Janice R., 2006n1146

Welsh, James M., 2006n1151

Wenborn, Neil, 2006n1246

Wendel, Christopher S., 2005n851, 2007n750

Wendel, Helmut F., 2005n851, 2007n750

Wepman, Dennis, 2009n772

Werlock, Abby H. P., 2007n940

Werlock, James P., 2007n940

Werneke, Diane, 2006n207, 2006n239, 2007n736, 2008n216

Werness, Hope B., 2005n939

Wertheim, Eric, 2006n674, 2008n599

Wertkin, Gerard C., 2005n935

Wesleyan holiness movement, 2006n1225

Wesson, Cameron B., 2005n344

West, Barbara A., 2009n305

West, Nigel, 2006n665, 2007n560, 2008n588, 2008n589

West's ency of American law, 2d ed, 2005n537

Westbrooks, Elaine L., 2005n630

Westcott, Rich, 2005n768

Westerman-Alkire, Cheryl, 2005n57, 2006n55

Western drama through the ages, 2008n894

Western Europe 2009, 2009n110

Western film series of the sound era, 2009n1068

Western lives, 2005n22

Western philosophy, 2005n1236

Westfahl, Gary, 2006n1025, 2006n1029

Westman, Stephen R., 2007n527

Westney, Lynn C. Hattendorf, 2005n278

Westwood, David, 2006n681

Wexler, Alan, 2005n525
Whale watcher, 2007n1211
Wharton, Peter, 2006n1311
What do children & YAs read next, v.6, 2005n1014
What do I read next? 2005 ed, 2007n920
What do I read next? v.1, 2004, 2005n1042
What do I read next? v.2, 2003, 2005n1041
What do I read next? v.2, 2008 ed, 2009n940
What is what in the nanoworld, 2006n1397
What ship is that? 2d ed, 2009n1351
What they didn't say, 2007n46
Wheeler, Maurice B., 2006n615
When in Rome or Rio or Riyadh, 2005n393
Wherry, Timothy Lee, 2008n541, 2009n562
Whitaker, John O., Jr., 2009n1207
Whitaker, Richard, 2005n1512
Whitaker, Russel, 2005n987, 2005n988, 2005n989, 2005n990
Whitaker's almanack 2006, 138th ed, 2006n9
Whitaker's almanack 2008, 2009n3
Whitburn, Joel, 2005n1143, 2005n1145
White court, 2005n557
White, E. B., 2006n887
White, Glenn D., 2006n1084
White, Hilary, 2009n1057
White, John, 2006n1353
White, Kevin, 2007n1234
White, Marilyn Domas, 2006n644
White, Phillip M., 2008n320
Whited, Tamara L., 2006n1545
Whitman, Sylvia, 2009n761
Whitney, Elspeth, 2005n1296
Whitson, Kathy J., 2006n985
Whittaker, Paul, 2006n1357
Who: a dir of prominent people, 2006n19
Who: a dir of prominent people, 2d ed, 2007n13
Who buys what, 2007n230
Who sang what on Broadway, 1866-1996, 2006n1171
Who was who in America 2006-07, 2008n19
Who was who in America, with world notables 2002-04, v.15, 2005n23
Who we are: Asians, 2008n752
Who we are: Blacks, 2008n753
Who we are: Hispanics, 2008n754
Who's buying for travel, 2006n165
Who's buying groceries, 2d ed, 2005n183
Who's buying series, 2008n259
Who's buying series, 2d ed, 2007n231
Who's who among African Americans, 17th ed, 2005n332
Who's who among African Americans, 18th ed, 2006n326
Who's who among African Americans, 21st ed, 2008n309
Who's who in ...
    America 2005, 59th ed, 2005n24
    America 2006, 60th ed, 2006n21

America 2007, 61st ed, 2007n17
American art 2005-06, 26th ed, 2006n918
American art 2007-08, 27th ed, 2007n812
American educ 2004-05, 6th ed, 2005n274
American law 2005-06, 14th ed, 2006n515
American law 2007-08, 30th ed, 2008n463
American pol 2005-06, 20th ed, 2006n702
American pol 2007-08, 21st ed, 2008n623
art, 31st ed, 2005n933
Asia 2007, 2008n21
Canadian business 2004, 24th ed [CD-ROM], 2005n143
Canadian business 2004, 24th ed, 2005n142
finance & business 2006-07, 35th ed, 2007n132
finance & business 2008-09, 36th ed, 2008n151
in art, 32d ed, 2007n813
intl affairs 2005, 4th ed, 2006n684
medicine & healthcare 2004-05, 5th ed, 2005n1416
medicine & healthcare 2006-07, 6th ed, 2007n1231
sci & engineering 2005-046 8th ed, 2006n1252
sci & engineering 2006-07, 9th ed, 2007n1131
sci & engineering 2008-09, 10th ed, 2008n1106
the Arab world 2005-06, 17th ed, 2005n26
the Arab world 2007-08, 18th ed, 2007n121
the Arab world 2009-10, 19th ed, 2009n17
the East 2008, 35th ed, 2008n20
the Jewish Bible, 2009n1118
the world 2005, 22d ed, 2005n20
the world, 24th ed, 2007n14
Who's who of American women 2006-07, 25th ed, 2006n853
Who's who of American women 2007, 26th ed, 2007n756
Who's who of British jazz, 2d ed, 2005n1150
Who's who of emerging leaders 2007, 2008n16
Whole digital lib hndbk, 2008n511
Whole lib hndbk 4, 2007n497
Whole person healthcare, 2008n1244
Whole school lib hndbk, 2006n607
Wich hazels, 2006n1356
Wiener, Roberta, 2006n448
Wiggins, David K., 2005n749
Wigoder, Geoffrey, 2005n1277
Wikipedia [Website], 2008n32
Wilbert, Warren N., 2006n784
Wild & sown grasses, 2006n1351
Wild flowers of Ohio, 2d ed, 2009n1181
Wild orchids of the NE, 2008n1154
Wild orchids of the prairies & great plains region of N America, 2008n1155
Wild orchids of the SE US North of peninsular Fla., 2006n1345
Wildavsky, Ben, 2006n279
Wildflowers of the Rocky Mountains, 2008n1158
Wildflowers of the western plains, paperback ed, 2009n1182
Wildlife & plants, 3d ed, 2007n1170

Wildlife-friendly plants, 2005n1323
Wiley electrical & electronics engineering dict, 2005n1410
Wiley ency of biomedical engineering, 2007n1222
Wiley ency of clinical trials, 2009n1224
Wiley, Keith, 2007n1162
Wiley's remediation technologies hndbk, 2005n1408
Wilford, Jane, 2006n397
Wilford, Richard, 2007n1163
Wilkens, Steve, 2008n1093
Wilkins, Jamie, 2007n1306
Wilkinson, Frances C., 2005n626
Wilkinson, Toby, 2007n400
Willbanks, James H., 2006n682
Willems, Jos, 2007n992
Williams, Amanda, 2007n511
Williams, Chris, 2005n487
Williams, Christian, 2005n782
Williams, D. Newell, 2006n1230
Williams, Deborah K., 2007n839
Williams, Greg H., 2007n361, 2007n569
Williams, Hywel, 2006n492
Williams, Joseph M., 2008n801, 2009n807
Williams, Mark E., 2008n1245
Williams, Randy, 2007n1052
Williams, Robert C., 2009n435
Williams, Robert G., 2009n1323
Williams, Roymond Leslie, 2008n942
Williams, Tyrone, 2009n954
Williamson, H. G. M., 2006n1222
Willie Mays, 2006n774
Willings press gd 2004, 2005n889
Willings press gd 2007, 133d ed, 2008n792
Willings press gd 2008, 134th ed, 2009n799
Willis, Barbara, 2006n764
Willis, Jim, 2005n1242, 2006n764
Willis, Martin, 2009n918
Willmott, H. P., 2005n519
Wilson, A. Paula, 2005n594, 2005n635
Wilson, Ann, 2005n185, 2005n220
Wilson, Charles E., Jr., 2006n988
Wilson, Charles Reagan, 2007n62, 2007n63
Wilson, Christopher R., 2007n961
Wilson, Don E., 2005n53, 2007n1209
Wilson, Donnie E., 2006n331
Wilson, Ellen Judy, 2005n524
Wilson, Feleta L., 2009n535
Wilson, Jeffrey, 2006n1440, 2007n445, 2008n678, 2009n703
Wilson, John D., 2007n948, 2008n878
Wilson, Katharina M., 2005n871
Wilson, Kevin, 2009n240
Wilson, Nigel, 2006n473
Wilson, R. Marshall, 2006n1496
Wilson, Ray W., 2009n580
Wilson, Raymond, 2009n308
Wilson, Steven Patrick, 2009n532

Win, May Kyi, 95, 2006n97
Windelspecht, Michael, 2005n1346
Wine atlas of Australia, 2008n1116
Wines & wineries of Calif. central coast, 2009n1149
Wines of the world, 2005n1308
Wink, Michael, 2005n1352
Winkle, Kenneth J., 2006n428
Winn, Peter A. S., 2006n802
Winning with lib leadership, 2005n643
Winokur, Jon, 2008n53
Winsberg, Morton D., 2007n64
Winship, Michael, 2008n570
Winston, Mark, 2009n563
Winston, Robert, 2005n53
Winter, Jay, 2007n378, 2007n379
Wintle, Justin, 2008n445
Wintz, Cary D., 2006n866
Wired [Website], 2009n1291
Wirtz, James J., 2006n676
Wise-Gervais, Cathryn, 2006n1368
Wishart, David J., 2005n77, 2008n324
Witalec, Janet, 2005n978, 2005n991, 2005n1012
Withgott, Jay, 2009n1345
Withner, Carl L., 2005n1359
Witte, Stephen S., 2009n396
Witzel, Morgen, 2006n263
Wives of the American presidents, 2d ed, 2007n597
Wizard of Oz catalog, 2006n995
Wlaschin, Ken, 2005n1200, 2007n1002, 2009n1060
Wnek, Gary E., 2005n1405
Wohl, Alice Sedgwick, 2008n832
Wojtanik, Andrew, 2007n58
Wokler, Robert, 2007n579
Wolbrink, Shelley, 2005n512
Wolf, Carolyn, 2007n498
Wolf, Kirsten, 2005n532
Wolfe, Gene, 2008n903
Wolfe, Lorne M., 2008n1145
Wolfe, Timothy W., 2006n576
Wolfinger, Anne, 2007n205
Wolfreys, Julian, 2005n1003, 2007n763
Wolpert, Stanley, 2006n91, 2007n96
Womack, Kenneth, 2009n938
Women & gender in Central & E Europe, Russia, & Eurasia, 2008n775
Women & gender in medieval Europe, 2007n759
Women & museums, 2006n54
Women & pol participation, 2005n715
Women & sci, 2006n863
Women & social movement in the US, 1775-2000 [Website], 2005n863
Women & war, 2007n760
Women adventurers 1750-1900, 2009n783
Women composers, v.7, 2005n1117
Women composers, v.8, 2007n984
Women during the Civil War, 2008n785
Women engaged in war in lit for youth, 2008n882

Women in America musical theatre, 2009n1080
Women in early America, 2006n857
Women in pol [Website], 2005n685
Women in pol [Website], 2008n776, 2008n777
Women in the American Civil War, 2009n789
Women in the American West, 2009n791
Women in the Middle Ages, 2005n871
Women Nobel Peace Prize winners, 2007n11
Women on US postage stamps, 2009n784
Women, sci, & myth, 2009n790
Women Vaudeville stars, 2007n1054
Women writers project [Website], 2005n995
Women writers project [Website], 2007n874
Women's adventures in sci series, 2006n1253
Women's health concerns sourcebk, 2d ed, 2005n1452
Women's human rights resources [Websites],
    2005n589
Women's movement today, 2006n859
Women's movement today, 2007n761
Women's rights, 2006n864
Women's rights, 2008n786
Women's roles in the renaissance, 2006n860
Women's studies, feminist, & gender periodicals
    [Website], 2005n875
Women's studies intl [Website], 2005n864
Women's studies section core jls for women's studies
    [Website], 2005n865
Women's suffrage, 2006n862
Women's suffrage in America, updated ed, 2006n861
Wong, Chi-Huey, 2008n1286
Wood, Donna, 2005n47, 2006n38
Wood, Elaine, 2006n1274, 2006n1520, 2007n1143,
    2008n1115, 2009n1139
Wood, M. Sandra, 2007n1253, 2009n529
Wood, Thalia, 2005n714
Woodall's N American campground dir 2005,
    2006n786
Woodall's tenting dir 2005, 2006n787
Woodbridge, John D., 2005n1263
Woodford, Chris, 2006n1275
Woodger, Elin, 2007n344
Woodham, Jonathan M., 2006n911
Woodland garden, rev ed, 2005n1325
Woods, Adrienne L., 2005n1475, 2006n1457,
    2007n1279
Woods, Damon L., 2007n101
Woods, Richard D., 2006n1063
Woods, Thomas E., Jr., 2008n397, 2009n377
Woodstock, 2006n1075
Woodstra, Chris, 2005n1147, 2005n1148, 2007n998
Woodward, John, 2007n1316
Woodward, Susan L., 2005n1343
Woodward, William McKenzie, 2005n82
Woodworker's illus ency, 2009n841
Woodworth, David, 2006n242
Woodworth, Steven E., 2006n428, 2009n386
Woodworth-Ney, Laura E., 2009n791

Woolley, A. R., 2006n1515
Woolley, John T., 2007n624, 2009n647
Woolls, Blanche, 2006n607, 2006n608, 2009n526
Wooster, Robert, 2006n337
Wooten, Deborah A., 2007n908
Word hists & mysteries, 2005n955
Word origins . . . & how we know them, 2006n948
Word parts dict, 2d ed, 2009n881
Word routes, 2006n949
Words of intelligence, 2007n595
Words to rhyme with, 3d ed, 2008n866
Words, words, words, 2007n836
Worek, Jordan, 2009n838
Worek, Michael, 2009n13, 2009n838
Work in America, 2005n227
Work your way around the world, 13th ed, 2008n248
Working Americans 1880-2005, v.6: women at work,
    2006n238
Working Americans 1880-2006, v.7: social
    movements, 2007n194
Working Americans 1880-2007, v.8: immigrants,
    2009n211
Working in America, 2008n233
World & its peoples: Eastern & Southern Asia,
    2009n97
World & its peoples: Mexico & Central America,
    2009n124
World & its peoples: Middle East, W Africa, & N
    Africa, 2007n124
World Almanac & bk of facts 2005, 2005n4
World Almanac & bk of facts 2006, 2007n2
World Almanac & bk of facts 2008, 2008n6
World Almanac world atlas, 2005n380
World art Web kiosk [Website], 2005n941
World atlas [Website], 2009n336
World atlas of great apes & their conservation,
    2006n1390
World authors 2000-05, 2008n876
World Bank Africa database 2005 [CD-ROM],
    2007n81
World Bk atlas, 2007n307
World Bk dict, 2007n27
World Bk discover [Website], 2009n24
World Bk discovery ency, 2009n25
World Bk ency, 2004 ed, 2005n34
World Bk ency, 2006 ed, 2006n30
World Bk ency, 2007 ed, 2007n28
World Bk ency, 2008 ed, 2008n33
World Bk ency, 2009 ed, 2009n26
World Bk ency of people & places, 2006n66
World Bk ency of people & places, 2007n55
World Bk lib of natural disasters, 2009n1320
World Bk myths & legends series, 2005n1171
World Bk of America's presidents, 2005 ed, 2006n737
World Bk student dict, 2005 ed, 2005n35
World Bk student discovery ency, 2d ed, 2008n34
World Bk student discovery sci ency, 2006n1264

World Bk's childcraft, 2005n36
World Bk's ency of flags, 2006n368
World Bk's human body works, 2007n1173
World Bk's sci & nature gds, 2005n1344
World Bk's yr in review: 2004, 2006n52
World Christianities, c.1815-c.1914, v.8, 2007n1116
World Christianities, c.1914-c.2000, v.9, 2007n1117
World consumer expenditure patterns 2003, 4th ed, 2005n268
World consumer income patterns 2003, 2005n269
World consumer lifestyles databk 2004, 3d ed, 2005n270
World consumer lifestyles databk 2008, 2009n237
World consumer spending 2004/05, 5th ed, 2005n271
World consumer spending 2006/07, 7th ed, 2007n232
World consumer spending 2009, 9th ed, 2009n238
World cookbk for students, 2008n1129
World cosmetics & toiletries mktg dir, 4th ed, 2006n187
World cultural leaders of the 20th & 21st centuries, 2d ed, 2008n788
World data analyst online [Website], 2009n54
World dir of ...
    business info libs 2007, 6th ed, 2008n509
    info Web sites 2007, 7th ed, 2008n164
    non-official statl sources 2007, 7th ed, 2008n763
    trade & business assns 2007, 5th ed, 2008n165
    trade & business jls 2007, 3d ed, 2008n166
    business info Websites 2003, 2005n164
World dvlpmt report 2006, 2007n184
World economic & social survey 2005, 2006n208
World economic & social survey 2006, 2007n178
World economic & social survey 2007, 60th ed, 2008n745
World economic factbk 2003/04, 2005n210
World economic factbk 2005/06, 13th ed, 2006n209
World economic factbk 2009, 16th ed, 2009n194
World ency of archaeology, 2008n382
World ency of pol systems & parties, 4th ed, 2008n613
World ency of police forces & correctional systems, 2d ed, 2007n473
World environmental databk 2006, 2007n1335
World environmental databk 2008/09, 2009n1346
World factbk 2005, 2006n68
World factbk 2006, 2007n59
World factbk 2007, 2008n67
World fascism, 2007n632
World fertility report: 2003, 2006n826
World food habits [Website], 2008n1117
World food mktg dir 2008, 5th ed, 2009n190
World gd to foundations, 3d ed, 2005n815
World geography [Website], 2009n339
World health databk 2006, 2007n1243
World health databk 2007/08, 2009n1233
World hist: ancient & medieval eras [Website], 2005n509

World hist: the modern era [Website], 2008n459
World hist [Website], 2009n431
World hist on file, updated ed, 2005n533
World hist on file, v.1: early civilizations, 2d ed, 2007n435
World hist on file, v.2: the expanding world, 2007n436
World hist on file, v.3: the age of revolution, 2d ed, 2007n437
World hist on file, v.4: the 20th century, 2d ed, 2007n438
World hunger, 2008n735
World income distribution 2004/05, 2d ed, 2005n172
World income distribution 2006/07, 4th ed, 2007n185
World income distribution 2008/09, 2009n239
World Internet UFO dir, 2006n765
World investment report 2005, 2006n210
World investment report 2007, 2008n217
World list of universities & other institutions of higher educ, 25th ed, 2007n250
World military leaders, 2008n574
World monarchies & dynasties, 2006n504
World monetary units, 2006n119
World mortality report 2005, 2007n726
World of ...
    animals: amphibians & reptiles, v.41-50, 2006n1392
    animals: fish, 2006n1383
    animals: index, 2007n1189
    animals: insects & other invertebrates, 2005n1395
    forensic sci, 2006n563
    Islam in lit for youth, 2007n892
    plants series, 2007n1175
    sports sci, 2007n672
World party, 2007n1035
World police ency, 2007n474
World population, 2d ed, 2007n721
World population ageing 2007, 2008n746
World population prospects: the 2004 revision, 2007n727
World poverty, 2009n761
World railways of the 19th century, 2006n1552
World religions series, 2007n1091
World religions: almanac, 2007n1088
World religions: biogs, 2007n1089
World religions: primary sources, 2007n1090
World retail data & stats 2008/09,, 2009n195
World Shakespeare bibliog online [Website], 2009n976
World shores & beaches, 2006n388
World stadiums [Website], 2005n760
World stats pocketbk, 2007n744
World War I, 2006n505
World War I, 2007n430, 2007n426
World War I, 2008n460
World War I, 2009n432
World War I sheet music, 2008n970
World War II, 2005n519, 2005n520

World War II, 2006n506
World War II, 2007n439
World War II, 2009n608
World War II almanac, 2009n419
World War II in lit for youth, 2006n999
World War II naval & maritime claims against the US,
    2007n569
World writers in English, 2005n996
World's protected areas, 2009n1347
Worldmark ency of religious practices, 2006n1209
Worldmark ency of the nations, 11th ed, 2005n72
Worldmark ency of the nations, 12th ed, 2007n56
Worldmark ency of the states, 7th ed, 2008n72
Worldwide govt dir with intl orgs 2005, 2006n690
Worth, Roland H., Jr., 2006n1218, 2009n369,
    2009n1095
Worthen, Dennis B., 2005n1477
Worthington, William E., Jr., 2006n1255
Woy, James, 2005n135
Wrede, Jan, 2006n1358
Wright, Christopher, 2008n846
Wright, David, 2005n1263, 2007n299
Wright, Edmund, 2007n1290
Wright, Jill, 2007n299
Wright, John D., 2007n370
Wright, John W., 2006n7
Wright, Jonathan A., 2006n516
Wright, Marshall D., 2005n770
Wright, N. T., 2007n1097
Wright, Raymond S., III, 2005n363
Wright, Richard A., 2006n557
Wright, Russell O., 2005n885, 2005n1545, 2007n236,
    2008n767, 2009n768
Wright, Sarah Bird, 2007n951
Wright-McLeod, Brian, 2006n1091
Write grants, get money, 2d ed, 2009n578
WriteExpress online rhyming [Website], 2009n1006
Writer's market, 2005, 2005n892
Writer's market, 2007, 2008n796
Writer's market 2009, 88th ed, 2009n804
Writer's market companion, 2d ed, 2006n881
Writers dir 2005, 20th ed, 2005n1000
Writers dir 2006, 21st ed, 2006n977
Writers dir 2007, 22d ed, 2007n877
Writers dir 2009, 24th ed, 2009n908
Writing African American women, 2007n945
Writing the critical essay series, 2009n806
Wrobel, Murray, 2005n1400
Wrolstad, Ronald E., 2005n1305
Wrong word dict, 2007n838
WSSLINKS: women, girls, & educ [Website],
    2005n273
WSSLINKS: women, girls, & educ [Website],
    2007n235
WTO analytical index, 2d ed, 2009n487
WTO case law of 2004-05, 2009n488
Wuthnow, Robert, 2007n575

Wyatt, Neal, 2008n946
Wyman, Bruce, 2008n1339
Wyman, David M., 2006n399
Wynbrandt, James, 2005n129, 2009n105, 2009n1242
Wynn, Graeme, 2008n1351
Wynn, Neil A., 2009n648

Xiong, Victor Cunrui, 2009n400
Xu, Lijuan, 2005n628

YA librarians' homepage [Website], 2007n518
Yaakov, Juliette, 2005n5
Yadon, Laurence, 2008n88
Yadon, Laurence J., 2009n83
Yager, Fred, 2006n259
Yager, Jan, 2006n259
Yale bk of quotations, 2007n48
Yamamoto, Sandra H., 2009n519
Yanak, Ted, 2005n443
Yankah, Kwesi, 2005n1153
Yanow, Scott, 2006n1107
Yates, Douglas A., 2007n86
Ye, Tan, 2009n1078
Year of programs for teens, 2007n510
Yearbook of intl orgs 2005-06, v.43, 2007n38
Yearbook of the UN 2005, v.59, 60th ed, 2009n41
Yearley, Steven, 2007n691
Yee, Martha M., 2009n545
Yeh, Christine, 2009n257
Yevgeny Mravinsky, 2006n1083
Yiddish given names, 2009n328
Yivo ency of Jews in E Europe, 2009n312
Yoga, 2008n714
Yon, Richard, 2007n588
Yorath, Chris, 2006n1517
York, Jennifer M., 2005n332
York, Michael, 2005n1243, 2008n1094, 2009n1116
York, Sherry, 2005n1021, 2006n1004
Yost, Jeffrey R., 2006n1482
You can write your family hist, repr ed, 2009n320
Young, A. M., 2006n1350
Young adult lit in action, 2009n547
Young, Christian C., 2008n1147
Young, Nancy K., 2005n1179, 2006n1077, 2008n404
Young person's Occupational Outlook Hndbk, 6th ed,
    2008n238
Young, Robert A., 2009n865
Young, William H., 2005n1179, 2006n1077,
    2008n404
Youngerman, Barry, 2008n105, 2009n1254
Yount, Lisa, 2005n1379, 2005n1413, 2006n1536,
    2008n499, 2008n780, 2008n1167, 2009n1219
Your lib goes virtual, 2009n516
Your military family network, 2008n724

Your rights in the workplace, 7th ed, 2007n486
Youth activism, 2006n688
Youth activism, 2007n578
Youth, educ, & sexualities, 2006n816
Youth gangs in lit, 2005n1030
Yrigoyen, Charles, Jr., 2006n1231
Yuan, Michael S., 2007n260
Yurkevich, Myroslav, 2006n106

Zacher, Christian, 2008n69
Zachos, Ellen, 2006n1332
Zafirovski, Milan, 2006n123
Žagar, Mitja, 2005n339
Zahn-Waxler, Carolyn, 2005n743
Zaprudnik, Jan, 2008n120
Zarian, Beth Bartleson, 2005n1022
Zbaracki, Matthew D., 2009n933
Zegura, Elizabeth Chesney, 2005n1086
Zelden, Charles L., 2008n648
Zeldin, Richard P., 2005n166, 2005n167, 2006n145,
    2006n146

Zelizer, Julian E., 2006n718
Zell, Hans M., 2009n589
Zemboy, James, 2009n944
Zeng, Marcia Lei, 2009n574
Zerbonia, Ralph G., 2005n327, 2005n328, 2006n111,
    2006n112, 2006n113
Zetterlund, Henrik, 2009n1160
Zhang, Yan, 2009n1294
Zhang, Yawei, 2009n1222
Zheng, Jun, 2009n1294
Zhou, Yuan, 2007n371
Zilinskas, Raymond A., 2006n751
Zils, Michael, 2005n815
Zipes, Jack, 2007n909
Ziporyn, Terra, 2005n1440
Zirpolo, Lilian H., 2008n837
Zoller, Curt J., 2005n721
Zorn, Elayne, 2009n307
Zuchowski, Willow, 2008n1152
Zvelebil, Marketa J., 2005n1411

Subject Index

ABBREVIATIONS
Acronym finder [Website], 2006n1
Acronyms, initialisms & abbrevs dict, 34th ed, 2005n1
Acronyms, initialisms & abbrevs dict, 39th ed, 2008n1
American Heritage abbrevs dict, 3d ed, 2006n2
Elsevier's dict of abbrevs, acronyms, synonyms, &
    symbols used in medicine, 2d ed, 2005n1434
Reverse acronyms, initialisms, & abbrevs dict, 39th
    ed, 2008n2

ABOLITION
Encyclopedia of antislavery & abolition, 2008n394

ABORTION
Abortion in the US, 2008n716
Encyclopedia of abortion in the US, 2d ed, 2009n740
Roe v. Wade, 2009n451

ABUSE. *See also* **DOMESTIC VIOLENCE**
Abuse & violence info for teens, 2009n764

ACADEMIC LIBRARIES. *see* **COLLEGE &
RESEARCH LIBRARIES**

ACCOUNTING
Dictionary of accounting terms, 4th ed, 2006n155
Law firm accounting & financial mgmt, 3d ed,
    2007n455
Lower taxes in 7 easy steps, 2007n152
Ultimate accountants' ref, 2d ed, 2008n173

**ACQUISITIONS (LIBRARIES) –
MANAGEMENT.** *See also* **COLLECTION
DEVELOPMENT (LIBRARIES)**
Buying & contracting for resources & servs, 2005n653
Complete gd to acquisitions mgmt, 2005n626

ACTING
Tools & techniques for character interpretation,
    2007n1038

ACTORS. *See also* **MOTION PICTURES**
Bob Hope films, 2006n1162
Casting might-have-beens, 2005n1202
Celebrity death certificates 2, 2006n1128
Christopher Lee filmography, 2005n1204
Encyclopedic dict of women in early American films
    1895-1930, 2005n1189
Enter the players: N.Y. stage actors in the 20th
    century, 2005n1218
Film stars & their awards, 2009n1062

Harrison Ford, 2006n1159
John Wayne filmography, 2005n1205
New biographical dict of film, updated ed, 2007n1040
Obituaries in the performing arts, 2003, 2005n1180
Obituaries in the performing arts, 2004, 2006n1127
Obituaries in the performing arts, 2005, 2007n1036
Obituaries in the performing arts, 2007, 2009n1049
Quinlan's character stars, rev ed, 2005n1192
Serial film stars, 2006n1136
Women Vaudeville stars, 2007n1054

ADMINISTRATIVE AGENCIES
Encyclopedia of fed agencies & commissions,
    2005n700

ADOPTION
Adoption, 2d ed, 2008n723
Children & youth in adoption, orphanages, & foster
    care, 2006n807
Encyclopedia of adoption, 3d ed, 2008n719

ADULT SERVICES IN PUBLIC LIBRARIES
Easy info sources for ESL, adult learners, & new
    readers, 2009n569
Nonfiction readers' advisory, 2006n601
Programming for adults, 2006n602
Readers' advisory serv in the public lib, 3d ed,
    2006n603

ADVERTISING. *See also* **MARKETING**
Co-op advertising programs sourcebk 2007, 2008n254
Plunkett's advertising & branding industry almanac,
    2005n257
Plunkett's advertising & branding industry almanac
    2006, 2007n228
Plunkett's advertising & branding industry almanac
    2007, 2008n256

AERONAUTICS
AIM/FAR 2006, 2006n1547
AIM/FAR 2008, 2008n1352
Aviation century: wings of change, 2006n1548

AERONAUTICS, MILITARY
Aviation century: WW II, 2005n1547
B-29 Superfortress, 2005n677
Graphic war, 2006n666
Military aircraft, origins to 1918, 2006n678
Naval Institute gd to the ships & aircraft of the US
    Fleet, 18th ed, 2006n675
One hundred yrs of world military aircraft, 2005n676

AFFIRMATIVE ACTION. *See also* **CIVIL RIGHTS**
Affirmative action, 2005n587

AFGHANISTAN
Brief hist of Afghanistan, 2008n105
Culture & customs of Afghanistan, 2006n88
Historical dict of Afghan wars, revolutions, &
     insurgencies, 2d ed, 2006n87
IntelCenter terrorism incident ref (TIR): Afghanistan:
     2000-07, 2009n685

AFRICA
Africa south of the Sahara 2007, 36th ed, 2008n96
Africa south of the Sahara [Website], 2008n91
African biogl dict, 2d ed, 2007n79
African households, 2007n723
African studies center [Website], 2008n93
African studies centre [Website], 2008n94
Bibliography of Africana per lit [Website], 2008n92
Biographical ency of the modern Middle East & N
     Africa, 2008n142
Cities of the Middle East & N Africa, 2008n143
Food culture in Sub-Saharan Africa, 2006n1294
New ency of Africa, 2008n95
Reference gd to Africa, 2d ed, 2006n78
Research, ref serv, & resources for the study of Africa,
     2006n79
Teen life in Africa, 2005n83
World & its peoples: Middle East, W Asia, & N
     Africa, 2008n145
World Bank Africa database 2005 [CD-ROM],
     2007n81

AFRICA, BUSINESS
Major companies of Africa S of the Sahara 2004, 9th
     ed, 2005n211
Major companies of Africa S of the Sahara 2005, 10th
     ed, 2006n211

AFRICA, ECONOMICS
Economic report on Africa 2007, 2008n218

AFRICA, HISTORY
Africa & the Americas, 2009n692
Africa south of the Sahara 2008, 37th ed, 2009n89
African placenames, 2d ed, 2009n342
African timelines [Website], 2005n463
Civilizations of Africa, 2009n85
Daily life of the Nubians, 2005n464
Encyclopedia of African hist, 2006n460
Encyclopedia of African hist & culture, 2006n461
Historical dict of Civil Wars in Africa, 2d ed,
     2009n398
Historical dict of Ghana, 3d ed, 2006n81
Historical dict of Guinea, 4th ed, 2006n82
Historical dict of Rwanda, new ed, 2008n98

Historical dict of the Central African Republic, 3d ed,
     2006n77
Historical dict of the Republic of Cape Verde, 4th ed,
     2008n97
Historical dict of Western Sahara, 3d ed, 2007n80
Historical dict of women in sub-Saharan Africa,
     2006n858
Historical dict of Zambia, 3d ed, 2008n99
New ency of Africa, 2009n88

AFRICA, NORTH
Atlas of the Middle East & N Africa, 2007n118
Cities of the Middle East & N Africa, 2007n122
World & its peoples: Middle East, W Africa, & N
     Africa, 2007n124

AFRICA, POLITICS & GOVERNMENT
African states & rulers, 3d ed, 2007n626
Political hndbk of Africa 2007, 2007n625

AFRICAN AMERICAN ARTS
Encyclopedia of the Harlem literary renaissance,
     2006n1034
Encyclopedia of the Harlem renaissance, 2006n866
Harlem renaissance, 2009n959
Historical dict of African American theater, 2009n1075
Historical dict of African-American TV, 2006n1149

AFRICAN AMERICAN AUTHORS
African American dramatists, 2005n1034
African American lit, 2006n1030
African American women writers of the 19th century
     [Website], 2005n1057
African American women writers of the 19th century
     [Website], 2007n934
African-American writers, 2005n1058
Alice Walker, 2006n1040
Black lit criticism, 2009n903
Columbia gd to contemporary African American
     fiction, 2006n1035
Coretta Scott King awards 1970-2004, 3d ed,
     2005n1056
Critical companion to Toni Morrison, 2009n963
Critical companion to Zora Neale Hurston, 2009n961
Encyclopedia of African American women writers,
     2008n911
Encyclopedia of African-American lit, 2009n956
Encyclopedia of the Harlem literary renaissance,
     2006n1034
Greenwood ency of African American lit, 2007n941
Masterplots II: African American lit, rev ed, 2009n954
Notable African American writers, 2007n943
100 most popular African American authors,
     2008n908
Richard Wright, 2008n926
Richard Wright ency, 2009n967
Writing African American women, 2007n945

AFRICAN AMERICAN BUSINESSPEOPLE
African-American business leaders & entrepreneurs, 2005n140
Encyclopedia of African American business, 2007n134

AFRICAN AMERICAN ENTERTAINERS
Historical dict of African American cinema, 2008n1014
Swingin' on the ether waves, 2006n890

AFRICAN AMERICAN FOLKLORE
Greenwood ency of African American folklore, 2007n1019

AFRICAN AMERICAN GENEALOGY
Free African Americans of N.C., Va., & S.C., 5th ed, 2006n357

AFRICAN AMERICAN HISTORY
African American experience [Website], 2009n298
African American hist, 2006n327
African American hist, 2007n269
Africana, 2d ed, 2006n328
Atlas of African-American hist, rev ed, 2008n308
Black submariners in the US Navy, 1940-75, 2006n672
Civil rights revolution, 2005n421
Columbia gd to African American hist since 1939, 2007n273
Encyclopedia of African American hist 1619-1895, 2007n270
Encyclopedia of African American hist, 1896 to the present, 2009n300
Encyclopedia of African American society, 2006n330
Encyclopedia of African-American culture & hist, 2d ed, 2006n329
Encyclopedia of slave resistance & rebellion, 2008n395
Encyclopedia of the great black migration, 2007n271
Encyclopedia of the middle passage, 2008n396
Greenwood ency of African American civil rights, 2005n334
Jim Crow ency, 2009n302
1001 things everyone should know about African American hist, 2d ed, 2007n275
Oxford African American studies center [Website], 2009n303
Slave revolts, 2009n397
Slavery in the south, 2005n454African American chronology, 2007n268
Voting rights act of 1965, 2009n392

AFRICAN AMERICAN NEWSPAPERS
Bibliographic checklist of African American newspapers, 2009n317

AFRICAN AMERICAN POLITICIANS
African-American pol leaders, 2005n695
African Americans in Congress, 2009n659

AFRICAN AMERICAN SOLDIERS
African Americans in the military, 2005n658
African Americans in the US Army in WW II, 2009n304
Black American military leaders, 2008n575
Encyclopedia of African American military hist, 2005n665
On the trail of the buffalo soldier, 2005n657

AFRICAN AMERICANS
African American almanac, 9th ed, 2005n335
African American almanac, 10th ed, 2008n307
African American biogs, 2007n267
African American issues, 2007n274
African American lives, 2005n326
African American natl biog, 2009n14
African American religious experience in America, 2007n1086
African Americans & pop culture, 2009n1047
Black Americans, 2007 ed, 2008n311
Contemporary black biog, v.42, 2005n327
Contemporary black biog, v.43, 2005n328
Contemporary black biog, v.44, 2005n329
Contemporary black biog, v.45, 2005n330
Encyclopedia of black studies, 2005n333
Encyclopedia of the African diaspora, 2009n301
Historical dict of African-American TV, 2007n1046
Martin Luther King, Jr., ency, 2009n299
Notable black American men, bk 2, 2009n297
Notable black American women, bk 3, 2005n331
Treasury of black quotations, 2006n331
Who we are: blacks, 2008n753
Who's who among African Americans, 17th ed, 2005n332
Who's who among African Americans, 18th ed, 2006n326
Who's who among African Americans, 21st ed, 2008n309

AFRICAN AMERICANS IN MASS MEDIA
African Americans in the media today, 2008n310

AFRICAN AMERICANS, RELIGION
African American religious experience in America, 2006n1216

AFRICAN AMERICANS, SOCIAL LIFE & CUSTOMS
African-American holidays, festivals, & celebrations, 2007n272

AFRICAN AMERICANS, SPORTS
African Americans in sports, 2005n749
Latino & African American athletes today, 2005n751

AFRICAN AUTHORS

African children's lit [Website], 2006n989
African letters [Website], 2006n1066
African lit in English [Website], 2006n1052
Anglophone & lusophone African women's writing [Website], 2006n1053
Bibliography of criticism on S African lit in English [Website], 2006n1054
Chinua Achebe ency, 2005n1082
Columbia gd to E African lit in English since 1945, 2009n977
Columbia gd to W African lit in English since 1945, 2009n978
Contemporary Africa database [Website], 2006n1055
Cultures & lits of Africa links [Website], 2005n1083
Literature of Africa, 2006n1056
Reading women writers & African lits [Website], 2006n1057
Rienner anthology of African lit, 2008n936
Student ency of African lit, 2009n979

AFRICAN FOLKLORE & MYTHOLOGY

African folklore, 2005n1153
African mythology A to Z, 2005n1161

AFRICANS

Encyclopedia of the African diaspora, 2009n301

AGED

Ageline database [Website], 2005n793
Encyclopedia of aging, 4th ed, 2007n693
Encyclopedia of elder care, 2005n794
Encyclopedia of health & aging, 2008n1207
Frauds against the elderly, 2005n797
Geriatric physical diagnosis, 2008n1245
Handbook of health psychology & aging, 2008n685
Internet gd to anti-aging & longevity, 2007n692
Mental health issues of older women, 2008n691
Older Americans info dir 2005, 5th ed, 2005n795
Older Americans info dir 2007, 6th ed, 2007n694
Older Americans info dir 2008, 7th ed, 2009n742
Older Americans info dir [Website], 2005n796
Online resources for senior citizens, 2d ed, 2007n695
Rights of the elderly, 2009n743
World population ageing 2007, 2008n746

AGNOSTICISM

Icons of unbelief, 2009n1089
New ency of unbelief, 2008n1058

AGRICULTURAL CHEMICALS

Pesticides, 2d ed, 2005n1298

AGRICULTURAL GEOGRAPHY

Handbook of agricultural geophysics, 2009n1143
Study of agricultural geography, 2006n1280

AGRICULTURAL SCIENCE

AGRICOLA (AGRICultural online access) [Website], 2006n1279

AIDS (DISEASE)

Global AIDS crisis, 2006n1441

AIRLINE INDUSTRY

Career opportunities in aviation & the aerospace industry, 2006n248
Plunkett's airline, hotel, & travel industry almanac, 2006 ed, 2006n190
Plunkett's airline, hotel, & travel industry almanac 2007, 2008n195

AIRLINE SECURITY

Aviation security mgmt, 2009n1348

AIRPLANES. *See also* AERONAUTICS; AVIATION

Aviation century: war & peace in the air, 2007n1336
Aviation century: wings of change, 2006n1548
Field gd to airplanes of N America, 3d ed, 2007n1337
50 aircraft that changed the world, 2008n1353
Military aircraft, 1919-45, 2009n615

ALBANIA

Historical dict of Albania, new ed, 2005n106

ALCOHOL ABUSE

Addiction counselor's desk ref, 2007n716
Alcohol & temperance in modern hist, 2005n820
Alcoholism sourcebk, 2d ed, 2007n715
Directory of drug & alcohol residential rehabilitation facilities, 2004, 2005n821
Directory of drug & alcohol residential rehabilitation facilities [Website], 2005n822
Encyclopedia of drugs, alcohol, & addictive behavior, 3d ed, 2009n762

ALGERIA

Historical dict of Algeria, 3d ed, 2007n82

ALLUSIONS

Facts on File dict of allusions, 2009n911

ALMANACS

Canadian almanac & dir 2006, 159th ed, 2006n3
Canadian almanac & dir 2007, 160th ed, 2008n3
Canadian almanac & dir 2008, 161st ed, 2009n2
Chambers bk of facts 2006, 2006n4
Chambers fact finder, 2005n2
Chase's calendar of events 2006, 49th ed, 2006n5
Chase's calendar of events 2007, 2008n4
Encyclopaedia Britannica almanac 2004, 2005n3
Encyclopaedia Britannica almanac 2006, 2007n1

New York Times almanac 2005, 2006n7
New York Times almanac 2008, 2008n5
Scott's Canadian sourcebk 2005, 40th ed, 2006n8
Whitaker's almanack 2006, 138th ed, 2006n9
Whitaker's almanack 2008, 2009n3
World Almanac & bk of facts 2005, 2005n4
World Almanac & bk of facts 2006, 2007n2
World Amanac & bk of facts 2008, 2008n6

ALTERNATIVE MEDICINE
A-Z of essential oils, 2005n1454
Ayurveda, 2009n1256
Ayurvedic herbs, 2008n1243
Book of alternative medicine, 2008n1239
Chinese natural cures, 2007n1264
Complementary & alternative medicine info for teens,
    2008n1240
Complementary & alternative medicine sourcebk, 3d
    ed, 2007n1262
Complete ency of natural healing, rev ed, 2007n1265
Complete natural gd to breast cancer, 2005n1462
Complete natural medicine gd to the 50 most common
    medicinal herbs, 2005n1453
Consumer's gd to dietary supplements & alternative
    medicines, 2008n1241
Duke ency of new medicine, 2008n1237
Encyclopedia of complementary & alternative
    medicine, 2005n1455
Encyclopedia of homeopathy, 2007n1263
Gale ency of alternative medicine, 2d ed, 2006n1439
Gale ency of alternative medicine, 3d ed, 2009n1255
Whole person healthcare, 2008n1244

AL-ZAWAHIRI, AYMAN
IntelCenter words of Ayman al-Zawahiri, v.1,
    2009n680

ALZHEIMER DISEASE
Alzheimer disease sourcebk, 4th ed, 2009n1260

AMERICAN LITERATURE. *See also* AUTHORS,
AMERICAN
Age of Milton, 2005n1002
American ethnic writers, 2009n949
American hist through lit 1820-70, 2007n937
American hist through lit 1870-1920, 2007n938
American writers, 2005n1060
American writers, suppl 17, 2009n950
American writers, suppl 18, 2009n951
Backgrounds to American lit series, 2007n946
Cambridge hist of American lit, v.3: prose writing,
    2007n947
Chicano & Chicana lit, 2007n972
Chronology of American lit, 2005n1062
Companion to the lits of Colonial America, 2006n1036
Early American nature writers, 2009n952
Encyclopedia of African-American lit, 2009n956

Encyclopedia of American Indian lit, 2008n913
Encyclopedia of American lit, rev ed, 2009n953
Encyclopedia of beat lit, 2007n939
Encyclopedia of the Chicago literary renaissance,
    2005n1064
Encyclopedia of the Harlem literary renaissance,
    2006n1034
Encyclopedia of transcendentalism, 2007n944
Facts on File companion to the American novel,
    2007n940
Greenwood ency of African American lit, 2007n941
Greenwood ency of multiethnic American lit,
    2007n942
Literary research & the American modernist era,
    2009n948
Literary research & the era of American nationalism &
    romanticism, 2009n958
Literary S Carolina, 2005n1059
Literature & the environment, 2005n1008
Magill's literary annual 2006, 2007n948
Magill's survey of American lit, 2007n935
Masterpieces of beat lit, 2008n914
Masterplots II: African American lit, rev ed, 2009n954
Notable African American writers, 2007n943
Notable American novelists, rev ed, 2008n907
100 great American novels you've (probably) never
    read, 2008n905
Oxford ency of American lit, 2005n1063
Race & racism in lit, 2006n988
Railroad in American fiction, 2006n1031
Southern writers, 2007n936
Student's ency of American literary characters,
    2009n957
Understanding the lit of WW I, 2006n987
Victorian lit hndbk, 2009n918
Washington, D.C. of fiction, 2007n919

AMERICAN SIGN LANGUAGE -
DICTIONARIES
Gallaudet dict of American sign lang, 2007n852

AMPHIBIANS
Elsevier's dict of amphibians, 2005n1400
Grzimek's student animal life resource: amphibians,
    2007n1218
Guide & ref to the amphibians of E & Central N
    America, 2007n1215
Reptiles & amphibians of the southern pine woods,
    2009n1211
World of animals: amphibians & reptiles, v.41-50,
    2006n1392

ANATOMY
Amazing baby, 2009n1174
Anatomy of exercise, 2009n735
Animal & plant anatomy, 2008n1148
Attorney's ref on human anatomy, 2009n1176

E.guides: human body, 2007n1171
First human body ency, 2006n1320
Gray's anatomy for students, 2006n1321
Handy anatomy answer bk, 2009n1175
Human body, 2007n1172
Netter's atlas of the human body, 2006n1322
World Bk's human body works, 2007n1173

ANCIENT HISTORY
Ancient Canaan & Israel, 2006n116
Ancient Greece, 2007n390
Ancient Greece, 2008n435
Ancient hist, 2006n494
Ancient Indus Valley, 2008n383
Ancient Mesopotamia, 2006n485
Ancient Mesopotamia, 3300-331 B.C.E., 2005n504
Ancient world, 2008n451
Aztecs, 2006n341
Complete royal families of ancient Egypt, 2006n484
Daily life in the medieval Islamic world, 2006n1243
Daily life in the N.T., 2009n433
Daily life of the ancient Egyptians, 2d ed, 2009n415
E.guides: Ancient Greece, 2007n391
Edinburgh companion to Ancient Greece & Rome,
     2007n384
Encyclopedia of ancient Asian civilizations, 2005n467
Encyclopedia of ancient Greece, 2006n473
Encyclopedia of society & culture in the ancient
     world, 2008n455
Encyclopedia of the ancient Greek world, rev ed,
     2006n474
Establishment of the Han Empire & Imperial China,
     2006n465
Global hist, 2005n527
Great empires of the past series, 2005n528
Great events from hist: the ancient world, prehist-476
     CE, 2005n515
Great lives from hist: the ancient world, prehist-476
     CE, rev ed, 2005n511
Greenhaven ency of Ancient Greece, 2008n436
Greenhaven ency of Ancient Mesopotamia, 2008n441
Historical atlas of Ancient Greece, 2007n392
Historical atlas of Acient Mesopotamia, 2005n502
Historical atlas of Ancient Rome, 2006n486
Historical dict of Ancient Israel, 2005126
Historical dict of Ancient S America, 2009n413
Historical dict of medieval India, 2009n101
Historical dict of the Hittites, 2005500
History of the ancient & medieval world, 2d ed,
     2009n428
Hstorical dict of ancient Egypt, 2d ed, 2009n414
Mycenaean civilization, rev ed, 2005n492
New dict of the hist of ideas, 2006n501
Oxford dict of the classical world, 2006n468
Penguin histl atlas of ancient civilizations, 2007n401
Perseus digital lib [Website], 2007n408
Reign of Cleopatra, 2006n482

Thames & Hudson dict of Ancient Egypt, 2007n400
Trojan War, 2006n514
World hist [Website], 2009n431

ANGELS
Angels A to Z, 2d ed, 2009n1091
Encyclopedia of angels, 2d ed, 2005n1240

ANGOLA
Culture & customs of Angola, 2007n83
Historical dict of Angola, new ed, 2005n84

ANIMAL RIGHTS
Animal rights, 2005n1379
Animal rights, rev ed, 2008n1167
Animals are the issue, 2005n1376

ANIMALS
Amazing animals of the world 1, 2008n1169
Amazing animals of the world 2, 2007n1184
Amazing animals of the world 3, 2007n1185
Animal & plant anatomy, 2008n1148
Animal atlas, 2007n1183
Atlas of endangered species, rev ed, 2009n1192
Carnivores of British Columbia, 2009n1204
Complete gd to artic wildlife, 2007n1188
DK 1st animal ency, 2006n1363
E.encyclopedia animal, 2007n1186
Encyclopedia of animal behavior, 2006n1364
Encyclopedia of animal sci, 2005n1333
Encyclopedia of animal sci [Website], 2005n1334
Encyclopedia of animals, 2005n1381
Encyclopedia of animals, 2006n1367
Encyclopedia of animals, 2007n1187
Encyclopedia of human-animal relationships, 2008n1165
Encyclopedia of mammals, 2d ed, 2007n1208
Extraordinary animals, 2008n1168
Field gd to N Atlantic wildlife, 2006n1366
Grzimek's student animal life resource: mammals,
     2006n1388
Nature's children, 2005n1382
Nature's children, set 1, rev ed, 2008n1170
Nature's children, set 2, 2008n1171
Nature's children, set 3, 2009n1193
Nature's children, set 4, 2009n1194
Primate family tree, 2009n1206
Storey's illus breed gd to sheep, goats, cattle, & pigs,
     2009n1168
Walker's marsupials of the world, 2006n1389
Wildlife & plants, 3d ed, 2007n1170
World atlas of great apes & their conservation,
     2006n1390
World of animals: index, 2007n1189

ANIMATED FILMS
Animated movie gd, 2007n1041
Encyclopedia of animated cartoons, 3d ed, 2009n1043

ANIME. *See also* **MANGA**
Anime ency, 2008n997

ANTACRCTIC
Antarctic fishes, 2008n1182
Canada & Arctic N America, 2008n1351
Encyclopedia of the Antarctic, 2008n148
Encyclopedia of the Arctic, 2005n90

ANTHROPOLOGY
Annual review of anthropology, v.32, 2003, 2005n322
Annual review of anthropology, v.32, 2008, 2009n290
ANSS reviews [Website], 2008n295
Anthropology of food [Website], 2008n296
Anthropology review database [Website], 2006n320
AnthroSource [Website], 2008n297
Biographical dict of social & cultural anthropology,
    2005n319
Cultural anthropology, 2d ed, 2009n292
Database of the Calif. Academy of Scis, Dept of
    Anthropology collection [Website], 2005n320
Encyclopedia of anthropology, 2007n259
Encyclopedia of medical anthropology, 2006n321
G. K. Hall bibliog gd to anthropology & archaeology
    2002, 2005n318
Human fossil record, v.3, 2007n260
Human fossil record, v.4, 2007n261
Realms of the sacred in daily life [Website], 2005n321
Visual Anthropology.net [Website], 2008n298

ANTIQUES. *See also* **COLLECTIBLES**
Antique & collectible dict, 2009n821
Antique Trader antiques & collectibles price gd 2005,
    20th ed, 2005n912
Antique Trader antiques & collectibles price gd 2006,
    2006n897
Antique Trader antiques & collectibles price gd 2007,
    2008n811
Antique Trader gd to fakes & reproductions, 4th ed,
    2008n812
Antiques 101, 2006n900
Antiques price gd 2008, 2009n820
Antiques Roadshow 20th-century collectibles,
    2005n910
Kovels' American antiques 1750-1900, 2006n899
Kovels' American Collectibles 1900 to 2000,
    2008n814
Kovels' antiques & collectibles price list 2006, 38th
    ed, 2007n795
Maloney's antiques & collectibles resource dir, 7th ed,
    2005n913
Miller's antiques price gd 2007, 2008n815
Miller's buying affordable antiques, 2008n816
Schroeder's antiques price gd 2005, 23d ed, 2005n914
Schroeder's antiques price gd 2006, 24th ed, 2006n901
Schroeder's antiques price gd 2008, 26th ed, 2008n819
Schroeder's antiques price gd 2009, 27th ed, 2009n822

Standard ency of carnival glass, 11th ed, 2009n815
Standard ency of carnival glass price gd, 16th ed,
    2009n816
Warman's antiques & collectibles price gd, 38th ed,
    2005n915
Warman's antiques & collectibles price gd, 40th ed,
    2007n796
Warman's antiques & collectibles 2009 price gd, 42d
    ed, 2009n823

ANTISEMITISM
Antisemitism, 2005n349
Antisemitism, 2006n346
Dictionary of antisemitism, 2008n457

ANTS
Ants of N America, 2008n1185
Urban ants of N America & Europe, 2009n1203

APPALACHIA
Encyclopedia of Appalachia, 2007n61

AQUARIUMS
Aquariums, 2006n1381
Focus on freshwater aquarium fish, 2005n1393
New ency of the saltwater aquarium, 2008n1183

ARAB AMERICANS
Arab Americans, 2006n332
Arab-American experience in the US & Canada,
    2008n312
Encyclopedia of Arab American artists, 2009n851

ARAB WORLD
Censorship in the Arab world, 2007n120

ARABIAN NIGHTS
Arabian Nights ency, 2005n1093

ARABIC LANGUAGE
Short ref grammar of Iraqi Arabic, repr ed, 2005n969

ARABS
Who's who in the Arab world 2009-10, 19th ed,
    2009n17

ARABS, FOLKLORE
Arab folklore, 2009n1032

ARCHAEOLOGY
ArchNet [Website], 2008n379
Concise Oxford dict of archaeology, 2d ed, 2009n357
Database of the Calif. Academy of Scis, Dept of
    Anthropology collection [Website], 2005n320
Dictionary of artifacts, 2009n358
eHRAF collection of ethnography/archaeology
    [Website], 2007n262

G. K. Hall bibliog gd to anthropology & archaeology
　　2002, 2005n318
Giza archives program [Website], 2006n419
Historical sites of Egypt, v.1, 2008n378
Milestones in archaeology, 2008n381
National archeological database (NADB) [Website],
　　2008n380
Unearthing the past, 2007n322
World ency of archaeology, 2008n382

ARCHITECTURE
Abrams gd to American house styles, 2005n945
Archiplanet [Website], 2009n857
Architectural inspiration, 2008n845
Architecture, 2007n816
Architecture of England, Scotland, & Wales,
　　2006n931
Architecture of France, 2007n817
Architecture of Greece, 2005n947
Architecture of Spain, 2006n932
Buildings of Rhode Island, 2005n82
Buildings of W.Va, 2006n76
Built in America [Website], 2009n858
Canadian churches, 2008n844
Cities & buildings collections [Website], 2009n859
Elements of style, new ed, 2006n927
Encyclopedia of 20th century architecture, 2005n948
First American women architects, 2009n856
Frank Lloyd Wright comp, rev ed, 2007n818
Global hist of architecture, 2008n843
Greenwood ency of homes through American hist,
　　2009n862
Grove ency of classical art & architecture, 2008n835
Historic preservation tech, 2009n865
Historical dict of architecture, 2009n863
Home Planner's ency of home designs, 3d ed,
　　2006n929
Home Planner's ultimate home plan ref, 2006n930
Mary Gilliatt's dict of architecture & interior design,
　　2006n928
National park architecture sourcebk, 2009n864
State houses, 2006n933
Understanding architecture, 2005n946
Visual dict of architecture, 2009n861
Vitruvio.com [Website], 2009n860

ARCHIVES
Archival info, 2005n600
Archives & archivists in the info age, 2006n613
Archives & the digital lib, 2008n522
Personal versus private: presidential records in a
　　legislative context, 2006n693
Preservation & conservation for libs & archives,
　　2006n612

ARCTIC REGIONS
Encyclopedia of the Arctic, 2005n90

ARGENTINA
Argentina, 2009n120
Argentina, rev ed, 2006n414

ARISTOTLE
Aristotle bibliog [Website], 2006n1180

ARMAGEDDON
Armageddon now, 2006n764

ARMS CONTROL
Historical dict of arms control & disarmament,
　　2006n744

ARMSTRONG, LOUIS
Louis Armstrong, 2005n1132
Satchmo: the Louis Armstrong ency, 2005n1131

ART
American art dir 2007-08, 61st ed, 2008n838
Art market research, 2007n815
Art museum image gallery [Website], 2009n848
Art nouveau, 2005n911
Artist's & graphic designer's market 2005, 2006n923
Artist's & graphic designer's market 2008, 2008n839
Artist's materials, 2006n925
Artwalks in New York, 3d ed, 2005n940
British & Irish paintings in public collections,
　　2008n846
Canadian paintings, prints, & drawings, 2008n842
Cesnola collection: terracottas [CD-ROM], 2005n951
Continuum ency of animal symbolism in art,
　　2005n939
Defining Latin American art, 2006n919
Dictionary of subjects & symbols in art, 2d ed,
　　2009n850
Encyclopedia of American folk art, 2005n935
Eye on art series, 2008n841
G. K. Hall annual bibliog of modern art 2001-02,
　　2005n930
Grove ency of classical art & architecture, 2008n835
Grove ency of materials & techniques in art, 2009n849
Inventory of paintings of Cardinal Pietro Ottoboni
　　(1667-1740), 2005n949
Looking at prints, drawings, & watercolours,
　　2007n814
National Gallery of Art: master paintings from the
　　collection, 2006n934
Oxford dict of American art & artists, 2008n836
Oxford dict of art, 3d ed, 2005n937
Queer ency of the visual arts, 2005n938
Steinway collection, repr ed, 2006n935
World art Web kiosk [Website], 2005n941

ART HISTORY
Age of Romanticism, 2008n430
America: a hist in art, 2009n855

Art & culture [Website], 2007n762
Art in world hist, 2005n943
Arts & humanities through the eras, 2005n880
Atlas of Egyptian art, paperback ed, 2009n847
Bibliographical hist of the study & use of color from
    Aristotle to Kandinsky, 2008n831
Facts on File ency of art, 2006n921
Historical dict of Renaissance art, 2008n837
Modern art: 1905-45, 2006n924
19th century French art: 1848-1905, 2006n926
Renaissance art, 2005n944
Thames & Hudson dict of design since 1900, 2d ed,
    2006n922

ART, ISLAMIC
Islam & the religious arts, 2005n1272

ART LIBRARIANSHIP
Art museum libs & librarianship, 2008n518
Guide to the lit of art hist 2, 2005n592

ARTHRITIS
Arthritis, 2009n1261
Arthritis sourcebk, 2d ed, 2005n1460

ARTISTS
African, Asian, & Middle Eastern artists' signatures &
    monographs from 1800, 2009n853
American artists II, 2008n840
Artists of Colonial America, 2005n932
Artists of the Renaissance, 2005n931
Artists of WW II, 2006n917
Authors & artists for YAs, v.73, 2008n787
Biographical ency of artists, 2006n916
Encyclopedia of Arab American artists, 2009n851
Encyclopedia of Asian American artists, 2008n833
Encyclopedia of Jewish American artists, 2008n834
Encyclopedia of Native American artists, 2009n307
Giovan Pietro Bellori: lives of the modern painters,
    sculptors, & architects, 2008n832
Oxford dict of American art & artists, 2008n836
Who's who in American art 2005-06, 26th ed,
    2006n918
Who's who in American art 2007-08, 27th ed,
    2007n812
Who's who in art, 31st ed, 2005n933
Who's who in art, 32d ed, 2007n813

ASIA
Annotated bibliog on the Mekong, 2009n94
East & SE Asia [Website], 2008n102
Historical atlas of central Asia, 2005n465
Historical dict of ancient SE Asia, 2008n100
Mapping the silk road & beyond, 2006n385
PAIR: portal to Asian Internet resources [Website],
    2008n103

Peoples of E Asia, 2005n91
Peoples of W Asia, 2008n101
Sources of E Asian tradition, 2009n95
South Asia: an environmental hist, 2009n1341
South Asia 2007, 4th ed, 2008n104
Southeast Asia, 2005n92
Southeast Asia, 2008n1345
Teen life in Asia, 2005n93
World & its peoples: Eastern & Southern Asia,
    2009n97
World & its peoples: Middle East, W Asia, & N
    Africa, 2008n145

ASIA, BUSINESS
Asian mktg data & stats 2007/08, 3d ed, 2009n196
Consumer Asia 2004, 11th ed, 2005n213
Consumer Asia 2006, 13th ed, 2006n212
Consumer Asia 2009, 2009n197
Consumer China 2005, 10th ed, 2006n213
Consumer China 2009, 14th ed, 2009n198
Directory of trade & investment-related orgs of
    developing countries & areas in Asia & the
    Pacific 2003, 2005n214
Major companies of SW Asia 2004, 8th ed, 2005n215
Major companies of SW Asia 2005, 9th ed, 2006n215
Major companies of the Far East & Australasia 2008,
    2008n219
South Asia 2009, 2009n98

ASIA, CENTRAL
Central Asia, 2006n85
Scholars' gd to Washington, D.C. for Central Asian &
    Caucasus studies, 2006n86
World & its peoples: Middle East, W Africa, & N
    Africa, 2007n124

ASIA, ECONOMICS
Economic & social survey of Asia & the Pacific 2005,
    2006n214

ASIA, FOREIGN RELATIONS
Historical dict of US-SE Asia relations, 2009n693

ASIA, LITERATURE
South Asian lit in English, 2005n1084

ASIA, POLITICS
Political hndbk of Asia 2007, 2008n653

ASIA, STATISTICS
Asian databk, 2005n839
Statistical indicators for Asia & the Pacific, v.34,
    2006n838

ASIAN AMERICAN ARTISTS
Encyclopedia of Asian American artists, 2008n833

ASIAN AMERICAN LITERATURE
Columbia gd to Asian American lit since 1945, 2007n962
Encyclopedia of Asian-American lit, 2009n955

ASIAN AMERICANS
Asian American children, 2005n336
Asian American issues, 2005n337
Asian Americans, 2007 ed, 2008n313
Student almanac of Asian American hist, 2005n338
Who we are: Asians, 2008n752

ASIAN AMERICANS, POLITICS & GOVERNMENT
East Asian Americans & pol participation, 2006n721

ASIAN THEATER
Encyclopedia of Asian theatre, 2008n1040

ASIANS
Encyclopedia of the peoples of Asia & Oceania, 2009n305
World & its peoples: Eastern & Southern Asia, 2009n97
Who's who in Asia 2007, 2008n21

ASSISTED SUICIDE
Right to die & euthanasia, rev ed, 2008n499

ASSOCIATIONS
Associationexecs.com [Website], 2007n29
AssocationExecs.com [Website], 2009n134
Associations Canada 2007, 28th ed, 2008n35
Associations USA, 2005n37
Associations USA, 2d ed, 2007n30
Associations yellow bk, Summer 2005 ed, 2006n31
Associations yellow book, 2008 ed, 2009n28
Encyclopedia of assns: intl orgs, 42d ed, 2007n31
National trade & professional assns of the US 2008, 2009n139
State & regional assns of the US 2008, 2009n33
Trade assns & professional bodies of Continental Europe, 2005 ed, 2005n221
Trade assns & professional bodies of the Continental European Union, 5th ed, 2009n202

ASTHMA
Asthma info for teens, 2006n1442
Asthma sourcebk, 2d ed, 2007n1268

ASTRONOAUTICAL ENGINEERING
Cambridge aerospace dict, 2006n1400

ASTRONOMY
A to Z of scientists in space & astronomy, 2006n1503
Ancient astronomy, 2006n1506
Astronomy, 2005n1505

Astronomy, 2007n1305
Atlas of the Messier objects, 2009n1303
Backyard astronomer's gd, 3d ed, 2009n1307
Birth of stars & planets, 2007n1304
Cambridge ency of stars, 2007n1300
Cambridge illus dict of astronomy, 2009n1304
Carolina starwatch, 2008n1298
Children's night sky atlas, 2005n1501
de Vaucouleurs atlas of galaxies, 2008n1297
E.guides: space travel, 2005n1504
Encyclopedia of space & astronomy, 2007n1299
Extrasolar planets, 2006n1504
Facts on File dict of astronomy, 5th ed, 2007n1301
Facts on File dict of space tech, rev ed, 2005n1502
Firefly atlas of the universe, 3d ed, 2006n1500
Firefly ency of astronomy, 2005n1503
Florida starwatch, 2008n1299
From luminous hot stars to starburst galaxies, 2009n1306
Frontiers of space exploration, 2d ed, 2005n1506
Great observatories of the world, 2006n1507
Handy astronomy answer bk, 2009n1308
History of astronomy, 2008n1304
Library of the 9 planets, 2006n1508
National Geographic ency of space, 2006n1505
New atlas of the moon, 2008n1301
New atlas of the stars, 2006n1501
New views of the solar system, 2008n1305
Next space age, 2009n1309
Night sky atlas, 2006n1502
Oxford companion to cosmology, 2009n1305
Space & astronomy, 2008n1302
Space exploration: almanac, 2005n1507
Space exploration: biogs, 2005n1508
Space exploration: primary sources, 2005n1509
Space sci, 2005n1510
Spacecraft launch sites worldwide, 2008n1303
Texas starwatch, 2008n1300
300 astronomical objects, 2007n1306
USA in space, 2007n1302
Visual ency of space, 2007n1303

ATHEISM
Dictionary of Atheism, skepticism, & humanism, 2007n1077
Icons of unbelief, 2009n1089
New ency of unbelief, 2008n1058

ATHLETES
African Americans in sports, 2005n749
Biography today: sports, v.12, 2005n750
Biography today: sports, v.13, 2006n767
Latino & African American athletes today, 2005n751
Native Americans in sports, 2005n752

ATHLETIC TRAINING
Quick ref dict for athletic training, 2d ed, 2006n1454
Sports sci hndbk, 2006n1455

ATLASES. *See also* **CHILDREN'S ATLASES**
America discovered, 2005n385
Atlas A to Z, rev ed, 2005n368
Atlas of US hist, rev ed, 2009n359
Chambers ref atlas, 8th ed, 2006n370
Comparative world atlas, 3d ed, 2006n371
Comparative world atlas, rev ed, 2009n329
DK compact atlas of the world, 3d ed, 2006n372
DK 1st atlas, 2006n373
Dorling Kindersley concise atlas of the world, 2d ed,
    2005n369
Dorling Kindersley concise atlas of the world, 3d ed,
    2006n374
Dorling Kindersley traveler's atlas, 2006n393
Dorling Kindersley world atlas, 3d ed, 2005n370
Dorling Kindersley world atlas, 6th ed, 2007n297
Encyclopaedia Britannica world atlas, 2007n298
Firefly atlas of N America, 2007n300
Firefly great world atlas, 2006n375
G. K. Hall bibliog gd to maps & atlases 2002,
    2005n381
G. K. Hall bibliog gd to maps & atlases 2003,
    2006n383
Gramercy family world atlas, 2008n350
Great world atlas, 3d ed, 2005n371
Hammond essential world atlas, 2009n330
Hammond world atlas, 5th ed, 2009n331
Hammond world travel atlas, 2005n392
Historical atlas of central Asia, 2005n465
Historical map & chart project [Website], 2006n376
Historical maps online [Website], 2005n372
Historical maps online [Website], 2007n301
Illustrated atlas, rev ed, 2005n373
Maps on file, 2005 ed, 2005n375
Maryland State Archives atlas of histl maps of Md.
    1608-1908, 2006n381
National Geographic atlas of the world, 8th ed,
    2006n377
National Geographic family ref atlas of the world, 2d
    ed, 2007n303
National Geographic histl atlas of the US, 2006n427
National Geographic US atlas for young explorers,
    updated ed, 2006n378
New concise world atlas, 2d ed, 2007n304
Oxford atlas of exploration, 2d ed, 2009n332
Oxford atlas of N America, 2006n379
Oxford atlas of the US, 2009n333
Oxford atlas of the world, 12th ed, 2005n376
Oxford atlas of the world, 13th ed, 2007n305
Oxford atlas of the world, 14th ed, 2008n351
Oxford atlas of the world, 15th ed, 2009n334
Oxford atlas of the world, deluxe ed, 2006n380
Oxford essential world atlas, 2009n335
Random House atlas of the world, 2005n378
Random House world atlas & ency, 2008n30
Reader's Digest illus world atlas, 2007n306
Scholastic new headline world atlas, 2006n382

Student atlas, 3d ed, 2005n379
World Almanac world atlas, 2005n380
World atlas [Website], 2009n336
World Bk atlas, 2007n307

ATMOSPHERE
Encyclopedia of the atmospheric environment
    [Website], 2005n1513

AUDIO RECORDINGS
Latino media resource gd 2004, 2005n908

AUDIOVISUAL MATERIALS. *See also* **VIDEO
RECORDINGS**
Audio visual market place 2009, 37th ed, 2009n811
AV market place 2006, 2007n784
Cataloging of audiovisual materials & other special
    materials, 5th ed, 2009n541

AUSTRALIA
Australia, 5th ed, 2008n370
Australia, rev 4th ed, 2006n404
Australia, New Zealand, & the Pacific, 2006n1542
Australia, Oceania, & Antarctica, 2005n1542
Culture & customs of Australia, 2005n103
Encyclopedia of Melbourne, 2007n104
Historical dict of Australia, 3d ed, 2008n110
Historical dict of Australian radio & TV, 2008n1019
Plants of the Kimberley region of W Australia, rev ed,
    2005n1354
Rough gd to Australia, 6th ed, 2005n402
Wine atlas of Australia, 2008n1116

AUSTRIA, HISTORY
Issues in Germany, Austria, & Switzerland, 2005n105

AUTHORS
Authors & artists for YAs, v.73, 2008n787
Biography today: authors, v.16, 2005n997
Biography today: authors, v.18, 2007n875
Black lit criticism, 2009n903
Bloom's literary ref online [Website], 2009n904
Books & writers [Website], 2006n975
Concise major 21st-century writers, 2007n871
Cyclopedia of world authors, 4th rev ed, 2005n984
Cyclopedia of YA authors, 2006n1001
Encyclopedia of world writers: beginnings through the
    13th century, 2006n980
Encyclopedia of world writers: 14th through 18th
    centuries, 2006n981
Encyclopedia of world writers: 19th & 20th centuries,
    2006n982
Franz Kafka ency, 2006n1058
Great world writers: 20th century, 2005n985
International who's who of authors & writers 2005,
    2006n976

International who's who of authors & writers 2007,
    22d ed, 2007n876
International who's who of authors & writers 2009,
    24th ed, 2009n907
Literary 100, rev ed, 2009n906
Literary ref online [Website], 2007n873
Multicultural writers since 1945, 2005n986
100 most popular genre fiction authors, 2007n921
100 most popular nonfiction authors, 2009n985
Popular contemporary writers, 2006n974
Short story writers, rev ed, 2008n875
Victorian women writers project [Website], 2005n994
Women writers project [Website], 2007n874
World authors 2000-05, 2008n876
World writers in English, 2005n996
Writers dir 2005, 20th ed, 2005n1000
Writers dir 2006, 21st ed, 2006n977
Writers dir 2007, 22d ed, 2007n877
Writers dir 2009, 24th ed, 2009n908

AUTHORS, AFRICAN

African children's lit [Website], 2006n989
African letters [Website], 2006n1066
African lit in English [Website], 2006n1052
Anglophone & lusophone African women's writing
    [Website], 2006n1053
Bibliography of criticism on S African lit in English
    [Website], 2006n1054
Chinua Achebe ency, 2005n1082
Contemporary Africa database [Website], 2006n1055
Cultures & lits of Africa links [Website], 2005n1083
Literature of Africa, 2006n1056
Reading women writers & African lits [Website],
    2006n1057
Rienner anthology of African lit, 2008n936

AUTHORS, AMERICAN

A to Z of American women writers, rev ed, 2008n909
African American women writers of the 19th century
    [Website], 2007n934
Alice Walker, 2006n1040
American ethnic writers, 2009n949
American writers, 2005n1060
American writers, suppl 17, 2009n950
American writers, suppl 18, 2009n951
Amy Tan, 2005n1071
Companion to Faulkner studies, 2005n1067
Critical companion to Arthur Miller, 2008n922
Critical companion to Edgar Allan Poe, 2008n923
Critical companion to Emily Dickinson, 2007n949
Critical companion to Ernest Hemingway, 2008n920
Critical companion to F. Scott Fitzgerald, 2008n917
Critical companion to Flannery O'Connor, 2009n964
Critical companion to Herman Melville, 2008n921
Critical companion to John Steinbeck, 2006n1039
Critical companion to Kurt Vonnegut, 2009n966
Critical companion to Mark Twain, 2008n924
Critical companion to Nathaniel Hawthorne, 2007n951
Critical companion to Robert Frost, 2008n918
Critical companion to T. S. Eliot, 2008n916
Critical companion to Tennessee Williams, 2006n1041
Critical companion to Toni Morrison, 2009n963
Critical companion to Walt Whitman, 2007n954
Critical companion to William Faulkner, 2009n960
Critical companion to Zora Neale Hurston, 2009n961
Dr. Seuss catalog, 2006n991
Early American nature writers, 2009n952
Encyclopedia of African American women writers,
    2008n911
Encyclopedia of beat lit, 2007n939
Encyclopedia of the Chicago literary renaissance,
    2005n1064
Gore Vidal, 2008n925
Henry Wadsworth Longfellow companion, 2005n1069
Jack Aubrey commands, 2005n1070
Jack Kerouac, 2005n1068
Jamaica Kincaid, 2009n962
James Welch, 2005n1073
John Steinbeck bibliog 1996-2006, 2009n965
John Steinbeck ency, 2007n953
Kaye Gibbons, 2008n919
Literary S Carolina, 2005n1059
Magill's survey of American lit, 2007n935
Mark Twain, 2005n1072
Masterplots II: African American lit, rev ed, 2009n954
Notable African American writers, 2007n943
Notable American novelists, rev ed, 2008n907
100 most popular African American authors,
    2008n908
Oxford W. E. B. Du Bois, 2008n915
Patrick O'Brian Muster bk, 2007n952
Richard Wright, 2008n926
Richard Wright ency, 2009n967
Robert E. Howard, 2008n906
Southern writers, 2007n936
Supplement to Ralph Waldo Emerson, 2007n950
Understanding Melville's short fiction, 2006n1038
Webster's new explorer dict of American writers,
    2005n1061
Wizard of Oz catalog, 2006n995
Writing African American women, 2007n945

AUTHORS, ARAB

Undergraduate's companion to Arab writers & their
    Web Sites, 2006n1064

AUTHORS, AUSTRALIAN

Australian writers, 1975-2000, 2007n963

AUTHORS, CANADIAN

Alice Munro, 2008n937
Margaret Atwood, 2005n1085
Margaret Atwood, 2008n938

AUTHORS, ENGLISH

Alexander Pope ency, 2005n1112
All things Austen, 2006n1048
All things Chaucer, 2008n929
Arthurian writers, 2009n969
British women romantic poets, 1789-1952 [Website], 2005n1100
British writers, suppl 14, 2009n968
Chronology of Jane Austen & her family, 2008n928
Class & society in Shakespeare, 2009n974
Contemporary writers in the UK [Website], 2006n1042
Critical companion to Charles Dickens, 2008n930
Critical companion to Chaucer, 2007n957
Critical companion to Jane Austen, 2009n973
Critical companion to William Shakespeare, 2006n1050
Dickens's nonfictional theatrical, & poetical writings, 2008n931
Encyclopedia of British writers, 2006n1043
Essential Shakespeare hndbk, 2005n1080
Everyone & everything in George Eliot, 2007n958
Everyone & everything in Trollope, 2005n1081
Field gd to Narnia, 2005n1078
General studies of Charles Dickens & his writings & collected eds of his works, 2005n1077
Greenwood companion to Shakespeare, 2006n1051
J. R. R. Tolkien companion & gd, 2008n934
J. R. R. Tolkien ency, 2008n935
John Buchan, 2009n942
Oxford companion to Chaucer, 2005n1076
Oxford companion to the Brontes, 2005n1075
Shakespeare for students, 2d ed, 2008n933
Shakespeare's lang, 2d ed, 2009n975
Shakespeare's religious lang, 2007n959
Student companion to Thomas Hardy, 2008n932
Undergraduate's companion to English Renaissance writers & their Web sites, 2005n1074
World Shakespeare bibliog online [Website], 2009n976

AUTHORS, FRENCH

Rabelais ency, 2005n1086

AUTHORS, IRISH

Cambridge hist of Irish lit, 2007n965
Critical companion to James Joyce, 2007n968
Critical companion to Jonathan Swift, 2007n967
Irish women writers, 2007n969

AUTHORS, LATIN AMERICAN

Latin American women writers, 2008n943
Notable Latino writers, 2006n1062

AUTHORS, RUSSIAN

Dostoevsky ency, 2005n1097
Leo Tolstoy, 2007n974

AUTHORS, SPANISH

Cervantes ency, 2005n1098
Merce Rodoreda, 2005n1099

AUTHORSHIP. *See also* PUBLISHERS & PUBLISHING; STYLE GUIDES

American dir of writer's gdlines, 5th ed, 2007n769
Author law A to Z, 2006n876
Author's hndbk, 2d ed, 2007n773
Bryson's dict for writers & editors, 2009n802
Children's writer's & illus market 2006, 18th ed, 2006n877
Children's writer's & illus market 2008, 2008n793
Christian writer's market gd 2007, 2008n797
Christian writers' market gd 2005, 2006n880
Cite right, 2007n779
Craft & business of writing, 2009n805
Dictionary of concise writing, 2d ed, 2007n768
Elements of style, 2006n887
Facts on File gd to good writing, 2006n882
Facts on File gd to style, 2007n777
Guide to literary agents 2005, 2005n891
Guide to literary agents 2007, 2007n770
Handbook of rhetorical devices [Website], 2009n803
Magazine writer's hndbk, 2d ed, 2007n774
Manual for writers of research papers, theses, & dissertations, 7th ed, 2008n801
MLA style manual & gd to scholarly publishing, 3d ed, 2009n808
Novel & short story writer's market, 2006, 25th ed, 2006n878
Novel & short story writer's market, 2007, 2008n794
Oxford American writer's thesaurus, 2d ed, 2009n895
Poet's market, 2006, 21st ed, 2006n879
Poet's market, 2008, 2008n795
Random House writer's ref, rev ed, 2005n895
Writer's market, 2005, 2005n892
Writer's market, 2007, 2008n796
Writer's market, 2009, 88th ed, 2009n804
Writer's market companion, 2d ed, 2006n881
Writing the critical essay series, 2009n806

AUTISM

Autism & pervasive developmental sourcebk, 2009n1262
Encyclopedia of autism spectrum disorders, 2007n1269

AUTOBIOGRAPHY

Autobiographical writings on Mexico, 2006n1063
Encyclopedia of women's autobiog, 2006n856
Remembered childhoods, 2008n945

AUTOMOBILE DRIVERS' RECORDS

MVR bk, 2006 ed, 2006n544
MVR bk, 2008 ed, 2009n455
MVR decoder digest, 2006 ed, 2006n545

MVR decoder digest, 2008 ed, 2009n456

AUTOMOBILE INDUSTRY
Career opportunities in the automotive industry,
    2006n254
Historical who's who of the automotive industry in
    Europe, 2007n1341
Plunkett's automobile industry almanac, 2005,
    2005n196
Plunkett's automobile industry almanac, 2007,
    2007n169
Plunkett's automobile industry almanac, 2009 ed,
    2009n176

AUTOMOBILES
American cars, 1946-59, 2009n1350
American cars, 1960 to 1972, 2005n1549
Automotive Websites, 2d ed, 2007n1340
Car & its future, 2005n1548
Cars & culture, 2005n1550
Great American hot rods, 2007n1339
Standard gd to American muscle cars, 4th ed,
    2006n1551

AVIATION
Aviation century: the golden age, 2005n1546
Aviation century: wings of change, 2006n1548
Aviation century: WW II, 2005n1547
Aviation security mgmt, 2009n1348
Military aircraft, origins to 1918, 2006n678

AWARDS & PRIZES
Awards, honors & prizes, 23d ed, 2005n38
Awards, honors & prizes, 24th ed, 2006n32
Awards, honors & prizes, 26th ed, 2008n36
Children's bks: awards & prizes, 2005 ed, 2006n1003
Coretta Scott King awards 1970-2004, 3d ed,
    2005n1056
Entertainment awards, 3d ed, 2005n1183
Ethnic bk awards, 2006n1004
Newbery & Caldecott awards, 2005n1033
Newbery & Caldecott awards, 2006 ed, 2007n899
Newbery & Caldecott awards, 2007 ed, 2008n885
Newbery & Caldecott awards, 2008 ed, 2009n926
Newbery/Printz companion, 3d ed, 2008n884
Nobel: a century of prize winners, 2009n13
Nobel e-museum [Website], 2005n15
Pura Belpre awards, 2007n906
Women Nobel Peace Prize winners, 2007n11

AZTECS
Aztecs, 2006n341
Handbook to life in the Aztec world, 2007n279

BACTERIA
Microterrors, 2005n1337

BAHAI FAITH
Historical dict of the Baha'i faith, 2d ed, 2007n1093

BALTIC STATES
Culture & customs of the Baltic States, 2007n109

BANGLADESH
Historical dict of Bangladesh, 3d ed, 2005n94

BANKING. *See also* FINANCE
Banking basics [Website], 2009n159
Banking tutor [Website], 2009n160
Dictionary of banking terms, 5th ed, 2007n162
Dictionary of finance & banking, 4th ed, 2009n164
Federal Reserve educ [Website], 2009n161
Federal Reserve system, 2006n166
Financial yellow bk, Summer 2005, 2006n169
Financial yellow bk, 2008 ed, 2009n168
First Bank of the US [Website], 2009n162
Maggie L. Walker natl historic site [Website],
    2009n163
Major financial institutions of the world 2004, 7th ed,
    2005n185
Major financial institutions of the world, 9th ed,
    2007n163
Plunkett's banking, mortgages, & credit industry
    almanac 2005, 2006n170
Plunkett's banking, mortgages, & credit industry
    almanac 2006, 2007n164
Plunkett's banking, mortgages, & credit industry
    almanac 2009, 2009n169
TheStreet.com ratings' gd to banks & thrifts, Fall
    2007, 2008n182
TheStreet.com ratings' gd to banks & thrifts, Spring
    2008, 2009n170
Weiss Ratings' gd to banks & thrifts, Fall 2005,
    2006n173
Weiss Ratings' gd to banks & thrifts, Summer 2004,
    2005n186

BASEBALL
African American pioneers of baseball, 2008n707
Ballparks of the deadball era, 2009n719
Baseball bibliog, 2d ed, 2007n675
Baseball bks, 2008n708
Baseball cyclopedia, repr ed, 2006n777
Baseball novel, 2009n939
Baseball prospectus 2005, 2006n779
Baseball's retired nos, 2005n763
Black stars who made baseball whole, 2006n783
Cultural ency of baseball, 2d ed, 2006n778
Diamonds around the globe, 2006n776Great World
    Series games, 2006n784
Early exits: the premature endings of baseball careers,
    2007n682
Encyclopedia of major league baseball clubs,
    2007n678

Encyclopedia of women & baseball, 2007n679
Hank Aaron, 2006n775
Iron men of baseball, 2007n676
Leadoff batters of major league baseball, 2007n681
Lou Gehrig, 2005n766
Negro Leagues chronology, 2007n677
Official Major League baseball fact bk, 2005 ed,
    2006n780
Pete Rose, 2005n765
Phillies ency, 3d ed, 2005n768
Roger Hornsby, 2005n764
Sporting News baseball gd 2006, 2007n683
Sporting News baseball gd, 2005 ed, 2006n781
Sporting News baseball register 2007, 2007n684
Sporting News baseball register, 2005 ed, 2006n782
Spring training hndbk, 2005n769
Team-by-team ency of major league baseball,
    2007n680
Ted Williams, 2005n767
Texas league in baseball, 1888-1958, 2005n770\
2006 ESPN baseball ency, 2007n685
Willie Mays, 2006n774

BASKETBALL
Atlantic coast conference men's basketball games,
    2008n709
Basketball, 2006n785
Clemson Univ men's basketball games, 2009n720
Duke Univ men's basketball games, 2009n721
Georgia Tech men's basketball games, 2009n722
National Basketball Assn ultimate basketball,
    2005n771
North Carolina State Univ men's basketball games,
    2009n723
Sporting News official NBA gd 2006-07, 2007n686
University of Maryland men's basketball games,
    2009n724
University of N.C. men's basketball games, 2008n710
University of Va. men's basketball games, 2009n725

BATTLESHIPS
Battleships, 2006n680
Cruisers & battle cruisers, 2005n679
Naval Institute gd to combat fleets of the world
    2005-06, 2006n674
Naval Institute gd to the ships & aircraft of the US
    Fleet, 18th ed, 2006n675
Russian & Soviet battleships, 2005n674

BEAT LITERATURE
Encyclopedia of beat lit, 2007n939
Masterpieces of beat lit, 2008n914

BED & BREAKFAST ACCOMMODATIONS
Bed & breakfast Ireland 2006, 2008n372
Irish bed & breakfast bk, 2009n352

BEES
Bees of the world, 2d ed, 2008n1186

BELARUS
Historical dict of Belarus, 2d ed, 2008n120

BELGIUM
Historical dict of Belgium, 2d ed, 2008n118
Historical dict of Brussels, 2005n107

BERBERS
Historical dict of the Berbers (Imazighen), 2009n306

BEST BOOKS
Best bks for boys, 2009n933
Best bks for children, 8th ed, 2007n886
Best bks for high school readers grades 9-12,
    2005n1017
Best bks for middle school & jr high readers grades
    6-9, 2005n1018
Best bks for YAs, 3d ed, 2008n881
More outstanding bks for the college bound, 2006n620

BIBLE & LITERATURE
Everyday biblical literacy, 2008n1070
Thematic gd to biblical lit, 2008n1072

BIBLE - ATLASES
IVP atlas of Bible hist, 2007n1094
Oxford Bible atlas, 4th ed, 2009n1093

BIBLE - BIBLIOGRAPHY
Ancient texts for the study of the Hebrew Bible,
    2006n1220
Biblical studies on the Internet, 2d ed, 2009n1095
Unbound Bible [Website], 2007n1095

BIBLE - BIOGRAPHY
All the people in the Bible, 2009n1096
Peoples of the N.T. world, 2009n1097
Who's who in the Jewish Bible, 2009n1118

BIBLE - DICTIONARIES & ENCYCLOPEDIAS
All things in the Bible, 2007n1100
Ancient Christian commentary on scripture CD-ROM
    [CD-ROM], 2006n1221
Baker ency of Bible people, 2007n1096
Concise dict of Bible origins & interpretation,
    2008n1069
Dictionary for theological interpretation of the Bible,
    2007n1097
Dictionary of biblical criticism & interpretation,
    2008n1067
Dictionary of major biblical interpreters, 2008n1068
Dictionary of the O.T.: histl bks, 2006n1222
Expository dict of Bible words, 2006n1223

Illustrated gd to the Bible, 2009n1098
IVP dict of the N.T., 2005n1248
New interpreter's dict of the Bible, v.1, 2008n1071
Theological dict of the O.T., v.14, 2005n1249
Theological dict of the O.T., v.15, 2007n1099

BIBLE - HANDBOOKS & YEARBOOKS
American Catholic Bible in the 19th century,
    2007n1103
Ancient texts for N.T. studies, 2007n1101
Art of The Saint John's Bible, 2009n1099
Handbook of patristic exegesis, 2005n1250
Interpreting the Bible, 2007n1098
IVP intro to the Bible, 2008n1073
Manners & customs in the Bible, 3d ed, 2007n1102
Mastering N.T. Greek, 2007n1104
Targum of Psalms, 2005n1251

BIBLE - QUOTATION BOOKS
On reading the Bible, 2006n1224

BIBLIOGRAPHIC RECORDS
Functional requirements for bibliog records (FRBR),
    2006n616

BIBLIOGRAPHY
Canadian bks in print, 2004: author & title index,
    2005n7
Canadian bks in print, 2004: subject index, 2005n8
Canadian bks in print, 2005: author & title index,
    2006n12
Canadian bks in print, 2005: subject index, 2006n13
CD-ROMs in print, 18th ed, 2005n9
Complete dir of large print bks & serials 2005,
    2006n14
Eighteenth-century current bibliog, 2007n4
Eighteenth-century current bibliog: n.s. v.26 for 2000,
    2006n10
Eighteenth-century current bibliog, n.s. v.27 for 2001,
    2006n11
Eighteenth-century current bibliog: n.s. v.29-for 2003,
    2008n8
Focus groups, v.1, 2009n5
Guide to microforms in print 2007, 2008n9
H-NET reviews in the humanities & social scis
    [Website], 2007n5
Online bks page [Website], 2005n10
Online bks page [Website], 2007n8
Public lib catalog, 12th ed, 2005n5
Reference Bks Bulletin 2002-03, 2005n6
Small press record of bks in print 2008, 33d ed
    [CD-ROM], 2008n10

BILL DRAFTING
Legislative drafter's desk ref, 2d ed, 2008n476

BIN LADEN, OSAMA
IntelCenter words of Osama Bin Laden, v.1, 2009n681

BIOETHICS
Bioethics & medical issues in lit, 2006n1012

BIOGRAPHY
African American lives, 2005n326
African American natl biog, 2009n14
Almanac of famous people, 8th ed, 2005n11
Almanac of famous people, 9th ed, 2008n11
American heroes, 2009n362
American natl biog, suppl 2, 2006n20
American natl biog [Website], 2008n17
American villains, 2009n461
Biographical connections series, 2007n9
Biography ref bank [Website], 2009n7
Biography resource center [Website], 2009n8
Biography today, v.12, 2003, 2005n12
Biography today, v.13, 2006n15
Biography today, v.14—2005 annual cumulation,
    2007n10
Biography today, v.15, 2008n12
Biography today, v.16—2007 annual cumulation,
    2009n9
Canadian who's who 2004, v.39, 2005n25
Canadian who's who 2005, v.40, 2006n22
Canadian who's who 2006, v.41, 2007n19
Canadian who's who 2007, v.42, 2008n22
Canadian who's who 2008, 2009n16
Contemporary black biog, v.42, 2005n327
Contemporary black biog, v.43, 2005n328
Contemporary black biog, v.44, 2005n329
Contemporary black biog, v.45, 2005n330
Current biog cumulated index 1940-2005, 2007n42
Current biog illus [Website], 2009n15
Current biog intl yrbk 2003, 2005n13
Current biog intl yrbk 2004, 2006n16
Current biog intl yrbk 2007, 2008n13
Current biog yrbk 2003, 2005n21
Current biog yrbk 2005, 2007n15
Current biog yrbk 2007, 2008n18
Dictionary of Canadian biog, v.25, 1921-30, 2006n23
Dictionary of Jewish biog, 2006n347
Encyclopedia of world biog suppl, v.24, 2005n14
Encyclopedia of world biography, suppl, v. 27,
    2009n10
Great lives from hist: notorious lives,
    2008n443International who's who [Website],
    2008n14
Great lives from hist: the ancient world, prehist-476
    CE, rev ed, 2005n511
Great lives from hist: the Middle Ages, 477-1453,
    2005n512
Great lives from hist: the 20th century, 1901-2000,
    2009n417

International who's who 2006, 69th ed, 2006n17
International who's who 2008, 2009n11
Marquis who's who on the Web [Website], 2008n15
Newsmakers 2005 cum ed, 2006n18
Newsmakers 2007, 2009n12
Nobel e-museum [Website], 2007n12
Nobel: a century of prize winners, 2009n13
Oxford dict of natl biog [Website], 2005n17
Oxford dict of natl biog, new ed, 2005n16
Remembered childhoods, 2008n945
Riverside dict of biography, 2005n18
Scribner ency of American lives, v.7, 2007n16
U*X*L Newsmakers, 2005n19
Western lives, 2005n22
Who was who in America 2006-07, 2008n19
Who was who in America, with world notables
    2002-04, v.15, 2005n23
Who: a dir of prominent people, 2006n19
Who: a dir of prominent people, 2d ed, 2007n13
Who's who in America 2005, 59th ed, 2005n24
Who's who in America 2006, 60th ed, 2006n21
Who's who in America 2007, 61st ed, 2007n17
Who's who in the Arab world 2005-06, 17th ed,
    2005n26
Who's who in the Arab world 2009-10, 19th ed,
    2009n17
Who's who in the East 2008, 35th ed, 2008n20
Who's who in the world 2005, 22d ed, 2005n20
Who's who in the world, 24th ed, 2007n14
Who's who of American women 2006-07, 25th ed,
    2006n853
Who's who of emerging leaders 2007, 2008n16
World cultural leaders of the 20th & 21st centuries, 2d
    ed, 2008n788

BIOLOGICAL HAZARDS
Microterrors, 2005n1337

BIOLOGICAL SCIENCES
Amazing baby, 2009n1174
Basics of biology, 2005n1342
Biology, 2008n1139
Biology matters! 2005n1339
Biology resources in the electronic age, 2005n1335
Biomes of Earth, 2005n1343
Cambridge dict of human biology & evolution,
    2006n1313
Chicago gd to landing a job in academic biology,
    2008n1145
Dictionary of biology, 6th ed, 2009n1170
Dictionary of microbiology & molecular biology, 3d
    ed, 2008n1142
E.guides: human body, 2007n1171
Elsevier's dict of zoology & general biology,
    2005n1380
Encyclopedia of biology, 2005n1338
Encyclopedia of life scis, 2d ed, 2005n1336

Essential atlas of biology, 2005n1341
Facts on File biology hndbk, rev ed, 2007n1168
Facts on File dict of biology, 4th ed, 2006n1314
Handbook of proteins, 2009n1173
Handy biology answer bk, 2005n1340
Invasive species in the Pacific NW, 2007n1169
McGraw-Hill concise ency of biosci, 2006n1315
New biology series, 2006n1318
Penguin dict of biology, 11th ed, 2006n1316
Wildlife & plants, 3d ed, 2007n1170
World Bk's human body works, 2007n1173
World Bk's sci & nature gds, 2005n1344

BIOLOGICAL WARFARE
Chemical & biological warfare, 2d ed, 2007n572

BIOMEDICAL ENGINEERING
Encyclopedia of biomaterials & biomedical
    engineering, 2005n1405
Encyclopedia of biomaterials & biomedical
    engineering [Website], 2005n1406
Sourcebook of models in biomedical research,
    2009n1212
Wiley ency of biomedical engineering, 2007n1222

BIOMETRIC TECHNOLOGY
Grey House biometric info dir 2006, 2006n180
Grey House biometric info dir online [Website],
    2006n181

BION, W. R.
Dictionary of the work of W. R. Bion, 2005n736

BIOTECHNOLOGY
Biotechnology, 2008n1140
Biotechnology & genetic engineering, rev ed,
    2005n1413
Plunkett's biotech & genetics industry almanac, 2006
    ed, 2006n191
Plunkett's biotech & genetics industry almanac, 2007
    ed, 2007n170
Plunkett's biotech & genetics industry almanac, 2009
    ed, 2009n177

BIOTERRORISM
Encyclopedia of bioterrorism defense, 2006n751

BIOTIC COMMUNITIES
Biomes of Earth, 2005n1343

BIRDS
Arizona breeding bird atlas, 2006n1368
Atlas of bird migration, 2008n1172
Bird almanac, rev ed, 2005n1384
Bird-finding gd to Panama, 2009n1195
Birder's companion, 2008n1179
Birds, 2007n1191

Birds of Australia, 7th ed, 2006n1375
Birds of Costa Rica, 2008n1176
Birds of the Carolinas, 2d ed, 2007n1195
Birds of the raincoast, 2005n1390
Birds of the world, 2007n1190
Birds of the world, 2008n1177
Birds of the world, 2009n1196
Clements checklist of birds of the world, 6th ed,
	2008n1173
Encyclopedia of birds, 2008n1174
Extreme birds, 2009n1198
Field gd to N Atlantic wildlife, 2006n1366
Finding birds of the great Tex. Coastal birding trail,
	2009n1199
Grzimek's student animal life resource: birds,
	2005n1385
Guide to backyard birds, 2006n1373
Guide to the birds of the SE states, 2007n1196
Gulls of N America, Europe, & Asia, 2005n1389
Gulls of the Americas, 2008n1178
Handbook of bird biology, 2d ed, 2005n1386
Introduction to birds of the S Calif. Coast, 2006n1372
Jim Burns' Ariz. birds, 2009n1197
National Geographic complete birds of N America,
	2007n1193
National Geographic field gd to the birds of N
	America, 5th ed, 2007n1194
National Geographic ref atlas to the birds of N
	America, 2006n1374
Nesting birds of a tropical frontier, 2006n1369
North American birdfeeder gd, 2006n1370
Oklahoma breeding bird atlas, 2005n1388
Pete Dunne's essential field gd companion, 2007n1192
Photographic gd to the birds of the Indian Ocean
	islands, 2008n1181
Raptors of N America, 2007n1197
Second atlas of breeding birds in N.Y. state,
	2009n1200
TOS hndbk of Tex. birds, 2005n1387
Waterfowl of eastern N America, 2006n1371

BLUES MUSIC
American popular music: blues, 2006n1099
Billboard illus ency of jazz & blues, 2007n1011
Encyclopedia of the blues, 2007n1007
Penguin gd to blues recordings, 2008n986

BODY, HUMAN - SOCIAL ASPECTS
Cultural ency of the body, 2009n291
Encyclopedia of body adornment, 2009n843

BODYBUILDING
Bodybuilding anatomy, 2009n726
Encyclopedia of muscle & strength, 2008n700
Sculpting her body perfect, 3d ed, 2009n727

BOOK COLLECTING
ABC for bk collectors, 8th ed, 2005n920
Antique Trader bk collector's price gd, 2d ed,
	2007n797
Antique Trader collectible paperback price gd,
	2009n824
Bookman's price index, v.76, 2005n916
Bookman's price index, v.77, 2005n917
Bookman's price index, v.78, 2005n918
Bookman's price index, v.79, 2005n919
Bookman's price index, v.88, 2009n825
Bookman's price index, v.89, 2009n826
Encyclopedia of collectible children's bks, 2009n827
Lewis Carroll among his bks, 2006n647
Warman's Little Golden Bks, 2007n798

BOOK INDUSTRIES & TRADE. *See also*
PUBLISHERS & PUBLISHING
American bk trade dir 2008-09, 54th ed, 2009n590
Bowker annual lib & bk trade almanac 2007, 52d ed,
	2008n510
Directory of pub 2008, 33d ed, 2008n566
International literary market place 2008, 2008n567
International literary market place 2009, 2009n595
Introduction to manuscript studies, 2009n598
Literary market place 2007, 67th ed, 2008n568
Literary market place 2009, 2009n596
Publishing, bks, & reading in Sub-Saharan Africa,
	2009n589

BOOK REVIEWS
Book review index, 2004 cum ed, 2005n55
Book review index, 2005 cum ed, 2006n53
Book review index, 2008 cum ed, 2009n42
Children's bk review index, v.29, 2003, 2005n1032
Literature of chemistry, 2006n1489
Reference Bks Bulletin 2002-03, 2005n6

BOOKS, HISTORY
Book: the life story of a tech, 2006n657
History of the bk in America, v.1: the Colonial bk in
	the Atlantic world, 2008n569
History of the bk in America, v.3: the industrial bk,
	1840-80, 2008n570
History of the bk in Canada, v.1, 2006n655
History of the bk in Canada, v.2, 2006n656
History of the bk in Canada, v.3, 2008n571

BOOKTALKS
Booktalking bonanza, 2009n549

BOSNIA & HERZEGOVINA
Historical dict of Bosnia & Herzegovina, 2d ed,
	2008n119

BOTANY. *See also* **PLANTS**
Animal & plant anatomy, 2008n1148
Atlas of woody plant stems, 2009n1180
Botany for gardeners, rev ed, 2006n1302
Crocosmia & chasmanthe, 2005n1361
eNature.com [Website], 2006n1328
Encyclopedia of plant & crop sci, 2005n1348
Encyclopedia of plant & crop sci [Website],
    2005n1349
Encyclopedia of psychoactive plants, translated ed,
    2006n1331
Field gd to ferns & their related families, 2d ed,
    2006n1333
Flora of N America N of Mexico, v.4, pt. 1,
    2005n1360
Flora of N America N of Mexico, v.19, 2007n1176
Flora of N America N of Mexico, v.20, 2007n1177
Flora of N America N of Mexico, v.21, 2007n1178
Flora of N America N of Mexico, v.24, 2008n1150
Flowering plant families of the world, 2008n1157
Flowering plants of the neotropics, 2005n1356
Fruit, 2005n1367
Genus lavandula, 2005n1351
Genus paeonia, 2005n1362
Gymnosperm database [Website], 2006n1340
Handbook of plant biotech, 2005n1353
Handbook of plant sci, 2008n1151
Hardy gingers, 2006n1344
International plant names index [Website], 2006n1341
Medicinal plants of N America, 2009n1178
Medicinal plants of the world, 2005n1352
Names of plants, 4th ed, 2009n1177
Native plants of the northeast, 2006n1335
North American wildland plants, 2005n1355
Passiflora, 2005n1358
Photosynthesis & the Web [Website], 2006n1323
Phylogeny of life [Website], 2006n1329
Plant, 2006n1330
Plant ontology consortium (POC) [Website],
    2006n1325
PlantGDB [Website], 2006n1324
Plants of the Kimberley region of W Australia, rev ed,
    2005n1354
PlantStress [Website], 2006n1326
Poisonous plants, 2d ed, 2006n1334
Rare plants of Tex., 2009n1179
Tree ferns, 2005n1374
WallBioNet [Website], 2006n1327
Waterlilies & lotuses, 2006n1347
Wildlife & plants, 3d ed, 2007n1170
World Bk's sci & nature gds, 2005n1344
World of plants series, 2007n1175

BOTSWANA
Culture & customs of Botswana, 2007n84
Historical dict of Botswana, 4th ed, 2009n90

BOXING IN MOTION PICTURES
Boxing filmography, 2005n1207

BRAHMS, JOHANNES, 1833-1897
Brahms & his world, 2007n994

BRAZIL
Brazil, 2008n139
Cambridge hist of Latin America, v.9: Brazil since
    1930, 2009n412

BREAST CANCER
Breast cancer sourcebk, 2d ed, 2006n1445
Complete natural gd to breast cancer, 2005n1462
Encyclopedia of breast cancer, 2005n1464

BRITISH MAGAZINES
Age of the storytellers, 2007n781

BROADCASTING. *See* **RADIO**
BROADCASTING; TELEVISION
Burrelle's transcripts [Website], 2005n907
Gale dir of pubs & broadcast media, 138th ed,
    2005n887
Gale dir of pubs & broadcast media, 140th ed,
    2006n872
Gale dir of pubs & broadcast media, 143d ed, 2009n797
Museum of Broadcast Communications ency of radio,
    2005n909

BUDDHISM
BuddhaNet [Website], 2007n1105
BuddhaNet: Buddhist studies [Website], 2005n1252
Buddhism in world cultures, 2007n1106
Buddhist experience in America, 2005n1253
Key words in Buddhism, 2007n1107
Encyclopedia of Buddhism, 2008n1075

BULBS
Bulbs in containers, 2006n1307
Timber Press pocket gd to bulbs, 2006n1300

BULGARIA
Historical dict of Bulgaria, 2d ed, 2007n112

BURMA
Historical dict of Burma (Myanmar), 2007n93

BURUNDI
Historical dict of Burundi, 3d ed, 2007n85

BUSH, GEORGE H. W.
George H. W. Bush yrs, 2007n589

BUSINESS - BIBLIOGRAPHY
Encyclopedia of business info sources, 19th ed,
    2005n135

Strauss's hndbk of business info, 2d ed, 2005n136
Encyclopedia of business info sources, 20th ed,
    2006n117

BUSINESS - BIOGRAPHY

African-American business leaders & entrepreneurs,
    2005n140
Biography today: business leaders, 2006n118
Icons of business, 2008n150
International dir of business biogs, 2005n139
Movers & shakers, 2005n141
Who's who in Canadian business 2004, 24th ed,
    2005n142
Who's who in Canadian business 2004, 24th ed
    [CD-ROM], 2005n143
Who's who in finance & business 2006-07, 35th ed,
    2007n132
Who's who in finance & business 2008-09, 36th ed,
    2008n151

BUSINESS COMMUNICATION

Strategic business letters & e-mail, 2005n272

BUSINESS - DICTIONARIES & ENCYCLOPEDIAS

Battleground: business, 2008n152
Bulls, bears, boom, & bust, 2007n133
Elsevier's dict of economics, business, finance, & law,
    2005n144
Encyclopedia of African American business,
    2007n134
Encyclopedia of American business, 2005n145
Encyclopedia of American business hist, 2007n137
Encyclopedia of American industries, 4th ed,
    2006n174
Encyclopedia of American women in business,
    2006n124
Encyclopedia of business & finance, 2d ed, 2007n160
Encyclopedia of business ethics & society, 2009n132
Encyclopedia of business info sources, 22d ed,
    2008n155
Encyclopedia of business info sources, 23d ed,
    2009n133
Encyclopedia of capitalism, 2005n146
Encyclopedia of mgmt, 5th ed, 2006n262
Encyclopedia of small business, 3d ed, 2007n136
Harrap's Spanish & English business dict, 2006n122
Understanding American business jargon, 2d ed,
    2006n121

BUSINESS - DIRECTORIES

Almanac of American employers 2004, 2005n228
Almanac of American employers 2007, 2008n225
American wholesalers & distributors dir, 13th ed,
    2005n188
American wholesalers & distributors dir, 14th ed,
    2006n176

American wholesalers & distributors dir, 16th ed,
    2008n190
AssocationExecs.com [Website], 2009n134
BEOnline: business & economics online [Website],
    2006n125
Brands & their companies, 27th ed, 2006n177
Business info resources [Website], 2006n127
Business orgs, agencies, & pubs dir, 16th ed,
    2005n148
Business orgs, agencies, & pubs dir, 19th ed,
    2006n129
Companies & their brands, 26th ed, 2005n189
Consultants & consulting orgs dir, 27th ed, 2005n149
Consultants & consulting orgs dir suppl, 27th ed,
    2005n150
Consultants & consulting orgs dir, 30th ed, 2008n157
Corporate yellow bk, Summer 2005, 2006n130
Directory of business info resources 2005, 12th ed,
    2005n151
Directory of business info resources 2006, 13th ed,
    2006n128
Directory of business info resources 2007, 14th ed,
    2008n158
Directory of business info resources 2008, 15th ed,
    2009n135
Directory of business info resources [Website],
    2005n152
Directory of business info resources [Website],
    2008n159
Directory of business to business catalogs 2005, 13th
    ed, 2006n178
Directory of business to business catalogs [Website],
    2005n191
Directory of convenience stores, 2005, 2006n179
Directory of foreign firms operating in the US,
    2007n166
Directory of mail order catalogs 2005, 19th ed,
    2006n161
Directory of mail order catalogs 2007, 21st ed,
    2007n155
Directory of mail order catalogs online [Website],
    2007n156
EconData [Website], 2005n153
ECONlinks [Website], 2005n154
Encyclopedia of products &
    industries—manufacturing, 2009n171
Hoover's hndbk of American business 2004,
    2005n155
Hoover's hndbk of American business 2005, 15th ed,
    2006n131
Hoover's hndbk of American business 2007,
    2007n139
Hoover's hndbk of emerging companies 2004,
    2005n156
Hoover's hndbk of emerging companies 2005,
    2006n132

Hoover's hndbk of emerging companies 2007, 2008n160

Hoover's hndbk of private companies 2004, 9th ed, 2005n157

Hoover's hndbk of private companies 2006, 2006n133

Hoover's hndbk of private companies 2007, 2008n161

Hoover's hndbk of world business 2004, 2005n208

Hoover's hndbk of world business 2005, 12th ed, 2006n201

Hoover's hndbk of world business 2007, 2008n213

Hoover's Masterlist of major US companies 2006, 2006n134

Hoover's Masterlist of US companies 2007, 2007n140

Hoover's MasterList: Ca. ed 2004, 2005n158

Hoover's MasterList: N.Y. metro ed 2004, 2005n159

International dir of co hists, v.71, 2006n135

International dir of co hists, v.72, 2006n136

International dir of co hists, v.73, 2006n137

International dir of co hists, v.74, 2006n138

Major companies of Africa South of the Sahara 2004, 9th ed, 2005n211

Major companies of Europe 2005, 24th ed, 2005n220

Major companies of SW Asia 2004, 8th ed, 2005n215

National dir of corporate public affairs 2004, 22d ed, 2005n160

National dir of corporate public affairs 2005, 23d ed, 2006n139

National dir of corporate public affairs 2006, 24th ed, 2007n141

National dir of corporate public affairs, Fall 2008, 2009n136

National dir of minority-owned business firms, 13th ed, 2006n140

National dir of minority-owned business firms, 14th ed, 2009n137

National dir of woman-owned business firms, 13th ed, 2006n141

National dir of woman-owned business firms, 14th ed, 2009n138

National trade & professional assns of the US 2008, 2009n139

Online business sourcebk, 8th ed, 2009n140

Plunkett's almanac of middle market companies 2007, 2008n162

Plunkett's apparel & textiles industry almanac, 2008 ed, 2009n175

Plunkett's automobile industry almanac, 2009 ed, 2009n176

Plunkett's biotech & genetics industry almanac, 2009 ed, 2009n177

Plunkett's consulting industry almanac 2005, 2006n192

Plunkett's consulting industry almanac 2006, 2007n171

Plunkett's consulting industry almanac, 2008 ed, 2009n178

Plunkett's e-commerce & Internet business almanac, 2008 ed, 2009n179

Plunkett's nanotech & MEMS industry almanac, 2008 ed, 2009n180

Plunkett's transportation, supply chain, & logistics industry almanac, 2008 ed, 2009n181

Plunkett's wireless, WI-FI, RFID, & cellular industry almanac, 2009 ed, 2009n182

Retail tenant dir 2006, 2007n176

Small business sourcebk, 18th ed, 2005n161

Small business sourcebk, 20th ed, 2006n143

Small business sourcebk, 22d ed, 2008n163

Small business sourcebk, 24th ed, 2009n141

Ward's business dir of US private & public companies, 47th ed, 2005n162

Ward's business dir of US private & public companies, suppl, 47th ed, 2005n163

Ward's business dir of US private & public companies, 48th ed, 2006n144

Ward's business dir of US private & public companies, 51st ed, 2009n142

World dir of business info Websites 2003, 2005n164

World dir of business info Websites 2007, 7th ed, 2008n164

World dir of trade & business assns 2007, 5th ed, 2008n165

World dir of trade & business jls 2007, 3d ed, 2008n166

BUSINESS EDUCATION

Barron's gd to graduate business schools, 13th ed, 2005n288

Barron's gd to graduate business schools, 14th ed, 2006n285

Business school buzz bk, 2005 ed, 2005n293

Complete bk of business schools, 2004 ed, 2005n297

Vault MBA career bible, 2005 ed, 2005n252

Wall Street Jl gd to the top business schools 2006, 2007n251

BUSINESS ETHICS

Encyclopedia of business ethics & society, 2008n154

BUSINESS FORMS

Business forms on file, 2004 ed, 2005n166

Business forms on file, 2006n145

Business forms on file 2006, rev ed, 2007n143

Business forms on file, 2007 ed, 2008n167

Personal & business forms online [Website], 2007n149

Small business legal forms simplified, 2005n558

BUSINESS - HANDBOOKS & YEARBOOKS

Administrative assistant's & secretary's hndbk, 3d ed, 2009n240

Business rankings annual 2006, 2006n147

Business rankings annual 2007, 2007n144

Business rankings annual 2009, 2009n143

Consumer USA 2006, 10th ed, 2006n268
Entrepreneur's info sourcebk, 2007n142
Global business etiquette, 2009n148
Market share reporter 2005, 2006n156
McGraw-Hill hndbk of business letters, 4th ed, 2007n233
Partnership, 2006n152
Sole proprietorship, 2006n153
United States foreign trade highlights, 2006n207

BUSINESS - INDEXES
F & S index—US, v.46, no.3, 6, 9, 10, 2007n151

BUSINESS LAW
Manager's legal hndbk, 3d ed, 2007n451

BUSINESS LIBRARIES
Strauss's hndbk of business info, 2d ed, 2005n136
World dir of business info libs 2007, 6th ed, 2008n509

BUSINESS MANAGEMENT
About.com [Website], 2006n260
All business [Website], 2006n261
Business background investigations, 2009n145
Business plans hndbk, v.14, 2009n230
Dictionary of strategy, 2005n254
Encyclopedia of leadership, 2005n147
Encyclopedia of mgmt, 5th ed, 2006n262
Encyclopedia of the hist of American mgmt, 2006n263
Greening your business, 2009n233
International ency of organization studies, 2009n231
MoreBusiness.com [Website], 2006n264
Safe hiring audit, 2009n232

BUSINESS - QUOTATION BOOKS
Elgar dict of economic quotations, 2005n173
Forbes bk of business quotations, repr ed, 2006n154

BUSINESS STATISTICS
BizStats.com [Website], 2006n126
Business rankings annual, 2004, 2005n168
Business stats of the US 2004, 9th ed, 2005n169
Business stats of the US 2005, 10th ed, 2006n148
Business stats of the US 2006, 11th ed, 2007n145
Business stats of the US 2007, 12th ed, 2008n168
Business stats of the US 2008, 13th ed, 2009n144
Direction of trade stats yrbk 2005, 2006n269
World consumer income patterns 2003, 2005n269
World dir of non-official statl sources 2007, 7th ed, 2008n763

BUSINESS STRATEGY
Knowledge mgmt & business strategies, 2008n170

BUTTERFLIES
Butterflies of W Africa, 2006n1386

Field gd to butterflies of the San Francisco Bay & Sacramento Valley regions, 2008n1187
Kaufman field gd to butterflies of N America, 2007n1204

BYZANTINE EMPIRE
Encyclopedia of the Byzantine empire, 2005n473

CALCULUS
Math on file: calculus, 2005n1535

CALIFORNIA
Backroads of S Calif., 2006n399
California cities, towns, & counties, 2007 ed, 2008n74
California pol almanac 2007-08, 2008n642
Historical atlas of Calif. with original maps, 2008n75
Natural hist of the Point Reyes Peninsula, rev ed, 2009n1190
Profiles of Calif., 2007, 2008n76

CAMEROON
Culture & customs of Cameroon, 2006n80

CAMPAIGN FUNDS
Campaign & election reform, 2005n717

CAMPING
Complete sportsman's ency, 2d repr ed, 2009n728
Woodall's N American campground dir 2005, 2006n786
Woodall's tenting dir 2005, 2006n787

CANADA
Associations Canada 2007, 28th ed, 2008n35
Associations Canada 2008, 29th ed, 2009n27
Canada & Arctic N America, 2008n1351
Canadian almanac & dir 2006, 159th ed, 2006n3
Canadian almanac & dir 2007, 160th ed, 2008n3
Canadian almanac & dir 2008, 161st ed, 2009n2
Canadian environmental dir 2007, 12th ed, 2008n1342
Canadian environmental dir 2008, 13th ed, 2008n1343
Geology of southern Vancouver Island, rev ed, 2006n1517
History of the bk in Canada, v.3, 2008n571
Junior Worldmark ency of the Canadian provinces, 5th ed, 2008n111
Scott's Canadian sourcebk 2005, 40th ed, 2006n8
USA & Canada 2008, 2009n70

CANADA - BIOGRAPHY
BC Almanac bk of greatest British Columbians, 2007n18
Canadian who's who 2004, v.39, 2005n25
Canadian who's who 2005, v.40, 2006n22
Canadian who's who 2006, v.41, 2007n19
Canadian who's who 2007, v.42, 2008n22

Canadian who's who 2008, 2009n16
Dictionary of Canadian biog, v.25, 1921-30, 2006n23

CANADA, BUSINESS
Financial servs Canada 2007/08, 10th ed, 2008n181
Who's who in Canadian business 2004, 24th ed,
    2005n142
Who's who in Canadian business 2004, 24th ed
    [CD-ROM], 2005n143

CANADA, HISTORY
Brief hist of Canada, 2d ed, 2008n426
Early Canadiana online [Website], 2005n470
Fitzhenry & Whiteside bk of Canadian facts & dates,
    3d ed, 2006n47

CANADA, LAW
Ontario legal dir 2005, 80th ed, 2006n531

CANADA, POLITICS & GOVERNMENT
Canada's Prime Ministers, MacDonald to Trudeau,
    2008n654
Canadian Parliamentary gd 2008, 2009n669

CANADA, TRAVEL
Explore Canada, rev ed, 2005n404
Great Canadian vacations, 2005n403

CANADIAN LITERATURE
Canadian bks in print 2004: author & title index,
    2005n7
Canadian bks in print 2004: subject index, 2005n8
Canadian bks in print 2005: author & title index,
    2006n12
Canadian bks in print 2005: subject index, 2006n13
Canadian bks in print 2006: author & title index,
    2007n6
Canadian bks in print 2006: subject index, 2007n7
Caribbean & S Asian writers in Canada, 2008n939
Crime fiction Canada [Website], 2006n1013

CANCER
Breast cancer sourcebk, 2d ed, 2006n1445
Cancer dict, 3d ed, 2008n1251
Cancer hndbk, 2d ed, 2008n1252
Cancer info for teens, 2005n1461
Cancer sourcebk, 5th ed, 2008n1253
Cancer sourcebk for women, 3d ed, 2007n1270
Cancer survivorship sourcebk, 2008n1254
Complete natural gd to breast cancer, 2005n1462
Encyclopedia of breast cancer, 2005n1464
Encyclopedia of cancer, 2006n1447
Encyclopedia of cancer & society, 2008n1250
Encyclopedia of men's reproductive cancer,
    2005n1463
Encyclopedia of women's reproductive cancer,
    2005n1465

Gale ency of cancer, 2d ed, 2006n1446
Medical Lib Assn gd to cancer info, 2008n1249
Salem health: cancer, 2009n1264

CAPITAL PUNISHMENT
Capital punishment, 3d ed, 2006n570
Death penalty on trial, 2006n541
Death sentences in Mo., 1803-2005, 2007n482
Encyclopedia of capital punishment in the US, 2d ed,
    2009n473
Greenhaven ency of capital punishment, 2007n469
Legal executions in Calif., 2007n483
Legal executions in N.J., 1691-1963, 2007n467

CAPITALISM
Encyclopedia of capitalism, 2005n146

CAPITOLS, UNITED STATES
State houses, 2006n933

CAREER EDUCATION
How to plan & develop a career center, 2d ed,
    2008n234

CAREERS
All in a day's work, 2d ed, 2009n1140
Almanac of American employers, 2006 ed, 2006n228
America's 101 fastest growing jobs, 8th ed, 2006n251
America's top 100 jobs for people without a 4-yr
    degree, 7th ed, 2005n241
America's top 101 computer & technical jobs, 2d ed,
    2005n242
America's top 101 jobs for college graduates, 6th ed,
    2006n252
America's top 300 jobs, 9th ed, 2005n238
Best career & educ Web sites, 5th ed, 2007n205
Best entry-level jobs, 2005n237
Best jobs for the 21st century, 4th ed, 2007n199
Book of US govt jobs, 9th ed, 2006n245
Book of US govt jobs, 10th ed, 2008n241
Career discovery ency, 6th ed, 2007n198
Career ideas for teens series, 2006n243
Career info center, 9th ed, 2007n209
Career opportunities in advertising & public relations,
    4th ed, 2006n244
Career opportunities in aviation & the aerospace
    industry, 2006n248
Career opportunities in banking, finance, & insurance,
    2d ed, 2008n246
Career opportunities in computers & cyberspace, 2d
    ed, 2005n249
Career opportunities in conservation & the
    environment, 2008n247
Career opportunities in educ & related servs, 2d ed,
    2007n212
Career opportunities in engineering, 2007n223
Career opportunities in forensic sci, 2009n216

Career opportunities in health care, 3d ed, 2008n245

Career opportunities in journalism, 2008n240

Career opportunities in law & the legal industry, 2d ed, 2008n243

Career opportunities in law enforcement, security, & protective servs, 2d ed, 2006n249

Career opportunities in lib & info sci, 2006n595

Career opportunities in photography, 2007n222

Career opportunities in pol, govt, & activism, 2d ed, 2009n213

Career opportunities in sci, 2d ed, 2009n217

Career opportunities in the armed forces, 2d ed, 2008n249

Career opportunities in the automotive industry, 2006n254

Career opportunities in the energy industry, 2009n228

Career opportunities in the fashion industry, 2d ed, 2008n253

Career opportunities in the Internet, video games, & multimedia, 2008n251

Career opportunities in the music industry, 5th ed, 2005n245

Career opportunities in the nonprofit sector, 2007n208

Career opportunities in the publishing industry, 2006n259

Career opportunities in the sports industry, 3d ed, 2005n246

Career opportunities in the travel industry, 2005n239

Career opportunities in the visual arts, 2007n210

Career opportunities in theater & the performing arts, 3d ed, 2007n221

Career opportunities in TV & cable, 2007n224

Career opportunities in writing, 2007n225

Careers in business, 5th ed, 2006n258

Careers in intl affairs, 8th ed, 2009n214

Careers in travel, tourism, & hospitality, 2d ed, 2006n247

Chicago gd to landing a job in academic biology, 2008n1145

Chicago gd to your career in sci, 2009n1135

College majors hndbk with real career paths & payoffs, 2d ed, 2005n247

Directory of executive recruiters, 14th corporate ed, 2006n229

Directory of executive recruiters 2005-06, 34th ed, 2006n230

Directory of executive recruiters 2007-08, 35th ed, 2007n192

Discovering careers for your future series, 2006n246

Discovering careers for your future series, 2009n215

ECO gd to careers that make a difference, 2006n250

Encyclopedia of career dvlpmt, 2007n190

Encyclopedia of careers & vocational guidance, 13th ed, 2006n226

Encyclopedia of careers & vocational guidance, 14th ed, 2008n223

Enhanced occupational outlook hndbk, 5th ed, 2005n233

Enhanced occupational outlook hndbk, 6th ed, 2008n229

Exploring careers, 3d ed, 2005n240

Exploring health care careers, 3d ed, 2007n213

Exploring tech careers, 4th ed, 2007n214

Extraordinary jobs in . . . Series, 2007n215

EZ occupational outlook hndbk, 2008n230

FBI careers, 2d ed, 2007n206

Federal law enforcement careers, 2d ed, 2007n207

Federal resume gdbk, 4th ed, 2008n237

Ferguson career coach: managing your career in educ, 2009n218

Ferguson career coach: managing your career in law enforcement, 2009n219

Ferguson career coach: managing your career in the art industry, 2009n220

Ferguson career coach: managing your career in the health care industry, 2009n1230

Ferguson career coach: managing your career in the music industry, 2009n221

Ferguson career coach: managing your career in the sports industry, 2009n223

Ferguson career coach: managing your career in theater & the performing arts, 2009n222

Ferguson career resource gd for people with disabilities, 3d ed, 2007n702

Ferguson career resource gd for women & minorities, 2007n201

Ferguson career resource gd to apprenticeship programs, 3d ed, 2007n202

Ferguson career resource gd to internships & summer jobs, 2007n203

Ferguson career skills lib series, 2005n243

Ferguson gd to resumes & job-hunting skills, 2006n241

Ferguson's career guidance center [Website], 2008n239

Ferguson's careers in focus series, 2005n244

Ferguson's careers in focus series, 2007n220

Ferguson's careers in focus series, 2009n224

40 best fields for your career, 2007n218

Gallery of best resumes, 4th ed, 2008n232

Great careers with a high school diploma series, 2009n225

Great jobs for biology majors, 2005n248

Great jobs for chemistry majors, 2d ed, 2006n257

Great jobs for math majors, 2d ed, 2006n253

Great jobs for pol sci majors, 2d ed, 2005n250

Guide to America's fed jobs, 3d ed, 2006n255

Guide to Internet job searching, 2006-07 ed, 2007n211

Health care job explosion! 4th ed, 2008n242

Health professions career & educ dir 2005-06, 33d ed, 2006n1418

Internships 2005, 2006n231

Job hunter's sourcebk, 6th ed, 2005n230

Job hunter's sourcebk, 7th ed, 2007n193
Job hunter's sourcebk, 8th ed, 2009n207
Jobs & careers abroad, 12th ed, 2006n232
New gd for occupational exploration, 4th ed,
	2007n218
Occupational outlook hndbk 2004-05 ed, 2005n236
Occupational outlook hndbk 2006-07, 2007n197
Occupational outlook hndbk 2008-09, 2009n210
145 things to be when you grow up, 2005n253
150 best jobs through military training, 2008n250
150 best jobs through military training, 2009n226
150 great tech prep careers, 2d ed, 2009n227
175 best jobs not behind a desk, 2008n244
People at work! a student's A-Z gd to 350 jobs,
	2006n256
Perfect resume, rev ed, 2005n235
Plunkett's companion to the almanac of American
	employers, 2004-05 ed, 2006n233
Plunkett's employers' Internet sites with careers info
	2004-05, 2005n231
Summer jobs abroad 2005, 36th ed, 2006n242
300 best jobs without a 4-yr degree, 2d ed, 2007n217
Top 100: the fastest growing careers for the 21st
	century, 4th ed, 2009n229
Top 300 careers, 10th ed, 2007n204
Top careers in 2 yrs series, 2008n252
200 best jobs for college graduates, 3d ed, 2007n200
219 best jobs for baby boomers, 2007n217
Vault college career bible, 2005 ed, 2005n251
Vault gd to top internships 2005 ed, 2005n232
Vault gd to top internships 2006, 2006n234
Vault MBA career bible, 2005 ed, 2005n252
Work your way around the world, 13th ed, 2008n248

CARIBBEAN
Brief hist of the Caribbean, 2008n440
Caribbean, 5th ed, 2006n415
Caribbean, updated ed, 2008n374
Caribbean & S Asian writers in Canada, 2008n939
Fodor's Caribbean 2006, 2006n416
Food culture in the Caribbean, 2006n1288
Peoples of the Caribbean, 2006n352

CARIBBEAN LITERATURE
Encyclopedia of Caribbean lit, 2007n970

CARIBBEAN MUSIC
Caribbean popular music, 2006n1108

CARIBBEAN, TRAVEL
100 best resorts of the Caribbean, 6th ed, 2005n409
Travel gd to the Jewish Caribbean & Latin America,
	2005n408

CARROLL, LEWIS
Lewis Carroll among his bks, 2006n647

CARTOGRAPHY
Guide to US map resources, 3d ed, 2006n384
Historical map & chart project [Website], 2006n376
Maps in the atlases of the British Lib, 2006n386
Historical map & chart project [Website], 2006n376
Mapping the silk road & beyond, 2006n385
Maps in the atlases of the British Lib, 2006n386

CARTOONS
Encyclopedia of animated cartoons, 3d ed, 2009n1043
Graphic novels, 2007n900
Supervillain bk, 2007n1031
U*X*L graphic novelists, 2007n910

CASTLES
Castles of Scotland, 2006n405
Medieval castles, 2006n513

CATALOGING & CLASSIFICATION
Bibliographic control of music, 1897-2000, 2007n505
Cataloging & classification, 3d ed, 2008n528
Cataloging & organizing digital resources, 2006n617
Cataloging cultural objects, 2008n527
Cataloging of audiovisual materials & other special
	materials, 5th ed, 2009n541
Education for lib cataloging, 2007n509
Fiction catalog, 2007 suppl, 2008n529
FRBR, 2008n530
Functional requirements for bibliog records (FRBR),
	2006n616
Introduction to tech servs, 7th ed, 2006n646
KidzCat, 2009n539
Maxwell's hndbk for AACR2, 4th ed, 2005n616
Middle & jr high school lib catalog, 2006 suppl,
	2008n531
Middle & jr high school lib catalog, 2007 suppl,
	2008n532
Moving image cataloging, 2009n545
Resources for teachers & students of the DDC
	[Website], 2009n542
Sears list of subject headings, 18th ed, 2005n617
Sears list of subject headings, 19th ed, 2008n512
Sears lista de encabezamientos de materia, 2009n544
Subject access to a multilingual museum database,
	2009n540
User's gd to Sears list of subject headings, 2009n543
Using XML, 2008n533

CATALOGS
Directory of business to business catalogs 2004, 12the
	ed, 2005n190
Directory of business to business catalogs [Website],
	2005n191
Directory of mail order catalogs 2004, 18th ed,
	2005n181

CATHOLIC CHURCH
American Catholic Bible in the 19th century, 2007n1103
Catholic bk of quotations, 2005n1268
Catholic experience in America, 2006n1238
Catholic spirit, 2009n1115
Catholicism & sci, 2009n1114
Deaths of the popes, 2005n1267
Encyclopedia of Catholic social thought, social sci, & social policy, 2008n1081
Encyclopedia of Catholicism, 2008n1082
John Paul II & the Jewish people, 2009n314
Modern Catholic ency, rev ed, 2005n1261
Official Catholic dir 2007, 2008n1085
OSV's ency of Catholic hist, rev ed, 2005n1262
Our Sunday Visitor's Catholic almanac 2004, 2005n1266
Our Sunday Visitor's Catholic almanac 2007, 2008n1092
Our Sunday Visitor's Catholic almanac 2008, 2009n1101

CATHOLIC LITERATURE
Encyclopedia of Catholic lit, 2006n979

CATHOLIC SCHOOLS
Catholic schools in the US, 2005n280

CATS
Cat owner's home veterinary hndbk, 3d ed, 2009n1164
Cats: eyewitness companions, 2007n1198
1001 things you always wanted to know about cats, 2006n1377

CATTLE BREEDS
Field gd to cattle, 2009n1167

CD-ROM BOOKS
CD-ROMs in print, 18th ed, 2005n9

CD-ROMS
Ancient Christian commentary on scripture CD-ROM [CD-ROM], 2006n1221
Cesnola collection: terracottas [CD-ROM], 2005n951
Contemporary Chinese Societies [CD-ROM], 2008n106
Directory of physicians in the US 2005 [CD-ROM], 2006n1416
Education dict [CD-ROM], 2006n274
Encyclopaedia Britannica 2005 [CD-ROM], 2005n30
Genealogist's address bk [CD-ROM], 5th ed, 2006n355
International ency of ergonomics & human factors, 2d ed [CD-ROM], 2007n1220
National Geographic natl park trail gds [CD-ROM], 2005n775

Oxford English dict, 2d ed on [CD-ROM], 2006n29
Oxford spellchecker & dict [CD-ROM], 2009n878
Small press record of bks in print 2008, 33d ed [CD-ROM], 2008n10
Who's who in Canadian business 2004, 24th ed [CD-ROM], 2005n143
World Bank Africa database 2005 [CD-ROM], 2007n81

CELEBRITIES. *See also* ACTORS
Almanac of famous people, 8th ed, 2005n11
Almanac of famous people, 9th ed, 2008n11
Celebrity culture in the US, 2009n1048
Celebrity death certificates 2, 2006n1128
Encyclopedia of Hollywood, 2d ed, 2005n1199
James Dean in death, 2006n1147
Movieland dir, 2005n1203

CELLULAR BIOLOGY
Handbook of proteins, 2009n1173

CELTIC CULTURE
Brewer's dict of Irish phrase & fable, 2006n1115
Celtic culture, 2006n104

CELTIC MYTHOLOGY
Celtic mythology A to Z, 2005n1163
Encyclopedia of Celtic mythology & folklore, 2005n1164

CENSORSHIP
Censorship, 2009n485
Censorship in the Arab world, 2007n120
Encyclopedia of censorship, new ed, 2006n632
Literature suppressed on political grounds, rev ed, 2007n868
Literature suppressed on religious grounds, rev ed, 2007n867
Literature suppressed on sexual grounds, rev ed, 2007n869
Literature suppressed on social grounds, rev ed, 2007n870

CENTRAL AMERICA
Brief hist of Central America, 2d ed, 2008n137
Central America, 2d ed, 2008n375
Historical atlas of Central America, 2005n119
History of Central America, 2007n399
Mexico & Central America hndbk 2009, 17th ed, 2009n354
World & its peoples: Mexico & Central America, 2009n124

CENTRAL INTELLIGENCE AGENCY
Central Intelligence Agency, 2007n605
Words of intelligence, 2007n595

CERVANTES SAAVEDRA, MIGUEL DE, 1547-1616
Cervantes ency, 2005n1098

CHEMICAL COMPANIES
Major chemical & petrochemical companies of the world 2004, 8th ed, 2005n193
Plunkett's chemicals, coatings, & plastics industry almanac 2007, 2008n196

CHEMICAL ENGINEERING
Dictionary of nanotech, colloid & interface sci, 2009n1215
Encyclopedic dict of polymers, 2009n1213
Handbook of fluorous chemistry, 2006n1402
Handbook of ion chromatography, 2006n1403
Nine-lang dict of polymers & composites, 2009n1214
Perry's chemical engineers' hndbk, 8th ed, 2008n1197
Petroleum tech, 2008n1198
Sax's dangerous properties of industrial materials, 11th ed, 2005n1407
Sittig's hndbk of toxic & hazardous chemicals & carcinogens, 5th ed, 2009n1218
Wiley's remediation technologies hndbk, 2005n1408

CHEMICAL LIBRARIES
Literature of chemistry, 2006n1489

CHEMICAL WARFARE
Chemical & biological warfare, 2d ed, 2007n572

CHEMICALS, ORGANIC
Handbook of industrial chemistry: organic chemicals, 2006n1494
Vocabulary & concepts of organic chemistry, 2d ed, 2006n1496

CHEMISTRY
Catalysis from A to Z, 3d ed, 2008n1286
Chemical composition of everyday products, 2006n1497
Chemical compounds, 2007n1292
Chemistry, 2005n1492
Chemistry, 2008n1285
Chemistry matters! 2008n1289
CRC hndbk of chemistry & physics 2007-08, 88th ed, 2008n1294
Dean's hndbk of organic chemistry, 2d ed, 2005n1497
Dictionary of chemistry, 6th ed, 2009n1296
Encyclopedia of chemistry, 2006n1492
Encyclopedia of chemical processing, 2006n1490
Encyclopedia of electrochemistry, v.7a: inorganic electrochemistry, 2008n1287
Encyclopedia of electrochemistry, v.7b: inorganic electrochemistry, 2008n1288

Encyclopedia of polymer sci & tech, concise 3d ed, 2008n1196
Encyclopedia of supramolecular chemistry, 2005n1493
Encyclopedia of supramolecular chemistry [Website], 2005n1494
Encyclopedia of the elements, 2005n1495
Facts on File chemistry hndbk, rev ed, 2007n1293
Facts on File dict of chemistry, 4th ed, 2006n1491
Forensic sci experiments on file, 2005n1286
Handbook of asymmetric heterogeneous catalysis, 2009n1297
Handbook of food analytical chemistry, 2005n1305
Hawley's condensed chemical dict, 15th ed, 2008n1292
Illustrated pocket dict of chromatography, 2007n1223
Japanese-English chemical dict, 2009n1298
Kirk-Othmer chemical tech & the environment, 2008n1290
Kirk-Othmer concise ency of chemical tech, 5th ed, 2008n1291
Lange's hndbk of chemistry, 16th ed, 2006n1495
McGraw-Hill concise ency of chemistry, 2005n1496
Merck index, 14th ed, 2007n1284
New chemistry series, 2008n1295
100 most important chemical compounds, 2008n1293
Van Nostrand's ency of chemistry, 5th ed, 2006n1493

CHESS
Chess results 1947-50, 2009n730
Chess world championships, 3d ed, 2009n731

CHICAGO
Encyclopedia of Chicago, 2007n65

CHILD ABUSE
Child abuse sourcebk, 2005n801
Childhood sexual abuse, 2d ed, 2008n479
Encyclopedia of child abuse, 3d ed, 2008n720

CHILD DEVELOPMENT. *See also* **YOUTH DEVELOPMENT**
Cambridge ency of child dvlpmt, 2006n822
Children & consumer culture in American society, 2009n765
Encyclopedia of applied developmental sci, 2005n825
Girl culture, 2009n766
Greenwood ency of children's issues worldwide, 2009n767
Scholarly resources for children & childhood studies, 2008n738

CHILD LABOR
Child labor, 2006n237

CHILD PSYCHOLOGY
Handbook of child psychology, 6th ed, 2007n663

CHILD WELFARE
Children & youth in adoption, orphanages, & foster care, 2006n807

CHILDREN, HEALTH & HYGIENE. *See also* **PEDIATRIC MEDICINE**
Children & youth in sickness & in health, 2005n826

CHILDREN, SOCIAL CONDITIONS
Child poverty in America today, 2008n733
Practical gd to the Indian Child Welfare Act, 2009n310

CHILDREN WITH DISABILITIES
Children with disabilities in America, 2007n698

CHILDREN'S ATLASES
DK 1st atlas, 2006n373
Facts on File children's atlas, 2006 ed, 2007n299
Illustrated atlas, rev ed, 2005n373
Kingfisher student atlas of N America, 2007n302
National Geographic US atlas for young explorers, updated ed, 2006n378
Scholastic new headline world atlas, 2006n382
Student atlas, 3d ed, 2005n379

CHILDREN'S ENCYCLOPEDIAS & DICTIONARIES
American Heritage children's dict, updated ed, 2007n848
American Heritage 1st dict, 2007n849
Britannica learning zone [Website], 2009n18
Children's illus ency, 6th ed, 2007n22
DK Merriam-Webster children's dict, rev ed, 2006n957
Kingfisher 1st dict, 2006n959
Kingfisher 1st thesaurus, 2006n960
Merriam-Webster's primary dict, 2006n961
My 1st Britannica, 2005n32
New bk of knowledge, 2008 ed, 2008n28
Scholastic children's ency, 2005n33
Webster's new explorer student dict, new ed, 2007n851
World Bk discover [Website], 2009n24
World Bk discovery ency, 2009n25
World Bk ency, 2008 ed, 2008n33
World Bk student dict, 2005 ed, 2005n35
World Bk student discovery ency, 2d ed, 2008n34
World Bk's childcraft, 2005n36

CHILDREN'S LIBRARY SERVICES
Big bk of children's reading lists, 2007n515
Box full of tales, 2009n554
Capturing readers with children's choice bk awards, 2007n517
Children's jukebox, 2d ed, 2008n963
Children's lit in action, 2009n557
Fiore's summer lib reading program hndbk, 2006n619
Fundamentals of children's servs, 2006n623
Get up & move with nonfiction, 2009n556

Going places with youth outreach, 2006n621
Growing & knowing: a selection gd for children's lit, 2005n620
Librarian's gd to developing Christian fiction collections for children, 2006n625
Once upon a time, 2009n552
Outstanding lib serv to children, 2007n511
Practical puppetry A-Z, 2006n618
Reading is funny! 546

CHILDREN'S LITERATURE. *See also* **YOUNG ADULT LITERATURE**
A to zoo, 7th ed, 2007n897
A to zoo, suppl to the 7th ed, 2009n924
Across cultures, 2009n921
African children's lit [Website], 2006n989
Around the world with histl fiction & folktales, 2005n1022
Best bks for boys, 2009n933
Best bks for children, 8th ed, 2007n886
Best bks for children, suppl to the 8th ed, 2009n919
Best bks for middle school & jr high readers grades 6-9, 2005n1018
Beyond picture bks, 3d ed, 2009n920
Big bk of children's reading lists, 2007n515
Book crush, 2008n891
Books kids will sit still for 3, 2007n891
Building character through multicultural lit, 2005n611
Capturing readers with children's choice bk awards, 2007n517
Children's & YA lit by Native Americans, 2005n1021
Children's & YA lit hndbk, 2007n893
Children's authors & illustrators too good to miss, 2005n1028
Children's bks: awards & prizes, 2005 ed, 2006n1003
Children's bk review index, v.29, 2003, 2005n1032
Children's catalog, 19th ed, 2007n502
Children's lit [Website], 2007n887
Children's lit in action, 2009n557
Children's lit review, v.96, 2005n1023
Children's lit review, v.97, 2005n1024
Children's lit review, v.98, 2005n1025
Companion to American children's picture bks, 2006n1002
Continuum ency of children's lit, 2005n1029
Core collection for children & YAs, 2009n930
Coretta Scott King awards 1970-2004, 3d ed, 2005n1056
Crossing boundaries with children's bks, 2007n888
Cultural journeys, 2007n912
Database of award-winning children's lit [Website], 2007n889
Dr. Seuss catalog, 2006n991
Educational paperback assn Website [Website], 2007n903
Ethnic bk awards, 2006n1004

Fairrosa cyber lib of children's lit [Website], 2007n890
Fantasy lit for children & YAs, 5th ed, 2006n992
Favorite children's authors & illustrators, 2005n1026
Favorite children's authors & illustrators, 2d ed, 2007n904
Find someone who: introducing 200 favorite picture bks, 2009n928
Four British fantasists, 2007n911
Get up & move with nonfiction, 2009n556
Growing & knowing: a selection gd for children's lit, 2005n620
Guide to collective biogs for children & YAs, 2006n990
Illustrators of The Wind in the Willows 1908-2008, 2009n935
International children's digital lib [Website], 2005n1019
International children's digital lib [Website], 2007n896
Jewish values finder, 2009n931
Middle & jr high school lib catalog, 9th ed, 2006n993
Ninth bk of jr authors & illustrators, 2006n1000
Middle ages in lit for youth, 2005n1015
Multicultural & ethnic children's lit in the US, 2008n889
Neal-Schuman gd to celebrations & holidays around the world, 2005n1176
Newbery & Caldecott awards, 2005n1033
Newbery & Caldecott awards, 2006 ed, 2007n899
Newbery & Caldecott awards, 2007 ed, 2008n885
Newbery & Caldecott awards, 2008 ed, 2009n926
Newbery/Printz companion, 3d ed, 2008n884
Oxford ency of children's lit, 2007n909
Poetry people, 2008n955
Popular series fiction for K-6, 2006n997
Pura Belpre awards, 2007n906
Reading about children's lit [Website], 2007n901
Recommended bks in Spanish for children & YAs, 2006n994
Recommended bks in Spanish for children & YAs 2004-08, 2009n929
60 years of notable children's bks, 2005n1020
Teaching bks [Website], 2007n905
Teaching with bks that heal, 2009n936
Tenth bk of jr authors & illustrators, 2009n934
TumbleBooks [Website], 2009n932
Undergraduate's companion to children's writer & their Web sites, 2006n996
Using picture story bks to teach literary devices, v.4, 2009n923
Vandergrift's children's & YA lit pages [Website], 2007n907
War & peace, 2008n887
What do children & YAs read next, v.6, 2005n1014
Wizard of Oz catalog, 2006n995
Women engaged in war in lit for youth, 2008n882

World of Islam in lit for youth, 2007n892
World War II in lit for youth, 2006n999

CHILDREN'S REFERENCE. *See also*
CHILDREN'S ENCYCLOPEDIAS & DICTIONARIES
Amazing animals of the world 2, 2007n1184
Amazing animals of the world 3, 2007n1185
Animal atlas, 2007n1183
Biology matters! 2005n1339
Children's night sky atlas, 2005n1501
Cobblestone online [Website], 2009n43
Concise dinosaur ency, 2005n1522
DK 1st animal ency, 2006n1363
Epidemics, 2005n1445
Explorer atlas, 2007n312
First human body ency, 2006n1320
History for kids [Website], 2005n523
InfoTrac kids [Website], 2008n51
Junior worldmark ency of the nations, 4th ed, 2005n71
Kidbits, 3d ed, 2005n54
Library of the 9 planets, 2006n1508
Nature's children, 2005n1382
Nature's children, set 1, rev ed, 2008n1170
Nature's children, set 2, 2008n1171
Nature's children, set 3, 2009n1193
Nature's children, set 4, 2009n1194
New 1st dict of cultural literacy, 2005n325
People at the center of ... series, 2006n491
U*X*L Newsmakers, 2005n19
Women's adventures in sci series, 2006n1253
World Bk's sci & nature gds, 2005n1344

CHILDREN'S SONGS
Children's jukebox, 2d ed, 2008n963

CHINA
China, 2008n368
China, 2009n99
China today, 2006n89
Contemporary Chinese Societies [CD-ROM], 2008n106
Historical dict of Chinese theater, 2009n1078
Historical dict of Hong Kong cinema, 2008n1022
Historical dict of US-China relations, 2006n745
Pop culture China! 2008n1002
State of China atlas, 2006n90
Twentieth century China, 2005n95

CHINA, BUSINESS
Consumer China 2005, 10th ed, 2006n213
Consumer China 2009, 14th ed, 2009n198

CHINA, FOREIGN RELATIONS
Encyclopedia of Chinese-American relations, 2007n636
Historical dict of US—China relations, 2007n639

World Christianities, c.1914-c.2000, v.9, 2007n1117

CHRISTIANITY & POLITICS
Conservative Christians & pol participation, 2006n735
Encyclopedia of modern Christian politics, 2007n574
Mainline Christians & US public policy, 2008n676
Religious right, 3d ed, 2008n1066

CHRISTMAS
Christmas ency, 2d ed, 2006n1120

CHROMOSOMES
Atlas of mammalian chromosomes, 2007n1207

CHURCH HISTORY
Birth of the church, 2005n1263
Charts of modern & postmodern church hist,
    2005n1265
Jesus in hist, thought, & culture, 2005n1260

CHURCH OF JESUS CHRIST OF LATTER-DAY SAINTS
Latter-day Saint experience in America, 2005n1264

CHURCHES
Canadian churches, 2008n844

CHURCHILL, WINSTON, SIR, 1874-1965
Annotated bibliog of works about Sir Winston S.
    Churchill, 2005n721
Bibliography of the writings of Sir Winston Churchill,
    2007n627

CITIES & TOWNS
America's top-rated cities 2004, 11th ed, 2005n852
America's top-rated cities 2005, 12th ed, 2006n847
America's top-rated cities 2006, 13th ed, 2007n751
America's top-rated cities 2007, 14th ed, 2008n769
America's top-rated cities 2008, 15th ed, 2009n778
America's top-rated smaller cities 2004-05, 5th ed,
    2005n853
America's top-rated smaller cities 2006/07, 6th ed,
    2007n752
America's top-rated smaller cities 2008/09, 7th ed,
    2009n779
Cities & growth, 2008n772
Cities & water, 2009n780
Cities of the Middle East & N Africa, 2007n122
Cities of the US, 6th ed, 2009n781
City profiles USA 2006-07, 8th ed, 2007n319
Comparative gd to American suburbs 2005, 3d ed,
    2006n848
Comparative gd to American suburbs 2007, 4th ed,
    2008n773
County & city extra 2004, 12th ed, 2005n854
County & city extra 2005, 13th ed, 2006n849
County & city extra 2007, 15th ed, 2008n774

County & city extra 2008, 16th ed, 2009n782
Encyclopedia of American urban hist, 2008n768
Historic cities of the Americas, 2006n845
Medieval city, 2006n469
Moving & relocation dir 2005-06, 5th ed, 2006n846
Moving & relocation dir 2007-08, 6th ed, 2008n770
Places, towns, & townships 2007, 4th ed, 2008n771

CIVIL DEFENSE
Grey House homeland security dir 2005, 2d ed, 2005n43
Grey House homeland security dir 2006, 3d ed, 2006n35
Grey House homeland security dir 2007, 4th ed, 2007n32
Grey House homeland security dir 2008, 5th ed, 2008n37
Grey House homeland security dir [Website], 2005n44
Grey House homeland security dir [Website], 2007n33
Grey House homeland security dir [Website], 2008n38
Homeland security, 2005n550
Homeland security, 2006n729
Homeland security hndbk for citizens & public
    officials, 2007n646
Homeland security law hndbk, 2005n551
Intelligence & natl security, 2008n592
International security & the US, 2009n696
McGraw-Hill Homeland Security hndbk, 2007n647
Researching natl security & intelligence, 2005n730
U.S. natl security, 2d ed, 2008n652
US Homeland Security, 2007n644

CIVIL RIGHTS. *See also* HUMAN RIGHTS
Affirmative action, 2005n587
America in revolt during the 1960s & 1970s,
    2008n405
Civil rights revolution, 2005n421
Encyclopedia of American civil liberties, 2007n442
Encyclopedia of American civil rights & liberties,
    2007n490
Encyclopedia of American race riots, 2008n301
Encyclopedia of civil liberties in America, 2006n582
Greenwood ency of African American civil rights,
    2005n334
Human & civil rights, 2007n491
Martin Luther King, Jr., ency, 2009n299
U.S. natl debate topic 2005-06: US civil liberties,
    2006n550
USA Patriot Act of 2001, 2005n542
Voting rights act of 1965, 2009n392

CIVILIZATION - ANCIENT
Ancient Canaan & Israel, 2006n116
Ancient Greece, 2007n390
Ancient hist, 2006n494
Ancient Indus Valley, 2008n383
Ancient Mesopotamia, 2006n485
Ancient Mesopotamia, 3300-331 B.C.E., 2005n504
Ancient world, 2008n451
Aztecs, 2006n341
Complete royal families of Ancient Egypt, 2006n484

Daily life in the medieval Islamic world, 2006n1243
Daily life in the N.T., 2009n433
Daily life of the Ancient Egyptians, 2d ed, 2009n415
E.guides: Ancient Greece, 2007n391
Edinburgh companion to Ancient Greece & Rome, 2007n384
Encyclopedia of Ancient Asian civilizations, 2005n467
Encyclopedia of Ancient Greece, 2006n473
Encyclopedia of society & culture in the ancient world, 2008n455
Encyclopedia of the Ancient Greek world, rev ed, 2006n474
Establishment of the Han Empire & Imperial China, 2006n465
Global hist, 2005n527
Great empires of the past series, 2005n528
Great events from hist: the ancient world, prehist-476 CE, 2005n515
Great lives from hist: the ancient world, prehist-476 CE, rev ed, 2005n511
Greenhaven ency of Ancient Greece, 2008n436
Greenhaven ency of Ancient Mesopotamia, 2008n441
Historical atlas of Ancient Greece, 2007n392
Historical atlas of Ancient Mesopotamia, 2005n502
Historical atlas of Ancient Rome, 2006n486
Historical dict of Ancient Egypt, 2d ed, 2009n414
Historical dict of Ancient Israel, 2005n126
Historical dict of Ancient S America, 2009n413
Historical dict of medieval India, 2009n101
Historical dict of the Hittites, 2005n500
History of the ancient & medieval world, 2d ed, 2009n428
Mycenaean civilization, rev ed, 2005n492
New dict of the hist of ideas, 2006n501
Oxford dict of the classical world, 2006n468
Penguin histl atlas of ancient civilizations, 2007n401
Perseus digital lib [Website], 2007n408
Reign of Cleopatra, 2006n482
Thames & Hudson dict of Ancient Egypt, 2007n400
Trojan War, 2006n514
World hist [Website], 2009n431

CLASSICAL HISTORY
Cambridge dict of classical civilization, 2007n377
Classical studies, 2d ed, 2007n403

CLASSICAL MUSIC. See also COMPOSERS (MUSIC)
All Music gd to classical music, 2007n998
American popular music: classical, 2006n1088
Billboard ency of classical music, 2005n1136
Boston symphony orchestra, 2009n1016
Dictionary of American classical composers, 2d ed, 2006n1079
Great instrumental works, 2006n1089
International who's who in classical music 2006, 2007n1000
Johann Nepomuk Hummel, 2008n972
Memento mori, 2008n977
Penguin companion to classical music, 2007n999
Penguin gd to compact discs & DVDs, 2003/04 ed, 2006n1090
Symphonic etudes, 2008n974
Symphonic repertoire, v.3, pt.A, 2008n975
Symphonic repertoire, v.3, pt.B, 2008n976

CLASSICISTS
Dictionary of British classicists, 2006n865

CLIMATOLOGY
Atlas of climate change, 2007n1307
Climate change, 2009n1321
Climate change 2007, 2008n1311
Climate change in context, 2009n1316
Clouds R Us.com [Website], 2009n1310
Encyclopedia of disasters, 2009n1318
Encyclopedia of hurricanes, typhoons, & cyclones, new ed, 2008n1308
Encyclopedia of weather & climate, rev ed, 2008n1307
Encyclopedia of world climatology, 2007n1308
Extreme weather, 2008n1313
Extreme weather & climate events [Website], 2009n1311
Facts on File dict of weather & climate, rev ed, 2007n1309
Firefly gd to weather, 2006n1509
Global climate change, 2007n1329
Hurricanes, 2d ed, 2006n1510
Interactive weather maker [Website], 2009n1312
Natural disasters, new ed, 2009n1317
Notable natural disasters, 2008n1309
Rough gd to climate change, 2008n1312
SciJinks weather laboratory [Website], 2009n1313
U*X*L ency of weather & natural disasters, 2008n1310
Weather & climate, 2008n1306
Weather glossary [Website], 2009n1319
Weather underground [Website], 2009n1314
Weather watch [Website], 2009n1315
World Bk lib of natural disasters, 2009n1320

CLINICAL TRIALS
Wiley ency of clinical trials, 2009n1224

CLOTHING. See also FASHION
Greenwood ency of clothing through world hist, 2009n844
History of fashion & costume, 2006n909

COGNITIVE LEARNING
Cambridge hndbk of the learning scis, 2007n53

COGNITIVE THERAPY
Encyclopedia of behavior modification & cognitive behavior therapy, 2006n755
Encyclopedia of cognitive behavior therapy, 2007n650

COIN & PAPER MONEY

Guide to coin collecting, 2009n828
Investor's gd to US coins, 2d ed, 2008n820
Paper money of the US, 17th ed, 2005n921
Paper money of the US, 18th ed, 2007n799
So-called dollars, 2009n829
Standard catalog of world coins: 1901-2000, 34th ed, 2007n800
Standard catalog of world coins 2001-date 2009, 3d ed, 2009n830
Standard catalog of world coins 2006, 33d ed, 2006n902
Standard catalog of world coins, 2009, 2009n831
Standard catalog of world paper money, 14th ed, 2009n832
U.S. coin digest 2006, 2006n903
U.S. coin digest 2009, 7th ed, 2009n833

COLD WAR

Chronology of the Cold War 1917-92, 2006n659
Cold War, 2007n563
Cold War, 2008n580
Cold War presidency, 2008n649
Encyclopedia of Cold War espionage, spies, & secret operations, 2005n664
Encyclopedia of the Cold War, 2008n583
Historical dict of Cold War counterintelligence, 2008n588
History in dispute, v.19: the red scare after 1945, 2005n451

COLLECTIBLES

Ancient Indian artifacts, v.1, 2009n837
Antique & collectible dict, 2009n821
Antique Trader antiques & collectibles price gd 2005, 20th ed, 2005n912
Antique Trader antiques & collectibles 2006 price gd, 2006n897
Antique Trader antiques & collectibles price gd 2007, 2008n811
Antique Trader collectible paperback price gd, 2009n824
Antique Trader furniture price gd, 3d ed, 2009n814
Antique Trader gd to fakes & reproductions, 4th ed, 2008n812
Antiques 101, 2006n900
Antiques price gd 2008, 2009n820
Antiques Roadshow 20th-century collectibles, 2005n910
Art nouveau, 2005n911
Arts & crafts, 2006n896
Collector's ency of American composition dolls, 1900-50, v.2, 2006n904
Collector's ency of Depression glass, 18th ed, 2008n813
Collector's gd to antique radios, 6th ed, 2005n926
Collector's gd to antique radios, 7th ed, 2008n823

Complete price gd to watches, 2007 ed, 2007n807
Complete price gd to watches, 2008 ed, 2008n826
Doll values, 9th ed, 2007n801
Doll values, 10th ed, 2009n834
Early American furniture, 2007n805
Elegant glassware of the depression era, 13th ed, 2009n817
Encyclopedia of collectible children's bks, 2009n827
English China, 2009n819
Indian artifacts, 2005n925
Investor's gd to US coins, 2d ed, 2008n820
Kovels' American antiques 1750-1900, 2006n899
Kovels' American collectibles 1900 to 2000, 2008n814
Kovels' antiques & collectibles price list 2006, 38th ed, 2007n795
Madame Alexander, 2008n821
Made in the 20th century, 2006n895
Maloney's antiques & collectibles resource dir, 7th ed, 2005n913
Miller's antiques price gd 2007, 2008n815
Miller's buying affordable antiques, 2008n816
Miller's ceramic figures buyer's gd, 2008n817
Miller's collectibles price gd 2007, 2008n809
Miller's companion to antiques & collectables, 2008n810
Miller's 20th-century glass, 2008n818
O'Brien's collecting toys, 12th ed, 2009n839
Official price gd to Disney collectibles, 2007n792
Official price gd to pottery & porcelain, 9th ed, 2007n793
Pocket gd to depression glass & more 1920s-60s, 2009n818
Rare & unusual Indian artifacts, 2008n822
Schroeder's antiques price gd 2005, 23d ed, 2005n914
Schroeder's antiques price gd 2006, 24th ed, 2006n901
Schroeder's antiques price gd 2008, 26th ed, 2008n819
Schroeder's antiques price gd 2009, 27th ed, 2009n822
Schroeder's collectible toys 2006, 10th ed, 2006n907
Schroeder's collectible toys antique to modern price gd 2008, 11th ed, 2008n825
Standard catalog of firearms 2004, 14th ed, 2005n923
Standard catalog of firearms 2005, 15th ed, 2006n905
Standard catalog of military firearms 1870 to the present, 2d ed, 2005n924
Standard catalog of military firearms, 3d ed, 2007n804
Standard catalog of world coins 2001-date 2009, 3d ed, 2009n830
Standard catalog of world coins 2006, 33d ed, 2006n902
Standard catalog of world coins 2009, 2009n831
Standard catalog of world paper money, 14th ed, 2009n832
Standard ency of carnival glass, 11th ed, 2009n815
Standard ency of carnival glass price gd, 16th ed, 2009n816

Standard ency of pressed glass 1860-1930, 4th ed, 2006n898

Standard ency of pressed glass 1860-1930, 5th ed, 2007n794

Standard knife collector's gd, 5th ed, 2007n806

Toys & prices, 12th ed, 2005n927

Tribal art, 2007n791

U.S. coin digest 2006, 2006n903

Warman's antiques & collectibles price gd, 38th ed, 2005n915

Warman's antiques & collectibles price gd, 40th ed, 2007n796

Warman's antiques & collectibles 2009 price gd, 42d ed, 2009n823

COLLECTION DEVELOPMENT (LIBRARIES)
Collection dvlpmt issues in the online environment, 2007n519

Collection dvlpmt policies, 2005n622

Complete gd to acquisitions mgmt, 2005n626

Evaluation of lib collections, access, & electronic resources, 2005n593

Fundamentals of collection dvlpmt & mgmt, 2005n623

Fundamentals of collection dvlpmt & mgmt, 2d ed, 2009n558

Growing & knowing: a selection gd for children's lit, 2005n620

Kovac's gd to electronic lib collection dvlpmt, 2005n591

Librarian's gd to developing Christian fiction collections for adults, 2006n624

Librarian's gd to developing Christian fiction collections for children, 2006n625

Librarian's gd to developing Christian fiction collections for YAs, 2006n626

Public lib catalog, 12th ed, 2005n5

Reference collection dvlpmt, 2006n643

Selecting materials for lib collections, 2005n625

Senior high core collection, 17th ed, 2008n515

COLLECTION MANAGEMENT - LIBRARIES
Analyzing lib collection use with Excel, 2008n565

Collection mgmt & strategic access to digital resources, 2006n597

Integrating print & digital resources in lib collections, 2007n533

Selecting & managing electronic resources, rev ed, 2007n520

COLLECTIVE SETTLEMENTS
Modern American communes, 2006n801

COLLEGE & RESEARCH LIBRARIES
Academic lib & the net gen student, 2008n513

Academic lib research, 2009n503

Collection mgmt & strategic access to digital resources, 2006n597

Digital info & knowledge mgmt, 2008n547

Directory of histl textbk & curriculum collections, 2006n593

Fostering community through digital storytelling, 2009n505

Improving Internet ref servs to distance learners, 2006n598

Information literacy collaborations that work, 2008n542

Information literacy programs in the digital age, 2009n566

Informed learning, 2009n504

Introduction to ref servs in academic libs, 2007n499

Libraries within their institutions, 2006n599

Library 2.0, 2009n506

Outreach servs in academic & special libs, 2005n604

Practical gd to info literacy assessment for academic librarians, 2009n568

Practical pedagogy for lib instructors, 2009n507

Real-life mktg & promotion strategies in college libs, 2007n500

Successful academic librarian, 2007n501

Teaching literacy, 2009n508

COLLEGE TEACHERS
Black academic's gd to winning tenure—without losing your soul, 2009n278

COMIC BOOKS
DC comics ency, 2006n1121

Encyclopedia of animated cartoons, 3d ed, 2009n1043

Encyclopedia of superheroes on film & TV, 2d ed, 2009n1044

500 comic bk villains, 2006n1119

Graphic novels, 2007n900

Marvel graphic novels & related pubs, 2009n1037

Superhero bk, 2005n1173

U*X*L graphic novelists, 2007n910

COMMUNICABLE DISEASES. *See also* **EPIDEMICS**
Contagious diseases sourcebk, 2005n1443

Infectious diseases in context, 2008n1229

Infectious diseases sourcebk, 2005n1448

COMMUNICATIONS. *See also* **MASS MEDIA**
Battleground: the media, 2009n795

Chronology of communication in the US, 2005n885

Encyclopedia of political communication, 2009n617

Encyclopedia of religion, communication, & media, 2008n1053

Gale dir of publications & broadcast media, 138th ed, 2005n887

Information & communications for dvlpmt 2006, 2007n182

International ency of communication, 2009n796

News media leadership dir online [Website], 2009n810

Nonverbal dict of gestures, signs, & body lang cues [Website], 2007n765

Poststructuralism & communication, 2006n1186

COMMUNISM

History in dispute, v.19: the red scare after 1945, 2005n451

COMMUNITY LIFE

Cambridge ency of hunters & gatherers, paperback ed, 2006n800

Encyclopedia of homelessness, 2005n807

Modern American communes, 2006n801

Rich & poor in America, 2009n760

COMPANIES

Brands & their companies, 27th ed, 2006n177

Business rankings annual 2007, 2007n144

Companies & their brands, 26th ed, 2005n189

Directory of foreign firms operating in the US, 2007n166

Hoover's hndbk of American business 2004, 2005n155

Hoover's hndbk of American business 2005, 15th ed, 2006n131

Hoover's hndbk of American business 2007, 2007n139

Hoover's hndbk of emerging companies 2004, 2005n156

Hoover's hndbk of emerging companies 2005, 2006n132

Hoover's hndbk of emerging companies 2007, 2008n160

Hoover's hndbk of private companies 2004, 9th ed, 2005n157

Hoover's hndbk of private companies 2006, 2006n133

Hoover's hndbk of private companies 2007, 2008n161

Hoover's hndbk of world business 2004, 2005n208

Hoover's hndbk of world business 2005, 12th ed, 2006n201

Hoover's hndbk of world business 2007, 2008n213

Hoover's MasterList of major US companies 2006, 2006n134

Hoover's MasterList of US companies 2007, 2007n140

Hoover's MasterList: Ca. ed 2004, 2005n158

Hoover's MasterList: N.Y. metro ed 2004, 2005n159

Major companies of Africa South of the Sahara 2004, 9th ed, 2005n211

Major companies of Europe 2005, 24th ed, 2005n220

Major companies of SW Asia 2004, 8th ed, 2005n215

International dir of co hists, v.71, 2006n135

International dir of co hists, v.72, 2006n136

International dir of co hists, v.73, 2006n137

International dir of co hists, v.74, 2006n138

Ward's business dir of US private & public companies, 47th ed, 2005n162

Ward's business dir of US private & public companies, suppl, 47th ed, 2005n163

Ward's business dir of US private & public companies, 48th ed, 2006n144

Ward's business dir of US private & public companies, 51st ed, 2009n142

COMPARATIVE GOVERNMENT. *See also* WORLD POLITICS

Governments of the world, 2006n685

Political hndbk of the world: 2005-06, 2007n583

Political hndbk of the world online ed [Website], 2007n584

COMPOSERS (MUSIC)

Brahms & his world, 2007n994

Cambridge Mozart ency, 2006n1080

Dictionary of American classical composers, 2d ed, 2006n1079

Exploring Haydn, 2006n1081

Johann Nepomuk Hummel, 2008n972

Lives & times of the great composers, 2005n1133

Mahler symphonies, 2005n1130

Memento mori, 2008n977

Musical AKAs, 2007n991

Piano music by women composers, v.2, 2005n1129

Steinway collection, repr ed, 2006n935

Women composers, v.8, 2007n984

Yevgeny Mravinsky, 2006n1083

COMPOSERS IN MOTION PICTURES

Great composers portrayed on film, 1913-2002, 2005n1190

COMPUTATIONAL BIOLOGY

Dictionary of bioinformatics & computational biology, 2005n1411

COMPUTER CRIMES

Cybercrime, 2005n582

Encyclopedia of high-tech crime & crime fighting, 2005n567

Internet predators, 2006n572

COMPUTER ENGINEERING

McGraw-Hill dict of electrical & computer engineering, 2005n1409

COMPUTER GAMES

A-Z of cool computer games, 2006n1480

COMPUTER NETWORK RESOURCES. *See* INTERNET (COMPUTER NETWORK)

COMPUTER SCIENCE
Academic search premier [Website], 2006n1474
ACM digital lib [Website], 2006n1475
Annotated computer vision bibliog [Website],
    2006n1471
Cetus links [Website], 2006n1470
Collection of computer sci bibliogs [Website],
    2006n1472
Computer industry, 2006n1482
Computers, 2006n1481
Computing reviews [Website], 2006n1473
Concise ency of computer sci, 2006n1476
Dictionary of computer vision & image processing,
    2006n1479
Dictionary of computing, 6th ed, 2009n1285
Elements of visual style, 2008n1276
Encyclopedia of computer sci & tech, rev ed,
    2009n1288
Encyclopedia of human computer interaction,
    2006n1477
Encyclopedia of human computer interaction
    [Website], 2006n1478
Encyclopedia of networked & virtual orgs, 2009n1286
FACCTs [Website], 2006n1463
Facts on File dict of computer sci, rev ed, 2007n1290
Handbook of info & computer ethics, 2009n1287
High definition, 2007n1285
1001 computer words you need to know, 2005n1483
Random House concise dict of sci & computers,
    2006n1261
TechInfoSource [Website], 2006n1464

COMPUTER SCIENTISTS
Leaders of the info age, 2005n1482

COMPUTER SECURITY
Advances in enterprise info tech security, 2008n1277
Information security & ethics, 2008n1274
Minoli-Cordovana's authoritative computer & network
    security dict, 2007n1291

COMPUTER SOFTWARE
Encyclopedia of visual effects, 2008n1275
Handbook of research on open source software,
    2008n1278

CONDUCTORS (MUSIC)
Directory of conductors' archives in American
    institutions, 2007n987
Maestros in America, 2009n1013

CONFLICT RESOLUTION
CRInfo: the conflict resolution info source [Website],
    2008n669

CONFUCIANISM
Illustrated ency of Confucianism, 2006n1198

CONNECTICUT
Connecticut municipal profiles, 2007 ed, 2008n77
Profiles of Conn. & R.I., 2008n79

CONSERVATION, ENVIRONMENTAL. *See also*
ENVIRONMENTALISM
American women conservationists, 2005n1536
Ecoterrorism, 2005n580
Russian far east, 2d ed, 2005n115
Shapers of the great debate on conservation,
    2005n1537

CONSERVATISM
American conservatism, 2008n625

CONSPIRACIES
Conspiracies & secret societies, 2007n1030
Conspiracy theories in American hist, 2005n424

CONSTANTINE I, EMPEROR OF ROME
Cambridge companion to the age of Constantine,
    2006n477

CONSTITUTIONAL LAW
Birth of the Bill of Rights, 2005n701
Constitutional amendments series, 2009n448
Constitutional convention of 1787, 2006n446
Constitutions of the world, 3d ed, 2008n481
Encyclopedia of the 1st amendment, 2009n437
Encyclopedia of world constitutions, 2007n444
100 Americans making constitutional hist, 2005n534
State constitutions of the US, 2d ed, 2006n543
U.S. Constitution A to Z, 2d ed, 2009n439

CONSTITUTIONS
Constitutions of the world, 3d ed, 2009n625

CONSTRUCTION INDUSTRY
Plunkett's real estate & construction industry almanac
    2007, 2008n260

CONSULTING INDUSTRY
Consultants & consulting orgs dir, 27th ed, 2005n149
Consultants & consulting orgs dir suppl, 27th ed,
    2005n150
Consultants & consulting orgs dir, 30th ed, 2008n157
Plunkett's consulting industry almanac 2005,
    2006n192
Plunkett's consulting industry almanac 2006,
    2007n171
Plunkett's consulting industry almanac, 2008 ed,
    2009n178

CONSUMER GUIDES
A to Z gd to American consumers, 2009n157
Children & consumer culture in American society,
    2009n765

Consumer sourcebk, 17th ed, 2005n180
Consumer sourcebk, 18th ed, 2006n160
Consumer sourcebk, 21st ed, 2009n155
Directory of business to business catalogs 2004, 12the
    ed, 2005n190
Directory of business to business catalogs [Website],
    2005n191
Directory of mail order catalogs 2004, 18th ed,
    2005n181
Directory of mail order catalogs 2005, 19th ed,
    2006n161
Directory of mail order catalogs 2007, 21st ed,
    2007n155
Directory of mail order catalogs 2008, 22d ed,
    2008n179
Directory of mail order catalogs online [Website],
    2007n156
Free stuff for baby! 2006-07 ed, 2007n158
Grey House safety & security dir, 2004 ed, 2005n182
Grey House safety & security dir, 2006 ed, 2006n162
Grey House safety & security dir, 2007 ed, 2007n157
Grey House safety & security dir, 2008, 2009n156
Grey House safety & security dir [Website], 2006n163
Purple bk, 2005 ed, 2006n164
Purple bk, 2006 ed, 2007n159
TheStreet.com Ratings' consumer box set, 2008 ed,
    2009n158
World consumer spending 2009, 9th ed, 2009n238

CONSUMER PROTECTION
Frauds against the elderly, 2005n797

CONSUMER SPENDING
American marketplace, 7th ed, 2006n829
American marketplace, 8th ed, 2008n748
American men, 2d ed, 2007n728
American women, 3d ed, 2007n729
Baby boom: Americans born 1946 to 1964, 4th ed,
    2005n267
Best customers, 3d ed, 2005n259
Consumer Asia 2004, 11th ed, 2005n213
Consumer E Europe 2004-05, 12th ed, 2005n216
Consumer intl 2003/04, 2005n206
Consumer intl 2005/06, 12th ed, 2006n202
Consumer Latin America 2004, 2005n222
Consumer USA 2004, 2005n261
Family spending, 2005 ed, 2007n725
Generation X, 4th ed, 2005n262
Household spending, 9th ed, 2005n834
Household spending, 11th ed, 2007n734
Household spending, 12th ed, 2008n750
Millennials: Americans born 1977 to 1994, 2d ed,
    2005n266
Older Americans, 4th ed, 2005n835
Who buys what, 2007n230
Who's buying for travel, 2006n165

Who's buying groceries, 2d ed, 2005n183
Who's buying series, 2d ed, 2007n231
Who's buying series, 2008n259
World consumer expenditure patterns 2003, 4th ed,
    2005n268
World consumer lifestyles databk 2004, 3d ed,
    2005n270
World consumer spending 2006/07, 7th ed, 2007n232

COOKERY. *See also* FOOD HABITS; FOOD SCIENCES
Contemporary ency of herbs & spices, 2007n1150
Cook's essential kitchen dict, 2006n1283
Encyclopedia of kitchen hist, 2005n1302
Food ency, 2007n1151
Oxford ency of food & drink in America, 2005n1301
Spice & herb bible, 2d ed, 2007n1154

COPTIC CHURCH
Historical dict of the Coptic Church, 2009n1109

COPYRIGHT
Author law A to Z, 2006n876
Carmack's gd to copyright & contracts, 2006n358
Center for intellectual property hndbk, 2007n521
Complete copyright, 2006n629
Copyright catechism, 2007n523
Copyright companion for writers, 2007n522
Copyright companion for writers, 2008n538
Copyright for administrators, 2009n561
Copyright for teachers & librarians, 2005n608
Copyright hndbk, 9th ed, 2008n539
Copyright in cyberspaace 2, 2006n628
Copyright law for librarians & educators, 2006n627
Copyright policies, 2009n560
Intellectual property, 2009n562
Internet & the law, 2006n521
Student plagiarism in an online world, 2008n540

CORETTA SCOTT KING AWARD
Coretta Scott King awards 1970-2004, 3d ed, 2005n1056

CORPORATE CULTURE
Financial hist of modern US corporate scandals,
    2007n148
Global business etiquette, 2009n148
Way we work, 2009n205

CORPORATIONS. *See* BUSINESS; INTERNATIONAL BUSINESS

CORRECTIONAL INSTITUTIONS
Encyclopedia of prisons & correctional facilities,
    2005n563
Prisons, 2007n481
Prisons & prison systems, 2006n561

COSTA RICA
Birds of Costa Rica, 2008n1176
Costa Rica 2008, 2008n376
Costa Rica, 2009n121
Fodor's Costa Rica 2006, 2006n417
Mammals of Costa Rica, 2008n1193
Tropical plants of Costa Rica, 2008n1152

COSTUME
Disruptive pattern material, 2006n908
Encyclopedia of clothing & fashion, 2005n928
History of fashion & costume, 2006n909

COUNTRY MUSIC
All Music gd to country, 2d ed, 2005n1147
American popular music: country, 2006n1100
Billboard illus ency of country music, 2009n1018
First generation of country music stars, 2008n987
Joel Whitburn presents hot country albums,
    2009n1020
Joel Whitburn's top country songs 1944-2005,
    2006n1101
New generation of country music stars, 2009n1019

COURT RECORDS
Directory of local court & county retrievers, 2005 ed,
    2006n524
Directory of state court clerks & county courthouses,
    2006 ed, 2006n525
History of the N.Y. Court of Appeals, 1932-2003,
    2007n458
Want's fed-state court dir, 2006 ed, 2006n533

COURTS, UNITED STATES. *See* LAW, UNITED STATES

CREATIONISM
Counter-creationism hndbk, 2006n1317
Evolution & creationism, 2008n1147
Evolution vs. creationism, 2005n1235
More than Darwin, 2009n1172

CRIME. *See also* TERRORISM
American murder, 2009n471
American villains, 2009n461
City crime rankings, 10th ed, 2005n571
City crime rankings, 12th ed, 2006n575
City crime rankings, 13th ed, 2007n477
City crime rankings, 14th ed, 2008n492
Corporate crime, 2009n479
Crime & punishment in America: almanac, 2005n572
Crime & punishment in America: biogs, 2005n573
Crime & punishment in America: primary sources,
    2005n574
Crime & punishment in the US, 2009n467
Crime scene, 2005n581
Crime scene investigations series, 2007n479

Crime scene investigations series, 2008n493
Crime state rankings 2004, 11th ed, 2005n575
Crime state rankings 2005, 12th ed, 2006n567
Crime state rankings 2006, 13th ed, 2007n480
Crime state rankings 2007, 14th ed, 2008n494
Crime state rankings 2008, 2009n476
Crimes & trials of the century, 2008n484
Cybercrime, 2005n582
Encyclopedia of conspiracies & conspiracy theories,
    2006n559
Encyclopedia of crime scene investigation, 2009n472
Encyclopedia of criminology, 2006n557
Encyclopedia of forensic sci, rev ed, 2009n466
Encyclopedia of gangs, 2009n468
Encyclopedia of high-tech crime & crime fighting,
    2005n567
Encyclopedia of interpersonal violence, 2009n469
Encyclopedia of intl organized crime, 2006n556
Encyclopedia of rape, 2006n558
Encyclopedia of serial killers, 2d ed, 2007n470
Encyclopedia of the FBI's 10 most wanted list,
    2005n569
Encyclopedia of unsolved crimes, 2005n568
Encyclopedia of white-collar & corporate crime,
    2005n564
Encyclopedia of white collar crime, 2008n487
Essentials of forensic sci series, 2009n478
Facts on File dict of forensic sci, 2005n565
Forensic sci, 2007n472
Forensic sci, 2009n470
Forensic sci timelines [Website], 2006n553
Great pictorial hist of world crime, 2005n566
Hate crimes, 2d ed, 2006n564
Historical atlas of American crime, 2006n560
Illicit trafficking, 2006n574
Internet predators, 2006n572
Jack the Ripper suspects, 2005n561
Mafia ency, 3d ed, 2006n562
Organized crime, 2008n490
Sage dict of criminology, 2d ed, 2007n471
World of forensic sci, 2006n563

CRIMINAL JUSTICE
American dict of criminal justice, 3d ed, 2006n554
Battleground: criminal justice, 2009n465
Crime & punishment, 2007n478
Criminal justice, 2006n555
Criminal justice, 2007n468
Criminal justice abstracts [Website], 2005n560
Criminal justice links [Website], 2007n475
Death sentences in Mo., 1803-2005, 2007n482
Defendant rights, 2005n579
DNA evidence & forensic sci, 2009n480
Encyclopedia of American law enforcement,
    2008n489
Encyclopedia of capital punishment in the US, 2d ed,
    2009n473

Encyclopedia of law enforcement, 2006n518
Encyclopedia of police studies, 3d ed, 2008n486
Greenhaven ency of capital punishment, 2007n469
Icons of crime fighting, 2009n462
International criminal law practitioners lib, v.1,
　　　2009n475
Juvenile justice, 2006n576
Legal executions in Calif., 2007n483
Legal executions in N.J., 1691-1963, 2007n467
National archive of criminal justice data (NACJD)
　　　[Website], 2007n476
Policing in America, 2008n495
Profiling & criminal justice in America, 2005n570
Punishment in America, 2006n565
Sentencing, 2008n491
World police ency, 2007n474

CRIME FICTION. *See also* **DETECTIVE &**
MYSTERY STORIES
Crime fiction Canada [Website], 2006n1013
Crime writers for Canada [Website], 2006n1014
Read on . . . crime fiction, 2009n943

CRIMINAL LAW
World ency of police forces & correctional systems, 2d
　　　ed, 2007n473

CRIMINAL RECORDS
Criminal records manual, 2005n577
Criminal records manual, 2d ed, 2006n573
Criminal records manual, 3d ed, 2009n477

CRUSADES
Crusades, 2005n530
Crusades, 2007n417
Crusades: almanac, 2005n505
Crusades: biog, 2005n506
Crusades: primary sources, 2005n507
Encyclopedia of the crusades, 2005n521

CRYPTOZOOLOGY
Encyclopedia of cryptozoology, 2006n1365

CUBA
Cuba, 2009n122
Encyclopedia of Cuban-US relations, 2005n727

CUBA, LITERATURE
Cuban-American fiction in English, 2006n1061

CUBA, MUSIC
Cuban music from A to Z, 2005n1121

CUBAN MISSILE CRISIS
National security archive: the Cuban missile crisis,
　　　1962 [Website], 2009n360

CULTS, UNITED STATES
Cults, 2d ed, 2006n1214
Introduction to new & alternative religions in America,
　　　2008n1065

CULTURES
Biographical dict of social & cultural anthropology,
　　　2005n319
Culture & customs of Afghanistan, 2006n88
Culture & customs of Angola, 2007n83
Culture & customs of Botswana, 2007n84
Culture & customs of Cameroon, 2006n80
Culture & customs of Germany, 2005n109
Culture & customs of Ireland, 2007n115
Culture & customs of Israel, 2005n128
Culture & customs of Italy, 2006n105
Culture & customs of Mexico, 2005n121
Culture & customs of Morocco, 2006n84
Culture & customs of Mozambique, 2007n89
Culture & customs of Pakistan, 2007n99
Culture & customs of Palestinians, 2005n124
Culture & customs of Saudi Arabia, 2007n128
Culture & customs of Thailand, 2005n102
Culture & customs of the Baltic States, 2007n109
Culture & customs of the US, 2008n73
Culture & customs of Zambia, 2007n91
CultureGrams [Website], 2009n67
Daily life online [Website], 2009n423
Discovering world cultures: the Middle East,
　　　2005n123
Encyclopedia of New Year's holidays worldwide,
　　　2009n1038
Encyclopedia of the world's nations & cultures,
　　　2008n64
Entertaining from ancient Rome to the Super Bowl,
　　　2009n1145
Greenwood ency of American regional cultures,
　　　2006n70
Greenwood ency of daily life, 2005n517
Human, 2005n53
Issues in the French-speaking world, 2005n108
Multiculturalism in the US, rev ed, 2006n324
New 1st dict of cultural literacy, 2005n325
Peoples, nations, & cultures, 2006n325
Sage dict of cultural studies, 2007n265
World Bk ency of people & places, 2006n66

CZECH LITERATURE
Franz Kafka ency, 2006n1058

DANCE
Classes in classical ballet, 2008n1011
International ency of dance, paperback ed, 2005n1188
Social dancing in America, 2007n1039

DANTE ALIGHIERI, 1265-1321
Critical companion to Dante, 2009n1005

DARWIN, CHARLES (1809-1882)
All things Darwin, 2008n1163
Darwin's fishes, 2006n1382
More than Darwin, 2009n1172

DATA MINING & WAREHOUSING
Encyclopedia of data warehousing & mining, 2006n1468
Encyclopedia of data warehousing & mining, 2d ed, 2009n1280
Encyclopedia of data warehousing & mining [Website], 2006n1469

DATA PROTECTION
Privacy in the info age, rev ed, 2007n1288

DATABASE MANAGEMENT
Encyclopedia of database technologies & applications, 2006n1486
Metadata in practice, 2005n630

DATABASES
Gale dir of databases, 2004, 2005n1489
Gale dir of databases, 2009 ed, 2009n29
Web lib, 2005n1488

DEAD SEA SCROLLS
Guide to the Dead Sea Scrolls & related lit, 2009n1094

DEAN, JAMES, 1931-1955
James Dean in death, 2006n1147

DEATH
Death & dying sourcebk, 2d ed, 2007n696
Encyclopedia of cremation, 2007n697
Encyclopedia of death & dying, 2006n802

DEBATES
Commission on presidential debates [Website], 2009n631

DECISION MAKING - DATA PROCESSING
Encyclopedia of decision making & decision support technologies, 2009n1281

DECORATIVE ARTS
Grove ency of decorative arts, 2007n790

DEER
Encyclopedia of deer, 2005n1397

DEMOGRAPHICS
A to Z gd to American consumers, 2009n157
African households, 2007n723
American attitudes, 5th ed, 2009n59
American generations, 5th ed, 2006n827
American generations, 6th ed, 2009n770
American incomes, 5th ed, 2006n828
American incomes, 6th ed, 2008n747
American marketplace, 7th ed, 2006n829
American marketplace, 8th ed, 2008n748
American men, 2d ed, 2007n728
American time use, 2008n764
American women, 3d ed, 2007n729
Americans & their homes, 2d ed, 2006n830
Baby boom: Americans born 1946 to 1964, 4th ed, 2005n267
Best customers, 3d ed, 2005n259
Community sourcebk of county demographics 2004, 16th ed, 2005n833
Community sourcebk of county demographics 2006, 18th ed, 2007n730
Community sourcebk of ZIP code demographics 2006, 20th ed, 2007n731
Counties USA, 3d ed, 2007n732
County & city extra 2004, 12th ed, 2005n854
County & city extra 2006, 14th ed, 2007n753
Demographic & health surveys [Website], 2008n742
Demographic yrbk 2001, 53d ed, 2005n830
Demographic yrbk 2002, 54th ed, 2006n825
Demographic yrbk 2003, 2007n724
Demographic yrbk 2004, 2008n743
Demographics of the US, 3d ed, 2008n749
Future demographic, 2005n831
Generation X, 4th ed, 2005n262
Household spending, 9th ed, 2005n834
Household spending, 11th ed, 2007n734
Household spending, 12th ed, 2008n750
Millennials: Americans born 1977 to 1994, 2d ed, 2005n266
New York state dir, 2005-06, 2006n833
Older Americans, 4th ed, 2005n835
Profiles of New York state, 2005-06, 2006n834
State profiles, 3d ed, 2007n736
Who we are: Asians, 2008n752
Who we are: Blacks, 2008n753
Who we are: Hispanics, 2008n754
World economic & social survey 2007, 60th ed, 2008n745
World fertility report: 2003, 2006n826
World mortality report 2005, 2007n726
World population, 2d ed, 2007n721
World population prospects: the 2004 revision, 2007n727

DENMARK
Historical dict of Denmark, 2d ed, 2009n111

DENTISTRY
Dental care & oral health sourcebk, 3d ed, 2009n1257

DERMATOLOGY
Encyclopedia of skin & skin disorders, 3d ed, 2007n1276
Pediatric dermatology, 2007n1266

DESCARTES, RENAE, 1596-1650
Historical dict of Descartes & Cartesian philosophy,
 2005n1228

DESERTS
Deserts, rev ed, 2008n1315
Firefly gd to deserts, 2007n1310

DESIGN. *See also* **GRAPHIC DESIGN;**
INTERIOR DESIGN
Thames & Hudson dict of design since 1900, 2d ed,
 2006n922

DETECTIVE & MYSTERY STORIES
ClueLass.com & the mysterious home page [Website],
 2005n1047
Crime fiction Canada [Website], 2006n1013
Crime writers for Canada [Website], 2006n1014
Critical survey of mystery & detective fiction, rev ed,
 2009n941
Detective novels of Agatha Christie, 2009n944
Gay detective novel, 2005n1048
Gay male sleuth in print & film, 2006n1015
Gumshoes: a dict of fictionary detectives, 2007n927
John Buchan, 2009n942
Murder in retrospect, 2007n928
Mystery women, rev ed, 2007n926
Poisons in mystery lit, 2008n900
Reference & research gd to mystery & detective
 fiction, 2d ed, 2005n1046
Ultimate mystery/detective Web gd [Website],
 2005n1049

DEVELOPING COUNTIRES
Atlas of global dvlpmt, 2009n107
Encyclopedia of the developing world, 2007n107
Historical dict of the non-aligned movement & third
 world, 2007n106
Least developed countries report 2006, 2007n108
Least developed countries report 2007, 2008n112

DIABETES
Diabetes ready-ref gd for health professionals, 2d ed,
 2005n1466

DICKENS, CHARLES
Dickens's nonfictional theatrical, & poetical writings,
 2008n931

DICKINSON, EMILY (1830-1886)
Critical companion to Emily Dickinson, 2007n949
Emily Dickinson, 2005n1066

DIETARY SUPPLEMENTS. *See also*
NUTRITION
Encyclopedia of dietary supplements, 2006n1282

Encyclopedia of vitamins, minerals, & supplements,
 2d ed, 2005n1419

DIGITAL LIBRARIES
Archives & the digital lib, 2008n522
Building digital libs, 2009n575
Cataloging & organizing digital resources, 2006n617
Global librarianship, 2005n633
Protecting your library's digital sources, 2005n631
Whole digital lib hndbk, 2008n511

DINOSAURS
Complete gd to prehistoric life, 2007n1315
Concise dinosaur ency, 2005n1522
Dinosaurs, 2008n1326
Dinosaurs, suppl 4, 2007n1314
Dinosaurs, suppl 5, 2008n1325
Dinosaur atlas, 2007n1316
Dinosauria, 2d ed, 2006n1521
E.guides: dinosaur, 2005n1523
Great dinosaur controversy, 2005n1524

DIRECTORIES
Associationexecs.com [Website], 2007n29
Associations Canada 2008, 29th ed, 2009n27
Associations USA, 2005n37
Associations yellow bk, Summer 2005 ed, 2006n31
Counties USA, 3d ed, 2007n732
Directories in print, 24th ed, 2005n39
Directories in print suppl, 24th ed, 2005n40
Directories in print, 25th ed, 2006n33
Directories in print, 28th ed, 2009n6
FaxUSA 2005, 12th ed, 2005n41
FaxUSA 2006, 13th ed, 2006n34
Gale dir of databases, 2009 ed, 2009n29
Government phone bk 2005, 13th ed, 2006n710
Government phone bk USA 2007, 15th ed, 200n635
Headquarters USA 2005, 27th ed, 2005n45
Headquarters USA 2006, 28th ed, 2006n36
Headquarters USA 2007, 29th ed, 2007n34
HQ online [Website], 2005n46
HQ online [Website], 2006n37
International dir of govt 2008, 5th ed, 2009n621
Leadership networks [Website], 2009n31
National dir of nonprofit orgs, 18th ed, 2006n39
National e-mail & fax dir 2005, 18th ed, 2006n40
National e-mail & fax dir 2006, 19th ed, 2007n35
Toll-free phone bk USA 2005, 9th ed, 2005n42
Toll-free phone bk USA 2006, 10th ed, 2006n41
Toll-free phone bk USA 2007, 11th ed, 2007n36
Toll-free phone bk USA 2008, 12th ed, 2008n41
Washington assns contacts dir 2008, 2009n34
Washington info dir online [Website], 2006n715Web
 site source bk 2005, 10th ed, 2006n42
Web site source bk 2004, 9th ed, 2005n48
Web site source bk 2006, 11th ed, 2007n37

Web site source bk 2007, 12th ed, 2008n42
Yearbook of intl orgs 2005-06, v.43, 2007n38

DISASTERS
Disasters, accidents, & crises in American hist,
  2009n366
Environmental disasters series, 2006n1540
Firefly gd to global hazards, 2005n1514

DISCOVERIES IN GEOGRAPHY
Encyclopedia of exploration, 2005n525

DISSERTATIONS
Dissertation abstracts intl [Website], 2007n3

DISTANCE EDUCATION
Distance educ, 2005n306
Encyclopedia of distance learning, 2006n284
Guide to distance learning programs 2005, 2006n293
Improving Internet ref servs to distance learners,
  2006n598
Online & distance learning, 2008n269

DIVORCE
Divorce without court, 2007n460
Nolo's essential gd to divorce, 2007n459

DOCUMENTARY FILMS
Encyclopedia of the documentary film, 2007n1045

DOGS
Dog owner's home veterinary hndbk, 4th ed,
  2009n1165
Dogs eyewitness companions, 2007n1200
Encyclopedia of dog breeds, 2d ed, 2006n1376
Planet dog, 2007n1199
Ultimate hunting dog ref bk, 2007n1201

DOMESTIC ANIMALS
Encyclopedia of human-animal relationships,
  2008n1165

DOMESTIC VIOLENCE
Child abuse sourcebk, 2005n801
Domestic violence, 2d ed, 2009n747
Domestic violence sourcebk, 2d ed, 2005n802
Encyclopedia of domestic violence, 2008n721
Encyclopedia of interpersonal violence, 2009n469
Violence against women online resources [Website],
  2005n803

DONNE, JOHN, 1572-1631
John Donne, 2006n1049

DOSTOEVSKY, FYODOR
Dostoevsky ency, 2005n1097

DRAMA
Banned plays, 2005n1039
Columbia ency of modern drama, 2008n1039
Drama for students, v.18, 2005n1037
Drama for students, v.19, 2005n1038
Drama for students, v.24, 2008n892
Drama 100, 2009n937
Facts on File companion to classical drama,
  2006n1005
Masterpieces of classic Greek drama, 2006n1007
Masterpieces of modern British & Irish drama,
  2006n1008
Masterpieces of 20th-century American drama,
  2006n1006
Play index 1998-2002, 2005n1222
Play index [Website], 2008n893
Poems, plays, & prose [Website], 2005n1006
Western drama through the ages, 2008n894

DRAMATISTS
African American dramatists, 2005n1034
Critical companion to Arthur Miller, 2008n922
Notable playwrights, 2005n1035
Tennessee Williams ency, 2005n1036

DREAMS
Watkins dict of dreams, 2008n680

DRUG ABUSE
Addiction counselor's desk ref, 2007n716
Directory of drug & alcohol residential rehabilitation
  facilities, 2004, 2005n821
Directory of drug & alcohol residential rehabilitation
  facilities [Website], 2005n822
Drug abuse sourcebk, 2d ed, 2006n820
Drug info for teens, 2d ed, 2007n717
Drugs & society, 2006n821
Encyclopedia of drug abuse, 2009n763
Encyclopedia of drugs, alcohol, & addictive behavior,
  3d ed, 2009n762
U*X*L ency of drugs & addictive substances,
  2007n718

DRUGS
AARP gd to pills, 2007n1280
Drug info, 3d ed, 2009n1273
Essential gd to prescription drugs, 2004 ed, 2005n1479
Essential gd to prescription drugs, 2006 ed, 2006n1461
Essential herb-drug-vitamin interaction gd, 2008n1261
Guide to off-label prescription drugs, 2007n1281
Handbook of drug-nutrient interactions, 2005n1480
Handbook of nonprescription drugs, 14th ed,
  2005n1481
Handbook of psychiatric drugs, 2007n1283
Litt's drug eruption ref manual including drug
  interactions, 13th ed, 2008n1262

Merck index, 14th ed, 2007n1284

PDR concise drug gd for advanced practice clinicians, 2008n1263

PDR concise drug gd for advanced practice clinicians, 2d ed, 2009n1274

PDR concise drug gd for pediatrics, 2008n1265

PDR concise drug gd for pediatrics, 2d ed, 2009n1275

PDR concise drug gd for pharmacists, 2008n1264

PDR drug gd for mental health professionals, 2d ed, 2006n1460

PDR drug gd for mental health professionals, 3d ed, 2008n1266

PDR for herbal medicines, 4th ed, 2008n1267

PDR for nonprescription drugs, dietary supplements, & herbs 2008, 29th ed, 2009n1276

PDR gd to drug interactions, side effects & indications, 63d ed, 2009n1277

PDR gd to drug interactions, side effects, & indications, 61st ed, 2008n1260

PDR nurse's drug hndbk, 2005 ed, 2005n1475

PDR nurse's drug hndbk, 2006 ed, 2006n1457

PDR nurse's drug hndbk, 2007 ed, 2007n1279

PDR nurse's drug hndbk, 2008 ed, 2008n1259

PDR nurse's drug hndbk, 2009 ed, 2009n1272

Physicians' desk ref 2006, 2006n1462

Physicians' desk ref 2007, 61st ed, 2008n1269

Physicians' desk ref 2009, 63d ed, 2009n1278

Pill bk, 11th ed, 2005n1478

Psychotropic drugs, 4th ed, 2009n1279

RX list [Website], 2007n1282

Springhouse nurse's drug gd, 7th ed, 2006n1458

DU BOIS, W. E. B.

Oxford W. E. B. Du Bois, 2008n915

DYE PLANTS

Dyes from American native plants, 2006n1337

DYLAN, BOB

Bob Dylan, 2d ed, 2009n1023

Keys to the rain: the definitive Bob Dylan ency, 2006n1111

EARTH SCIENCE

Dictionary of earth scis, 3d ed, 2009n1301

E.guides: Earth, 2005n1499

Earth sci, 2009n1299

Earth sci resources in the electronic age, 2005n1498

Encyclopedia of Earth, 2009n1300

Encyclopedia of earth & physical scis, 2007n1294

Encyclopedia of earth & physical scis, 2d ed, 2006n1498

Encyclopedia of earth sci, 2006n1499

Encyclopedia of geomagnetism & paleomagnetism, 2008n1296

Encyclopedia of geomorphology, 2005n1515

Facts on File dict of earth sci, rev ed, 2007n1295

Facts on File earth sci hndbk, rev ed, 2007n1297

Hazardous Earth series, 2009n1302

Life on Earth series, 2005n1291

Our living world: Earth's biomes, 2007n1298

Student's gd to earth sci, 2005n1500

EARTHQUAKES

Encyclopedia of earthquakes & volcanoes, 3d ed, 2008n1318

EASTERN EUROPE

Eastern Europe, Russia, & Central Asia 2009, 2009n109

G. K. Hall bibliog gd to Slavic, Baltic, & Eurasian studies 2002, 2005n104

G. K. Hall bibliog gd to Slavic, Baltic, & Eurasian studies 2003, 2006n101

Palgrave atlas of Byzantine hist, 2006n466

EASTERN EUROPEAN LITERATURE

Columbia lit hist of E Europe since 1945, 2009n980

EATING DISORDERS

Eating disorders, rev ed, 2005n1467

Eating disorders sourcebk, 2d ed, 2008n1255

Encyclopedia of obesity & eating disorders, 3d ed, 2007n1272

ECOLOGY

Ecology, rev ed, 2009n1337

Habitats of the world, 2006n1511

New atlas of planet mgmt, 3d ed, 2006n1537

Our Earth's changing land, 2007n1332

Russian far east, 2d ed, 2005n115

ECONOMIC DEVELOPMENT

Information tech & economic dvlpmt, 2008n171

ECONOMIC GEOGRAPHY

Firefly gd to the state of the world, 2006n67

ECONOMICS

Basics of economics, 2005n171

Cambridge economic hist of Latin America, 2007n188

Economic & social survey of Asia & the Pacific 2005, 2006n214

EconWPA [Website], 2005n131

Elsevier's dict of economics, business, finance, & law, 2005n144

Encyclopedia of the global economy, 2007n138

Eponymous dict of economics, 2006n120

Federal Reserve system, 2006n166

Global economic prospects 2006, 2007n147

Guide to economic indicators, 4th ed, 2007n146

IDEAS (Internet docs in economics access serv) [Website], 2005n132

International ency of econ sociology, 2006n123

International lib of the new institutional economics, 2006n150

LogEc [Website], 2005n133

Nations of the world 2005, 5th ed, 2005n74

RePEc (Research papers in economics) [Website], 2005n134

State of working America 2004/05, 2006n151

Value of a dollar, 3d ed, 2005n170

Value of a dollar: Colonial era to the Civil War, 2006n149

World dvlpmt report 2006, 2007n184

World income distribution 2004/05, 2d ed, 2005n172

World income distribution 2006/07, 4th ed, 2007n185

ECONOMISTS

Biographical dict of American economists, 2007n130

Biographical dict of Australian & New Zealand economists, 2008n149

Biographical dict of British economists, 2005n137

Biographies: lib of economics & liberty [Website], 2005n138

Nobel memorial laureates in economics, 2007n131

EDUCATION - BIBLIOGRAPHY

Social studies teaching activities bks, 2007n240

WSSLINKS: women, girls, & educ [Website], 2007n235

EDUCATION - BIOGRAPHY

Who's who in American educ 2004-05, 6th ed, 2005n274

EDUCATION, CAREERS

Career opportunities in educ & related servs, 2d ed, 2007n212

EDUCATION - CHRONOLOGY

Chronology of educ in the US, 2007n236

EDUCATION - DICTIONARIES & ENCYCLOPEDIAS

Battleground: schools, 2009n242

Catholic schools in the US, 2005n280

Critical thinking & learning, 2005n275

Dictionary of disruption, 2008n262

Early childhood educ, 2008n270

Education dict [CD-ROM], 2006n274

Encyclopedia of American educ, 3d ed, 2008n263

Encyclopedia of bilingual educ, 2009n243

Encyclopedia of distance learning, 2006n284

Encyclopedia of educ & human dvlpmt, 2006n275

Encyclopedia of educ law, 2009n244

Encyclopedia of educl leadership & admin, 2007n237

Encyclopedia of special educ, 2008n290

Encyclopedia of the social & cultural foundations of educ, 2009n246

Moral educ, 2009n260

EDUCATION - DIRECTORIES

Complete learning disabilities dir 2004/05, 11th ed, 2005n313

Complete learning disabilities dir 2005-06, 12th ed, 2006n314

Complete learning disabilities dir [Website], 2005n314

Educators gd to free multicultural materials 2007-08, 10th ed, 2008n271

Educators gd to free sci materials 2007-08, 48th ed, 2008n272

Educators gd to free social studies materials, 2007-08, 47th ed, 2008n273

Educators resource dir 2007/08, 7th ed, 2008n265

Educators resource dir, 2005/06, 6th ed, 2006n276

Funding sources for K-12 educ 2004, 6th ed, 2005n284

National faculty dir, 35th ed, 2005n303

National faculty dir, 39th ed, 2008n281

New research centers, 36th ed, 2009n247

Research centers dir, 36th ed, 2009n248

WSSLINKS: women, girls, & educ [Website], 2005n273

EDUCATION, ELEMENTARY

Comparative gd to American elem & secondary schools 2005, 3d ed, 2005n285

Comparative gd to American elem & secondary schools 2006, 4th ed, 2007n241

Comparative gd to American elem & secondary schools 8th ed, 5th ed, 2008n264

Educators gd to free Internet resources 2007-08, elem/middle school ed, 7th ed, 2008n291

Education gd to free Internet resources 2008-09, 8th ed, 2009n287

Educator's gd to solving common behavior problems, 2009n271

Educators gd to free videotapes 2004-05: elem/middle school, 5th ed, 2005n281

Educators gd to free videotapes 2005-06, 6th ed, 2006n318

Educators gd to free videotapes 2007-08, elem/middle school ed, 8th ed, 2008n293

Elementary educ, 2006n283

English lang arts units for grades 9-12, 2009n270

More than 100 brain friendly tools & strategies for literacy instruction, 2009n268

More than 100 ways to learner-centered literacy, 2d ed, 2009n267

100 experiential learning activities for social studies, lit, & the arts, grades 5-12, 2009n269

Teaching lib media skills in grades K-6, 2005n610

Visual arts units for all levels, 2009n266

EDUCATION - HANDBOOKS & YEARBOOKS

Academic bill of rights debate, 2008n266

Distance educ, 2005n306

Education facility security hndbk, 2009n261

Education state rankings 2003-04, 2d ed, 2005n277
Education state rankings 2008-09, 7th ed, 2009n250
Educational adequacy & the courts, 2006n280
Elementary educ, 2006n283
Handbook of educ pol & policy, 2009n253
Handbook of moral & character educ, 2009n254
Handbook of research in educ finance & policy, 2008n267
Handbook of school counseling, 2009n257
International perspectives on educ, 2008n268
Nourishing vocabulary, 2009n259
Reinventing project-based learning, 2009n249
Science for girls, 2008n274
Seventeenth mental measurements yrbk, 2009n262
Tablet PCs in K-12 educ, 2009n264
Teaching students with learning disabilities, 2009n283
10 langs you'll need most in the classroom, 2009n263
U.S. News & World Report ultimate gd to becoming a teacher, 2006n279
Urban educ, 2005n276

EDUCATION, HIGHER

Accredited institutions of postsecondary educ, 2006-07, 2008n275
All-American colleges, 2008n276
America's best value colleges, 2007 ed, 2007n247
Barron's best buys in college educ, 8th ed, 2005n287
Barron's best buys in college educ, 9th ed, 2007n248
Barron's gd to graduate business schools, 14th ed, 2006n285
Barron's gd to the most competitive colleges, 3d ed, 2005n290
Barron's gd to the most competitive colleges, 4th ed, 2006n286
Barron's profiles of American colleges 2005, 26th ed, 2005n291
Barron's profiles of American colleges 2007, 27th ed, 2007n243
Best 170 law schools, 2007 ed, 2007n244
Best 357 colleges, 2005 ed, 2005n292
Black academic's gd to winning tenure—without losing your soul, 2009n278
Business school buzz bk, 2005 ed, 2005n293
Choosing the right college 2008-2009, 2008n284
College blue bk, 31st ed, 2005n294
College blue bk, 32d ed, 2006n287
College blue bk, 34th ed, 2008n277
College Board bk of majors, 2006n288
College Board college hndbk 2005, 42d ed, 2005n295
College Board college hndbk 2006, 43d ed, 2006n289
College buzz bk, 2005n296
College majors & careers, 6th ed, 2009n277
College majors hndbk with real career paths & payoffs, 2d ed, 2005n247
Commonwealth universities yrbk 2005, 79th ed, 2007n245
Community colleges, 2006n301

Competitive colleges 2006, 2006n300
Culinary schools 2005, 8th ed, 2006n290
Europa world of learning 2008, 58th ed, 2008n278
Europa world of learning 2009, 59th ed, 2009n273
Fiske gd to colleges 2006, 22d ed, 2007n246
Fiske gd to colleges 2008, 24th ed, 2008n279
Four-yr colleges 2006, 36th ed, 2006n292
Graduate study in psychology 2008, 2008n682
Guide to distance learning programs 2005, 2006n293
Handbook of design research methods in educ, 2009n274
Insider's gd to graduate programs in clinical & counseling psychology, 2008/09 ed, 2009n706
International hndbk of univs, 17th ed, 2005n300
International hndbk of univs, 18th ed, 2006n294
International hndbk of univs, 19th ed, 2008n280
K & W gd to colleges for students with learning disabilities or attention deficit disorder, 7th ed, 2005n315
Law of higher education, 4th ed, 2009n275
MBA programs 2006, 11th ed, 2006n295
National dir to college & univ student records, 2005n302
National faculty dir, 35th ed, 2005n303
National faculty dir, 37th ed, 2006n296
Philosophical gourmet report [Website], 2006n297
Princeton Review gd to college majors, 2006 ed, 2008n285
Professional degree programs in the visual and performing arts 2006, 2006n298
References on chilly climate for women faculty in academe [Website], 2005n286
Research centers dir, 31st ed, 2005n304
Transitioning to college [Website], 2009n272
Two-yr colleges 2005, 36th ed, 2006n299
U.S. News & World Report ultimate college dir, 2004 ed, 2005n305
U.S. News & World Report ultimate gd to medical schools, 2d ed, 2008n283
US News & World Report ultimate college dir, 2007 ed, 2007n249
Wall Street Jl gd to the top business schools 2006, 2007n251
World list of universities & other institutions of higher educ, 25th ed, 2007n250

EDUCATION - HIGHER - GRADUATE WORK

Barron's gd to graduate business schools, 13th ed, 2005n288
Barron's gd to law schools 2005, 16th ed, 2005n289
Complete bk of business schools, 2004 ed, 2005n297
Complete bk of law schools, 2004 ed, 2005n298
Complete bk of medical schools, 2004 ed, 2005n299
Insider's gd to graduate programs in clinical & counseling psychology, 2004/05 ed, 2005n742

Law school buzz bk, 2005 ed, 2005n301

EDUCATION. INTERNATIONAL PROGRAMS
College Board intl student hndbk 2005, 18th ed,
    2005n310
College Board intl student hndbk 2007, 2007n254
Princeton Review gd to studying abroad, 2005n311
Study abroad 2004-05, 32d ed, 2005n312
Study abroad 2006, 13th ed, 2006n313
Succeeding as an intl student in the US & Canada,
    2009n276

EDUCATION, LEADERSHIP
Handbook of data-based decision making in educ,
    2009n251
International hndbk on the preparation & dvlpmt of
    school leaders, 2009n258

EDUCATION LIBRARIES
Acquiring & organizing curriculum materials, 2d ed,
    2005n624

EDUCATION, SECONDARY
Comparative gd to American elem & secondary
    schools 2005, 3d ed, 2005n285
Cosmeo [Website], 2009n285
Educators gd to free Internet resources 2007-08,
    secondary ed, 25th ed, 2008n292
Educators gd to free videotapes 2004-05: secondary
    ed, 21st ed, 2005n282
Educators gd to free videotapes 2005-06: secondary
    ed, 52d ed, 2006n319
Educators gd to free videotapes 2007-08, secondary
    ed, 54th ed, 2008n294
English lang arts units for grades 9-12, 2009n270
Finding an online high school, 2007n242
500 best ways for teens to spend the summer,
    2005n283
Handbook of research in social studies educ, 2009n252
100 experiential learning activities for social studies,
    lit, & the arts, grades 5-12, 2009n269
Private secondary schools 2006, 2006n281
Visual arts units for all levels, 2009n266

EDUCATION STATISTICS
Almanac of American educ 2005, 2006n277
Almanac of American educ 2006, 2007n238
Educational rankings annual 2005, 2005n278
Education state rankings 2005-06, 4th ed, 2006n278
Education state rankings 2006-07, 5th ed, 2007n239
National Center for Education Stats [Website],
    2005n279

EDUCATIONAL CONSULTANTS
Handbook of research in school consultation,
    2009n255

EDUCATIONAL PSYCHOLOGY
Encyclopedia of educ & human dvlpmt, 2006n275
Encyclopedia of educl psychology, 2009n245

EDUCATIONAL TECHNOLOGY
Best new media, K-12, 2009n284
Educational media & tech yrbk 2003, v.28, 2005n317
Educational media & tech yrbk 2005, v.30, 2006n317
Educational media & tech yrbk 2008, v.33, 2009n288
Educators gd to free Internet resources 2007-08,
    elem/middle school ed, 7th ed, 2008n291
Educators gd to free Internet resources 2007-08,
    secondary ed, 25th ed, 2008n292
Education gd to free Internet resources 2008-09, 8th
    ed, 2009n287
Educators gd to free Internet resources 2008-09, 26th
    ed, 2009n286
Encyclopedia of info tech curriculum integration,
    2009n1282
Handbook of research on instructional systems & tech,
    2008n1273
Web literacy for educators, 2009n289

EGYPT
Atlas of Egyptian art, paperback ed, 2009n847
Brief hist of Egypt, 2009n416
British military operations in Egypt & the Sudan,
    2009n600
Complete royal families of ancient Egypt, 2006n484
Daily life of the ancient Egyptians, 2d ed, 2009n415
Historical dict of ancient Egypt, 2d ed, 2009n414
Historical dict of Egypt, 3d ed, 2005n85
Historical sites of Egypt, v.1, 2008n378
History of Egypt, 2005n86
Reign of Cleopatra, 2006n482
Thames & Hudson dict of ancient Egypt, 2007n400

EGYPTIAN MYTHOLOGY
Egyptian mythology A to Z, rev ed, 2007n1027

EL SALVADOR
Salvadoran Americans, 2007n283

ELECTIONS
ACE electoral knowledge network [Website],
    2008n614
Almanac of state legislative elections, 3d ed,
    2008n650
Almanac of the unelected 2004, 17th ed, 2005n713
Almanac of the unelected 2006, 19th ed, 2007n586
Almanac of the unelected 2008, 21st ed, 2009n655
America at the polls 1960-2004, 2007n616
America votes 25, 2005n719
America votes 26, 2003-04, 2006n732
America votes 2005-06, 2008n643
Annenberg pol fact check [Website], 2009n629
Campaign & election reform, 2005n717

Campaign & election reform, 2d ed, 2009n668
Campaign ads [Website], 2009n630
Democracy project [Website], 2009n632
Electing Congress, 2d ed, 2009n657
ElectionGd [Website], 2008n615
Elections A to Z, 3d ed, 2008n628
Electoral voter predictor [Website], 2009n633
Encyclopedia of US campaigns, elections, & electoral
    behavior, 2009n640
Geography of presidential elections in the US,
    1868-2004, 2006n730
Green papers [Website], 2009n634
Guide to pol campaigns in America, 2006n726
Historical atlas of US presidential elections,
    1789-2004, 2007n585
Legislative women, 2009n662
National party conventions 1831-2004, 2007n617
Party affiliations in the state legislatures, 2008n624
PollingReport.com [Website], 2009n636
Presidential elections, 1789-2004, 2007n619
Project vote smart [Website], 2009n637
Race for the presidency, 2008n644
Student's gd to elections, 2009n667
United States election system, 2005n720
United States presidential primary election 2000-04,
    2007n609

ELECTORAL COLLEGE
Electoral voter predictor [Website], 2009n633

ELECTRICAL ENGINEERING
McGraw-Hill dict of electrical & computer
    engineering, 2005n1409
Standard hndbk for electrical engineers, 15th ed,
    2007n1225
Wiley electrical & electronics engineering dict,
    2005n1410

ELECTRONIC COMMERCE
Encyclopedia of e-commerce, e-govt, & mobile
    commerce, 2007n1286
Plunkett's e-commerce & Internet business almanac
    2006, 2007n172
Plunkett's e-commerce & Internet business almanac,
    2008 ed, 2009n179

ELECTRONIC GOVERNMENT INFORMATION
Encyclopedia of digital govt, 2007n39
Encyclopedia of e-commerce, e-govt, & mobile
    commerce, 2007n1286

ELECTRONIC INFORMATION RESOURCES
Collection dvlpmt issues in the online environment,
    2007n519
Integrating print & digital resources in lib collections,
    2007n533

Selecting & managing electronic resources, rev ed,
    2007n520

ELECTRONIC JOURNALS
E-journals, 2006n641
Electronic jl mgmt systems, 2006n642

ELECTRONIC MAIL
Glossary of netspeak & textspeak, 2005n1485

ELECTRONIC PUBLISHING
CD-ROMs in print, 18th ed, 2005n9

ELECTRONIC REFERENCE SERVICES
Assessing ref & user servs in a digital age, 2008n557
Collection mgmt & strategic access to digital
    resources, 2006n597
Cooperative ref, 2005n647
Digital ref serv, 2005n648
Digital resources & librarians, 2005n629
Evolving Internet ref resources, 2007n539
Improving Internet ref servs to distance learners,
    2006n598
Introduction to ref work in the digital age, 2005n650
Kovac's gd to electronic lib collection dvlpmt,
    2005n591
Library Web sites, 2005n635
Virtual ref desk, 2006n644
Virtual ref librarian's hndbk, 2005n651
Virtual ref serv, 2008n558
Virtual ref training, 2005n649

ELECTRONICS
Electronics, 2005n1292

ELLIS ISLAND IMMIGRATION STATION
Encyclopedia of Ellis Island, 2005n433

EMBLEMS
Book of emblems, 2005n942
Companion to emblem studies, 2009n327

EMERGENCY MANAGEMENT
Emergency mgmt, 2009n447

EMIGRATION & IMMIGRATION
Atlas of human migration, 2008n740
Chronology of immigration in the US, 2009n768
Daily life in immigrant America, 1820-70, 2009n387
Encyclopedia of diasporas, 2006n823
Encyclopedia of Ellis Island, 2005n433
Encyclopedia of immigration & migration in the
    American west, 2007n733
Encyclopedia of N American immigration, 2006n824
Encyclopedia of the great black migration, 2007n271
Illegal immigration, 2008n480
Immigration, 2007n722

Immigration, 2008n741
Immigration, 2009n772
Immigration & asylum, 2006n832
Immigration & migration, 2009n771
Immigration & multiculturalism, 2008n751
Immigration in America today, 2009n769
Immigration in US hist, 2007n735
Immigration to the US series, 2005n324
Migration & immigration, 2005n832
U.S. immigration & migration: almanac, 2005n836
U.S. immigration & migration: biogs, 2005n837
U.S. immigration & migration: primary sources,
    2005n838
Welcome to America: the complete gd for immigrants,
    2006n831
Working Americans 1880-2007, v.8: immigrants,
    2009n211

EMPLOYMENT LAW
Covenants not to compete, 3d ed, 2005n584
Covenants not to compete, 2003 suppl, 3d ed,
    2005n585
Employer legal forms simplified, 2008n235
Employer's legal hndbk, 7th ed, 2007n487
Essential gd to fed employment laws, 2007n485
Wage & hour laws, 2006n578
Your rights in the workplace, 7th ed, 2007n486

ENCYCLOPEDIAS & DICTIONARIES. *See also*
CHILDREN'S ENCYCLOPEDIAS &
DICTIONARIES
American Heritage student dict, updated ed, 2007n850
Annals of America, 2005n27
Britannica concise ency, rev ed, 2007n21
Britannica learning zone [Website], 2009n18
Britannica online [Website], 2008n23
Compton's by Britannica 2007, 2008n24
Compton's by Britannica 2008, 2009n19
Compton's by Encyclopaedia Britannica 2005,
    2007n23
DK online ency, 2007n24
Encyclopedia Americana, 2004 ed, 2005n31
Encyclopaedia Britannica 2005 [CD-ROM], 2005n30
Encyclopedia Americana, intl ed, 2006n24
Encyclopedia Americana [Website], 2006n25
Encyclopedia Americana [Website], 2008n25
Famous 1st facts, 6th ed, 2008n26
La nueva enciclopedia cumbre [Website], 2009n20
Marshall Cavendish digital [Website], 2009n21
MSN Encarta [Website], 2008n27
New bk of knowledge, 2006n26
New bk of knowledge, 2007 ed, 2007n25
New bk of knowledge, 2008 ed, 2008n28
New bk of knowledge online [Website], 2006n27
New Oxford American dict, 2d ed, 2006n28
Oxford concise ency, 2d ed, 2008n29
Oxford English dict, 2d ed on CD-ROM, 2006n29

Spanish ref center [Website], 2009n23
Wikipedia [Website], 2008n32
World Bk discover [Website], 2009n24
World Bk discovery ency, 2009n25
World Bk ency, 2006 ed, 2006n30
World Bk ency, 2007 ed, 2007n28
World Bk ency, 2008 ed, 2008n33
World Bk ency, 2009 ed, 2009n26
World Bk student dict, 2005 ed, 2005n35
World Bk student discovery ency, 2d ed, 2008n34
World Book ency 2004, 2005n34

ENDANGERED SPECIES
Atlas of endangered species, rev ed, 2009n1192
Endangered species, 2d ed, 2005n1377

ENERGY
Alternative energy, 2007n1322
Energy stats yrbk, 2002, 2006n1534
Energy stats yrbk 2003, 2007n1323
Energy stats yrbk 2004, 2008n1334
Energy supply, 2006n1536
Energy supply & renewable resources, 2008n1335
Energy use worldwide, 2008n1336
Natural resources & sustainable dvlpmt, 2009n1328
Renewable & alternative energy resources, 2009n1329
U.S. natl debate topic 2008-09: alternative energy,
    2009n1330

ENERGY INDUSTRY
Major energy companies of the world 2005, 8th ed,
    2006n183
Plunkett's energy industry almanac, 2006 ed,
    2006n1535
Plunkett's energy industry almanac 2007, 2008n197

ENGINEERING
Building the world, 2007n1224
Cambridge aerospace dict, 2006n1400
Career opportunities in engineering, 2007n223
Dekker ency of nanosci & nanotech, 2005n1401
Dekker ency of nanosci & nanotech [Website],
    2005n1402
Dictionary of engineering materials, 2005n1404
Elsevier's dict of engineering, 2005n1403
Encyclopedia of biomaterials & biomedical
    engineering, 2005n1405
Encyclopedia of biomaterials & biomedical
    engineering [Website], 2005n1406
Encyclopedia of chromatography, 2d ed, 2006n1401
Encyclopedia of computational mechanics, 2006n1393
Encyclopedia of corrosion tech, 2d ed, 2005n1414
Encyclopedia of nonlinear sci, 2006n1394
Encyclopedia of RF & microwave engineering,
    2006n1395
Encyclopedia of stats in quality & reliability,
    2009n1220

Encyclopedic dict of polymers, 2009n1213
Handbook of optical systems, v. 1, 2006n1407
Handbook of optical systems, v.2, 2006n1408
Handbook of polymer reaction engineering, 2006n1398
Illustrated pocket dict of chromatography, 2007n1223
International ency of ergonomics & human factors, 2d ed, 2007n1220
International ency of ergonomics & human factors, 2d ed [CD-ROM], 2007n1221
Marks' standard hndbk for mechanical engineers, 11th ed, 2007n1228
McGraw-Hill concise ency of engineering, 2006n1396
Mechanical engineers' hndbk, 3d ed, 2008n1201
Nine-lang dict of polymers & composites, 2009n1214
NTIS [Website], 2006n1277
Perry's chemical engineers' hndbk, 8th ed, 2008n1197
Plunkett's engineering & research industry almanac, 2005 ed, 2006n1399
Plunkett's engineering & research industry almanac 2007, 2008n198
Science of microscopy, 2007n1229
Standard hndbk for electrical engineers, 15th ed, 2007n1225
Using the engineering lit, 2008n1195
Wiley electrical & electronics engineering dict, 2005n1410
Wiley ency of biomedical engineering, 2007n1222

ENGINEERS

Who's who in sci & engineering 2005-06 8th ed, 2006n1252
Who's who in sci & engineering 2008-09, 10th ed, 2008n1106

ENGLAND. *See also* GREAT BRITAIN

Architecture of England, Scotland, & Wales, 2006n931
Cambridge dict of English place-names, 2006n390
Other British Isles, 2007n389

ENGLISH LANGUAGE

Lexicons of early modern English [Website], 2009n869
Varieties of English, 2009n873

ENGLISH LANGUAGE - DICTIONARIES

American Heritage children's dict, updated ed, 2008n863
American Heritage college dict, 4th ed, 2008n854
American Heritage desk dict & thesaurus, 2006n941
American Heritage dict define-a-thon for the high school freshman, 2008n855
American Heritage dict define-a-thon for the high school graduate, 2008n856
American Heritage dict of the English lang, 4th ed, 2007n20
American Heritage 1st dict, 2008n864
American Heritage high school dict, 4th ed, 2008n857
Cambridge advanced learner's dict, 2d ed, 2006n943
Cambridge English pronouncing dict, 17th ed, 2007n825
Cambridge essential English dict, 2006n944
Cambridge phrasal verbs dict, 2007n826
Chambers concise dict, 2005n953Concise Oxford English dict, 11th ed, 2005n28
Concise Oxford American dict, 2007n827
Divided by a common lang, 2006n938
DK illus Oxford dict, rev ed, 2005n29
Facts on File student's dict of American English, 2008n865
Facts on File student's thesaurus, 3d ed, 2006n958
First English dict, 1604, 2008n851
Gabby's wordspeller phonetic dict, 2d ed, 2009n874
Kingfisher 1st dict, 2006n959
Little Oxford English dict & thesaurus, 2d ed, 2009n875
Merriam-Webster's advanced learner's English dict, 2009n876
Merriam-Webster's primary dict, 2006n961
New Oxford American dict, 2d ed, 2006n28
100 words almost everyone confuses & misuses, 2005n960
100 words to make you sound smart, 2007n828
Oxford American large print dict, 2007n829
Oxford American large print dict, 2009n877
Oxford English dict, 2d ed on CD-ROM, 2006n29
Oxford spellchecker & dict [CD-ROM], 2009n878
Pocket Oxford American dict, 2d ed, 2009n880
Random House Webster's large print crossword puzzle dict, 2008n858
Right, wrong, & risky: a dict of today's American English usage, 2006n963
Shorter Oxford English dict, 6th ed, 2008n31
Webster's all-in-one dict & thesaurus, 2009n882
Webster's contemporary school & office dict, 2009n883
Webster's desk ref set, 2007n831
Webster's dict & thesaurus for students, 2007n832
Webster's dict for students, new ed, 2008n859
Webster's II new college dict, 3d ed, 2006n947
Webster's new explorer college dict, new ed, 2008n861
Webster's new explorer dict, new ed, 2006n945
Webster's new explorer dict & thesaurus, new ed, 2006n946
Webster's new explorer encyclopedic dict, 2007n26
Webster's new explorer gd to English usage, 2005n961
Webster's new explorer large print dict, new ed, 2007n834
Word parts dict, 2d ed, 2009n881
World Bk dict, 2007n27
Wrong word dict, 2007n838

ENGLISH LANGUAGE - DICTIONARIES - ARABIC
Short ref grammar of Iraqi Arabic, repr ed, 2005n969

ENGLISH LANGUAGE - DICTIONARIES - CHINESE
ABC Chinese-English comprehensive dict, 2005n970
250 essential Chinese characters for everyday use, 2005n971

ENGLISH LANGUAGE - DICTIONARIES - FRENCH
Barron's French-English dict, 2007n858
Bilingual visual dict: French/English, 2007n859
Harrap's French & English college dict, 2007n860
Oxford Hachette French dict, 4th ed, 2008n872
Webster's French-English dict, 2006n967

ENGLISH LANGUAGE - DICTIONARIES - GERMAN
Bilingual visual dict: German/English, 2007n861
Concise Oxford-Duden German dict, 3d ed, 2006n968
Oxford-Duden German dict, 3d ed, 2006n969

ENGLISH LANGUAGE - DICTIONARIES - INDONESIAN
Comprehensive Indonesian-English dict, 2005n973

ENGLISH LANGUAGE - DICTIONARIES - ITALIAN
Oxford color Italian dict plus, 2009n899
Oxford-Paravia Italian dict, 2d ed, 2009n900

ENGLISH LANGUAGE - DICTIONARIES - JUVENILE
American Heritage children's dict, updated ed, 2007n848
American Heritage 1st dict, 2007n849
American Heritage student dict, updated ed, 2007n850
Webster's new explorer student dict, new ed, 2007n851
World Bk student dict, 2005 ed, 2005n35

ENGLISH LANGUAGE - DICTIONARIES - RHYMING
Oxford rhyming dict, 2005n956
Words to rhyme with, 3d ed, 2008n866

ENGLISH LANGUAGE - DICTIONARIES - RUSSIAN
Elsevier's dict of economics, business, finance, & law, 2005n144
Elsevier's dict of zoology & general biology, 2005n1380

ENGLISH LANGUAGE - DICTIONARIES - SLANG
American slang dict, 2007n846

Encyclopedia of swearing, 2007n844
FUBAR: soldier slang of WW II, 2008n868
New Partridge dict of slang & unconventional English, 2007n845
Slanguage, new ed, 2005n957
Stone the crows: Oxford dict of modern slang, 2d ed, 2009n891
Talk the talk: the slang of 65 American subcultures, 2008n867

ENGLISH LANGUAGE - DICTIONARIES - SPANISH
Barron's Spanish-English dict, 2007n863
Bilingual visual dict: Spanish/English, 2007n864
Elsevier's dict of medicine: Spanish-English & English-Spanish, 2005n1435
Harrap's Spanish & English business dict, 2006n122
Larousse unabridged dict: Spanish-English, English-Spanish, 2005n974
New ref grammar of modern Spanish, 2006n971
Oxford Spanish dict, 4th ed, 2009n901
Spanish word histories & mysteries, 2008n874
Vocabulario Vaquero/cowboy talk, 2005n975
Webster's family Spanish-English dict, deluxe ed, 2007n865
Webster's new explorer Spanish-English dict, new ed, 2007n866

ENGLISH LANGUAGE – DICTIONARIES – VISUAL
DK ultimate visual dict, 2005n967
Firefly 5 lang visual dict, 2006n965
Firefly jr visual dict, 2008n870
Heinle picture dict, 2005n968
Merriam-Webster's visual dict, 2007n857

ENGLISH LANGUAGE - ETYMOLOGY
Analytic dict of English etymology, 2009n887
Facts on File ency of word & phrase origins, 4th ed, 2009n885
Last word, 2009n886
Life of lang, 2007n824
More word histories & mysteries, 2007n837
Movers & shakers, 2007n835
Webster's new explorer dict of word origins, 2005n954
Word hists & mysteries, 2005n955
Word origins . . . & how we know them, 2006n948
Word routes, 2006n949
Words, words, words, 2007n836

ENGLISH LANGUAGE - GRAMMAR
American Heritage gd to contemporary usage & style, 2006n950
Between you & I: a little bk of bad English, 2006n952
Cambridge gd to English usage, 2006n883
Dictionary of disagreeable English, 2005n958

Glossary of morphology, 2006n951
McGraw-Hill dict of misspelled & easily confused
    words, 2007n839

ENGLISH LANGUAGE - HOMONYMS
Homophones & homographs, 4th ed, 2007n840

ENGLISH LANGUAGE - IDIOMS
Cambridge idioms dict, 2d ed, 2007n841
Dictionary of American idioms, 4th ed, 2006n953
McGraw-Hill's American idioms dict, 4th ed,
    2008n862
McGraw-Hill's dict of American idioms & phrasal
    verbs, 2006n954
Oxford dict of idioms, 2d ed, 2006n956
Weasel words, 2007n847

ENGLISH LANGUAGE - SYNONYMS &
ANTONYMS
American Heritage college thesaurus, 2005n962
American Heritage desk dict & thesaurus, 2006n941
Chambers synonyms & antonyms, 2005n963
Chambers thesaurus, 2005n964
Concise Oxford American thesaurus, 2007n855
Facts on File student's thesaurus, 3d ed, 2006n958
Kingfisher first thesaurus, 2006n960
Little Oxford English dict & thesaurus, 2d ed,
    2009n875
Oxford American large print thesaurus, 2007n830
Oxford American writer's thesaurus, 2005n965
Oxford American writer's thesaurus, 2d ed, 2009n895
Oxford large print thesaurus, 2005n966
Pocket Oxford thesaurus, 2d ed, 2009n879
Thinker's thesaurus, 2007n856
Webster's all-in-one dict & thesaurus, 2009n882
Webster's contemporary school & office thesaurus,
    2009n884
Webster's dict & thesaurus for students, 2007n832
Webster's new explorer crossword puzzle dict, 2d ed,
    2007n833
Webster's new explorer dict & thesaurus, new ed,
    2006n946
Webster's thesaurus for students, new ed, 2008n860

ENGLISH LANGUAGE - TERMS & PHRASES
American Heritage dict of phrasal verbs, 2006n962
Common phrases & where they came from, 2d ed,
    2009n894
Descriptionary, 3d ed, 2006n964
Dimwit's dict, 2d ed, 2007n842
Eyes like butterflies: a treasury of similes &
    metaphors, 2007n853
Facts on File dict of cliches, 2d ed, 2007n854
Facts on File dict of foreign words & phrases, 2d ed,
    2009n893
Foyle's philavery, repr ed, 2009n888

Handbook of commonly used American idioms, 4th
    ed, 2005n959
100 words almost everyone mispronounces, 2009n889
100 words for lovers, 2009n890
Real McCoy: the true stories behind our everyday
    phrases, 2007n843
Sticklers, sideburns & bikinis, 2009n892

ENGLISH LANGUAGE – VOCABULARY
Cure for the common word, 2008n871
Vocabulary of success, 2009n896
Webster's new explorer vocabulary skill builder,
    2009n897

ENGLISH LITERATURE. See also AUTHORS,
ENGLISH
Age of Milton, 2005n1002
Alexander Pope ency, 2005n1112
Arthurian writers, 2009n969
British women romantic poets, 1789-1952 [Website],
    2005n1100
British writers, suppl 14, 2009n968
Cambridge gd to lit in English, 3d ed, 2007n878
Cambridge hist of English lit, 1660-1780, 2006n1045
Companion to the 18th-century English novel &
    culture, 2006n1046
Critical companion to Jane Austen, 2009n973
Encyclopedia of British writers, 2006n1043
English lit in context, 2009n970
Essential Shakespeare hndbk, 2005n1080
Everyone & everything in Trollope, 2005n1081
Facts on File companion to the British novel,
    2006n1044
Facts on File companion to the British short story,
    2008n927
Field gd to Narnia, 2005n1078
General studies of Charles Dickens & his writings &
    collected eds of his works, 2005n1077
Literary research & the British Romantic Era,
    2006n1047
Masterpieces of modern British & Irish drama,
    2006n1008
Oxford companion to Chaucer, 2005n1076
Oxford companion to English lit, 6th rev ed, 2007n955
Oxford companion to the Brontes, 2005n1075
Oxford concise companion to English lit, 3d ed,
    2009n971
Oxford ency of British lit, 2007n956
Oxford hndbk of English lit & theology, 2009n972
Undergraduate's companion to English Renaissance
    writers & their Web sites, 2005n1074
Understanding the lit of WW I, 2006n987
Victorian lit hndbk, 2009n918

ENGLIGHTENMENT
Encyclopedia of the Enlightenment, rev ed, 2005n524

ENTERTAINING
Entertaining from ancient Rome to the Super Bowl, 2009n1145

ENTERTAINMENT INDUSTRY
Entertainment awards, 3d ed, 2005n1183
Hollywood creative dir, Spring 2004, 50th ed, 2005n1186
Hollywood creative dir, Spring 2008, 62d ed, 2008n1006
Hollywood creative dir, Spring 2009, 65th ed, 2009n1051
Hollywood creative dir online [Website], 2008n1007
Hollywood creative dir online [Website], 2009n1052
Hollywood distribution dir 2007-08, 18th ed, 2008n1008
Hollywood music industry dir, premier ed 2004, 2005n1122
Hollywood music industry dir 2008, 5th ed, 2008n968
Hollywood representation dir, Summer 2004, 27th ed, 2005n1187
Hollywood representation dir, Winter 2007, 34th ed, 2008n1009
Plunkett's entertainment & media industry almanac 2004, 2005n888
Plunkett's entertainment & media industry almanac 2006, 2007n173
Plunkett's entertainment & media industry almanac 2007, 2008n199

ENTREPRENEURSHIP
African-American business leaders & entrepreneurs, 2005n140
Entrepreneur's info sourcebk, 2007n142
International hndbk of research on indigenous entrepreneurship, 2009n294

ENVIRONMENTAL CAREERS
Career opportunities in conservation & the environment, 2008n247
ECO gd to careers that make a difference, 2006n250

ENVIRONMENTAL DISASTERS. *See also* NATURAL DISASTERS
Environmental disasters series, 2006n1540

ENVIRONMENTAL ENGINEERING
Environmental engineering dict, 4th ed, 2006n1404

ENVIRONMENTAL HISTORY
Annual review of environment & resources, v.28, 2003, 2005n1540
Annual review of environment & resources, v.29, 2004, 2006n1538
Australia, New Zealand, & the Pacific, 2006n1542
Canada & Arctic N America, 2008n1351
Climate change 2007, 2008n1311

Environmental issues in American hist, 2008n1346
Global climate change, 2007n1329
Historical dict of the green movement, 2d ed, 2008n1341
Mediterranean: an environmental hist, 2006n1543
Northeast & Midwest United States: an environmental hist, 2006n1539
Our Earth's changing land, 2007n1332
Southeast Asia, 2008n1345
Southern US, 2007n1327
Sub-Saharan Africa, 2007n1331
United States west coast, 2008n1348

ENVIRONMENTAL INDUSTRY
World environmental databk 2006, 2007n1335
World environmental databk 2008/09, 2009n1346

ENVIRONMENTAL LAW
Environmental law hndbk, 18th ed, 2007n488
Environmental law hndbk, 19th ed, 2009n481
Environmental regulatory dict, 4th ed, 2006n579
Environmental statutes, 2004 ed, 2005n586
Environmental statutes, 2005 ed, 2006n580
Environmental statutes, 2008 ed, 2009n482
International environmental disputes, 2007n1333
International environmental law reports, v.5, 2009n483

ENVIRONMENTAL LEADERS
American environmental leaders, 2d ed, 2009n1331
American women conservationists, 2005n1536
Shapers of the great debate on conservation, 2005n1537

ENVIRONMENTAL LITERATURE
Literature & the environment, 2005n1008

ENVIRONMENTAL PROTECTION
Africa & the Middle East: a continental overview of environmental issues, 2005n1541
Australia, Oceania, & Antarctica, 2005n1542
Conservation dir 2005-06, 50th ed, 2007n1326
Environmental Protection Agency, 2007n645
Indigenous peoples & environmental issues, 2005n1538
International environmental disputes, 2007n1333
Latin America & the Caribbean, 2005n1543
State of the wild 2006, 2007n1334

ENVIRONMENTAL PROTECTION AGENCY
Environmental Protection Agency, 2006n722

ENVIRONMENTAL SCIENCE
Clean air hndbk, 4th ed, 2009n1338
Climate change, 2009n1321
Earth's changing environment, 2009n1339
Encyclopedia of environmental ethics & philosophy, 2009n1333

Encyclopedia of global warming & climate change, 2009n1334
Environment: the sci behind the stories, 2009n1345
Environmental regulatory calculations hndbk, 2009n1342
Environmental sci in context, 2009n1335
Teen gds to environmental sci, 2005n1544

ENVIRONMENTALISM
Battleground: environment, 2009n1332
Canadian environmental dir 2007, 12th ed, 2008n1342
Canadian environmental dir 2008, 13th ed, 2008n1343
Conflicts over natural resources, 2008n1350
Dictionary of environment & conservation, 2008n1340
Ecology, rev ed, 2009n1337
Ecoterrorism, 2005n580
Encyclopedia of environment & society, 2008n1338
Environmental issues: essential primary sources, 2007n1328
Environmental resource hndbk 2005/06, 3d ed, 2006n1541
Environmental resource hndbk 2008-09, 4th ed, 2008n1344
Facts on File dict of environmental sci, 3d ed, 2008n1339
Grasslands of the US, 2008n1347
Great debates in American environmental hist, 2009n1340
International yrbk of environmental & resource economics 2006/07, 2007n1330
Living green, 2009n1336
New atlas of planet mgmt, 3d ed, 2006n1537
South Asia: an environmental hist, 2009n1341
State of the environ in Asia & the Pacific 2005, 2008n1349
World's protected areas, 2009n1347

EPIDEMICS
Black death, 2005n475
Encyclopedia of pestilence, pandemics, & plagues, 2009n1223
Encyclopedia of plague & pestilence, 3d ed, 2008n454
Epidemics, 2005n1445
Epidemics & pandemics, 2006n1423
Infectious diseases in context, 2008n1229
Pandemics & global health, 2009n1254

EPIDEMIOLOGY
Encyclopedia of epidemiology, 2008n1225

ERGONOMICS
International ency of ergonomics & human factors, 2d ed, 2007n1220
International ency of ergonomics & human factors, 2d ed [CD-ROM], 2007n1221

EROTIC LITERATURE
Encyclopedia of erotic lit, 2007n922

ESPIONAGE
Encyclopedia of Cold War espionage, spies, & secret operations, 2005n664
Encyclopedia of intelligence & counterintelligence, 2006n661
Literary spy, 2005n59

ESSENTIAL OILS
A-Z of essential oils, 2005n1454

ESTATE PLANNING
Estate planning simplified, 2007n463
Plan your estate, 9th ed, 2009n484

ETHICS
Encyclopedia of business ethics & society, 2008n154
Ethics, rev ed, 2006n1192
Ethics updates [Website], 2006n1201
ETHX on the Web [Website], 2006n1185
Historical dict of ethics, 2009n1084
Moral educ, 2009n260

ETHIOPIA
Historical dict of Ethiopia, new ed, 2005n87

ETHNIC RELATIONS
African American issues, 2007n274
Encyclopedia of racism in the US, 2007n263
Encyclopedia of race & racism, 2008n302
Prejudice in the modern world: almanac, 2008n304
Prejudice in the modern world: biogs, 2008n305
Prejudice in the modern world: primary sources, 2008n306

ETHNIC STUDIES
eHRAF collection of ethnography/archaeology [Website], 2007n262
Encyclopedia of race & ethnic studies, 2005n323
Encyclopedia of race, ethnicity, & society, 2009n293
Encyclopedia of the world's minorities, 2006n323
Former Yugoslavia's diverse peoples, 2005n339
Global gateway: world culture & resources [Website], 2008n299
Historical dict of the peoples of the SE Asian massif, 2007n264
Lands & peoples, 2006n65
Multiculturalism in the US, rev ed, 2006n324
Nationalism & ethnicity terminologies, v.3, 2006n63
Native web [Website], 2008n300
New ency of southern culture, v.6: ethnicity, 2008n303
Peoples, nations, & cultures, 2006n325
Peoples of W Asia, 2007n92
Racial & ethnic diversity, 5th ed, 2007n266

Sage dict of cultural studies, 2007n265
South Africa's diverse peoples, 2007n90

ETIQUETTE
Global business etiquette, 2009n148
Latitia Baldrige's new manners for new times, 2005n800
Metrosexual gd to style, 2005n1175

EUGENICS
Eugenics movement, 2006n1191

EUROPE
Teen life in Europe, 2006n102
European integration current contents [Website], 2008n113

EUROPE, BUSINESS
Consumer E Europe 2004-05, 12th ed, 2005n216
Consumer E Europe 2008/09, 2009n199
Consumer Europe 2004/05, 20th ed, 2005n217
Consumer W Europe 2006/07, 22d ed, 2007n187
Consumer W Europe 2008/09, 2009n200
European mktg data & stats 2004, 39th ed, 2005n218
European mktg data & stats 2006, 41st ed, 2006n218
European mktg forecasts 2004/05, 8th ed, 2005n219
European mktg forecasts 2005/06, 9th ed, 2006n219
European mktg forecasts 2009, 12th ed, 2009n201
Major companies of Central & E Europe & the Commonwealth of Independent States 2005, 14th ed, 2006n220
Major companies of Europe 2005, 24th ed, 2005n220
Trade assns & professional bodies of Continental Europe, 2005 ed, 2005n221
Trade assns & professional bodies of the Continental European Union, 5th ed, 2009n202
Western Europe 2009, 2009n110

EUROPE, EASTERN & CENTRAL
Access to E European & Eurasian culture, 2009n527
Biographical dict of Central & E Europe in the 20th century, 2009n108
Central & S Eastern Europe 2007, 7th ed, 2008n116
Consumer E Europe 2005/06, 13th ed, 2006n217
Consumer E Europe 2006/07, 14th ed, 2007n186
Eastern Europe, 2006n100
Eastern Europe, Russia, & Central Asia 2007, 7th ed, 2008n117
Eastern Europe, Russia, & Central Asia 2009, 2009n109
Encyclopedia of the Byzantine empire, 2005n473
G. K. Hall bibliog gd to Slavic, Baltic, & Eurasian studies 2002, 2005n104
G. K. Hall bibliog gd to Slavic, Baltic, & Eurasian studies 2003, 2006n101
Guide to Slavic collections in the US, 2006n611

Historical dict of Bosnia & Herzegovina, 2d ed, 2008n119
Major companies of Central & E Europe & the Commonwealth of Independent States 2008, 2008n221
Palgrave atlas of Byzantine hist, 2006n466
Virtual Slavica, 2007n506
Women & gender in Central & E Europe, Russia, & Eurasia, 2008n775

EUROPE, ENVIRONMENTAL CONDITIONS
Northern Europe: an environmental hist, 2006n1545

EUROPE, HISTORY
A to Z of Byzantium, 2007n382
Age of Romanticism, 2008n430
Black death, 2005n475
Cultural exchange in early modern Europe, 2008n429
Daily life in the Byzantine Empire, 2007n386
Encyclopedia of European peoples, 2007n111
Encyclopedia of the age of Imperialism, 1800-1914, 2009n402
Encyclopedia of the age of pol revolutions & new ideologies 1760-1815, 2008n657
Encyclopedia of the Renaissance & the Reformation, rev ed, 2005n472
EuroDocs [Website], 2005n476
Eurominority [Website], 2008n114
Europe, 1789-1914, 2007n378
Europe since 1914, 2007n379
Exploring the Middle Ages, 2007n380
Handbook to life in prehistoric Europe, 2007n385
Handbook to life in renaissance Europe, 2006n470
Historical dict of the Renaissance, 2005n474
Key figures in Medieval Europe, 2007n381
Medieval cathedrals, 2007n383
Online ref bk for medieval studies [Website], 2005n479

EUROPE, POLITICS & GOVERNMENT
Political hndbk of Europe 2007, 2007n628

EUROPE, RELIGIOUS HISTORY
Encyclopedia of the crusades, 2005n521

EUROPE, TRAVEL
Greece, 5th ed, 2005n405
Italy, new ed, 2008n373
Mediterranean cruises, 2005n407
Russia: Belarus & Ukraine, updated ed, 2009n353
Spain 2008, 2008n377

EUROPEAN UNION
European Union, 2006n738
European Union ency & dir 2008, 2008n115
Historical dict of the European Union, 2007n110

EUTHANASIA
Euthanasia, 2d ed, 2008n498

EVALUATION
Encyclopedia of evaluation, 2005n64

EVOLUTION
Counter-creationism hndbk, 2006n1317
Encyclopedia of evolution, 2007n1166
Evolution, 2007n1167
Evolution, 2008n1144
Evolution & creationism, 2008n1147
Evolution vs. creationism, 2005n1235
Evolving Eden: an illus gd to the evolution of the
      African large-mammal fauna, 2005n1383
Icons of evolution, 2009n1169
More than Darwin, 2009n1172
Scopes "Monkey Trial," 2007n453

EXHIBITIONS
Encyclopedia of world's fairs & expositions,
      2009n1039

EXPLORERS & EXPLORATION
America discovered, 2005n385
Discovery & exploration series, 2006n389
Encyclopedia of exploration, 2005n525
Exploration & sci, 2007n1145
Explorer atlas, 2007n312
Explorers & exploration, 2005n382
Historical dict of the discovery & exploration of the
      NW coast of America, 2009n380
North American jls of Prince Maximilian of Wied, v.1,
      2009n396
Oxford atlas of exploration, 2d ed, 2009n332
Oxford companion to world exploration, 2008n359

FAIRY TALES. *See also* **FOLKLORE**
Greenwood ency of folktales & fairy tales, 2009n1030
Tales online [Website], 2009n1029

FAITH DEVELOPMENT
Encyclopedia of religion & spiritual dvlpmt,
      2007n1079

FAMILY
American families in crisis, 2009n748
Blackwell companion to the sociology of families,
      2006n806
Family in society, 2007n703
Family life in 17th- & 18th-century America,
      2006n809
Family life in 20th-century America, 2008n722
International hndbk of stepfamilies, 2009n746
Oxford companion to family & local hist, 2009n324
Your military family network, 2008n724

FAMILY VIOLENCE.
Child abuse sourcebk, 2005n801
Domestic violence, 2d ed, 2009n747
Domestic violence sourcebk, 2d ed, 2005n802
Encyclopedia of domestic violence, 2008n721
Encyclopedia of interpersonal violence, 2009n469
Violence against women online resources [Website],
      2005n803

FANTASY LITERATURE
Encountering enchantment, 2008n883
Field gd to Harry Potter, 2009n945
Fluent in fantasy, 2009n946
Four British fantasists, 2007n911
Greenwood ency of sci fiction & fantasy, 2006n1025
Historical dict of fantasy lit, 2006n1027
J. R. R. Tolkien companion & gd, 2008n934
J. R. R. Tolkien ency, 2008n935
Read on . . . fantasy fiction, 2008n904
Supernatural lit of the world, 2007n932

FASCISM
World fascism, 2007n632

FASHION
Color answer bk, 2006n914
Disruptive pattern material, 2006n908
Encyclopedia of clothing & fashion, 2005n928
Encyclopedia of hair, 2007n809
Greenwood ency of clothing through world hist,
      2009n844
History of fashion & costume, 2006n909
Thames & Hudson dict of fashion & fashion designers,
      2d ed, 2009n845
Visual dict of fashion design, 2009n842

FAULKNER, WILLIAM
Companion to Faulkner studies, 2005n1067

FEDERAL BUREAU OF INVESTIGATION
Encyclopedia of the FBI's 10 most wanted list,
      2005n569
FBI careers, 2d ed, 2007n206

FEDERAL GOVERNMENT - UNITED STATES
Encyclopedia of fed agencies & commissions,
      2005n700
Federal leadership dir online [Website], 2009n649
Federal staff dir, fall 2004, 46th ed, 2005n706
Federal staff dir [Website], 2005n707
Federalism in America, 2007n594
Legislative branch of fed govt, 2009n660

FEMINISM
Documents from the women's liberation movement
      [Website], 2005n858
Feminism & women's issues [Website], 2005n859

Historical dict of feminism, 2d ed, 2005n869
Historical dict of feminist philosophy, 2007n758
Women's studies, feminist, & gender periodicals
    [Website], 2005n875

FEMINISM & LITERATURE
Encyclopedia of feminist lit, 2006n985
Feminist theory Website [Website], 2006n850

FERNS
Field gd to ferns & their related families, 2d ed,
    2006n1333
Tree ferns, 2005n1374

FESTIVALS. *See also* **HOLIDAYS**
Traditional festivals, 2006n1124
World party, 2007n1035

FICTION
Anatomy of wonder, 5th ed, 2006n1018
Baseball novel, 2009n939
BiblioTravel [Website], 2006n1009
Bioethics & medical issues in lit, 2006n1012
Blood, bedlam, bullets, & badguys: a reader's gd to
    adventure/suspense fiction, 2005n1040
Bookreporter.com [Website], 2006n972
Books & beyond, 2009n938
Canadian romance authors' networks (CRAN)
    [Website], 2006n1017
Chambers dict of literary characters, 2005n104
ClueLass.com & the mysterious home page [Website],
    2005n1047
Crime fiction Canada [Website], 2006n1013
Critical survey of mystery & detective fiction, rev ed,
    2009n941
Detective novels of Agatha Christie, 2009n944
Encountering enchantment, 2008n883
Encyclopedia of fantasy & horror fiction, 2007n929
Encyclopedia of gothic lit, 2005n1045
Encyclopedia of sci fiction, 2006n1024
Facts on File companion to the American novel,
    2007n940
Facts on File companion to the British novel,
    2006n1044
Fantastic fiction [Website], 2006n1010
Fiction catalog, 15th ed, 2007n916
Fluent in fantasy, 2009n946
Gay detective novel, 2005n1048
Historical dict of sci fiction lit, 2005n1051
Genreflecting, 6th ed, 2007n917
Gothic lit, 2007n930
Greenwood ency of sci fiction & fantasy, 2006n1025
Guide to the gothic 3, 2006n1016
Gumshoes: a dict of fictionary detectives, 2007n927
Historical dict of fantasy lit, 2006n1027
Historical dict of sci fiction lit, 2005n1051
Historical fiction, 2007n918

Historical fiction for young readers (grades 4-8),
    2009n922
Horror readers' advisory, 2005n1050
Internet speculative fiction database [Website],
    2006n1019
Latin American sci fiction writers, 2005n1091
Literary themes for students: race & prejudice,
    2007n923
Literary themes for students: war & peace, 2007n924
Locus online [Website], 2006n1020
Masterplots II: short story series, rev ed, 2005n1053
More bk lust, 2006n1011
Murder in retrospect, 2007n928
Mystery women, rev ed, 2007n926
Novels for students, v.19, 2005n1043
Novels for students, v.25, 2008n897
100 most popular genre fiction authors, 2007n921
Poisons in mystery lit, 2008n900
Primer of the novel, rev ed, 2007n925
Read on . . . fantasy fiction, 2008n904
Read on . . . histl fiction, 2008n901
Read on . . . horror fiction, 2007n931
Read the high country, 2007n933
Reference & research gd to mystery & detective
    fiction, 2d ed, 2005n1046
Rocked by romance, 2005n1016
Short stories for students, v.19, 2005n1054
Short stories for students, v.20, 2005n1055
Short stories for students, v.25, 2008n898
Short story index [Website], 2008n899
Short story writers, rev ed, 2008n875
Student's ency of American literary characters,
    2009n957
Supernatural lit of the world, 2007n932
Twentieth-century short story explication new series,
    v.6, 2005n1052
Ultimate mystery/detective Web gd [Website],
    2005n1049
Washington, D.C. of fiction, 2007n919
What do I read next? 2005 ed, 2007n920
What do I read next? v.1, 2004, 2005n1042
What do I read next? v.1, 2004, 2005n1042
What do I read next? v.2, 2003, 2005n1041
What do I read next? v.2, 2008 ed, 2009n940

FILM FESTIVALS
Ultimate film festival survival gd, 3d ed, 2005n1201

FILMS. *See* **MOTION PICTURES**

FINANCE
American Bar Assn gd to credit & bankruptcy,
    2006n534
Budgeting & debt mgmt, 2008n183
Cash & credit info for teens, 2006n171
Debt info for teens, 2008n184
Dictionary of finance & banking, 4th ed, 2009n164

Directory of venture capital & private equity firms
    2004, 8th ed, 2005n184
Directory of venture capital & private equity firms
    2005, 9th ed, 2006n167
Directory of venture capital & private equity firms
    2008, 12th ed, 2009n166
Directory of venture capital & private equity firms
    [Website], 2009n167
Encyclopedia of business & finance, 2d ed, 2007n160
Encyclopedia of finance, 2007n161
Everyday finance, 2009n165
Financial servs Canada 2007/08, 10th ed, 2008n181
Financial yellow bk, Summer 2005, 2006n169
Financial yellow bk, 2008 ed, 2009n168
First Bank of the US [Website], 2009n162
Major financial institutions of the world 2004, 7th ed,
    2005n185
Major financial institutions of the world, 9th ed,
    2007n163
Plunkett's banking, mortgages, & credit industry
    almanac 2005, 2006n170
Plunkett's banking, mortgages & credit industry
    almanac 2006, 2007n164
Plunkett's banking, mortgages, & credit industry
    almanac, 2009 ed, 2009n169
Plunkett's investment & securities industry almanac
    2005, 2006n157
Reaching financial goals, 2008n185
Savings & investment info for teens, 2006n172
TheStreet.com ratings' gd to banks & thrifts, Fall
    2007, 2008n182
TheStreet.com ratings' gd to banks & thrifts, Spring
    2008, 2009n170
Venture capital dir [Website], 2006n168
Weiss Ratings' gd to banks & thrifts, Summer 2004,
    2005n186
Weiss Ratings' gd to bond & money market mutual
    funds, Summer 2005, 2006n158
Weiss Ratings' gd to stock mutual funds, Summer
    2005, 2006n159

FINANCIAL AID & SCHOLARSHIPS. *See also*
GRANTS-IN-AID

Career resource gd to grants, scholarships, & other
    financial resources, 2008n286
College Board college cost & financial aid hndbk
    2005, 25th ed, 2006n311
College Board scholarship hndbk 2005, 8th ed,
    2005n307
College Board scholarship hndbk 2006, 9th ed,
    2006n302
College financing info for teens, 2009n279
College money hndbk 2006, 23d ed, 2006n312
Directory of financial aid for women 2005-07,
    2006n304
Financial aid for Hispanic Americans 2003-05,
    2006n305
Financial aid for Native Americans 2003-05,
    2006n306
Financial aid for research & creative activities abroad
    2006-08, 2006n307
Financial aid for studying & training abroad 2006-08,
    2006n308
Financial aid for the disabled & their families 2004-06,
    2005n316
Financial aid for the disabled & their families 2006-08,
    2007n252
Financial aid for veterans, military personnel, & their
    dependents 2004-06, 2006n309
Grants register 2004, 22d ed, 2005n308
Grants register 2006, 24th ed, 2006n303
RSP funding for nursing students & nurses 2004-06,
    4th ed, 2005n1476
RSP funding for nursing students & nurses 2006-08,
    2007n253
Scholarships, fellowships, & loans, 21st ed, 2005n309
Scholarships, fellowships, & loans, 22d ed, 2006n310
Scholarships, fellowships, & loans, 23d ed, 2008n287

FINLAND

Historical dict of Finland, 2d ed, 2007n113

FIREARMS

Exploring gun use in America, 2005n548
Firearms, 2005n680
Flayderman's gd to antique American firearms, 9th ed,
    2009n835
Machine guns, 2006n682
Modern guns, 15th ed, 2005n922
Modern guns, 16th ed, 2007n803
Modern guns, 17th ed, 2009n836
Official Gun Digest bk of guns & prices, 2007n802
Rifles, 2006n681
Single action sixguns, 2006n906
Standard catalog of firearms 2004, 14th ed, 2005n923
Standard catalog of firearms 2005, 15th ed, 2006n905
Standard catalog of military firearms, 3d ed, 2007n804
Standard catalog of military firearms 1870 to the
    present, 2d ed, 2005n924

FISHES

Antarctic fishes, 2008n1182
Aquariums, 2006n1381
Cutthroat, 2d ed, 2009n1202
Darwin's fishes, 2006n1382
Early stages of Atlantic fishes, 2006n1379
Encyclopedia of aquarium & pond fish, 2006n1378
Field gd to freshwater fishes of Calif., rev ed,
    2007n1203
Field gd to N Atlantic wildlife, 2006n1366
Fishes of Ala., 2005n1392
Fishes of the Tex. Laguna Madre, 2009n1201
500 freshwater aquarium fish, 2007n1202
Focus on freshwater aquarium fish, 2005n1393

Grzimek's student animal life resource: fishes, 2006n1380

New ency of the saltwater aquarium, 2008n1183

World of animals: fish, 2006n1383

FITNESS

Anatomy of exercise, 2009n735

Athletic dvlpmt, 2009n733

Bodybuilding anatomy, 2009n726

Essentials of strength training & conditioning, 3d ed, 2009n732

Fitness info for teens, 2005n1428

Fitness info for teens, 2d ed, 2009n1231

Fitness professional's hndbk, 5th ed, 2009n734

Stretching anatomy, 2009n736

FLAGS

Flags of all countries [Website], 2005n365

Flags of all countries [Website], 2007n295

World Bk's ency of flags, 2006n368

FLORIDA

Atlas of race, ancestry, & religion in 21st-century Fla., 2007n64

Complete Fla. beach gd, 2009n349

Florida almanac 2007-08, 17th ed, 2008n80

Florida landscape plants, 2d rev ed, 2006n1339

Florida municipal profiles, 2007 ed, 2009n72

Profiles of Fla., 2006n73

Profiles of Fla., 2009n73

FLOWERS. *See also* GARDENING

American azaleas, 2005n1331

American Horticultural Society garden plants & flowers, 2005n1319

Armitage's garden annuals, 2005n1312

Best rose gd, 2005n1357

Bleeding hearts, corydalis, & their relatives, 2009n1160

Bulbs for garden habitats, 2006n1304

Cattleyas & their relatives, 2005n1359

Complete hydrangeas, 2008n1137

Crocosmia & chasmanthe, 2005n1361

Daylily, 2005n1328

Dictionary of common wildflowers of Tex. & the Southern Great Plains, 2006n1343

Encyclopedia of dahlias, 2005n1315

Encyclopedia of hydrangeas, 2005n1321

Field gd to the wild orchids of Tex., 2008n1153

Field gd to the wild orchids of Thailand, 4th ed, 2006n1348

Flora of N America N of Mexico, v.4, pt. 1, 2005n1360

Flora of N America N of Mexico, v.19, 2007n1176

Flora of N America N of Mexico, v.20, 2007n1177

Flora of N America N of Mexico, v.21, 2007n1178

Flora's orchids, 2006n1342

Flowering plant families of the world, 2008n1157

Flowering plants of the neotropics, 2005n1356

Gardener's A-Z gd to growing flowers from seed to bloom, 2005n1317

Gardener's peony, 2006n1309

Gardening with hardy geraniums, 2006n1296

Genus paeonia, 2005n1362

Hardy gingers, 2006n1344

Hydrangeas, rev ed, 2006n1306

Hydrangeas for American gardens, 2005n1324

Illustrated ency of orchids, repr ed, 2007n1179

Irises, 2006n1295

Lewis Clark's field gd to wild flowers of the sea coast in the Pacific NW, 3d ed, 2006n1346

Lilies, 2005n1366

Marie Selby Botanical Gardens illus dict of orchid genera, 2009n1183

Mountain wildflowers of the southern Rockies, 2008n1156

Orchid grower's companion, 2006n1301

Orchids to know & grow, 2008n1159

Passiflora, 2005n1358

Peonies, 2007n1161

Perennials for the SW, 2007n1157

Rose, 2005n1363

Success with rhododendrons & azaleas, rev ed, 2005n1329

Timber Press pocket gd to clematis, 2007n1159

Timber Press pocket gd to shade perennials, 2006n1299

Tulips, 2007n1163

Waterlilies & lotuses, 2006n1347

Wild flowers of Ohio, 2d ed, 2009n1181

Wild orchids of the NE, 2008n1154

Wild orchids of the prairies & great plains region of N America, 2008n1155

Wildflowers of the Rocky Mountains, 2008n1158

Wildflowers of the western plains, paperback ed, 2009n1182

FLUTE MUSIC

Flute on record, 2007n995

FOLK ART

Encyclopedia of American folk art, 2005n935

FOLK MUSIC

American folk songs, 2009n1021

American popular music: folk, 2006n1102

Folk music, 2006n1103

History of folk music festivals in the US, 2009n1022

FOLKLORE

African folklore, 2005n1153

American regional folklore, 2005n1156

Arab folklore, 2009n1032

Archetypes & motifs in folklore & lit, 2006n1116
Brewer's dict of Irish phrase & fable, 2006n1115
Campus legends, 2006n1117
Caribbean folklore, 2008n991
Children's folklore, 2009n1033
Encyclopedia of American folklife, 2007n1018
Encyclopedia of American folklore, 2008n992
Encyclopedia of Celtic mythology & folklore,
      2005n1164
Encyclopedia of vampires, werewolves, & other
      monsters, 2005n1154
Fabulous creatures, mythical monsters, & animal
      power symbols, 2009n1034
Fairy lore, 2007n1020
Fantasy ency, 2007n1017
Film, folklore, & urban legends, 2008n1032
Gems in myth, legend, & lore, rev ed, 2008n996
Greenwood ency of African American folklore,
      2007n1019
Greenwood ency of folktales & fairy tales, 2009n1030
Greenwood ency of world folklore & folklife,
      2006n1114
Greenwood lib of American folktales, 2007n1021
Greenwood lib of world folktales, 2009n1031
Holy bingo, the lingo of Eden, jumpin' jehosophat, &
      the land of nod, 2007n1111
Jewish story finder, 2006n1113
Oxford dict of phrase & fable, 2d ed, 2006n867
Proverbs, 2005n1155
South Asian folklore, 2007n1022
Storytelling, 2009n1035
Tales online [Website], 2009n1029

FOOD HABITS & HISTORY
American Indian food, 2006n1285
Atlas of food, rev ed, 2009n1144
Cooking in America 1840-1945, 2008n1131
Encyclopedia of kitchen hist, 2005n1302
Entertaining from ancient Rome to the Super Bowl,
      2009n1145
Food culture in Great Britain, 2005n1306
Food culture in Italy, 2005n1307
Food culture in Japan, 2005n1304
Food culture in Mexico, 2006n1289
Food culture in Russia & Central Asia, 2006n1291
Food culture in S America, 2006n1290
Food culture in Spain, 2006n1292
Food culture in Sub-Saharan Africa, 2006n1294
Food culture in the Caribbean, 2006n1288
Food culture in the Near East, Middle East, & N
      Africa, 2006n1287
Food in colonial & fed America, 2006n1293
Food in medieval times, 2005n1303
Food in the ancient world, 2007n1152
Foodways & folklore, 2009n1154
History of food, new ed, 2009n1155
Jewish American food culture, 2009n1151

Latino food culture, 2009n1152
New ency of southern culture, v.7: foodways,
      2008n1120
Oxford companion to American food & drink,
      2009n1146
Oxford companion to food, 2d ed, 2009n1147
Oxford companion to Italian food, 2009n1148
Oxford ency of food & drink in America, 2005n1301
World cookbk for students, 2008n1129
World food habits [Website], 2008n1117

FOOD INDUSTRY
Culinary schools 2005, 8th ed, 2006n290
Food & beverage market place 2007, 6th ed, 2007n167
Food & beverage market place 2008, 7th ed,
      2008n1125
Food & beverage market place 2009, 2009n174
Market scope 2004, 2005n200
Plunkett's food industry almanac 2007, 2008n200
Thomas food & beverage market place 2005, 4th ed,
      2006n185
Thomas food & market place online [Website],
      2006n186
World food mktg dir 2008, 5th ed, 2009n190

FOOD SCIENCE
Contemporary ency of herbs & spices, 2007n1150
Cook's essential kitchen dict, 2006n1283
Dictionary of food sci & tech, 2006n1281
Encyclopedia of junk food & fast food, 2008n1122
Food alert! 2d ed, 2009n1153
Food & drug dict, 2005n1299
Food biotech, 2d ed, 2006n1286
Food ency, 2007n1151
Food plants of the world, 2006n1338
Food safety, 2d ed, 2008n1132
Gardener's A-Z gd to growing organic food,
      2005n1313
Handbook of food analytical chemistry, 2005n1305
Handbook of food products manufacturing, 2008n1128
Herbalist in the kitchen, 2008n1118
Kirk-Othmer food & feed tech, 2008n1130
Oxford ency of food & drink in America, 2005n1301
Spice & herb bible, 2d ed, 2007n1154

FOOTBALL
Best bks of football facts & stats, rev ed, 2005n772
ESPN pro football ency, 2d ed, 2008n711
Pro football prospectus 2005, 2006n789
Sporting news pro football gd, 2005 ed, 2006n790
Sporting News pro football register, 2005 ed,
      2006n791
Uniform numbers of the NFL, 2006n788

FORENSIC SCIENCE. *See also* **CRIME**
DNA evidence & forensic sci, 2009n480
Encyclopedia of forensic sci, rev ed, 2009n466

Essentials of forensic sci series, 2009n478
Facts on File dict of forensic sci, 2005n565
Forensic art [Website], 2006n577
Forensic sci, 2007n472
Forensic sci, 2009n470
Forensic sci experiments on file, 2005n1286
Forensic sci timelines [Website], 2006n553
International Assn of Forensic Linguists [Website], 2006n552
World of forensic sci, 2006n563

FOREST FIRES
Encyclopedia of fire protection, 2d ed, 2007n1325
Forest fires, 2006n1544

FORESTS & FORESTRY
Temperate forests, rev ed, 2008n1314
Tropical forests, 2008n1316

FORTUNE-TELLING
Fortune-telling bk, 2005n744

FOUNDATIONS. *See* **GRANTS-IN-AID**

FOURTH OF JULY
Fourth of July ency, 2008n1000

FRANCE
Architecture of France, 2007n817
France & the Americas, 2006n747
Issues in the French-speaking world, 2005n108
Placenames of France, 2005n391

FRANCE, HISTORY
Age of Napoleon, 2005n481
Cultures in conflict: the French Revolution, 2005n480
Encyclopedia of the French Revolutionary & Napoleonic wars, 2007n553
Historical dict of France, 2d ed, 2009n403
Joan of Arc & the hundred yrs war, 2006n471

FRANCE, INTELLECTUAL LIFE
Columbia hist of 20th-century French thought, 2007n1064
Encyclopedia of modern French thought, 2005n1230

FREE PRESS & FREE TRIAL
Freedom of the press, 2005n546
Media & American courts, 2005n539

FREEDOM OF ASSOCIATION
Freedom of association, 2005n544

FREEDOM OF INFORMATION
Opportunity for leadership, 2009n563

FREEDOM OF RELIGION
Shapers of the great debate on the freedom of religion, 2006n516

FRENCH & INDIAN WAR
French & Indian War, 2005n439

FRENCH LANGUAGE - DICTIONARIES – ENGLISH
Barron's French-English dict, 2007n858
Bilingual visual dict: French/English, 2007n859
Harrap's French & English college dict, 2007n860
Oxford Hachette French dict, 4th ed, 2008n872
Webster's French-English dict, 2006n967

FRENCH LITERATURE
Facts on File companion to the French novel, 2008n940
Masterpieces of French lit, 2005n1087
Rabelais ency, 2005n1086

FRENCH REVOLUTION
A to Z of the French Revolution, 2008n431
Cultures in conflict: the French Revolution, 2005n480
Encyclopedia of the French Revolutionary & Napoleonic wars, 2007n553
French Revolution, 2005n482
Historical dict of the French Revolution, 2005n483

FROST, ROBERT, 1874-1963
Critical companion to Robert Frost, 2008n918

FRUIT
Fruit, 2005n1367
Fruit, 2009n1184
Fruit & nuts, 2007n1180
Vegetables, herbs, & fruit, 2007n1149

FUNGI
Field gd to the fungi of Australia, 2006n1350
IndexFungorum [Website], 2006n1349
Mushrooms & other fungi of N America, repr ed, 2007n1182
North American mushrooms, 2007n1181

FURNITURE
Antique Trader furniture price gd, 3d ed, 2009n814
Early American furniture, 2007n805
Encyclopedia of wood, 2006n910
History of interior design & furniture, 2d ed, 2007n810
Sourcebook of modern furniture, 3d ed, 2006n915

GABON
Historical dict of Gabon, 3d ed, 2007n86

GAMBIA
Historical dict of The Gambia, 4th ed, 2009n91

GAMBLING
Legalized gambling, 2007n687

GANDHI, MAHATMA, 1869-1948
Comprehensive, annotated bibliog on Mahatma
Gandhi, v.2, 2008n109

GANGS
Encyclopedia of gangs, 2009n468

GARDENING. *See also* **PLANTS**
Agapanthus for gardeners, 2005n1320
Alpine plants of Europe, 2006n1298
American azaleas, 2005n1331
American Horticultural Society A-Z ency of garden
plants, rev ed, 2005n1310
American Horticultural Society AHS great plant gd,
rev ed, 2005n1311
American Horticultural Society garden plants &
flowers, 2005n1319
Armitage's garden annuals, 2005n1312
Armitage's native plants for N American gardens,
2007n1155
Bleeding hearts, corydalis, & their relatives,
2009n1160
Blueberries, cranberries, & other vacciniums,
2005n1332
Botany for gardeners, rev ed, 2006n1302
Bulbs for garden habitats, 2006n1304
Bulbs in containers, 2006n1307
Classic garden plans, 2005n1330
Color ency of hostas, 2005n1350
Complete compost gardening gd, 2009n1159
Complete hydrangeas, 2008n1137
Daylily, 2005n1328
Designer plant combinations, 2009n1157
Dryland gardening, 2006n1297
Easy orchids, 2006n1305
Elegant silvers, 2006n1303
Encyclopedia of dahlias, 2005n1315
Encyclopedia of garden design & structure,
2007n1156
Encyclopedia of hardy plants, 2008n1134
Encyclopedia of hydrangeas, 2005n1321
Encyclopedia of water garden plants, 2005n1318
Garden insects of N America, 2005n1394
Garden plants of Japan, 2005n1314
Gardener's A-Z gd to growing flowers from seed to
bloom, 2005n1317
Gardener's A-Z gd to growing organic food,
2005n1313
Gardener's peony, 2006n1309
Gardening with hardy geraniums, 2006n1296
Growing hardy orchids, 2006n1310

Hydrangeas, rev ed, 2006n1306
Hydrangeas for American gardens, 2005n1324
Illustrated dict of gardening, 2007n1158
Irises, 2006n1295
Jade garden, 2006n1311
Knott's hndbk for vegetable growers, 5th ed,
2008n1138
Lilies, 2005n1366
Native plants of the northeast, 2006n1335
New bk of herbs, 2005n1316
New York Times 1000 gardening questions &
answers, 2005n1327
Old-fashioned & David Austin roses, 2005n1365
Orchid grower's companion, 2006n1301
Organic gardener's hndbk, 2009n1161
Ornamental foliage plants, 2005n1326
Peonies, 2007n1161
Perennial vegetables, 2009n1156
Perennials for the SW, 2007n1157
Plant finder, 2008n1136
Plant locator: western region, 2005n1322
Planting design, 2006n1308
Reliable roses, 2005n1364
Restoring American gardens, 2005n1309
Shade, 2007n1162
Success with rhododendrons & azaleas, rev ed,
2005n1329
Timber Press pocket gd to bulbs, 2006n1300
Timber Press pocket gd to clematis, 2007n1159
Timber Press pocket gd to ground covers, 2007n1160
Timber Press pocket gd to shade perennials,
2006n1299
Tulips, 2007n1163
Uses of wild plants, 2009n1162Vegetable grower's
hndbk, 2009n1163
Vegetables, herbs, & fruit, 2007n1149
Veggie gardener's answer bk, 2009n1158
Wildlife-friendly plants, 2005n1323
Woodland garden, rev ed, 2005n1325

GASTROINTESTINAL SYSTEM
Encyclopedia of the digestive system & digestive
disorders, 2005n1439
Gastrointestinal diseases & disorders sourcebk, 2d ed,
2007n1258

GAYS
Encyclopedia of gay & lesbian popular culture,
2009n1046
Encyclopedia of lesbian, gay, bisexual, & transgender
hist in America, 2005n804
Gay & lesbian issues, 2005n806
Gay rights, rev ed, 2006n810
Great events from hist: gay, lesbian, bisexual,
transgender events, 2007n705
Handbook of gay, lesbian, bisexual, & transgender
admin & policy, 2005n805

Leading the parade, 2008n725
Our own voices [Website], 2009n45
Queer America, 2009n749
Queer ency of film & TV, 2007n1048
Queer ency of music, dance, & musical theater,
    2005n1181
Queer ency of the visual arts, 2005n938
Rights of lesbians, gay men, bisexuals, & transgender
    people, 4th ed, 2006n583
Routledge intl ency of queer culture, 2007n706
Youth, educ, & sexualities, 2006n816

GAYS IN LITERATURE
Gay detective novel, 2005n1048
Gay male sleuth in print & film, 2006n1015

GEHRIG, LOU
Lou Gehrig, 2005n766

GEMSTONES
Firefly gd to gems, 2005n1516

GENEALOGY
Adventurers of purse & person Va. 1607-24/5, v.1, 4th
    ed, 2008n338
Adventurers of purse & person Va. 1607-24/5, v.2, 4th
    ed, 2008n339
Adventurers of purse & person Va. 1607-24/5, v.3, 4th
    ed, 2008n340
Ancestors in German archives, 2005n363
Ancestral trails, 2d ed, 2007n290
Ancestry lib ed [Website], 2009n325
Bibliographic checklist of African American
    newspapers, 2009n317
Bounty & donation land grants in British colonial
    America, 2008n341
Carmack's gd to copyright & contracts, 2006n358
Clans & families of Ireland, 2005n360
Companions of Champlain, 2009n318
County Longford residents prior to the famine,
    2005n364
Cyndi's list of genealogy sites on the Internet
    [Website], 2007n286
Denizations & naturalizations in the British colonies in
    America, 1607-1775, 2006n362
Emigration from the UK to America, v.1, 2007n293
Emigration from the UK to America, v.2, 2007n294
Emigration from the UK to America, v.3, 2008n343
Erin's sons, 2009n326
Flemish DNA & ancestry, 2009n321
Free African Americans of N.C., Va., & S.C., 5th ed,
    2006n357
Genealogist's address bk, 5th ed, 2006n355
Genealogist's address bk [CD-ROM], 5th ed,
    2006n356
Genealogy for the first time, 2005n358

Genealogy of the wives of the American presidents &
    their 1st two generations of descent,
    2006n359
Germans to America series II, v.7, 2006n363
Getting started in genealogy online, 2007n288
In search of your German roots, 4th ed, 2009n319
Italians to America, v.17, 2006n364
Italians to America, v.18, 2006n365
Italians to America, v.19, 2006n366
Italians to America, v.20, 2006n367
Italians to America, v.21, 2008n344
Italians to America, v.22, 2008n345
Jamestown ancestors 1607-99, 2007n292
Magna Carta ancestry, 2006n361
Michigan genealogy sources & resources, 2d ed,
    2006n360
My Family.com [Website], 2007n287
Oxford companion to family & local hist, 2009n324
Plantagenet ancestry, 2005n362
Pocket gd to Irish genealogy, 3d ed, 2009n323
Red bk, 3d ed, 2005n361
Roots for kids, 2008n336
Royal descents of 600 immigrants to the American
    colonies or the US, 2005n356
Royal families, v.3, 2008n337
Searching for Flemish (Belgian) ancestors, 2009n322
Source, 3d ed, 2007n291
Sourcebook for genealogical research, 2005n357
Tracing your Irish Ancestors, 3d ed, 2007n289
Tracing your Scottish ancestry, 3d ed, 2005n359
Virginia immigrants & adventurers 1607-35,
    2008n346
You can write your family hist, repr ed, 2009n320

GENEALOGY LIBRARIANSHIP
Basics of genealogy ref, 2009n537
Librarian's gd to genealogical servs & research,
    2005n603

GENETIC DISORDERS
Encyclopedia of genetic disorders & birth defects, 3d
    ed, 2009n1242
Gale ency of genetic disorders, 2d ed, 2006n1360
Genetic disorders sourcebk, 3d ed, 2005n1446

GENETIC ENGINEERING
Biotechnology & genetic engineering, rev ed,
    2005n1413
Biotechnology & genetic engineering, 3d ed,
    2009n1219
Dictionary of bioinformatics & computational biology,
    2005n1411
Dictionary of gene tech, 3d ed, 2005n1412
Encyclopedia of genetics, rev ed, 2005n1375
Encyclopedia of medical genomics & proteomics,
    2006n1405
GenBank [Website], 2006n1361

Genetic engineering, 2d ed, 2007n1226
Genetics revolution, 2006n1362
Handbook of genome research, 2006n1406
Handbook of statl genetics, 3d ed, 2008n1199
Human genome sourcebk, 2006n1359

GENETICS INDUSTRY
Plunkett's biotech & genetics industry almanac, 2006 ed, 2006n191
Plunkett's biotech & genetics industry almanac 2007, 2007n170
Plunkett's biotech & genetics industry almanac, 2009 ed, 2009n177

GENOCIDE
Dictionary of genocide, 2009n474
Encyclopedia of genocide & crimes against humanity, 2005n588
Encyclopedia of war crimes & genocide, 2007n422

GEOGRAPHY
America discovered, 2005n385
Atlas A to Z, rev ed, 2005n368
Boundary-related links [Website], 2008n352
Columbia gazetteer of the world, 2d ed, 2009n337
Columbia gazetteer of the world [Website], 2008n349
Companion ency of geography, 2d ed, 2008n358
Countries of the world series, 2005n73
Dictionary of Greek & Roman geography, 2007n310
Encyclopedia of historic places, rev ed, 2008n357
Encyclopedia of world geography, 2006n387
Essential atlas of physical geography, 2005n383
Firefly world factbk, 2d ed, 2008n360
G. K. Hall bibliog gd to maps & atlases 2002, 2005n381
G. K. Hall bibliog gd to maps & atlases 2003, 2006n383
Geographers, v.25, 2007n308
Geographic info, 2005n387
Geography action [Website], 2008n353
Geography basics, 2005n384
Geography on file, updated ed, 2007n313
Geography zone [Website], 2008n354
Geography4Kids [Website], 2008n355
Guide to US map resources, 2007n309
Historical gazetteer of the US, 2005n386
Historical maps online [Website], 2005n372
Historical maps online [Website], 2007n301
Indian Placenames in America, v.2, 2005n390
Interactive Mediterranean project [Website], 2005n374
Junior worldmark ency of the nations, 4th ed, 2005n71
Lands & peoples, 2006n65
Maps in the atlases of the British Lib, 2006n386
Maps on file, 2005 ed, 2005n375
Maps on file, 2008 ed, 2008n361
National Geographic almanac of geography, 2007n314
Native American placenames of the US, 2005n389

New ency of southern culture, v.2: geography, 2007n311
Outline maps on file, rev ed, 2008n362
Perry Castaneda lib map collection [Website], 2005n377
Random House world atlas & ency, 2008n30
Statistical abstract: geography & environment [Website], 2008n356
Study of agricultural geography, 2006n1280
Timeless Earth, 2009n348
U*X*L ency of landforms & other geologic features, 2005n1517
United States geography [Website], 2009n338
World Almanac world atlas, 2005n380
World geography [Website], 2009n339

GEOLOGY
Encyclopedia of coastal sci, 2006n1518
Encyclopedia of Earth, 2009n1300
Encyclopedia of geomorphology, 2005n1515
Exploring the geology of the Carolinas, 2008n1321
Field gd to geology, new ed, 2008n1319
Field gd to rocks & minerals of southern Africa, 2006n1513
Firefly gd to minerals rocks & fossils, 2006n1515
Firefly gd to mountains, 2007n1311
Geology of southern Vancouver Island, rev ed, 2006n1517
Handy geology answer bk, 2005n1519
Rocks & fossils, 2006n1514
Sourcebook of decorative stone, 2008n1320
Tundra, 2008n1317
U*X*L ency of landforms & other geologic features, 2005n1517
USGS educ resources for teachers [Website], 2008n1322

GEOPHYSICS
Handbook of agricultural geophysics, 2009n1143

GEORGIA (REPUBLIC)
Historical dict of Georgia, 2008n122

GERIATRICS. *See also* **AGED**
Geriatric physical diagnosis, 2008n1245

GERMAN GENEALOGY
Ancestors in German archives, 2005n363
Germans to America series II, v.7, 2006n363

GERMAN LANGUAGE DICTIONARIES
Bilingual visual dict: German/English, 2007n861
Concise Oxford-Duden German dict, 3d ed, 2006n968
Oxford-Duden German dict, 3d ed, 2006n969

GERMAN THEATER
Historical dict of German theater, 2007n1056

GERMANY
Cultural chronicle of the Weimar Republic, 2009n404
Culture & customs of Germany, 2005n109
Events that changed Germany, 2006n472
Germany, 3d ed, 2006n408
Germany & the Americas, 2006n748
Historical dict of contemporary Germany, 2008n123
Hitler & the Nazis, 2007n387
Issues in Germany, Austria, & Switzerland, 2005n105
Pop Culture Germany! 2007n1033
Regions of Germany, 2006n103

GEYSERS
Geysers of Yellowstone, 4th ed, 2009n1322

GHANA
Historical dict of Ghana, 3d ed, 2006n81

GIRLS, SOCIAL CONDITIONS. *See also* CHILD DEVELOPMENT
Girl culture, 2009n766

GLOBAL WARMING
Climate change, 2009n1321
Earth's changing environment, 2009n1339
Encyclopedia of global warming & climate change, 2009n1334
Environment: the sci behind the stories, 2009n1345
Water supply, 2009n1344

GLOBALIZATION. *See also* INTERNATIONAL TRADE
Dictionary of globalization, 2007n577
Encyclopedia of globalization, 2007n135
Globalization, 2009n192
Globalization & free trade, 2008n258

GOLD MINES
Silver & gold mining camps of the old west, 2008n401

GOLF
Golf Digest best places to play, 2005n773
Golf Digest's golf weekends, 2006n793
Golfing communities in the SE, 2005n774
Historical dict of golfing terms, repr ed, 2006n792

GOSPEL MUSIC
Encyclopedia of American gospel music, 2006n1112
Historical dict of sacred music, 2007n1016
Uncloudy days: the gospel music ency, 2007n1015

GOTHIC LITERATURE
Encyclopedia of gothic lit, 2005n1045

GOVERNMENT INFORMATION
Electronic govt, 2009n36
Encyclopedia of digital govt, 2008n43

Encyclopedia of govtl advisory orgs, 19th ed, 2005n705
Encyclopedia of govtl advisory orgs, 20th ed, 2006n705
Encyclopedia of govtl advisory orgs, 22d ed, 2008n632
Federal regulatory dir, 12th ed, 2007n598
Government affairs yellow bk, Summer 2005, 2006n709
Government research dir, 18th ed, 2005n689
Government research dir, 19th ed, 2006n689
Government research dir, 21st ed, 2008n616
Government research dir, 22d ed, 2009n620
International govt info & country info, 2005n50
Local & regional govt info, 2006n43
Managing electronic govt info in libs, 2009n534
Worldwide govt dir with intl orgs 2005, 2006n690

GOVERNMENT LEADERS
American pol leaders 1789-2005, 2006n719
Annotated bibliog of works about Sir Winston S. Churchill, 2005n721
Biographical dict of modern world leaders 1900 to 1991, 2005n683
Kennedy yrs, 2005n697
Leadership, 2008n446
People in power [Website], 2008n609
Profiles of worldwide govt leaders 2004, 2005n684
Shapers of the great debate at the Constitutional Convention of 1787, 2006n431
Shapers of the great debate on the great society, 2006n694
Who's who in American pol 2005-06, 20th ed, 2006n702
Who's who in intl affairs 2005, 4th ed, 2006n684
Women in pol [Website], 2005n685

GOVERNMENT PUBLICATIONS
Changing face of govt info, 2008n519
Guide to US govt pubs, 2007 ed, 2008n44
Guide to US govt pubs, 2005 ed, 2005n49
Guide to US govt pubs, 2008 ed, 2009n37

GRANTS-IN-AID
Annual register of grant support 2004, 37th ed, 2005n809
Annual register of grant support 2006, 39th ed, 2007n707
Annual register of grant support 2007, 40th ed, 2008n729
Annual register of grant support 2009, 42d ed, 2009n750
Big bk of lib grant money 2006, 2006n591
Corporate giving dir, 26th ed, 2005n810
Corporate giving dir, 29th ed, 2008n730
Corporate giving dir, 30th ed, 2009n751

Directory of biomedical & health care grants 2006, 20th ed, 2006n811

Directory of grants in the humanities 2004/05, 18th ed, 2005n882

Directory of grants in the humanities 2005/06, 19th ed, 2006n868

Directory of research grants 2006, 2006n812

Europa intl foundation dir 2005, 2006n813

Europa intl foundation dir 2008, 17th ed, 2009n752

Financial aid for research & creative activities abroad 2006-08, 2006n307

Financial aid for studying & training abroad 2006-08, 2006n308

Financial aid for the disabled & their families 2004-06, 2005n316

Foundation reporter, 37th ed, 2005n811

Foundation reporter 2008, 40th ed, 2009n753

Funding sources for children & youth programs 2004, 3d ed, 2005n812

Funding sources for community & economic dvlpmt 2004/05, 10th ed, 2005n813

Funding sources for K-12 educ 2004, 6th ed, 2005n284

Government assistance almanac 2004-05, 18th ed, 2005n817

Grants register 2004, 22d ed, 2005n308

Grants register 2006, 24th ed, 2006n303

Proposal planning & writing, 4th ed, 2009n754

Rich register 2004, 2005n814

RSP funding for nursing students & nurses 2004-06, 4th ed, 2005n1476

World gd to foundations, 3d ed, 2005n815

Write grants, get money, 2d ed, 2009n578

GRAPHIC DESIGN

Artist's & graphic designer's market 2005, 2006n923

Artist's & graphic designer's market 2008, 2008n839

GRASSES

Grasses of Colo., 2009n1185

Timber Press pocket gd to ornamental grasses, 2005n1368

Wild & sown grasses, 2006n1351

GREAT BRITAIN

Bosworth Field to Bloody Mary, 2005n486

Britain & the Americas, 2006n746

British military operations in Egypt & the Sudan, 2009n600

Companion to 19th-century Britain, 2005n487

Early peoples of Britain & Ireland, 2009n405

Eleanor of Aquitaine, courtly love, & the Troubadours, 2005n491

Elizabethan world: almanac, 2008n432

Elizabethan world: biogs, 2008n433

Elizabethan world: primary sources, 2008n434

Encyclopedia of the Victorian era, 2005n485

Events that changed Great Britain from 1066 to 1714, 2005n489

Food culture in Great Britain, 2005n1306

Historical dict of British intelligence, 2006n665

History of Great Britain, 2005n490

Magna Carta, 2005n488

Other British Isles, 2007n389

Oxford companion to black British hist, 2009n406

Queen Victoria, 2005n484

Victorians at war 1815-1914, 2005n663

GREAT BRITAIN, POLITICS

Annotated bibliog of works about Sir Winston S. Churchill, 2005n721

GREAT BRITAIN - ROYAL NAVY

Ships of the Royal Navy, rev ed, 2007n566

GREAT PLAINS - UNITED STATES

Dictionary of common wildflowers of Tex. & the Southern Great Plains, 2006n1343

Encyclopedia of the great plains, 2005n77

Wild orchids of the prairies & great plains region of N America, 2008n1155

GREECE

Architecture of Greece, 2005n947

Greece, 5th ed, 2005n405

Peloponnesian War, 2005n493

GREEK HISTORY

A to Z of ancient Greek & Roman women, rev ed, 2009n785

Ancient Greece, 2007n390

Daily life in the Hellenistic age, 2009n408

Dictionary of Greek & Roman culture, 2009n407

Dictionary of Greek & Roman geography, 2007n310

E.guides: Ancient Greece, 2007n391

Edinburgh companion to Ancient Greece & Rome, 2007n384

Encyclopedia of ancient Greece, 2006n473

Encyclopedia of the ancient Greek world, rev ed, 2006n474

Greenhaven ency of Ancient Greece, 2008n436

Historical atlas of Ancient Greece, 2007n392

Land battles in 5th century BC Greece, 2009n602

Oxford dict of the classical world, 2006n468

GREEK LITERATURE

Early Christian Greek & Latin lit, 2006n1236

Encyclopedia of modern Greek lit, 2005n1088

Hellenistic bibliog [Website], 2007n964

Masterpieces of classic Greek drama, 2006n1007

GREEK MYTHOLOGY. *See also* MYTHOLOGY

Dictionary of Greek & Roman biog & mythology, 2008n993

Greek mythology link [Website], 2007n1025

GREEK PHILOSOPHY
Historical dict of ancient Greek philosophy, 2008n1047

GUINEA
Historical dict of Guinea, 4th ed, 2006n82

GUN CONTROL
Exploring gun use in America, 2005n548
Gun control, rev ed, 2006n571

GUNS
Firearms, 2005n680
Flayderman's gd to antique American firearms, 9th ed, 2009n835
Machine guns, 2006n682
Modern guns, 15th ed, 2005n922
Modern guns, 16th ed, 2007n803
Modern guns, 17th ed, 2009n836
Official Gun Digest bk of guns & prices, 2007n802
Rifles, 2006n681
Single action sixguns, 2006n906
Standard catalog of firearms 2004, 14th ed, 2005n923
Standard catalog of firearms 2005, 15th ed, 2006n905
Standard catalog of military firearms, 3rd ed, 2007n804
Standard catalog of military firearms 1870 to the present, 2d ed, 2005n924

GUSTAV, MAHLER
Mahler symphonies, 2005n1130

GYPSIES
Historical dict of the Gypsies, 2d ed, 2008n314

HAIRSTYLES
Encyclopedia of hair, 2007n809

HANDBOOKS, VADE MECUMS, ETC.
Annual register, 2008, 2009n38
Encyclopaedia Britannica bk of the yr 2006, 2007n40
Europa world yr bk 2005, 2006n45
Europa world yr bk 2007, 48th ed, 2008n45
Europa world yr bk 2008, 49th ed, 2009n39
Financial Times world desk ref, 6th ed, 2005n51
Firefly's world of facts, 2d ed, 2009n40
Guinness world records 2004, 2005n52
Kidbits, 3d ed, 2005n54
New Penguin factfinder, 2006n49
New York Times gd to essential knowledge, 2006n50
Notable last facts, 2006n44
Top 10 of everything 2006, 2006n51

Trivia lover's lists of nearly everything in the universe, 2007n41
Vital stats, 2006n48
World Bk's yr in review: 2004, 2006n52
Yearbook of the UN 2005, v.59, 60th ed, 2009n41

HARDY, THOMAS, 1840-1928
Student companion to Thomas Hardy, 2008n932

HARLEM RENAISSANCE
Encyclopedia of the Harlem literary renaissance, 2006n1034
Encyclopedia of the Harlem renaissance, 2006n866
Harlem renaissance, 2009n959

HAWAII
Fodor's Hawai'i 2006, 2006n396

HAWTHORNE, NATHANIEL, 1804-1864
Critical companion to Nathaniel Hawthorne, 2007n951

HAYDN, JOSEPH, 1732-1809
Exploring Haydn, 2006n1081

HAZARDOUS WASTE MANAGEMENT
Handbook on household hazardous waste, 2009n1216
Waste mgmt, 2009n1343

HEADS OF STATE. *See* **GOVERNMENT LEADERS; POLITICAL LEADERS**

HEALTH CARE
Encyclopedia of family health & wellness, 2009n1236
Encyclopedia of global health, 2009n1222
Encyclopedia of health & aging, 2008n1207
Encyclopedia of obesity, 2009n1265
Health ref center [Website], 2008n1228
Medicine, health, & bioethics, 2007n1242
PubMed [Website], 2008n1204
Teen health & wellness [Website], 2007n1235

HEALTH CARE - BIBLIOGRAPHY
Bibliography of medical & biomedical biog, 3d ed, 2007n1230
Medical & health care bks & serials in print 2005, 2006n1409

HEALTH CARE - BIOGRAPHY
Dictionary of medical biog, 2008n1205
Who's who in medicine & healthcare 2004-05, 5th ed, 2005n1416
Who's who in medicine & healthcare 2006-07, 6th ed, 2007n1231

HEALTH CARE CAREERS
Career opportunities in health care, 3d ed, 2008n245
Exploring health care careers, 3d ed, 2007n213

Ferguson career coach: managing your career in the
    health care industry, 2009n1230
Health care job explosion! 4th ed, 2008n242
Health professions career & educ dir 2005-06, 33d ed,
    2006n1418

HEALTH CARE - DICTIONARIES & ENCYCLOPEDIAS
Encyclopedia of health & behavior, 2005n1417
Nutrition & well-being A to Z, 2005n1420
Quick ref for health care providers, 2005n1421
Sage dict of health & society, 2007n1234

HEALTH CARE - DIRECTORIES
America's cosmetic doctors & dentists, 2d ed,
    2006n1411
America's top doctors, 5th ed, 2006n1412
America's top doctors, 7th ed, 2008n1208
Chronic illness dir [Website], 2006n1414
Comparative gd to American hospitals 2005,
    2006n1415
Comparative gd to American hospitals, 2d ed,
    2008n1209
Complete dir for pediatric disorders 2008, 4th ed,
    2008n1246
Complete dir for pediatric disorders 2005, 3d ed,
    2005n1457
Complete dir for pediatric disorders [Website],
    2005n1458
Complete dir for pediatric disorders [Website],
    2008n1247
Complete dir for people with chronic illness 2005/06,
    7th ed, 2006n1413
Complete dir for people with chronic illness 2007/08,
    8th ed, 2008n1210
Directory of hospital personnel 2006, 18th ed,
    2007n1236
Directory of hospital personnel 2007, 19th ed,
    2008n1211
Directory of hospital personnel 2008, 20th ed,
    2009n1225
Directory of hospital personnel [Website], 2007n1237
Directory of hospital personnel [Website], 2008n1212
Directory of physicians in the US 2005 [CD-ROM],
    2006n1416
Encyclopedia of medical orgs & agencies, 14th ed,
    2005n1422
Encyclopedia of medical orgs & agencies, 15th ed,
    2006n1417
Encyclopedia of medical orgs & agencies, 18th ed,
    2009n1226
Encyclopedic gd to searching & finding health info on
    the Web, 2005n1423
Grey House rare disorders dir 2006-07, 2007n1238
Medical & health info dir, 16th ed, 2005n1426
Medical & health info dir, 17th ed, 2006n1421
Medical & health info dir, 20th ed, 2008n1214

Medical & health info dir, 21st ed, 2009n1228
Plunkett's health care industry almanac 2006,
    2006n1426
Plunkett's health care industry almanac 2007,
    2008n1218

HEALTH CARE, EDUCATION
Complete bk of medical schools, 2004 ed, 2005n299
Nursing programs 2006, 11th ed, 2006n1456
RSP funding for nursing students & nurses 2004-06,
    4th ed, 2005n1476
Ultimate gd to medical schools, 2006n291
U.S. News & World Report ultimate gd to medical
    schools, 2d ed, 2008n283

HEALTH CARE GRANTS
Directory of biomedical & health care grants 2006,
    20th ed, 2006n811

HEALTH CARE - HANDBOOK & YEARBOOKS
Annual review of public health, v.25, 2004,
    2005n1427
Annual review of public health, v.29, 2009,
    2009n1229
Diseases & disorders series, 2009n1245
Global AIDS crisis, 2006n1441
Global epidemics, 2008n1220
Handbook of obesity, 2d ed, 2005n1447
Health care policy & politics A to Z, 3d ed, 2009n697
Health care state rankings 2008, 2009n1232
International travel & health, 2005n1430
Pandemics & global health, 2009n1254
Perspectives on diseases & disorders series,
    2009n1249
U.S. natl debate topic 2007-08: health care in
    Sub-Saharan Africa, 2008n1222

HEALTH CARE REFORM
Healthcare reform in America, 2005n1431

HEALTH CARE STATISTICS
American health, 2006n1422
American health, 2d ed, 2008n1219
Demographic & health surveys [Website], 2008n742
Health care state rankings 2004, 12th ed, 2005n1429
Health care state rankings 2005, 13th ed, 2006n1424
Health care state rankings 2006, 2007n1241
Health care state rankings 2007, 15th ed, 2008n1221
State of health atlas, 2009n1221
World health databk 2006, 2007n1243
World health databk 2007/08, 2009n1233

HEALTH ECONOMICS
Dictionary of health economics & finance, 2007n1232

HEALTH INSURANCE
HMO/PPO dir 2005, 17th ed, 2005n1424

HMO/PPO dir 2006, 18th ed, 2007n1239
HMO/PPO dir 2007, 19th ed, 2008n1213
HMO/PPO dir 2009, 21st ed, 2009n1227
HMO/PPO dir [Website], 2005n1425
HMO/PPO dir [Website], 2006n1420
HMO/PPO dir [Website], 2007n1240
TheStreet.com ratings' gd to health insurers, Summer
    2007, 2008n210
TheStreet.com ratings' gd to health insurers, Spring
    2008, 2009n187
TheStreet.com ratings' gd to life & annuity insurers,
    Fall 2007, 2008n211
Weiss Ratings' gd to HMOs & health insurers,
    Summer 2004, 2005n201
Weiss Ratings' gd to HMOs & health insurers, Winter
    2005-06, 2006n197
Weiss Ratings' gd to life, health, & annuity insurers,
    Summer 2004, 2005n202

HEAT
Heat & thermodynamics, 2009n1136

HEBREW PRINTING
Hebrew printing in America 1735-1926, 2007n545

HEGEL, GEORG WILHELM FRIEDRICH, 1770-1831
Historical dict of Hegelian philosophy, 2d ed,
    2009n1081

HELICOPTERS
Helicopters, 2006n677

HEMINGWAY, ERNEST, 1899-1961
Critical companion to Ernest Hemingway, 2008n920

HEPATITIS
Encyclopedia of hepatitis & other liver diseases,
    2007n1273
Hepatitis, 2007n1274

HERADLRY
Companion to emblem studies, 2009n327
Flags of all countries [Website], 2005n365

HERBAL MEDICINE. See also NATURAL MEDICINE
Complete natural medicine gd to the 50 most common
    medicinal herbs, 2005n1453
Internet gd to herbal remedies, 2008n1236

HERBS
Complete natural medicine gd to the 50 most common
    medicinal herbs, 2005n1453
Essential herb-drug-vitamin interaction gd, 2008n1261
Herbalist in the kitchen, 2008n1118
Incense bible, 2008n1242

Internet gd to herbal remedies, 2008n1236
New bk of herbs, 2005n1316

HIKING
Mountain ency, 2006n794
National Geographic natl park trail gds [CD-ROM],
    2005n775

HINDI LANGUAGE - DICTIONARIES
Hindi-English, English-Hindi: dict & phrasebk,
    2005n972

HINDUISM
Contemporary Hindu, 2005n1269
Encyclopedia of Hinduism, 2008n1094
Encyclopedia of Hinduism, 2008n1095
Encyclopedia of Hinduism, 2009n1116
Key words in Hinduism, 2007n1118

HIP-HOP MUSIC
All Music gd to hip-hop, 2005n1148
Encyclopedia of rap & hip hop culture, 2007n1009
Hip hop culture, 2007n1010
Icons of hip-hop, 2008n988

HIROSHIMA-SHI (JAPAN) - HISTORY
Columbia gd to Hiroshima & the bomb, 2008n413

HISPANIC AMERICANS
A to Z of Latino Americans series, 2008n333
Columbia hist of Latinos in the US since 1960,
    2005n353
Encyclopedia Latina, 2006n350
Encyclopedia of Latin American hist & culture, 2d ed,
    2009n118
Encyclopedia of Latino popular culture, 2005n354
Great Hispanic-Americans, 2006n349
HAPI: Hispanic American per index online [Website],
    2008n50
Hispanic Americans, 2007 ed, 2008n334
Hispanic Americans, 2008n335
Hispanic American biogs, 2007n284
Hispanics in the American West, 2006n353
Icons of Latino America, 2009n315
Latinas in the US, 2007n285
Latino & African American athletes today, 2005n751
Latino American experience [Website], 2009n316
Latino chronology, 2008n332
Latino food culture, 2009n1152
Mexican American experience, 2005n355
100 Hispanics you should know, 2008n331
Oxford ency of Latinos & Latinas in the US, 2006n351
Who we are: Hispanics, 2008n754

HISPANIC AMERICANS & LIBRARIES
Bienvenidos! Welcome! A handy resource gd for mktg
    your lib to Latinos, 2006n633

HISTORIC DOCUMENTS
American colonist's lib [Website], 2005n437
Historic documents cumulative index 1972-2005,
    2007n582
Historic documents of 2005, 2007n581
National Archives & Records Admin (NARA)
    [Website], 2005n718

HISTORIC PRESERVATION
Historic preservation tech, 2009n865

HISTORIC SITES
Encyclopedia of American natl parks, 2005n75
Landmarks of American women's hist, 2005n873

HISTORY – AMERICAN
A to Z of revolutionary America, 2008n400
A to Z of the Civil War, 2007n355
America in revolt during the 1960s & 1970s,
    2008n405
America: a hist in art, 2009n855
America's founding charters, 2007n362
American Civil War, 2005n456
American Civil War, 2009n386
American colonist's lib [Website], 2005n437
American generals of the Revolutionary War,
    2008n572
American heroes, 2009n362
American hist [Website], 2009n371
American hist album, 2009n838
American Revolution, 2008n406
American Revolution, updated ed, 2008n407
American Revolutionary War, 2007n345
American Revolutionary War, 2008n392
Antebellum era, 2005n442
Antebellum period, 2005n461
Atlas of American hist, 2007n336
Atlas of US hist, rev ed, 2009n359
Books on early American hist & culture 1961-70,
    2008n387
British Colonial America, 2009n388
Chronology of American hist, 2009n368
Chronology of the American Revolution, 2009n370
Civil War, 2005n423
Civil War, 2005n459
Civil War & reconstruction, 2009n367
Civil War almanac, 2008n384
Civil War America, 1850 to 1875, 2008n420
Civil War Medal of Honor recipients, 2008n573
Civil War suits in the US court of claims, 2007n361
Colonial America, 2007n347
Colonial America, 2007n365
Colonial America, 2008n408
Columbia hist of post-WW II America, 2008n409
Companion to the American west, 2005n440
Companion to the Civil War & Reconstruction,
    2005n441

Conspiracy theories in American hist, 2005n424
Daily life America [Website], 2009n373
Daily life in immigrant America, 1820-70, 2009n387
Daily life in the early American republic, 1790-1820,
    2005n449
Daily life in the industrial US, 1870-1900, 2005n453
Day by day: the 1930s, 2008n391
Debatable issues in US hist, 2005n444
Development of the industrial US: almanac, 2007n326
Development of the Industrial US: biogs, 2007n327
Development of the industrial US: primary sources,
    2007n328
Disasters, accidents, & crises in American hist,
    2009n366
Early natl period, 2005n458
Early republic, 2009n389
Early republic [Website], 2009n365
Encyclopedia of American histl docs, 2005n425
Encyclopedia of American studies [Website],
    2009n375
Encyclopedia of Civil War medicine, 2009n383
Encyclopedia of N American colonial conflicts to
    1775, 2009n605
Encyclopedia of the American Revolution, 2d ed,
    2007n350
Encyclopedia of the American Revolutionary War,
    2007n349
Encyclopedia of the jazz age, 2009n376
Encyclopedia of the new American nation, 2007n351
Essential Civil War, 2007n363
Exploring American hist, 2008n397
Famous 1st facts, 6th ed, 2008n26
Forts of the US, 2007n353
Frontier America, 2005n427
Gale ency of US hist: war, 2009n378
Gilded age & progressive era, 2007n368
Gilded age & progressive era: almanac, 2007n329
Gilded age & progressive era: biogs, 2007n330
Gilded age & progressive era: primary sources,
    2007n331
Gilded age, 2005n460
Gilded age, rev ed, 2007n364
Great American hist fact-finder, 2d ed, 2005n443
Great Depression & the New Deal, 2009n391
Great Depression in America, 2008n404
Greenhaven ency of the Civil War, 2005n428
Historical atlas of the US, 2007n335
Historical dict of the Civil War & Reconstruction,
    2005n434
Historical dict of the discovery & exploration of the
    NW coast of America, 2009n380
Historical dict of the early American Republic,
    2007n346
Historical dict of the gilded age, 2005n431
Historical dict of the Jacksonian era & Manifest
    Destiny, 2007n348
Historical dict of the 1940s, 2007n354

Historical dict of the old south, 2007n359
Historical dict of the Roosevelt-Truman era, 2009n648
Historical dict of the War of 1812, 2007n357
History in dispute, v.19: the red scare after 1945, 2005n451
Home front heroes, 2007n337
Icons of the American west, 2009n364
Industrial revolution in America, 2008n411
Industrial revolution in America, 2008n412
Industrial revolution, 2007n366
Industrial revolution, 2009n393
Issues & controversies in American hist [Website], 2009n381
Jacksonian & antebellum age, 2009n394
Jamestown colony, 2008n398
Landmarks of the American Revolution, 2d ed, 2007n356
Making of the American West, 2008n414
Media scandals, 2009n800
Milestone docs in American hist, 2009n395
More Okla. Renegades, 2008n89
National Geographic almanac of American hist, 2007n342
New Deal network [Website], 2005n420
New ency of southern culture, v.3: history, 2007n62
New York Public Library American hist desk ref, 2d ed, 2005n457
9/11 ency, 2009n372
1920s, 2005n1174
1940s, 2005n1178
1950s, 2005n1179
1970s, 2007n341
1980s, 2007n344
1990s, 2005n1177
1990s, 2007n343
North American jls of Prince Maximilian of Wied, v.1, 2009n396
Old West, 2009n382
1001 events that made America, 2007n338
1001 people who made America, 2008n389
1001 things you didn't know about the Civil War, 2008n423
Opposing viewpoints in American hist, 2008n416
Political hist of America's wars, 2007n561
Postwar America, 2007n358
Presidents were here, 2009n390
Progressive era, 2005n438
Quotable founding fathers, 2005n462
Reconstruction era, 2005n445
Reconstruction era: almanac, 2005n413
Reconstruction era: biogs, 2005n414
Reconstruction era: primary sources, 2005n415
Reference sources in hist, 2d ed, 2005n510
Revolutionary era, 2005n452
Revolutionary War almanac, 2007n340
Roaring 20s, rev ed, 2008n422

Second great awakening & the transcendentalists, 2005n448
Seventies in America, 2007n360
Shapers of the great debate on Jacksonian democracy, 2005n696
Shaping of America, 1783-1815: almanac, 2007n332
Shaping of America, 1783-1815: biogs, 2007n333
Shaping of America, 1783-1815: primary sources, 2007n334
Ship Island, Miss., 2008n388
Sixties in America: almanac, 2005n416
Sixties in America: biogs, 2005n417
Sixties in America: primary sources, 2005n418
Slavery in America, 2007n369
This day in American hist, 3d ed, 2009n369
Trans-Mississippi West 1804-1912, 2009n361
U*X*L ency of US hist, 2009n385
USA twenties, 2005n435
USCivilWar.Net [Website], 2005n419
Women during the Civil War, 2008n785
Women in the American Civil War, 2009n789

HISTORY - ANCIENT
Ancient Canaan & Israel, 2006n116
Ancient Greece, 2007n390
Ancient Greece, 2008n435
Ancient hist, 2006n494
Ancient Indus Valley, 2008n383
Ancient Mesopotamia, 2006n485
Ancient Mesopotamia, 3300-331 B.C.E., 2005n504
Ancient world, 2008n451
Aztecs, 2006n341
Complete royal families of ancient Egypt, 2006n484
Daily life in the medieval Islamic world, 2006n1243
Daily life in the N.T., 2009n433
Daily life of the ancient Egyptians, 2d ed, 2009n415
E.guides: Ancient Greece, 2007n391
Edinburgh companion to Ancient Greece & Rome, 2007n384
Encyclopedia of ancient Asian civilizations, 2005n467
Encyclopedia of ancient Greece, 2006n473
Encyclopedia of society & culture in the ancient world, 2008n455
Encyclopedia of the ancient Greek world, rev ed, 2006n474
Establishment of the Han Empire & Imperial China, 2006n465
Global hist, 2005n527
Great empires of the past series, 2005n528
Great events from hist: the ancient world, prehist-476 CE, 2005n515
Great lives from hist: the ancient world, prehist-476 CE, rev ed, 2005n511
Greenhaven ency of Ancient Greece, 2008n436
Greenhaven ency of Ancient Mesopotamia, 2008n441
Historical atlas of Ancient Greece, 2007n392
Historical atlas of Acient Mesopotamia, 2005n502

Historical atlas of Ancient Rome, 2006n486
Historical dict of Ancient Israel, 2005n126
Historical dict of Ancient S America, 2009n413
Historical dict of medieval India, 2009n101
Historical dict of the Hittites, 2005n500
History of the ancient & medieval world, 2d ed,
    2009n428
Hstorical dict of ancient Egypt, 2d ed, 2009n414
Mycenaean civilization, rev ed, 2005n492
New dict of the hist of ideas, 2006n501
Oxford dict of the classical world, 2006n468
Penguin histl atlas of ancient civilizations, 2007n401
Perseus digital lib [Website], 2007n408
Reign of Cleopatra, 2006n482
Thames & Hudson dict of Ancient Egypt, 2007n400
Trojan War, 2006n514
World hist [Website], 2009n431

HISTORY - ASIAN
Encyclopedia of ancient Asian civilizations, 2005n467
Historical atlas of central Asia, 2005n465
Historical dict of ancient SE Asia, 2008n100
Mapping the silk road & beyond, 2006n385
South Asia: an environmental hist, 2009n1341

HISTORY - MEDIEVAL
Atlas of the medieval world, 2006n487
Daily life in the medieval Islamic world, 2006n1243
Encyclopedia of society & culture in the medieval
    world, 2009n425
Handbook to life in the medieval world, 2009n401
Historical dict of medieval China, 2009n400
Historical dict of medieval India, 2009n101
History of the ancient & medieval world, 2d ed,
    2009n428
Key figures in Medieval Europe, 2007n381
Kingfisher atlas of the medieval world, 2008n427
Knights Templar ency, 2008n428
Medieval castles, 2006n513
Medieval cathedrals, 2007n383
Medieval city, 2006n469
Medieval Ireland, 2006n475
New Cambridge medieval hist, 2007n432
New Cambridge medieval hist, v.4, 2006n511
Penguin histl atlas of the medieval world, 2007n376

HISTORY - MIDDLE AGES
Daily life of Jews in the Middle Ages, 2006n348
Encyclopedia of the Byzantine empire, 2005n473
Exploring the Middle Ages, 2006n467
Great events from hist: the Middle Ages, 477-1453,
    2005n516
Great lives from hist: the Middle Ages, 477-1453,
    2005n512
Palgrave atlas of Byzantine hist, 2006n466

HISTORY - RENAISSANCE
Artists of the Renaissance, 2005n931
Great events from hist: the Renaissance & early
    modern era, 2006n500
Great lives from hist: the Renaissance & early modern
    era, 1454-1600, 2006n489
Encyclopedia of the Renaissance & the Reformation,
    rev ed, 2005n472
Handbook to life in renaissance Europe, 2006n470
Historical dict of Renaissance art, 2008n837
Historical dict of the Renaissance, 2005n474
Renaissance art, 2005n944

HISTORY, RESEARCH
Historian's toolbox, 2d ed, 2009n435

HISTORY - WORLD
A to Z of the Renaissance, 2007n423
ABZU: a gd to study of the ancient Near East on the
    Web [Website], 2005n526
ACLS hist e-bk project [Website], 2007n402
Ancient hist, 2006n494
APIS: advanced papryological info system [Website],
    2007n407
Berkshire ency of world hist, 2007n416
Best of hist web sites, 2008n442
Cambridge ancient hist, v.12: the crisis of empire,
    A.D. 193-337, 2d ed, 2007n429
Cassell's chronology of world hist, 2006n492
Chambers hist factfinder, 2006n509
Classical studies, 2d ed, 2007n403
Crusades, 2007n417
Daily life online [Website], 2009n423
Day by day: the twenties, 2009n418
Day by day: the 90s, 2005n513
Dictionary of world hist, 2d ed, 2007n418
Eighties in America, 2009n374
Encyclopedia idiotica, 2006n503
Encyclopedia of society & culture in the ancient
    world, 2008n455
Encyclopedia of the modern world, 2008n456
Encyclopedia of war crimes & genocide, 2007n422
Encyclopedia of world hist, 2009n426
Gale ency of world hist: war, 2009n427
Global hist, 2005n527
Great events from hist: the 17th century, 2006n493
Great events from hist: the 17th century, 2007n409
Great events from hist: the 18th century, 2007n410
Great events from hist: the 19th century, 1801-1900,
    2007n411
Great events from hist: the 19th century, 2008n449
Great events from hist: the 20th century, 1940-70,
    2009n421
Great events from hist: the 20th century, 1971-2000,
    2009n420

Great events from hist: the 20th century, 2008n450
Great events from hist: the ancient world, prehist-476 CE, 2005n515
Great events from hist: the Middle Ages 477-1453, 2005n516
Great lives from hist: notorious lives, 2008n443
Great lives from hist: the 17th century, 2006n490
Great lives from hist: the 17th century, 2007n404
Great lives from hist: the 18th century, 2007n405
Great lives from hist: the 19th century, 1801-1900, 2007n406
Great lives from hist: the 19th century, 1801-1900, 2008n444
Great lives from hist: the 20th century, 1901-2000, 2009n417
Great lives from hist: the ancient world, prehist-476 CE, rev ed, 2005n511
Great lives from hist: the Middle Ages, 477-1453, 2005n512
Greenwood daily life online [Website], 2005n508
Greenwood dict of world hist, 2007n420
Greenwood ency of daily life, 2005n517
Handy hist answer bk, 2d ed, 2006n510
Historic events of the 20th century [Website], 2005n522
Historical dict of the enlightenment, 2006n496
History for kids [Website], 2005n523
History highway, 4th ed, 2007n427
History of fashion & costume, 2006n909
History of the world in photographs, 2009n422
History resource center [Website], 2007n421
Modern world hist online [Website], 2009n429
Mysteries in hist, 2006n507
National Geographic concise hist of the world, 2007n412
National Geographic visual hist of the world, 2007n413
Nations & nationalism, 2009n434
New 1st dict of cultural literacy, 2005n325
New makers of modern culture, 2008n445
Oxford dict of contemporary world hist, 3d ed, 2009n430
Oxford dict of the classical world, 2008n458
People at the center of ... series, 2006n491
Reference sources in hist, 2d ed, 2005n510
Reformation, exploration, & empire, 2006n502
Renaissance & reformation, 2007n425
Revolutionary movements in world hist, 2007n414
Timelines of hist, 2006n495
Timelines on file: nations & states, updated ed, 2007n415
WebChron [Website], 2005n518
World fascism, 2007n632
World hist [Website], 2009n431
World hist on file, updated ed, 2005n533
World hist on file, v.1: early civilizations, 2d ed, 2007n435
World hist on file, v.2: the expanding world, 2007n436
World hist on file, v.3: the age of revolution, 2d ed, 2007n437
World hist on file, v.4: the 20th century, 2d ed, 2007n438
World hist: the modern era [Website], 2008n459
World monarchies & dynasties, 2006n504

HITLER, ADOLF, 1889-1945
Hitler & the Nazis, 2007n387

HMONG (ASIAN PEOPLE)
Hmong-related works, 1996-2006, 2008n315

HOCKEY
Sporting News hockey gd & register 2006-07, 2007n688

HOLIDAYS
African-American holidays, festivals, & celebrations, 2007n272
Chase's calendar of events 2006, 49th ed, 2006n5
Christmas ency, 2d ed, 2006n1120
Encyclopedia of American holidays & natl days, 2008n998
Encyclopedia of holidays & celebrations, 2007n1029
Encyclopedia of New Year's Holidays Worldwide, 2009n1038
Fourth of July ency, 2008n1000
Holiday symbols & customs, 4th ed, 2009n1042
Holidays, festivals, & celebrations of the world dict, 3d ed, 2006n1123
International bk of days, 2006n6
Neal-Schuman gd to celebrations & holidays around the world, 2005n1176
Patriotic holidays of the US, 2006n1122
Religious holidays & calendars, 3d ed, 2005n1172
Thanksgiving bk, 2008n1001
Traditional festivals, 2006n1124
World party, 2007n1035

HOLOCAUST, JEWISH (1939-1945)
A to Z of the Holocaust, 2006n499
Holocaust, 2007n431
Holocaust lit, 2009n912
Holocaust survivors, 2008n447
United States Holocaust Memorial Museum [Website], 2008n448

HOMELESSNESS
Encyclopedia of homelessness, 2005n807

HOPE, BOB (1903-2003)
Bob Hope films, 2006n1162

HORROR FILMS
British horror film locations, 2009n1058

Horror films of the 1980s, 2008n1026
Television fright films of the 1970s, 2008n1024
Universal horrors, 2d ed, 2008n1030

HORROR LITERATURE
Encyclopedia of fantasy & horror fiction, 2007n929
Gothic lit, 2007n930
Guide to the gothic 3, 2006n1016
Horror readers' advisory, 2005n1050
Icons of horror & the supernatural, 2008n902
Read on . . . horror fiction, 2007n931

HORSES
Horseman's illus dict, 2005n1391
International ency of horse breeds, paperback ed,
    2008n1189
Lyon's Press horseman's dict, rev ed, 2008n1190

HORTICULTURE. *See also* BOTANY; PLANTS; GARDENING
Landscape architectural graphic standards, 2008n1135

HOUSING DEVELOPMENT. *See also* URBAN STUDIES
Chronology of housing in the US, 2008n767
Urban sprawl, 2007n754

HUMAN ANATOMY
Amazing baby, 2009n1174
Anatomy of exercise, 2009n735
Attorney's ref on human anatomy, 2009n1176
E.guides: human body, 2007n1171
Firefly gd to the human body, 2005n1345
First human body ency, 2006n1320
Gray's anatomy for students, 2006n1321
Handy anatomy answer bk, 2009n1175
Human body, 2007n1172
Human body systems, 2005n1346
Netter's atlas of the human body, 2006n1322
World Bk's human body works, 2007n1173

HUMAN DEVELOPMENT
Encyclopedia of human dvlpmt, 2007n651

HUMAN ECOLOGY
Encyclopedia of environment & society, 2008n1338
Great debates in American environmental hist,
    2009n1340

HUMAN EVOLUTION
Cambridge dict of human biology & evolution,
    2006n1313
Counter-creationism hndbk, 2006n1317
Encyclopedia of the life course & human dvlpmt,
    2009n739
Human, 2005n53

Human evolution, 2006n1319

HUMAN GENOME
Human genome sourcebk, 2006n1359

HUMAN GEOGRAPHY
Companion to cultural geography, 2005n68
Encyclopedia of human geography, 2005n66
Encyclopedia of human geography, 2007n50

HUMAN RESOURCES
National dir to college & univ student records, 2005n302

HUMAN RIGHTS
Eleanor Roosevelt papers, v.1, 2008n496
Encyclopedia of genocide & crimes against humanity,
    2005n588
Euthanasia, 2d ed, 2008n498
Historical dict of human rights & humanitarian orgs,
    2d ed, 2008n497
Human & civil rights, 2007n491
Human rights worldwide, 2007n489
New slavery, 2d ed, 2006n581
Rights of lesbians, gay men, bisexuals, & transgender
    people, 4th ed, 2006n583
Unreasonable searches & seizures, 2006n546
Women's human rights resources [Websites],
    2005n589

HUMANITIES
Art & culture [Website], 2007n762
Arts & humanities through the eras, 2005n880
Continuum ency of modern criticism & theory,
    2007n763
Directory of grants in the humanities 2005/06, 19th ed,
    2006n868
Electronic links for classicists [Website], 2005n876
Electronic links for classicists [Website], 2009n792
Film & media resources from Artslynx [Website],
    2006n869
Film & media resources from Artslynx [Website],
    2009n793
Focus groups, v.1, 2009n5
Humbul humanities hub [Website], 2005n883
Intute: arts & humanities [Website], 2009n794
Oxford dict of phrase & fable, 2d ed, 2006n867
World cultural leaders of the 20th & 21st centuries, 2d
    ed, 2008n788

HUME, DAVID, 1711-1776
Historical dict of Hume's philosophy, 2009n1085

HUNTING
Complete sportsman's ency, 2d repr ed, 2009n728
Encyclopedia of tracks & scats, 2005n776
Field gd to animal tracks, 3d ed, 2006n795

HURRICANES
Hurricanes, 2d ed, 2006n1510

HYDROLOGICAL SCIENCES
Encyclopedia of hydrological scis, 2007n1227
Processing water, 2009n1327
Texas water atlas, 2009n1326
U*X*L ency of water sci, 2005n1539
Water ency, 3d ed, 2008n1337
Water supply, 2009n1344

HYPERTENSION
Hypertension sourcebk, 2005n1469

ICELAND
Historical dict of Iceland, 2d ed, 2009n112

IDEOLOGIES
Encyclopedia of the age of pol revolutions & new
    ideologies 1760-1815, 2008n657
Isms & ologies, 2008n60

ILLEGAL ALIENS. *See also* EMIGRATION & IMMIGRATION
Illegal immigration, 2008n480

ILLINOIS
Encyclopedia of Chicago, 2007n65
Place names of Ill., 2009n340
Profiles of Ill., 2009n74

IMMIGRATION. *See* EMIGRATION & IMMIGRATION

IMMUNOTOXICOLOGY
Encyclopedic ref of immunotoxicology, 2007n1251

IMPERIALISM
Encyclopedia of western colonialism since 1450,
    2007n419

INCA MYTHOLOGY
Handbook of Inca mythology, 2005n1169

INDEXES
Author index to little mags of the mimeograph
    revolution, 2009n44
Book review index, 2004 cum ed, 2005n55
Book review index, 2005 cum ed, 2006n53
Bookman's price index, v.76, 2005n916
Bookman's price index, v.77, 2005n917
Bookman's price index, v.78, 2005n918
Bookman's price index, v.79, 2005n919
Current biog cumulated index 1940-2005, 2007n42
Gallup poll cumulative index, 1998-2007, 2009n63
Historic documents cumulative index 1972-2005,
    2007n581

World of animals: index, 2007n1189

INDIA
Brief hist of India, 2006n92
Comprehensive, annotated bibliog on Mahatma
    Gandhi, v.2, 2008n109
Conflict between India & Pakistan, 2009n96
Encyclopaedia of Indian events & dates, 5th rev ed,
    2007n95
Encyclopedia of India, 2006n91
Encyclopedia of the India diaspora, 2009n100
Historical dict of ancient India, 2009n399
Historical dict of India, 2d ed, 2007n97
Historical dict of medieval India, 2009n101
Historical dict of the Tamils, 2008n424
India, 5th ed, 2005n401
India, 7th ed, 2006n401
India, 8th ed, 2008n369
Pop culture India! 2007n1034

INDIANA
Native American place-names of Ind., 2009n341
Profiles of Ind., 2008n81

INDIANS OF NORTH AMERICA
A to Z of American Indian women, rev ed, 2008n317
American Indian biogs, rev ed, 2006n334
American Indian chronology, 2008n320
American Indian contributions to the world series,
    2006n338
American Indian culture, 2006n335
American Indian food, 2006n1285
American Indian hist online [Website], 2007n277
American Indian law deskbk, 2007 suppl, 2008n472
American Indian religious traditions, 2006n336
American Indian wars, 2008n318
American Indians in the early west, 2009n309
Ancient Indian artifacts, v.1, 2009n837
Cherokee ency, 2008n322
Chronology of American Indian hist, updated ed,
    2007n276
Encyclopedia of American Indian hist, 2008n323
Encyclopedia of American Indian lit, 2008n913
Encyclopedia of Native American artists, 2009n307
Encyclopedia of Native American tribes, 3d ed,
    2007n278
Encyclopedia of Native American wars & warfare,
    2006n337
Encyclopedia of native tribes of N America, 2008n325
Encyclopedia of the great plains Indians, 2008n324
Great Plains illus index, 2005n348
Handbook of N American Indians, Southeast, v.14,
    2005n345
Handbook of N American Indians, v.3: environment,
    origins, & population, 2008n327
Handbook of Native American mythology, 2006n1118
Handbook to life in the Aztec world, 2007n279

Historical dict of early N America, 2005n344
Historical dict of Native American movements, 2009n308
Historical dict of the Inuit, 2005n343
Incas, 2007n280
Index of Native American bk resources on the Internet [Website], 2006n1037
Indian artifacts, 2005n925
Indian placenames in America, v.2, 2005n390
Native America from prehist to 1st contact, 2008n328
Native America from prehist to first contact, 2007n281
Native American issues, 2d ed, 2006n340
Native American mythology A to Z, 2005n1162
Native American placenames of the US, 2005n389
Native American sites [Website], 2008n316
Native Americans & pol participation, 2006n339
Native Americans in sports, 2005n752
Navajo as seen by the Franciscans, 1898-1921, 2005n346
North American jls of Prince Maximilian of Wied, v.1, 2009n396
Pawnee nation, 2005n340
Practical gd to the Indian Child Welfare Act, 2009n310
Praeger hndbk on contemporary issues in Native America, 2008n329
Puebloan society of Chaco Canyon, 2005n347
Rare & unusual Indian artifacts, 2008n822
Reference ency of the American Indian, 11th ed, 2005n342
Theodor de Bry's engravings of Native American life [Website], 2005n341
Travel gd to the Plains Indian wars, 2007n320
Treaties with American Indians, 2008n326

INDIANS OF NORTH AMERICA, LEGAL STATUS
American Indian law deskbk, 3d ed, 2005n540

INDIANS OF NORTH AMERICA - LIBRARIES
Tribal libs in the US, 2008n508

INDIANS OF NORTH AMERICA, LITERATURE
James Welch, 2005n1073

INDIANS OF NORTH AMERICA, MUSIC
Encyclopedia of native music, 2006n1091

INDIANS OF SOUTH AMERICA
Early civilizations in the Americas: almanac, 2006n342
Early civilizations of the Americas: biogs & primary sources, 2006n343
Guide to documentary sources for Andean studies, 1530-1900, 2009n119
South & meso-American mythology A to Z, 2005n1157

INDIANS OF THE WEST INDIES
Peoples of the Caribbean, 2006n352

INDIGENOUS PEOPLES
Indigenous peoples & environmental issues, 2005n1538
International hndbk of research on indigenous entrepreneurship, 2009n294

INDONESIA
Historical dict of Indonesia, 2d ed, 2005n96
History of Indonesia, 2007n374
Indonesia, 2005n97

INDONESIAN LANGUAGE DICTIONARIES
Comprehensive Indonesian-English dict, 2005n973

INDUSTRIAL ENGINEERING
Building of the world, 2007n1224

INDUSTRIAL RELATIONS
Glossary of labour law & industrial relations, 2006n227

INDUSTRIAL REVOLUTION - UNITED STATES
Development of the industrial US: almanac, 2006n420
Development of the industrial US: biogs, 2006n421
Development of the industrial US: primary sources, 2006n422
Industrial revolution, 2007n366
Industrial revolution, 2009n393
Industrial revolution in America, 2006n456
Industrial revolution in America, 2008n411
Industrial revolution in America, 2008n412

INDUSTRIAL STATISTICS
Industry research using the economic census, 2005n165

INDUSTRY. *See also* **BUSINESS; INTERNATIONAL BUSINESS**
American wholesalers & distributors dir, 14th ed, 2006n176
American wholesalers & distributors dir, 16th ed, 2008n190
American wholesalers & distributors dir, 17th ed, 2009n172
Brands & their companies, 27th ed, 2006n177
Brands & their companies, 29th ed, 2008n191
Companies & their brands, 26th ed, 2005n189
Companies & their brands, 29th ed, 2008n192
Directory of business to business catalogs 2004, 12the ed, 2005n190
Directory of business to business catalogs 2005, 13th ed, 2006n178
Directory of convenience stores, 2005, 2006n179

Plunkett's wireless, WI-FI, RFID, & cellular industry almanac 2008, 2008n206
Plunkett's wireless, WI-FI, RFID, & cellular industry almanac, 2009 ed, 2009n182
Sports market place dir 2008, 2009n718
U.S. industry & market outlook 2007, 2008n209
Ward's business dir of US private & public companies, 51st ed, 2009n142
World cosmetics & toiletries mktg dir, 4th ed, 2006n187

INDUSTRY - SECURITY
PSI hdnbk of business security, 2009n149

INFORMATION ETHICS
Encyclopedia of info ethics & security, 2008n1270

INFORMATION LITERACY
Creating a comprehensive info literacy plan, 2007n525Learning to learn, 2d ed, 2007n526
Developing an info literacy program K-12, 2d ed, 2005n627
Disciplinary blueprint for the assessment of info lit, 2009n570
Guided inquiry, 2009n567
Information literacy assessment, 2008n543
Information literacy assessment in K-12 settings, 2009n565
Information literacy collaborations that work, 2008n542
Information literacy programs in the digital age, 2009n566
Learning to lead & manage info literacy instruction, 2006n630
Motivating students in info literacy classes, 2005n628
Partners in literacy, 2009n564
Practical gd to info literacy assessment for academic librarians, 2009n568
Proven strategies for building an info literacy program, 2008n544
Teaching lib media skills in grades K-6, 2005n610
Teen girls & tech, 2009n550
Web literacy for educators, 2009n289

INFORMATION ORGANIZATION
Metadata in practice, 2005n630

INFORMATION RESOURCES MANAGEMENT
Encyclopedia of knowledge mgmt, 2006n1465

INFORMATION SCIENCE
Dictionary for lib & info sci, 2005n595
Encyclopedia of info sci & tech, 2006n586
Foundations of lib & info sci, 2d ed, 2005n602
Fundamentals of info studies, 2d ed, 2008n545
Information sci 101, 2009n571
Portable MLIS, 2009n502

Understanding info systems, 2005n632

INFORMATION SERVICES
Information industry dir, 27th ed, 2005n598
Information industry dir, 28th ed, 2006n594
Information industry dir, 30th ed, 2008n507
Leadership basics for librarians & info professionals, 2008n555

INFORMATION STORAGE & RETRIEVAL SYSTEMS
Understanding info systems, 2005n632

INFORMATION TECHNOLOGY
Advances in enterprise info tech security, 2008n1277
Encyclopedia of E-collaboration, 2009n1284
Encyclopedia of gender & info tech, 2007n1287
Encyclopedia of info sci & tech, 2006n586
Encyclopedia of info tech curriculum integration, 2009n1282
Fundamentals of info studies, 2d ed, 2008n545
Information security & ethics, 2008n1274
Information tech & economic dvlpmt, 2008n171
Major info tech companies of the world, 5th ed, 2005n194
Major info tech companies of the world 2005, 7th ed, 2006n184
Major info tech companies of the world 2007, 9th ed, 2008n193
Neal-Schuman lib tech companion, 2d ed, 2007n529
Plunkett's infotech industry almanac, 2006 ed, 2006n193
Plunkett's infotech industry almanac 2007, 2008n201
Technology & the school lib, 2007n503
Technology made simple, 2007n528
Web based instruction, 2d ed, 2006n631

INFORMATION WARFARE. *See also* INTELLIGENCE SERVICE
Information operations—doctrine & practice, 2009n610

INSECTS
Ants of N America, 2008n1185
Bees of the world, 2d ed, 2008n1186
Butterflies of W Africa, 2006n1386
Evolution of the insects, 2007n1205
Field gd to insects of southern Africa, updated ed, 2006n1387
Garden insects of N America, 2005n1394
Grzimek's student animal life resource: insects & spiders, 2006n1385
Identification & geographical distribution of the mosquitoes of N America, 2006n1384
Insects, 2007n1206
Kaufman field gd to butterflies of N America, 2007n1204
Kaufman field gd to insects of N America, 2008n1184

Urban ants of N America & Europe, 2009n1203
World of animals: insects & other invertebrates, 2005n1395

INSTRUCTIONAL MATERIALS CENTERS - COLLECTION DEVELOPMENT
Acquiring & organizing curriculum materials, 2d ed, 2005n624

INSTRUCTIONAL SYSTEMS
Handbook of research on instructional systems & tech, 2008n1273

INSTRUMENTS
Origins & dvlpmt of musical instruments, 2008n973

INSURANCE
Canadian insurance claims dir 2008, 76th ed, 2009n185
HMO/PPO dir 2005, 17th ed, 2006n1419
HMO/PPO dir 2006, 18th ed, 2007n1239
HMO/PPO dir 2007, 19th ed, 2008n1213
HMO/PPO dir 2009, 21st ed, 2009n1227
HMO/PPO dir [Website], 2006n1420
HMO/PPO dir [Website], 2007n1240
Plunkett's insurance industry almanac 2005, 2006n196
Plunkett's insurance industry almanac 2006, 2007n179
Plunkett's insurance industry almanac, 2009 ed, 2009n186
TheStreet.com Ratings' consumer box set, 2008 ed, 2009n158
TheStreet.com ratings' gd to health insurers, Spring 2008, 2009n187
TheStreet.com ratings' gd to health insurers, Summer 2007, 2008n210
TheStreet.com ratings' gd to life & annuity insurers, Fall 2007, 2008n211
TheStreet.com ratings' gd to life & annuity insurers, Spring 2008, 2009n188
TheStreet.com ratings' gd to property & casualty insurers, Fall 2007, 2008n212
TheStreet.com ratings' gd to property & casualty insurers, Spring 2008, 2009n189
Weiss Ratings' gd to HMOs & health insurers, Summer 2004, 2005n201
Weiss Ratings' gd to HMOs & health insurers, Winter 2005-06, 2006n197
Weiss Ratings' gd to life, health, & annuity insurers, Summer 2004, 2005n202
Weiss Ratings' gd to life, health, & annuity insurers, Fall 2005, 2006n198
Weiss Ratings' gd to property & casualty insurers, Spring 2004, 2005n203
Weiss Ratings' gd to property & casualty insurers, Fall 2005, 2006n199

INTELLECTUAL FREEDOM
Censorship in the Arab world, 2007n120
Encyclopedia of censorship, new ed, 2006n632
Intellectual freedom manual, 7th ed, 2007n530

INTELLECTUAL PROPERTY
Center for intellectual property hndbk, 2007n521
Intellectual property, 2008n482
Intellectual property, 2008n541
McCarthy's desk ency of intellectual property, 3d ed, 2005n590

INTELLIGENCE SERVICE
Encyclopedia of intelligence & counterintelligence, 2006n661
Historical dict of British intelligence, 2006n665
Historical dict of Cold War counterintelligence, 2008n588
Historical dict of intl intelligence, 2007n560
Historical dict of Israeli intelligence, 2007n629
Historical dict of Russian & Soviet intelligence, 2007n558
Historical dict of US intelligence, 2006n663
Researching natl security & intelligence, 2005n730
Words of intelligence, 2007n595

INTERIOR DESIGN
Color answer bk, 2006n914
Design, 2008n830
Dictionary of modern design, 2006n911
Elements of design, 2005n929
Green design, 2009n846
History of interior design & furniture, 2d ed, 2007n810
Interior materials & surfaces, 2006n912
Mary Gilliatt's dict of architecture & interior design, 2006n928

INTERNATIONAL AFFAIRS
Careers in intl affairs, 8th ed, 2009n214
Worldmark ency of the nations, 11th ed, 2005n72

INTERNATIONAL BUSINESS. *See also* INTERNATIONAL TRADE
Consumer Asia 2004, 11th ed, 2005n213
Consumer E Europe 2004-05, 12th ed, 2005n216
Consumer Europe 2004/05, 20th ed, 2005n217
Consumer intl 2003/04, 2005n206
Consumer Latin America 2004, 2005n222
Craighead's intl business, travel, & relocation gd 2004-05, 12th ed, 2005n204
Doing business in 2004, 2005n207
Economic survey of Latin America & the Caribbean, 2004-05, 2007n189
Encyclopedia of the global economy, 2007n138
Global market share planner, 4th ed, 2007n181

Global market share planner, 6th ed, 2009n193
Historical dict of Japanese business, 2008n220
Hoover's hndbk of world business 2005, 12th ed,
    2006n201
Hoover's hndbk of world business 2007, 2008n213
Inside Wash.: govt resources for intl business,
    2005n205
Major companies of Africa S of the Sahara 2004, 9th
    ed, 2005n211
Major companies of Africa S of the Sahara 2005, 10th
    ed, 2006n211
Major companies of Central & E Europe & the
    Commonwealth of Independent States 2005,
    14th ed, 2006n220
Major companies of Central & E Europe & the
    Commonwealth of Independent States 2008,
    2008n221
Major companies of Europe 2005, 24th ed, 2005n220
Major companies of Latin America & the Caribbean
    2004, 2005n224
Major companies of Latin America & the Caribbean
    2005, 10th ed, 2006n222
Major companies of SW Asia 2004, 8th ed, 2005n215
Major companies of SW Asia 2005, 9th ed, 2006n215
Major companies of the Arab world 2006, 29th ed,
    2006n224
Major companies of the Arab world 2008, 31st ed,
    2008n222
Major companies of the Far East & Australasia 2008,
    2008n219
National accounts stats, 2001, 2005n209
World cosmetics & toiletries mktg dir, 4th ed,
    2006n187
World dvlpmt report 2006, 2007n184
World economic & social survey 2005, 2006n208
World economic & social survey 2006, 2007n178
World economic factbk 2003/04, 2005n210
World economic factbk 2009, 16th ed, 2009n194
World income distribution 2006/07, 4th ed, 2007n185
World investment report 2005, 2006n210

INTERNATIONAL LAW
Electronic info system for intl law (EISIL) [Website],
    2008n500
Handbook of intl law, 2006n538
International criminal law practitioners lib, v.1,
    2009n475
International law, 2006n517
International law in domestic courts [Website],
    2007n492
Max Planck ency of public intl law online [Website],
    2009n486
Treaties & intl agreements online [Website], 2008n502
WTO case law of 2004-05, 2009n488

INTERNATIONAL LIBRARIANSHIP
Global librarianship, 2005n633

Impact of tech on Asian, African, & Middle Eastern
    lib collections, 2008n549
International librarianship, 2008n550
Politics of promoting freedom of info & expression in
    intl librarianship, 2008n548

INTERNATIONAL ORGANIZATIONS
A to Z of multinational peacekeeping, 2007n633
Chronology of intl orgs, 2009n672
Encyclopedia of the United Nations, 2d ed, 2009n673
Europa dir of intl orgs 2005, 7th ed, 2006n740
Europa dir of intl orgs 2007, 2008n658
Europa dir of intl orgs 2008, 2009n676
Guide to the world bank, 2005n722
Historical dict of human rights & humanitarian orgs,
    2d ed, 2008n497
Historical dict of multinational peacekeeping, 2d ed,
    2005n723
Historical dict of NATO & other intl security orgs,
    2009n674
Historical dict of the League of Nations, 2007n635
Historical dict of the UN, new ed, 2008n659
International orgs, 6th ed, 2007n634
Non-governmental orgs research gd [Website],
    2008n660
Treaties & alliances of the world, 8th ed, 2009n675
U.S. natl debate topic 2004-05: the United Nations,
    2005n724
Who's who in intl affairs 2005, 4th ed, 2006n684
Worldwide govt dir with intl orgs 2005, 2006n690

INTERNATIONAL RELATIONS
Africa & the Americas, 2009n692
Annual review of global peace operations 2008,
    2009n694
Anti-Americanism, 2008n667
Britain & the Americas, 2006n746
Chronology of US—Iraqi relations, 1920-2006,
    2008n662
CIAO: Columbia Intl Affairs online [Website],
    2005n725
Encyclopedia of American foreign policy, 2005n726
Encyclopedia of Arab-Israeli conflict, 2009n127
Encyclopedia of Chinese-American relations,
    2007n636
Encyclopedia of histl treaties & alliances, 2d ed,
    2007n424
Encyclopedia of intl relations & global pol, 2006n743
Facts on intl relations & security trends (FIRST)
    [Website], 2008n661
Foreign relations of the US (FRUS) [Website],
    2009n678
France & the Americas, 2006n747
Germany & the Americas, 2006n748
Global perspectives on the US, v.3, 2008n668
Historical dict of the US diplomacy since the Cold
    War, 2008n664

Historical dict of US-China relations, 2006n745
Historical dict of US diplomacy from the Civil War to
    WW I, 2006n742
Historical dict of US-Japan relations, 2008n666
Historical dict of US-Latin American relations,
    2007n638
Historical dict of US-Middle East relations, 2008n663
Historical dict of US-SE Asia relations, 2009n693
Iberia & the Americas, 2006n749
IntelCenter terrorism incident ref (TIR): Afghanistan:
    2000-07, 2009n685
IntelCenter terrorism incident ref (TIR): Algeria,
    2000-07, 2009n687
IntelCenter terrorism incident ref (TIR): Arabian
    Peninsula, 2000-07, 2009n686
IntelCenter terrorism incident ref (TIR): Iraq: 2000-05,
    2009n689
IntelCenter terrorism incident ref (TIR): Iraq: 2006,
    2009n690
IntelCenter terrorism incident ref (TIR): Iraq: 2007,
    2009n691
IntelCenter terrorism incident ref (TIR): Pakistan:
    2000-07, 2009n684
IntelCenter terrorism incident ref (TIR): Philippines,
    2000-07, 2009n688
International relations, intl security, & comparative
    pol, 2009n677
International security & counter terrorism ref center
    [Website], 2009n682
Nation-building, 2005n729
Regional gd to intl conflict & mgmt from 1945 to
    2003, 2006n741
Research gd to US & intl interest groups, 2005n728
Routledge pol & intl relations resource [Website],
    2008n612
US presidents & foreign policy, 2007n592

INTERNATIONAL SECURITY

Praeger security intl online [Website], 2008n665

INTERNATIONAL TRADE

Asian mktg data & stats 2007/08, 3d ed, 2009n196
Asia-Pacific mktg info sourcebk, 2005n212
Commodity yrbk 2003, 2005n260
Consumer Asia 2004, 11th ed, 2005n213
Consumer Asia 2006, 13th ed, 2006n212
Consumer Asia 2009, 2009n197
Consumer China 2005, 10th ed, 2006n213
Consumer China 2009, 14th ed, 2009n198
Consumer E Europe 2004-05, 12th ed, 2005n216
Consumer E Europe 2005/06, 13th ed, 2006n217
Consumer E Europe 2006/07, 14th ed, 2007n186
Consumer E Europe 2008/09, 2009n199
Consumer Europe 2004/05, 20th ed, 2005n217
Consumer intl 2003/04, 2005n206
Consumer intl 2005/06, 12th ed, 2006n202

Consumer intl 2008/09, 2009n191
Consumer Latin America 2004, 2005n222
Consumer Latin America 2006, 13th ed, 2006n221
Consumer Latin America 2009, 2009n203
Consumer Middle East 2006, 8th ed, 2006n223
Consumer USA 2006, 10th ed, 2006n268
Consumer USA 2009, 13th ed, 2009n236
Consumer W Europe 2006/07, 22d ed, 2007n187
Consumer W Europe 2008/09, 2009n200
Direction of trade stats yrbk 2005, 2006n269
Directory of trade & investment-related orgs of
    developing countries & areas in Asia & the
    Pacific 2003, 2005n214
Encyclopedia of world trade, 2006n200
European mktg data & stats 2006, 41st ed, 2006n218
European mktg forecasts 2005/06, 9th ed,
    2006n219Free trade, 2006n203
European mktg forecasts 2009, 12th ed, 2009n201
Globalization, 2007n180
Globalization, 2009n192
Globalization & free trade, 2008n258
History of world trade since 1450, 2006n265
International investment agreements, 2006n204
International mktg data & stats 2004, 2005n263
International mktg data & stats 2006, 30th ed,
    2006n270
International mktg forecasts 2003/04, 2005n264
International mktg forecasts 2005/06, 9th ed,
    2006n271
International trade stats yrbk 2002, 51st ed, 2005n265
International trade stats yrbk 2003, 2006n272
International trade stats yrbk 2004, 2007n183
Nations of the world 2006, 6th ed, 2007n57
Retail trade intl 2005, 14th ed, 2006n205
Retail trade intl 2007, 15th ed, 2008n214
Statistical yrbk for Asia & the Pacific 2003, 2006n216
Trade & dvlpmt report, 2005, 2006n206
Trade & dvlpmt report 2007, 2008n215
Trade assns & professional bodies of the Continental
    European Union, 5th ed, 2009n202
United States foreign trade highlights, 2006n207
United States foreign trade highlights 2007, 2d ed,
    2008n216
Who buys what, 2007n230
World consumer lifestyles databk 2008, 2009n237
World consumer spending 2004/05, 5th ed, 2005n271
World consumer spending 2006/07, 7th ed, 2007n232
World consumer spending 2009, 9th ed, 2009n238
World dir of trade & business assns 2007, 5th ed,
    2008n165
World economic factbk 2005/06, 13th ed, 2006n209
World food mktg dir 2008, 5th ed, 2009n190
World income distribution 2008/09, 2009n239
World investment report 2007, 2008n217
World retail data & stats 2008/09, 2009n195

INTERNET (COMPUTER NETWORK). *See also* WORLD WIDE WEB

Digital resources & librarians, 2005n629
DK online ency, 2007n24
Extreme searcher's Internet hndbk, 2005n1486
Find it online, 4th ed, 2006n1483
Glossary of netspeak & textspeak, 2005n1485
Internet, 2006n1485
Internet & society, 2008n1281
Internet revolution, 2006n1484
Internet tech hndbk, 2005n1487
Librarian's Internet survival gd, 2d ed, 2007n540
Net effects, 2005n634
100 ready-to-use pathfinders for the Web, 2005n594
Pew Internet & American life project [Website], 2009n1289
Real-world network troubleshooting manual, 2005n1484
Search engine watch [Website], 2009n1290
Social sci resources in the electronic age, 2005n63
Web lib, 2005n1488
Wired [Website], 2009n1291

INTERNET (COMPUTER NETWORK) - DIRECTORIES

ALA best free ref Web sites [Website], 2008n7
Automotive Websites, 2d ed, 2007n1340
Best career & educ Web sites, 5th ed, 2007n205
Best of hist web sites, 2008n442
Biology resources in the electronic age, 2005n1335
E.encyclopedia sci, 2005n1284
E.guides: dinosaur, 2005n1523
E.guides: Earth, 2005n1499
E.guides: space travel, 2005n1504
Earth sci resources in the electronic age, 2005n1498
History highway, 4th ed, 2007n427
Internet gd to anti-aging & longevity, 2007n692
Internet gd to cosmetic surgery for men, 2007n1253
Internet gd to herbal remedies, 2008n1236
Internet gd to medical diets & nutrition, 2008n1124
Internet sources on each US state, 2006n71
Librarians' Internet index [Website], 2008n46
Online resources for senior citizens, 2d ed, 2007n695
Plunkett's employers' Internet sites with careers info 2004-05, 2005n231
Purple bk, 2005 ed, 2006n164
Purple bk, 2006 ed, 2007n159
Refdesk.com: ref desk [Website], 2008n1280
United States govt Internet manual 2003-04, 2005n710
United States govt Internet manual 2005-06, 2007n602
United States govt Internet manual 2007, 2008n638
United States govt Internet manual 2008, 2009n651
Web site source bk 2004, 9th ed, 2005n48
Web site source bk 2005, 10th ed, 2006n42
Web site source bk 2006, 11th ed, 2007n37
Web site source bk 2007, 12th ed, 2008n42
Web site source bk 2008, 13th ed, 2009n35
World dir of business info Web sites 2007, 7th ed, 2008n164

INTERNET (COMPUTER NETWORK) - LAW & LEGISLATION

Internet & the law, 2006n521

INTERNSHIPS

Ferguson career resource gd to internships & summer jobs, 2007n203
Internships 2005, 2006n231
Vault gd to top internships 2006, 2006n234

INTERPERSONAL RELATIONS

Cambridge hndbk of personal relationships, 2007n662

INVENTORS & INVENTIONS

Cool stuff & how it works, 2006n1275
Groundbreaking scientific experiments, inventions, & discoveries of the Middle Ages & the Renaissance, 2005n1290
History of invention series, 2005n1288
How it happens, 2006n1271
Inventors & inventions, 2008n1108
New dict of the hist of ideas, 2006n501
100 greatest sci inventions of all time, 2007n1142
Origin of everyday things, 2008n1110

INVESTMENTS. *See also* BANKING; FINANCE

Complete gd to market breadth indicators, 2007n153
Concise ency of investing, 2008n174
Corporate finance sourcebk 2008, 2008n180
Directory of venture capital & private equity firms 2004, 8th ed, 2005n184
Market share reporter 2005, 2006n156
Market share reporter, 2009 ed, 2009n150
Plunkett's investment & securities industry almanac 2005, 2006n157
Plunkett's investment & securities industry almanac 2006, 2007n154
Reaching financial goals, 2008n185
Savings & investment info for teens, 2006n172
Standard & Poor's MidCap 400 gd, 2003 ed, 2005n174
Standard & Poor's small cap 600 gd, 2003 ed, 2005n175
TheStreet.com ratings' gd to bond & money market mutual funds, Summer 2007, 2008n176
TheStreet.com ratings' gd to bond & money market mutual funds, Spring 2008, 2009n151
TheStreet.com ratings' gd to common stocks, Summer 2007, 2008n177
TheStreet.com ratings' gd to common stocks, Spring 2008, 2009n152
TheStreet.com ratings' gd to exchange-traded funds, Summer 2007, 2008n178

TheStreet.com ratings' gd to exchange-traded funds, Spring 2008, 2009n153

TheStreet.com ratings' gd to stock mutual funds, Summer 2007, 2009n154

TheStreet.com ratings' ultimate guided tour of stock investing, 2008n175

Weiss Ratings' gd to bond & money market mutual funds, Spring 2004, 2005n176

Weiss Ratings' gd to bond & money market mutual funds, Summer 2005, 2006n158

Weiss Ratings' gd to brokerage firms, Winter 2003-04, 2005n177

Weiss Ratings' gd to stock mutual funds, Spring 2004, 2005n178

Weiss Ratings' gd to stock mutual funds, Summer 2005, 2006n159

Weiss Ratings' ultimate guided tour of stock investing, Summer 2004, 2005n179

IRAN
Historical dict of Iran, 2d ed, 2007n126
Iran's diverse peoples, 2006n344

IRAQ
Ancient Mesopotamia, 2006n485
Chronology of US—Iraqi relations, 1920-2006, 2008n662
Greenhaven ency of ancient Mesopotamia, 2008n441Brief hist of Iraq, 2009n129
Historical dict of Iraq, 2005n125
History of Iraq, 2006n114
IntelCenter terrorism incident ref (TIR): Iraq: 2000-05, 2009n689
IntelCenter terrorism incident ref (TIR): Iraq: 2006, 2009n690
IntelCenter terrorism incident ref (TIR): Iraq: 2007, 2009n691

IRAQ WAR, 2003
Iraq War, 2005n666
Iraq War, updated ed, 2008n591

IRELAND
CELT: Corpus of electronic texts. The online resource for Irish hist [Website], 2005n494
Celt culture, 2007n114
Celtic culture, 2006n104
Culture & customs of Ireland, 2007n115
Early peoples of Britain & Ireland, 2009n405
Encyclopedia of Irish hist & culture, 2005n110
Everything Irish, 2005n111
Historical dict of the Northern Ireland conflict, 2008n437
Ireland, 2007n393
Ireland, 6th ed, 2006n409
Ireland & the Americas, 2009n113
Irish bed & breakfast bk, 2009n352

Medieval Ireland, 2006n475

IRISH AMERICANS
Columbia gd to Irish American hist, 2006n345

IRISH FOLKLORE
Brewer's dict of Irish phrase & fable, 2006n1115

IRISH GENEALOGY
Clans & families of Ireland, 2005n360
County Longford residents prior to the famine, 2005n364

IRISH LITERATURE
Cambridge hist of Irish lit, 2007n965
Critical companion to James Joyce, 2007n968
Critical companion to Jonathan Swift, 2007n967
Irish women writers, 2006n1059
Literary research & Irish lit, 2009n981

ISLAM
Biographical ency of Islamic philosophy, 2007n1062
Columbia world dict of Islamism, 2008n1097
Dictionary of Islamic philosophical terms [Website], 2006n1239
Encyclopedia of Islam in the US, 2008n1098
Encyclopedia of women & Islamic cultures, v.1, 2005n870
Encyclopedia of women & Islamic cultures, v.2, 2006n854
Encyclopedia of women & Islamic cultures, v.3, 2006n855
Encyclopedia of women & Islamic cultures, v.4, 2007n757
Encyclopedia of women & Islamic cultures, v.5: practices, interpretations, & representations, 2008n782
Encyclopedia of women & Islamic cultures, v.6: suppl & index, 2008n783
Historical atlas of Islam, 2005n1271
Historical atlas of the Islamic world, 2005n1270
Historical dict of Sufism, 2006n1240
Islam & the religious arts, 2005n1272
Islam in world cultures, 2006n1242
Islamic civilization, 2007n1123
Islamic world, 2005n1274
Islamism, 2008n1096
Key words in Islam, 2007n1120
New ency of Islam, 3d ed, 2009n1117
Qur'an, 2007n1122
Rise of Islam, 2006n1241
Understanding Islam & Muslim traditions, 2005n1273
Voices of Islam, 2008n1099

ISLAM, LITERATURE
Literature of Islam, 2007n973
World of Islam in lit for youth, 2007n892

ISLAMIC EMPIRE
Daily life in the medieval Islamic world, 2006n1243
Encyclopedia of the crusades, 2005n521
Medieval Islamic civilization, 2007n1121

ISRAEL
Aerial atlas of the Holy Land, 2009n125
Ancient Canaan & Israel, 2006n116
Brief hist of Israel, 2005n127
Brief hist of Israel, 2d ed, 2009n131
Culture & customs of Israel, 2005n128
Dictionary of the Israeli-Palestinian conflict, 2006n115
Encyclopedia of Arab-Israeli conflict, 2009n127
Historical dict of ancient Israel, 2005n126
Historical dict of Israel, 2d ed, 2009n130
Historical dict of Israeli intelligence, 2007n629
Historical dict of the Arab-Israeli conflict, 2007n123

ITALIAN GENEALOGY
Italians to America, v.17, 2006n364
Italians to America, v.18, 2006n365
Italians to America, v.19, 2006n366
Italians to America, v.20, 2006n367

ITALIAN LANGUAGE DICTIONARIES
Oxford color Italian dict plus, 2009n899
Oxford-Paravia Italian dict, 2d ed, 2009n900

ITALIAN LITERATURE
Encyclopedia of Italian literary studies, 2008n941
Italian lit & its times, v.7, 2006n1060

ITALY
Culture & customs of Italy, 2006n105
Food culture in Italy, 2005n1307
Italy, 2005n406
Italy, 2005n497
Italy, new ed, 2008n373
Historical dict of modern Italy, 2d ed, 2008n124

ITALY, HISTORY
Cambridge companion to the age of Constantine, 2007n394

ITALY, TRAVEL
Fodor's Italy 2006, 2006n406
Italy, updated ed, 2006n410
Venice, 4th ed, 2006n413

JACK, THE RIPPER
Jack the Ripper suspects, 2005n561

JACKSON, ANDREW
Shapers of the great debate on Jacksonian democracy, 2005n696

JAPAN
Companion to Japanese hist, 2007n372
Food culture in Japan, 2005n1304
Handbook to life in medieval & early modern Japan, 2007n373
Historical dict of Japanese traditional theatre, 2007n1057
Sources of Japanese tradition, v.2, 2d ed, 2007n98

JAPAN, COMMERCE
Historical dict of Japanese business, 2008n220

JAPAN, FOREIGN RELATIONS
Historical dict of US-Japan relations, 2008n666

JAPAN, MOTION PICTURES
Toho studios story, 2009n1067

JAPAN, TRAVEL
Tokyo, 2006n403

JAPANESE AMERICANS
Japanese American relocation digital archives [Website], 2006n333

JAPANESE LANGUAGE - DICTIONARIES
Berlitz Japanese dict, 2006n970
Classical Japanese reader & essential dict, 2008n873
Japanese-English chemical dict, 2009n1298

JAPANESE LITERATURE
Classical Japanese reader & essential dict, 2008n873

JAZZ MUSIC
All of me: the complete discography of Louis Armstrong, 2007n992
American popular music: jazz, 2006n1105
Billboard illus ency of jazz & blues, 2007n1011
Free jazz & free improvisation, 2005n1151
Jazz: a regional exploration, 2006n1107
Jazz fiction, 2008n990
Jazz musicians, 1945 to the present, 2007n1012
Penguin gd to jazz on CD, 7th ed, 2006n1106
Richard Cook's jazz ency, 2008n989
Who's who of British jazz, 2d ed, 2005n1150

JEHOVAH'S WITNESSES
Historical dict of Jehovah's Witnesses, 2009n1107

JEWELRY
Jeweler's dir of gemstones, 2007n808
Jewelrymaking through hist, 2008n829

JEWISH ARTISTS
Encyclopedia of Jewish American artists, 2008n834

JEWISH FOLKLORE
Jewish story finder, 2006n1113

JEWISH LITERATURE
Jewish American lit, 2006n1032
Jewish values finder, 2009n931

JEWS
Ancient Canaan & Israel, 2006n116
Bibliography of the Samaritans, 3d ed, 2006n1245
Columbia hist of Jews & Judaism in America, 2009n313
Daily life of Jews in the Middle Ages, 2006n348
Dictionary of Jewish biog, 2006n347
Encyclopedia of American Jewish hist, 2008n330
Encyclopedia of modern Jewish culture, 2007n282
Encyclopedia of the Jewish diaspora, 2009n311
Historical dict of ancient Israel, 2005n126
Jewish yr bk 2005, 2006n1247
Jewish yr bk 2007, 2008n1101
Judaica ref sources, 3d rev ed, 2005n350
These are the names: studies in Jewish onomastics, v.4, 2005n351
Travel gd to the Jewish Caribbean & Latin America, 2005n408
Yivo ency of Jews in E Europe, 2009n312

JOAN, OF ARC, SAINT (1412-1432)
Joan of Arc & the hundred yrs war, 2006n471

JOBS. *See* CAREERS

JOURNALISM
Career opportunities in journalism, 2008n240
Encyclopedia of American journalism, 2008n802
1stHeadlines [Website], 2005n898
High school journalism, 2008n803
Journalism, 3d ed, 2005n897
JournalismNet [Website], 2005n900
News media yellow bk, Summer 2005 ed, 2006n888
Power of the news media, 2005n899
Poynter online [Website], 2005n901

JUDAISM
Bibliography of the Samaritans, 3d ed, 2006n1245
Cambridge companion to American Judaism, 2006n1244
Columbia hist of Jews & Judaism in America, 2009n313
Dictionary of ancient Rabbis, 2005n1275
Dictionary of Jewish-Christian relations, 2006n1246
Encyclopaedia Judaica, 2d ed, 2007n1124
Encyclopedia of Jewish myth, magic, & mysticism, 2008n1100
Encyclopedia of Judaism, 2006n1248
Encyclopedia of modern Jewish culture, 2007n282
Historical dict of Judaism, 2d ed, 2008n1102

Jewish yr bk 2004, 2005n1276
Jewish yr bk 2007, 2008n1101
John Paul II & the Jewish people, 2009n314
Judaica ref sources, 3d rev ed, 2005n350
Key words in Judaism, 2007n1125
Maven in blue jeans, 2009n1092
Student's ency of Judaism, 2005n1277
These are the names: studies in Jewish onomastics, v.4, 2005n351
Who's who in the Jewish Bible, 2009n1118

JUDGES, UNITED STATES. *See also* LAW, UNITED STATES
Great American judges, 2005n535

JUVENILE DELINQUENCY. *See also* CRIME; CRIMINAL JUSTICE
Encyclopedia of juvenile violence, 2008n485
Juvenile justice, 2006n576

KANT, IMMANUEL, 1724-1804
Historical dict of Kant & Kantianism, 2006n1194

KING, MARTIN LUTHER, JR., 1929-1968
Martin Luther King, Jr., ency, 2009n299

KNIGHTS TEMPLAR
Knights Templar ency, 2008n428

KNOWLEDGE MANAGEMENT
Digital info & knowledge mgmt, 2008n547
Encyclopedia of communities of practice in info & knowledge mgmt, 2006n584
Encyclopedia of communities of practice in info & knowledge mgmt [Website], 2006n585
Encyclopedia of knowledge mgmt, 2006n1465
Encyclopedia of portal technologies & applications, 2008n1282
Knowledge mgmt, 2008n169
Knowledge mgmt, 2009n146
Knowledge mgmt, 2009n573
Knowledge mgmt & business strategies, 2008n170

KOREA
Historical dict of the Republic of Korea, 2d ed, 2005n98
History of Korea, 2006n93
Korea, updated ed, 2006n402
North Korea in quotation, 2006n94
Two Koreas, 2005n99

KOREAN WAR, 1950-1953
A to Z of the Korean War, 2006n462
Hill wars of the Korean conflict, 2006n463
Korean battle chronology, 2005n659
Korean War, 2005n447
Korean War, 2008n578

Korean War almanac, 2007n339

KOSOVA
Historical dict of Kosova, 2005n112

KU KLUX KLAN
Ku Klux Klan, 2007n367

KURDS
Historical dict of the Kurds, 2005n352

KYRGYZSTAN
Historical dict of Kyrgyzstan, 2005n100

LABOR
Almanac of American employers 2004, 2005n228
Almanac of American employers 2007, 2008n225
American salaries & wages survey, 8th ed, 2006n235
Child labor, 2006n237
Directory of executive recruiters 2005-06, 34th ed, 2006n230
Directory of executive recruiters 2007-08, 35th ed, 2007n192
Directory of executive recruiters, 14th corporate ed, 2006n229
Directory of US labor orgs, 2004 ed, 2005n229
Directory of US labor orgs, 2008 ed, 2009n206
Employment, hours, & earnings 2005, 2006n239
Employment, hours, & earnings, 2007 ed, 2008n228
Employment, hours, & earnings 2008, 2009n208
Encyclopedia of career dvlpmt, 2007n190
Encyclopedia of US labor & working class hist, 2007n191
Enhanced occupational outlook hndbk, 5th ed, 2005n233
Essential gd to fed employment laws, 2007n485
Glossary of labour law & industrial relations, 2006n227
Handbook of U.S. labor stats 2004, 7th ed, 2005n234
Handbook of US labor stats 2005, 8th ed, 2006n240
Handbook of US labor stats 2006, 9th ed, 2007n195
Handbook of US labor stats 2007, 10th ed, 2008n231
Handbook of US labor stats 2008, 11th ed, 2009n209
Healthy work, 2006n225
Historical dict of organized labor, 2d ed, 2005n225
Historical dir of trade unions, v.5, 2008n226
Historical ency of American labor, 2005n226
Job hunter's sourcebk, 6th ed, 2005n230
Job hunter's sourcebk, 8th ed, 2009n207
Jobs in America, 2007n196
Labor relations, 2006n236
Occupational outlook hndbk, 2004-05 ed, 2005n236
Occupational outlook hndbk 2006-07, 2007n197
Occupational outlook hndbk 2008-09, 2009n210
Plunkett's companion to the almanac of American employers: mid-size firms, 2007 ed, 2008n227

State of working America 2004/05, 2006n151
State of working America 2006-07, 2008n236
Way we work, 2009n205
Work in America, 2005n227
Working Americans 1880-2005, v.6: women at work, 2006n238
Working Americans 1880-2006, v.7: social movements, 2007n194
Working Americans 1880-2007, v.8: immigrants, 2009n211
Working in America, 2008n233
Young person's Occupational Outlook Hndbk, 6th ed, 2008n238

LABORATORY TESTS
Mosby's diagnostic & lab test ref, 7th ed, 2006n1425

LANDSCAPING
Landscape architectural graphic standards, 2008n1135

LANGUAGE & LINGUISTICS
Atlas of the world's langs, 2d ed, 2008n848
Bibliography of modern Romani linguistics, 2005n952
Dictionary of linguistics & phonetics, 6th ed, 2009n870
Encyclopedia of fictional & fantastic langs, 2007n822
Encyclopedia of linguistics, 2006n939
Encyclopedia of the world's endangered langs, 2008n850
Ethnologue [Website], 2008n849
First English dict, 1604, 2008n851
History of the English lang, 2008n853
Key terms in syntax & syntactic theory, 2009n871
Lexicons of early modern English [Website], 2009n869
New ency of southern culture: v.5, lang, 2008n852
Omniglot [Website], 2006n940
One thousand langs, 2009n872
Varieties of English, 2009n873

LAOS
Historical dict of Laos, 3d ed, 2009n102

LATIN AMERICA
G. K. Hall bibliog gd to Latin American studies 2002, 2005n118
G. K. Hall bibliog gd to Latin American studies 2003, 2006n107
LANIC: Latin American network & info center [Website], 2008n134
Latin American database (LADB) [Website], 2008n135
Latin American network info center (LANIC) [Website], 2008n136
Political databases of the Americas (PDBA) [Website], 2008n655
Social panorama of Latin America 2006, 2008n138

LATIN AMERICA, ART
Defining Latin American art, 2006n919

LATIN AMERICA, BUSINESS
Cambridge economic hist of Latin America, 2007n188
Consumer Latin America 2004, 2005n222
Consumer Latin America 2006, 13th ed, 2006n221
Consumer Latin America 2009, 2009n203
Economic survey of Latin America & the Caribbean, 2004-05, 2007n189
Latin American mktg data & stats 2007/08, 2009n204
Latin American mktg info sourcebk, 2005n223
Major companies of Latin America & the Caribbean 2004, 2005n224
Major companies of Latin America & the Caribbean 2005, 10th ed, 2006n222

LATIN AMERICA, ENVIRONMENTAL CONDITIONS
Latin America & the Caribbean, 2005n1543

LATIN AMERICA, HISTORY
Atlas & survey of Latin American hist, 2007n117
Historical atlas of Central America, 2005n119
Historical dict of the "Dirty Wars," 2005n499

LATIN AMERICAN AUTHORS
Autobiographical writings on Mexico, 2006n1063
Columbia gd to the Latin American novel since 1945, 2008n942
Chicano & Chicana lit, 2007n972
Cuban-American fiction in English, 2006n1061
Encyclopedia of Hispanic-American lit, 2009n984
Feminist ency of Spanish lit, 2005n1089
Greenwood ency of Latino lit, 2009n982
Hispanic lit of the US, 2005n1065
Latin American sci fiction writers, 2005n1091
Latin American women writers, 2008n943
Latino lit in America, 2005n1090
Literature of Latin America, 2005n1092
Literature of the Caribbean, 2009n983
Notable Latino writers, 2006n1062

LATIN AMERICAN DRAMA
Encyclopedia of Latin American theater, 2005n1219

LATIN AMERICAN MOTION PICTURES
Film in Latin America [Website], 2006n1135

LATIN AMERICANS
A to Z of Latino Americans series, 2008n333
Columbia hist of Latinos in the US since 1960, 2005n353
Encyclopedia Latina, 2006n350
Encyclopedia of Latin American hist & culture, 2d ed, 2009n118
Encyclopedia of Latino popular culture, 2005n354

Great Hispanic-Americans, 2006n349
HAPI: Hispanic American per index online [Website], 2008n50
Hispanic Americans, 2007 ed, 2008n334
Hispanic Americans, 2008n335
Hispanic American biogs, 2007n284
Hispanics in the American West, 2006n353
Icons of Latino America, 2009n315
Latinas in the US, 2007n285
Latino & African American athletes today, 2005n751
Latino American experience [Website], 2009n316
Latino chronology, 2008n332
Latino food culture, 2009n1152
Mexican American experience, 2005n355
100 Hispanics you should know, 2008n331
Oxford ency of Latinos & Latinas in the US, 2006n351
Who we are: Hispanics, 2008n754

LATIN AMERICANS, POLITICAL PARTICIPATION
Latino Americans & pol participation, 2006n727

LATIN LITERATURE
Early Christian Greek & Latin lit, 2006n1236

LATVIA
Historical dict of Latvia, 2d ed, 2009n114

LAW - BIBLIOGRAPHY
HeinOnline [Website], 2008n462

LAW - BIOGRAPHY
Who's who in American law 2005-06, 14th ed, 2006n515
Who's who in American law 2007-08, 30th ed, 2008n463

LAW - DICTIONARIES & ENCYCLOPEDIAS
Burton's legal thesaurus, 4th ed, 2007n441
Elgar ency of comparative law, 2008n501
Encyclopedia of law & society, 2008n466
Encyclopedia of the 1st amendment, 2009n437
Gale ency of everyday law, 2d ed, 2007n445
International law, 2006n517
Internet & the law, 2006n521
Oran's dict of law, 4th ed, 2008n468
U.S. Constitution A to Z, 2d ed, 2009n439
U.S. legal system, 2005n536
West's ency of American law, 2d ed, 2005n537

LAW - DIRECTORIES
All business [Website], 2006n261
BNA's dir of state & fed courts, judges, & clerks, 2006n522
BNA's dir of state & fed courts, judges, & clerks online [Website], 2006n523

Directory of local court & county retrievers, 2005 ed, 2006n524

Global legal info network [Website], 2008n470

Judicial staff dir, winter 2005, 25th ed, 2006n526

Judicial staff dir online [Website], 2006n527

Judicial yellow bk, Spring 2005, 2006n528

Judicial yellow bk, 2008 ed, 2009n441

Law & legal info dir, 15th ed, 2005n538

Law & legal info dir, 16th ed, 2006n529

Law & legal info dir, 18th ed, 2008n471

Law & legal info dir, 19th ed, 2009n442

Law firms yellow bk, Summer 2005, 2006n530

Law firms yellow bk, 2008 ed, 2009n443

Ontario legal dir 2005, 80th ed, 2006n531

Ontario legal dir 2008, 83d ed, 2009n444

Want's fed-state court dir, 2006 ed, 2006n533

LAW ENFORCEMENT

Career opportunities in law enforcement, security, & protective servs, 2d ed, 2006n249

Encyclopedia of American law enforcement, 2008n489

Encyclopedia of law enforcement, 2006n518

Encyclopedia of police studies, 3d ed, 2008n486

Federal law enforcement careers, 2d ed, 2007n207

Policing in America, 2008n495

World ency of police forces & correctional systems, 2d ed, 2007n473

World police ency, 2007n474

LAW, EDUCATION

Barron's gd to law schools 2005, 16th ed, 2005n289

Best 170 law schools, 2007 ed, 2007n244

Complete bk of law schools, 2004 ed, 2005n298

Law school buzz bk, 2005 ed, 2005n301

LAW – HANDBOOKS & YEARBOOKS

American Bar Assn gd to credit & bankruptcy, 2006n534

American Bar Assn legal gd for women, 2006n535

American Indian law deskbk, 2007 suppl, 2008n472

American law yrbk 2008, 2009n446

Capital punishment, 3d ed, 2006n570

Covenants not to compete, 3d ed, 2005n584

Covenants not to compete, 2003 suppl, 3d ed, 2005n585

Death penalty on trial, 2006n541

Defendant rights, 2005n579

Divorce without court, 2007n460

Employer's legal hndbk, 7th ed, 2007n487

Environmental statutes, 2004 ed, 2005n586

Essential gd to fed employment laws, 2007n485

Estate planning simplified, 2007n46

Flying solo: a survival gd for the solo & small firm lawyer, 4th ed, 2006n540

Internet & the law, 2007n447

Invasion of privacy, 2006n542

Issues on trial series, 2009n452

Law: key concepts in philosophy, 2007n1070

Law firm accounting & financial mgmt, 3d ed, 2007n455

Legal forms for starting & running a small business, 4th ed, 2007n465

Legal terminology, 2006n539

Manager's legal hndbk, 3d ed, 2007n451

Marriage on trial, 2006n551

Medicine on trial, 2005n545

MVR bk, 2006 ed, 2006n544

MVR bk, 2008 ed, 2009n455

MVR decoder digest, 2006 ed, 2006n545

MVR decoder digest, 2008 ed, 2009n456

National survey of state laws, 6th ed, 2009n457

Nolo's essential gd to divorce, 2007n459

Plan your estate, 9th ed, 2009n484

Right to counsel & privilege against self-incrimination, 2005n559

Rights of lesbians, gay men, bisexuals, & transgender people, 4th ed, 2006n583

Social Security hndbk 2005-06, 15th ed, 2007n464

Voting rights act, 2007n466

Wage & hour laws, 2006n578

We the students, 3d ed, 2009n459

Your rights in the workplace, 7th ed, 2007n486

LAW - INDEXES

WTO analytical index, 2d ed, 2009n487

LAW, INTERNATIONAL

Handbook of intl law, 2006n538

International law, 2006n517

International law in domestic courts [Website], 2007n492

LAW, UNITED STATES

American Indian law deskbk, 3d ed, 2005n540

American law yrbk 2003, 2005n541

American law yrbk 2005, 2006n536

American rights series, 2006n537

Avalon project at Yale Law School [Website], 2006n508

Brown v. Board of Educ, 2006n547

Chase court, 2005n552

Documentary hist of the Supreme Court of the US 1789-1800, v.7, 2005n547

Documentary hist of the Supreme Court of the US 1789-1800, v.8, 2008n474

Encyclopedia of American civil liberties, 2007n442

Encyclopedia of American civil rights & liberties, 2007n490

Encyclopedia of the Supreme Court, 2006n520

Encyclopedia of the Supreme Court of the US, 2009n438

Freedom of association, 2005n544

Guide to the U.S. Supreme Court, 4th ed, 2005n556

Handy Supreme Court answer bk, 2008n477

History of the N.Y. Court of Appeals, 1932-2003, 2007n458

Jay & Ellsworth, the 1st courts, 2009n450

Judicial branch of state govt, 2007n454

Judiciary & responsible govt 1910-1921, v. 9, 2008n478

Landmark decisions of the US Supreme Court, 2d ed, 2008n464

Landmark Supreme Court cases, 2005n549

Library of American laws & legal principles, 2007n456

Major acts of Congress, 2005n553

Media & American courts, 2005n539

National survey of state laws, 5th ed, 2005n554

Oxford companion to the Supreme Court of the US, 2d ed, 2006n519

Public debate over controversial Supreme Court decisions, 2007n461

Punishment in America, 2006n565

Roe v. Wade, 2009n451

Scopes "Monkey Trial," 2007n453

Sexual harassment decisions of the US Supreme Court, 2007n462

Supreme Court compendium, 4th ed, 2008n475

Supreme Court of the US, 3d ed, 2009n458

Taft court, 2005n555

U.S. natl debate topic 2005-06: US civil liberties, 2006n550

U.S. Supreme Court, 2008n469

United States Supreme Court, 2006n548

United States Supreme Court, 2006n549

Unreasonable searches & seizures, 2006n546

Vinson court, 2005n543

White court, 2005n557

LAWRENCE, T. E. (1888-1935)

Lawrence of Arabia, 2005n503

LEADERSHIP

Encyclopedia of leadership, 2005n147

LEAGUE OF NATIONS

Historical dict of the League of Nations, 2007n635

LEARNING

Critical thinking & learning, 2005n275

Informed learning, 2009n504

LEARNING DISABILITIES

Complete learning disabilities dir 2004/05, 11th ed, 2005n313

Complete learning disabilities dir 2005-06, 12th ed, 2006n314

Complete learning disabilities dir 2007, 13th ed, 2007n255

Complete learning disabilities dir 2008, 14th ed, 2008n288

Complete learning disabilities dir 2009, 15th ed, 2009n280

Complete learning disabilities dir [Website], 2005n314

Complete learning disabilities dir [Website], 2007n256

Complete learning disabilities dir [Website], 2008n289

Encyclopedia of learning disabilities, 2d ed, 2007n257

Encyclopedia of special educ, 2008n290

K & W gd to colleges for students with learning disabilities or attention deficit disorder, 7th ed, 2005n315

Learning disabilities dir [Website], 2006n316

Learning disabilities info for teens, 2006n315

Learning disabilities sourcebk, 3d ed, 2009n282

Teaching students with learning disabilities, 2009n283

Transition to postsecondary educ for students with disabilities, 2009n281

LEGAL FORMS. *See also* **BUSINESS FORMS**

Employer legal forms simplified, 2008n235

Landlord legal forms simplified, 2008n261

Real estate forms simplified, 2007n234

LEGAL WRITING

Pocket gd to legal writing, 2006n886

LEGISLATIVE BODIES

Party affiliations in the state legislatures, 2008n624

LEGISLATIVE BRANCH

Legislative branch of fed govt, 2009n660

State yellow bk, 2008 ed, 2009n650

LEISURE

Encyclopedia of leisure & outdoor recreation, 2005n754

Encyclopedia of recreation & leisure in America, 2005n755

LESBIAN LITERATURE

Historical dict of lesbian lit, 2007n881

LESBIAN STUDIES

Encyclopedia of gay & lesbian popular culture, 2009n1046

Encyclopedia of lesbian, gay, bisexual, & transgender hist in America, 2005n804

Gay & lesbian issues, 2005n806

Great events from hist: gay, lesbian, bisexual, transgender events, 2007n705

Handbook of gay, lesbian, bisexual, & transgender admin & policy, 2005n805

Leading the parade, 2008n725

Our own voices [Website], 2009n45

Queer America, 2009n749

Queer ency of music, dance, & musical theater, 2005n1181
Queer ency of the visual arts, 2005n938
Routledge intl ency of queer culture, 2007n706

LESOTHO
Historical dict of Lesotho, new ed, 2005n88

LEWIS & CLARK EXPEDITION
Lewis & Clark expedition, 2005n446
Lewis & Clark lexicon of discovery, 2005n430

LIBERTARIANISM
Encyclopedia of libertarianism, 2009n671

LIBRARIANS IN MOTION PICTURES
Image of librarians in cinema, 1917-99, 2006n1166

LIBRARIANSHIP
Basic lib skills, 5th ed, 2007n498
Harrod's librarian's glossary & ref bk, 10th ed, 2006n588
Institute of museum & lib servs [Website], 2009n489
Internet lib for librarians [Website], 2009n494
Librarian's yellow pages [Website], 2009n497
LibrarySpot [Website], 2009n498
New on the job: a school lib media specialist's gd to success, 2008n516
NextGen librarian's survival gd, 2007n507
On account of sex: an annotated bibliog on the status of women in librarianship, 2007n493
Oxford gd to lib research, 3d ed, 2006n596
Portable MLIS, 2009n502
WebJunction [Website], 2009n490
Whole lib hndbk 4, 2007n497

LIBRARIES
American lib dir 2004-05, 57th ed, 2005n596
American lib dir 2005-06, 58th ed, 2006n589
American lib dir 2007-08, 60th ed, 2008n505
American lib dir 2008-09, 61st ed, 2009n491
American lib dir [Website], 2006n590
Bowker annual 2004, 49th ed, 2005n601
Bowker annual lib & bk trade almanac 2007, 52d ed, 2008n510
Directory of special libs & info centers, 30th ed, 2005n597
Directory of special libs & info centers, 34th ed, 2009n493
Subject dir of special libs, 34th ed, 2009n499
World dir of business info libs 2007, 6th ed, 2008n509

LIBRARIES & COMMUNITY
From outreach to equity, 2005n641
How libs & librarians help, 2006n635
Libraries beyond their institutions, 2006n645

LIBRARIES & MINORITIES
Achieving diversity, 2008n554

LIBRARIES & THE INTERNET
Library Web sites, 2005n635
Net effects, 2005n634
Public libs & Internet serv roles, 2009n512
Web 2.0 for librarians & info professionals, 2009n572
Your lib goes virtual, 2009n516

LIBRARIES, CANADA
Directory of libs in Canada 2008/09, 23d ed, 2009n492

LIBRARIES, EUROPE
Directory of univ libs in Europe, 3d ed, 2008n506

LIBRARIES, EVALUATION
Using benchmarking, needs assessment, quality improvement, outcome measurement, & lib standards, 2008n520

LIBRARIES, INVENTORY CONTROL
Complete RFID hndbk, 2009n559

LIBRARIES, PUBLIC RELATIONS
Bienvenidos! Welcome! A handy resource gd for mktg your lib to Latinos, 2006n633
Blueprint for your lib mktg plan, 2006n636
Creating your lib brand, 2009n581
Even more great ideas for libs & friends, 2009n515
Family-centered lib hndbk, 2009n551
High tech, high touch: lib customer serv through tech, 2005n642
Library contests, 2009n582
Outreach servs in academic & special libs, 2005n604
Real-life mktg & promotion strategies in college libs, 2007n500

LIBRARY AUTOMATION
Neal-Schuman lib tech companion, 2d ed, 2007n529

LIBRARY CAREERS
Career opportunities in lib & info sci, 2006n595
Day in the life: career options in lib & info sci, 2008n523
Good match, 2008n526
Is consulting for you? 2008n524
Librarian's career gdbk, 2006n614
Rethinking info work, 2008n525

LIBRARY EDUCATION
Education for lib cataloging, 2007n509
Global evolution, 2008n503
Unfinished business: race, equity, & diversity in lib & info sci educ, 2006n615

LIBRARY EMPLOYEES
Human resources for results, 2009n510
Neal-Schuman dir of public lib job descriptions, 2006n592
New librarian, new job, 2007n508
NextGen librarian's survival gd, 2007n507

LIBRARY FACILITIES
Designing a school lib media center for the future, 2d ed, 2008n514
Heart of the community, 2008n552
Library security & safety gd to prevention, planning, & response, 2009n577
Managing facilities for results, 2009n509
Planning the modern public lib bldg, 2005n636
Teen spaces, 2d ed, 2009n576

LIBRARY FUNDRAISING
Big bk of lib grant money 2006, 2006n591
Grants for libs, 2007n524
Write grants, get money, 2d ed, 2009n578

LIBRARY HISTORY
Cambridge hist of libs in Britain & Ireland, 2007n495
History of the lib in western civilization, 2005n637
History of the lib in western civilization, 2007n531
Libraries & librarianship, 2008n551
Library as place, 2008n553

LIBRARY LEGISLATION
Professional liability issues for librarians & info professionals, 2009n501

LIBRARY MANAGEMENT
Accidental lib manager, 2006n638
Branch librarians' hndbk, 2005n638
Complete gd to acquisitions mgmt, 2005n626
Creating your library's business plan, 2009n579
Empowering your lib, 2005n639
Fundamentals of lib supervision, 2006n637
Leadership basics for librarians & info professionals, 2008n555
Management basics for info professionals, 2d ed, 2008n556
Managing budgets & finances, 2006n639
Managing change, rev ed, 2007n532
Managing the 21st-century ref department, 2005n652
Managing 21st century libs, 2006n640
Performance mgmt & appraisal, 2005n640
Public lib manager's forms, policies, & procedures hndbk w/CD-ROM, 2005n605
Quality lib, 2009n580
Running a small lib, 2007n534
Small change, big problems, 2007n535
Staffing the modern lib, 2006n634
Supervising staff, 2007n536

Training paraprofessionals for ref serv, 2d ed, 2009n586
Winning with lib leadership, 2005n643

LIBRARY MATERIALS, CONSERVATION & RESTORATION
Archives & archivists in the info age, 2006n613
Preservation & conservation for libs & archives, 2006n612
Protecting your library's digital sources, 2005n631

LIBRARY OF CONGRESS
Encyclopedia of the Lib of Congress, 2006n587

LIBRARY ORIENTATION
Practical pedagogy for lib instructors, 2009n507

LIBRARY SCIENCE
Dictionary for lib & info sci, 2005n595
Dictionary of info sci & tech, 2008n504
Foundations of lib & info sci, 2d ed, 2005n602
Subject dir of special libs & info centers 29th ed, 2005n599

LIBRARY USE STUDIES
Analyzing lib collection use with Excel, 2008n565

LIBRARY WEBSITES
Creating database-backed lib web pages, 2007n527

LIBYA
Historical dict of Libya, 4th ed, 2007n87

LIFE INSURANCE
TheStreet.com ratings' gd to life & annuity insurers, Fall 2007, 2008n211
TheStreet.com ratings' gd to life & annuity insurers, Spring 2008, 2009n188
Weiss Ratings' gd to life, health, & annuity insurers, summer 2004, 2005n202
Weiss Ratings' gd to life, health, & annuity insurers, Fall 2005, 2006n198

LIFE SCIENCES
Encyclopedia of life scis, 2d ed, 2005n1336
Life on Earth series, 2005n1291

LINCOLN, ABRAHAM, 1809-1865
Abraham Lincoln companion, 2009n638
Abraham Lincoln on screen, 2d ed, 2009n1059

LITERACY
Collaborative strategies for teaching reading comprehension, 2009n523
Library research with emergent readers, 2009n520
Literacy for young children, 2009n265

More than 100 brain friendly tools & strategies for literacy instruction, 2009n268
More than 100 ways to learner-centered literacy, 2d ed, 2009n267
Motivating readers in the middle grades, 2009n517
Reading is funny! 2009n546

LITERARY AGENTS
Guide to literary agents 2005, 2005n891

LITERARY AWARDS
Children's bks: awards & prizes, 2005 ed, 2006n1003
Coretta Scott King awards 1970-2004, 3d ed, 2005n1056
Newbery & Caldecott awards, 2005n1033
Newbery & Caldecott awards, 2006 ed, 2007n899
Newbery & Caldecott awards, 2007 ed, 2008n885
Newbery & Caldecott awards, 2008 ed, 2009n926
Newbery/Printz companion, 3d ed, 2008n884
Pura Belpre awards, 2007n906

LITERARY THEORY
Literary theory, 2008n790

LITERATURE - BIBLIOGRAPHY
African American lit, 2006n1030
Anatomy of wonder, 5th ed, 2006n1018
Autobiographical writings on Mexico, 2006n1063
Best bks for middle school & jr high readers grades 6-9, 2005n1018
Children's catalog, 19th ed, 2007n502
Encountering enchantment, 2008n883
Faith reads, 2009n986
Fantasy lit for children & YAs, 5th ed, 2006n992
Fiction catalog, 15th ed, 2007n916
General studies of Charles Dickens & his writings & collected eds of his works, 2005n1077
Genrefied classics, 2008n895
Jewish American lit, 2006n1032
Literary research & Irish lit, 2009n981
Literary research & the American modernist era, 2009n948
Literary research & the era of American nationalism & romanticism, 2009n958
Literary research gd, 5th ed, 2009n902
Literature suppressed on pol grounds, rev ed, 2007n868
Literature suppressed on religious grounds, rev ed, 2007n867
Literature suppressed on sexual grounds, rev ed, 2007n869
Literature suppressed on social grounds, rev ed, 2007n870
Merce Rodoreda, 2005n1099
100 great American novels you've (probably) never read, 2008n905
Popular series fiction for K-6, 2006n997
Popular series fiction for middle school & teen readers, 2006n998

Real story, 2007n977
Supplement to Ralph Waldo Emerson, 2007n950
Thematic gd to popular nonfiction, 2007n976
Undergraduate's companion to Arab writers & their Web Sites, 2006n1064
Undergraduate's companion to children's writer & their Web sites, 2006n996
Undergraduate's companion to English Renaissance writers & their Web sites, 2005n1074

LITERATURE - BIO-BIBLIOGRAPHY
American writers, suppl 17, 2009n950
American writers, suppl 18, 2009n951
Best bks for high school readers grades 9-12, 2005n1017
Black lit criticism, 2009n903
Bloom's literary ref online [Website], 2009n904
British writers, suppl 14, 2009n968
Children's authors & illustrators too good to miss, 2005n1028
Concise major 21st-century writers, 2007n871
Contemporary postcolonial & postimperial lit in English [Website], 2006n973
Cyclopedia of world authors, 4th rev ed, 2005n984
Favorite children's authors & illustrators, 2005n1026
John Donne, 2006n1049
Literary newsmakers for students, 2007n872
Literary ref online [Website], 2007n873
Literary ref center [Website], 2009n905
Masterplots II: African American lit, rev ed, 2009n954
Masterplots II: Christian lit, 2009n916
Middle Eastern lit & their times, 2005n1094
Multicultural writers since 1945, 2005n986
Ninth bk of jr authors & illustrators, 2006n1000
Popular contemporary writers, 2006n974
Women writers project [Website], 2005n995
World writers in English, 2005n996

LITERATURE - BIOGRAPHY
African-American writers, 2005n1058
American ethnic writers, 2009n949
American writers, 2005n1060
Arthurian writers, 2009n969
Biography today: authors, v.16, 2005n997
Early American nature writers, 2009n952
Feminism in lit, 2005n999
International who's who of authors and writers 2005, 2006n976
Jack Kerouac, 2005n1068
Literary 100, rev ed, 2009n906
Mark Twain, 2005n1072
Webster's new explorer dict of American writers, 2005n1061
Writers dir 2005, 20th ed, 2005n1000
Writers dir 2006, 21st ed, 2006n977
Writers dir 2009, 24th ed, 2009n908

LITERATURE - CRITICISM

Children's lit review, v.96, 2005n1023
Children's lit review, v.97, 2005n1024
Children's lit review, v.98, 2005n1025
Classical & medieval lit criticism, v.66, 2005n977
Classical & medieval lit criticism, v.67, 2005n978
Classical & medieval lit criticism, v.68, 2005n979
Classical & medieval lit criticism, v.69, 2005n980
Contemporary literary criticism, v.189, 2005n981
Contemporary literary criticism, v.190, 2005n982
Contemporary literary criticism, v.191, 2005n983
Continuum ency of modern criticism & theory,
    2005n1003
Johns Hopkins gd to literary theory & criticism, 2d ed,
    2005n1005
Literature criticism from 1400 to 1800, v.100,
    2005n1009
Literature criticism from 1400 to 1800, v.101,
    2005n1010
Literature criticism from 1400 to 1800, v.102,
    2005n1011
Literature criticism from 1400 to 1800, v.103,
    2005n1012
Nineteenth-century lit criticism, v.138, 2005n987
Nineteenth-century lit criticism, v.139, 2005n988
Nineteenth-century lit criticism, v.140, 2005n989
Nineteenth-century lit criticism, v.141, 2005n990
Short stories for students, v.19, 2005n1054
Short stories for students, v.20, 2005n1055
Short stories for students, v.25, 2008n878
Twentieth-century literary criticism, v.149, 2005n991
Twentieth-century literary criticism, v.150, 2005n992
Twentieth-century literary criticism, v.151, 2005n993

LITERATURE - DICTIONARIES & ENCYCLOPEDIAS

Age of Milton, 2005n1002
Cambridge gd to lit in English, 3d ed, 2007n878
Chambers dict of literary characters, 2005n1044
Cyclopedia of YA authors, 2006n1001
Dictionary of American YA fiction, 1997-2001,
    2005n1027
Dictionary of literary & thematic terms, 2d ed, 2007n882
Dostoevsky ency, 2005n1097
Encyclopedia of African-American lit, 2009n956
Encyclopedia of American lit, rev ed, 2009n953
Encyclopedia of ancient lit, 2009n909
Encyclopedia of Catholic lit, 2006n979
Encyclopedia of erotic lit, 2007n922
Encyclopedia of Hispanic-American lit, 2009n984
Encyclopedia of lit & politics, 2007n880
Encyclopedia of medieval lit, 2006n984
Encyclopedia of modern Greek lit, 2005n1088
Encyclopedia of renaissance lit, 2006n978
Encyclopedia of renaissance lit, 2007n879
Encyclopedia of world writers: beginnings through the
    13th century, 2006n980

Encyclopedia of world writers: 14th through 18th
    centuries, 2006n981
Encyclopedia of world writers: 19th & 20th centuries,
    2006n982
Facts on File companion to the world novel, 2009n910
Feminist ency of Spanish lit, 2005n1089
Greenwood ency of Latino lit, 2009n982
Historical dict of lesbian lit, 2007n881
Holocaust lit, 2009n912
Johns Hopkins gd to literary theory & criticism
    [Website], 2009n913
Literary ency [Website], 2006n983
Oxford concise companion to English lit, 3d ed,
    2009n971
Oxford dict of literary terms, 3d ed, 2009n914
Oxford ency of American lit, 2005n1063
Poems, plays, & prose [Website], 2005n1006
Shakespeare's non-standard English, 2005n1079
South Asian lit in English, 2005n1084
Student ency of African lit, 2009n979
Student's ency of American literary characters,
    2009n957

LITERATURE – FICTION

Anatomy of wonder, 5th ed, 2006n1018
Baseball novel, 2009n939
BiblioTravel [Website], 2006n1009
Bioethics & medical issues in lit, 2006n1012
Blood, bedlam, bullets, & badguys: a reader's gd to
    adventure/suspense fiction, 2005n1040
Bookreporter.com [Website], 2006n972
Books & beyond, 2009n938
Canadian romance authors' networks (CRAN)
    [Website], 2006n1017
Chambers dict of literary characters, 2005n104
ClueLass.com & the mysterious home page [Website],
    2005n1047
Crime fiction Canada [Website], 2006n1013
Critical survey of mystery & detective fiction, rev ed,
    2009n941
Detective novels of Agatha Christie, 2009n944
Encountering enchantment, 2008n883
Encyclopedia of fantasy & horror fiction, 2007n929
Encyclopedia of gothic lit, 2005n1045
Encyclopedia of sci fiction, 2006n1024
Facts on File companion to the American novel,
    2007n940
Facts on File companion to the British novel,
    2006n1044
Fantastic fiction [Website], 2006n1010
Fiction catalog, 15th ed, 2007n916
Fluent in fantasy, 2009n946
Gay detective novel, 2005n1048
Historical dict of sci fiction lit, 2005n1051
Genreflecting, 6th ed, 2007n917
Gothic lit, 2007n930
Greenwood ency of sci fiction & fantasy, 2006n1025

Guide to the gothic 3, 2006n1016
Gumshoes: a dict of fictionary detectives, 2007n927
Historical dict of fantasy lit, 2006n1027
Historical dict of sci fiction lit, 2005n1051
Historical fiction, 2007n918
Historical fiction for young readers (grades 4-8),
    2009n922
Horror readers' advisory, 2005n1050
Internet speculative fiction database [Website],
    2006n1019
Latin American sci fiction writers, 2005n1091
Literary themes for students: race & prejudice,
    2007n923
Literary themes for students: war & peace, 2007n924
Locus online [Website], 2006n1020
Masterplots II: short story series, rev ed, 2005n1053
More bk lust, 2006n1011
Murder in retrospect, 2007n928
Mystery women, rev ed, 2007n926
Novels for students, v.19, 2005n1043
Novels for students, v.25, 2008n897
100 most popular genre fiction authors, 2007n921
Poisons in mystery lit, 2008n900
Primer of the novel, rev ed, 2007n925
Read on . . . fantasy fiction, 2008n904
Read on . . . histl fiction, 2008n901
Read on . . . horror fiction, 2007n931
Read the high country, 2007n933
Reference & research gd to mystery & detective
    fiction, 2d ed, 2005n1046
Rocked by romance, 2005n1016
Short stories for students, v.19, 2005n1054
Short stories for students, v.20, 2005n1055
Short stories for students, v.25, 2008n898
Short story index [Website], 2008n899
Short story writers, rev ed, 2008n875
Student's ency of American literary characters,
    2009n957
Supernatural lit of the world, 2007n932
Twentieth-century short story explication new series,
    v.6, 2005n1052
Ultimate mystery/detective Web gd [Website],
    2005n1049
Washington, D.C. of fiction, 2007n919
What do I read next? 2005 ed, 2007n920
What do I read next? v.1, 2004, 2005n1042
What do I read next? v.1, 2004, 2005n1042
What do I read next? v.2, 2003, 2005n1041
What do I read next? v.2, 2008 ed, 2009n940

LITERATURE - HANDBOOKS & YEARBOOKS
Bookshelf of our own, 2005n1007
Columbia gd to E African lit in English since 1945,
    2009n977
Columbia gd to W African lit in English since 1945,
    2009n978
Everyone & everything in Trollope, 2005n1081

Italian lit & its times, v.7, 2006n1060
Labor & workplace issues in lit, 2007n885
Literary newsmakers for students, v.2, 2008n877
Literary newsmakers for students, v.3, 2009n915
Literary themes for students, 2007n924
Literary themes for students: race & prejudice,
    2007n923
Literary themes for students: the American dream,
    2008n896
Literature & sci, 2006n986
Literature & the environment, 2005n1008
Literature of Africa, 2006n1056
Literature of the Caribbean, 2009n983
Magill's literary annual 2006, 2007n948
Magill's literary annual 2007, 2008n878
Magill's survey of American lit, 2008n910
Masterpieces of French lit, 2005n1087
New hndbk of literary terms, 2008n880
Novels for students, v.25, 2008n897
Oxford hndbk of English lit & theology, 2009n972
Primer of the novel, rev ed, 2007n925
Research gd for undergraduate students, 6th ed,
    2007n494
Social issues in lit series, 2009n917
Victorian lit hndbk, 2009n918
Youth gangs in lit, 2005n1030

LITERATURE - INDEXES
Index of Native American bk resources on the Internet
    [Website], 2006n1037

LITERATURE - MEDIEVAL
Classical & medieval lit criticism, v.66, 2005n977
Classical & medieval lit criticism, v.67, 2005n978
Classical & medieval lit criticism, v.68, 2005n979
Classical & medieval lit criticism, v.69, 2005n980

LITERATURE - QUOTATION BOOKS
Oxford dict of literary quotations, 2d ed, 2005n1013

LITERATURE - 20TH CENTURY
Beat culture, 2006n1033
Columbia gd to contemporary African American
    fiction, 2006n1035
Contemporary literary criticism, v.189, 2005n981
Contemporary literary criticism, v.190, 2005n982
Contemporary literary criticism, v.191, 2005n983
Critical companion to Tennessee Williams,
    2006n1041
Dictionary of literary influences, 2005n998
Encyclopedia of literary modernism, 2005n1004
Encyclopedia of the Harlem literary renaissance,
    2006n1034
Great world writers: 20th century, 2005n985
Historical dict of postmodernist lit & theater,
    2008n789
History in lit, 2005n1001

Masterpieces of 20th-century American drama,
    2006n1006
Twentieth-century literary criticism, v.149, 2005n991
Twentieth-century literary criticism, v.150, 2005n992
Twentieth-century literary criticism, v.151, 2005n993

LOBBYING, UNITED STATES
Research gd to US & intl interest groups, 2005n728

LOUISIANA
Louisiana almanac, 2006-07 ed, 2007n67
Louisiana almanac, 2008-09 ed, 2008n82
Louisiana coast, 2009n1191

MADAGASCAR
Historical dict of Madagascar, 2d ed, 2006n83

MAGAZINES
Age of the storytellers, 2007n781
British poetry mags 1914-2000, 2008n948

MAGIC
Encyclopedia of Jewish myth, magic, & mysticism,
    2008n1100

MAGNA CARTA
Magna Carta, 2005n488

MALI
Historical dict of mali, 4th ed, 2009n92

MAMMALS. *See also* ANIMALS
Atlas of mammalian chromosomes, 2007n1207
Carnivores of British Columbia, 2009n1204
Cats of Africa, 2008n1191
Encyclopedia of animal behavior, 2006n1364
Encyclopedia of mammals, 2d ed, 2007n1208
Evolving Eden: an illus gd to the evolution of the
    African
Exploring mammals, 2008n1188
Field gd to mammals of N America N of Mexico, 4th
    ed, 2007n1210
Field gd to N Atlantic wildlife, 2006n1366
Grzimek's student animal life resource: mammals,
    2006n1388
Mammal species of the world, 2007n1209
Mammals of Costa Rica, 2008n1193
Mammals of Ind., 2009n1207
Mammals of S America, 2008n1192
Mammals of S America, v.1, 2009n1205
Primate family tree, 2009n1206
Storey's illus breed gd to sheep, goats, cattle, & pigs,
    2009n1168
World atlas of great apes & their conservation,
    2006n1390
Large-mammal fauna, 2005n1383
Mammals of Calif., rev ed, 2005n1396

MANAGEMENT. *See* BUSINESS
MANAGEMENT; LIBRARY MANAGEMENT
Encyclopedia of mgmt, 5th ed, 2006n262
Encyclopedia of the hist of American mgmt, 2006n263

MANGA
Graphic novels, 2008n886

MANUFACTURERS. *See also* INDUSTRY
American wholesalers & distributors dir, 14th ed,
    2006n176
American wholesalers & distributors dir, 16th ed,
    2008n190
American wholesalers & distributors dir, 17th ed,
    2009n172
Directory of business to business catalogs 2004, 12the
    ed, 2005n190
Encyclopedia of products &
    industries—manufacturing, 2008n189
Manufacturing & distribution USA, 3d ed, 2005n199
Manufacturing & distribution USA, 5th ed, 2009n184

MANUSCRIPTS - MEDIEVAL
Catalogue of Medieval & Renaissance ms in the
    Beinecke rare bk & ms lib Yale Univ,
    2005n614

MAP COLLECTIONS
Guide to US map resources, 3d ed, 2006n384
Historical map & chart project [Website], 2006n376
Maps in the atlases of the British Lib, 2006n386
Historical map & chart project [Website], 2006n376
Mapping the silk road & beyond, 2006n385
Maps in the atlases of the British Lib, 2006n386

MARINE ANIMALS
Coastal gd to S Africa, 2009n1209
Firefly gd to seashells of the world, 2005n1398
Grzimek's student animal life resource: corals,
    jellyfishes, sponges, & other simple animals,
    2007n1212
Marine life of the Pacific NW, 2007n1214
Two oceans, 2009n1208

MARINE BIOLOGY
Facts on File dict of marine sci, new ed, 2008n1324

MARKETING
Asia-Pacific mktg info sourcebk, 2005n212
Best customers, 4th ed, 2007n229
Consumer USA 2004, 2005n261
Dictionary of mktg communications, 2005n255
Direct mktg market place 2008, 2009n234
Directory of mail order catalogs 2008, 22d ed,
    2008n179
Encyclopedia of major mktg campaigns, v.2,
    2007n227

European mktg data & stats 2004, 39th ed, 2005n218
European mktg forecasts 2004/05, 8th ed, 2005n219
European mktg forecasts 2005/06, 9th ed, 2006n219
International mktg data & stats 2004, 2005n263
International mktg forecasts 2003/04, 2005n264
International mktg forecasts 2005/06, 9th ed,
    2006n271
Latin American mktg data & stats 2007/08, 2009n204
Latin American mktg info sourcebk, 2005n223
Marketing gdbk, 2005, 2005n256
Marketing gdbk, 2008, 2008n255
Marketing gdbk, 2009, 2009n235
Marketing guidebk 2006, 2006n266
Plunkett's advertising & branding industry almanac,
    2005n257
Plunkett's advertising & branding industry almanac
    2006, 2007n228
Plunkett's advertising & branding industry almanac
    2007, 2008n256
Sports market place dir 2004, 2005n758
Trade shows worldwide, 20th ed, 2005n258
Trade shows worldwide, 22d ed, 2006n267
Trade shows worldwide, 23d ed, 2008n257
Who's buying series, 2d ed, 2007n231
World consumer expenditure patterns 2003, 4th ed,
    2005n268
World consumer lifestyles databk 2004, 3d ed,
    2005n270
World consumer lifestyles databk 2008, 2009n237
World consumer spending 2004/05, 5th ed, 2005n271

MARRIAGE CUSTOMS
Marriage customs of the world, 2006n808

MARRIAGE LAW
Marriage on trial, 2006n551

MARSUPIALS
Walker's marsupials of the world, 2006n1389

MARXISM
Historical dict of Marxism, 2007n1071

MARYLAND
Maryland State Archives atlas of histl maps of Md.
    1608-1908, 2006n381

MASKS
Masks & masking, 2007n258

MASS MEDIA
African Americans in the media today, 2008n310
AV market place 2006, 2007n784
Bacon's media calendar dir 2004, 22d ed, 2005n902
Bacon's newspaper dir 2004, 52d ed, 2005n903
Bacon's TV/cable dir 2004, 18th ed, 2005n906
Battleground: the media, 2009n795

Encyclopedia of children, adolescents, & the media,
    2007n764
Encyclopedia of media & pol, 2008n610
Encyclopedia of public relations, 2005n886
Gale dir of publications & broadcast media, 138th ed,
    2005n887
Gale dir of publications & broadcast media, 140th ed,
    2006n872
Gale dir of pubs & broadcast media, 143d ed,
    2009n797
Hudson's Washington news media contacts dir 2008,
    41st ed, 2009n798
International ency of communication, 2009n796
Latino media resource gd 2005, 2d ed, 2006n873
Media scandals, 2009n800
News media leadership dir online [Website],
    2009n810
News media yellow bk, Summer 2005 ed, 2006n888
Plunkett's entertainment & media industry almanac
    2004, 2005n888
Plunkett's entertainment & media industry almanac
    2006, 2007n173
Power of the news media, 2005n899
Skinny about dollies, best boys, green rooms, leads, &
    other media lingo, 2007n767
Violence in the media, 2006n875
Willings press gd 2004, 2005n889
Willings press gd 2007, 133d ed, 2008n792
Willings press gd 2008, 134th ed, 2009n799

MASS MEDIA & CRIMINAL JUSTICE
Media & American courts, 2005n539

MASSACHUSETTS
Massachusetts municipal profiles, 2007 ed, 2008n83
Profiles of Mass., 2006, 2007n68

MATERIALS SCIENCE
Encyclopedia of corrosion tech, 2d ed, 2005n1414

MATHEMATICIANS
A to Z of mathematicians, 2006n1525
Biographies of women mathematicians [Website],
    2005n1527
Biographies of women mathematicians [Website],
    2007n1319
Combined membership list 2004-05, 2006n1529
Mathematical scis professional dir 2005, 2006n1530

MATHEMATICS
Assistantships & graduate fellowships in the
    mathematical scis 2005, 2006n1528
Cornell Univ lib of histl mathematics monographs
    [Website], 2005n1529
Cornell Univ Lib of histl mathematics monographs
    [Website], 2008n1330

Distributed digital lib of mathematical monographs [Website], 2005n1530
Distributed digital lib of mathematical monographs [Website], 2008n1331
Encyclopedia of mathematics, 2006n1527
Essential atlas of mathematics, 2006n1532
Facts on File dict of mathematics, 4th ed, 2006n1526
Guide to info sources in mathematics & stats, 2006n1524
Handbook of intl research in mathematics educ, 2d ed, 2009n1325
Handy math answer bk, 2006n1531
History of mathematics series, 2005n1534
Jahrbuch-Project, electronic research archive for mathematics [Website], 2005n1531
MacTutor hist of mathematics [Website], 2005n1528
MacTutor hist of mathematics archive [Website], 2008n1332
Math archives [Website], 2005n1532
Math forum Internet mathematics lib [Website], 2005n1533
Math forum Internet mathematics lib [Website], 2008n1333
Math on file: calculus, 2005n1535
Mathematics on the Web [Website], 2005n1526
Mathematics on the Web [Website], 2007n1320
Project euclid [Website], 2005n842
Real-life math, 2007n1321

MAURITANIA
Historical dict of Mauritania, 3d ed, 2009n86

MECHANICAL ENGINEERING
Encyclopedia of computational mechanics, 2006n1393
Marks' standard hndbk for mechanical engineers, 11th ed, 2007n1228
Mechanical engineers' hndbk, 3d ed, 2008n1201
Mechanisms & mechanical devices sourcebk, 4th ed, 2008n1202

MEDIA LIBRARIANSHIP
Handbook for media librarians, 2009n528

MEDICAL ANTHROPOLOGY
Encyclopedia of medical anthropology, 2006n321

MEDICAL ECONOMICS
Dictionary of health economics, 2006n1410

MEDICAL EDUCATION
Complete bk of medical schools, 2004 ed, 2005n299
Nursing programs 2006, 11th ed, 2006n1456
RSP funding for nursing students & nurses 2004-06, 4th ed, 2005n1476
Ultimate gd to medical schools, 2006n291
U.S. News & World Report ultimate gd to medical schools, 2d ed, 2008n283

MEDICAL INSTRUMENTS
Encyclopedia of medical devices & instrumentation, 2d ed, 2007n1233
Medical device register 2007, 27th ed, 2008n1215
Medical device register 2008, 28th ed, 2008n1216

MEDICAL LAWS
Medicine on trial, 2005n545

MEDICAL LIBRARIES
Answering consumer health questions, 2009n587
Answers to the health questions people ask in libs, 2009n532
Drug info, 3d ed, 2009n1273
Essential gd to becoming an expert searcher, 2009n531
Guide to developing end user educ programs in medical libs, 2006n610
Introduction to health scis librarianship, 2009n529
Introduction to ref sources in the health sci, 5th ed, 2009n530
Medical Lib Assn gd to health literacy, 2009n535
Using benchmarking, needs assessment, quality improvement, outcome measurement, & lib standards, 2008n520

MEDICAL TESTS
Consumer's gd to lab tests, 2006n1427
Gale ency of surgery & medical tests, 2d ed, 2009n1238
Medical tests sourcebk, 3d ed, 2009n1247
Mosby's diagnostic & lab test ref, 7th ed, 2006n1425
PDR lab advisor 2007, 2008n1217

MEDICINAL PLANTS
Medicinal plants in folk tradition, 2005n1347
Medicinal plants of the world, 2005n1352
Medicinal plants of N America, 2009n1178

MEDICINE - BIBLIOGRAPHY
Introduction to ref sources in the health scis, 4th ed, 2005n1415

MEDICINE - BIOGRAPHIES
Parkinson's disease, 2009n1234
Who's who in medicine & healthcare 2004-05, 5th ed, 2005n1416

MEDICINE - DICTIONARIES & ENCYCLOPEDIAS
American Heritage medical dict, new ed, 2008n1223
American Heritage Stedman's medical dict, 2d ed, 2005n1432
American Medical Assn concise medical ency, 2007n1245
Black's medical dict, 40th ed, 2005n1433
Black's medical dict, 41st ed, 2007n1246
Cancer dict, 3d ed, 2008n1251

Concise dict of modern medicine, 2007n1250
Dictionary of clinical trials, 2d ed, 2008n1206
Dictionary of orthopedic terminology, 2009n1259
Diseases, 3d ed, 2007n1248
Diseases & disorders, 2008n1224
Elsevier's dict of abbrevs, acronyms, synonyms, &
　　　symbols used in medicine, 2d ed, 2005n1434
Elsevier's dict of medicine: Spanish-English &
　　　English-Spanish, 2005n1435
Encyclopedia of autism spectrum disorders,
　　　2007n1269
Encyclopedia of breast cancer, 2005n1464
Encyclopedia of cancer, 2006n1447
Encyclopedia of children's health & wellness,
　　　2005n1459
Encyclopedia of endocrine diseases & disorders,
　　　2006n1430
Encyclopedia of epidemiology, 2008n1225
Encyclopedia of family health, 3d ed, 2005n1436
Encyclopedia of family health & wellness, 2009n1236
Encyclopedia of genetic disorders & birth defects, 3d
　　　ed, 2009n1242
Encyclopedia of hepatitis & other liver diseases,
　　　2007n1273
Encyclopedia of infectious diseases, 2008n1226
Encyclopedia of infectious diseases, 3d ed, 2008n1232
Encyclopedia of men's health, 2006n1431
Encyclopedia of men's reproductive cancer,
　　　2005n1463
Encyclopedia of multiple sclerosis, 2006n1451
Encyclopedia of obesity & eating disorders, 3d ed,
　　　2007n1272
Encyclopedia of Parkinson's disease, 2005n1471
Encyclopedia of sexually transmitted diseases,
　　　2005n1472
Encyclopedia of skin & skin disorders, 3d ed,
　　　2007n1276
Encyclopedia of sports medicine, 2005n1473
Encyclopedia of stress & stress-related diseases, 2d ed,
　　　2007n1247
Encyclopedia of the back & spine systems &
　　　disorders, 2008n1248
Encyclopedia of the digestive system & digestive
　　　disorders, 2005n1439
Encyclopedia of the heart & heart disease, 2005n1468
Encyclopedia of the muscle & skeletal systems &
　　　disorders, 2006n1432
Encyclopedia of women's health, 5th ed, 2006n1428
Encyclopedia of women's reproductive cancer,
　　　2005n1465
Encyclopedic ref of immunotoxicology, 2007n1251
Facts on File ency of health & medicine, 2008n1227
Gale ency of alternative medicine, 2d ed, 2006n1439
Gale ency of cancer, 2d ed, 2006n1446
Gale ency of children's health, 2006n1440
Gale ency of genetic disorders, 2d ed, 2006n1360
Gale ency of medicine, 3d ed, 2007n1249

Gale ency of neurological disorders, 2005n1437
Gale ency of surgery & medical tests, 2d ed,
　　　2009n1238
Health ref center [Website], 2008n1228
Infectious diseases in context, 2008n1229
Magill's medical gd, 3d rev ed, 2005n1438
Magill's medical gd, 4th rev ed, 2008n1230
Merck manual of diagnosis & therapy [Website],
　　　2008n1234
Merriam-Webster's medical desk dict, rev ed,
　　　2006n1429
New Harvard gd to women's health, 2005n1440
Salem health [Website], 2008n1231
Salem health: cancer, 2009n1263
Webster's new explorer medical dict, new ed,
　　　2007n1252

MEDICINE - HANDBOOKS & YEARBOOKS

A-Z common symptom answer gd, 2005n1451
American College of Physicians complete home
　　　medical gd, 2d ed, 2005n1442
American Medical Assn family medical gd, 4th ed,
　　　2006n1434
Current medical diagnosis & treatment 2004, 43d ed,
　　　2005n1444
Current medical diagnosis & treatment 2007, 46th ed,
　　　2007n1255
Infectious diseases sourcebk, 2005n1448
Johns Hopkins medical gd to health after 50,
　　　2005n1449
Medicine, health, & bioethics, 2007n1242
Merck manual of diagnosis & therapy, 18th ed,
　　　2007n1259

MEDICINE - HISTORY

Medical marvels, 2007n1261
Medicina Antiqua [Website], 2007n1244

MEDICINE IN LITERATURE

Bioethics & medical issues in lit, 2006n1012

MEDICINE - POPULAR

Accident & safety info for teens, 2009n1268
Adolescent health sourcebk, 2d ed, 2007n1254
Adult health concerns sourcebk, 2009n1243
Allergy info for teens, 2007n1267
Alzheimer disease sourcebk, 4th ed, 2009n1260
Arthritis, 2009n1261
Arthritis sourcebk, 2d ed, 2005n1460
Asthma info for teens, 2006n1442
Asthma sourcebk, 2d ed, 2007n1268
Back & neck sourcebk, 2d ed, 2006n1435
Blood & circulatory disorders sourcebk, 2d ed,
　　　2006n1443
Brain disorders sourcebk, 2d ed, 2006n1444
Breast cancer sourcebk, 2d ed, 2006n1445
Cancer info for teens, 2005n1461

Cancer sourcebk, 5th ed, 2008n1253
Cancer sourcebk for women, 3d ed, 2007n1270
Cancer survivorship sourcebk, 2008n1254
Cardiovascular diseases & disorders sourcebk, 3d ed, 2006n1449
Congenital disorders sourcebk, 2d ed, 2008n1233
Contagious diseases sourcebk, 2005n1443
Dermatological disorders sourcebk, 2d ed, 2006n1452
Diabetes info for teens, 2007n1271
Disease mgmt sourcebk, 2009n1244
Diseases & disorders series, 2009n1245
Ear, nose & throat disorders sourcebk, 2d ed, 2007n1257
Eating disorders, rev ed, 2005n1467
Eating disorders info for teens, 2006n1448
Eating disorders sourcebk, 2d ed, 2008n1255
Eye care sourcebk, 3d ed, 2009n1258
Gastrointestinal diseases & disorders sourcebk, 2d ed, 2007n1258
Genetic disorders sourcebk, 3d ed, 2005n1446
Healthy woman, 2009n1246
Hepatitis, 2007n1274
Hepatitis sourcebk, 2006n1450
Hypertension sourcebk, 2005n1469
Immune system disorders sourcebk, 2d ed, 2006n1436
Infectious diseases sourcebk, 2005n1448
Internet gd to cosmetic surgery for men, 2007n1253
Men's health concerns sourcebk, 2d ed, 2005n1450
Menopause bible, 2006n1437
Muscular dystrophy sourcebk, 2005n1470
Pain sourcebk, 3d ed, 2009n1248
Perspectives on diseases & disorders series, 2009n1249
Podiatry sourcebk, 2d ed, 2008n1235
Pregnancy & birth sourcebk, 2d ed, 2005n1456
Prostate & urological disorders sourcebk, 2007n1260
Respiratory disorders sourcebk, 2d ed, 2009n1266
Sexually transmitted diseases sourcebk, 3d ed, 2007n1275
Sleep disorders sourcebk, 2d ed, 2006n1438
Sports injuries info for teens, 2d ed, 2009n1269
Stress info for teens, 2009n1251
Stroke sourcebk, 2d ed, 2009n1252
Surgery sourcebk, 2d ed, 2009n1253
Thyroid disorders sourcebk, 2006n1453
Urinary tract & kidney diseases & disorders sourcebk, 2d ed, 2006n1433
Women's health concerns sourcebk, 2d ed, 2005n1452

MEDIEVAL HISTORY
Atlas of the medieval world, 2006n487
Daily life in the medieval Islamic world, 2006n1243
Encyclopedia of society & culture in the medieval world, 2009n425
Handbook to life in the medieval world, 2009n401
Historical dict of medieval China, 2009n400
Historical dict of medieval India, 2009n101

History of the ancient & medieval world, 2d ed, 2009n428
Key figures in Medieval Europe, 2007n381
Kingfisher atlas of the medieval world, 2008n427
Knights Templar ency, 2008n428
Medieval castles, 2006n513
Medieval cathedrals, 2007n383
Medieval city, 2006n469
Medieval Ireland, 2006n475
New Cambridge medieval hist, 2007n432
New Cambridge medieval hist, v.4, 2006n511
Penguin histl atlas of the medieval world, 2007n376

MEDIEVAL LITERATURE
Encyclopedia of medieval lit, 2007n883

MELVILLE, HERMAN, 1819-1891
Understanding Melville's short fiction, 2006n1038

MEN'S HEALTH
Encyclopedia of men's health, 2006n1431
Encyclopedia of men's reproductive cancer, 2005n1463
Men's health concerns sourcebk, 2d ed, 2005n1450

MEN'S STUDIES
International ency of men & masculinities, 2008n726
Metrosexual gd to style, 2005n1175

MENTAL HEALTH. *See also* **PSYCHOLOGY**
Complete mental health dir 2004, 4th ed, 2005n739
Complete mental health dir 2008, 6th ed, 2009n704
Complete mental health dir [Website], 2005n740
Depression sourcebk, 2d ed, 2009n712
Encyclopedia of counseling, 2009n701
Encyclopedia of mental health, 3d ed, 2008n679
Gale ency of mental health, 2d ed, 2008n678
Insider's gd to mental health resources online, rev ed, 2005n741
Mental health disorders sourcebk, 3d ed, 2006n759
Mental health in America, 2008n690
Mental health issues of older women, 2008n691

MENTAL HEALTH PERSONNEL IN MOTION PICTURES
Psychotherapists on film, 1899-1999, 2005n1194

MERTON, THOMAS, 1915-1968
More than silence: a bibliog of Thomas Merton, 2009n1102

METADATA
Metadata, 2009n574

METEOROLOGY. *See* **CLIMATOLOGY; WEATHER**

MEXICAN WAR, 1846-1848
Mexican War, 2006n452

MEXICO
Brief hist of Mexico, rev ed, 2005n498
Culture & customs of Mexico, 2005n121
Fodor's Mexico 2006, 2006n418
Food culture in Mexico, 2006n1289
Junior worldmark ency of the Mexican states, 2006n108
Junior worldmark ency of the Mexican states, 2d ed, 2008n140
Mexico, 2005n120
Mexico, 2009n123
Mexico & Central America hndbk 2009, 17th ed, 2009n354
World & its peoples: Mexico & Central America, 2009n124

MICHIGAN
Profiles of Mich., 2007n69
Profiles of Mich. 2008, 2d ed, 2009n75

MICROSCOPY
Dictionary of microscopy, 2006n1257

MIDDLE AGES, HISTORY
Daily life of Jews in the Middle Ages, 2006n348
Encyclopedia of the Byzantine empire, 2005n473
Exploring the Middle Ages, 2006n467
Great events from hist: the Middle Ages, 477-1453, 2005n516
Great lives from hist: the Middle Ages, 477-1453, 2005n512
Palgrave atlas of Byzantine hist, 2006n466

MIDDLE AGES IN LITERATURE
Middle Ages in lit for youth, 2005n1015

MIDDLE EAST
Aerial atlas of the Holy Land, 2009n125
Atlas of the Middle East & N Africa, 2007n118
Biographical ency of the modern Middle East & N Africa, 2008n142
Cities of the Middle East & N Africa, 2007n122
Companion to the hist of the Middle East, 2006n483
Discovering world cultures: the Middle East, 2005n123
Historical dict of the Gulf Arab States, 2d ed, 2008n144
History in dispute, v.14: the Middle East since 1945, 2005n501
Middle East, 10th ed, 2006n110
Middle East conflict: almanac, 2006n111
Middle East conflict: biogs, 2006n112
Middle East conflict: primary sources, 2006n113
100 myths about the Middle East, 2007n125

Peoples of W Asia, 2007n92
Pop culture Arab world! 2006n1126
State of the Middle East, 2007n119
Who's who in the Arab world 2007-08, 18th ed, 2007n121
World & its peoples: Middle East, W Africa, & N Africa, 2007n124
World & its peoples: Middle East, W Asia, & N Africa, 2008n145

MIDDLE EAST, BUSINESS
Consumer Middle East 2006, 8th ed, 2006n223
Major companies of the Arab world 2006, 29th ed, 2006n224
Major companies of the Arab world 2008, 31st ed, 2008n222

MIDDLE EAST, INTERNATIONAL RELATIONS. *See also* INTERNATIONAL RELATIONS
Encyclopedia of Arab-Israeli conflict, 2009n127
Historical dict of the Arab-Israeli conflict, 2007n123

MIDDLE EAST, POLITICS
Contemporary Middle East, 2008n146
Historical dict of US-Middle East relations, 2008n663
Middle East, 11th ed, 2008n147
Middle East strategic balance 2004-05, 2008n656
Middle East studies Internet resources [Website], 2008n141
Political hndbk of the Middle East 2006, 2007n630
Political hndbk of the Middle East 2008, 2009n670
State of the Middle East, updated 2d ed, 2009n126

MIDDLE EASTERN LITERATURE
Arabian Nights ency, 2005n1093
Middle Eastern lit & their times, 2005n1094

MILITARY AIRCRAFT
Aviation century: WW II, 2005n1547
B-29 Superfortress, 2005n677
F-15 Eagle engaged, 2008n602
Graphic war, 2006n666
Military aircraft, origins to 1918, 2006n678
Naval Institute gd to the ships & aircraft of the US Fleet, 18th ed, 2006n675
One hundred yrs of world military aircraft, 2005n676

MILITARY FAMILIES
Your military family network, 2008n724

MILITARY HISTORY
A to Z of the Korean War, 2006n462
Age of sail, v.2, 2005n672
Age of wars of religion, 2008n587
American generals of the Revolutionary War, 2008n572

American Naval hist, 3d ed, 2005n675
American soldiers' lives: WW I, 2007n564
Atlas of American military hist, 2006n658
Battle of Iwo Jima, 2006n488
Battlefield, 2008n590
Brassey's D-day ency, 2005n660
Chronology of the Cold War 1917-92, 2006n659
Chronology of the war at sea, 1939-45, 3d rev ed,
     2006n669
Civil wars of the world, 2008n579
Dictionary of wars, 3d ed, 2008n581
Empires at war, 2006n662
Encyclopedia of African American military hist,
     2005n665
Encyclopedia of conflicts since WWII, 2008n582
Encyclopedia of invasions & conquests from the
     ancient times to the present, 2d ed, 2007n550
Encyclopedia of warrior peoples & fighting groups, 2d
     ed, 2007n549
Encyclopedia of WW I, 2006n497
Encyclopedia of WW II, 2006n498
Fatal Army Air Forces aviation accidents in the US
     1941-45, 2007n548
Fortress America, 2005n455
Greenwood lib of American war reporting, 2007n562
Hill wars of the Korean conflict, 2006n463
Historical dict of the Russo-Japanese War, 2007n557
History in dispute, v.18: The Spanish Civil War,
     2006n481
History of WW II, 2005n529
Home front ency, 2008n584
Home front heroes, 2007n337
International ency of military hist, 2007n555
Land battles in 5th century BC Greece, 2009n602
Medal of Honor citations [Website], 2008n576
Military aircraft, 1919-45, 2009n615
Military ink [Website], 2009n599
Military medicine, 2009n606
On the trail of the buffalo soldier, 2005n657
Soldiers' lives through hist: ancient world, 2008n593
Soldiers' lives through hist: the early modern world,
     2008n597
Soldiers' lives through hist: the Middle Ages,
     2008n595
Uniforms, arms, & equipment, 2008n607
United States at war [Website], 2009n607
Victorians at war 1815-1914, 2005n663
Warfare & armed conflicts, 3d ed, 2009n604
Warrior, 2009n609
Wars of the Americas, 2d ed, 2009n601
Women & war, 2007n760
World military leaders, 2008n574
World War I, 2006n505
World War II, 2005n519
World War II, 2006n506
World War II, 2009n608

MILITARY INTELLIGENCE
Encyclopedia of Cold War espionage, spies, & secret
     operations, 2005n664
Historical dict of British intelligence, 2006n665
Historical dict of US intelligence, 2006n663
Historical dict of WW II intelligence, 2008n589
Intelligence & natl security, 2008n592
Military communications, 2008n594
Researching natl security & intelligence, 2005n730

MILITARY STUDIES
Air Univ Lib index to military per [Website], 2005n670
Aircraft carriers, 2007n571
Aircraft markings of the Strategic Air Command,
     1946-53, 2007n565
Armed conflict database [Website], 2008n577
Black American military leaders, 2008n575
Civilian's gd to the U.S military, 2008n596
Dictionary of battles & sieges, 2007n556
Dictionary of wars, 3d ed, 2007n551
Encyclopedia of the American armed forces,
     2006n660
Encyclopedia of US natl security, 2007n642
Encyclopedia of wars, 2005n662
Historical dict of nuclear, biological, & chemical
     warfare, 2008n601
Iraq War, 2005n666
Space warfare & defense, 2009n603
United States at war, 2006n664
US military serv, 2008n598
Weapons of mass destruction, 2007n570

MILITARY WEAPONS
Aircraft carriers, 2007n571
Battleships, 2006n680
Chemical & biological warfare, 2d ed, 2007n572
Cruisers & battle cruisers, 2005n679
Destroyers, 2006n679
Encyclopedia of military tech & innovation, 2005n661
Helicopters, 2006n677
Historical dict of nuclear, biological, & chemical
     warfare, 2008n601
Machine guns, 2006n682
Medieval weapons, 2008n603
Naval Institute gd to combat fleets of the world
     2005-06, 2006n674
Naval Institute gd to the ships & aircraft of the US
     Fleet, 18th ed, 2006n675
Naval Institute gd to world naval weapon systems, 5th
     ed, 2007n573
Nuclear weapons & nonproliferation, 2d ed, 2008n604
Rifles, 2006n681
Rockets & missiles, 2005n682
Submarines, 2008n605
Tanks, 2005n681
Uniforms, arms, & equipment, 2008n607
US destroyers, rev ed, 2005n678

MINERALOGY

Field gd to gold, gemstone, & mineral sites of British
    Columbia, v.2, rev ed, 2007n1312
Firefly gd to gems, 2005n1516
Minerals, 2006n1516
Rock & gem, 2006n1512
Rocks & fossils, 2006n1514

MOBILE COMMUNICATIONS SYSTEMS

Encyclopedia of mobile computing & commerce,
    2008n1271
Handbook of research on mobile multimedia, 2d ed,
    2009n1293

MOLDOVA

Historical dict of Moldova, 2d ed, 2008n125

MONARCHY, HISTORY

World monarchies & dynasties, 2006n504

MONEY

World monetary units, 2006n119

MONGOLIA

Culture & customs of Mongolia, 2009n103
Daily life in the Mongol Empire, 2007n375
Encyclopedia of Mongolia & the Mongol empire,
    2005n466
Genghis Khan & Mongol rule, 2005n468

MONROE, JAMES, 1758-1831

Papers of James Monroe, v. 2, 2007n618

MOON

New atlas of the moon, 2008n1301

MORMONISM

Historical dict of Mormonism, 3d ed, 2009n1106

MOROCCO

Culture & customs of Morocco, 2006n84
Historical dict of Morocco, 2d ed, 2007n88

MOTION PICTURE ACTORS & ACTRESSES.
See ACTORS

MOTION PICTURE DIRECTORS

Brothers grim, 2008n1034
Dictionary of African filmmakers, 2009n1061
Directors up close, 2d ed, 2006n1163
Encyclopedia of Arab American filmmakers,
    2007n1047
Italian horror film directors, 2005n1191

MOTION PICTURE - DIRECTORIES

Blu-bk production dir, 2004, 2005n1182
Blu-bk production dir 2005, 2006n1129

Blu-bk production dir 2006, 2007n1037
Hollywood creative dir, Spring 2004, 50th ed,
    2005n1186
Hollywood creative dir, Spring 2006, 56th ed,
    2006n1130
Hollywood distributors dir 2005, 16th ed, 2006n1131
Hollywood representation dir, 30th ed, 2006n1132
Movieland dir, 2005n1203
Ultimate film festival survival gd, 3d ed, 2005n1201

MOTION PICTURE MUSIC

Best songs of the movies, 2006n1164

MOTION PICTURE THEATERS

Historic movie theatres in Ill., 1883-1960, 2008n1010

MOTION PICTURES

Abraham Lincoln on screen, 2d ed, 2009n1059
All movie gd [Website], 2006n1138
American frontiersmen on film, 2006n1158
American plays & musicals on screen, 2005n1197
Animated movie gd, 2007n1041
Batman filmography, 2005n1206
BFI film & TV hndbk 2004, 21st ed, 2005n1209
Bob Hope films, 2006n1162
Boxing filmography, 2005n1207
British film noir gd, 2009n1056
British horror film locations, 2009n1058
Casting might-have-beens, 2005n1202
Chambers film factfinder, 2007n1050History in the
    media, 2007n1051
Cinema spot [Website], 2006n1152
Cinema yr by yr 1894-2004, 2005n1195
CineMedia [Website], 2006n1153
Columbia companion to American hist on film,
    2005n1210
Controversial cinema, 2009n1070
Creature features, 2009n1069
Encyclopedia of early cinema, 2006n1148
Encyclopedia of film noir, 2008n1018
Encyclopedia of Hollywood, 2d ed, 2005n1199
Encyclopedia of novels into film, 2d ed, 2006n1151
Encyclopedia of opera on screen, 2005n1200
Encyclopedia of superheroes on film & TV,
    2005n1198
Encyclopedia of war movies, 2005n1196
Enser's filmed bks & plays, 6th ed, 2005n1193
Epic films, 2d ed, 2005n1214
Film, folklore, & urban legends, 2008n1032
Film in Latin America [Website], 2006n1135
Film studies resources—academic info [Website],
    2006n1154
Filmography of social issues, 2006n1161
Filmography of world hist, 2008n1028
Flickipedia, 2008n1013
Frame by frame III, 2008n1025

Great composers portrayed on film, 1913-2002, 2005n1190

Great Spanish films since 1950, 2009n1071

Guerilla film makers hndbk, 2005n1211

Harrison Ford, 2006n1159

Historical dict of African American cinema, 2008n1014

Historical dict of Australian & New Zealand cinema, 2006n1150

Historical dict of French cinema, 2008n1016

Historical dict of Hong Kong cinema, 2008n1022

Historical dict of Irish cinema, 2008n1015

Historical dict of Italian cinema, 2009n1063

Historical dict of Polish cinema, 2008n1017

Historical dict of westerns in cinema, 2009n1066

Historical Dictionary of German cinema, 2009n1064

Horror films of the 1980s, 2008n1026

Image of librarians in cinema, 1917-99, 2006n1166

Internet movie database [Website], 2006n1155

John Wayne filmography, 2005n1205

Literary filmography, 2007n104

Magill's cinema annual 2004, 23d ed, 2005n1212

Magill's cinema annual 2008, 27th ed, 2009n1057

Movie archive [Website], 2006n1141

Movie tome [Website], 2006n1156

Multicultural films, 2006n1146

1001 movies you must see before you die, 2005n1213

Plato & popcorn: a philosopher's gd to 75 thought-provoking movies, 2005n1215

Prehistoric humans in film & TV, 2007n1043

Psychotherapists on film, 1899-1999, 2005n1194

Queer ency of film & TV, 2007n1048

Reel women, 2008n1029

Rock & roll film ency, 2008n1020

Saints, clergy, & other religious figures on film & TV, 1895-2003, 2006n1143

Schirmer ency of film, 2008n1021

Serial film stars, 2006n1136

Shakespeare: a hundred yrs on film, 2005n1208

Show me the money! 2006n1144

Silent cinema in song, 1896-1929, 2009n1060

Special effects artists, 2009n1053

Sports cinema 100 movies, 2007n1052

Stars & stripes on screen, 2006n1145

Teachers in the movies, 2008n1027

Television fright films of the 1970s, 2008n1024

Toho studios story, 2009n1067

Universal horrors, 2d ed, 2008n1030

Western film series of the sound era, 2009n1068

MOTION PICTURES - REVIEWS

Best DVDs you've never seen, just missed, or almost forgotten, 2006n1167

DVD & video gd 2004, 2005n1216

Flickipedia, 2009n1054

Greatest films [Website], 2006n1160

Leonard Maltin's movie gd, 2006 ed, 2006n1168

Metacritic [Website], 2006n1169

Movie review query engine (MRQE) [Website], 2006n1142

VideoHound's golden movie retriever 2005, 2005n1217

VideoHound's golden movie retriever 2006, 2006n1170

VideoHound's golden movie retriever, 2009 ed, 2009n1072

MOUNTAINS

Firefly gd to mountains, 2007n1311

First ascent, 2009n737

Mountain ency, 2006n794

MOZAMBIQUE

Culture & customs of Mozambique, 2007n89

MOZART, WOLFGANG AMADEUS, 1756-1791

Cambridge Mozart ency, 2006n1080

MULTICULTURALISM. *See also* CULTURES

Achieving diversity, 2008n554

Educators gd to free multicultural materials 2007-08, 10th ed, 2008n271

Multicultural & ethnic children's lit in the US, 2008n889

MULTICULTURALISM IN LITERATURE

Across cultures, 2009n921

Building character through multicultural lit, 2005n611

Children's & YA lit by Native Americans, 2005n1021

Crossing boundaries with children's bks, 2007n888

Cultural journeys, 2007n912

Ethnic bk awards, 2006n1004

Greenwood ency of multiethnic American lit, 2007n942

International children's digital lib [Website], 2005n1019

Recommended bks in Spanish for children & YAs, 2006n994

MULTIMEDIA COMMUNICATIONS

Encyclopedia of multimedia tech & networking, 2006n1466

Encyclopedia of multimedia tech & networking [Website], 2006n1467

New media, 2007n1289

MULTIMEDIA TECHNOLOGY

Encyclopedia of multimedia tech & networking, 2d ed, 2009n1283

MUSCULAR DYSTROPHY

Encyclopedia of the muscle & skeletal systems & disorders, 2006n1432

Muscular dystrophy sourcebk, 2005n1470

MUSEUMS

Art museum image gallery [Website], 2009n848
Halls of fame, 2005n56
Institute of museum & lib servs [Website], 2009n489
International dir of arts 2003, 27th ed, 2005n884
Museums, libs, & urban vitality, 2009n536
Museums of the world, 14th ed, 2008n47
Official museum dir 2007, 37th ed, 2008n48
Sports museums & halls of fame worldwide, 2006n769
Women & museums, 2006n54

MUSHROOMS

Mushrooms & other fungi of N America, repr ed,
    2007n1182
North American mushrooms, 2007n1181

MUSIC - BIBLIOGRAPHY

American pol music, 2006n1072
Analyses of 19th- & 20th-century music, 2008n962
Archives of traditional music [Website], 2008n961
Children's jukebox, 2d ed, 2008n963
Confederate sheet music, 2005n1116
Grawemeyer award for music composition, 2008n966
Historical dict of sacred music, 2007n1016
Orchestral music, 4th ed, 2006n1093
Penguin gd to compact discs & DVDs, 2003/2004 ed,
    2006n1090
Popular music teaching hndbk, 2005n1138

MUSIC - BIO-BIBLIOGRAPHY

Recent American art song, 2009n1010

MUSIC - BIOGRAPHIES

Exploring Haydn, 2006n1081
Icons of hip-hop, 2008n988
International who's who in classical music 2006,
    2007n1000
International who's who in popular music 2006, 8th
    ed, 2007n1005
International who's who in popular music 2009,
    2009n1017
Lives & times of the great composers, 2005n1133
Louis Armstrong, 2005n1132
Maestros in America, 2009n1013
New generation of country music stars, 2009n1019
Rock band name origins, 2009n1026
Satchmo: the Louis Armstrong ency, 2005n1131
Stan Getz, 2005n1128
Who's who of British jazz, 2d ed, 2005n1150
Women composers, v.7, 2005n1117
Yevgeny Mravinsky, 2006n1083

MUSIC - CATALOGS & COLLECTIONS

All Music gd to country, 2d ed, 2005n1147
Catalogue of music for organ & instruments,
    2006n1085
Naxos music lib [Website], 2009n1011

Sousa at Ill.: a catalogue of the collections, 2006n1078
Twentieth-century countertenor repertoire, 2009n1012

MUSIC - DICTIONARIES & ENCYCLOPEDIAS

A to X of alternative music, 2005n1141
Art of the piano, 3d ed, 2005n1134
Billboard ency of classical music, 2005n1136
Billboard illus ency of country music, 2009n1018
Billboard illus ency of music, 2005n1139
Continuum ency of popular music of the world, v.3-7,
    2006n1094
Cuban music from A to Z, 2005n1121
Encyclopedia of American gospel music, 2006n1112
Encyclopedia of native music, 2006n1091
Encyclopedia of rap & hip hop culture, 2007n1009
Encyclopedia of recorded sound, 2d ed, 2005n1119
Facts on File dict of music, 2005n1118
Free jazz & free improvisation, 2005n1151
Greenwood ency of rock hist, 2007n1014
Harvard dict of music, 4th ed, 2005n1120
Keys to the rain: the definitive Bob Dylan ency,
    2006n1111
Later swing era, 1942 to 1955, 2005n1140
Music abbrevs, 2006n1073
Penguin companion to classical music, 2007n999
Performance practice, 2006n1074

MUSIC - DIRECTORIES

Directory of conductors' archives in American
    institutions, 2007n987
Hollywood music industry dir, premier ed 2004,
    2005n1122
Hollywood music industry dir 2006, 3d ed, 2006n1076
Hollywood music industry dir 2008, 5th ed, 2008n968
Music publishers' intl ISMN dir 2003, 4th ed,
    2005n1123

MUSIC - DISCOGRAPHY

American political music, 2007n985
New York philharmonic, 2007n986

MUSIC - HANDBOOKS & YEARBOOKS

American songbk, 2007n1004
English glee in the reign of George III, 2005n1126
Guide to musical temperament, 2006n1087
Hit singles, 5th ed, 2006n1095
Joel Whitburn presents hot country albums,
    2009n1020
Joel Whitburn presents rock tracks 1981-2008,
    2009n1025
Joel Whitburn's music yrbk, 2003, 2005n1145
Joel Whitburn's 2004 music yrbk, 2006n1096
Music lust, 2007n990
Music of the Civil War era, 2005n1124
Music of the colonial & revolutionary era, 2005n1125
Music of the counterculture era, 2005n1146
Musical biog, 2007n983

National anthems of the world, 11th ed, 2008n969
Oxford hist of western music, 2005n1127
Sourcebook for research in music, 2d ed, 2007n989

MUSIC, HISTORY
Cambridge hist of 17th-century music, 2007n988
Folk music, 2006n1103
Music of the Great Depression, 2006n1077
Music of the postwar era, 2008n971
Smithsonian global sound [Website], 2008n967
World War I sheet music, 2008n970

MUSIC - INDEXES
Hit records, 1950-75, 2006n1097
Popular song index, 4th suppl: 1988-2002, 2006n1098
Rock song index, 2006n1110

MUSIC LIBRARIANSHIP
American music librarianship, 2006n609
Bibliographic control of music, 1897-2000, 2007n505
Manual for the performance lib, 2008n521
Uniform titles for music, 2009n533

MUSIC - POPULAR
All Music gd to hip-hop, 2005n1148
American popular music: blues, 2006n1099
American popular music: country, 2006n1100
American popular music: folk, 2006n1102
American popular music: jazz, 2006n1105
American popular music: rhythm & blues, rap, &
    hip-hop, 2006n1104
American popular music: rock & roll, 2006n1109
American songbk, 2007n1004
Billboard albums, 6th ed, 2007n1003
Billboard hot 100 annual 1955-2005, 2008n981
Billboard illus ency of country music, 2009n1018
Billboard illus ency of jazz & blues, 2007n1011
Billboard illus ency of music, 2005n1139
Billboard top adult songs 1961-2006, 2008n982
Billboard's hottest hot 100 hits, 4th ed, 2008n983
Caribbean popular music, 2006n1108
Continuum ency of popular music of the world, v.3-7,
    2006n1094
Encyclopedia of the blues, 2007n1007
Hip hop culture, 2007n1010
Hit records, 1950-75, 2006n1097
Hit singles, 5th ed, 2006n1095
Hot dance disco 1974-2003, 2005n1143
Icons of R&B & soul, 2009n1024
Icons of rock, 2009n1027
International who's who in popular music 2006, 8th
    ed, 2007n1005
International who's who in popular music 2009,
    2009n1017
Jazz: a regional exploration, 2006n1107
Joel Whitburn presents Christmas in the charts
    1920-2004, 2005n1144

Joel Whitburn presents hot country albums,
    2009n1020
Joel Whitburn presents rock tracks 1981-2008,
    2009n1025
Joel Whitburn presents top R&B/hip-hop singles
    1942-2004, 2005n1149
Joel Whitburn's 2004 music yrbk, 2006n1096
Joel Whitburn's music yrbk 2005-06, 2008n984
Joel Whitburn's top country songs 1944-2005,
    2006n1101
Joel Whitburn's top pop singles 1955-2006, 2008n985
Later swing era, 1942 to 1955, 2005n1140
Music of the counterculture era, 2005n1146
New generation of country music stars, 2009n1019
100 albums that changed popular music, 2008n980
Popular music teaching hndbk, 2005n1138
Popular song index, 4th suppl: 1988-2002, 2006n1098
Rock & roll yr by yr, 2005n1152
Rock band name origins, 2009n1026
Story behind the song, 2005n1142

MUSIC - VOCATIONAL GUIDANCE
Career opportunities in the music industry, 5th ed,
    2005n245
Music in Shakespeare, 2007n961

MUSICALS
American plays & musicals on screen, 2005n1197
Broadway musicals, 1943-2004, 2006n1173
Historical dict of the Broadway musical, 2008n1041
Oxford companion to the American musical,
    2009n1077
Rodgers & Hammerstein ency, 2008n1042
Theater mania gd to musical theater recordings,
    2006n1174
Who sang what on Broadway, 1866-1996, 2006n1171
Women in America musical theatre, 2009n1080

MUSICIANS
All of me: the complete discography of Louis
    Armstrong, 2007n992
Bob Dylan, 2d ed, 2009n1023
Bob Dylan ency, 2007n1008
Contemporary musicians, v.60, 2008n964
Contemporary musicians, v.61, 2008n965
Icons of R&B & soul, 2009n1024
Icons of rock, 2009n1027
Jazz musicians, 1945 to the present, 2007n1012
Lives & times of the great composers, 2005n1133
Louis Armstrong, 2005n1132
Musical AKAs, 2007n991
New histl anthology of music by women, 2006n1082
Satchmo: the Louis Armstrong ency, 2005n1131
Stan Getz, 2005n1128
Who's who of British jazz, 2d ed, 2005n1150
Women composers, v.7, 2005n1117

MYTHOLOGY

African mythology A to Z, 2005n1161
Celtic mythology A to Z, 2005n1163
Chinese mythology A to Z, 2005n1165
Dictionary of gods & goddesses, 2d ed, 2005n1160
Dictionary of Greek & Roman biog & mythology, 2008n993
Egyptian mythology A to Z, rev ed, 2007n1027
Encyclopedia mythica [Website], 2007n1024
Encyclopedia of Celtic mythology & folklore, 2005n1164
Fabulous creatures, mythical monsters, & animal power symbols, 2009n1034
Facts on File ency of world mythology & legend, 2d ed, 2005n1158
Gems in myth, legend, & lore, rev ed, 2008n996
Gods, goddesses, & mythology, 2005n1159
Greek mythology link [Website], 2007n1025
Handbook of Inca mythology, 2005n1169
Handbook of Native American mythology, 2006n1118
Handbook of Polynesian mythology, 2005n1166
Intoxication in mythology, 2007n1023
Myth: a hndbk, 2005n1167
Mythology in our midst, 2005n1168
Native American mythology A to Z, 2005n1162
Oxford companion to world mythology, 2007n1026
South & meso-American mythology A to Z, 2005n1157
Storytelling, 2009n1035
Tales online [Website], 2009n1029
Thematic gd to world mythology, 2005n1170
U*X*L ency of world mythology, 2009n1036
World Bk myths & legends series, 2005n1171

NAMES, PERSONAL

Beyond Jennifer & Jason, Madison & Montana, rev ed, 2005n367
Complete bk of baby names, 2008n347
First name reverse dict, 2d ed, 2008n348
German-American names, 3d ed, 2007n296
Goldenballs & the iron lady: a little bk of nicknames, 2006n369

NANOTECHNOLOGY

Dekker ency of nanosci & nanotech, 2005n1401
Dekker ency of nanosci & nanotech [Website], 2005n1402
Plunkett's nanotech & MEMS industry almanac 2006, 2007n174
Plunkett's nanotech & MEMS industry almanac, 2008 ed, 2009n180
What is what in the nanoworld, 2006n1397

NAPOLEON, BONAPARTE

Age of Napoleon, 2005n481

NAPOLEONIC WARS, 1800-1815

Encyclopedia of the French Revolutionary & Napoleonic wars, 2007n553

NARRATION (RHETORIC)

Routledge ency of narrative theory, 2006n871

NASCAR

Day-by-day in NASCAR hist, 2005n783

NATIONAL ANTHEMS

National anthems of the world, 11th ed, 2008n969

NATIONAL SECURITY

Grey House homeland security dir 2005, 2d ed, 2005n43
Grey House homeland security dir 2008, 5th ed, 2008n37
Grey House homeland security dir [Website], 2005n44
Grey House homeland security dir [Website], 2008n38
Homeland security, 2005n550
Homeland security, 2005n550
Homeland security law hndbk, 2005n551
Intelligence & natl security, 2008n592
Researching natl security & intelligence, 2005n730
U.S. natl debate topic 2006-07: natl service, 2007n648
U.S. natl security, 2d ed, 2008n652

NATIONALISM

Nationalism & ethnicity terminologies, v.3, 2006n63
Nations & nationalism, 2009n434

NATURAL DISASTERS

Encyclopedia of disasters, 2009n1318
Firefly gd to global hazards, 2005n1514
Hazardous Earth series, 2009n1302
Natural disasters, new ed, 2009n1317
World Bk lib of natural disasters, 2009n1320

NATURAL HISTORY

All things Darwin, 2008n1163
Animal rights, 2005n1379
Animal rights, rev ed, 2008n1167
Atlas of endangered species, rev ed, 2009n1192
Encyclopedia of religion & nature, paperback ed, 2009n1090
Encyclopedia of tidepools & rocky shores, 2008n1166
Field gd to the natural world of NYC, 2008n1164
Field gd to the plants & animals of the Middle Rio Grande Bosque, 2009n1189
Kingfisher illus nature ency, 2005n1378
Louisiana coast, 2009n1191
More than Darwin, 2009n1172
Natural hist of the Point Reyes Peninsula, rev ed, 2009n1190

NATURAL MEDICINE. *See also* **ALTERNATIVE**
MEDICINE
A-Z of essential oils, 2005n1454
Ayurveda, 2009n1256
Book of alternative medicine, 2008n1239
Chinese natural cures, 2007n1264
Complementary & alternative medicine sourcebk, 3d
        ed, 2007n1262
Complete ency of natural healing, rev ed, 2007n1265
Complete natural gd to breast cancer, 2005n1462
Complete natural medicine gd to the 50 most common
        medicinal herbs, 2005n1453
Duke ency of new medicine, 2008n1237
Encyclopedia of complementary & alternative
        medicine, 2005n1455
Encyclopedia of homeopathy, 2007n1263
Gale ency of alternative medicine, 2d ed, 2006n1439
Gale ency of alternative medicine, 3d ed, 2009n1255
Incense bible, 2008n1242
Internet gd to herbal remedies, 2008n1236
New ency of flower remedies, 2008n1238
Whole person healthcare, 2008n1244

NATURAL RESOURCES
Natural resources & sustainable dvlpmt, 2009n1328
Russian far east, 2d ed, 2005n115

NAVAJO LANGUAGE
Navajo/English dict of verbs, 2007n862

NAVY
Age of sail, v.2, 2005n672
American Naval hist, 3d ed, 2005n675
Black submariners in the US Navy, 1940-75,
        2006n672
Chronology of the war at sea, 1939-45, 3d rev ed,
        2006n669
Civil War navies 1855-83, 2007n568
Dictionary of naval abbrevs, 4th ed, 2006n670
Dictionary of naval terms, 6th ed, 2006n671
Falconer's new universal dict of the Marine, repr ed,
        2007n567
Naval ceremonies, customs, & traditions, 6th ed,
        2005n673
Naval Institute almanac of the US Navy, 2006n673
Naval Institute gd to combat fleets of the world
        2005-06, 2006n674
Naval Institute gd to combat fleets of the world, 15th
        ed, 2008n599
Naval Institute gd to the ships & aircraft of the US
        Fleet, 18th ed, 2006n675
Oxford ency of maritime hist, 2008n600
Russian & Soviet battleships, 2005n674
Ships of the Royal Navy, rev ed, 2007n566
US destroyers, rev ed, 2005n678
World War II naval & maritime claims against the US,
        2007n569

NEEDLEWORK
Needlework through hist, 2008n827

NERVOUS SYSTEM DISEASES
Gale ency of neurological disorders, 2005n1437

NETHERLANDS
Brief hist of The Netherlands, 2009n409
Historical dict of The Netherlands, 2d ed, 2008n126

NEW AGE MOVEMENT
Encyclopedic sourcebk of new age religions,
        2005n1239
Historical dict of new age movements, 2005n1243

NEW ENGLAND
Encyclopedia of New England, 2006n69
Historical dict of New England, 2005n78

NEW JERSEY
Encyclopedia of New Jersey, 2005n81
New Jersey municipal data bk, 2007 ed, 2008n78
Profiles of N.J., 2006, 2007n70

NEW MEXICO, HISTORY
Western lives, 2005n22

NEW YORK CITY
Almanac of New York City, 2009n76
Artwalks in New York, 3d ed, 2005n940
Field gd to the natural world of NYC, 2008n1164
New York City, 2005n398
New York City 2008, 2008n366

NEW YORK PHILHARMONIC
New York Philharmonic, 2007n986

NEW YORK STATE
Encyclopedia of N.Y. state, 2007n71
New York state dir, 2005-06, 2006n833
New York state dir, 2006-07, 2007n72
New York state dir, 2007/08, 2008n84
New York state dir, 2008-09, 2009n77
Profiles of N.Y. state, 2005-06, 2006n834
Profiles of N.Y. state 2006, 2007n73
Profiles of N.Y. state 2008-09, 2009n78
Profiles of N.Y. state, 2007/08, 2008n85

NEW ZEALAND
Australia, New Zealand, & the Pacific, 2006n1542
Historical dict of New Zealand, 2d ed, 2007n105
History of New Zealand, 2005n469

NEWSPAPERS
Bacon's media calendar dir 2004, 22d ed, 2005n902
Bacon's newspaper dir 2004, 52d ed, 2005n903
Newsletters in print, 18th ed, 2005n904

ProQuest histl newspapers [Website], 2005n905
ProQuest histl newspapers [Website], 2008n804
Willings press gd 2004, 2005n889

NIETZSCHE, FRIEDRICH WILHELM, 1844-1900
Historical dict of Nietzscheanism, 2d ed, 2007n1067

NOBEL PRIZE WINNERS
Nobel: a century of prize winners, 2009n13
Nobel e-museum [Website], 2005n15
Nobel e-museum [Website], 2007n12
Women Nobel Peace Prize winners, 2007n11

NON-ENGLISH-LANGUAGE DICTIONARIES
Oxford lang dicts online [Website], 2009n898

NONFICTION LITERATURE
Encyclopedia of women's autobiog, 2006n856
Real story, 2007n977
Remembered childhoods, 2008n945
Thematic gd to popular nonfiction, 2007n976

NONPROFIT ORGANIZATIONS
Dictionary of civil society, philanthropy, & the
    nonprofit sector, 2008n727
Dictionary of nonprofit terms & concepts, 2008n728
National dir of nonprofit orgs, 18th ed, 2006n39
National dir of nonprofit orgs, 20th ed, 2008n40
Nonprofit sector yellow bk, Summer 2005, 2006n142

NORTH CAROLINA
Encyclopedia of N Carolina, 2007n74
North Carolina cities, towns & counties, 2007 ed,
    2008n86
Profiles of N Carolina & S Carolina, 2008n87

NORTHERN IRELAND
Historical dict of the Northern Ireland conflict,
    2008n437

NORTHWEST PASSAGE
Historical dict of the discovery & exploration of the
    NW passage, 2007n129

NORWAY
Historical dict of Norway, 2009n115

NUBIANS
Daily life of the Nubians, 2005n464

NUCLEAR ENGINEERING
Nuclear power, 2007n1324
Nuclear tech, 2006n1265

NUCLEAR WEAPONS
Nuclear nonproliferation, 2009n614

Nuclear weapons & nonproliferation, 2d ed, 2008n604

NURSERY RHYMES
Nursery rhymes [Website], 2009n993

NURSING
Cumulative index to nursing & allied health lit
    [Website], 2005n1474
Gale ency of nursing & allied health, 2d ed,
    2007n1278
Nursing programs 2006, 11th ed, 2006n1456
PDR nurse's drug hndbk, 2005 ed, 2005n1475
PDR nurse's drug hndbk, 2006 ed, 2006n1457
PDR nurse's drug hndbk, 2007 ed, 2007n1279
PDR nurse's drug hndbk, 2008 ed, 2008n1259
PDR nurse's drug hndbk, 2009 ed, 2009n1272
RSP funding for nursing students & nurses 2004-06,
    4th ed, 2005n1476
RSP funding for nursing students & nurses 2006-08,
    2007n253
Springhouse nurse's drug gd, 7th ed, 2006n1458

NUTRITION
Complete gd to nutrition in primary care, 2008n1127
Diet & nutrition sourcebk, 3d ed, 2007n1153
Diet info for teens, 2d ed, 2007n1256
Encyclopedia of dietary supplements, 2006n1282
Encyclopedia of vitamins, minerals, & supplements,
    2d ed, 2005n1419
Endurance sports nutrition, 2d ed, 2008n703
Gale ency of diets, 2008n1119
Handbook of drug-nutrient interactions, 2005n1480
Internet gd to medical diets & nutrition, 2008n1124
Nutrition & diet therapy ref dict, 5th ed, 2005n1418
Nutrition & well-being A to Z, 2005n1420
Nutrition at a glance, 2008n1126
Simplified diet manual, 10th ed, 2008n1133

OBESITY
ABC of obesity, 2008n1256
Encyclopedia of obesity, 2009n1265
Encyclopedia of obesity & eating disorders, 3d ed,
    2007n1272
Handbook of obesity, 2d ed, 2005n1447

O'BRIAN, PATRICK
Jack Aubrey commands, 2005n1070

OCCULTISM
Cults, 2d ed, 2006n1214
Encyclopedia of magic & alchemy, 2008n694
Encyclopedia of occultism, 2005n745
Encyclopedia of witchcraft, 2007n666
Encyclopedic sourcebk of Satanism, 2009n715
Fortune-telling bk, 2005n744
Modern paganism in world cultures, 2006n1215
Spirit bk, 2006n762

OCEANIA
Australia, Oceania, & Antarctica, 2005n1542
Encyclopedia of the peoples of Asia & Oceania,
    2009n305
Historical dict of the discovery & exploration of the
    Pacific Islands, 2006n99

OCEANOGRAPHY
Encyclopedia of coastal sci, 2006n1518
Encyclopedia of marine sci, 2009n1323
Encyclopedia of tidepools & rocky shores, 2008n1166
Facts on File dict of marine sci, new ed, 2008n1324
Firefly gd to the oceans, 2005n1521
Life in the sea series, 2006n1520
Ocean, 2009n1324
Oceans, 2006n1519
Oceans, 2007n1313
Oceans, rev ed, 2008n1323

OFFICE PRACTICES
Administrative assistant's & secretary's hndbk, 3d ed,
    2009n240
Greening your business, 2009n233
Safe hiring audit, 2009n232

OHIO
Profiles of Ohio, 2006, 2007n75
Profiles of Ohio, 2d ed, 2009n79

OKLAHOMA
Historical atlas of Okla., 4th ed, 2007n76
Oklahoma, 2009n80

OLYMPICS
A to Z of the Olympic movement, 2008n712
Encyclopedia of the modern Olympic movement,
    2005n777
Olympic Games, 2005n778

OPERA
American opera singers & their recordings, 2005n1137
Billboard illus ency of opera, 2006n1092
Encyclopedia of American opera, 2007n1002
Encyclopedia of opera on screen, 2005n1200
Grove bk of operas, 2d ed, 2007n1001
Opera, 2008n979
Start-up at the new Met, 2008n978
Symphonic etudes, 2008n974

OPHTHALMIC MEDICINE
PDR for ophthalmic medicines 2007, 35th ed,
    2008n1268

OPTICAL ENGINEERING
Handbook of optical systems, v.1, 2006n1407
Handbook of optical systems, v.2, 2006n1408
Science of microscopy, 2007n1229

ORATORS
American voices, 2006n870

ORCHESTRAL MUSIC
Orchestral music, 4th ed, 2006n1093

ORCHIDS
Cattleyas & their relatives, 2005n1359
Easy orchids, 2006n1305
Field gd to the wild orchids of Tex., 2008n1153
Field gd to the wild orchids of Thailand, 4th ed, 2006n1348
Flora's orchids, 2006n1342
Growing hardy orchids, 2006n1310
Illustrated ency of orchids, repr ed, 2007n1179
Marie Selby Botanical Gardens illus dict of orchid
    genera, 2009n1183
Orchid grower's companion, 2006n1301
Orchids to know & grow, 2008n1159
Wild orchids of the NE, 2008n1154
Wild orchids of the prairies & great plains region of N
    America, 2008n1155
Wild orchids of the SE US North of peninsular Fla.,
    2006n1345

ORGAN MUSIC
Catalogue of music for organ & instruments,
    2006n1085
Organ, 2007n996
Understanding the pipe organ, 2009n1014

ORGANIZATION STUDIES
International ency of organization studies, 2009n231

ORTHODOX EASTERN CHURCH
Eastern Orthodox churches, 2006n1227

ORTHOPEDIC MEDICINE
Dictionary of orthopedic terminology, 2009n1259

OWLS
Field gd to owls of Calif. & the west, 2008n1180

PACIFIC ISLANDS
Historical dict of the discovery & exploration of the
    Pacific Islands, 2006n99

PAGANISM
Modern paganism in world cultures, 2006n1215

PAINTING, ITALIAN
Inventory of paintings of Cardinal Pietro Ottoboni
    (1667-1740), 2005n949

PAKISTAN
Brief hist of Pakistan, 2009n105
Conflict between India & Pakistan, 2009n96
Culture & customs of Pakistan, 2007n99

Historical dict of Pakistan, 3d ed, 2007n127
History of Pakistan, 2009n104
IntelCenter terrorism incident ref (TIR): Pakistan:
    2000-07, 2009n684
Pakistan, 2007n100

PALEONTOLOGY
Complete gd to prehistoric life, 2007n1315
Concise dinosaur ency, 2005n1522
Dinosaur atlas, 2007n1316
Dinosauria, 2d ed, 2006n1521
Dinosaurs, 2008n1326
Dinosaurs, suppl 5, 2008n1325
E.guides: dinosaur, 2005n1523
Great dinosaur controversy, 2005n1524

PALESTINIAN ARABS
Culture & customs of Palestinians, 2005n124
Dictionary of the Israeli-Palestinian conflict, 2006n115
Encyclopedia of the Palestinians, rev ed, 2006n354

PAPACY
Deaths of the popes, 2005n1267

PARAPSYCHOLOGY
Armageddon now, 2006n764
Encyclopedia of ghosts & spirits, 3d ed, 2008n696
Greenhaven ency of paranormal phenomena,
    2007n668
Unexplained: an ency of curious phenomena,
    2008n695
Unnatural phenomena, 2006n763
World Internet UFO dir, 2006n765

PARKINSON'S DISEASE
Encyclopedia of Parkinson's disease, 2005n1471

PEACE
Annual review of global peace operations 2008,
    2009n694
CRInfo: the conflict resolution info source [Website],
    2008n669
Historical dict of multinational peacekeeping, 2d ed,
    2005n723

PEDIATRIC MEDICINE
Children & youth in sickness & in health, 2005n826
Complete dir for pediatric disorders 2005, 3d ed,
    2005n1457
Complete dir for pediatric disorders [Website],
    2005n1458
Encyclopedia of children's health & wellness,
    2005n1459
Gale ency of children's health, 2006n1440
Pediatric dermatology, 2007n1266

PENNSYLVANIA
Profiles of Pa., 2006, 2007n77

PERCUSSION MUSIC
Practical percussion, rev ed, 2006n1086

PERFORMING ARTS
Grey House performing arts dir 2005, 4th ed,
    2005n1184
Grey House performing arts dir 2007, 5th ed, 2008n1005
Grey House performing arts dir [Website], 2005n1185
Obituaries in the performing arts, 2003, 2005n1180
Obituaries in the performing arts, 2004, 2006n1127
Obituaries in the performing arts, 2005, 2007n1036
Obituaries in the performing arts, 2007, 2009n1049
Professional degree programs in the visual and
    performing arts 2006, 2006n298
Queer ency of music, dance, & musical theater,
    2005n1181

PERIODICALS
Access, 2008n49
Author index to little mags of the mimeograph
    revolution, 2009n44
Bibliography of Africana per lit [Website], 2008n92
Cobblestone online [Website], 2009n43
E-journals, 2006n641
Electronic jl mgmt systems, 2006n642
From A to Zine: building a winning zine collection in
    your lib, 2005n644
HAPI: Hispanic American per index online [Website],
    2008n50
InfoTrac kids [Website], 2008n51
International dir of little mags & small presses
    2008-09, 44th ed, 2009n594
Introduction to serials work for lib technicians, 2005n645
Newsletters in print, 18th ed, 2005n904
Our own voices [Website], 2009n45
Periodical title abbrevs, 15th ed, 2005n57
Periodical title abbrevs, 16th ed, 2006n55
Periodicals index online [Website], 2007n43
RAND pubs [Website], 2007n44
Standard per dir 2004, 27th ed, 2005n58
Standard per dir 2008, 31st ed, 2009n46
Ulrich's per dir 2005, 44th ed, 2006n56
Ulrich's per dir [Website], 2006n57
Ulrich's per dir [Website], 2008n52
Willings press gd 2004, 2005n889
Women's studies, feminist, & gender periodicals
    [Website], 2005n875
Women's studies section core jls for women's studies
    [Website], 2005n865
World dir of trade & business jls 2007, 3d ed,
    2008n166

PERSIAN GULF WAR, 1991
A to Z of the Persian Gulf War, 1990-91, 2008n586
War in the Persian Gulf: almanac, 2005n667
War in the Persian Gulf: biogs, 2005n668
War in the Persian Gulf: primary sources, 2005n669

PERSONAL FORMS
Personal & business forms online [Website], 2007n150
Personal forms on file, 2004 ed, 2005n167
Personal forms on file, 2006n146
Personal forms on file 2006, rev ed, 2007n149
Personal forms on file, 2007 ed, 2008n172

PERSONAL NAMES
Beyond Jennifer & Jason, Madison & Montana, rev
    ed, 2005n367
Complete bk of baby names, 2008n347
First name reverse dict, 2d ed, 2008n348
German-American names, 3d ed, 2007n296
Goldenballs & the iron lady: a little bk of nicknames,
    2006n369
Oxford dict of nicknames, 2005n366

PERSONS WITH DISABILITIES. *See also*
LEARNING DISABILITIES
Children with disabilities in America, 2007n698
Complete dir for people with disabilities 2003/04, 12th
    ed, 2005n798
Complete dir for people with disabilities 2005, 13th
    ed, 2006n803
Complete dir for people with disabilities 2006, 14th
    ed, 2007n699
Complete dir for people with disabilities 2008, 16th
    ed, 2008n717
Complete dir for people with disabilities 2009, 17th
    ed, 2009n744
Complete dir for people with disabilities [Website],
    2005n799
Complete dir for people with disabilities [Website],
    2007n700
Complete dir for people with disabilities [Website],
    2008n718
Complete dir of disabilities [Website], 2006n804
Encyclopedia of disability, 2006n805
Ferguson career resource gd for people with
    disabilities, 3d ed, 2007n702
Rights of the disabled, 2009n745
Transition to postsecondary educ for students with
    disabilities, 2009n281

PERU
Brief hist of Peru, 2005n122

PESTICIDES
Pesticides, 2d ed, 2005n1298

PETROLEUM TECHNOLOGY
Petroleum tech, 2008n1198

PHARMACEUTICAL SCIENCES. *See also*
DRUGS
Dictionary of pharmacy, 2005n1477
Drug info, 3d ed, 2009n1273
Essential gd to prescription drugs, 2004 ed, 2005n1479
Essential herb-drug-vitamin interaction gd, 2008n1261
Handbook of drug-nutrient interactions, 2005n1480
Handbook of nonprescription drugs, 14th ed,
    2005n1481
Handbook of psychiatric drugs, 2007n1283
Litt's drug eruption ref manual including drug
    interactions, 13th ed, 2008n1262
Major pharmaceutical & biotech companies of the
    world 2005, 7th ed, 2006n1459
Merck index, 14th ed, 2007n1284
PDR concise drug gd for advanced practice clinicians,
    2008n1263
PDR concise drug gd for advanced practice clinicians,
    2d ed, 2009n1274
PDR concise drug gd for pediatrics, 2008n1265
PDR concise drug gd for pediatrics, 2d ed, 2009n1275
PDR concise drug gd for pharmacists, 2008n1264
PDR drug gd for mental health professionals, 3d ed,
    2008n1266
PDR for herbal medicines, 4th ed, 2008n1267
PDR for nonprescription drugs, dietary supplements,
    & herbs 2008, 29th ed, 2009n1276
PDR gd to drug interactions, side effects &
    indications, 63d ed, 2009n1277
PDR gd to drug interactions, side effects, &
    indications, 61st ed, 2008n1260
PDR nurse's drug hndbk, 2005 ed, 2005n1475
PDR nurse's drug hndbk, 2008 ed, 2008n1259
PDR nurse's drug hndbk, 2009 ed, 2009n1272
Physicians' desk ref 2006, 2006n1462
Physicians' desk ref 2007, 61st ed, 2008n1269
Physicians' desk ref 2009, 63d ed, 2009n1278
Pill bk, 11th ed, 2005n1478
Psychotropic drugs, 4th ed, 2009n1279

PHILADELPHIA PHILLIES (BASEBALL TEAM)
Phillies ency, 3d ed, 2005n768

PHILANTHROPY. *See also* GRANTS-IN-AID
Corporate giving dir, 26th ed, 2005n810
Dictionary of civil society, philanthropy, & the
    nonprofit sector, 2008n727
Dictionary of nonprofit terms & concepts, 2008n728
Europa intl foundation dir 2007, 2008n731
Foundation reporter, 37th ed, 2005n811
Philanthropy in America, 2005n808
Rich register 2004, 2005n814
Rich register 2006, 2006n814

PHILIPPINES
Historical dict of the Philippines, 2d ed, 2006n95
Philippines, 2007n101

PHILOSOPHERS
Aristotle bibliog [Website], 2006n1180
Bibliography of modern American philosophers, 2006n1181
Bibliography of modern British philosophers, 2005n1223
Bio-bibliography for Biruni, 2007n1060
Dictionary of Irish philosophers, 2005n1225
Dictionary of modern American philosophers, 2006n1188
Dictionary of 20th-century British philosophers, 2006n1189
Directory of women philosophers [Website], 2006n1200
Great thinkers A-Z, 2005n1226
Historical dict of Hegelian philosophy, 2d ed, 2009n1081
Historical dict of Hume's philosophy, 2009n1085
Historical dict of Husserl's philosophy, 2009n1083
Historical dict of Wittgenstein's philosophy, 2005n1233
One hundred philosophers, 2005n1227
Satre dict, 2009n1082

PHILOSOPHY
APA online [Website], 2006n1199
Basics of western philosophy, 2005n1234
Biographical ency of Islamic philosophy, 2007n1062
Cambridge companion to Renaissance philosophy, 2008n1049
Cambridge hist of 18th-century philosophy, 2007n1072
Christian philosophy A-Z, 2008n1045
Columbia companion to 20th-century philosophies, 2008n1050
Columbia hist of 20th-century French thought, 2007n1064
Columbia hist of 20th-century French thought, paperback ed, 2008n1051
Companion to contemporary pol philosophy, 2d ed, 2009n623
Contemporary philosophy of the mind [Website], 2006n1182
Continuum ency of British philosophy, 2007n1065
Dictionary of alternatives, 2008n1046
Dictionary of Atheism, skepticism, & humanism, 2007n1077
Dictionary of continental philosophy, 2007n1066
Dictionary of Islamic philosophical terms [Website], 2006n1239
Dictionary of philosophical terms & names [Website], 2006n1190
Encyclopedia of modern French thought, 2005n1230

Encyclopedia of philosophy, 2007n1068
Encyclopedia of religious phenomena, 2008n1056
Encyclopedia of the Enlightenment, rev ed, 2005n524
EpistemeLinks.com: philosophy resources on the Internet [Website], 2006n1183
Erratic impact's philosophy research base [Website], 2006n1184
Ethics, rev ed, 2006n1192
Great voyages [Website], 2005n1224
Historical companion to postcolonial thought in English, 2006n1193
Historical dict of Descartes & Cartesian philosophy, 2005n1228
Historical dict of epistemology, 2007n1061
Historical dict of existentials, 2009n1086
Historical dict of feminist philosophy, 2007n758
Historical dict of Kant & Kantianism, 2006n1194
Historical dict of Leibniz's philosophy, 2007n1063
Historical dict of logic, 2007n1069
Historical dict of Marxism, 2007n1071
Historical dict of medieval philosophy & theology, 2008n1044
Historical dict of Nietzscheanism, 2d ed, 2007n1067
Internet ency of philosophy [Website], 2005n1231
Law: key concepts in philosophy, 2007n1070
101 key terms in philosophy & their importance for theology, 2005n1229
Online papers in philosophy [Website], 2006n1202
Oxford companion to philosophy, 2d ed, 2006n1196
Philosophical gourmet report [Website], 2006n297
Philosophy, 3d ed, 2007n1059
Philosophy in cyberspace [Website], 2006n1203
Philosophy of mind A-Z, 2008n1048
Philosophy of sci, 2007n1137
PHILTAR: philosophy, theology, & religion [Website], 2006n1204
POIESIS: philosophy online serials [Website], 2006n1187
Political philosophy A-Z, 2009n1087
Poststructuralism & communication, 2006n1186
Routledge ency of philosophy [Website], 2006n1197
Unpublished ms in British idealism, 2006n1205
Western philosophy, 2005n1236

PHOTOGRAPHY
Abrams ency of photography, 2005n950
Career opportunities in photography, 2007n222
Encyclopedia of 19th-century photography, 2008n847
Encyclopedia of 20th-century photography, 2007n819
Fundamentals of photography, 2009n866
Photographer's market 2006, 29th ed, 2006n937
Photography bks index 3, 2007n820
Pioneer photographers from the Miss. To the Continental Divide, 2006n936
Twentieth century US photographers, 2009n867
Ultimate field gd to photography, 2007n821

PHYSICAL EDUCATION
Sport discus [Website], 2005n747

PHYSICAL FITNESS
Fitness & exercise sourcebk, 3d ed, 2008n706

PHYSICAL SCIENCES
Encyclopedia of earth & physical scis, 2d ed, 2006n1498

PHYSICS
Basics of physics, 2008n1329
CRC hndbk of chemistry & physics 2007-08, 88th ed, 2008n1294
Dictionary of physics, 2005n1525
Encyclopedia of physics, 2006n1523
Encyclopedia of physics, 3d ed, 2007n1317
Facts on File dict of physics, 4th ed, 2006n1522
Facts on File physics hndbk, rev ed, 2008n1328
McGraw-Hill concise ency of physics, 2007n1318
Physics, 2008n1327

PIANO MUSIC
Art of the piano, 3d ed, 2005n1134
Guide to musical temperament, 2006n1087
Pianist's dict, 2005n1135
Piano in chamber ensemble, 2d ed, 2007n997
Piano music by women composers, v.2, 2005n1129

PLACE-NAMES
African placenames, 2d ed, 2009n342
Cambridge dict of English place-names, 2006n390
Getty thesaurus of geographic names online [Website], 2007n315
International glossary of place name elements, 2006n391
Native American place-names of Ind., 2009n341
Nicknames of places, 2007n316
Place names of Ill., 2009n340
Placenames of the world, 2d ed, 2006n392
Pronunciation of placenames, 2009n343

PLAGIARISM
Plagiarism plague, 2005n646
Student plagiarism in an online world, 2008n540

PLANT SCIENCE
Encyclopedia of plant & crop sci, 2005n1348
Encyclopedia of plant & crop sci [Website], 2005n1349
Handbook of plant biotech, 2005n1353
North American wildland plants, 2005n1355

PLANTS. *See also* **BOTANY; GARDENING**
Alpine plants of Europe, 2006n1298
American Horticultural Society A-Z ency of garden plants, rev ed, 2005n1310

American Horticultural Society AHS great plant gd, rev ed, 2005n1311
American Horticultural Society garden plants & flowers, 2005n1319
Animal & plant anatomy, 2008n1148
Armitage's native plants for N American gardens, 2007n1155
Atlas of woody plant stems, 2009n1180
Blueberries, cranberries, & other vacciniums, 2005n1332
Color ency of hostas, 2005n1350
Complete houseplant survival manual, 2006n1336
Dryland gardening, 2006n1297
Dyes from American native plants, 2006n1337
E.guides: plant, 2007n1174
Elegant silvers, 2006n1303
eNature.com [Website], 2006n1328
Encyclopedia of hardy plants, 2008n1134
Encyclopedia of psychoactive plants, translated ed, 2006n1331
Encyclopedia of water garden plants, 2005n1318
Florida landscape plants, 2d rev ed, 2006n1339
Food plants of the world, 2006n1338
Fruit & nuts, 2007n1180
Garden plants of Japan, 2005n1314
Gymnosperm database [Website], 2006n1340
Handbook of plant sci, 2008n1151
International plant names index [Website], 2006n1341
Jade garden, 2006n1311
Medicinal plants in folk tradition, 2005n1347
Medicinal plants of N America, 2009n1178
Medicinal plants of the world, 2005n1352
Names of plants, 4th ed, 2009n1177
Native plants of the northeast, 2006n1335
Ornamental foliage plants, 2005n1326
Phylogeny of life [Website], 2006n1329
Plant, 2006n1330
Plant finder, 2008n1136
Plant Locator: western region, 2005n1322
Plant ontology consortium (POC) [Website], 2006n1325
PlantGDB [Website], 2006n1324
Plants of the Kimberley region of W Australia, rev ed, 2005n1354
PlantStress [Website], 2006n1326
Rare plants of Tex., 2009n1179
Restoring American gardens, 2005n1309
Tempting tropicals, 2006n1332
Tropical plants of Costa Rica, 2008n1152
Uses of wild plants, 2009n1162
WallBioNet [Website], 2006n1327
Wildlife & plants, 3d ed, 2007n1170
Wildlife-friendly plants, 2005n1323
World of plants series, 2007n1175

POETRY
African letters [Website], 2006n1066
American verse project [Website], 2009n988

Bartleby verse [Website], 2009n989
British women romantic poets, 1789-1952 [Website], 2005n1100
Cambridge companion to 20th-century English poetry, 2009n1007
Cambridge hist of American lit, v.4: 19th-century poetry, 2006n1070
Directory of poetry pubs 2008-09, 24th ed, 2009n591
Electronic poetry center [Website], 2009n990
Elizabethan poetry, 2005n1102
Facts on File companion to American poetry, 2008n957
Facts on File companion to British poetry before 1600, 2009n1001
Facts on File companion to British poetry: 17th & 18th centuries, 2009n1002
Facts on File companion to British poetry: 1900 to the present, 2009n1003
Facts on File companion to 20th-century American poetry, 2006n1069
Facts on File companion to world poetry 1900 to the present, 2008n956
Favorite poem project [Website], 2009n991
Giggle poetry [Website], 2008n947
Glossary of poetic terms [Website], 2009n1004
Greenwood ency of American poets & poetry, 2007n979
Henry Wadsworth Longfellow companion, 2005n1069
Modern American poetry [Website], 2009n992
Poems, plays, & prose [Website], 2005n1006
Poet's corner [Website], 2008n951
Poet's market 2006, 21st ed, 2006n879
Poetry archive [Website], 2009n994
Poetry archives [Website], 2009n995
Poetry criticism, v.54, 2005n1104
Poetry criticism, v.55, 2005n1105
Poetry criticism, v.56, 2005n1106
Poetry criticism, v.57, 2005n1107
Poetry daily [Website], 2008n949
Poetry daily [Website], 2009n996
Poetry for students, v.18, 2005n1108
Poetry for students, v.19, 2005n1109
Poetry for students, v.20, 2005n1110
Poetry in lit for youth, 2007n980
Poetry 180 [Website], 2008n950
Poetry Society of America [Website], 2009n997
Poets & writers [Website], 2009n998
Poets.org [Website], 2009n999
Undergraduates companion to women poets of the world & their Web sites, 2005n1101
Verse—anthologies [Website], 2009n1000
WriteExpress online rhyming [Website], 2009n1006

POETRY - INDEXES

Columbia Granger's index to poetry in anthologies, 13th ed, 2008n959
Columbia Granger's index to poetry in collected & selected works, 2d ed, 2005n1113
Index of American per verse 2003, 2006n1071
Index of American per verse 2004, 2007n982
Index of American per verse 2005, 2008n960
Index of American periodical verse 2001, 2005n1114
Index of American periodical verse 2002, 2005n1115
Index of American periodical verse 2006, 2009n1009
New index of middle English verse, 2007n981

POETS

Academy of American poets [Website], 2008n952
Alexander Pope ency, 2005n1112
All things Chaucer, 2008n929
British & Irish poets, 2008n954
Concordance to the major poems of Edward Taylor, 2009n1008
Contemporary American ethnic poets, 2005n1103
Critical companion to Dante, 2009n1005
Critical companion to T. S. Eliot, 2008n916
Critical companion to Walt Whitman, 2007n954
Edwin Arlington Robinson ency, 2008n958
Emily Dickinson, 2005n1066
Ezra Pound ency, 2006n1068
International who's who in poetry 2005, 13th ed, 2006n1067
International who's who in poetry 2007, 14th ed, 2007n978
International who's who in poetry 2009, 2009n987
Poetry people, 2008n955
Poets for YAs, 2008n953
W. H. Auden ency, 2005n1111

POISONOUS PLANTS

Poisonous plants, 2d ed, 2006n1334

POLAR REGIONS

Antarctic fishes, 2008n1182
Canada & Arctic N America, 2008n1351
Encyclopedia of the Antarctic, 2008n148
Encyclopedia of the Arctic, 2005n90
Historical dict of the discovery & exploration of the NW passage, 2007n129

POLICE

Encyclopedia of American law enforcement, 2008n489
Encyclopedia of police studies, 3d ed, 2008n486
Policing in America, 2008n495
World ency of police forces & correctional systems, 2d ed, 2007n473
World police ency, 2007n474

POLITICAL ACTIVISM

Research gd to US & intl interest groups, 2005n728
Youth activism, 2007n578

POLITICAL CAREERS
Great jobs for pol sci majors, 2d ed, 2005n250

POLITICAL CORRUPTION, UNITED STATES
Political corruption in America, 2005n699

POLITICAL LEADERS
American pol leaders 1789-2005, 2006n719
Annotated bibliog of works about Sir Winston S.
     Churchill, 2005n721
Biographical dict of modern world leaders 1900 to
     1991, 2005n683
Leadership, 2008n446
People in power [Website], 2008n609
Profiles of worldwide govt leaders 2004, 2005n684
Shapers of the great debate at the Constitutional
     Convention of 1787, 2006n431
Shapers of the great debate on the great society,
     2006n694
Who's who in American pol 2005-06, 20th ed,
     2006n702
Who's who in intl affairs 2005, 4th ed, 2006n684
Women in pol [Website], 2005n685

POLITICAL MOVEMENTS
History in dispute, v.16: 20th-century European social
     & pol movements, 1st series, 2005n477
History in dispute, v.17: 20th-century European social
     & pol movements, 2d series, 2005n478

POLITICAL PARTICIPATION
Conservative Christians & pol participation, 2006n735
Latino Americans & pol participation, 2006n727
Native Americans & pol participation, 2006n339
Youth activism, 2006n688

POLITICAL PARTIES
American political parties in the 21st century,
     2007n593
Encyclopedia of politics, 2006n703
Party affiliations in the state legislatures, 2008n624
Political parties [Website], 2008n611
Political parties of the world, 6th ed, 2006n687
World ency of pol systems & parties, 4th ed,
     2008n613

POLITICAL SCIENCE
Annenberg pol fact check [Website], 2009n629
Annual review of pol sci, v.6, 2003, 2005n690
Annual review of pol sci, v.11, 2008, 2009n622
Bibliography of pol sci resources on the study of pol
     violence [Website], 2008n670
Book of rule, 2005n691
California pol almanac 2007-08, 2008n642
Cambridge hist of 18th-century political thought,
     2007n579
Campaign ads [Website], 2009n630

Commission on presidential debates [Website],
     2009n631
Companion to contemporary pol philosophy, 2d ed,
     2009n623
Encyclopedia of governance, 2007n641
Encyclopedia of govt & pols, 2d ed, 2005n687
Encyclopedia of media & pol, 2008n610
Encyclopedia of political communication, 2009n617
Green papers [Website], 2009n634
Information sources of pol sci, 5th ed, 2006n683
Political resources on the net [Website], 2008n608
PollingReport.com [Website], 2009n636
Pro/con 3, 2005n692
Pro/con 4, 2006n691
Project vote smart [Website], 2009n637
Routledge pol & intl relations resource [Website],
     2008n612
Safire's pol dict, updated ed, 2009n619
Statesman's yrbk 2004, 140th ed, 2005n70
Statesman's yrbk 2008, 2008n63
Women & pol participation, 2005n715

POLITICAL VIOLENCE
Historical dict of the "Dirty Wars", 2005n499

POLLING
Polling the nations [Website], 2008n744

POLO
Polo ency, 2005n779
Profiles in polo, 2008n713

POPULAR CULTURE
African Americans & pop culture, 2009n1047
American icons, 2007n1028
American presidents in popular culture, 2007n1032
Antebellum period, 2005n461
Born this day, 2d ed, 2008n1004
Conspiracies & secret societies, 2007n1030
Encyclopedia of gay & lesbian popular culture,
     2009n1046
Encyclopedia of Latino popular culture, 2005n354
Gilded age, 2005n460
Great Depression in America, 2008n404
Greenwood ency of world popular culture, 2008n999
Material culture in America, 2008n1003
1920s, 2005n1174
1940s, 2005n1178
1950s, 2005n1179
1990s, 2005n1177
Pop culture Arab world! 2006n1126
Pop culture China! 2008n1002
Pop Culture Germany! 2007n1033
Pop culture India! 2007n1034
Pop culture Russia! 2006n1125
Pop culture universe [Website], 2009n1045

POPULAR MEDICINE

Accident & safety info for teens, 2009n1268
Adolescent health sourcebk, 2d ed, 2007n1254
Adult health concerns sourcebk, 2009n1243
Allergy info for teens, 2007n1267
Alzheimer disease sourcebk, 4th ed, 2009n1260
Arthritis, 2009n1261
Arthritis sourcebk, 2d ed, 2005n1460
Asthma info for teens, 2006n1442
Asthma sourcebk, 2d ed, 2007n1268
Back & neck sourcebk, 2d ed, 2006n1435
Blood & circulatory disorders sourcebk, 2d ed, 2006n1443
Brain disorders sourcebk, 2d ed, 2006n1444
Breast cancer sourcebk, 2d ed, 2006n1445
Cancer info for teens, 2005n1461
Cancer sourcebk, 5th ed, 2008n1253
Cancer sourcebk for women, 3d ed, 2007n1270
Cancer survivorship sourcebk, 2008n1254
Cardiovascular diseases & disorders sourcebk, 3d ed, 2006n1449
Congenital disorders sourcebk, 2d ed, 2008n1233
Contagious diseases sourcebk, 2005n1443
Dermatological disorders sourcebk, 2d ed, 2006n1452
Diabetes info for teens, 2007n1271
Disease mgmt sourcebk, 2009n1244
Diseases & disorders series, 2009n1245
Ear, nose & throat disorders sourcebk, 2d ed, 2007n1257
Eating disorders, rev ed, 2005n1467
Eating disorders info for teens, 2006n1448
Eating disorders sourcebk, 2d ed, 2008n1255
Eye care sourcebk, 3d ed, 2009n1258
Gastrointestinal diseases & disorders sourcebk, 2d ed, 2007n1258
Genetic disorders sourcebk, 3d ed, 2005n1446
Healthy woman, 2009n1246
Hepatitis, 2007n1274
Hepatitis sourcebk, 2006n1450
Hypertension sourcebk, 2005n1469
Immune system disorders sourcebk, 2d ed, 2006n1436
Infectious diseases sourcebk, 2005n1448
Internet gd to cosmetic surgery for men, 2007n1253
Men's health concerns sourcebk, 2d ed, 2005n1450
Menopause bible, 2006n1437
Muscular dystrophy sourcebk, 2005n1470
Pain sourcebk, 3d ed, 2009n1248
Perspectives on diseases & disorders series, 2009n1249
Podiatry sourcebk, 2d ed, 2008n1235
Pregnancy & birth sourcebk, 2d ed, 2005n1456
Prostate & urological disorders sourcebk, 2007n1260
Respiratory disorders sourcebk, 2d ed, 2009n1266
Sexually transmitted diseases sourcebk, 3d ed, 2007n1275
Sleep disorders sourcebk, 2d ed, 2006n1438
Sports injuries info for teens, 2d ed, 2009n1269

Stress info for teens, 2009n1251
Stroke sourcebk, 2d ed, 2009n1252
Surgery sourcebk, 2d ed, 2009n1253
Thyroid disorders sourcebk, 2006n1453
Urinary tract & kidney diseases & disorders sourcebk, 2d ed, 2006n1433
Women's health concerns sourcebk, 2d ed, 2005n1452

POPULAR MUSIC

All Music gd to hip-hop, 2005n1148
American popular music: blues, 2006n1099
American popular music: country, 2006n1100
American popular music: folk, 2006n1102
American popular music: jazz, 2006n1105
American popular music: rhythm & blues, rap, & hip-hop, 2006n1104
American popular music: rock & roll, 2006n1109
American songbk, 2007n1004
Billboard albums, 6th ed, 2007n1003
Billboard hot 100 annual 1955-2005, 2008n981
Billboard illus ency of country music, 2009n1018
Billboard illus ency of jazz & blues, 2007n1011
Billboard illus ency of music, 2005n1139
Billboard top adult songs 1961-2006, 2008n982
Billboard's hottest hot 100 hits, 4th ed, 2008n983
Caribbean popular music, 2006n1108
Continuum ency of popular music of the world, v.3-7, 2006n1094
Encyclopedia of the blues, 2007n1007
Hip hop culture, 2007n1010
Hit records, 1950-75, 2006n1097
Hit singles, 5th ed, 2006n1095
Hot dance disco 1974-2003, 2005n1143
Icons of R&B & soul, 2009n1024
Icons of rock, 2009n1027
International who's who in popular music 2006, 8th ed, 2007n1005
International who's who in popular music 2009, 2009n1017
Jazz: a regional exploration, 2006n1107
Joel Whitburn presents Christmas in the charts 1920-2004, 2005n1144
Joel Whitburn presents hot country albums, 2009n1020
Joel Whitburn presents rock tracks 1981-2008, 2009n1025
Joel Whitburn presents top R&B/hip-hop singles 1942-2004, 2005n1149
Joel Whitburn's 2004 music yrbk, 2006n1096
Joel Whitburn's music yrbk 2005-06, 2008n984
Joel Whitburn's top country songs 1944-2005, 2006n1101
Joel Whitburn's top pop singles 1955-2006, 2008n985
Later swing era, 1942 to 1955, 2005n1140
Music of the counterculture era, 2005n1146
New generation of country music stars, 2009n1019
100 albums that changed popular music, 2008n980

Popular music teaching hndbk, 2005n1138
Popular song index, 4th suppl: 1988-2002, 2006n1098
Rock & roll yr by yr, 2005n1152
Rock band name origins, 2009n1026
Story behind the song, 2005n1142

POPULATION
Future demographic, 2005n831
Politics & population control, 2005n734
Population index on the Web [Website], 2005n828
Population ref bureau [Website], 2005n829
World fertility report: 2003, 2006n826
World population, 2d ed, 2007n721
World population ageing 2007, 2008n746
World population prospects: the 2004 revision,
    2007n727

PORTUGAL
Spain & Portugal, 2008n131

POSTAGE STAMPS
American hist album, 2009n838
United States as depicted on its postage stamps,
    2008n824
Women on US postage stamps, 2009n784

POSTCOLONIAL THOUGHT
Historical companion to postcolonial thought in
    English, 2006n1193

POSTMODERNISM
Historical dict of postmodernist lit & theater,
    2008n789

POULTRY BREEDS
Storey's illus gd to poultry breeds, 2008n1175

POVERTY
Child poverty in America today, 2008n733
Encyclopedia of world poverty, 2007n713
Poverty in America, 2008n734
Poverty in the US, 2005n818
World poverty, 2009n761

PREGNANCY
Pregnancy & birth sourcebk, 2d ed, 2005n1456

PREJUDICES. *See also* RACE RELATIONS
Prejudice in the modern world: almanac, 2008n304
Prejudice in the modern world: biogs, 2008n305
Prejudice in the modern world: primary sources,
    2008n306

PRESIDENTS - UNITED STATES
Abraham Lincoln companion, 2009n638
American presidents, 3d ed, 2007n588
American presidents attend the theatre, 2007n1058

American presidents in popular culture, 2007n1032
Carter yrs, 2007n590
Childhoods of the American presidents, 2006n696
Clinton yrs, 2005n702
Cold War presidency, 2008n649
Domestic programs of the American Presidents,
    2009n658
Encyclopedia of the American presidency, 2005n698
FDR yrs, 2008n621
Geography of presidential elections in the US,
    1868-2004, 2006n730
George H. W. Bush yrs, 2007n589
Guide to the presidency, 4th ed, 2008n629
Handy presidents answer bk, 2006n728
Historical atlas of US presidential elections,
    1789-2004, 2007n585
Historical dict of the Eisenhower era, 2009n646
Historical dict of the Reagan-Bush era, 2008n626
Historical dict of the Roosevelt-Truman era, 2009n648
Johnson yrs, 2007n591
Kennedy yrs, 2005n697
Life & presidency of Franklin Delano Roosevelt,
    2006n692
Papers of Dwight David Eisenhower [Website],
    2009n635
Papers of James Monroe, v. 2, 2007n618
Personal versus private: presidential records in a
    legislative context, 2006n693
Powers of the presidency, 2009n664
Presidency A to Z, 4th ed, 2009n647
Presidency, the public, & the parties, 3d ed, 2009n665
Presidential facts, 2007n621
Presidents, 2d ed, 2006n697
Presidents from Adams through Polk, 1825-49,
    2006n733
Presidents from Eisenhower through Johnson,
    1953-69, 2007n614
Presidents were here, 2009n390
Presidents, first ladies, & vice presidents, 2006n695
Race for the presidency, 2008n644
Reagan era, 2008n418
Reagan yrs, 2006n699
Ronald Reagan, 2009n628
Shapers of the great debate on Jacksonian democracy,
    2005n696
State of the Union, 2007n623
Truman yrs, 2006n700
US presidents & foreign policy, 2007n592
US presidents factbk, 2007n613
World Bk of America's presidents, 2005 ed, 2006n737

PRESIDENTS' SPOUSES
American first ladies, 2d ed, 2007n587
First ladies fact bk, 2006n698
Genealogy of the wives of the American presidents &
    their 1st two generations of descent,
    2006n359

Presidents, first ladies, & vice presidents, 2006n695
Wives of the American presidents, 2d ed, 2007n597

PRIMATES
Primate family tree, 2009n1206

PRINTS, AMERICAN
Bibliography on American prints of the 17th through
the 19th centuries, 2007n811
Hebrew printing in America 1735-1926, 2007n545

PRISONS
Encyclopedia of prisons & correctional facilities,
2005n563
Prisons, 2006n568
Prisons & prison systems, 2006n561

PRISONERS OF WAR
Encyclopedia of prisoners of war & internment, 2d ed,
2007n552

PRIVACY, RIGHT OF
Encyclopedia of privacy, 2007n443
Invasion of privacy, 2006n542
Privacy in the info age, rev ed, 2007n1288

PROPAGANDA
Historical dict of American propaganda, 2005n432

PROTESTANTISM. *See also* **CHRISTIANITY**
Encyclopedia of Protestantism, 2005n1258

PROVERBS
Facts on File dict of proverbs, 2d ed, 2008n869
Oxford dict of proverbs, new ed, 2005n60
Proverbs, 2005n1155

PSYCHOLOGY
Adult psychopathology & diagnosis, 5th ed, 2009n708
Annual review of psychology, v.55, 2004, 2005n743
Annual review of psychology, v.60, 2009, 2009n709
APA dict of psychology, 2007n649
Biographical dict of psychologists, psychiatrists, &
psychotherapists, 2009n698
Cambridge hndbk of personal relationships, 2007n662
Classic experiments in psychology, 2006n760
Complete mental health dir 2004, 4th ed, 2005n739
Complete mental health dir 2006, 5th ed, 2007n659
Complete mental health dir 2008, 6th ed, 2009n704
Complete mental health dir [Website], 2005n740
Complete mental health dir [Website], 2007n660
Comprehensive hndbk of clinical health psychology,
2009n711
Comprehensive hndbk of personality &
psychopathology, 2008n683
Comprehensive hndbk of psychological assessment,
2006n758

Concise Corsini ency of psychology & behavioral sci,
3d ed, 2006n753
Consumer's gd to mental health servs, 2008n684
Counseling & psychotherapy transcripts, client
narrative, & ref works [Website], 2009n699
Depression sourcebk, 2d ed, 2009n712
Dictionary of existential psychotherapy & counseling,
2007n658
Dictionary of multicultural psychology, 2007n656
Dictionary of the work of W. R. Bion, 2005n736
Directory of unpublished experimental mental
measures, v.9, 2008n681
Encyclopedia of applied developmental sci, 2005n825
Encyclopedia of behavior modification & cognitive
behavior therapy, 2006n755
Encyclopedia of cognitive behavior therapy, 2007n650
Encyclopedia of counseling, 2009n701
Encyclopedia of educl psychology, 2009n245
Encyclopedia of human dvlpmt, 2007n651
Encyclopedia of industrial & organizational
psychology, 2007n652
Encyclopedia of mental health, 3d ed, 2008n679
Encyclopedia of multicultural psychology, 2007n653
Encyclopedia of phobias, fears, & anxieties, 3d ed,
2009n700
Encyclopedia of psychological trauma, 2009n702
Encyclopedia of schizophrenia & other psychotic
disorders, 3d ed, 2007n657
Encyclopedia of school psychology, 2006n756
Encyclopedia of social psychology, 2008n677
Encyclopedia of stats in behavioral sci, 2007n654
Ethics desk ref for psychologists, 2009n710
Gale ency of mental health, 2d ed, 2008n678
Handbook of child psychology, 6th ed, 2007n663
Handbook of clinical psychology, 2009n713
Handbook of health psychology & aging, 2008n685
Handbook of multicultural assessment, 3d ed,
2008n686
Handbook of personality assessment, 2009n714
Handbook of psychological assessment, case
conceptualization, & treatment, 2008n687
Handbook of psychopathy, 2008n688
Handbook of sport psychology, 3d ed, 2008n689
Insider's gd to graduate programs in clinical &
counseling psychology, 2004/05 ed,
2005n742
Insider's gd to graduate programs in clinical &
counseling psychology, 2006-07 ed,
2007n661
Insider's gd to graduate programs in clinical &
counseling psychology, 2008/09 ed,
2009n706
Insider's gd to mental health resources online, rev ed,
2005n741
International dict of psychoanalysis, 2006n757
International hndbk of creativity, 2007n664
Mental health disorders sourcebk, 3d ed, 2006n759

Mental health in America, 2008n690
Mental health info for teens, 2d ed, 2007n665
Oxford companion to the mind, 2d ed, 2005n737
Popular psychology, 2006n754
Praeger hndbk on stress & coping, 2008n692
Psychologists & their theories for students, 2005n735
Psychology basics, rev ed, 2005n738
Student's A-Z of psychology, 2007n655
Tests, 6th ed, 2009n707

PSYCHOLOGY - GRADUATE SCHOOL
Graduate study in psychology 2008, 2008n682

PUBLIC ADMINISTRATION
Encyclopedia of governance, 2007n641
Encyclopedia of public admin & public policy,
    2005n733
Encyclopedia of public admin & public policy, 1st
    updated suppl, 2006n752
International dict of public mgmt & governance,
    2006n750

PUBLIC AFFAIRS GROUPS
National dir of corporate public affairs 2004, 22d ed,
    2005n160
National dir of corporate public affairs 2005, 23d ed,
    2006n139
National dir of corporate public affairs 2006, 24th ed,
    2007n141

PUBLIC HEALTH
Annual review of public health, v.25, 2004,
    2005n1427
Annual review of public health, v.29, 2009,
    2009n1229
Encyclopedia of family health, 3d ed, 2005n1436

PUBLIC INTEREST GROUPS
Public interest group profiles 2004-05, 11th ed,
    2005n731
Public interest group profiles 2006-07, 2007n600

PUBLIC LIBRARIES
Human resources for results, 2009n510
Introduction to public librarianship, 2005n607
Managing facilities for results, 2009n509
Neal-Schuman dir of public lib job descriptions,
    2006n592
Nonfiction readers' advisory, 2006n601
Programming for adults, 2006n602
Public libs & Internet serv roles, 2009n512
Public lib catalog, 12th ed, 2005n5
Public lib manager's forms, policies, & procedures
    hndbk w/CD-ROM, 2005n605
Public lib start-up gd, 2005n606

Readers' advisory serv in the public lib, 3d ed,
    2006n603
Small public lib survival gd, 2009n511
Strategic planning for results, 2009n514
Technology for results, 2006n600

PUBLIC OPINION POLLS
American attitudes, 4th ed, 2005n67
Gallup poll: pubic opinion 2003, 2005n69
Gallup poll, 2007, 2009n62
Gallup poll cumulative index, 1998-2007, 2009n63
Polling America, 2006n686
Polling the nations [Website], 2008n744
PollingReport.com [Website], 2009n636
Public opinion & polling around the world, 2005n688

PUBLIC POLICY
Encyclopedia of bioterrorism defense, 2006n751
Encyclopedia of public admin & public policy,
    2005n733
Encyclopedia of public admin & public policy, 1st
    updated suppl, 2006n752
Evolution of US counterterrorism policy, 2009n695
Health care policy & politics A to Z, 3d ed, 2009n697
Mainline Christians & US public policy, 2008n676
Research skills for policy & dvlpmt, 2008n674
Think tank dir, 2d ed, 2008n673

PUBLIC RECORDS
Manual to online public records, 2009n454
Personal versus private: presidential records in a
    legislative context, 2006n693
Public record research system-Web [Website],
    2007n448
Public record research tips bk, 2009n460
Public records online, 5th ed, 2005n732
Public records online, 6th ed, 2007n643
Sourcebook to public record info, 5th ed, 2005n709
Sourcebook to public record info, 6th ed, 2006n532
Sourcebook to public record info, 7th ed, 2007n449
Sourcebook to public record info, 9th ed, 2009n445

PUBLIC RELATIONS
Encyclopedia of public relations, 2005n886

PUBLIC WELFARE
Child poverty in America today, 2008n733
Encyclopedia of world poverty, 2007n713
Poverty in America, 2008n734
Poverty in the US, 2005n818
World poverty, 2009n761

PUBLISHERS & PUBLISHING. *See also*
AUTHORSHIP
Alternative publishers of bks in N America, 6th ed,
    2007n547

American bk trade dir 2005-06, 51st ed, 2006n648
American bk trade dir 2006-07, 52d ed, 2007n546
Author law A to Z, 2006n876
Book: the life story of a tech, 2006n657
Bowker annual lib & bk trade almanac 2007, 52d ed,
 2008n510
Canadian bks in print 2006: author & title index, 2007n6
Canadian bks in print 2006: subject index, 2007n7
Career opportunities in the publishing industry,
 2006n259
Craft of research, 3d ed, 2009n807
Directory of poetry pubs 2005-06, 21st ed, 2006n649
Directory of poetry pubs 2008-09, 24th ed, 2009n591
Directory of pub 2004, 29th ed, 2005n654
Directory of pub 2008, 33d ed, 2008n566
Directory of publishing 2009, 34th ed, 2009n592
Directory of small press/mag editors & pubs 2005-06,
 36th ed, 2006n650
Directory of small press/mag editors & pubs 2008-09,
 39th ed, 2009n593
History of the bk in America, v.1: the Colonial bk in
 the Atlantic world, 2008n569
History of the bk in America, v.3: the industrial bk,
 1840-80, 2008n570
History of the bk in Canada, v.1, 2005n656
History of the bk in Canada, v.1, 2006n655
History of the bk in Canada, v.2 1840-1918, 2006n656
History of the bk in Canada, v.3, 2008n571
International dir of little mags & small presses
 2005-06, 41st ed, 2006n651
International dir of little mags & small presses
 2008-09, 44th ed, 2009n594
International literary marketplace 2004, 2005n655
International literary market place 2006, 2006n652
International literary market place 2008, 2008n567
International literary market place 2009, 2009n595
Introduction to manuscript studies, 2009n598
Literary market place 2006, 2006n653
Literary market place 2007, 67th ed, 2008n568
Literary market place 2009, 2009n596
Publishers dir 2005, 28th ed, 2006n654
Publishers dir, 32d ed, 2009n597
Publishing, bks, & reading in Sub-Saharan Africa,
 2009n589

PUNK ROCK MUSIC
Encyclopedia of punk music & culture, 2007n1013

PUPPET THEATER
Practical puppetry A-Z, 2006n618

PURITANS
Historical dict of the Puritans, 2008n1084
Puritans & puritanism in Europe & America,
 2007n1115

QUILTS
Crazy quilts, 2009n840
Quilt, 2008n828

QUOTATION BOOKS
Big curmudgeon, 2008n53
Born this day, 2d ed, 2008n1004
Call to America, 2006n58
Catholic bk of quotations, 2005n1268
Dictionary of contemporary quotations, v.10, 5th rev
 ed, 2006n59
Dow's dict of railway quotations, 2007n1338
Elgar dict of economic quotations, 2005n173
Forbes bk of business quotations, repr ed, 2006n154
Founders on religion, 2007n1092
Glimpses of God through the ages, 2005n1247
Great quotations that shaped the western world,
 2009n48
High impact quotations, 2007n45
i-Quote, 2008n54
Literary spy, 2005n59
Little Oxford dict of quotations, 3d ed, 2006n60
Little Oxford dict of quotations, 4th ed, 2009n49
North Korea in quotation, 2006n94
On reading the Bible, 2006n1224
Oscar Wilde in quotation, 2007n966
Oxford dict of American quotations, 2006n61
Oxford dict of Civil War quotations, 2007n370
Oxford dict of humorous quotations, 3d ed, 2006n62
Oxford dict of humorous quotations, 4th ed, 2009n51
Oxford dict of literary quotations, 2d ed, 2005n1013
Oxford dict of phrase, saying, & quotation, 3d ed,
 2007n47
Oxford dict of proverbs, new ed, 2005n60
Oxford dict of quotations, 6th ed, 2005n61
Quotable American Civil War, 2009n50
Quotable founding fathers, 2005n462
Quotable John Adams, 2009n52
Quotable soldier, 2006n667
Treasury of black quotations, 2006n331
Vietnam War, 2006n459
We hold these truths, 2009n47
What they didn't say, 2007n46
Yale bk of quotations, 2007n48

QUR'AN
Qur'an, 2007n1122

RACE RELATIONS
Encyclopedia of American race riots, 2008n301
Encyclopedia of race & racism, 2008n302
Jim Crow ency, 2009n302
Martin Luther King, Jr., ency, 2009n299
Multiracial America, 2006n322
Race relations in the US, 2006n437

Race relations in the US, 1980-2000, 2009n295
Voting rights act of 1965, 2009n392

RACIAL PROFILING IN LAW ENFORCEMENT
Profiling & criminal justice in America, 2005n570

RACISM IN LITERATURE
Encyclopedia of racism in the US, 2007n263
Race & racism in lit, 2006n988

RADICALISM
Encyclopedia of modern worldwide extremists &
    extremist groups, 2005n686

RADIO BROADCASTING
Encyclopedia of American radio, 1920-60, 2d ed,
    2009n813
Great radio sitcoms, 2008n808
Historical dict of American radio soap operas,
    2006n891
Historical dict of Australian radio & TV, 2008n1019
Historical dict of British radio, 2007n783
Historical dict of old-time radio, 2008n805
Museum of Broadcast communications ency of radio,
    2005n909
Music radio, 2006n889
Radio, 2006n894
Radio series scripts, 1930-2001, 2007n782
Swingin' on the ether waves, 2006n890
This day in network radio, 2009n812

RADIOLOGY
A-Z of chest radiology, 2009n1241

RADIOS
Collector's gd to antique radios, 6th ed, 2005n926

RAILROADS
Dow's dict of railway quotations, 2007n1338
Encyclopedia of N American railroads, 2008n1354
Field gd to southern New England railroad depots &
    freight houses, 2008n1356
Railroad, 2006n1550
Railroad atlas of the US in 1946, v.2: N.Y. & New
    England, 2006n1549
Railroad atlas of the US in 1946, v.3, 2009n1349
Regional railroads of the Midwest, 2008n1355
Tourist trains gdbk, 2008n367
World railways of the 19th century, 2006n1552

RAP MUSIC
All Music gd to hip-hop, 2005n1148
Encyclopedia of rap & hip hop culture, 2007n1009
Hip hop culture, 2007n1010
Icons of hip-hop, 2008n988

RAPE
Encyclopedia of rape, 2006n558

RAWANDA
Historical dict of Rwanda, new ed, 2008n98

READERS' ADVISORY SERVICES
African American lit, 2006n1030
Best bks for boys, 2009n933
Blood, bedlam, bullets, & badguys: a reader's gd to
    adventure/suspense fiction, 2005n1040
Book crush, 2008n891
Encountering enchantment, 2008n883
Genrefied classics, 2008n895
Genreflecting, 6th ed, 2007n917
Gentle reads, 2009n925
Graphic novels, 2007n900
Historical fiction, 2007n918
Horror readers' advisory, 2005n1050
Jewish American lit, 2006n1032
More bk lust, 2006n1011
Nonfiction readers' advisory, 2006n601
Read on . . . crime fiction, 2009n943
Read on . . . fantasy fiction, 2008n904
Read on . . . histl fiction, 2008n901
Read the high country, 2007n933
Readers' advisory gd to nonfiction, 2008n946
Readers' advisory serv in the public lib, 3d ed,
    2006n603
Real story, 2007n977
Research-based readers' advisory, 2009n513
Rocked by romance, 2005n1016
Serving teens through readers' advisory, 2008n535
Teen reader's advisor, 2007n513
What do children & YAs read next, v.6, 2005n1014
What do I read next? v.2, 2003, 2005n1041
What do I read next? v.1, 2004, 2005n1042
What do I read next? 2005 ed, 2007n920
What do I read next? v.2, 2008 ed, 2009n940

READING. *See also* LITERACY
Books & beyond, 2009n938

REAGAN, RONALD
Reagan yrs, 2006n699
Ronald Reagan, 2009n628

REAL ESTATE
Encyclopedia of real estate terms, 3d ed, 2009n241
Landlord legal forms simplified, 2008n261
Plunkett's real estate & construction industry almanac
    2005, 2006n273
Plunkett's real estate & construction industry almanac
    2007, 2008n260
Real estate forms simplified, 2007n234

RECREATION

Encyclopedia of leisure & outdoor recreation, 2005n754

Encyclopedia of recreation & leisure in America, 2005n755

REFERENCE BOOKS

Reference sources for small & medium-sized libs, 7th, 2009n4

Reference sources in hist, 2d ed, 2005n510

REFERENCE SERVICES

Answering consumer health questions, 2009n587

Assessing ref & user servs in a digital age, 2008n557

Cooperative ref, 2005n647

Crash course in ref, 2009n584

Desk & beyond, 2009n583

Digital ref serv, 2005n648

Essential ref servs for today's school media specialists, 2005n612

Evolving Internet ref resources, 2007n539

Internet public lib [Website], 2009n495

Introduction to ref servs in academic libs, 2007n499

Introduction to ref work in the digital age, 2005n650

Librarians Internet index [Website], 2009n496

Librarian's Internet survival gd, 2d ed, 2007n540

Managing the 21st-century ref department, 2005n652

New Directions in ref, 2007n541

100 ready-to-use pathfinders for the Web, 2005n594

Reference & info servs in the 21st century, 2007n538

Reference collection, 2007n542

Reference collection dvlpmt, 2006n643

Reference librarian's policies, forms, guidelines, & procedures hndbk, 2007n537

Research within the disciplines, 2008n561

Training paraprofessionals for ref serv, 2d ed, 2009n586

Virtual ref best practices, 2009n585

Virtual ref desk, 2006n644

Virtual ref librarian's hndbk, 2005n651

Virtual ref on a budget, 2009n588

Virtual ref serv, 2008n558

Virtual ref training, 2005n649

RELIGION & POLITICS

Encyclopedia of modern Christian politics, 2007n574

Encyclopedia of politics & religion, 2d ed, 2007n575

RELIGION & SCIENCE

Catholicism & sci, 2009n1114

Encyclopedia of religion & nature, paperback ed, 2009n1090

Evangelicals & sci, 2009n1138

RELIGION - BIOGRAPHY

Dictionary of evangelical biog 1730-1860, 2005n1254

RELIGION, CHRISTIANITY

A to Z of Lutheranism, 2008n1083

Anglican young people's dict, 2005n1259

Augustana Evangelical Lutheran church in print, 2008n1076

Birth of the church, 2005n1263

Cambridge hist of Christianity, v.6: reform & expansion 1500-1660, 2009n1113

Cambridge hist of Christianity, v.7, 2008n1086

Charts of modern & postmodern church hist, 2005n1265

Christian chronology [Website], 2005n1255

Christian philosophy A-Z, 2008n1045

Christianity reader, 2008n1087

Chronology of world Christianity, 2009n1105

Dictionary of evangelical biog 1730-1860, 2005n1254

Dictionary of Jewish-Christian relations, 2006n1246

Dictionary of mission theology, 2008n1080

Eastern Orthodox churches, 2006n1227

Encyclopedia of Christian theology, 2005n1256

Encyclopedia of Christianity, 2006n1228

Encyclopedia of Christianity, v.4, 2006n1229

Encyclopedia of Christianity, v.5, 2009n1108

Encyclopedia of Pentecostal & charismatic Christianity, 2007n1109

Encyclopedia of prayer & praise, 2005n1257

Encyclopedia of Protestantism, 2005n1258

Encyclopedia of Protestantism, 2006n1233

Encyclopedia of the Stone-Campbell movement, 2006n1230

Faith seeking action, 2008n1090

Fathers of the church, 2008n1088

Global dict of theology, 2009n1110

Handbook of patristic exegesis, 2005n1250

Historical dict of Anglicanism, 2007n1108

Historical dict of Jehovah's Witnesses, 2009n1107

Historical dict of Methodism, 2d ed, 2006n1231

Historical dict of Mormonism, 3d ed, 2009n1106

Historical dict of Seventh-day Adventists, 2006n1232

Historical dict of the Coptic Church, 2009n1109

Historical dict of the Shakers, 2009n1112

History of Christianity in Asia, Africa, & Latin America, 1450-1990, 2008n1089

Holiness-Pentecostal movement, 2009n1103

Holy bingo, the lingo of Eden, jumpin' jehosophat, & the land of nod, 2007n1111

Jesus in hist, thought, & culture, 2005n1260

John Wesley's ecclesiology, 2008n1091

Key words in Christianity, 2007n1110

Latter-day Saint experience in America, 2005n1264

New dict of Christian apologetics, 2007n1113

New dict of saints, 2008n1079

New Westminster dict of Christian spirituality, 2007n1114

New Westminster dict of church hist, v.1, 2009n1111

Original Dr. Steve's almanac of Christian trivia, 2008n1093

Oxford dict of the Christian church, 3d ed, 2006n1234
Oxford hist of Christian worship, 2006n1237
Pocket dict of N American denominations, 2006n1235
Puritans & puritanism in Europe & America,
    2007n1115
Reading Jonathan Edwards, 2009n1104
Religious right, 3d ed, 2008n1066
Wesleyan holiness movement, 2006n1225
World Christianities, c.1815-c.1914, v.8, 2007n1116
World Christianities, c.1914-c.2000, v.9, 2007n1117

**RELIGION - DICTIONARIES &
ENCYCLOPEDIAS**
Encyclopedia of prayer & praise, 2005n1257
Encyclopedia of religion & war, 2005n1238
Encyclopedic sourcebk of new age religions,
    2005n1239
Historical dict of new age movements, 2005n1243
Religion bk, 2005n1242

RELIGION IN AMERICA
African American religious experience in America,
    2006n1216
American Indian religious traditions, 2006n336
American religion data archive [Website], 2006n1219
Atlas of race, ancestry, & religion in 21st-century Fla.,
    2007n64
Cambridge companion to American Judaism, 2006n1244
Catholic experience in America, 2006n1238
Columbia documentary hist of religion in America
    since 1945, 2006n1211
Cults, 2d ed, 2006n1214
Encyclopedia of American religions, 7th ed,
    2005n1241
Encyclopedia of religious revivals in America,
    2008n1054
Encyclopedia of women & religion in N America,
    2007n1080
Introduction to new & alternative religions in America,
    2008n1065
New ency of southern culture, v. 1: religion,
    2007n1083
New religious movement experience in America,
    2005n1244
Puritans & puritanism in Europe & America,
    2007n1115
Religion & the law in America, 2008n1057
Religion in America, 2008n1062
Shapers of the great debate on the freedom of religion,
    2006n516

RELIGION IN THE PUBLIC SCHOOLS
Educator's classroom gd to America's religious beliefs
    & practices, 2008n1064

RELIGION - INDEXES
ATLA religion database [Website], 2005n1245

Internet sacred text archive [Website], 2005n1246

RELIGION - QUOTATIONS
Glimpses of God through the ages, 2005n1247

RELIGIONS
A to Z of new religious movements, 2007n1076
Atlas of the world's religions, 2d ed, 2009n1088
Baker pocket gd to new religions, 2007n1074
Brill dict of religion, 2007n1075
Cyber worship in multifaith perspectives, 2007n1087
Dictionary of Atheism, skepticism, & humanism,
    2007n1077
Encyclopedia of love in world religions, 2008n1052
Encyclopedia of religion, 2d ed, 2006n1207
Encyclopedia of religion & nature, 2006n1208
Encyclopedia of religion & spiritual dvlpmt,
    2007n1079
Encyclopedia of religion, communication, & media,
    2008n1053
Encyclopedia of religious phenomena, 2008n1056
Encyclopedia of world religions, rev ed, 2007n1081
Founders on religion, 2007n1092
Geography of religion, 2006n1212
Global dict of theology, 2009n1110
Handbook of ancient religions, 2008n1063
Historical atlas of religions, 2007n1073
Holy people of the world, 2006n1206
Introduction to the world's major religions, 2006n1213
Key words in religious studies, 2007n1082
Maven in blue jeans, 2009n1092
Messiahs & Messianic movements through 1899,
    2006n1218
Pocket gd to world religions, 2007n1078
Religion past & present, v.1, 2008n1059
Religions of the ancient world, 2006n1217
Religions of the world, rev ed, 2006n1210
Routledge religion resource [Website], 2008n1060
World religions: almanac, 2007n1088
World religions: biogs, 2007n1089
World religions: primary sources, 2007n1090
World religions series, 2007n1091
Worldmark ency of religious practices, 2006n1209

RELIGIOUS FUNDAMENTALISM
Conservative Christians & pol participation, 2006n735
Encyclopedia of modern worldwide extremists &
    extremist groups, 2005n686
Fundamentalism, 2008n1061
Religious right, 3d ed, 2008n1066

RENAISSANCE
A to Z of the Renaissance, 2007n423
Encyclopedia of renaissance lit, 2007n879
Encyclopedia of the Renaissance & the Reformation,
    rev ed, 2005n472

Great events from hist: the Renaissance & early modern era, 2006n500
Handbook to life in renaissance Europe, 2006n470
Historical atlas of the Renaissance, 2005n471
Historical dict of the Renaissance, 2005n474
Renaissance & reformation, 2007n425
Sports & games of the Renaissance, 2005n762

RENAISSANCE LITERATURE
Encyclopedia of Renaissance lit, 2006n978

RENEWABLE ENERGY
Renewable & alternative energy resources, 2009n1329

REPTILES
Complete gd to the snakes of southern Africa, 2d ed, 2006n1391
Guide & ref to the crocodilians, turtles, & lizards of E & Central N America, 2007n1216
Guide to the reptiles of southern Africa, 2009n1210
Reptiles & amphibians of the southern pine woods, 2009n1211
Venomous reptiles of the western hemisphere, 2005n1399
Venomous snakes of the world, 2007n1219
World of animals: amphibians & reptiles, v.41-50, 2006n1392

REPUBLIC OF CAPE VERDE
Historical dict of the Republic of Cape Verde, 4th ed, 2008n97

RESEARCH
A-Z of social research, 2005n65
Academic lib research, 2009n503
Beyond the Internet, 2008n560
College student's research companion, 4th ed, 2008n564
Craft of research, 3d ed, 2009n807
Elements of lib research, 2009n500
Encyclopedic gd to searching & finding health info on the Web, 2005n1423
Essential gd to becoming an expert searcher, 2009n531
Evidence explained, 2008n563
Extreme searcher's Internet hndbk, 2005n1486
Facts on File gd to research, 2006n46
Find it online, 4th ed, 2006n1483
Focus groups, v.1, 2009n5
Handbook of design research methods in educ, 2009n274
Historian's toolbox, 2d ed, 2009n435
Industry research using the economic census, 2005n165
Literary research & the British Romantic Era, 2006n1047
Literature search strategies for interdisciplinary research, 2007n543

Oxford gd to lib research, 3d ed, 2006n596
Practical research methods for librarians & info professionals, 2008n559
Research gd for undergraduate students, 6th ed, 2007n494
Research, ref serv, & resources for the study of Africa, 2006n79
Research skills for policy & dvlpmt, 2008n674
Research within the disciplines, 2008n561
Researching leisure, sport, & tourism, 2008n704
Researching WW I, 2005n531
Sage dict of social research methods, 2007n51
Sage ency of qualitative research methods, 2009n57
Sourcebook for research in music, 2d ed, 2007n989

RESEARCH CENTERS
Government research dir, 21st ed, 2008n616
International research centers dir, 18th ed, 2005n47
International research centers dir, 19th ed, 2006n38
International research centers dir, 21st ed, 2008n39
New research centers, 36th ed, 2009n247
Research centers dir, 31st ed, 2005n304
Research centers dir, 35th ed, 2008n282
Research centers dir, 36th ed, 2009n248
Subject dir of special libs & info centers 29th ed, 2005n599

RESOURCE SCIENCE
Annual review of environmental & resources, v.29, 2004, 2006n1538

RETAIL INDUSTRY
Directory of convenience stores, 2005, 2006n179
Directory of convenience stores, 2008, 2009n173
High-volume retailers 2005, 2005n192
High-volume retailers 2006, 2006n182
Plunkett's retail industry almanac, 2006 ed, 2006n194
Plunkett's retail industry almanac 2007, 2008n203
Retail tenant dir 2008, 2008n207
Retail trade intl 2005, 14th ed, 2006n205
Retail trade intl 2007, 15th ed, 2008n214
World retail data & stats 2008/09, 2009n195

REVIEWS. *See also* BOOK REVIEWS
H-NET reviews in the humanities & social scis [Website], 2007n5

RHODE ISLAND
Buildings of Rhode Island, 2005n82
Profiles of Conn. & R.I., 2008n79

RHYTHM & BLUES MUSIC
Icons of R&B & soul, 2009n1024

RIGHT TO COUNSEL
Right to counsel & privilege against self-incrimination, 2005n559

RITES & CEREMONIES
Life events & rites of passage, 2009n1040

RIVERS
River systems of the world [Website], 2005n1518

ROCK MUSIC
A to X of alternative music, 2005n1141
American popular music: rock & roll, 2006n1109
Encyclopedia of indie rock, 2009n1028
Encyclopedia of punk music & culture, 2007n1013
Greenwood ency of rock hist, 2007n1014
Icons of rock, 2009n1027
Joel Whitburn presents rock tracks 1981-2008, 2009n1025
Rock & roll yr by yr, 2005n1152
Rock band name origins, 2009n1026
Rock song index, 2006n1110

ROCKETRY
Rockets & missiles, 2005n682

ROMAN HISTORY
A to Z of ancient Greek & Roman women, rev ed, 2009n785
Cambridge companion to the age of Constantine, 2006n477
Chronicle of the Roman Republic, 2005n495
Daily life in the Roman city, 2006n476
De Imperatoribus Romani [Website], 2007n395
Decline & fall of the Roman Empire, 2006n478
Dictionary of Greek & Roman culture, 2009n407
Dictionary of Greek & Roman geography, 2007n310
Edinburgh companion to Ancient Greece & Rome, 2007n384
Historical atlas of Ancient Rome, 2006n486
Oxford dict of the classical world, 2006n468
Roman army, 2007n396
Romans, 2005n496

ROMAN MYTHOLOGY
Dictionary of Greek & Roman biog & mythology, 2008n993

ROMANCE LITERATURE
Canadian romance authors' networks (CRAN) [Website], 2006n1017
Rocked by romance, 2005n1016

ROMANIES
Historical dict of the Gypsies, 2d ed, 2008n314

ROMANTICISM
Encyclopedia of the romantic era, 1760-1850, 2005n881

ROOSEVELT, ELEANOR (1884-1962)
Eleanor Roosevelt papers, v.1, 2008n496

ROOSEVELT, FRANKLIN D. (1882-1945)
FDR yrs, 2008n621
Life & presidency of Franklin Delano Roosevelt, 2006n692

ROSES
Best rose gd, 2005n1357
Old-fashioned & David Austin roses, 2005n1365
Reliable roses, 2005n1364
Rose, 2005n1363

ROWLING, J. K.
Field gd to Harry Potter, 2009n945

RUNNING
Running well, 2009n738

RUSSIA
Brief hist of Russia, 2009n116
Cambridge hist of Russia, v.1, 2007n397
Cambridge hist of Russia, v.2, 2007n398
Cambridge hist of Russia: v.3, the 20th century, 2008n438
Daily life in Imperial Russia, 2009n410
Encyclopedia of contemporary Russian culture, 2008n127
Food culture in Russia & Central Asia, 2006n1291
Historical dict of Russian & Soviet intelligence, 2007n558
Joseph Stalin, 2008n439
Pop culture Russia! 2006n1125
Russia, 2005n113
Russia, updated ed, 2006n411
Russian far east, 2d ed, 2005n115
St. Petersburg, new ed, 2006n412
Supplement to The Modern Ency of Russian, Soviet & Eurasian Hist, v.5, 2006n480
Territories of the Russian Federation 2007, 8th ed, 2008n128

RUSSIAN LANGUAGE DICTIONARIES
Elsevier's dict of economics, business, finance, & law, 2005n144
Elsevier's dict of zoology & general biology, 2005n1380

RUSSIAN LITERATURE
From the ends to the beginning: a bilingual anthology of Russian verse [Website], 2005n1095
Russian lit pages at Northwestern Univ early 20th-century Russian drama [Website], 2005n1096

RUSSO-JAPANESE WAR, 1904-1905
Historical dict of the Russo-Japanese War, 2007n557

SACRED MUSIC
Encyclopedia of American gospel music, 2006n1112
Historical dict of sacred music, 2007n1016
Uncloudy days: the gospel music ency, 2007n1015

SACRED SITES
Oracles of the ancient world, 2005n1237

SAILING
Encyclopedia of yacht designers, 2007n1342
Farwell's rules of the nautical road, 8th ed, 2006n1553
Sailor's illus dict, 2005n780

SAINTS
Butler's lives of the saints, v.1, 2006n1226
New dict of saints, 2008n1079
Saints & their symbols, 2005n936
Saints of Asia, 2008n1078

SALVATION ARMY
Historical dict of The Salvation Army, 2007n1112

SAUDI ARABIA
Brief hist of Saudi Arabia, 2005n129
Culture & customs of Saudi Arabia, 2007n128

SCANDINAVIAN LITERATURE
Historical dict of Scandinavian lit & theater, 2007n975

SCHOOL COUNSELING
Handbook of school counseling, 2009n257

SCHOOL LIBRARIES
Building character through multicultural lit, 2005n611
Children's catalog, 19th ed, 2007n502
Collaborating for project-based learning for grades 9-12, 2009n519
Collaboration & the school lib media specialist, 2006n604
Collection mgmt for youth, 2006n605
Copyright catechism, 2007n523
Copyright for teachers & librarians, 2005n608
Designing a school lib media center for the future, 2d ed, 2008n514
Developing an info literacy program K-12, 2d ed, 2005n627
Enhancing teaching & learning, 2d ed, 2005n609
Enhancing teaching & learning, 2d ed, 2009n518
Essential ref servs for today's school media specialists, 2005n612
Essential school lib glossary, 2006n606
Essentials of elem school lib mgmt, 2005n613
Leadership for excellence, 2009n522
Library research with emergent readers, 2009n520
Motivating readers in the middle grades, 2009n517
Motivating students in info literacy classes, 2005n628
New on the job: a school lib media specialist's gd to success, 2008n516

No school lib left behind, 2009n521
Resources for school librarians [Website], 2007n504
Resources for school librarians [Website], 2009n524
School lib media manager, 2009n526
School lib media manager, 3d ed, 2006n608
School-Libraries.net [Website], 2009n525
Senior high core collection, 17th ed, 2008n515
Story celebrations, 2009n553
Teaching lib media skills in grades K-6, 2005n610
Teaching with bks that heal, 2009n936
Technology & the school lib, 2007n503
Teen bk discussion groups @ the lib, 2005n618
Toward a 21st-century school lib media program, 2008n517
Whole school lib hndbk, 2006n607
Your lib goes virtual, 2009n516

SCHOOL PSYCHOLOGY
Encyclopedia of school psychology, 2006n756

SCIENCE
Access sci [Website], 2009n1124
Chicago gd to your career in sci, 2009n1135
Computer & info systems abstracts [Website], 2006n1276
eLibrary sci [Website], 2009n1120
Exploration & sci, 2007n1145
Gale ency of sci, 4th ed, 2008n1107
Growing up with sci, 3d ed, 2007n1141
Imperialism & sci, 2007n1147
Inventors & inventions, 2009n1128
KidHaven sci lib, 2008n1112
NTIS [Website], 2006n1277
100 greatest sci discoveries of all time, 2008n1111
Origin of everyday things, 2008n1110
ProQuest AP sci [Website], 2009n1121
Research & discovery, 2009n1137
Science & tech in modern European life, 2009n1141
Scientific thought, 2009n1133
Search it! Science [Website], 2009n1122
Timelines of sci & tech, 2007n1132
Web of sci [Website], 2006n1278

SCIENCE & LITERATURE
Literature & sci, 2006n986

SCIENCE & RELIGION
Science & nonbelief, 2006n1268
Science & religion, 400 BC to AD 1550, 2006n1269
Science & religion, 1450-1900, 2005n1294

SCIENCE - DICTIONARIES & ENCYCLOPEDIAS
American Heritage sci dict, 2005n1282
Battleground: sci & tech, 2009n1125
Britannica illus sci lib, 2009n1126
Dictionary of microscopy, 2006n1257

Encyclopedia sci, 2005n1284
Encyclopaedia of the hist of sci, tech, & medicine in
        non-Western cultures, 2d ed, 2009n1127
Encyclopedia of nonlinear sci, 2006n1394
Encyclopedia of sci, tech, & ethics, 2006n1254
Encyclopedia of scientific principles, laws, & theories,
        2009n1129
Exploring technology, 2005n1283
McGraw-Hill concise ency of sci & tech, 5th ed,
        2006n1259
McGraw-Hill ency of sci & tech, 10th ed, 2008n1109
New bk of popular sci, 2007n1135
New bk of popular sci, 2008 ed, 2009n1131
New bk of popular sci [Website], 2009n1132
100 sci words every college graduate should know,
        2007n1136
Philosophy of sci, 2007n1137
Random House concise dict of sci & computers,
        2006n1261
Science & scientists, 2007n1138
Science fact & sci fiction, 2007n1139
Science in the contemporary world, 2006n1263
Science in the early 20th century, 2006n1256
Science, tech, & society, 2006n1262
Van Nostrand's scientific ency, 10th ed, 2009n1134
World Bk student discovery sci ency, 2006n1264

SCIENCE EDUCATION
Science for girls, 2008n274

SCIENCE EXPERIMENTS
Experiment central, v.5 & 6, 2005n1293
Forensic sci experiments on file, 2005n1286
Junior nature experiments on file, 2007n1143
Junior sci experiments on file, new ed, 2005n1289
Junior sci experiments on file, v.2, 2006n1270
Junior sci experiments on file, v.3, 2007n1144
Science experiments on file, v.2, 2006n1274
Science experiments on file, v.4, 2008n1115
Science experiments on file, v.5, 2009n1139

SCIENCE FICTION
A to Z of sci fiction lit, 2006n1026
Anatomy of wonder, 5th ed, 2006n1018
Brave new words, 2008n903
Companion to sci fiction, 2006n1028
Encountering enchantment, 2008n883
Encyclopedia of sci fiction, 2006n1024
Greenwood ency of sci fiction & fantasy, 2006n1025
Historical dict of sci fiction lit, 2005n1051
Internet speculative fiction database [Website],
        2006n1019
Latin American sci fiction writers, 2005n1091
Locus online [Website], 2006n1020
Science fiction & fantasy research database [Website],
        2006n1021
Science fiction quotations, 2006n1029

Science fiction studies [Website], 2006n1022
Science fiction TV series, 1990-2004, 2009n1055
SF Canada [Website], 2006n1023
Women & sci, 2006n863

SCIENCE - HANDBOOKS & YEARBOOKS
Cool stuff & how it works, 2006n1275
Discover sci almanac, 2005n1285
Handy sci answer bk, centennial ed, 2005n1287
History of invention series, 2005n1288
How it happens, 2006n1271
McGraw-Hill yrbk of sci & tech 2005, 2006n1272
McGraw-Hill yrbk of sci & tech 2008, 2008n1113

SCIENCE - HISTORY
Cambridge hist of sci, v.3: early modern sci,
        2007n1140
Chronology of sci, 2007n1133
Encyclopedia of 20th-century tech, 2006n1255
Groundbreaking scientific experiments, inventions, &
        discoveries of the Middle Ages & the
        Renaissance,
2005n1290
History of sci & tech, 2005n1281
History of sci, tech, & medicine [Website], 2005n1297
Medieval sci & tech, 2005n1296
Medieval sci, tech, & medicine, 2006n1260
100 greatest sci inventions of all time, 2007n1142
Science & society in the 20th century, 2005n1295
Science & tech in Colonial America, 2006n1267
Science & tech in 19th-century America, 2006n1273
Science in the ancient world, 2006n1258
Scientific revolution & the foundations of modern sci,
        2006n1266
Theories for everything, 2007n1146

SCIENCE LIBRARIES
Innovations in sci & tech libs, 2005n615

SCIENTISTS
American men & women of sci, 22d ed, 2005n1279
American men & women of sci, 23d ed, 2007n1128
American scientists, 2006n1251
Biography today: scientists & inventors, v.10,
        2006n1250
Biography today: scientists & inventors, v.11,
        2007n1129
Encyclopedia of world scientists, rev ed, 2008n1105
Inventors & inventions, 2009n1128
Ladies in the lab II, 2005n1280
New dict of scientific biog, 2008n1104
Who's who in sci & engineering 2005-046 8th ed,
        2006n1252
Who's who in sci & engineering 2006-07, 9th ed,
        2007n1131
Who's who in sci & engineering 2008-09, 10th ed,
        2008n1106

Women's adventures in sci series, 2006n1253

SCOTLAND
Biographical dict of Scottish women, 2007n388
Biographical dict of Scottish women, paperback ed, 2008n778
Castles of Scotland, 2006n405
Illustrated ency of Scotland, 2005n116

SCOTTISH GENEALOGY
Tracing your Scottish ancestry, 3d ed, 2005n359

SCUBA DIVING
Dive, 2005n781

SCULPTURE
Cesnola collection: terracottas [CD-ROM], 2005n951

SEASHELLS
Firefly gd to seashells of the world, 2005n1398

SEASHORE
World shores & beaches, 2006n388

SEGREGATION IN EDUCATION
Brown v. Board of Educ, 2006n547

SENEGAL
Culture & customs of Senegal, 2009n93

SERIAL MURDERS. *See also* **CRIME**
Jack the Ripper suspects, 2005n561

SEVENTH-DAY ADVENTISTS
Historical dict of Seventh-day Adventists, 2006n1232

SEX CRIMES
Encyclopedia of rape, 2006n558
Sexual misconduct & the clergy, 2006n569

SEX STUDIES
American sexual behavior, 2007n708
Continuum complete intl ency of sexuality, updated ed, 2005n816
Encyclopedia of prostitution & sex work, 2007n709
Encyclopedia of sex & gender, 2006n815
Gender issues & sexuality, 2007n710
Greenwood ency of love, courtship, & sexuality through hist, 2009n755
Handbook of sexual & gender identity disorders, 2009n756
Sex from Plato to Paglia, 2007n711
Youth, educ, & sexualities, 2006n816

SEXUALLY TRANSMITTED DISEASES
Encyclopedia of sexually transmitted diseases, 2005n1472

Sexual health info for teens, 2d ed, 2009n1267

SHAKERS
Historical dict of the Shakers, 2009n1112

SHAKESPEARE, WILLIAM
Class & society in Shakespeare, 2009n974
Critical companion to William Shakespeare, 2006n1050
Essential Shakespeare hndbk, 2005n1080
Greenwood companion to Shakespeare, 2006n1051
Music in Shakespeare, 2007n961
Shakespeare: a hundred yrs on film, 2005n1208
Shakespeare for students, 2d ed, 2008n933
Shakespeares after Shakespeare, 2007n960
Shakespeare's lang, 2d ed, 2009n975
Shakespeare's non-standard English, 2005n1079
Shakespeare's religious lang, 2007n959
World Shakespeare bibliog online [Website], 2009n976

SHAMANISM
Historical dict of Shamanism, 2008n1103
Shamanism, 2005n1278

SHINTO
A to Z of Shinto, 2007n1127

SHIPS
Oxford companion to ships & the sea, 2d ed, 2006n1554
Ship, 2005n1551
What ship is that? 2d ed, 2009n1351

SHIPWRECKS
Titanic in print & on screen, 2006n1133

SHOOTING, MILITARY
Marksmanship in the US Army, 2005n671

SHORT STORIES
Masterplots II: short story series, rev ed, 2005n1053
Short stories for students, v.19, 2005n1054
Short stories for students, v.20, 2005n1055
Short stories for students, v.25, 2008n898
Short story index [Website], 2008n899
Short story writers, rev ed, 2008n875
Understanding Melville's short fiction, 2006n1038

SIERRA LEONE
Historical dict of Sierra Leone, new ed, 2009n87

SIKHISM
Historical dict of Sikhism, 2d ed, 2006n1249

SILVER MINES
Silver & gold mining camps of the old west, 2008n401

SINGAPORE
Encyclopedia of Singapore, 2007n102

SKIING
Rough Guide to skiing & snowboarding in N America, 2005n782

SKIN DISEASES
Dermatological disorders sourcebk, 2d ed, 2006n1452

SLAVERY
Encyclopedia of antislavery & abolition, 2008n394
Encyclopedia of emancipation & abolition in the transatlantic world, 2008n453
Encyclopedia of slave resistance & rebellion, 2008n395
Encyclopedia of the middle passage, 2008n396
Encyclopedia of the Underground Railroad, 2008n399
New slavery, 2d ed, 2006n581
People of the Underground Railroad, 2009n363
Slave revolts, 2009n397
Slavery in America, 2007n369
Slavery in America, 2008n419
Slavery in America, 2008n421
Slavery in the south, 2005n454
Slavery in the US, 2008n403
Underground Railroad, 2009n384

SLEEP DISORDERS
Sleep disorders sourcebk, 2d ed, 2006n1438

SLOVAKIA
Historical dict of Slovakia, 2d ed, 2008n129

SLOVENIA
Historical dict of Slovenia, 2d ed, 2008n130

SMALL LIBRARIES
New OPL sourcebk, 2007n496
Technology made simple, 2007n528

SMOKING
Smoking concerns sourcebk, 2005n823
Tobacco in hist & culture, 2005n824

SNAKES
Complete gd to the snakes of southern Africa, 2d ed, 2006n1391
Guide & ref to the snakes of E & Central N America, 2007n1217
New ency of snakes, 2008n1194
Venomous snakes of the world, 2007n1219

SOCCER
Soccer yrbk 2004-05, 2006n796

SOCIAL CLASSES
Class in America, 2008n58

SOCIAL CONDITIONS. *See also* **UNITED STATES – SOCIAL CONDITIONS**
Greenwood daily life online [Website], 2005n508

SOCIAL ISSUES
At issue series, 2009n60
Current controversies series, 2008n62
Current controversies series, 2009n61
Current issues [Website], 2009n53
History of issues series, 2008n461
Issues [Website], 2008n57
Pro/con 3, 2005n692
Pro/con 4, 2006n691

SOCIAL JUSTICE
Encyclopedia of activism & social justice, 2008n59

SOCIAL POLICY
International ency of social policy, 2008n672
Social policy, 2007n54

SOCIAL SCIENCES
A-Z of social research, 2005n65
Allyn & Bacon social atlas of the US, 2008n55
American attitudes, 4th ed, 2005n67
Avalon project at Yale Law School [Website], 2006n508
Companion to cultural geography, 2005n68
Encyclopedia of human geography, 2005n66
Encyclopedia of human geography, 2007n50
Encyclopedia of social problems, 2009n55
Focus groups, v.1, 2009n5
Gallup poll, 2007, 2009n62
Gallup poll cumulative index, 1998-2007, 2009n63
General social survey bibliog [Website], 2005n62
Human dvlpmt report 2007/08, 2009n64
International ency of the social scis, 2d ed, 2008n61
Introducing issues with opposing viewpoints series, 2009n65
Intute: social scis [Website], 2008n56
Isms & ologies, 2008n60
Issues on trial series, 2009n452
Sage dict of social research methods, 2007n51
Sage ency of qualitative research methods, 2009n57
SIRS researcher [Website], 2009n58
Social issues firsthand series, 2009n66
Social issues in America, 2007n52
Social sci research network (SSRN) electronic lib [Website], 2007n49
Social sci resources in the electronic age, 2005n63
Statesman's yrbk 2004, 140th ed, 2005n70
Statesman's yrbk 2008, 2008n63
World data analyst online [Website], 2009n54

SOCIAL SECURITY
Social Security, 2008n473
Social security, 2009n449

Social Security hndbk 2005-06, 15th ed, 2007n464
US social security, 2009n453

SOCIAL STUDIES
Social studies teaching activities bks, 2007n240

SOCIAL SURVEYS
Encyclopedia of survey research methods, 2009n56

SOCIAL WELFARE
Child poverty in America today, 2008n733
Comprehensive hndbk of social work & social welfare,
    2009n759
Encyclopedia of social welfare hist in N America,
    2006n818
Encyclopedia of world poverty, 2007n713
Government assistance almanac 2005-06, 19th ed,
    2006n817
Government assistance almanac 2006-07, 20th ed,
    2007n712
Government assistance almanac 2009, 21st ed,
    2009n758
Historical dict of the welfare state, 2d ed, 2007n714
Poverty in America, 2008n734
Rich & poor in America, 2009n760
Statistical hndbk on the social safety net, 2006n819

SOCIAL WORK
Comprehensive hndbk of social work & social welfare,
    2009n759
Encyclopedia of social work, 20th ed, 2009n757
Social work dict, 5th ed, 2005n819

SOCIALISM
Historical dict of socialism, 2d ed, 2007n631

SOCIOLOGY
Annual review of sociology, v.29, 2003, 2005n791
Annual review of sociology, v.30, 2004, 2005n792
Basics of sociology, 2006n799
Blackwell companion to the sociology of families,
    2006n806
Blackwell ency of sociology, 2007n689
Cambridge dict of sociology, 2008n715
Dictionary of sociology, 3d ed, 2006n797
Encyclopedia of social theory, 2005n788
Encyclopedia of social theory, 2007n690
Encyclopedia of the life course & human dvlpmt,
    2009n739
Sage dict of sociology, 2007n691
Sociological collection [Website], 2005n786
Sociological tour through cyberspace [Website],
    2005n789
Sociology: a Sage full-text collection [Website],
    2005n787
SocioWeb [Website], 2005n790
SocioWeb [Website], 2006n798

SOIL SCIENCE
Encyclopedia of soil sci, 2d ed, 2007n1148
Encyclopedia of soil sci, 2009n1142

SOUND - RECORDING & REPRODUCING
Audio dict, 3d ed, 2006n1084
Encyclopedia of recorded sound, 2d ed, 2005n1119

SOUSA, JOHN PHILIP, 1854-1932
Sousa at Ill.: a catalogue of the collections, 2006n1078

SOUTH AFRICA
Coastal gd to S Africa, 2009n1209
Culture & customs of S Africa, 2005n89
South Africa's diverse peoples, 2007n90

SOUTH AMERICA
Guide to documentary sources for Andean studies,
    1530-1900, 2009n119
Historical dict of ancient S America, 2009n413

SOUTH ASIA
Historical dict of ancient SE Asia, 2008n100
Historical dict of the peoples of the SE Asian massif,
    2007n264
South Asia 2007, 4th ed, 2008n104
South Asia 2009, 2009n98
South Asia: an environmental hist, 2009n1341
South Asian folklore, 2007n1022
Southeast Asia, 2008n1345
World & its peoples: Eastern & Southern Asia,
    2009n97

SOUTH CAROLINA
Profiles of N Carolina & S Carolina, 2008n87

SOUTHERN STATES, HISTORY
Historical dict of the Old South, 2006n443

SOVIET UNION, HISTORY
Daily life in the Soviet Union, 2005n114
Documents of Soviet hist, v.6, 2006n479
Joseph Stalin, 2008n439
Supplement to The Modern Ency of Russian, Soviet &
    Eurasian Hist, v.5, 2006n480

SPACE SCIENCE
A to Z of scientists in space & astronomy, 2006n1503
Ancient astronomy, 2006n1506
Astronomy, 2007n1305
Atlas of the Messier objects, 2009n1303
Backyard astronomer's gd, 3d ed, 2009n1307
Birth of stars & planets, 2007n1304
Cambridge ency of stars, 2007n1300
Cambridge illus dict of astronomy, 2009n1304
Carolina starwatch, 2008n1298
Children's night sky atlas, 2005n1501

de Vaucouleurs atlas of galaxies, 2008n1297
E.guides: space travel, 2005n1504
Encyclopedia of space & astronomy, 2007n1299
Extrasolar planets, 2006n1504
Facts on File dict of astronomy, 5th ed, 2007n1301
Facts on File dict of space tech, rev ed, 2005n1502
Firefly atlas of the universe, 3d ed, 2006n1500
Firefly ency of astronomy, 2005n1503
Florida starwatch, 2008n1299
From luminous hot stars to starburst galaxies,
    2009n1306
Frontiers of space exploration, 2d ed, 2005n1506
Great observatories of the world, 2006n1507
Handy astronomy answer bk, 2009n1308
History of astronomy, 2008n1304
Library of the 9 planets, 2006n1508
National Geographic ency of space, 2006n1505
New atlas of the moon, 2008n1301
New atlas of the stars, 2006n1501
New views of the solar system, 2008n1305
Next space age, 2009n1309
Night sky atlas, 2006n1502
Oxford companion to cosmology, 2009n1305
Space & astronomy, 2008n1302
Space exploration: almanac, 2005n1507
Space exploration: biogs, 2005n1508
Space exploration: primary sources, 2005n1509
Space sci, 2005n1510
Spacecraft launch sites worldwide, 2008n1303
Texas starwatch, 2008n1300
300 astronomical objects, 2007n1306
USA in space, 2007n1302
Visual ency of space, 2007n1303

SPAIN
Architecture of Spain, 2006n932
Fodor's Spain 2006, 2006n407
Food culture in Spain, 2006n1292
History in dispute, v.18: The Spanish Civil War,
    2006n481
Iberia & the Americas, 2006n749
Spain 2008, 2008n377
Spain & Portugal, 2008n131

SPANISH LANGUAGE BOOKS
Recommended bks in Spanish for children & YAs
    2004-08, 2009n929

SPANISH LANGUAGE DICTIONARIES
Barron's Spanish-English dict, 2007n863
Bilingual visual dict: Spanish/English, 2007n864
Elsevier's dict of medicine: Spanish-English &
    English-Spanish, 2005n1435
Harrap's Spanish & English business dict, 2006n122
La nueva enciclopedia cumbre [Website], 2009n20
Larousse unabridged dict: Spanish-English,
    English-Spanish, 2005n974

New ref grammar of modern Spanish, 2006n971
Oxford Spanish dict, 4th ed, 2009n901
Spanish ref center [Website], 2009n23
Spanish word histories & mysteries, 2008n874
Vocabulario Vaquero/cowboy talk, 2005n975
Webster's family Spanish-English dict, deluxe ed,
    2007n865
Webster's new explorer Spanish-English dict, new ed,
    2007n866

SPANISH LITERATURE
Cambridge hist of Spanish lit, 2006n1065
Cervantes ency, 2005n1098
Merce Rodoreda, 2005n1099

SPECIAL COLLECTIONS (LIBRARIES)
Access to E European & Eurasian culture, 2009n527
American music librarianship, 2006n609
Answers to the health questions people ask in libs,
    2009n532
Art museum libs & librarianship, 2008n518
Catalogue of Medieval & Renaissance ms in the
    Beinecke rare bk & ms lib Yale Univ,
    2005n614
Directory of special libs & info centers, 30th ed,
    2005n597
Directory of special libs & info centers, 34th ed,
    2009n493
Guide to developing end user educ programs in
    medical libs, 2006n610
Guide to Slavic collections in the US, 2006n611
Innovations in sci & tech libs, 2005n615
Managing electronic govt info in libs, 2009n534
Manual for the performance lib, 2008n521
Outreach servs in academic & special libs, 2005n604
Subject access to a multilingual museum database,
    2009n540
Subject dir of special libs, 34th ed, 2009n499
Subject dir of special libs & info centers 29th ed,
    2005n599
Tribal libs in the US, 2008n508

SPECIAL EDUCATION
Encyclopedia of special educ, 2008n290

SPEECHES, ADDRESSES
American voices, 2006n870
Representative American speeches 2002-03, 2005n890
Representative American speeches 2004-05, 2006n874
Representative American speeches 2005-06, 2007n766
Representative American speeches 2007-08, 2009n801

SPORTING GOODS INDUSTRY
Career opportunities in the sports industry, 3d ed,
    2005n246
Plunkett's sports industry almanac, 2006n770
Plunkett's sports industry almanac 2007, 2008n204

Sports market place dir 2004, 2005n758
Sports market place dir 2005, 2006n771
Sports market place dir 2008, 2009n718
Sports market place dir [Website], 2005n759
Sports market place dir [Website], 2006n772

SPORTS. *See also* **ATHLETES**
Athletic dvlpmt, 2009n733
Berkshire ency of extreme sports, 2008n697
Berkshire ency of world sport, 2007n670
Biography today: sports, v.13, 2006n767
Biography today: sports, v.14, 2007n669
Chambers sports factfinder, 2006n773
Drugs & sports, 2008n705
Encyclopedia of intl sports studies, 2007n671
Encyclopedia of the modern Olympic movement, 2005n777
Encyclopedia of title IX & sports, 2009n717
ESPN sports almanac 2004, 2005n761
Olympic Games, 2005n778
Researching leisure, sport, & tourism, 2008n704
Scholarly sport sites [Website], 2005n757
SIRC's sport quest [Website], 2005n746
Sport discus [Website], 2005n747
Sport in American culture, 2006n768
Sporting News archives [Website], 2005n748
Sports & games of the renaissance, 2005n762
Sports, exercise, & fitness, 2006n766
Sports in America, 2005n753
Sports market place dir 2006, 2007n673
Sports market place dir 2007, 2008n702
Sports market place dir [Website], 2007n674
Sports museums & halls of fame worldwide, 2006n769
Statistical ency of N American professional sports, 2d
    ed, 2008n698
World of sports sci, 2007n672
World stadiums [Website], 2005n760

SPORTS MEDICINE
Clinical sports medicine, 3d ed, 2007n1277
Encyclopedia of sports medicine, 2005n1473
Key topics in sports medicine, 2009n1270
Quick ref dict for athletic training, 2d ed, 2006n1454
Sports injuries gdbk, 2009n1271
Sports medicine, 2008n1258
Sports sci hndbk, 2006n1455

SPORTS NUTRITION
Endurance sports nutrition, 2d ed, 2008n703

SPORTS PSYCHOLOGY
Handbook of sport psychology, 3d ed, 2008n689

SRI LANKA
Encyclopedia of Sri Lanka, 2d rev ed, 2007n103

STALIN, JOSEPH, 1879-1953
Joseph Stalin, 2008n439

STAMPS. *See* **POSTAGE STAMPS**

STATESMEN - UNITED STATES
American statesmen, 2005n694
Statesman's yrbk 2004, 140th ed, 2005n70
Statesman's yrbk 2008, 2008n63

STATISTICS
America's top-rated cities 2005, 12th ed, 2006n847
Annual abstract of stats, no.141, 2005 ed, 2006n835
Asian databk, 2005n839
Business stats of the US 2004, 9th ed, 2005n169
Business stats of the US 2005, 10th ed, 2006n148
Business stats of the US 2006, 11th ed, 2007n145
CQ's state fact finder 2004, 2005n846
CQ's state fact finder 2005, 2006n842
CQ's state fact finder 2006, 2007n745
Crime state rankings 2004, 11th ed, 2005n575
Crime state rankings 2005, 12th ed, 2006n567
Datapedia of the US 2004, 3d ed, 2005n847
Datapedia of the US 2007, 4th ed, 2009n774
Dictionary of stats & methodology, 3d ed, 2007n739
Education state rankings 2003-04, 2d ed, 2005n277
Encyclopedia of measurements & stats, 2007n737
Encyclopedia of statl scis, 2d ed, 2007n1134
Encyclopedia of stats in behavioral sci, 2007n654
Encyclopedia of stats in quality & reliability,
    2009n1220
Handbook of US labor stats 2004, 7th ed, 2005n234
Handbook of US labor stats 2005, 8th ed, 2006n240
Health care state rankings 2005, 13th ed, 2006n1424
Household surveys in developing & transition
    countries, 2006n836
Industrial commodity stats yrbk 2004, 2008n208
International histl stats: Africa, Asia & Oceania
    1750-2000, 4th ed, 2005n840
International histl stats: Europe 1750-2000, 5th ed,
    2005n841
International histl stats: the Americas 1750-2000, 5th
    ed, 2005n848
International trade stats yrbk 2002, 51st ed, 2005n265
International trade stats yrbk, 2003, 2006n272
International yrbk of industrial stats 2005, 2006n189
International yrbk of industrial stats 2008, 2009n183
Key population & vital stats, series VS no.30,
    2007n740
Monthly bulletin of stats [Website], 2008n756
National accounts stats 2003-04, 2007n741
National accounts stats 2004, 2008n758
National accounts stats 2004-05, 2008n757
National Center for Education Stats [Website],
    2005n279
NationMaster.com [Website], 2008n759
OECD factbk 2006, 2007n742
Oxford dict of stats, 2009n773
Project euclid [Website], 2005n842
Racial & ethnic diversity, 5th ed, 2007n266

Regional trends, 2007n743
Sage dict of stats, 2007n738
Social change in America, 2006, 2007n746
Social trends, no.35, 2005 ed, 2006n837
State rankings 2005, 16th ed, 2006n843
State rankings 2006, 2007n747
State rankings 2007, 2008n765
State trends, 2005n849
State trends, 2d ed, 2006n844
State trends, 3d ed, 2007n748
State trends, 2008 ed, 2009n776
Statistical abstract of the US 2003, 123d ed, 2005n850
Statistical abstract of the US 2004-05, 124th ed,
    2007n749
Statistical abstract of the US 2007, 126th ed, 2008n766
Statistical abstract of the US 2009, 128th ed, 2009n777
Statistical hndbk on the social safety net, 2006n819
Statistical yrbk 2001, 48th ed, 2005n843
Statistical yrbk 2002-04, 49th ed, 2006n839
Statistical yrbk, 50th ed, 2008n760
Statistical yrbk for Asia & the Pacific 2003, 2006n216
Statistics sources 2005, 28th ed, 2005n844
Statistics sources 2006, 29th ed, 2006n840
Statistics sources, 31st ed, 2008n761
UNCTAD hndbk of stats 2003, 2005n845
UNCTAD hndbk of stats 2004, 2006n841
UNCTAD hndbk of stats 2006-07, 2008n762
Vital stats, 2006n48
Vital stats of the US 2006, 2d ed, 2007n750
Vital stats of the US, 2004, 2005n851
Vital stats on American politics 2005-06, 2007n622
Vital stats on American politics [Website], 2007n623
World dir of non-official statl sources 2007, 7th ed,
    2008n763
World stats pocketbk, 2007n744

STEINBECK, JOHN, 1902-1968
Critical companion to John Steinbeck, 2006n1039
John Steinbeck bibliog 1996-2006, 2009n965
John Steinbeck ency, 2007n953

STEINEM, GLORIA
Gloria Steinem, 2005n867

STEM CELL RESEARCH
Encyclopedia of stem cell research, 2009n1171
Stem cell research, 2008n1146

STOCK CAR RACING
Day-by-day in NASCAR hist, 2005n783

STOCK MARKET. *See also* INVESTMENTS
Market share reporter, 2009 ed, 2009n150
Standard & Poor's MidCap 400 gd, 2003 ed,
    2005n174
Standard & Poor's small cap 600 gd, 2003 ed,
    2005n175

TheStreet.com ratings' gd to bond & money market
    mutual funds, Spring 2008, 2009n151
TheStreet.com ratings' gd to bond & money market
    mutual funds, Summer 2007, 2008n176
TheStreet.com ratings' gd to common stocks, Spring
    2008, 2009n152
TheStreet.com ratings' gd to common stocks, Summer
    2007, 2008n177
TheStreet.com ratings' gd to exchange-traded funds,
    Spring 2008, 2009n153
TheStreet.com ratings' gd to exchange-traded funds,
    Summer 2007, 2008n178
TheStreet.com ratings' gd to stock mutual funds,
    Summer 2007, 2009n154
TheStreet.com ratings' ultimate guided tour of stock
    investing, 2008n175
Weiss Ratings' ultimate guided tour of stock investing,
    Summer 2004, 2005n179

STORYTELLING
Box full of tales, 2009n554
Fostering community through digital storytelling,
    2009n505
Once upon a time, 2009n552
Story celebrations, 2009n553
Storytelling, 2009n1035
Tales online [Website], 2009n1029

STRESS
Praeger hndbk on stress & coping, 2008n692
Stress-related disorders sourcebk, 2d ed, 2008n693

STYLE GUIDES. *See also* WRITING
AMA manual of style, 10th ed, 2008n798
Associated Press stylebk & briefing on media law,
    39th ed, 2005n893
Associated Press stylebk & briefing on media law,
    2008n799
Cambridge gd to English usage, 2006n883
Chicago gd to writing about numbers, 2005n894
Chicago manual of style online [Website], 2007n775
Cite it right, 2d ed, 2007n778
Cite it right, 3d ed, 2008n800
Cite right, 2007n779
Columbia gd to online style, 2d ed, 2007n780
Concise rules of APA style, 2007n776
Cooper Hill stylebk, 2d ed, 2006n885
Copyeditor's hndbk, 2d ed, 2006n884
Copywriter's hndbk, 3d ed, 2007n771
Elements of style, 2006n887
Facts on File gd to style, 2007n777
Manual for writers of research papers, theses, &
    dissertations, 7th ed, 2008n801
McGraw-Hill desk ref for editors, writers, &
    proofreaders, 2007n772
MLA style manual & gd to scholarly publishing, 3d
    ed, 2009n808

Pocket gd to legal writing, 2006n886
Random House writer's ref, rev ed, 2005n895
UPI stylebk & gd to newswriting, 4th ed, 2005n896
Webster's new explorer gd to English usage,
    2005n961
Writer's market companion, 2d ed, 2006n881

SUBJECT HEADINGS. *See also* CATALOGING & CLASSIFICATION
Sears list of subject headings, 18th ed, 2005n617
Sears list of subject headings, 19th ed, 2008n512
Sears lista de encabezamientos de materia, 2009n544
Thesaurus of psychological index terms, 10th ed,
    2006n761
User's gd to Sears list of subject headings, 2009n543

SUBMARINES
Submarines, 2008n605

SUBSTANCE ABUSE
Addiction counselor's desk ref, 2007n716
Directory of drug & alcohol residential rehabilitation
    facilities, 2004, 2005n821
Directory of drug & alcohol residential rehabilitation
    facilities [Website], 2005n822
Drug abuse sourcebk, 2d ed, 2006n820
Drug info for teens, 2d ed, 2007n717
Drugs & society, 2006n821
Encyclopedia of drug abuse, 2009n763
Encyclopedia of drugs, alcohol, & addictive behavior,
    3d ed, 2009n762
U*X*L ency of drugs & addictive substances,
    2007n718

SUCCULENTS
500 cacti, 2008n1160

SUDAN
British military operations in Egypt & the Sudan,
    2009n600

SUFFRAGISTS
Women's suffrage, 2006n862
Women's suffrage in America, updated ed, 2006n861

SUMMER PROGRAMS
500 best ways for teens to spend the summer,
    2005n283
Summer opportunities for kids & teenagers 2006,
    2006n282

SUPERNATURAL IN LITERATURE
Icons of horror & the supernatural, 2008n902

SURVIVAL TECHNIQUES
Encyclopedia of survival techniques, new ed,
    2009n729

SWEDEN
Historical dict of Sweden, 2d ed, 2007n116

SWITZERLAND
Historical dict of Switzerland, 2008n132
Issues in Germany, Austria, & Switzerland, 2005n105

SYMBOLS
Complete dict of symbols, 2006n920
Continuum ency of animal symbolism in art,
    2005n939
Dictionary of subjects & symbols in art, 2d ed,
    2009n850
Elsevier's dict of symbols & imagery, 2d ed,
    2005n934
Fabulous creatures, mythical monsters, & animal
    power symbols, 2009n1034
Saints & their symbols, 2005n936

SYRIA
Historical dict of Syria, 2d ed, 2005n130

TAIWAN
Historical dict of Taiwan, 3d ed, 2008n107

TAMILS
Historical dict of the Tamils, 2008n424

TANKS
Tanks, 2005n681

TAROT CARDS
Encyclopedia of tarot, v.4, 2007n667

TATOOS
Encyclopedia of body adornment, 2009n843

TAXATION
Lower taxes in 7 easy steps, 2007n152

TEACHING
U.S. News & World Report ultimate gd to becoming a
    teacher, 2006n279

TECHNICAL SERVICES (LIBRARIES)
Fundamentals of tech servs mgmt, 2009n538
Teams in lib tech servs, 2007n544

TECHNOLOGY
Battleground: sci & tech, 2009n1125
Computer & info systems abstracts [Website],
    2006n1276
Encyclopedia of multimedia tech & networking
    [Website], 2006n1467
Encyclopedia of multimedia tech & networking,
    2006n1466
Encyclopedia of sci, tech, & ethics, 2006n1254

Encyclopedia of 20th-century tech, 2006n1255
Exploring technology, 2005n1283
High definition, 2007n1285
History of sci, tech, & medicine [Website], 2005n1297
McGraw-Hill concise ency of sci & tech, 5th ed, 2006n1259
McGraw-Hill ency of sci & tech, 10th ed, 2008n1109
McGraw-Hill yrbk of sci & tech 2005, 2006n1272
McGraw-Hill yrbk of sci & tech 2008, 2008n1113
Medieval sci, tech, & medicine, 2006n1260
New media, 2007n1289
Plunkett's nanotechnology & MEMS industry almanac, 2005n197
Science & tech in Colonial America, 2006n1267
Science, tech, & society, 2006n1262
Timelines of sci & tech, 2007n1132

TECHNOLOGY - VOCATIONAL GUIDANCE

America's top 101 computer & technical jobs, 2d ed, 2005n242

TEENAGERS

Contemporary youth culture, 2007n719
International ency of adolescence, 2007n720
Greenwood ency of children's issues worldwide, 2009n767
Teen life in Africa, 2005n83
Teen life in Asia, 2005n93
Using lit to help troubled teenagers cope with abuse issues, 2005n1031
Teen life in Europe, 2006n102
Teen's gds series, 2008n739

TEENAGERS - FINANCE, PERSONAL

Cash & credit info for teens, 2006n171
Savings & investment info for teens, 2006n172

TEENAGERS - HEALTH & HYGIENE

Abuse & violence info for teens, 2009n764
Accident & safety info for teens, 2009n1268
Adolescent health sourcebk, 2d ed, 2007n1254
Allergy info for teens, 2007n1267
Asthma info for teens, 2006n1442
Cancer info for teens, 2005n1461
Children & youth in sickness & in health, 2005n826
Complementary & alternative medicine info for teens, 2008n1240
Diabetes info for teens, 2007n1271
Diet info for teens, 2d ed, 2007n1256
Drug info for teens, 2d ed, 2007n717
Eating disorders info for teens, 2006n1448
Fitness info for teens, 2005n1428
Fitness info for teens, 2d ed, 2009n1231
Mental health info for teens, 2d ed, 2007n665
Sexual health info for teens, 2d ed, 2009n1267
Sleep info for teens, 2009n1250
Sports injuries info for teens, 2d ed, 2009n1269

Stress info for teens, 2009n1251
Teen health & wellness [Website], 2007n1235
Tobacco info for teens, 2008n736

TELECOMMUNICATIONS

Encyclopedia of info communication tech, 2009n1292
FaxUSA 2005, 12th ed, 2005n41
Glossary of netspeak & textspeak, 2005n1485
Handbook of research on wireless security, 2009n1294
Headquarters USA 2005, 27th ed, 2005n45
Major telecommunications companies of the world 2004, 7th ed, 2005n1490
Major telecommunications companies of the world 2007, 10th ed, 2008n194
National e-mail & fax dir 2005, 18th ed, 2006n40
National e-mail & fax dir, 21st ed, 2009n32
Plunkett's telecommunications industry almanac, 2006 ed, 2006n195
Plunkett's telecommunications industry almanac 2008, 2008n205
Plunkett's wireless, WI-FI, RFID, & cellular industry almanac, 2006n1488
Plunkett's wireless, WI-FI, RFID, & cellular industry almanac 2008, 2008n206
Plunkett's wireless, WI-FI, RFID, & cellular industry almanac, 2009 ed, 2009n182
Telecommunications & data communications hndbk, 2008n1283
Telecommunications dir, 14th ed, 2005n1491
Telecommunications dir, 17th ed, 2008n1284
Telecommunications fact bk & illus dict, 2d ed, 2006n1487
Toll-free phone bk USA 2005, 9th ed, 2005n42

TELEVISION

Bacon's TV/cable dir 2004, 18th ed, 2005n906
BFI film & TV hndbk 2004, 21st ed, 2005n1209
Blu-bk production dir, 2004, 2005n1182
Columbia hist of American TV, 2008n1031
Daytime serials of TV, 1946-60, 2007n786
Emmy Award winning nighttime TV shows, 1948-2004, 2007n1042
Encyclopedia of early TV crime fighters, 2007n1044
Encyclopedia of TV shows, 1925-2007, 2009n1065
Encyclopedia of TV subjects, themes, & settings, 2008n1023
From daytime to primetime, 2006n1165
Historical dict of African-American TV, 2006n1149
Movies made for TV 1964-2004, 2006n1140
Queer ency of film & TV, 2007n1048
Science fiction TV series, 1990-2004, 2009n1055
Swingin' on the ether waves, 2006n890
Television characters, 2006n1137
Television game show hosts, 2008n1012
Television in American society: almanac, 2007n787
Television in American society: biogs, 2007n788

Television in American society: primary sources, 2007n789
Television variety shows, 2006n1139
TV yr, v.1, 2008n1033
TV.com [Website], 2006n1157

TEMPERANCE
Alcohol & temperance in modern hist, 2005n820

TENNIS
Language of tennis, 2005n784

TERRORISM
Chronologies of modern terrorism, 2009n464
Chronology of world terrorism, 1901-2001, 2005n562
Counterterrorism, 2005n583
Ecoterrorism, 2005n580
Encyclopedia of bioterrorism defense, 2006n751
Encyclopedia of terrorism, rev ed, 2008n483
Evolution of US counterterrorism policy, 2009n695
Extremist groups, 2007n576
Global terrorism, rev ed, 2005n576
Greenhaven ency of terrorism, 2008n488
IntelCenter al-Qaeda messaging/attacks timeline 1992-2007, 2009n683
IntelCenter terrorism incident ref (TIR): Afghanistan: 2000-07, 2009n686
IntelCenter terrorism incident ref (TIR): Algeria, 2000-07, 2009n687
IntelCenter terrorism incident ref (TIR): Arabian Peninsula, 2000-07, 2009n686
IntelCenter terrorism incident ref (TIR): Iraq: 2000-05, 2009n689
IntelCenter terrorism incident ref (TIR): Iraq: 2006, 2009n690
IntelCenter terrorism incident ref (TIR): Iraq: 2007, 2009n691
IntelCenter terrorism incident ref (TIR): Pakistan: 2000-07, 2009n684
IntelCenter terrorism incident ref (TIR): Philippines, 2000-07, 2009n688
IntelCenter terrorist & rebel logo identification gd, 2009n679
IntelCenter words of Ayman al-Zawahiri, v.1, 2009n680
IntelCenter words of Osama bin laden, v.1, 2009n681
International security & counter terrorism ref center [Website], 2009n682
9/11 ency, 2009n372
Patterns of global terrorism, 1985-2005, 2007n433
Terrorism, 2005n578
Terrorism, 2006n566
Terrorism, 2007n484
Terrorism 2005-07, 2009n463
Terrorism & global security, 2008n675
USA Patriot Act of 2001, 2005n542

TEXAS
Dictionary of common wildflowers of Tex. & the Southern Great Plains, 2006n1343
Profiles of Tex. 2005-06, 2006n74
Profiles of Tex. 2008, 2009n81
Texas almanac 2006-07, 2006n75
Texas almanac 2008-09, 64th, 2009n82
Texas water atlas, 2009n1326
200 Tex. outlaws & lawmen 1835-1935, 2009n83

TEXTBOOKS
Directory of histl textbk & curriculum collections, 2006n593

TEXTILE INDUSTRY
Plunkett's apparel & textiles industry almanac, 2005n195

THAILAND
Atlas of Thailand, 2005n101
Culture & customs of Thailand, 2005n102
Historical dict of Thailand, 2d ed, 2006n97
Thailand, 2006n96

THANKSGIVING
Thanksgiving bk, 2008n1001

THEATER
American presidents attend the theatre, 2007n1058
American women stage directors of the 20th century, 2009n1073
Banned plays, 2005n1039
Blood on the stage, 2009n1079
Broadway musicals, 1943-2004, 2006n1173
Cambridge hist of British theatre, 2006n1178
Columbia ency of modern drama, 2008n1039
Directory of theatre training programs 2003-05, 9th ed, 2006n1175
Encyclopedia of Asian theatre, 2008n1040
Encyclopedia of Latin American theater, 2005n1219
Enter the players: N.Y. stage actors in the 20th century, 2005n1218
Enter the playmakers, 2007n1055
Grey House performing arts dir 2009, 6th ed, 2009n1050
Historical dict of African American theater, 2009n1075
Historical dict of American theater: modernism, 2009n1074
Historical dict of Chinese theater, 2009n1078
Historical dict of German theater, 2007n1056
Historical dict of Japanese traditional theatre, 2007n1057
Historical dict of postmodernist lit & theater, 2008n789
Historical dict of Russian theater, 2008n1043
Historical dict of the Broadway musical, 2008n1041

Oxford companion to American theatre, 3d ed,
    2005n1220
Oxford companion to the American musical, 2009n1077
Oxford dict of plays, 2006n1172
Play index 1998-2002, 2005n1222
Queer ency of music, dance, & musical theater,
    2005n1181
Regional theatre dir 2003-04, 2006n1176
Rodgers & Hammerstein ency, 2008n1042
Sherlock Holmes on the stage, 2009n1076
Summer theatre dir 2004, 2005n1221
Summer theatre dir 2005, 2006n1177
Theater mania gd to musical theater recordings,
    2006n1174
Theatre as human interaction, 2006n1179
Tools & techniques for character interpretation,
    2007n1038
Who sang what on Broadway, 1866-1996, 2006n1171
Women in America musical theatre, 2009n1080

THEOLOGY
Donald G. Bloesch, 2008n1077
Encyclopedia of Christian theology, 2005n1256
Historical dict of medieval philosophy & theology,
    2008n1044

THERMODYNAMICS
Heat & thermodynamics, 2009n1136

TITANIC (STEAMSHIP)
Titanic in print & on screen, 2006n1133

TOBACCO INDUSTRY
Smoking concerns sourcebk, 2005n823
Tobacco in hist & culture, 2005n824
Tobacco info for teens, 2008n736

TOLKIEN, J. R. R. (1892-1973)
J. R. R. Tolkien companion & gd, 2008n934
J. R. R. Tolkien ency, 2008n935

TOLSTOY, LEO (1828-1910)
Leo Tolstoy, 2007n974

TOOLS
Tools, 2006n913

TOYS
O'Brien's collecting toys, 12th ed, 2009n839
Schroeder's collectible toys 2006, 10th ed, 2006n907

TRADE ASSOCIATIONS
Trade assns & professional bodies of Continental
    Europe, 2005 ed, 2005n221

TRADE SHOWS
Trade shows worldwide, 20th ed, 2005n258

Trade shows worldwide, 22d ed, 2006n267
Trade shows worldwide, 23d ed, 2008n257

TRADE UNIONS
Historical dir of trade unions, v.5, 2008n226

TRADE. *See* **INTERNATIONAL TRADE**

TRANSCENDENTALISM
Second great awakening & the transcendentalists,
    2005n448

TRANSPORTATION HISTORY
Chronology of transportation in the US, 2005n1545
Ship, 2005n1551

TRANSPORTATION INDUSTRY
Grey House transportation security dir & hndbk,
    2006n1546
Plunkett's transportation, supply chain, & logistics
    industry almanac, 2005n198
Plunkett's transportation, supply chain, & logistics
    industry almanac 2007, 2007n175
Plunkett's transportation, supply chain, & logistics
    industry almanac, 2008 ed, 2009n181

TRAVEL
Australia, 5th ed, 2008n370
Australian bed & breakfast bk 2007, 2008n371
Backroads of S Calif., 2006n399
Bed & breakfast Ireland 2006, 2008n372
Berlitz complete gd to cruising & cruise ships 2008,
    2008n363
Berlitz complete gd to cruising & cruise ships 2009,
    18th ed, 2009n344
Caribbean, updated ed, 2008n374
Central America, 2d ed, 2008n375
China, 2008n368
City profiles USA 2006-07, 8th ed, 2007n319
City profiles USA 2008-09, 9th ed, 2009n350
Complete Fla. beach gd, 2009n349
Complete gd to cruising & cruise ships 2006, 16th ed,
    2007n318
Costa Rica 2008, 2008n376
Dorling Kindersley traveler's atlas, 2006n393
Eco-travel gd, 2009n345
Fodor's escape to nature without roughing it,
    2005n395
From Agincourt to Zanzibar, 2009n346
Globe trekker's world, 2006n394
Great Canadian vacations, 2005n403
Greece, 5th ed, 2005n405
Hammond world travel atlas, 2005n392
India, 8th ed, 2008n369
Irish bed & breakfast bk, 2009n352
Italy, new ed, 2008n373
Lewis & Clark Columbia River water trail, 2005n397

Mediterranean cruises, 2005n407
Mexico & Central America hndbk 2009, 17th ed,
    2009n354
National Geographic gd to the natl parks of the US,
    5th ed, 2007n321
New traveler's atlas, 2008n364
New York City 2008, 2008n366
Ocean cruising & cruise ships 2005, 2006n395
100 best family resorts in N America, 7th ed,
    2006n397
100 best resorts of the Caribbean, 6th ed, 2005n409
100 best resorts of the Caribbean, new ed, 2009n356
1,000 places to see before you die, 2005n394
1001 historic sites you must see before you die,
    2009n347
Peru, 5th ed, 2009n355
Plunkett's airline, hotel, & travel industry almanac
    2007, 2008n195
Russia: Belarus & Ukraine, updated ed, 2009n353
Sierra Club gd to the ancient forests of the NE,
    2005n399
Spain 2008, 2008n377
Stern's gd to the cruise vacation 2008, 2008n365
10 best of everything: an ultimate gd for travelers,
    2007n317
Timeless Earth, 2009n348
Tourist trains gdbk, 2008n367
Travel gd to the Jewish Caribbean & Latin America,
    2005n408
Travel gd to the Plains Indian wars, 2007n320
US natl parks west, 2006n398
USA: the new south, 2005n400
Washington D.C., 5th ed, 2009n351
When in Rome or Rio or Riyadh, 2005n393

TRAVEL INDUSTRY
Careers in travel, tourism, & hospitality, 2d ed,
    2006n247
Plunkett's airline, hotel, & travel industry almanac,
    2006 ed, 2006n190
Who's buying for travel, 2006n165

TREATIES
Encyclopedia of histl treaties & alliances, 2d ed,
    2007n424

TREES & SHRUBS
Dogwoods, 2006n1355
Firefly ency of trees, 2006n1352
Hardy bamboos, 2006n1357
Homeowner's complete tree & shrub hndbk,
    2008n1162
Illustrated ency of trees, 2d ed, 2006n1353
Maples, 2005n1372
Native trees for N American landscapes, 2005n1371
Pruning of trees, shrubs, & conifers, 2d ed, 2005n1373
Timber Press pocket gd to palms, 2009n1187

Tree ferns, 2005n1374
Trees, 2009n1188
Trees for the small garden, 2006n1354
Trees of Guatemala, 2009n1186
Trees of the Calif. Landscape, 2008n1161
Trees, shrubs, & vines of the Texas Hill Country,
    2006n1358
Tropical & subtropical trees, 2005n1369
Variegated trees & shrubs, 2005n1370
Witch hazels, 2006n1356

TRIALS (WITCHCRAFT)
Salem witch trials, 2009n379

TROJAN WAR
Images of the Trojan War myth [Website], 2008n994
Trojan War, 2006n514
Was there a Trojan War? [Website], 2008n995

TRUMAN, HARRY S., 1884-1972
Truman yrs, 2006n700

TURKEY
Cambridge hist of Turkey, v.4, 2009n411

TURKMENISTAN
Historical dict of Turkmenistan, 2006n98

UKRAINE
Historical dict of Ukraine, 2006n106

UNDERGROUND RAILROAD. *See also*
SLAVERY
Encyclopedia of the Underground Railroad, 2008n399
People of the Underground Railroad, 2009n363
Underground Railroad, 2009n384

UNIDENTIFIED FLYING OBJECTS (UFO)
World Internet UFO dir, 2006n765

UNITED KINGDOM. *See also* **GREAT BRITAIN**
Historical dict of the contemporary United Kingdom,
    2009n117

UNITED NATIONS
A to Z of multinational peacekeeping, 2007n633
Encyclopedia of the United Nations, 2d ed, 2009n673
Historical dict of the UN, new ed, 2008n659
U.S. natl debate topic 2004-05: the United Nations,
    2005n724
United Nations system, 2006n739
Yearbook of the UN 2005, v.59, 60th ed, 2009n41

UNITED STATES
Almanac of the 50 states, 2007 ed, 2008n68
American Midwest, 2008n69
City profiles USA 2008-09, 9th ed, 2009n350

Counties USA, 3d ed, 2007n732
CQ's state fact finder 2004, 2005n846
CQ's state fact finder 2005, 2006n842
CQ's state fact finder 2006, 2007n745
Encyclopaedia Britannica discover America, 2007n60
Encyclopedia of American studies [Website], 2005n76
Encyclopedia of N.Y. state, 2007n71
Encyclopedia of N Carolina, 2007n74
Encyclopedia of rural America, 2009n71
Encyclopedia of the great plains, 2005n77
50 states, 2d ed, 2008n70
Greenwood ency of American regional cultures,
    2006n70
Historical gazetteer of the US, 2005n386
Internet sources on each US state, 2006n71
Junior worldmark ency of the states, 4th ed, 2005n79
Junior worldmark ency of the states, 5th ed, 2008n71
New ency of southern culture, v.2: geography,
    2007n311
New ency of southern culture, v.4: myth, manners, &
    memory, 2007n63
State rankings 2005, 16th ed, 2006n843
State rankings 2007, 2008n765
State rankings 2008, 2009n775
State trends, 2d ed, 2006n844
State trends, 3d ed, 2007n748
State trends, 2008 ed, 2009n776
Statistical abstracts of the US 2009, 128th ed,
    2009n777
Uniting states, 2005n80
USA & Canada 2008, 2009n70
Worldmark ency of the states, 7th ed, 2008n72

UNITED STATES AIR FORCE

Aircraft markings of the Strategic Air Command,
    1946-53, 2007n565
Aircraft record cards of the US Air Force, 2009n611

UNITED STATES ARMY

Marksmanship in the US Army, 2005n671

UNITED STATES - ARMED FORCES - AFRICAN AMERICANS

African Americans in the military, 2005n658
African Americans in the US Army in WW II,
    2009n304
Black American military leaders, 2008n575
Encyclopedia of African American military hist,
    2005n665
On the trail of the buffalo soldier, 2005n657

UNITED STATES - BOUNDARIES

State & natl boundaries of the US, 2005n388

UNITED STATES - CIVIL WAR, 1861-1865

A to Z of the Civil War, 2007n355
American Civil War, 2005n456
American Civil War, 2009n386
Atlas of the Civil War, 2006n428
Civil War, 2005n423
Civil War, 2005n459
Civil War & reconstruction, 2009n367
Civil War almanac, 2008n384
Civil War America, 1850 to 1875, 2008n420
Civil War Medal of Honor recipients, 2008n573
Civil War suits in the US court of claims, 2007n361
Companion to the Civil War & Reconstruction,
    2005n441
Encyclopedia of Civil War medicine, 2009n383
Essential Civil War, 2007n363
Greenhaven ency of the Civil War, 2005n428
Guide to Civil War Philadelphia, 2005n436
Historical dict of the Civil War & Reconstruction,
    2005n434
Music of the Civil War era, 2005n1124
1001 things you didn't know about the Civil War,
    2008n423
"Out of the Mouth of Hell": Civil War prisons &
    escapes, 2006n450
Oxford dict of Civil War quotations, 2007n370
Quotable American Civil War, 2009n50
Shapers of the great debate on the Civil War,
    2006n430
Ship Island, Miss., 2008n388
USCivilWar.Net [Website], 2005n419
Women during the Civil War, 2008n785
Women in the American Civil War, 2009n789

UNITED STATES - CONGRESS

African Americans in Congress, 2009n659
Almanac of the unelected 2005, 18th ed, 2006n717
Almanac of the unelected 2007, 20th ed, 2008n630
American Congress, 2006n718
Congress A to Z, 5th ed, 2009n639
Congress & the nation series 1945-2004 [Website],
    2007n607
Congress & the nation XI: 2001-04, 2007n606
Congress of the US, 3d ed, 2007n620
Congressional districts in the 2000s, 2005n716
Congressional roll call 2004, 2006n723
Congressional roll call 2005, 2007n608
Congressional roll call 2007, 2009n656
Congressional staff dir: summer 2004, 70th ed,
    2005n703
Congressional staff dir [Website], 2005n704
Congressional yellow bk, Summer 2005, 2006n704
CQ's politics in America 2006, 2006n724
CQ's politics in America 2006: online ed [Website],
    2007n611
Directory of congressional voting scores & interest
    group ratings, 4th ed, 2007n601
Electing Congress, 2d ed, 2009n657
Encyclopedia of the US Congress, 2008n627
Guide to Congress, 6th ed, 2008n647

How Congress works, 4th ed, 2009n661
Legislative branch of fed govt, 2009n660
Legislative women, 2009n662
Major acts of Congress, 2005n553
109th congressional district atlas, 2006n731
110th Congressional district atlas, 2009n663
Student's gd to Congress, 2009n666
THOMAS: legislative info on the Internet [Website], 2008n637

UNITED STATES CONSTITUTION
Birth of the Bill of Rights, 2005n701
Constitutional amendments series, 2009n448
Constitutional convention of 1787, 2006n446
Constitutions of the world, 3d ed, 2008n481
Encyclopedia of the 1st amendment, 2009n437
Encyclopedia of world constitutions, 2007n444
100 Americans making constitutional hist, 2005n534
State constitutions of the US, 2d ed, 2006n543
U.S. Constitution A to Z, 2d ed, 2009n439

UNITED STATES DEPARTMENT OF HOMELAND SECURITY
Encyclopedia of US natl security, 2007n642
Grey House homeland security dir 2005, 2d ed, 2005n43
Grey House homeland security dir 2006, 3d ed, 2006n35
Grey House homeland security dir 2007, 4th ed, 2007n32
Grey House homeland security dir 2008, 5th ed, 2008n37
Grey House homeland security dir [Website], 2005n44
Grey House homeland security dir [Website], 2007n33
Grey House homeland security dir [Website], 2008n38
Homeland security, 2005n550
Homeland security, 2006n729
Homeland security hndbk for citizens & public officials, 2007n646
Homeland security law hndbk, 2005n551
Intelligence & natl security, 2008n592
International security & the US, 2009n696
McGraw-Hill Homeland Security hndbk, 2007n647
Researching natl security & intelligence, 2005n730
US Homeland Security, 2007n644
U.S. natl security, 2d ed, 2008n652

UNITED STATES - ECONOMIC CONDITIONS
Value of a dollar: Colonial era to the Civil War, 2006n149

UNITED STATES - FOREIGN RELATIONS
Africa & the Americas, 2009n692
American statesmen, 2005n694
Britain & the Americas, 2006n746
Chronology of US—Iraqi relations, 1920-2006, 2008n662

Encyclopedia of American foreign policy, 2005n726
Encyclopedia of Cuban-US relations, 2005n727
Foreign relations of the US (FRUS) [Website], 2009n678
France & the Americas, 2006n747
Germany & the Americas, 2006n748
Historical dict of the US diplomacy since the Cold War, 2008n664
Historical dict of US-China relations, 2006n745
Historical dict of US diplomacy from the Civil War to WW I, 2006n742
Historical dict of US-Japan relations, 2008n666
Historical dict of US-Latin American relations, 2007n638
Historical dict of US-Middle East relations, 2008n663
Historical dict of US-SE Asia relations, 2009n693
Iberia & the Americas, 2006n749
Nation-building, 2005n729

UNITED STATES - HISTORY
America: a hist in art, 2009n855
America in revolt during the 1960s & 1970s, 2008n405
America speaks, 2006n447
America the beautiful [Website], 2005n422
America's founding charters, 2007n362
American colonist's lib [Website], 2005n437
American counties, 5th ed, 2006n429
American heroes, 2009n362
American hist [Website], 2009n371
American hist album, 2009n838
Antebellum era, 2005n442
Antebellum period, 2005n461
Atlas of American hist, 2007n336
Atlas of US hist, rev ed, 2009n359
Books on early American hist & culture 1961-70, 2008n387
British Colonial America, 2009n388
Chronology of American hist, 2009n368
Colonial America, 2007n347
Colonial America, 2007n365
Colonial America, 2008n408
Columbia hist of post-WW II America, 2008n409
Columbia River Basin ethnic hist archives [Website], 2006n432
Companion to the American west, 2005n440
Companion to the Civil War & Reconstruction, 2005n441
Conspiracy theories in American hist, 2005n424
Constitutional convention of 1787, 2006n446
Daily life America [Website], 2009n373
Daily life in immigrant America, 1820-70, 2009n387
Daily life in the early American republic, 1790-1820, 2005n449
Daily life in the industrial US, 1870-1900, 2005n453
Day by day: the 1930s, 2008n391
Debatable issues in US hist, 2005n444

Decades of American hist series, 2006n438

Development of the industrial US: almanac, 2006n420

Development of the industrial US: biogs, 2006n421

Development of the industrial US: primary sources, 2006n422

Disasters, accidents, & crises in American hist, 2009n366

Early natl period, 2005n458

Early republic, 2006n451

Early republic, 2009n389

Early republic [Website], 2009n365

Encyclopedia of American histl docs, 2005n425

Encyclopedia of American studies [Website], 2009n375

Encyclopedia of Ellis Island, 2005n433

Encyclopedia of the gilded age & progressive era, 2006n440

Encyclopedia of the jazz age, 2009n376

Encyclopedia of the new American nation, 2007n351

Exploring American hist, 2008n397

Family life in 17th- & 18th-century America, 2006n809

Famous 1st facts, 6th ed, 2008n26

Food in colonial & fed America, 2006n1293

Frontier America, 2005n427

Gale ency of US hist: war, 2009n378

Geostat Center: histl census browser [Website], 2006n433

Gilded age, 2005n460

Gilded age, rev ed, 2007n364

Gilded age & progressive era, 2007n368

Gilded age & progressive era: almanac, 2007n329

Gilded age & progressive era: biogs, 2007n330

Gilded age & progressive era: primary sources, 2007n331

Great American hist fact-finder, 2d ed, 2005n443

Great Depression, updated ed, 2006n449

Great Depression & the New Deal, 2009n391

Great Depression in America, 2008n404

Historical atlas of the US, 2007n335

Historical dict of the Civil War & Reconstruction, 2005n434

Historical dict of the discovery & exploration of the NW coast of America, 2009n380

Historical dict of the early American Republic, 2007n346

Historical dict of the gilded age, 2005n431

Historical dict of the Jacksonian era & Manifest Destiny, 2007n348

Historical dict of the 1940s, 2007n354

Historical dict of the old south, 2007n359

Historical dict of the Roosevelt-Truman era, 2009n648

Historical maps on file, updated ed, 2006n454

History in dispute, v.19: the red scare after 1945, 2005n451

History of the American West [Website], 2006n434

Home front heroes, 2008n390

Icons of the American west, 2009n364

Industrial revolution, 2006n448

Industrial revolution, 2007n366

Industrial revolution, 2009n393

Industrial revolution in America, 2006n456

Industrial revolution in America, 2008n411

Industrial revolution in America, 2008n412

Issues & controversies in American hist [Website], 2009n381

Jacksonian & antebellum age, 2009n394

Jamestown colony, 2008n398

Making of America—Cornell [Website], 2006n435

Making of America—Michigan [Website], 2006n436

Making of the American West, 2008n414

Media scandals, 2009n800

Milestone docs in American hist, 2009n395

More Okla. Renegades, 2008n89

National Geographic almanac of American hist, 2007n342

National Geographic histl atlas of the US, 2006n427

New Deal network [Website], 2005n420

New ency of southern culture, v.3: history, 2007n62

New York Public Library American hist desk ref, 2d ed, 2005n457

9/11 ency, 2009n372

1920s, 2005n1174

1940s, 2005n1178

1950s, 2005n1179

1970s, 2007n341

1980s, 2007n344

1990s, 2005n1177

1990s, 2007n343

North American jls of Prince Maximilian of Wied, v.1, 2009n396

Northwest hist database [Website], 2006n72

Old West, 2009n382

100 Okla. Outlaws, gangsters, & lawmen 1839-1939, 2008n88

1001 events that made America, 2007n338

1001 people who made America, 2008n389

Opposing viewpoints in American hist, 2008n416

Postwar America, 2007n358

Presidents were here, 2009n390

Progressive era, 2005n438

Progressive era, 2006n457

Prohibition, 2006n453

Quotable founding fathers, 2005n462

Reconstruction era, 2005n445

Reconstruction era: almanac, 2005n413

Reconstruction era: biogs, 2005n414

Reconstruction era: primary sources, 2005n415

Reference sources in hist, 2d ed, 2005n510

Roaring 20s, rev ed, 2008n422

Roaring twenties ref lib, 2006n423

Science & tech in Colonial America, 2006n1267

Second great awakening & the transcendentalists, 2005n448

Seventies in America, 2006n444
Shapers of the great debate at the Constitutional
    Convention of 1787, 2006n431
Shapers of the great debate on Jacksonian democracy,
    2005n696
Shaping of America, 1783-1815: almanac, 2006n424
Shaping of America, 1783-1815: biogs, 2006n425
Shaping of America, 1783-1815: primary sources,
    2006n426
Sixties in America: almanac, 2005n416
Sixties in America: biogs, 2005n417
Sixties in America: primary sources, 2005n418
Slavery in America, 2007n369
Thirteen colonies series, 2006n458
This day in American hist, 3d ed, 2009n369
Trans-Mississippi West 1804-1912, 2009n361
U*X*L ency of US hist, 2009n385
USA fifties, 2006n445
USA twenties, 2005n435

UNITED STATES - HISTORY – MILITARY. *See also* MILITARY HISTORY

American soldiers' lives: WW I, 2007n564
Americans at war, 2006n439
Atlas of American military hist, 2006n658
Encyclopedia of African American military hist,
    2005n665
Encyclopedia of the American armed forces,
    2006n660
United States at war, 2006n664
Fortress America, 2005n455
Forts of the US, 2007n353
Historical dict of the War of 1812, 2007n357
Home front ency, 2008n584
Home front heroes, 2007n337
Political hist of America's wars, 2007n561
United States at war [Website], 2009n607

UNITED STATES - HISTORY - REVOLUTION

A to Z of revolutionary America, 2008n400
American generals of the Revolutionary War,
    2008n572
American Revolution, 2008n406
American Revolution, updated ed, 2008n407
American Revolutionary War, 2007n345
Chronology of the American Revolution, 2009n370
Encyclopedia of N American colonial conflicts to
    1775, 2009n605
Encyclopedia of the American Revolution, 2d ed,
    2007n350
Encyclopedia of the American Revolutionary War,
    2007n349
Historical dict of revolutionary America, 2006n442
Landmarks of the American Revolution, 2d ed,
    2007n356
Revolutionary era, 2005n452
Revolutionary War almanac, 2007n340

Revolutionary War era, 2006n455
We hold these truths, 2009n47

UNITED STATES MARINE CORP

Leaders of men, 2009n613
United States Marine Corps Generals of WWII,
    2009n612
United States Marine Corps Medal of Honor
    recipients, 2006n668

UNITED STATES NATIONAL PARKS

Encyclopedia of American natl parks, 2005n75
National Geographic gd to the natl parks of the US,
    5th ed, 2007n321
National Geographic natl park trail gds [CD-ROM],
    2005n775
Parks dir of the US, 4th ed, 2005n756
Parks dir of the US, 5th ed, 2008n701
US natl parks west, 2006n398

UNITED STATES NAVY

American Naval hist, 3d ed, 2005n675
Black submariners in the US Navy, 1940-75,
    2006n672
Chronology of the war at sea, 1939-45, 3d rev ed,
    2006n669
Civil War navies 1855-83, 2007n568
Dictionary of naval abbrevs, 4th ed, 2006n670
Dictionary of naval terms, 6th ed, 2006n671
Naval ceremonies, customs, & traditions, 6th ed,
    2005n673
Naval Institute almanac of the US Navy, 2006n673
Naval Institute gd to combat fleets of the world
    2005-06, 2006n674
Naval Institute gd to combat fleets of the world, 15th
    ed, 2008n599
Naval Institute gd to the ships & aircraft of the US
    Fleet, 18th ed, 2006n675
US destroyers, rev ed, 2005n678
World War II naval & maritime claims against the US,
    2007n569

UNITED STATES - POLITICS & GOVERNMENT

Almanac of American pol 2008, 2008n619
Almanac of state legislative elections, 3d ed,
    2008n650
Almanac of the unelected 2004, 17th ed, 2005n713
Almanac of the unelected 2006, 19th ed, 2007n586
Almanac of the unelected 2008, 21st ed, 2009n655
America at the polls 1960-2004, 2007n616
America votes 25, 2005n719
America votes 26, 2003-04, 2006n732
America votes 2005-06, 2008n643
American conservatism, 2008n625
American got on file, rev ed, 2005n714
American govt leaders, 2008n620

American pol leaders 1789-2005, 2006n719
Ben's gd to govt for kids [Website], 2008n631
Birth of the Bill of Rights, 2005n701
Campaign & election reform, 2d ed, 2009n668
Checks & balances, 2006n720
Clinton yrs, 2005n702
Congressional districts in the 2000s, 2005n716
Democracy project [Website], 2009n632
Domestic programs of the American Presidents,
    2009n658
East Asian Americans & pol participation, 2006n721
Elections A to Z, 3d ed, 2008n628
Encyclopedia of American govt & civics, 2009n643
Encyclopedia of fed agencies & commissions,
    2005n700
Encyclopedia of politics, 2006n703
Encyclopedia of the American presidency, 2005n698
Encyclopedia of US campaigns, elections, & electoral
    behavior, 2009n640
Encyclopedia of women & American pol, 2009n641
Executive branch of state govt, 2007n612
Executive branch of the fed govt, 2008n645
Federal leadership dir online [Website], 2009n649
Federal regional yellow bk, Summer 2005, 2006n706
Federal regulatory dir, 13th ed, 2008n633
Federal staff dir, fall 2004, 46th ed, 2005n706
Federal staff dir [Website], 2005n707
Federal yellow bk, Summer 2005, 2006n707
Flash focus: the one-stop study gd to American
    politics, 2006n725
Foreign representatives in the US yellow bk, Summer
    2005, 2006n708
Forms of local govt, 2008n646
From suffrage to the senate, 2d ed, 2007n596
Future of state [Website], 2008n634
Gale ency of US hist: govt & politics, 2009n642
Geography of presidential elections in the US,
    1868-2004, 2006n730
Government affairs yellow bk, Summer 2005,
    2006n709
Government phone bk USA 2004, 12th ed, 2005n708
Government phone bk USA 2005, 13th ed, 2006n710
Government phone bk USA 2007, 15th ed, 2008n635
Government phone bk USA 2008, 16th ed, 2009n30
Guide to pol campaigns in America, 2006n726
Guide to the presidency, 4th ed, 2008n629
Handy presidents answer bk, 2006n728
Historic docs of 2006, 2008n618
Historical atlas of US presidential elections,
    1789-2004, 2007n585
Historical dict of the Eisenhower era, 2009n646
Historical dict of the Jacksonian era & Manifest
    Destiny, 2007n348
Historical dict of the Kennedy-Johnson era, 2008n393
Historical dict of the Reagan-Bush era, 2008n626
Judicial branch of the fed govt, 2008n648
Kids.gov [Website], 2008n636

Latino Americans & pol participation, 2006n727
Legislative branch of fed govt, 2009n660
Legislative branch of state govt, 2007n615
Lobbyists.info [Website], 2007n599
Lobbyists.info [Website], 2009n654
Municipal yellow bk, Summer 2005, 2006n711
National Archives & Records Admin (NARA)
    [Website], 2005n718
National party conventions 1831-2004, 2007n617
Political corruption in America, 2005n699
Political corruption in America, 2d ed, 2009n644
Political hist of America's wars, 2007n561
Powers of the presidency, 2009n664
Presidency A to Z, 4th ed, 2009n647
Presidency, the public, & the parties, 3d ed, 2009n665
Presidential elections, 1789-2004, 2007n619
Presidents from Adams through Polk, 1825-49,
    2006n733
Presidents from Eisenhower through Johnson,
    1953-69, 2007n614
Reagan era, 2008n418
Shapers of the great debate on the great society,
    2006n694
State constitutions of the US, 2d ed, 2006n543
State yellow bk, 2008 ed, 2009n650
State yellow bk, Summer 2005, 2006n712
Student's gd to elections, 2009n667
U.S. govt manual [Website], 2008n639
United States election system, 2005n720
United States govt Internet manual 2003-04, 2005n710
United States govt Internet manual 2004-05, 2006n713
United States govt Internet manual 2005-06, 2007n602
United States govt Internet manual 2007, 2008n638
United States govt Internet manual 2008, 2009n651
United States presidential primary election 2000-04,
    2007n609
US presidents factbk, 2007n613
USA.gov [Website], 2008n640
Vital stats on American pol 2005-06, 2006n734
Vital stats on American pol 2007-08, 2008n651
Vital stats on American pol [Website], 2007n623
Washington info dir 2004-05, 2005n711
Washington info dir 2005-06, 2006n714
Washington info dir 2006-07, 2007n603
Washington info dir 2007-08, 2008n641
Washington info dir 2008-09, 2009n652
Washington info dir online [Website], 2006n715
Washington representatives 2004, 28th ed, 2005n712
Washington representatives 2005, 2006n716
Washington representatives 2006, 30th ed, 2007n604
Washington representatives, Spring 2008, 2009n653
Watergate, 2005n450
Watergate & the resignation of Richard Nixon,
    2006n736
Who's who in American pol 2005-06, 20th ed,
    2006n702

Who's who in American pol 2007-08, 21st ed,
    2008n623

UNITED STATES - SOCIAL CONDITIONS
American home front in WW II: almanac, 2005n410
American home front in WW II: biogs, 2005n411
American home front in WW II: primary sources,
    2005n412
American social reform movements: almanac,
    2007n323
American social reform movements: biogs, 2007n324
American social reform movements: primary sources,
    2007n325
Americans at war, 2006n439
Class in America, 2008n58
Culture & customs of the US, 2008n73
Encyclopedia of American social movements,
    2005n426
Encyclopedia of social problems, 2009n55
Encyclopedia of war & American society, 2007n352
Family life in 17th- & 18th-century America,
    2007n704
Fifties in America, 2006n441
Seventies in America, 2006n444
Social issues in America, 2007n52
Working Americans 1880-2006, v.7: social
    movements, 2007n194

UNITED STATES - SOCIAL LIFE & CUSTOMS.
See also **HOLIDAYS**
Girl culture, 2009n766
Life events & rites of passage, 2009n1040

UNITED STATES SUPREME COURT
Biographical ency of the Supreme Court, 2007n440
Chase court, 2005n552
Documentary hist of the Supreme Court of the US
    1789-1800, v.7, 2005n547
Documentary hist of the Supreme Court of the US,
    1789-1800, v.8, 2008n474
Encyclopedia of the Supreme Court, 2006n520
Encyclopedia of the Supreme Court of the US,
    2009n438
Guide to the U.S. Supreme Court, 4th ed, 2005n556
Handy Supreme Court answer bk, 2008n477
Illustrated great decisions of the Supreme Court, 2d ed,
    2007n457
Jay & Ellsworth, the 1st courts, 2009n450
Judiciary & responsible govt 1910-1921, v. 9,
    2008n478
Landmark decisions of the US Supreme Court, 2d ed,
    2008n464
Landmark Supreme Court cases, 2005n549
100 Americans making constitutional hist, 2005n534
Oxford companion to the Supreme Court of the US, 2d
    ed, 2006n519

Public debate over controversial Supreme Court
    decisions, 2007n461
Rehnquist Court, 2007n452
Sexual harassment decisions of the US Supreme Court,
    2007n462
Supreme Court A to Z, 4th ed, 2007n446
Supreme Court compendium, 4th ed, 2008n475
Supreme Court of the US, 3d ed, 2009n458
Taft court, 2005n555
U.S. Supreme Court, 2008n469
United States Supreme Court, 2006n548
United States Supreme Court, 2006n549
Vinson court, 2005n543
We the students, 3d ed, 2009n459
White court, 2005n557

UNITED STATES - TRAVEL
Backroads of S Calif., 2006n399
Fodor's Hawai'i 2006, 2006n396
Fodor's San Francisco 2005, 2005n396
Lewis & Clark Columbia River water trail, 2005n397
New York City, 2005n398
100 best family resorts in N America, 7th ed,
    2006n397
Sierra Club gd to the ancient forests of the NE,
    2005n399
USA: the new south, 2005n400

UNIVERSITIES & COLLEGES. *See*
EDUCATION, HIGHER

URBAN STUDIES. *See also* CITIES & TOWNS
America's top-rated cities 2004, 11th ed, 2005n852
America's top-rated cities 2006, 13th ed, 2007n751
America's top-rated smaller cities 2004-05, 5th ed,
    2005n853
America's top-rated smaller cities 2006/07, 6th ed,
    2007n752
America's top-rated smaller cities 2008/09, 7th ed,
    2009n779
Chronology of housing in the US, 2008n767
Cities & growth, 2008n772
Cities & water, 2009n780
Cities of the US, 6th ed, 2009n781
Comparative gd to American suburbs 2005, 3d ed,
    2006n848
County & city extra 2006, 14th ed, 2007n753
County & city extra 2008, 16th ed, 2009n782
Encyclopedia of American urban hist, 2008n768
Historic cities of the Americas, 2006n845
Urban sprawl, 2007n754

UTOPIAS
Historical dict of utopianism, 2005n1232
Modern American communes, 2006n801

VAMPIRES
Encyclopedia of vampires, werewolves, & other monsters, 2005n1154

VEGETABLES
Knott's hndbk for vegetable growers, 5th ed, 2008n1138
Vegetable grower's hndbk, 2009n1163
Vegetables, herbs, & fruit, 2007n1149
Veggie gardener's answer bk, 2009n1158

VENEZUELA
History of Venezuela, 2006n109

VERMONT
Vermont, 2007n78

VETERINARY SCIENCE
Cat owner's home veterinary hndbk, 3d ed, 2009n1164
Dog owner's home veterinary hndbk, 4th ed, 2009n1165
Encyclopedia of animal sci, 2005n1333
Encyclopedia of animal sci [Website], 2005n1334
Illustrated gd to veterinary medical terminology, 2d ed, 2006n1312
Merck veterinary manual, 9th ed, 2007n1164
Plumb's veterinary drug hndbk, 5th ed, 2007n1165
Plumb's veterinary drug hndbk, 6th ed, 2009n1166
Storey's illus breed gd to sheep, goats, cattle, & pigs, 2009n1168

VICE PRESIDENTS - UNITED STATES
Vice Presidents, 3d ed, 2006n701

VICTORIA, QUEEN OF GREAT BRITAIN, 1819-1901
Queen Victoria, 2005n484

VIDEO GAMES
Classic home video games 1972-84, 2008n1272
Gamers in the lib?! 2008n537

VIDEO RECORDINGS
AV market place 2005, 33d ed, 2006n892
AV market place 2007, 2008n806
Best DVDs you've never seen, just missed, or almost forgotten, 2006n1167
DVD & video gd 2004, 2005n1216
Educators gd to free videotapes 2004-05: elem/middle school, 5th ed, 2005n281
Educators gd to free videotapes 2004-05: secondary ed, 21st ed, 2005n282
Educators gd to free videotapes 2005-06, 6th ed, 2006n318
Educators gd to free videotapes 2005-06: secondary ed, 52d ed, 2006n319

Educators gd to free videotapes 2007-08, elem/middle school ed, 8th ed, 2008n293
Educators gd to free videotapes 2007-08, secondary ed, 54th ed, 2008n294
Latino media resource gd 2004, 2005n908
Metacritic [Website], 2006n1169
Video source bk, 34th ed, 2006n893
Video source bk, 36th ed, 2007n785
Video source bk, 38th ed, 2008n807
VideoHound's golden movie retriever 2005, 2005n1217
VideoHound's golden movie retriever 2006, 2006n1170
VideoHound's golden movie retriever 2007, 2007n1053
VideoHound's golden movie retriever 2008, 2008n1038

VIETNAM
History of Vietnam, 2009n106

VIETNAM WAR 1961-1975
Greenhaven ency of the Vietnam War, 2005n429
Vietnam online [Website], 2008n425
Vietnam War, 2006n459
Vietnam War, 2008n417

VIKINGS
Daily life of the Vikings, 2005n532

VIOLENCE. *See also* **DOMESTIC VIOLENCE**
Abuse & violence info for teens, 2009n764
Domestic violence, 2d ed, 2009n747
Encyclopedia of interpersonal violence, 2009n469
Violence against women online resources [Website], 2005n803

VIOLENCE ON TELEVISION
Violence in the media, 2006n875

VIRGINIA
Profiles of Va., 2009n84

VIRTUAL REALITY
Agent & Web serv techs in virtual enterprises, 2008n1279

VIRTUAL WORK TEAMS
Encyclopedia of E-collaboration, 2009n1284

VOCATIONAL GUIDANCE. *See* **CAREERS**

VOLCANOES
Encyclopedia of earthquakes & volcanoes, 3d ed, 2008n1318
Volcanoes, 2005n1520

WAR & SOCIETY
Encyclopedia of religion & war, 2005n1238
Encyclopedia of war & American society, 2007n352
Home front ency, 2007n554

WAR CRIMES
Encyclopedia of war crimes & genocide, 2007n422

WAR OF 1812
Historical dict of the War of 1812, 2007n357

WAR SONGS
World War I sheet music, 2008n970

WARS. *See also* MILITARY HISTORY
Age of wars of religion, 2008n587
Armed conflict database [Website], 2008n577
Battlefield, 2008n590
Dictionary of battles & sieges, 2007n556
Dictionary of wars, 3d ed, 2007n551
Encyclopedia of conflicts since WW II, 2008n582
Encyclopedia of N American colonial conflicts to
    1775, 2009n605
Gale ency of US hist: war, 2009n378
Gale ency of world hist: war, 2009n427
United States at war [Website], 2009n607
Warfare & armed conflicts, 3d ed, 2009n604
Warrior, 2009n609
Wars of the Americas, 2d ed, 2009n601

WASHINGTON (D.C.)
Inside Wash.: govt resources for intl business,
    2005n205
Washington assns contacts dir 2008, 2009n34
Washington D.C., 5th ed, 2009n351
Washington info dir 2004-05, 2005n711

WASTE MANAGEMENT
Handbook on household hazardous waste, 2009n1216
Waste mgmt, 2009n1343

WATER SCIENCE
Processing water, 2009n1327
Texas water atlas, 2009n1326
U*X*L ency of water sci, 2005n1539
Water ency, 2006n1533
Water ency, 3d ed, 2008n1337
Water supply, 2009n1344

WATERGATE AFFAIR (1972-1974)
Eyewitness to Watergate, 2008n410
Watergate, 2005n450
Watergate & the resignation of Richard Nixon,
    2006n736

WEAPONS
Aircraft carriers, 2007n571

Battleships, 2006n680
Chemical & biological warfare, 2d ed, 2007n572
Cruisers & battle cruisers, 2005n679
Destroyers, 2006n679
Encyclopedia of military tech & innovation, 2005n661
Helicopters, 2006n677
Historical dict of nuclear, biological, & chemical
    warfare, 2008n601
Machine guns, 2006n682
Medieval weapons, 2008n603
Naval Institute gd to combat fleets of the world
    2005-06, 2006n674
Naval Institute gd to the ships & aircraft of the US
    Fleet, 18th ed, 2006n675
Naval Institute gd to world naval weapon systems, 5th
    ed, 2007n573
Nuclear weapons & nonproliferation, 2d ed, 2008n604
Rifles, 2006n681
Rockets & missiles, 2005n682
Submarines, 2008n605
Tanks, 2005n681
Uniforms, arms, & equipment, 2008n607
US destroyers, rev ed, 2005n678
Weapons of mass destruction, 2006n676

WEATHER
Atlas of climate change, 2007n1307
Change in the weather, 2005n1511
Climate change, 2009n1321
Climate change in context, 2009n1316
Clouds R Us.com [Website], 2009n1310
Encyclopedia of disasters, 2009n1318
Encyclopedia of hurricanes, typhoons, & cyclones,
    new ed, 2008n1308
Encyclopedia of weather & climate, rev ed,
    2008n1307
Encyclopedia of world climatology, 2007n1308
Extreme weather, 2008n1313
Extreme weather & climate events [Website],
    2009n1311
Facts on File dict of weather & climate, rev ed,
    2007n1309
Firefly gd to global hazards, 2005n1514
Firefly gd to weather, 2006n1509
Global climate change, 2007n1329
Hurricanes, 2d ed, 2006n1510
Interactive weather maker [Website], 2009n1312
Natural disasters, new ed, 2009n1317
Notable natural disasters, 2008n1309
Rough gd to climate change, 2008n1312
SciJinks weather laboratory [Website], 2009n1313
U*X*L ency of weather & natural disasters,
    2008n1310
Weather, 2005n1512
Weather & climate, 2008n1306
Weather glossary [Website], 2009n1319
Weather underground [Website], 2009n1314

Weather watch [Website], 2009n1315
World Bk lib of natural disasters, 2009n1320

WEBSITES
About.com [Website], 2006n260
ABZU: a gd to study of the ancient Near East on the Web [Website], 2005n526
Academic search premier [Website], 2006n1474
Academy of American poets [Website], 2008n952
Access sci [Website], 2009n1124
ACE electoral knowledge network [Website], 2008n614
ACLS hist e-bk project [Website], 2007n402
Acronym finder [Website], 2006n1
Africa south of the Sahara [Website], 2008n91
African American experience [Website], 2009n298
African American women writers of the 19th century [Website], 2005n1057
African American women writers of the 19th century [Website], 2007n934
African children's lit [Website], 2006n989
African letters [Website], 2006n1066
African lit in English [Website], 2006n1052
African studies centre [Website], 2008n94
African timelines [Website], 2005n463
AGRICOLA (AGRICultural online access) [Website], 2006n1279
Air Univ Lib index to military per [Website], 2005n670
ALA best free ref Web sites [Website], 2008n7
All business [Website], 2006n261
All movie gd [Website], 2006n1138
AM digital lib [Website], 2006n1475
America the beautiful [Website], 2005n422
American colonist's lib [Website], 2005n437
American hist [Website], 2009n371
American Indian hist online [Website], 2007n277
American Indian hist online [Website], 2008n321
American lib dir [Website], 2006n590
American natl biog [Website], 2008n17
American verse project [Website], 2009n988
American women's hist [Website], 2005n855
American women's hist online [Website], 2009n786
Ancestry lib ed [Website], 2009n325
Anglophone & lusophone African women's writing [Website], 2006n1053
Annenberg pol fact check [Website], 2009n629
Annotated computer vision bibliog [Website], 2006n1471
ANSS reviews [Website], 2008n295
Anthropology of food [Website], 2008n296
Anthropology review database [Website], 2006n320
AnthroSource [Website], 2008n297
APA online [Website], 2006n1199
APIS: advanced papryological info system [Website], 2007n407
Archiplanet [Website], 2009n857

Archives of traditional music [Website], 2008n961
ArchNet [Website], 2008n379
Aristotle bibliog [Website], 2006n1180
Armed conflict database [Website], 2008n577
Art & culture [Website], 2007n762
Art museum image gallery [Website], 2009n848
AssocationExecs.com [Website], 2009n134
Associationexecs.com [Website], 2007n29
ATLA religion database [Website], 2005n1245
Avalon project at Yale Law School [Website], 2006n508
Banking basics [Website], 2009n159
Banking tutor [Website], 2009n160
Bartleby verse [Website], 2009n989
Ben's gd to govt for kids [Website], 2008n631
BEOnline: business & economics online [Website], 2006n125
Bibliography of Africana per lit [Website], 2008n92
Bibliography of criticism on S African lit in English [Website], 2006n1054
Bibliography of pol sci resources on the study of pol violence [Website], 2008n670
BiblioTravel [Website], 2006n1009
Biographies of women mathematicians [Website], 2005n1527
Biographies of women mathematicians [Website], 2007n1319
Biographies: lib of economics & liberty [Website], 2005n138
Biography ref bank [Website], 2009n7
Biography resource center [Website], 2009n8
BizStats.com [Website], 2006n126
BNA's dir of state & fed courts, judges, & clerks online [Website], 2006n523
Bookreporter.com [Website], 2006n972
Books & writers [Website], 2006n975
Boston women's health bk collective [Website], 2005n1441
Boundary-related links [Website], 2008n352
Britannica learning zone [Website], 2009n18
Britannica online [Website], 2008n23
British women romantic poets, 1789-1952 [Website], 2005n1100
BuddhaNet [Website], 2007n1105
BuddhaNet: Buddhist studies [Website], 2005n1252
Built in America [Website], 2009n858
Burrelle's transcripts [Website], 2005n907
Business info resources [Website], 2006n127
Campaign ads [Website], 2009n630
Canadian romance authors' networks (CRAN) [Website], 2006n1017
Celebration of women writers [Website], 2005n976
CELT: Corpus of electronic texts. The online resource for Irish hist [Website], 2005n494
Cetus links [Website], 2006n1470
Chicago manual of style online [Website], 2007n775
Children's lit [Website], 2007n887

Chronic illness dir [Website], 2006n1414
CIAO: Columbia Intl Affairs online [Website], 2005n725
Cinema spot [Website], 2006n1152
Cities & buildings collections [Website], 2009n859
Clouds R Us.com [Website], 2009n1310
ClueLass.com & the mysterious home page [Website], 2005n1047
Cobblestone online [Website], 2009n43
Collection of computer sci bibliogs [Website], 2006n1472
Columbia gazetteer of the world [Website], 2008n349
Columbia River Basin ethnic hist archives [Website], 2006n432
Commission on presidential debates [Website], 2009n631
Complete dir for pediatric disorders [Website], 2005n1458
Complete dir for pediatric disorders [Website], 2008n1247
Complete dir for people with disabilities [Website], 2005n799
Complete dir for people with disabilities [Website], 2007n700
Complete dir for people with disabilities [Website], 2008n718
Complete dir of disabilities [Website], 2006n804
Complete learning disabilities dir [Website], 2005n314
Complete learning disabilities dir [Website], 2007n256
Complete learning disabilities dir [Website], 2008n289
Complete mental health dir [Website], 2005n740
Complete mental health dir [Website], 2007n660
Computer & info systems abstracts [Website], 2006n1276
Computing reviews [Website], 2006n1473
Congress & the nation series 1945-2004 [Website], 2007n607
Congressional staff dir [Website], 2005n704
Contemporary Africa database [Website], 2006n1055
Contemporary philosophy of the mind [Website], 2006n1182
Contemporary postcolonial & postimperial lit in English [Website], 2006n973
Contemporary women's issues [Website], 2005n856
Contemporary writers in the UK [Website], 2006n1042
Cornell Univ lib of histl mathematics monographs [Website], 2005n1529
Cornell Univ Lib of histl mathematics monographs [Website], 2008n1330
Cosmeo [Website], 2009n285
Counseling & psychotherapy transcripts, client narrative, & ref works [Website], 2009n699
Crime fiction Canada [Website], 2006n1013
Crime writers for Canada [Website], 2006n1014
Criminal justice abstracts [Website], 2005n560
Criminal justice links [Website], 2007n475

CRInfo: the conflict resolution info source [Website], 2008n669
CultureGrams [Website], 2009n67
Cultures & lits of Africa links [Website], 2005n1083
Cumulative index to nursing & allied health lit [Website], 2005n1474
Current biog illus [Website], 2009n15
Current issues [Website], 2009n53
Cyndi's list of genealogy sites on the Internet [Website], 2007n286
Daily life America [Website], 2009n373
Daily life online [Website], 2009n423
Database of award-winning children's lit [Website], 2007n889
Database of the Calif. Academy of Scis, Dept of Anthropology collection [Website], 2005n320
De Imperatoribus Romani [Website], 2007n395
Dekker ency of nanosci & nanotech [Website], 2005n1402
Democracy project [Website], 2009n632
Demographic & health surveys [Website], 2008n742
Dictionary of Islamic philosophical terms [Website], 2006n1239
Dictionary of philosophical terms & names [Website], 2006n1190
Diotima: materials for the study of women & gender in the ancient world [Website], 2005n857
Directory of business info resources [Website], 2005n152
Directory of business info resources [Website], 2008n159
Directory of business to business catalogs [Website], 2005n191
Directory of drug & alcohol residential rehabilitation facilities [Website], 2005n822
Directory of hospital personnel [Website], 2007n1237
Directory of hospital personnel [Website], 2008n1212
Directory of venture capital & private equity firms [Website], 2009n167
Directory of women philosophers [Website], 2006n1200
Distributed digital lib of mathematical monographs [Website], 2005n1530
Distributed digital lib of mathematical monographs [Website], 2008n1331
Documents from the women's liberation movement [Website], 2005n858
Early Canadiana online [Website], 2005n470
Early republic [Website], 2009n365
East & SE Asia [Website], 2008n102
EconData [Website], 2005n153
ECONlinks [Website], 2005n154
EconWPA [Website], 2005n131
Educational paperback assn Website [Website], 2007n903
eHRAF collection of ethnography/archaeology [Website], 2007n262

ElectionGd [Website], 2008n615
Electronic info system for intl law (EISIL) [Website],
  2008n500
Electronic links for classicists [Website],
  2005n876Encyclopedia of American studies
  [Website], 2005n76
Electronic links for classicists [Website], 2009n792
Electronic poetry center [Website], 2009n990
eLibrary sci [Website], 2009n1120
eNature.com [Website], 2006n1328
Encyclopedia [Website], 2006n25
Encyclopedia Americana [Website], 2008n25
Encyclopedia mythica [Website], 2007n1024
Encyclopedia of American studies [Website],
  2009n375
Encyclopedia of animal sci [Website], 2005n1334
Encyclopedia of biomaterials & biomedical
  engineering [Website], 2005n1406
Encyclopedia of communities of practice in info &
  knowledge mgmt [Website], 2006n585
Encyclopedia of data warehousing & mining
  [Website], 2006n1469
Encyclopedia of human computer interaction
  [Website], 2006n1477
Encyclopedia of multimedia tech & networking
  [Website], 2006n1467
Encyclopedia of plant & crop sci [Website],
  2005n1349
Encyclopedia of supramolecular chemistry [Website],
  2005n1494
Encyclopedia of the atmospheric environment
  [Website], 2005n1513
EpistemeLinks.com: philosophy resources on the
  Internet [Website], 2006n1183
Erratic impact's philosophy research base [Website],
  2006n1184
Ethics updates [Website], 2006n1201
Ethnologue [Website], 2008n849
ETHX on the Web [Website], 2006n1185
EuroDocs [Website], 2005n476
Eurominority [Website], 2008n114
European integration current contents [Website],
  2008n113
Extreme weather & climate events [Website],
  2009n1311
Eyewitness accounts [Website], 2005n514FemBio
  [Website], 2005n866
FACCTs [Website], 2006n1463
Facts on intl relations & security trends (FIRST)
  [Website], 2008n661
Fairrosa cyber lib of children's lit [Website],
  2007n890
Fantastic fiction [Website], 2006n1010
Favorite poem project [Website], 2009n991
Federal leadership dir online [Website], 2009n649
Federal Reserve educ [Website], 2009n161
Feminism & women's issues [Website], 2005n859

Feminist theory Website [Website], 2006n850
Ferguson's career guidance center [Website],
  2008n239
Ferguson's career guidance center [Website],
  2009n212
Film & media resources from Artslynx [Website],
  2006n869
Film & media resources from Artslynx [Website],
  2009n793
Film in Latin America [Website], 2006n1135
Film studies resources—academic info [Website],
  2006n1154
First Bank of the US [Website], 2009n162
1stHeadlines [Website], 2005n898
Flags of all countries [Website], 2005n365
Flags of all countries [Website], 2007n295
Foreign relations of the US (FRUS) [Website],
  2009n678
Forensic art [Website], 2006n577
Forensic sci timelines [Website], 2006n553
From the ends to the beginning: a bilingual anthology
  of Russian verse [Website], 2005n1095
Future of state [Website], 2008n634
GenBank [Website], 2006n1361
GenderReach [Website], 2005n860GenderWatch
  [Website], 2005n861
General social survey bibliog [Website], 2005n62
Geographic gd to uncovering women's hist in archival
  collections [Website], 2005n862
Geography action [Website], 2008n353
Geography zone [Website], 2008n354
Geography4Kids [Website], 2008n355
Geostat Center: histl census browser [Website],
  2006n433
Giggle poetry [Website], 2008n947
Giza archives program [Website], 2006n419
Global gateway: world culture & resources [Website],
  2008n299
Global issues in context [Website], 2009n68
Global legal info network [Website], 2008n470
Glossary of poetic terms [Website], 2009n1004
Great voyages [Website], 2005n1224
Greatest films [Website], 2006n1160
Greek mythology link [Website], 2007n1025
Green papers [Website], 2009n634
Greenwood daily life online [Website], 2005n508
Grey House biometric info dir online [Website],
  2006n181
Grey House homeland security dir [Website], 2005n44
Grey House homeland security dir [Website], 2008n38
Grey House performing arts dir [Website], 2005n1185
Grey House safety & security dir [Website], 2006n163
Handbook of rhetorical devices [Website], 2009n803
HAPI: Hispanic American per index online [Website],
  2008n50
Health ref center [Website], 2008n1228
Health ref center [Website], 2009n1239

HeinOnline [Website], 2008n462
Hellenistic bibliog [Website], 2007n964
Historic events of the 20th century [Website], 2005n522
Historical map & chart project [Website], 2006n376
Historical maps online [Website], 2005n372
Historical mps online [Website], 2007n301
History for kids [Website], 2005n523
History of sci, tech, & medicine [Website], 2005n1297
History of the American West [Website], 2006n434
History resource center [Website], 2007n421
HMO/PPO dir [Website], 2005n1425
HMO/PPO dir [Website], 2006n1420
HMO/PPO dir [Website], 2007n1240
H-NET reviews in the humanities & social scis [Website], 2007n5
Hollywood creative dir online [Website], 2008n1007
Hollywood creative dir online [Website], 2009n1051
HQ online [Website], 2005n46
HQ online [Website], 2006n37
Humbul humanities hub [Website], 2005n883
IDEAS (Internet docs in economics access serv) [Website], 2005n132
Images of the Trojan War myth [Website], 2008n994
Index of Native American bk resources on the Internet [Website], 2006n1037
IndexFungorum [Website], 2006n1349
Industry research desk [Website], 2006n175
InfoTrac kids [Website], 2008n51
Institute of museum & lib servs [Website], 2009n489
Interactive Mediterranean project [Website], 2005n374
Interactive weather maker [Website], 2009n1312International security & counter terrorism ref center [Website], 2009n682
International Assn of Forensic Linguists [Website], 2006n552
International children's digital lib [Website], 2005n1019
International children's digital lib [Website], 2007n896
International law in domestic courts [Website], 2007n492
International who's who [Website], 2008n14
Internet ency of philosophy [Website], 2005n1231
Internet ency of philosophy [Website], 2006n1195
Internet lib for librarians [Website], 2009n494
Internet movie database [Website], 2006n1155
Internet public lib [Website], 2009n495
Internet sacred text archive [Website], 2005n1246
Internet speculative fiction database [Website], 2006n1019
Intute: arts & humanities [Website], 2009n794
Intute: social scis [Website], 2008n56
Issues & controversies in American hist [Website], 2009n381
Issues [Website], 2008n57

Jahrbuch-Project, electronic research archive for mathematics [Website], 2005n1531
Japanese American relocation digital archives [Website], 2006n333
Johns Hopkins gd to literary theory & criticism [Website], 2009n913
JournalismNet [Website], 2005n900
Judicial staff dir online [Website], 2006n527
Kids.gov [Website], 2008n636
La nueva enciclopedia cumbre [Website], 2009n20
LANIC: Latin American network & info center [Website], 2008n134
Latin American database (LADB) [Website], 2008n135
Latin American network info center (LANIC) [Website], 2008n136
Latino American experience [Website], 2009n316
Leadership networks [Website], 2009n31
Learning disabilities dir [Website], 2006n315
Lexicons of early modern English [Website], 2009n869
Librarian's yellow pages [Website], 2009n497
Librarians Internet index [Website], 2009n496
Librarians' Internet index [Website], 2008n46
LibrarySpot [Website], 2009n498
Literary ency [Website], 2006n983
Literary ref center [Website], 2009n905
Literary ref online [Website], 2007n873
Lobbyists.info [Website], 2007n599
Lobbyists.info [Website], 2009n654
Locus online [Website], 2006n1020
LogEc [Website], 2005n133
MacTutor hist of mathematics [Website], 2005n1528
MacTutor hist of mathematics archive [Website], 2008n1332
Maggie L. Walker natl historic site [Website], 2009n163
Making of America—Cornell [Website], 2006n435
Making of America—Michigan [Website], 2006n436
Marquis who's who on the Web [Website], 2008n15
Marshall Cavendish digital [Website], 2009n21
Math archives [Website], 2005n1532
Math forum Internet mathematics lib [Website], 2005n1533
Math forum Internet mathematics lib [Website], 2008n1333
Mathematics on the Web [Website], 2005n1526
Max Planck ency of public intl law online [Website], 2009n486
Medal of Honor citations [Website], 2008n576
Medicina Antiqua [Website], 2007n1244
Merck manual of diagnosis & therapy [Website], 2008n1234
Metacritic [Website], 2006n1169
Middle East studies Internet resources [Website], 2008n141

Military ink [Website], 2009n599Modern American poetry [Website], 2009n992
Modern world hist online [Website], 2009n429
Monthly bulletin of stats [Website], 2008n756
MoreBusiness.com [Website], 2006n264
Movie archive [Website], 2006n1141
Movie review query engine (MRQE) [Website], 2006n1142
Movie tome [Website], 2006n1156
MSN Encarta [Website], 2008n27
My Family.com [Website], 2007n287
National archeological database (NADB) [Website], 2008n380
National archive of criminal justice data (NACJD) [Website], 2007n476
National Center for Education Stats [Website], 2005n279
National security archive: the Cuban missile crisis, 1962 [Website], 2009n360
NationMaster.com [Website], 2008n759
Native American sites [Website], 2008n316
Native web [Website], 2008n300
Navajo code talkers' dict [Website], 2008n585
Naxos music lib [Website], 2009n1011
New bk of knowledge online [Website], 2006n27
New bk of popular sci [Website], 2009n1132
New Deal network [Website], 2005n420
Nobel e-museum [Website], 2005n15
Nobel e-museum [Website], 2007n12
Non-governmental orgs research gd [Website], 2008n660
Nonverbal dict of gestures, signs, & body lang cues [Website], 2007n765
Northwest hist database [Website], 2006n72
NTIS [Website], 2006n1277
Nursery rhymes [Website], 2009n993
Older Americans info dir [Website], 2005n796
Omniglot [Website], 2006n940
Online bks page [Website], 2005n10
Online bks page [Website], 2007n8
Online papers in philosophy [Website], 2006n1202
Online ref bk for medieval studies [Website], 2005n479
Oxford African American studies center [Website], 2009n303
Oxford dict of natl biog [Website], 2005n17
Oxford lang dicts online [Website], 2009n898
PAIR: portal to Asian Internet resources [Website], 2008n103
Papers of Dwight David Eisenhower [Website], 2009n635
People in power [Website], 2008n609
Periodicals index online [Website], 2007n43
Perry Castaneda lib map collection [Website], 2005n377
Perseus digital lib [Website], 2007n408
Personal & business forms online [Website], 2007n149

Pew Internet & American life project [Website], 2009n1289
Philosophical gourmet report
Philosophy in cyberspace [Website], 2006n1203
PHILTAR: philosophy, theology, & religion [Website], 2006n1204
Photosynthesis & the Web [Website], 2006n1323
Phylogeny of life [Website], 2006n1329
Plant ontology consortium (POC) [Website], 2006n1325
PlantGDB [Website], 2006n1324
Play index [Website], 2008n893
Poems, plays, & prose [Website], 2005n1006
Poet's corner [Website], 2008n951
Poetry archive [Website], 2009n994
Poetry archives [Website], 2009n995
Poetry daily [Website], 2008n949
Poetry daily [Website], 2009n996
Poetry 180 [Website], 2008n950
Poetry Society of America [Website], 2009n997
Poets & writers [Website], 2009n998
Poets.org [Website], 2009n999
POIESIS: philosophy online serials [Website], 2006n1187
Political databases of the Americas (PDBA) [Website], 2008n655
Political hndbk of the world online ed [Website], 2007n584
Political parties [Website], 2008n611
Political resources on the net [Website], 2008n608
Polling the nations [Website], 2008n744
PollingReport.com [Website], 2009n636
Pop culture universe [Website], 2009n1045
Population index on the Web [Website], 2005n828
Population ref bureau [Website], 2005n829
Poynter online [Website], 2005n901
Praeger security intl online [Website], 2008n665
Project euclid [Website], 2005n842
Project vote smart [Website], 2009n637
ProQuest AP sci [Website], 2009n1121
ProQuest histl newspapers [Website], 2005n905
ProQuest histl newspapers [Website], 2008n804
Public record research system-Web [Website], 2007n448
PubMed [Website], 2008n1204
RAND pubs [Website], 2007n44
Reading about children's lit [Website], 2007n901
Reading women writers & African lits [Website], 2006n1057
Realms of the sacred in daily life [Website], 2005n321
Refdesk.com: ref desk [Website], 2008n1280
References on chilly climate for women faculty in academe [Website], 2005n286
RePEc (Research papers in economics) [Website], 2005n134
Resources for school librarians [Website], 2007n504
Resources for school librarians [Website], 2009n524

Resources for teachers & students of the DDC [Website], 2009n542

River systems of the world [Website], 2005n1518

Routledge ency of philosophy [Website], 2006n1197

Routledge pol & intl relations resource [Website], 2008n612

Routledge religion resource [Website], 2008n1060

Russian lit pages at Northwestern Univ early 20th-century Russian drama [Website], 2005n1096

Salem health [Website], 2008n1231

Salem health [Website], 2009n1263

Scholarly sport sites [Website], 2005n757

School-Libraries.net [Website], 2009n525

Science fiction & fantasy research database [Website], 2006n1021

Science fiction studies [Website], 2006n1022

SciJinks weather laboratory [Website], 2009n1313

Search engine watch [Website], 2009n1290

Search it! Science [Website], 2009n1122

SF Canada [Website], 2006n1023

Short story index [Website], 2008n899

SIRC's sport quest [Website], 2005n746

SIRS researcher [Website], 2009n58

Smithsonian global sound [Website], 2008n967

Social sci research network (SSRN) electronic lib [Website], 2007n49

Sociological collection [Website], 2005n786

Sociological tour through cyberspace, 2005n789

Sociology: a Sage full-text collection [Website], 2005n787

SocioWeb [Website], 2005n790

SocioWeb [Website], 2006n798

Spanish ref center [Website], 2009n23

Sport discus [Website], 2005n747

Sporting News archives [Website], 2005n748

Sports market place dir [Website], 2005n759

Sports market place dir online [Website], 2006n772

Statistical abstract: geography & environment [Website], 2008n356

Tales online [Website], 2009n1029

Teaching bks [Website], 2007n905

TechInfoSource [Website], 2006n1464

Teen health & wellness [Website], 2007n1235

Theodor de Bry's engravings of Native American life [Website], 2005n341

Thomas food & market place online [Website], 2006n186

THOMAS: legislative info on the Internet [Website], 2008n637

Transitioning to college [Website], 2009n272

Treaties & intl agreements online [Website], 2008n502

TumbleBooks [Website], 2009n932

TV.com [Website], 2006n1157

U.S. govt manual [Website], 2008n639

Ulrich's per [Website], 2006n57

Ulrich's per dir [Website], 2008n52

Ultimate mystery/detective Web gd [Website], 2005n1049

Unbound Bible [Website], 2007n1095

United States at war [Website], 2009n607

United States geography [Website], 2009n338

United States Holocaust Memorial Museum [Website], 2008n448

USA.gov [Website], 2008n640

USCivilWar.Net [Website], 2005n419

USGS educ resources for teachers [Website], 2008n1322

Vandergrift's children's & YA lit pages [Website], 2007n907

Venture capital dir [Website], 2006n168

Verse—anthologies [Website], 2009n1000

Victorian women writers project [Website], 2005n994

Vietnam online [Website], 2008n425

Violence against women online resources [Website], 2005n803

Visual Anthropology.net [Website], 2008n298

Vital stats on American politics [Website], 2007n624

Vitruvio.com [Website], 2009n860

Was there a Trojan War? [Website], 2008n995

Weather glossary [Website], 2009n1319

Weather underground [Website], 2009n1314

Weather watch [Website], 2009n1315

Web of sci [Website], 2006n1278

WebChron [Website], 2005n518

WebJunction [Website], 2009n490

Wikipedia [Website], 2008n32

Wired [Website], 2009n1291

Women & social movement in the US, 1775-2000 [Website], 2005n863

Women in pol [Website], 2005n685Women writers project [Website], 2005n995

Women in pol [Website], 2008n776

Women in pol [Website], 2008n777

Women writers project [Website], 2007n874

Women's human rights resources [Websites], 2005n589

Women's studies intl [Website], 2005n864

World art Web kiosk [Website], 2005n941

World atlas [Website], 2009n336

World Bk discover [Website], 2009n24

World data analyst online [Website], 2009n54

World food habits [Website], 2008n1117

World geography [Website], 2009n339

World hist [Website], 2009n431

World hist: ancient & medieval eras [Website], 2005n509

World hist: the modern era [Website], 2008n459

World Shakespeare bibliog online [Website], 2009n976

World stadiums [Website], 2005n760

WriteExpress online rhyming [Website], 2009n1006

WSSLINKS: women, girls, & educ [Website], 2005n273

YA librarians' homepage [Website], 2007n518

WEREWOLVES
Encyclopedia of vampires, werewolves, & other
  monsters, 2005n1154

WESLEY, JOHN, 1703-1791
John Wesley's ecclesiology, 2008n1091

WEST VIRGINIA
Buildings of W.Va, 2006n76

WESTERN FILMS
Historical dict of westerns in cinema, 2009n1066
Western film series of the sound era, 2009n1068

WHALE WATCHING
Whale watcher, 2007n1211

WILDE, OSCAR, 1854-1900
Oscar Wilde in quotation, 2007n966

WILLIAMS, TED (1918-)
Ted Williams, 2005n767

WILLIAMS, TENNESSEE
Tennessee Williams ency, 2005n1036

WINE & WINEMAKING
New wine lover's companion, 2d ed, 2005n1300
Oxford companion to wine, 3d ed, 2008n1121
Pacific pinot noir, 2009n1150
Sotheby's wine ency, 4th ed, 2008n1123
Vino Italiano buying gd, 2006n1284
Wine atlas of Australia, 2008n1116
Wines & wineries of Calif. central coast, 2009n1149
Wines of the world, 2005n1308

WISCONSIN
Profiles of Wis., 2008n90

WITCHCRAFT
Encyclopedia of witchcraft, 2007n666
Encyclopedia of witches, witchcraft & Wicca, 3d ed,
  2009n716
Salem witch trials, 2009n379

WITTGENSTEIN, LUDWIG, 1889-1951
Historical dict of Wittgenstein's philosophy,
  2005n1233

WOMEN & RELIGION
Encyclopedia of women & religion in N America,
  2007n1080

WOMEN & WAR
Women & war, 2007n760

Women during the Civil War, 2008n785
Women in the American Civil War, 2009n789

WOMEN AUTHORS
A to Z of American women writers, rev ed, 2008n909
African American women writers of the 19th century
  [Website], 2005n1057
Alice Munro, 2008n937
All things Austen, 2006n1048
Amy Tan, 2005n1071
Bookshelf of our own, 2005n1007
Celebration of women writers [Website], 2005n976
Chronology of Jane Austen & her family, 2008n928
Critical companion to Flannery O'Connor, 2009n964
Critical companion to Zora Neale Hurston, 2009n961
Encyclopedia of African American women writers,
  2008n911
Encyclopedia of feminist lit, 2006n985
Encyclopedia of women's autobiog, 2006n856
Feminism in lit, 2005n999
Feminist ency of Spanish lit, 2005n1089
Irish women writers, 2006n1059
Jamaica Kincaid, 2009n962
Kaye Gibbons, 2008n919
Latin American women writers, 2008n943
Margaret Atwood, 2005n1085
Undergraduates companion to women poets of the
  world & their Web sites, 2005n1101
Victorian women writers project [Website], 2005n994
Women adventurers 1750-1900, 2009n783
Women writers project [Website], 2005n995
Women writers project [Website], 2007n874

WOMEN - BIOGRAPHY
FemBio [Website], 2005n866
Gloria Steinem, 2005n867
Notable American women, 2006n851
Notable black American women, bk 3, 2005n331
Palgrave Macmillan dict of women's biog, 4th ed,
  2006n852
Profiles of Ohio women 1803-2003, 2005n868
Who's who of American women 2006-07, 25th ed,
  2006n853
Who's who of American women 2007, 26th ed,
  2007n756

WOMEN COMPOSERS
Women composers, v.7, 2005n1117
Women composers, v.8, 2007n984

WOMEN IN BUSINESS
Encyclopedia of American women in business,
  2006n124

WOMEN IN COMPUTER SCIENCE
Encyclopedia of gender & info tech, 2007n1287

WOMEN IN EDUCATION
References on chilly climate for women faculty in
    academe [Website], 2005n286

WOMEN IN MUSIC
New histl anthology of music by women, 2006n1082

WOMEN IN POLITICS
Encyclopedia of women & American pol, 2009n641
From suffrage to the senate, 2d ed, 2007n596
Legislative women, 2009n662
Suffragists in lit for youth, 2007n898
Women & pol participation, 2005n715
Women in pol [Website], 2008n776
Women in pol [Website], 2008n777

WOMEN IN SCIENCE
A to Z of women in sci & math, rev ed, 2008n780
Ladies in the lab II, 2005n1280
Women & sci, 2006n863
Women's adventures in sci series, 2006n1253

WOMEN IN SPORTS
SIRC's sport quest [Website], 2005n746

**WOMEN IN THE MOTION PICTURE
INDUSTRY**
Encyclopedic dict of women in early American films
    1895-1930, 2005n1189

WOMEN MATHEMATICIANS
A to Z of women in sci & math, rev ed, 2008n780

WOMEN PHILOSOPHERS
Directory of women philosophers [Website], 2006n1200

WOMEN'S HEALTH
Boston women's health bk collective [Website],
    2005n1441
Cancer sourcebk for women, 3d ed, 2007n1270
Encyclopedia of women's health, 5th ed, 2006n1428
Encyclopedia of women's reproductive cancer,
    2005n1465
Healthy woman, 2009n1246
Menopause bible, 2006n1437
New Harvard gd to women's health, 2005n1440
Pregnancy & birth sourcebk, 2d ed, 2005n1456
Women's health concerns sourcebk, 2d ed, 2005n1452

WOMEN'S RIGHTS
Women's human rights resources [Websites], 2005n589
Women's rights, 2006n864
Women's rights, 2008n786

WOMEN'S STUDIES
A to Z of Ancient Greek & Roman women, rev ed,
    2009n785

A to Z of feminism, 2008n781
American women's hist [Website], 2005n855
American women's hist online [Website], 2009n786
Battleground: women, gender, & sexuality, 2009n787
Biographical dict of Scottish women, paperback ed,
    2008n778
Contemporary women's issues [Website], 2005n856
Dictionary of women worldwide, 2007n755
Diotima: materials for the study of women & gender in
    the ancient world [Website], 2005n857
Documents from the women's liberation movement
    [Website], 2005n858
Encyclopedia of women & Islamic cultures, v.1,
    2005n870
Encyclopedia of women & Islamic cultures, v.2,
    2006n854
Encyclopedia of women & Islamic cultures, v.3,
    2006n855
Encyclopedia of women & Islamic cultures, v.4,
    2007n757
Encyclopedia of women & Islamic cultures, v.5:
    practices, interpretations, & representations,
    2008n782
Encyclopedia of women & Islamic cultures, v.6: suppl
    & index, 2008n783
Encyclopedia of women in the renaissance, 2008n784
Feminism & women's issues [Website], 2005n859
Feminist theory Website [Website], 2006n850
First American women architects, 2009n856
GenderReach [Website], 2005n860
GenderWatch [Website], 2005n861
Geographic gd to uncovering women's hist in archival
    collections, 2005n862
Historical dict of feminism, 2d ed, 2005n869
Historical dict of feminist philosophy, 2007n758
Historical dict of women in sub-Saharan Africa,
    2006n858
History of women in the US, 2005n872
Landmarks of American women's hist, 2005n873
Medieval feminist index or Feminae: medieval women
    & gender index [Website], 2005n874
Oxford ency of women in world hist, 2009n788
Women & gender in Central & E Europe, Russia, &
    Eurasia, 2008n775
Women & gender in medieval Europe, 2007n759
Women & museums, 2006n54
Women & social movement in the US, 1775-2000
    [Website], 2005n863
Women in early America, 2006n857
Women in the American West, 2009n791
Women in the middle ages, 2005n871
Women on US postage stamps, 2009n784
Women, sci, & myth, 2009n790
Women's movement today, 2006n859
Women's roles in the renaissance, 2006n860
Women's studies, feminist, & gender periodicals
    [Website], 2005n875

Women's studies intl [Website], 2005n864
Women's studies section core jls for women's studies [Website], 2005n865
Women's suffrage, 2006n862
Women's suffrage in America, updated ed, 2006n861
Working Americans 1880-2005, v.6: women at work, 2006n238

WOODSTOCK FESTIVAL
Woodstock, 2006n1075

WOODWORKING
Encyclopedia of wood, 2006n910
Woodworker's illus ency, 2009n841

WORLD BANK
Guide to the world bank, 2005n722

WORLD HISTORY
A to Z of the Renaissance, 2007n423
ABZU: a gd to study of the ancient Near East on the Web [Website], 2005n526
ACLS hist e-bk project [Website], 2007n402
Ancient hist, 2006n494
APIS: advanced papryological info system [Website], 2007n407
Atlas of the medieval world, 2006n487
Berkshire ency of world hist, 2007n416
Best of hist web sites, 2008n442
Cambridge ancient hist, v.12: the crisis of empire, A.D. 193-337, 2d ed, 2007n429
Cassell's chronology of world hist, 2006n492
Chambers hist factfinder, 2006n509
Classical studies, 2d ed, 2007n403
Crusades, 2007n417
Daily life in the N.T., 2009n433
Daily life online [Website], 2009n423
Day by day: the 90s, 2005n513
Day by day: the twenties, 2009n418
Dictionary of world hist, 2d ed, 2007n418
Eighties in America, 2009n374
Encyclopedia idiotica, 2006n503
Encyclopedia of society & culture in the ancient world, 2008n455
Encyclopedia of the modern world, 2008n456
Encyclopedia of war crimes & genocide, 2007n422
Encyclopedia of world hist, 2009n426
Eyewitness accounts [Website], 2005n514
Gale ency of world hist: war, 2009n427
Global hist, 2005n527
Great events from hist: the ancient world, prehist-476 CE, 2005n515
Great events from hist: the Middle Age 477-1453, 2005n516
Great events from hist: the Renaissance & early modern era, 2006n500
Great events from hist: the 17th century, 2006n493

Great events from hist: the 17th century, 2007n409
Great events from hist: the 18th century, 2007n410
Great events from hist: the 19th century, 1801-1900, 2007n411
Great events from hist: the 19th century, 2008n449
Great events from hist: the 20th century, 1940-70, 2009n421
Great events from hist: the 20th century, 1971-2000, 2009n420
Great events from hist: the 20th century, 2008n450
Great lives from hist: notorious lives, 2008n443
Great lives from hist: the ancient world, prehist-476 CE, rev ed, 2005n511
Great lives from hist: the Middle Ages, 477-1453, 2005n512
Great lives from hist: the renaissance & early modern era, 1454-1600, 2006n489
Great lives from hist: the 17th century, 2006n490
Great lives from hist: the 17th century, 2007n404
Great lives from hist: the 18th century, 2007n405
Great lives from hist: the 19th century, 1801-1900, 2007n406
Great lives from hist: the 19th century, 1801-1900, 2008n444
Great lives from hist: the 20th century, 1901-2000, 2009n417
Greenwood daily life online [Website], 2005n508
Greenwood dict of world hist, 2007n420
Greenwood ency of daily life, 2005n517
Handy hist answer bk, 2d ed, 2006n510
Historic events of the 20th century [Website], 2005n522
Historical dict of the enlightenment, 2006n496
History for kids [Website], 2005n523
History highway, 4th ed, 2007n427
History of fashion & costume, 2006n909
History of the world in photographs, 2009n422
History resource center [Website], 2007n421
Modern world hist online [Website], 2009n429
Mysteries in hist, 2006n507
National Geographic concise hist of the world, 2007n412
National Geographic visual hist of the world, 2007n413
Nations & nationalism, 2009n434
New 1st dict of cultural literacy, 2005n325
New makers of modern culture, 2008n445
Oxford dict of contemporary world hist, 3d ed, 2009n430
Oxford dict of the classical world, 2008n458
People at the center of … series, 2006n491
Reference sources in hist, 2d ed, 2005n510
Reformation, exploration, & empire, 2006n502
Renaissance & reformation, 2007n425
Revolutionary movements in world hist, 2007n414
Timelines of hist, 2006n495

Timelines on file: nations & states, updated ed,
    2007n415
WebChron [Website], 2005n518
World fascism, 2007n632
World hist [Website], 2009n431
World hist on file, updated ed, 2005n533
World hist on file, v.1: early civilizations, 2d ed,
    2007n435
World hist on file, v.2: the expanding world, 2007n436
World hist on file, v.3: the age of revolution, 2d ed,
    2007n437
World hist on file, v.4: the 20th century, 2d ed,
    2007n438
World hist: ancient & medieval eras [Website],
    2005n509
World hist: the modern era [Website], 2008n459
World monarchies & dynasties, 2006n504

WORLD HUNGER
World hunger, 2008n735

WORLD LEADERS. *See also* **GOVERNMENT**
LEADERS; POLITICAL LEADERS
Leadership, 2008n446

WORLD POLITICS
Afghanistan to Zimbabwe, 2007n58
Annual register 2007, 248th ed, 2008n617
Annual register 2008, 2009n38
Cold War, 2007n563
Constitutions of the world, 3d ed, 2009n625
Countries of the world & their leaders 2009, 2009n616
CultureGrams [Website], 2009n67
Dictionary of globalization, 2007n577
Encyclopedia of intl relations & global pol, 2006n743
Encyclopedia of the age of pol revolutions & new
    ideologies 1760-1815, 2008n657
Encyclopedia of the world's nations & cultures,
    2008n64
Europa world yr bk 2005, 2006n45
Europa world yr bk 2008, 49th ed, 2009n39
Firefly gd to the state of the world, 2006n67
Gale ency of world hist: govts, 2009n618
Global issues in context [Website], 2009n68
Globalization, 2007n180
Government, politics, & protest, 2007n580
Governments of the world, 2006n685
Historic docs of 2006, 2008n618
Historic docs of 2007, 2009n624
International dir of govt 2008, 5th ed, 2009n621
International relations, intl security, & comparative
    pol, 2009n677
Junior Worldmark ency of the nations, 5th ed,
    2008n65
Nations of the world 2005, 5th ed, 2005n74
Nations of the world 2006, 6th ed, 2007n57
Nations of the world 2007/08, 7th ed, 2008n66

Nations of the world 2009, 8th ed, 2009n69
Political hndbk of the Americas 2008, 2009n626
Political hndbk of the world: 2005-06, 2007n583
Political hndbk of the world 2008, 2009n627
Political hndbk of the world online ed [Website],
    2007n584
Political resources on the net [Website], 2008n608
Regional gd to intl conflict & mgmt from 1945 to
    2003, 2006n741
Revolutionary & dissident movements of the world,
    4th ed, 2005n693
World Bk ency of people & places, 2007n55
World ency of pol systems & parties, 4th ed,
    2008n613
World factbk 2005, 2006n68
World factbk 2006, 2007n59
World factbk 2007, 2008n67
Worldmark ency of the nations, 11th ed, 2005n72
Worldmark ency of the nations, 12th ed, 2007n56

WORLD TRADE
Encyclopedia of world trade, 2006n200

WORLD TRADE ORGANIZATION
WTO analytical index, 2d ed, 2009n487
WTO case law of 2004-05, 2009n488

WORLD WAR, 1914-1918
American soldiers' lives: WW I, 2007n564
Encyclopedia of WW I, 2006n498
Home front ency, 2007n554
Personal perspectives: WW I, 2007n434
Researching WW I, 2005n531
Understanding the lit of WW I, 2006n987
World War I, 2006n505
World War I, 2007n426
World War I, 2007n430
World War I, 2008n460
World War I, 2009n432

WORLD WAR, 1939-1945
African Americans in the US Army in WW II,
    2009n304
American home front in WW II: almanac, 2005n410
American home front in WW II: biogs, 2005n411
American home front in WW II: primary sources,
    2005n412
Battle of Iwo Jima, 2006n488
Brassey's D-day ency, 2005n660
Chronology of the war at sea, 1939-45, 3d rev ed,
    2006n669
Columbia gd to Hiroshima & the bomb, 2008n413
Encyclopedia of WW II, 2006n498
Encyclopedia of WW II, 2008n452
Graphic war, 2006n666
Historical dict of WW II intelligence, 2008n589
History of WW II, 2005n529

Hitler & the Nazis, 2007n387
Home front ency, 2007n554
Home front ency, 2008n584
Personal perspectives: WW II, 2006n512
World War II, 2005n519
World War II, 2005n520
World War II, 2006n506
World War II, 2007n439
World War II, 2009n608
World War II almanac, 2009n419
World War II naval & maritime claims against the US,
    2007n569

**WORLD WAR, 1939-1945 - JUVENILE
LITERATURE**
World War II in lit for youth, 2006n999

**WORLD WAR, 1939-1945 - PERSONAL
NARRATIVES**
Great stories of WW II, 2008n944

WORLD WIDE WEB. *See also* **INTERNET
(COMPUTER NETWORK)**
Agent & Web serv techs in virtual enterprises,
    2008n1279
Encyclopedia of portal technologies & applications,
    2008n1282
Internet & society, 2008n1281

WRIGHT, FRANK LLOYD
Frank Lloyd Wright comp, rev ed, 2007n818

WRITING
American dir of writer's gdlines, 5th ed, 2007n769
Author's hndbk, 2d ed, 2007n773
Bryson's dict for writers & editors, 2009n802
Career opportunities in writing, 2007n225
Chicago gd to writing about numbers, 2005n894
Children's writer's & illus market 2006, 18th ed,
    2006n877
Children's writer's & illus market 2008, 2008n793
Christian writers' market gd 2005, 2006n880
Christian writer's market gd 2007, 2008n797
Cooper Hill stylebk, 2d ed, 2006n885
Copywriter's hndbk, 3d ed, 2007n771
Craft & business of writing, 2009n805
Dictionary of concise writing, 2d ed, 2007n768
Elements of style, 2006n887
Facts on File gd to good writing, 2006n882
Guide to literary agents 2005, 2005n891
Guide to literary agents 2007, 2007n770
Handbook of rhetorical devices [Website], 2009n803
Magazine writer's hndbk, 2d ed, 2007n774
Manual for writers of research papers, theses, &
    dissertations, 7th ed, 2008n801
McGraw-Hill desk ref for editors, writers, &
    proofreaders, 2007n772

MLA style manual & gd to scholarly publishing, 3d
    ed, 2009n808
Novel & short story writer's market 2006, 25th ed,
    2006n878
Novel & short story writer's market 2007, 2008n794
Oxford American writer's thesaurus, 2d ed, 2009n895
Poet's market, 2008, 2008n795
Random House writer's ref, rev ed, 2005n895
UPI stylebk & gd to newswriting, 4th ed, 2005n896
Writer's market, 2005, 2005n892
Writer's market, 2007, 2008n796
Writer's market 2009, 88th ed, 2009n804
Writer's market companion, 2d ed, 2006n881
Writing the critical essay series, 2009n806

YELLOWSTONE NAITONAL PARK
Geysers of Yellowstone, 4th ed, 2009n1322

YOGA
Hatha yoga illustrated, 2005n785
Yoga, 2008n714

YOUNG ADULT LIBRARY SERVICES
Best bks for YAs, 3d ed, 2008n881
Big bk of teen reading lists, 2007n516
Building character through multicultural lit, 2005n611
Connecting YAs & libs, 3d ed, 2005n619
Crash course in teen servs, 2009n555
Dynamic youth servs through outcome-based planning
    & educ, 2007n512
Fiore's summer lib reading program hndbk, 2006n619
From A to Zine: building a winning zine collection in
    your lib, 2005n644
Gamers in the lib?!, 2008n537
Get connected, 2008n536
Going places with youth outreach, 2006n621
Hipster librarian's gd to teen craft projects, 2009n548
Historical fiction for young readers (grades 4-8),
    2009n922
Librarian's gd to developing Christian fiction
    collections for YAs, 2006n626
More outstanding bks for the college bound,
    2006n620
More teen programs that work, 2006n622
Official YALSA awards gdbk, 2009n927
Serving teens through readers' advisory, 2008n535
Sizzling summer reading programs for YAs, 2d ed,
    2007n514
Teen bk discussion groups @ the lib, 2005n618
Teen girls & tech, 2009n550
Teen reader's advisor, 2007n513
Teen spaces, 2d ed, 2009n576
Teens & libs, 2005n621
YA librarians' homepage [Website], 2007n518
Year of programs for teens, 2007n510
Young adult lit in action, 2009n547

YOUNG ADULT LITERATURE
A to zoo, 7th ed, 2007n897
Across cultures, 2009n921
American Indian themes in YA lit, 2007n913
Authors & artists for YAs, v.55, 2005n877
Authors & artists for YAs, v.56, 2005n878
Authors & artists for YAs, v.57, 2005n879
Best bks for boys, 2009n933
Best bks for high school readers grades 9-12, 2005n1017
Best bks for high school readers grades 9-12, suppl, 2007n894
Best bks for middle school & jr high readers grades 6-9, 2005n1018
Best bks for middle school & jr high readers, suppl, 2007n895
Best bks for YAs, 3d ed, 2008n881
Book crush, 2008n891
Children's & YA lit by Native Americans, 2005n1021
Children's & YA lit hndbk, 2007n895
Children's bks: awards & prizes, 2005 ed, 2006n1003
Continuum ency of YA lit, 2007n908
Core collection for children & YAs, 2009n930
Cultural journeys, 2007n912
Cyclopedia of YA authors, 2006n1001
Dictionary of American YA fiction, 1997-2001, 2005n1027
Educational paperback assn Website [Website], 2007n903
Encountering enchantment, 2008n883
Ethnic bk awards, 2006n1004
Fantasy lit for children & YAs, 5th ed, 2006n992
500 great bks for teens, 2007n902
Gentle reads, 2009n925
Historical fiction for young readers (grades 4-8), 2009n922
Middle & jr high school lib catalog, 9th ed, 2006n993
Middle ages in lit for youth, 2005n1015
Names & naming in YA lit, 2008n890
Newbery & Caldecott awards, 2007 ed, 2008n885
Newbery/Printz companion, 3d ed, 2008n884
Ninth bk of jr authors & illustrators, 2006n1000
Official YALSA awards gdbk, 2009n927
Poets for YAs, 2008n953
Popular series fiction for middle school & teen readers, 2006n998

Recommended bks in Spanish for children & YAs 2004-08, 2009n929
Suffragists in lit for youth, 2007n898
Teaching bks [Website], 2007n905
Tenth bk of jr authors & illustrators, 2009n934
Thematic gd to YA lit, 2007n914
Using lit to help troubled teenagers cope with abuse issues, 2005n1031
Using picture story bks to teach literary devices, v.4, 2009n923
Vandergrift's children's & YA lit pages [Website], 2007n907
What do children & YAs read next, v.6, 2005n1014
Women engaged in war in lit for youth, 2008n882
Young adult lit in action, 2009n547
Youth gangs in lit, 2005n1030

YOUTH DEVELOPMENT
Encyclopedia of applied developmental sci, 2005n825
Truth about series, 2005n827

YOUTH, SOCIAL CONDITIONS
Contemporary youth culture, 2007n719
Encyclopedia of children, adolescents, & the media, 2007n764
Youth activism, 2007n578

YUGOSLAVIA, ETHNIC RELATIONS
Breakup of Yugoslavia & its aftermath, rev ed, 2005n117
Former Yugoslavia's diverse peoples, 2005n339

ZAMBIA
Culture & customs of Zambia, 2007n91
Historical dict of Zambia, 3d ed, 2008n99

ZIONISM
Historical dict of Zionism, 2d ed, 2009n1119

ZOOLOGY. *See also* ANIMALS; MAMMALS
Elsevier's dict of zoology & general biology, 2005n1380
Encyclopedia of animals, 2005n1381
World Bk's sci & nature gds, 2005n1344

DATE DUE

HIGHSMITH 45230